Claudia Maienborn, Klaus von Heusinger and Paul Portner (Eds.)
Semantics – Theories

This volume is part of a larger set of handbooks to Semantics

1 **Semantics: Foundations, History and Methods**
Klaus von Heusinger, Claudia Maienborn, Paul Portner (eds.)

2 **Semantics: Lexical Structures and Adjectives**
Claudia Maienborn, Klaus von Heusinger, Paul Portner (eds.)

3 **Semantics: Theories**
Claudia Maienborn, Klaus von Heusinger, Paul Portner (eds.)

4 **Semantics: Noun Phrases and Verb Phrases**
Paul Portner, Klaus von Heusinger, Claudia Maienborn (eds.)

5 **Semantics: Sentence and Information Structure**
Paul Portner, Claudia Maienborn, Klaus von Heusinger (eds.)

6 **Semantics: Interfaces**
Claudia Maienborn, Klaus von Heusinger, Paul Portner (eds.)

7 **Semantics: Typology, Diachrony and Processing**
Klaus von Heusinger, Claudia Maienborn, Paul Portner (eds.)

Semantics
Theories

Edited by
Claudia Maienborn
Klaus von Heusinger
Paul Portner

DE GRUYTER
MOUTON

ISBN 978-3-11-058703-6
e-ISBN (PDF) 978-3-11-058924-5
e-ISBN (EPUB) 978-3-11-058714-2

Library of Congress Cataloging-in-Publication Data
Names: Maienborn, Claudia, editor. | Heusinger, Klaus von, editor. | Portner,
  Paul, editor.
Title: Semantics : theories / edited by Claudia Maienborn, Klaus von Heusinger,
  Paul Portner.
Description: Berlin ; Boston : De Gruyter, [2019] | Series: Mouton reader |
  Includes bibliographical references and index.
Identifiers: LCCN 2018031253 (print) | LCCN 2018047132 (ebook) | ISBN
  9783110589245 (electronic Portable Document Format (pdf)) | ISBN
  9783110587036 (paperback) | ISBN 9783110589245 (e-book pdf) | ISBN
  9783110587142 (e-book epub)
Subjects: LCSH: Semantics. | BISAC: LANGUAGE ARTS & DISCIPLINES / Linguistics
  / Semantics.
Classification: LCC P325 (ebook) | LCC P325 .S37998 2019 (print) | DDC
  401/.43--dc23
LC record available at https://lccn.loc.gov/2018031253

Bibliographic information published by the Deutsche Nationalbibliothek
The Deutsche Nationalbibliothek lists this publication in the Deutsche Nationalbibliografie;
detailed bibliographic data are available in the Internet at http://dnb.dnb.de.

© 2019 Walter de Gruyter GmbH, Berlin/Boston
Cover image: blackred/E+/ Getty Images
Typesetting: Integra Software Services Pvt. Ltd.
Printing and binding: CPI books GmbH, Leck

www.degruyter.com

Contents

	Leonard Talmy	
1	**Cognitive Semantics: An overview** —— 01	
	John R. Taylor	
2	**Prototype theory** —— 29	
	Jean-Mark Gawron	
3	**Frame Semantics** —— 57	
	Ray Jackendoff	
4	**Conceptual Semantics** —— 86	
	Ewald Lang and Claudia Maienborn	
5	**Two-level Semantics: Semantic Form and Conceptual Structure** —— 114	
	Jerry R. Hobbs	
6	**Word meaning and world knowledge** —— 154	
	Thomas Ede Zimmermann	
7	**Model-theoretic semantics** —— 181	
	Claudia Maienborn	
8	**Event semantics** —— 232	
	Jonathan Ginzburg	
9	**Situation Semantics and the ontology of natural language** —— 267	
	Jonathan Ginzburg	
10	**Situation Semantics: From indexicality to metacommunicative interaction** —— 295	
	Hans Kamp and Uwe Reyle	
11	**Discourse Representation Theory** —— 321	

Paul Dekker
12   Dynamic semantics —— 385

Henk Zeevat
13   Rhetorical relations —— 413

Index —— 441

Leonard Talmy
1 Cognitive Semantics: An overview

1   Introduction —— 1
2   The semantics of grammar —— 4
3   Schematic structure —— 7
4   Conceptual organization —— 13
5   Interactions among semantic structures —— 17
6   Conclusion —— 26
7   References —— 27

Abstract: The linguistic representation of conceptual structure is the central concern of the two-to-three decades old field that has come to be known as "cognitive linguistics". Its approach is concerned with the patterns in which and processes by which conceptual content is organized in language. It addresses the linguistic structuring of such basic conceptual categories as space and time, scenes and events, entities and processes, motion and location, and force and causation. To these it adds the basic ideational and affective categories attributed to cognitive agents, such as attention and perspective, volition and intention, and expectation and affect. It addresses the semantic structure of morphological and lexical forms, as well as of syntactic patterns. And it addresses the interrelationships of conceptual structures, such as those in metaphoric mapping, those within a semantic frame, those between text and context, and those in the grouping of conceptual categories into large structuring systems. Overall, its aim is to ascertain the global integrated system of conceptual structuring in language.

1 Introduction

The linguistic representation of conceptual structure is the central concern of the two-to-three decades old field that has come to be known generally as "cognitive linguistics" through such defining works as Fauconnier (1985), Fauconnier & Turner (2002), Fillmore (1975, 1976), Lakoff (1987, 1992), Langacker (1987, 1991), and Talmy (2000a, 2000b), as well as through edited collections like Geeraerts & Cuyckens (2007). This field can first be characterized by contrasting its "conceptual" approach with two other approaches, the "formal" and the "psychological".

Leonard Talmy, Buffalo, NY, USA

Particular research traditions have largely based themselves within one of these approaches, while aiming – with greater or lesser success – to address the concerns of the other two approaches.

The formal approach focuses on the overt structural patterns exhibited by linguistic forms, largely abstracted away from or regarded as autonomous from any associated meaning. This approach thus includes the study of syntactic, morphological, and morphemic structure. The tradition of generative grammar has been centered in the formal approach. But its relations to the other two approaches have remained limited. It has all along referred to the importance of relating its grammatical component to a semantic component, and there has indeed been much good work on aspects of meaning, but this enterprise has generally not addressed the overall conceptual organization of language. The formal semantics that has been adopted within the generative tradition (e.g., Lappin 1997) has largely included only enough about meaning to correlate with the formal categories and operations that the main body of the tradition has focused on. And the reach of generative linguistics to psychology has largely considered only the kinds of cognitive structure and processing that might be needed to account for its formal categories and operations.

The psychological approach regards language from the perspective of general cognitive systems such as perception, memory, attention, and reasoning. Centered in this approach, the field of psychology has also addressed the other two approaches. Its conceptual concerns (see e.g., Neely 1991) have in particular included semantic memory, the associativity of concepts, the structure of categories, inference generation, and contextual knowledge. But it has insufficiently considered systematic conceptual structuring – the global integrated system of schematic structures with which language organizes conceptual content.

By contrast, the conceptual approach of cognitive linguistics is concerned with the patterns in which and processes by which conceptual content is organized in language. It has thus addressed the linguistic structuring of such basic conceptual categories as space and time, scenes and events, entities and processes, motion and location, and force and causation. To these it adds the basic ideational and affective categories attributed to cognitive agents, such as attention and perspective, volition and intention, and expectation and affect. It addresses the semantic structure of morphological and lexical forms, as well as of syntactic patterns. And it addresses the interrelationships of conceptual structures, such as those in metaphoric mapping, those within a semantic frame, those between text and context, and those in the grouping of conceptual categories into large structuring systems. Overall, the aim of cognitive linguistics is to ascertain the global integrated system of conceptual structuring in language.

Cognitive linguistics, further, addresses the concerns of the other two approaches to language. First, it examines the formal properties of language from its conceptual perspective. Thus, it aims to account for grammatical structure in terms of the functions this serves in the representation of conceptual structure. Second, as one of its most distinguishing characteristics, cognitive linguistics aims to relate its findings to the cognitive structures that concern the psychological approach. It aims both to help account for the behavior of conceptual phenomena within language in terms of those psychological structures, and at the same time, to help work out some of the properties of those structures themselves on the basis of its detailed understanding of how language realizes them. It is this trajectory toward unification with the psychological that motivates the term "cognitive" within the name of this linguistic tradition. In the long term, its aim is to integrate the linguistic and the psychological perspectives on cognitive organization in a unified understanding of human conceptual structure.

With its focus on the conceptual, cognitive linguistics regards "meaning" or "semantics" simply as conceptual content as it is organized by language. Thus, general conception as experienced by individuals – i.e., thought – includes linguistic meaning within its greater compass. And while linguistic meaning – whether that expressible by an individual language or by language in general – apparently involves a selection from or constraints upon general conception, it is nevertheless qualitatively of a piece with it.

Cognitive linguistics is as ready as other linguistic approaches to represent an aspect of language abstractly with a symbolic formula or schematic diagram, provided that that aspect is judged both to consist of discrete components in crisp relationships and to be clearly understood. But most cognitive linguists share the sensibility that such formal representations poorly accord with the gradients, partial overlaps, interactions that lead to mutual modification, processes of fleshing out, inbuilt forms of vagueness, and the like that they observe in semantics. They instead aim to set forth such phenomena through descriptive means that provide precision and rigor without formalisms. They further find that formal accounts present their representations of language organization with premature exhaustiveness and mistakenly uniform certainty. We might propose developing a field of "theoryology" that taxonomizes types of theories, according to their defining properties. In such a field, a formal theory of language, at any given phase of its grasp of language phenomena, would be of the type that requires encompassive and perfected mechanisms to account for those phenomena. But cognitive linguistics rests on a type of theory that, at its foundation, builds in gradients for the stage of development to which any given aspect of language under analysis has been brought, and for the certainty with which the analysis is held.

While cognitive linguists largely share the approach to language outlined here, they may differ in more limited respects. For example, Ronald Langacker generally stresses the contribution of every morpheme and construction in a sentence to the unified meaning of the sentence, while George Lakoff and I see certain interactions among the elements as overriding such contributions. And Lakoff stresses a theory of embodiment that Langacker and I break into subtheories and in part challenge (see section 5.1).

Terminologically, "cognitive linguistics" refers to the field as a whole. Within that field, "cognitive grammar" is largely associated with Langacker's work, while "cognitive semantics" is largely associated with my own work (the main focus below), though it is sometimes used more extendedly.

Externally, cognitive linguistics is perhaps closest to functional linguistics (e.g., Givon 1989). Discourse is central to the latter while more peripheral to the former, but both approach language with similar sensibilities. Jackendoff's approach is comparable in spirit to cognitive linguistics, as seen in article 4 [this volume] (Jackendoff) *Conceptual Semantics*. Thus, he assumes a mentalist, rather than a cognition-avoiding logical, basis for meaning. And he critiques the approaches of Fodor, Wierzbicka, and Levin and Rappaport (see article 4 [Semantics: Lexical Structures and Adjectives] (Levin & Rappaport Hovav) *Lexical Conceptual Structure*) much as does cognitive linguistics. But his reliance on an algebraic features-based formalism to represent meaning differs from the cognitive-linguistic view of its inadequacy in handling the semantic gradience and modulation cited above. And his privileging of spatial structure in semantics is at variance with the significance that cognitive linguistics sees in such further domains as temporal structure, force-dynamic/causal structure, cognitive state (including purpose, expectation, affect, familiarity), and reality status (including factual, counterfactual, conditional, potential), as well as domains that he himself cites, like social relations.

2 The semantics of grammar

To turn to the specific contents of Cognitive Semantics, then, this outline opens with the semantics of grammar because it is the key to conceptual structuring in language. A universal design feature of languages is that their meaning-bearing forms are divided into two different subsystems, the open-class, or lexical, and the closed-class, or grammatical (see Talmy 2000a: ch. 1). Open classes have many members and can readily add many more. They commonly include (the roots of) nouns, verbs, and adjectives. Closed classes have relatively few members and are difficult to augment. They include bound forms – inflections, derivations, and clitics and such free forms as prepositions, conjunctions, and determiners. In addition to such overt closed classes, a language can have certain implicit closed classes such as word order patterns, a set of lexical categories (e.g., nounhood, verbhood, etc. per se), a set of grammatical relations (e.g., subject status, direct object status, etc.), and grammatical constructions.

2.1 Semantic constraint on grammar

Within this formal distinction, the crucial semantic finding is that the meanings that open-class forms can express are virtually unrestricted, whereas those of closed-class forms are highly constrained. This constraint applies both to the conceptual categories they can refer to and to the particular member notions within any such category. For example, many languages around the world have closed-class forms in construction with a noun that indicate the number of the noun's referent, but no languages have closed-class forms indicating its color. And even closed-class forms referring to number can indicate such notions as singular, dual, plural, paucal, and the like, but never such notions as even, odd, a dozen, or countable. By contrast, open-class forms can refer to all such notions, as the very words just used demonstrate.

The total set of conceptual categories with their member notions that closed-class forms can ever refer to thus constitutes an approximately closed inventory. Individual languages draw in different patterns from this universally available inventory for their particular set of grammatically expressed meanings. The inventory is graduated, progressing from categories and notions that may well appear universally in all languages (a candidate is "polarity" with its members 'positive' and 'negative'), through ones appearing in many but not all languages (a candidate is "number"), down to ones appearing in just a few languages (an example is "rate" with its members 'fast' and 'slow').

2.2 Topological principle for grammar

The next issue is what determines the conceptual categories and member notions included in the inventory as against those excluded from it. No single global principle is evident, but several semantic constraints with broad scope have been found. One of these, the "topology principle", applies to the meanings – or "schemas" – of closed-class forms referring to space, time or certain other domains. This principle largely excludes Euclidean properties such as absolutes of distance, size, shape, or angle from such schemas. Instead, these schemas exhibit such topological properties as "magnitude neutrality" and "shape neutrality".

To illustrate magnitude neutrality, the spatial schema of the English preposition *across* prototypically represents motion along a path from one edge of a bounded plane perpendicularly to its opposite. But this schema is abstracted away from magnitude so the preposition can be used equally well in *The ant crawled across my palm*, and in *The bus drove across the country*. Likewise in time, the temporal schema of the past tense morpheme *-ed* represents occurrence at a point on the time line before that of the current speech event, but the magnitude of the interval between the two points is irrelevant. Thus, *Alexander died young* can refer to an acquaintance a year ago or to Alexander the Great over two millennia ago.

The topological property of shape neutrality is seen in the preposition *through*. In one usage, its schema represents motion along a linear path located within a medium. But this path can be of any shape, as seen in *I made a bee-line / circled / zigzagged through the woods*.

2.3 Concept-structuring function of grammar

Based on their formal and semantic differences, a further major finding is that the two types of form classes exhibit a functional difference. In the conceptual complex evoked by any portion of discourse, the open-class forms contribute most of the *content*, while the closed-class forms determine most of the *structure*.

For illustration, consider the sentence *A rustler lassoed the steers* (a "rustler" being a cowboy who steals another's livestock). Its three open-class morphemes – *rustle, lasso, steer* – are conceptually rich. Thus, *rustle* includes concepts of property ownership, illegality, theft, and livestock. *Lasso* includes the concepts of twirling a looped rope, casting the loop over an animal's head, and tautening and drawing the rope's end. *Steer* includes the concepts of breeding for human consumption, a certain type of animal, and castration. These morphemes seem to provide most of the conceptual content.

By contrast, the more numerous closed-class forms are conceptually spare. They include: *-ed* 'occurring before the present moment'; *-s* 'multiple instantiation'; *-ø* 'unitary instantiation'; *the* 'speaker infers that the addressee can identify the referent'; *a* 'speaker infers that the addressee cannot identify the referent'; *-er* 'performer of the represented action'; noun status for *rustler* and *steer* 'thing'; verb status for *lasso* 'process'; subject status for *rustler* 'Agent'; and direct object status for *steer* 'affected Patient'. These seem to set most of the conceptual structure.

Shifting one class of forms while keeping the other class intact highlights their content/structure division of labor. A shift in all the closed-class forms – as in *Will the lassoers rustle a steer?* – restructures the conception, but leaves the cowboy-landscape content largely intact. By contrast, a shift in the open-class forms – as in *A machine stamped the envelopes* – changes content while leaving the structure intact.

The crucial conclusion is that the closed-class subsystem is perhaps the most fundamental conceptual structuring system of language. The fact that language may thus have a formally distinct subsystem dedicated to representing conceptual structure may give it a central role in the larger aim of examining conceptual structure across human cognition overall.

3 Schematic structure

The structuring of conception just outlined for language is also termed "schematic" in cognitive linguistics. When schematic structure pertains to the meaning of a single morpheme – as above for *across* – it is termed a "schema" in my own work and an "image-schema" in Lakoff's (e.g., 1987) work. Schematic structure extends further, though. At a first level, closed-class notions group into conceptual categories ("number" was an initial example), each with its own distinctive schematic structure. Such categories also largely share certain structural properties, such as the capacity for converting from one category member to another, the multiple nesting of such conversions, and a structural parallelism between objects in space and events in time. At a second level, these categories join in extensive "schematic systems" that structure major sectors of conception. Four of these schematic systems are outlined next.

3.1 Configurational structure

One schematic system, "configurational structure", comprehends all the respects in which closed-class schemas represent structure for space or time or other conceptual domains often in virtually geometric patterns (see Talmy 2000a: ch. 3, 2003, 2006; Herskovits 1986; article 5 [Semantics: Typology, Diachrony and Processing] (Pederson) *The expression of space*; article 13 [Semantics: Typology, Diachrony and Processing] (Landau) *Space in semantics and cognition*). It thus includes much that is within the schemas represented by spatial prepositions, by temporal conjunctions, and by tense and aspect markers, as well as by markers that otherwise interact with open-class forms with respect to object and event structure. This last type of schema is seen in the categories of "plexity" and "state of boundedness", treated next.

3.1.1 Plexity

The conceptual category of plexity pertains to a quantity's state of articulation into equivalent elements. Its two main member notions are "uniplexity" and "multiplexity". The novel term "plexity" was chosen to capture an underappreciated generalization present across the traditional categories of "number" for objects in space and "aspect" for events in time. In turn, uniplexity thus covers both the singular and the semelfactive, while multiplexity covers both plural and iterative. If an open-class form is intrinsically lexicalized for a uniplex referent, a closed-class form in construction with it can trigger a cognitive operation of "multiplexing" that copies its original solo referent onto various points of space or time. Thus, in English, the noun *bird* and the verb *(to) sigh* intrinsically have a uniplex referent. But this can be multiplexed by adding -s to the noun, as in *birds*, or by adding *keep -ing* to the verb, as in *keep sighing*. (True, English *keep* is open-class, but parallel forms in other languages are closed-class iterative forms.)

An operation of "unit excerpting" can perform the reverse conversion from multiplexity to uniplexity on an intrinsically multiplex open-class form. In English, this operation is performed only by grammatical complexes, as in going from *furniture* to *(a) piece of furniture* or from *breathe* to *take a breath*. But other languages have simplex forms. Thus, Yiddish goes from *groz* 'grass' to *(a) grezl* '(a) blade of grass'. And Russian goes from *čixat'* 'sneeze a multiplex number of times' to *čixnut'* 'sneeze once'.

3.1.2 State of boundedness

A second conceptual category is "state of boundedness", with two main member notions, "unboundedness" and "boundedness". An unbounded quantity is conceptualized as able to continue on indefinitely without intrinsic finiteness. A bounded quantity is conceptualized as an individuated unit entity with a boundary around it. As with plexity, these new terms are intended to capture the commonality across the space and time domains, and to generalize over such usually separate distinctions as mass and imperfective on the one hand, and count and perfective on the other. An English noun and verb lexicalized for a bounded referent are *lake* and *(to) dress*, as seen by their compatibility with *in*, as in: *We flew over a lake in 1 hour* and *I dressed in 8 minutes*. But *water* and *(to) sleep* express unbounded referents, as seen by their incompatibility with *in*, as in: **We flew over water in 1 hour. / *I slept in 8 hours*. But a closed-class form can trigger a cognitive operation of "bounding" or "portion excerpting" on these morphemes, as seen in: *We flew over some water in 1 hour. / I slept some.*

The reverse operation of "debounding" to convert a bounded referent into an unbounded one is also represented, at least for objects in space. Thus, the English count nouns *(a) shrub / panel* can take closed-class suffixes to yield the mass nominals *shrubbery / paneling*.

3.1.3 Configurational nesting

Schemas from all the schematic systems and the cognitive operations they trigger can be nested to form intricate structural patterns. Specifically, schemas from the plexity and boundedness categories of the configurational schematic system can nest in this way. Nesting can be illustrated first for events in time with the verb *(to) flash*. The basic uniplex status of this verb is seen in *The beacon flashed (once)*. This uniplex event can be multiplexed as in *The beacon kept flashing*. This can be bounded as in *The beacon flashed 5 times in a row*. This can then be treated as a new uniplexity and remultiplexed as in *The beacon kept flashing 5 times at a stretch*. And this can in turn be rebounded, as in *The beacon flashed 5 times at a stretch for 3 hours*.

A homologous set of structures can be represented for objects in space. This is seen in the following sequence of sentences:*I saw a duck. / I saw ducks. / I saw a group of 5 ducks. / I saw groups of 5 ducks each. / I saw 3 acres of groups of 5 ducks each*.

The progressively greater structural nesting common across these sentence-sets can be represented as follows:

(1) a. !
    b. ...!!!!!...
    c. [!!!!!]
    d. ... [!!!!!] – [!!!!!] ...
    e. [[!!!!!] – [!!!!!] ... [!!!!!] – [!!!!!]]

3.2 Perspective point

While the first schematic system, configurational structure, establishes the basic delineations by which a scene or event being referred to is structured, a second schematic system, "perspective point", directs one as to where to place one's "mental eyes" to look out at the structured scene or event (see Talmy 2000a: ch. 1). This perspectival system includes a number of conceptual categories, three of which are outlined next.

3.2.1 Perspectival location

One conceptual category, "perspectival location" is a perspective point's spatial or temporal positioning within a larger frame. The following two sentences are a spatial example: *The lunchroom door slowly opened and two men walked in. / Two men slowly opened the lunchroom door and walked in.* The first sentence induces the listener to locate her perspective point inside the room, whereas the second sentence is conducive to an external perspectival location (or perhaps to a non-specific one). How is this accomplished? The cognitive calculations at work appear to combine a rule of English with geometric knowledge. Though often breached, an apparent general rule in English is that if the initiator of an event is visible, it must be included in the clause expressing the event, but if not visible, it must be omitted. Thus, in the first sentence, no initiator of the door's opening is mentioned, hence none must have been visible. But the second clause indicates that the apparent initiator, the two men, moved from outside to inside the lunchroom. Assuming opaque walls and door, the only way that an entering initiator could not be visible to an observer during the door's opening is if that observer were located inside the lunchroom. In the second sentence, by contrast, the initiator is mentioned, hence must be visible. The only way a door-opening initiator who moves from the outside to the inside can be visible to an observational perspective point is if that perspective point is outside.

3.2.2 Perspectival distance and motive state

Two further conceptual categories here are "perspectival distance", with three main member notions: a perspective point's distal, medial, or proximal distance from a referent entity; and "perspectival motive state", with two main member notions: a perspective point's remaining stationary or moving along a path. Both can be illustrated at once by the following two sentences: *There are some houses in the valley. / There is a house every now and then through the valley.* Both sentences could refer to the exact same physical scene, and that circumstance will be assumed here. But the closed-class forms in the first sentence – the plural subject, the collective quantifier *some*, and the stationary preposition *in* – direct a listener to cognize the scene as if from a stationary distal perspective point with global scope of attention. By contrast, the closed-class forms of the second sentence – the singular subject, the distributive temporal phrase, and the motion preposition *through* – direct a listener to cognize the scene as if with a moving proximal perspective point with local scope of attention, that is, as if with a series of close-up views of successive houses.

3.2.3 Perspectival nesting

As with configurational nesting earlier, the perspectival schematic system also exhibits nesting. Its illustration here shows that perspective applies to time as well as to space as above, and introduces a further category, "direction of viewing". Consider the sentence *At the punchbowl, John was about to meet his first wife-to-be*. The expression *be about to* establishes a perspective point for the speaker shortly before John's encounter with a particular woman and a direction of viewing prospectively aimed toward that encounter. Next, the expression *(wife-)to-be* establishes a second prospective viewing that looks ahead to the time when the woman whom John encounters will be his wife. The originating point of this viewing can be taken either as the speaker's from the same earlier perspective point or as John's at the time of his encounter, nested within the speaker's earlier perspective. Then, triggered by the word *first*, a further prospective viewing, or family of viewings, points ahead to a subsequent wife or wives following John's marriage with the woman at the punchbowl. Finally, a perspective point of the speaker at the present moment of speech is established by the past tense of the main verb *was*. It is this perspective point at which the speaker's cumulative knowledge of the reported sequence of events is stored as memory and, in turn, which functions as the origin of a retrospective direction of viewing over the earlier sequence. The earlier perspective points are here nested within the scope of the viewing from the current perspective point.

3.3 Distribution of attention

A third schematic system, "distribution of attention", directs a listener's attention differentially over the structured scene from the established perspective point (see Talmy 2000a: ch. 4, 2007). Grammatical and other devices set up regions with different degrees of salience, arrange these regions into different patterns, and map these patterns in one or another way over the components of the structured scene. Several patterns are outlined here.

3.3.1 Focal attention

One attentional arrangement is a center-surround pattern with the center foregrounded as the focus and with the surround backgrounded. The grammatical relation of subject status can direct focal attention to the referent of the subject nominal, and alternative selections of subject can place the center of the pattern over different referents, even ones within the same event. Thus, focal attention can be mapped either onto the seller in a commercial transaction, with lesser attention on the remainder, as in *The clerk sold the vase to the customer*, or onto the buyer, with lesser attention on the new remainder, as in *The customer bought the vase from the clerk* (see Talmy 2000a: ch. 1).

For another realization of this pattern, Fillmore's (1976) term "frame" and Langacker's (1987) term "base" refer to a structured set of coentailed concepts in the attentional background. Their respective terms "highlighting" and "profiling" then refer to the foregrounding of the portion of the set that a morpheme refers to directly. A Husserl (1970) example can illustrate. The nouns *husband* and *wife* both presuppose the conception of a married couple in the background of attention, while each focuses attention on one or the other member of such a pair in the foreground.

3.3.2 Level of synthesis

In expressions referring to the same scene, different grammatical forms can direct greater attention to either of two main "levels of synthesis" or of granularity, the Gestalt level or the componential level. Thus, the head status of *pyramid* in the sentence *The pyramid of bricks came crashing down*, raises its salience over that of *bricks* with its dependent status. More attention is at the Gestalt level of the whole pyramid, conceptually tracking its overall movement. But the dependency relations are reversed in the sentence *The bricks in the pyramid came crashing down*. Here, more attention is at the componential level of the constituent bricks, tracking their multiple movements (see Talmy 2000a: ch. 1).

3.3.3 Window of attention

A third pattern is the "window of attention". Here, one or more (discontinuous) portions of a referent scene are foregrounded in attention (or "windowed") by the basic device of their explicit mention, while the remainder of the scene is backgrounded in attention (or "gapped") by their omission from mention. To illustrate, the sentence *The pen kept rolling off the uneven table* conveys the conception of an iterating cycle in which a pen progresses through the phases of lying on a table, falling down, lying on the ground, and being placed back on the table. But the overt linguistic material refers only to the departure phase of the pen's cyclic path. Accordingly, only this portion of the total referent is foregrounded in attention, while the remainder of the cycle is relatively backgrounded. With enough context, the alternative sentence *I kept placing the pen back on the uneven table* could refer to the same cycle. But here, the presence of overt material referring to the return phase of that cycle foregrounds that phase in attention, while now the departure phase is backgrounded (see Talmy 2000a: ch. 4).

3.3.4 Attentional nesting

Nesting was shown for configuration and for perspective, and it can also be seen in the schematic system of attention. It appears in the second of the following two sentences: *The customer bought a vase. / The customer was sold a vase.* In the second sentence, focal attention is first directed to the seller by the lexical choice of *sell* but is then redirected to the buyer by the passive voice. If this redirection of attention were total, then the second sentence would be semantically indistinguishable from the first sentence, but in fact it is not. Rather, the redirection of attention is only partial: it leaves intact the foregrounding of the seller's active intentional role, but it shifts the main focus onto the buyer as target. Altogether, then, it can be said that attention on the seller is hierarchically embedded within a more dominant attention on the buyer.

4 Conceptual organization

In addition to schematic systems, language has many other forms of extensive and integrated conceptual organization, such as the three presented next. Although Figure/Ground organization and factive/fictive organization could be respectively comprehended under the attentional and the configurational schematic systems, and force dynamic organization has elsewhere been treated as a fourth schematic system, these are all extensive enough and cut across enough distinctions to be presented here as separate bodies of conceptual organization.

4.1 Figure/ground organization

In representing many spatial, temporal, equational, and other situations, language is so organized as to single out two portions of the situation, the "Figure" and the "Ground", and to relate the former to the latter (see Talmy 2000a: ch. 5). In particular, the Figure is a conceptually movable entity; its location or path is conceived as a variable whose particular value is at issue. The Ground is a reference entity with a stationary setting relative to a reference frame; the Figure's variable is characterized with respect to it.

For a spatial example, consider the sentence *The bike is near the house*. The bike functions as Figure as a movable object whose location is characterized in terms of the house's location. The stationary house, set within the implicit reference frame of the neighborhood, etc., correspondingly functions as Ground. The presence of these Figure / Ground functions is demonstrated by the fact that the sentence with the nominals reversed – *The house is near the bike*– in which the house is now the Figure and the bike is the Ground, clearly has a different meaning and is odd to boot. Since the 'near' concept is symmetrical, the meaning difference must be attributed to something like the reversed Figure / Ground roles. Since prototypically a house is not conceptually movable and a bike is not a fixed reference point, these new role assignments clash with our background knowledge and the sentence is flagged as different and odd.

The temporal form of Figure / Ground roles can be seen in two events represented by the clauses of a complex sentence. Thus, in the sentence *He exploded after he touched the button*, the button-touching event, occurring earlier in time, functions as a Ground with its presumptively known location on the time line, while the explosion event functions as a Figure, getting localized on the time line with respect to the button-touching event. As before, these Figure / Ground roles are reversed in the otherwise synonymous sentence *He touched the button before he exploded*. And as before, these new role assignments clash with the prototypical bases for characterizing such temporal locations and so again flag the sentence as semantically different and unusual.

4.2 Factive/fictive organization

At least in language and visual perception (see Talmy 2000a: ch. 2), a pervasive cognitive pattern can be posited in which two different cognitive subsystems in an individual form discrepant representations of the same entity. Further, a third subsystem in the individual assesses one of those representations as more veridical, or "factive", and the other as less veridical, or "fictive". In particular, language abounds in "fictive motion", in which a factively stationary situation is represented in terms of motion. Of the many categories of fictive motion, two are outlined next.

4.2.1 Coextension paths

The category of fictive motion previously most noticed, "coextention paths", depicts the form, orientation, or location of a spatially extended object in terms of a path over the object's extent. An example is the sentence *The fence zigzags from the plateau down into the valley*. Here, one cognitive subsystem in a listener has the world knowledge that the fence is stationary. But another subsystem responds to the literal wording – specifically, the motion words *zigzag, from, down*, and *into* – to evoke a sense of motion along the linear extent of the fence that serves to characterize the fence's contour and positioning. A parallel sentence *The fence zigzags from the valley up onto the plateau*, evokes a sense of motion in the opposite direction. These two sentences together show how a concept – here, that of a sense of directed motion – can be imposed on or imputed to concepts of phenomena in the world through linguistic devices (see 5.1). By contrast, the factive stationariness of the fence might be represented, if poorly, by a sentence like *The fence stands in a zigzag pattern at an angle between the plateau and the valley*.

4.2.2 Emanation paths

Another category of fictive motion, "emanation paths", involves the fictive conceptualization of an intangible line emerging from a source object, passing in a straight line through space, and terminating on a target object, where factively nothing is in motion. In one subtype, "demonstrative paths", a directed line emerges from the pointed front of a source object. This is seen in *The arrow points toward / past / away from the town*.

In the "radiation paths" subtype, a beam of radiation emanates from a radiant object and terminates on an irradiated object. This is seen in *Light shone from the sun into the cave*. It might be claimed that photons do factively emanate from a radiant object, so that fictive motion need not be invoked. However, we do not see photons, so any representation of motion is cognitively imputed. In any case, in a related subtype, "shadow paths", none will claim the existence of "shadowons", and yet once again fictive motion is seen in a sentence like *The pole threw its shadow on the wall*.

Finally, a "sensory path" is represented as moving from the experiencer to the experienced object in a sentence like *I looked into / past / away from the tunnel*. Such an emanating "line of sight" can also be represented as moving laterally. Both these forms of fictivity – first lateral, then axial – are represented in *I slowly looked down into the well*.

One question for this fictive category, though, is what determines the direction of the intangible emanation. Logically, since motion is imagined, it should be possible to conceptualize a reversed path. Attempts at representing such reversed paths appear in sentences like **Light shone from my hand onto the sun*, or **The *shadow jumped from the wall onto the pole*, or **I looked from that distant mountain into my eyes*. But such formulations do not exist in any language that represents such events fictively. Rather, an "active-determinative" principle appears to govern the direction of emanation. Of the two objects, the more active or determinative one is conceptualized as the source. Thus, relative to my hand, the sun is brighter, hence, more active, and must be treated as the source of radiative emanation. My agency in looking is more active than the inanimate perceived object, so I am treated as the source of sensory emanation. And the pole is more determinative – I can move the pole and the shadow will also move, but I cannot perform the opposite operation of moving the shadow and getting the pole to move – so the pole is treated as the source of shadow emanation.

4.3 Force dynamics

Language has an extensive conceptual system of "force dynamics" for representing the patterns in which one entity, the "Agonist", has force exerted on it by another entity, the "Antagonist" (see Talmy 2000a: ch. 7). It covers such concepts as an Agonist's natural tendency toward action or rest, an Antagonist's opposition to such a tendency, the Agonist's resistance to this opposition, and the Antagonist's overcoming of such resistance. It includes the concepts of causing and letting, helping and hindering, and blockage and the removal of blockage. It generalizes over the causative concepts of traditional linguistics, placing them naturally within a matrix of finer distinctions. It also cuts across conceptual domains, from the physical, to the psychological, to the social, as illustrated next.

4.3.1 The physical domain

A contrast between two sentences can illustrate the physical domain. The sentence *The ball rolled along the green* represents motion in a force-dynamically neutral way. But *The ball kept rolling along the green* adds force dynamics to the otherwise same spatial movement. In fact, it has readings for two different force dynamic patterns. Interpreted under the "extended causing of motion" pattern, the ball as Agonist has a natural tendency toward rest but is being overcome by a stronger Antagonist such as the wind. Alternatively, interpreted under one of the "despite" patterns, the ball as Agonist has a natural tendency toward motion and is overcoming a weaker Antagonist such as stiff grass – that is, it moves along despite opposition from the grass.

4.3.2 The psychological domain

An individual's psyche can be conceptualized and linguistically represented as a "divided self" in which two different components are in force dynamic opposition. To illustrate, the sentence *I didn't respond* is force dynamically neutral. But the sentence *I refrained from responding*, though it still represents a lack of response, now adds in the force dynamic pattern "extended causing of rest". Specifically, a more central part of me, the Agonist, has a tendency toward responding, while a more peripheral part of me, the Antagonist, opposes this tendency, is stronger, and so blocks a response. The two opposing parts are explicitly represented in the corresponding sentence *I held myself back from responding*.

4.3.3 The social domain

Much as the closed-class category of prepositions is largely associated with a specific semantic category, that of paths or sites in relation to a Ground object, so the closed-class category of modals is largely associated with the semantic category of force dynamics – in particular, with its social application. Here, certain interpersonal interactions, mediated solely through communication, can be metaphorically represented in terms of force or pressure exerted by one individual or group on another.

For example, *must*, as in *You must go to school*, represents one of the "causing" force dynamic patterns between individuals. It sets the subject up as an Agonist whose desire – taken as a kind of tendency – is to do the opposite of the predicate's referent. And it sets up an implicit Antagonist – for example, I, your mother, people at large – that exerts psychological pressure on the Agonist toward performance of the undesired action.

The modal *may*, as in *You may go to the playground*, instead represents a "letting" force dynamic pattern. Here, the subject as Agonist has a desire or tendency toward the stated action that could have been blocked by an implicit stronger Antagonist, but this potential blockage is withheld.

5 Interactions among semantic structures

The preceding discussion has mostly dealt with conceptual structures each in its own terms. But a major aspect of language organization is that conceptual structures, from small to large, can also interact with each other in accordance with certain principles. Such interactions are grouped together below under four extensive categories.

5.1 Conceptual imposition

A widespread view about the contents and structures of cognition is that they ultimately derive from real properties of external phenomena, through processes of perception and abstraction, in what John Searle has called the "world-to-mind direction of fit". While acknowledging such processes, cognitive linguistics calls attention instead to intrinsic content and structure in cognition – presumably mainly of innate origin – and to how extensive they are. Such native cognitive properties certainly apply to the general functioning of cognition. But they also apply in many forms of "conceptual imposition" – the imputation of certain contents and structures to our conceptions and perceptions of the world in a "mind-to-world direction of fit". Several realizations of such conceptual imposition are outlined next.

5.1.1 The imputation of content or structure

An initial non-linguistic example of autochthonous cognition is "affect". Emotions such as anger or affection are experienced either as such or as applied to outside entities. But it is difficult to see how such feelings could arise from a process of abstraction from the external world. Linguistic examples of course abound. Fictive motion offers some immediately striking ones, such as the "shadow path" in *The pole threw its shadow onto the wall*. As described in 4.2.2, the literal wording here depicts a movement from pole to wall that is not overtly perceived as occurring "out there". That is, at least the language-related portion of our cognition imposes the conceptualization of motion onto what would be perceived as static.

Actually, though, virtually all the semantic structures described so far are forms of conceptual imposition. Thus, in the scene represented by the sentence *The post office is near the bank*, based on the discussion in 4.1, it could hardly be claimed that the post office is inherently Figure-like and the bank Ground-like, beyond our cognitive imputation of those roles to those objects. And houses dispersed over a valley, as described in 3.2.2, could scarcely possess an associated moving or stationary perspective point from which they are viewed, apart from the linguistic forms that ascribe such perspective to the represented scene.

5.1.2 Alternatives of conceptualization

A consequence of the fact that a particular structural or contentful conception can be imputed to a phenomenon is that a range of alternative conceptions could also be imputed to it. These are alternatives of what my work has termed the "conceptualization" and Langacker's has termed the "construal" of a phenomenon. For example, as seen in 4.2.1, the fictive motion that could be imputed to a fence along one coextension path, as in *The fence goes from the plateau down into the valley* could also be imputed to it along the reverse path, as in *The fence goes from the valley up onto the plateau.*

Or consider the deictics *this* and *that*, which establish a conceptual boundary in space and depict an indicated object as being respectively either on the speaker's side of the boundary or on the side opposite the speaker. Then, referring to the exact same bicycle standing, say, some 8 feet away, a speaker could opt to say either *This bike is in my way*, or *That bike is in my way*. The speaker can thus impose alternatives of conceptualization on the scene, imputing a conceptual boundary either between himself and the bike or on the other side of the bike.

5.1.3 Embodiment

The notion of "embodiment" extends the idea of conceptual imposition. It assumes that such imposed concepts are largely based on experiences humans have of their bodies interacting with environments or on psychological or neural structure. It proposes that such experiences are imputed to, or form the basis of, our understanding of most phenomena (Lakoff & Johnson 1999). In my view, though, the linguistic literature has largely applied the blanket term "embodiment" to a range of insufficiently distinguished ideas that differ in their validity. Four such distinct ideas of embodiment in current use are outlined here.

First, in what might be called the "bulk encounter" idea of embodiment, phenomena are grouped and categorized in terms of the way in which our bodies – with their particular shape and mesoscopic size – can interact with them. But this idea is either incorrect or limited. For example, many languages have closed-class representation for a linear configuration, as English does with the preposition *along*. This preposition applies to a Ground object schematizable as linear. But due to magnitude neutrality (see 1.2), this schema can be applied to objects of quite different sizes, as in *The ant climbed up along the matchstick*, and *The squirrel climbed up along the tree trunk*. Yet, although the *along* schema can group a matchstick and a tree trunk together, we bodily interact with those objects in quite different ways. Accordingly, the bulk encounter idea of embodiment does not account for this and perhaps much else in the structure of linguistically represented conception.

Second, in what could be called the "neural infrastructure" idea of embodiment, it is the organization and operation of our neural structure that determines how we conceptualize phenomena. Thus, the linear schematization just cited might arise from neurally based processes of visual perception that function to abstract out just such one-dimensional contours. Comparably, the concept evoked on hearing a word such as *bicycle* or *coffee* might arise from the reactivation of the visual, motor, and olfactory areas that were previously active during interaction with those objects, in the manner of Damasio's "convergence zones". The problem with this idea of embodiment is that, although generally correct, it is simply subsumed by psychology and needs no separate statement of its own.

Third, in what could be called the "concreteness as basic" idea of embodiment, the view is that experience with the tangible world is developmentally earlier and provides the basis for later conceptions of intangible phenomena, much as in Piagetian theory. A commonly cited example is concepts of time based on those of space. Another is the conception of purpose based on that of destination, that is, one's destination in a physical journey in what Lakoff (1992) terms the "event structure metaphor". While something of this directional bias is evident in metaphoric mapping (see below), it is not clear that it correctly characterizes cognitive organization. On the contrary, we may well have an innate cognitive system dedicated to temporal processing – perhaps already evident very early – that includes perception of and control over duration; starting, continuing, and stopping; interrupting and resuming; repeating; waiting; and speeding up and slowing down. We may likewise have an innate cognitive system for intention or purpose. In any case, "purpose" cannot be derived from "destination". After all, the concept that a person moving from point X to point Y has Y as a "destination" already includes a component of purpose. When such a component is lacking, we do not say that a person has point Y as her destination but rather that her motion simply "stops" at that point. Accordingly, the notion of purpose present in the concept of "destination" could not derive from perceptions of concrete motion patterns, but might originate in an innate cognitive system for the enactment and conception of intention or purpose.

In a fourth and final type here, what can be called the "anti-objectivism" idea of embodiment faults the view that there exists an autonomous truth, uniform and pervasive, in such realms as logic and mathematics that the human mind taps into for its understandings and activities in those realms. Rather, we deal with such realms by imputing or mapping onto them various of our conceptual schemas, motor programs, or other cognitive structures. On this view, we do much of our thinking and reasoning in terms of such experientially derived structures. For example, our sense of the meaning of the word *angle* is not derived from some independent ideal mathematical realm, but is rather built up from our experience, e.g., from perceptions of a static forking branch, from moving two sticks axially until their ends touch, or from rotating one stick while its end touches that of another. This view of how we think may be largely correct. But if applied too broadly, it might obscure the possible existence of an actual cognitive system for objectivity and reason. Such a system might have the capacity to check for coherence across concepts, for global consistency across conceptual and cognitive domains, and for consistency across inferences and reasoning, – whether or not the assessed components themselves arose through otherwise embodied processes – and it might be the source of the very conception of an objective domain.

5.2 Cognitive recruitment

I propose the term "recruitment" for a pervasive cognitive process in which a cognitive configuration with a certain original function or conceptual content gets used to perform another function or to represent some other concept. That is, the basic function or concept is appropriated or co-opted in the service of manifesting another one.

Such recruitment would certainly cover all tropes, including fictivity and metaphor. Thus, in a coextension path example of fictive motion like *The fence goes from the plateau to the valley* (see 4.2.1), the morphemes *go, from,* and *to* originally and basically refer to motion, but this reference is conscripted in the service of representing a stationary configuration.

And metaphor can also be understood in terms of recruitment. In cognitive linguistics, metaphor has been mainly studied not for its salient poetic form familiar from literature but – under the term "conceptual metaphor" – for its largely unconscious pervasive structuring of everyday expression (see e.g., Lakoff 1992; article 11 [Semantics: Lexical Structures and Adjectives] (Tyler & Takahashi) *Metaphors and metonymies*). In the basic analysis, certain structural elements of a conceptual "source domain" are mapped onto the content of a conceptual "target domain". But in our present terms, it can also be said that the conceptual structures and morphemic meanings original to the source domain are recruited for use as structures and meanings within the target domain. The directionality of the mapping – based on the "concrete as basic" view of embodiment (see 5.1.3) – is typically from a more concrete domain grounded in bodily experience to a more abstract domain. Thus, the more palpable domain of space is systematically mapped onto the more abstract domain of time in such everyday expressions as *Christmas is ahead / near / almost here / upon us / past.*

Recruitment can be seen as well in the appropriation of one type of construction to serve as another type. For example, the English question construction with certain modals can serve as a request, as in *Could you pass me the salt?*. Fictivity terminology could be extended to label the host construction here as a fictive question, and the parasitic construction as a factive request. Or it could be said that a request construction has recruited a question construction.

Finally, to illustrate functional recruitment, repair mechanisms in discourse, in their basic function, comprise a variety of devices that a speaker uses to remedy hitches that arise in the production of an utterance. Talmy (2000b: ch. 6) cites a recorded example of a young woman rejecting a suitor in which she uses an inordinate density of repair mechanisms, including false starts, interruptions, corrections, and repetitions. But it is evident that these originally corrective devices have been co-opted to perform a different function: to manifest embarrassed concern for the addressee's sensitive feelings. And, built in turn upon that function is the further function of the speaker's signaling to the addressee that she did have his feelings in mind.

5.3 Semantic conflict resolution

A conflict or incompatibility often exists between the references of two constituents in a sentence, or between the reference of a constituent and the context or one's general knowledge (see Talmy 2000b: ch. 5). The treatment of such semantic conflict thus complements treatments of semantic "unification" in which the referents of constituents integrate unproblematically. A hearer of a conflict generally applies one out of a set of resolutions to it. These include shifts, blends, juxtapositions, and juggling. Of these, the first two are characterized next.

5.3.1 Shifts

In the type of resolution Talmy (1977) termed a "shift" – now largely called "coercion" after Pustejovsky (1993) – the reference of one of the two conflicting forms changes so as to accord with the reference of the other form. A shift can involve the cancellation, stretching, or replacement of a semantic feature. Each of these three types of shifts is illustrated next.

The *across* schema cited in 2.2 can illustrate component cancellation. This schema prototypically involves a horizontal path on a bounded plane from one edge perpendicularly to its opposite. But the path's termination on the distal edge can be canceled, as in a sentence like *The shopping cart rolled across the boulevard and was hit by an oncoming car*. Here, the English preposition is not blocked from usage, or replaced by some preposition referring to partial planar traversal, but continues on with one of its semantic components missing. In fact, the preposition can continue in usage even with both of the path's edge contacts canceled, as seen in *The tumbleweed rolled across the desert for an hour*.

The *across* schema can also illustrate component stretching. A prototypical constraint on this schema, not mentioned earlier, is that the main axis of the plane, which is perpendicular to the path, may be longer than the path or of the same length, but cannot be shorter. Accordingly, I can swim "across" a square swimming pool from one edge to the other, or "across" a canal from one bank to the other, but if my path parallels a canal's banks, I am not swimming "across" the canal but "along" it. But what if I am at an oblong pool and swim from one of the narrow edges to its opposite? In referring to this situation, the acceptability of the sentence *I swam across the pool* is great where the pool is only slightly longer than a square shape, and decreases as its relative length increases. The *across* schema thus permits the path length within the relative-axis constraint to be stretched moderately but not too far.

Finally, component replacement can be seen in a sentence like *She is somewhat pregnant*. Here, the gradient specification of *somewhat* conflicts with the basic all-or-none specification of *pregnant*. A hearer might resolve this conflict through the mechanism of juxtaposition, to yield the "incongruity effect" of humor. If not, though, the hearer can shift *pregnant* into accord with *somewhat* by replacing its 'all-or-none' component with that of 'gradience'. Then the overall meaning of *pregnant* shifts as well from involving the presence or absence of a fetus to involving the length of gestation.

5.3.2 Blends

An incompatibility between two sets of specifications in a sentence can also be resolved as a "blend", in which a hearer generates an often imaginative conceptual hybrid that accommodates both of the original conceptual inputs in some novel relation to each other. Talmy (1977) distinguished two types of blends, superimposition and introjection, and illustrated the former with the sentence *My sister wafted through the party*. The conflict here is between *waft* suggesting something like a leaf moving gently in an irregular pattern through the air, and the rest of the sentence suggesting a person (moving) through a group of other people. In myself, this sentence evokes the blended conceptualization of my sister wandering aimlessly through the party, somewhat unconscious of the events around her, and of the party somehow suffused with a slight rushing sound of air.

Fauconnier & Turner (2002) have greatly elaborated on this process, also terming it a "blend" or a "conceptual integration". In their terms, two separate mental spaces (see below) can map elements of their content and structure into a third mental space that constitutes a blend of the two inputs, with potentially novel structure. Thus, in referring to a modern catamaran reenacting a century-old voyage by an early clipper, a speaker can say *At this point, the catamaran is barely maintaining a 4 day lead over the clipper*. The speaker here conceptually superimposes the two treks and generates the apparency of a race.

5.4 Semantic interrelations

In the preceding three subsections, semantic structures have in effect "acted on" each other to yield a novel conceptual derivative. But semantic elements and structures can also simply relate to each other in particular patterns. Four such patterns are outlined next.

5.4.1 Within one sense of a morpheme

Several bodies of research within cognitive linguistics address the structured relations among the semantic components of the meaning of a morpheme in one of its polysemous senses. Two of these are "frame semantics" and "prototype theory", outlined next.

Fillmore's (e.g., 1976) Frame Semantics (see article 3 [this volume] (Gawron) *Frame Semantics*) shows that the meaning of a morpheme does not simply consist of a central concept – the main concern of a speaker in using the morpheme – but extends out indefinitely with ever further conceptual associations that bear particular relations to each other and to the central concept. In fact, several different morphemes can share roughly the same extended frame while foregrounding different portions in the center. Thus, such "commercial frame" verbs as *sell, buy, spend, charge,* and *cost* all share in their frames a seller, a buyer, money, and goods, as well as the transfer of money from the buyer to the seller and, in return for that, the transfer of the goods from the seller to the buyer. Each of these concepts in turn rests on a further conceptual infrastructure. For example, the 'money' concept rests on notions of governmental minting and socially agreed value, while the 'in return for' concept rests on notions of reciprocity and equity.

In Lakoff's (1987) prototype theory (see article 2 [this volume] (Taylor) *Prototype theory*), a morpheme's meaning can generally be viewed as a category whose members differ in privilege, whose properties can vary in number and strength, and whose boundary can vary in scope. In its most prototypical usage, then, the morpheme refers to the most privileged category member, assigns the fullest set of its properties at their greatest strength to that member, and tightens its boundary to enclose the smallest scope. For an example from Fillmore (1976), the meaning of *breakfast* – in its most prototypical usage – consists of eating certain foods, namely, eggs, bacon, toast, coffee, orange juice, and the like, at a certain time of day, namely, in the morning. But the meaning can be extended to less prototypical values, for example, either to different foods – *The Joneses eat liver and onions for breakfast* – or to different times of the day – *Breakfast is served all day*.

5.4.2 Across different senses of a morpheme

Brugman (1981) was the first to show that for a polysemous morpheme, one sense can function as the prototype to which the other senses are progressively linked by conceptual increments within a "radial category". Thus, for the preposition *over*, the prototype sense may be 'horizontal motion above an object' as in *The bird flew over the hill*. But linked to this by "endpoint focus" is the sense in *Sam lives over the hill*.

5.4.3 Relations from within a morpheme to across a sentence

The "Motion typology" of Talmy (2000b: ch. 1) proposes a universal semantic framework for an event of motion or location. This consists of four components in the main event proper – the moving or stationary "Figure", its state of "Motion" (moving or being located), its "Path" (path or site), and the "Ground" that serves as its reference point – plus an outside "Co-event" typically of Manner or of Cause. Languages differ typologically as to which of these components they characteristically include within the verb of a sentence, and which they locate elsewhere in the sentence. And these two sets of allocations are correlated.

Thus, a "verb-framed" language like Spanish characteristically places the components of Motion and Path together in the verb, and so has an extensive series of "path verbs" with meanings like 'enter', 'exit', 'ascend', 'descend', 'cross', 'pass', and 'return'. In correlation with this lexicalization pattern for the verb, the language has a ready colloquial construction for representing the Co-event – typically a gerund form that can appear right after the path verb. For example, 'I ran into the cave' might be expressed as *Entré corriendo a la cueva* – literally, "I entered running to the cave".

By contrast, a "satellite-framed" language like English characteristically places the components of Motion and Co-event together in the verb, and so has a series of "Manner verbs" like *run, limp, scuttle* and *speed*. In correlation with this lexicalization pattern for the verb, the language also has an extensive series of "path satellites" – e.g., *in, out, up, down, past, across* and *back* – as well as a partially overlapping set of path prepositions, together with the syntactic construction for their inclusion after the verb. The English sentence corresponding to the preceding Spanish one is thus: *I ran into the cave*.

This correlation within a language between a verb's lexicalization pattern and the rest of the syntax in a motion sentence can be put into relief by noting minimally occurring patterns (see Slobin 1996). Thus, Spanish does not have a path satellite category or an extensive set of path prepositions, and in fact can largely not use the prepositions it does have to represent a path. For instance, it could not do so for the cave example. For its part, English does not have a colloquial gerund construction for use with its few path verbs (which in any case are mostly borrowed from Romance languages, where they are native). Thus, a sentence like *I entered the cave running* is fully awkward.

5.4.4 Across a sentence

Fauconnier (1985) shows how different portions of a sentence can set up distinct "mental spaces" with particular relations to each other. Each such space is a relatively self-contained conceptual domain with its component elements in a particular arrangement; two spaces can share many of the same elements; and a mapping can be established between corresponding elements. The mapping is directional, going from a "base" space – a conceptual domain generally factual for the speaker – to a "subordinate" space that can be counterfactual, representational, at a different time, etc. Thus, in *Max thinks Harry's name is Joe*, the speaker's base space includes 'Max' and 'Harry' as elements; the word *thinks* sets up a subordinate space for a portion of Max's belief system; and this contains an element 'Joe' that corresponds to 'Harry'.

6 Conclusion

In this survey, the field of cognitive linguistics in general and of Cognitive Semantics in particular is seen to have as its central concern the representation of conceptual structure in language. The field addresses properties of conceptual structure both local and global, both autonomous and interactive, and both typological and universal. And it relates these linguistic properties to more general properties of cognition. While much has already been done in this relatively young linguistic tradition, it remains quite dynamic and is extending its explorations in a number of new directions.

7 References

Brugman, Claudia 1981. *The Story of 'Over'*. MA thesis. University of California, Berkeley, CA.
Fauconnier, Gilles 1985. *Mental Spaces. Aspects of Meaning Construction in Natural Language*. Cambridge, MA: The MIT Press.
Fauconnier, Gilles & Mark Turner 2002. *The Way We Think. Conceptual Blending and the Mind's Hidden Complexities*. New York: Basic Books.
Fillmore, Charles 1975. An alternative to checklist theories of meaning. In: C. Cogen, et al. (eds.). *Proceedings of the First Annual Meeting of the Berkeley Linguistics Society (= BLS)*. Berkeley, CA: Berkeley Linguistics Society, 155–159.
Fillmore, Charles 1976. Frame semantics and the nature of language. *Annals of the New York Academy of Sciences* 280, 20–32.
Geeraerts, Dirk & Hubert Cuyckens (eds.) 2007. *The Oxford Handbook of Cognitive Linguistics*. Oxford: Oxford University Press.
Givón, Talmy 1989. *Mind, Code, and Context. Essays in Pragmatics*. Hillsdale, NJ: Erlbaum.
Herskovits, Annette 1986. *Language and Spatial Cognition. An Interdisciplinary Study of the Prepositions in English*. Cambridge: Cambridge University Press.
Husserl, Edmund 1900-01/1970. *Logische Untersuchungen*. 2nd edn. Halle/Saale: Niemeyer. English translation in: J. N. Findlay. *Logical Investigations, vol. 2*. London: Routledge & Kegan Paul, 1970.
Lakoff, George 1987. *Women, Fire, and Dangerous Things. What Categories Reveal about the Mind*. Chicago, IL: The University of Chicago Press.
Lakoff, George 1992. The contemporary theory of metaphor. In: A. Ortony (ed.). *Metaphor and Thought*. 2nd edn. Cambridge: Cambridge University Press. 1st edn. 1979.
Lakoff, George & Mark Johnson 1999. *Philosophy in the Flesh. The Embodied Mind and its Challenge to Western Thought*. New York: Basic Books.
Langacker, Ronald 1987. *Foundations of Cognitive Grammar, vol. 1. Theoretical Prerequisites*. Stanford, CA: Stanford University Press.
Langacker, Ronald 1991. *Foundations of Cognitive Grammar, vol. 2. Descriptive Application*. Stanford, CA: Stanford University Press.
Lappin, Shalom (ed.) 1997. *The Handbook of Contemporary Semantic Theory*. Oxford: Blackwell.
Neely, James H. 1991. Semantic priming effects in visual word recognition. A selective review of current findings and theories. In: D. Besner & G. W. Humphreys (eds.). *Basic Processes in Reading. Visual Word Recognition*. Hillsdale, NJ: Erlbaum, 264–336.
Pustejovsky, James 1995. Linguistic constraints on type coercion. In: P. Saint-Dizier & E. Viegas (eds.). *Computational Lexical Semantics*. Cambridge: Cambridge University Press, 71–97.
Slobin, Dan 1996. Two ways to travel. Verbs of motion in English and Spanish. In: M. Shibatani & S. Thompson (eds.). *Grammatical Constructions. Their Form and Meaning*. Oxford: Clarendon Press, 195–219.
Talmy, Leonard 1977. Rubber-sheet cognition in language. In: W. Beach, S. Fox & S. Philosoph (eds.). *Papers from the Thirteenth Regional Meeting of the Chicago Linguistic Society (= CLS)*. Chicago, IL: Chicago Linguistic Society, 612–628.
Talmy, Leonard 2000a. *Toward a Cognitive Semantics, vol. 1. Concept Structuring Systems*. Cambridge, MA: The MIT Press.
Talmy, Leonard 2000b. *Toward a Cognitive Semantics, vol. 2. Typology and Process in Concept Structuring*. Cambridge, MA: The MIT Press.

Talmy, Leonard 2003. The representation of spatial structure in spoken and signed language. In: K. Emmorey (ed.). *Perspectives on Classifier Constructions in Sign Language*. Mahwah, NJ: Erlbaum, 169–195.
Talmy, Leonard 2006. The fundamental system of spatial schemas in language. In: B. Hampe (ed.). *From Perception to Meaning. Image Schemas in Cognitive Linguistics*. Berlin: Mouton de Gruyter, 199–234.
Talmy, Leonard 2007. Attention phenomena. In: D. Geeraerts & H. Cuyckens (eds.). *The Oxford Handbook of Cognitive Linguistics*. Oxford: Oxford University Press, 264–293.

John R. Taylor
2 Prototype theory

1   Introduction —— 29
2   Prototype effects —— 32
3   Prototypes and the basic level —— 35
4   The cultural context of categories —— 38
5   Prototypes and categories —— 40
6   Objections to prototypes —— 45
7   Words and the world —— 47
8   Prototypes and polysemy —— 49
9   References —— 52

Abstract: According to a long-established theory, categories are defined in terms of a set of features. Entities belong in the category if, and only if, they exhibit each of the defining features. The theory is problematic for a number of reasons. Many of the categories which are lexicalized in language are incompatible with this kind of definition, in that category members do not necessarily share the set of defining features. Moreover, the theory is unable to account for prototype effects, that is, speakers' judgements that some entities are 'better' examples of a category than others. These findings led to the development of prototype theory, whereby a category is structured around its good examples. This article reviews the relevant empirical findings and discusses a number of different ways in which prototype categories can be theorized, with particular reference to the functional basis of categories and their role in broader conceptual structures. The article concludes with a discussion of how the notion of prototype category has been extended to handle polysemy, where the various senses of a word can be structured around, and can be derived from, a more central, prototypical sense.

1 Introduction

In everyday discourse, the term 'prototype' refers to an engineer's model which, after testing and possible improvement, may then go into mass production.

In linguistics and in cognitive science more generally, the term has acquired a specialized sense, although the idea of a basic unit, from which other examples

---

John R. Taylor, Dunedin, New Zealand

https://doi.org/10.1515/9783110589245-002

can be derived, may still be discerned. The term, namely, refers to the best, most typical, or most central member of category. Things belong in the category in virtue of their sharing of commonalities with the prototype. Prototype theory refers to this view on the nature of categories.

This article examines the role of prototypes in semantics, especially in lexical semantics. To the extent that words can be said to be names of categories, prototype theory becomes a theory of word meaning.

Prototype theory contrasts with the so-called classical, or Aristotelian theory of categorization (Lakoff 1982, 1987; Taylor 2003a). According to the classical theory, a category is defined in terms of a set of properties, or features, and an entity is a member of the category if it exhibits each of the features. Each of the features is necessary, jointly they are sufficient. The classical theory captures the 'essence' of a category in contrast to the 'accidental' properties of category members. The theory entails that categories have clear-cut boundaries and that all members, in their status as category members, have equal status within the category.

An example which is often cited to illustrate the classical theory is the category 'bachelor', defined in terms of the features [+human], [+adult], [+male], and [−married]. Any entity which exhibits each of the four defining features is, by definition, a member of the category and thus can bear the designation *bachelor*. Something which exhibits only three or fewer of the features is not a member. In their status as bachelors, all members of the category are equal (though they may, of course, differ with respect to non-essential, accidental features, such as their height, wealth, and such like).

The classical theory is attractive for a number of reasons. First, the theory neatly accounts for the relation of entailment. If X is a bachelor, then necessarily X is unmarried, because 'unmarried' is a property already contained in the definition of *bachelor*. Second, the theory explains why some expressions are contradictions. In *married bachelor*, or *This bachelor is married*, the property designated by *married* conflicts with a definitional feature of *bachelor*. Third, the theory accounts for the distinction between analytic and synthetic statements. *This bachelor is a man* is synthetic; it is necessarily true in virtue of the definitions of the words. *This man is a bachelor* is analytic; its truth is contingent on the facts of the matter. The theory also goes some way towards explaining concept combination. *A rich bachelor* refers to an entity which exhibits the features of *bachelor* plus the features of *rich*.

In spite of these obvious attractions, there are many problems associated with the classical theory. First, the theory is unable to account for the well-documented prototype effects, to be discussed in section 2. Another problem is that the theory says nothing about the function of categories. Organisms categorize in order to manage the myriad impressions of the environment. If something looks like an X, then it may well be an X, and we should behave towards it as we would towards other Xs. The classical theory is unable to accommodate this everyday kind of inferencing. According to the classical theory, the only way to ascertain whether something is an X is to check it out for each of the defining features of X. Having done that, there is nothing further to say about the matter. Categorization of the entity serves no useful purpose to the organism. A related matter is that the theory makes no predictions as to which categories are likely to be lexicalized in human languages. In principle, any random set of features can define a category. But many of these possible categories – for example, a category defined by the features [is red], [was manufactured before 1980], [weighs 8 kg] – although perfectly well-formed in terms of the theory, are not likely to be named in the lexicon of any human language.

A further set of problem arises in regard to the features. In terms of the theory, the features are more basic than the categories which they define. In many cases, however, the priority of the features might be questioned. [Having feathers] may well be a necessary feature of 'bird'. But do we comprehend the category 'bird' on the basis of a prior understanding of what it means for a creature to have feathers, in contrast, say, to having fur, hair, scales, or spines? Probably not. Rather, we understand 'feathers' in consequence of our prior acquaintance with birds. Another point to bear in mind is that each feature will itself define a category, namely, the category of entities exhibiting that feature. The feature [+adult] – one component of the definition of *bachelor* – singles out the category of adults. We will need to provide a classical definition of the category 'adult', whose features will in turn need to be given classical definitions. Unless we are prepared to postulate a set of universal, primitive features, out of which all possible categories are constructed – such as the controversial programme pursued by Wierzbicka and her associates (see Wierzbicka 1996; also article 6 [Semantics: Lexical Structures and Adjectives] (Cann) *Sense relations*) – we are faced with an infinite regress.

Not the least of the problems associated with the classical theory is that it is difficult to find convincing examples of words which designate classical categories. The word *bachelor* is cited with such depressing regularity in expositions of the classical theory – the present article is no exception – because it is one of the few words which might be amenable to this kind of analysis. (However, as we shall see, even the case of *bachelor* is not so straightforward.) Of course, scientists, bureaucrats, and various other kinds of experts may attempt to give rigorous definitions of categories relevant to their activities. But even technical and scientific terms may turn out to be problematic for the classical theory. Consider the recent discussions as to whether Pluto is a planet or some other kind of solar object, such as a comet or an asteroid. That such an issue could arise amongst the experts (in this case, the astronomers) demonstrates that 'planet' may not be susceptible to a classical definition, and, even if it were, there may still be uncertainty over whether a given entity exhibits each of the defining features.

As we shall see, prototype theory is able to accommodate, with varying degrees of success, the objections raised above, and therefore offers itself as an alternative to the classical theory. The starting point is the observation that for many categories, certain members seem to be more central, more basic, more typical than others; categories, therefore, have an internal structure, in that their members are not all of equal status. Given this approach, we need not stipulate that members of a category have to share a set of category-defining features. Moreover, the boundary of the category (the distinction between what is in and what is outside the category) may not be clear-cut. The possibility also arises that categories are learned and represented, not as combinations of features, but, in the first instance, on the basis of good examples.

Before proceeding, a word of caution is called for. In spite of the title of this article and the introductory remarks above, it may be inappropriate to speak of 'prototype theory' *tout court*. What we have, in the first instance, are prototype effects – very robust and undisputed empirical findings concerning goodness-of example ratings of members of a category. These are discussed below. The interpretation of prototype effects and their theoretical significance, however, are far from uncontroversial, in both psychology and linguistic semantics; for overviews, see Geeraerts (1989), Kleiber (1990), Lewandowska-Tomaszczyk (2007), MacLaury (1991), Murphy (2002), and Violi (1997). The common ground is that prototype effects impose a condition on a theory of categorization; the theory, namely, must be able to accommodate, and even predict these effects. But instead of there being a single 'theory of prototypes', there are, as we shall see, a number of distinct theoretical approaches to the issue.

2 Prototype effects

Prototype effects have been documented by many researchers, for many different kinds of categories. An early and well-known study is Labov (1973) on the names of household receptacles like *cup, mug, bowl, vase, pitcher*. Labov showed subjects line drawings of receptacles which varied in a number of ways, such as the ratio of height to depth, the shape of the cross-section (circular, square, or triangular), whether tapering towards the bottom or not, whether with or without a handle. The finding was that certain receptacles were unanimously called cups, others bowls or vases, whereas others elicited variable judgements. Judgements could also be shifted by asking subjects to imagine the receptacles holding coffee, mashed potato, or flowers. The upshot for Labov was that words such as *cup, bowl*, and *vase* could not be defined by clear-cut criteria, but rather in terms of what typical exemplars might look like and what they might typically be used for.

Cups usually have a handle, though some cups do not; they are usually tapering towards the bottom, though need not be; they are typically used for drinking hot tea or coffee, but could also be used for drinking soup or cold milk; they usually come with a saucer, though not necessarily. None of these properties, though typical and expected, is strictly speaking a necessary feature of 'cup'. There is, as Labov asserts, no 'essence' (in the classical theoretical sense) of 'cup'.

The idea that category membership may not be dependent on the sharing of features had also been argued by Wittgenstein (1978: 33–34) in his remarks on *game* (more precisely, since Wittgenstein was writing in German, on *Spiel*). Features such as 'for amusement', 'requires two or more players', 'involves competition between players', 'requires skill', 'depends on chance' are distributed over members of the category rather like the characteristics of a family (the family chin, the family nose, and the like) are distributed over the family members. Each game does not have to exhibit the full set of game-like features, just as a family member does not have to exhibit each of the family attributes in order to be recognized as such. Wittgenstein's analogy has given rise the concept of the 'family resemblance category'. It is worth noting, however, that Wittgenstein did not propose that certain games might be 'better', or more prototypical examples than others.

The researcher who is perhaps best known to linguists for work on prototype effects is the cognitive psychologist, Eleanor Rosch. Rosch's earliest work (published under the name of Heider) addressed colour categories and their encoding in language. The fact that different languages carve up the colour spectrum in different ways has long fascinated scholars, and was cited by Gleason (1955: 4) as an illustration of the essentially arbitrary way in which semantic domains are structured by language. This view was questioned by Berlin & Kay's (1969) cross-linguistic survey of colour terminology. They confirmed that languages do indeed differ with respect to the number of their colour categories and the extensional range of their colour terms. However, when speakers of different languages are asked to identify 'good examples' of their colour words, the amount of cross-linguistic diversity is greatly reduced. Speakers of different languages, when asked to pick out a 'good red', tend to select colours from a very limited area of the colour spectrum. Rather than corroborating the cross-linguistic diversity of colour terminology, Berlin & Kay's research strongly suggested the existence of a universal set of focal colours (eleven, to be precise), from which all languages make their selection. It also suggested that the sequence in which languages elaborate their colour terminology tends to follow a universal path, with black, white, and red lexicalized first, pink, brown, purple, and grey appearing last.

Heider (1971, 1972) found other experimental correlates of what she referred to as focal colours. For example, subjects were faster in naming focal than non-focal colours, and focal colours were better remembered on a short-term memory task. Speakers of a language with a very restricted colour vocabulary (the Dani, of Irian Jaya) were able to learn terms for focal colours faster than terms for non-focal colours. The evidence led Rosch to suppose that colour categories were learned and structured around their focal, or prototypical exemplars:

> [c]olor categories are processed by the human mind (learned, remembered, denoted, and evolved in languages) in terms of their internal structure; color categories appear to be represented in cognition not as a set of criterial features with clear-cut boundaries but rather in terms of a prototype (the clearest cases, best examples) of the category, surrounded by other colors of decreasing similarity to the prototype and of decreasing degree of membership.
> (Rosch 1975: 193)

Subsequently, Rosch extended her research to the categories encoded by other linguistic items, specifically, names for natural kind terms such as *fruit* and *bird*, and nominal kind terms such as *furniture* and *vehicle* (Rosch 1975; Rosch et al. 1976). The basic experimental paradigm was very simple. A group of subjects is presented with a category name, e.g. *furniture*. They are then given a list of possible members of the category, and asked to rate on a 7-point scale the extent to which each item "represented their idea or image of the meaning of the category name" (Rosch 1975: 198). A principal finding was that subjects tended to rank the category members rather similarly, with *chair* and *sofa* being judged good examples of 'furniture', *chest* and *bookcase* less good, and *clock* and *vase* as very poor examples. These are the goodness-of-example ratings referred to above.

Prototype effects – the finding that members of a category can be rated in terms of how good they are – are now very well documented. They pertain to natural kind terms (*bird*, *tree*, etc.), names of artifacts (*furniture*, *vehicle*), emotion concepts (Fehr & Russel 1984), as well as artificial categories (such as displays of dots, or sequences of letters and numbers). They show up on ad hoc categories (such as 'things that can fall on your head': Barsalou 1983) and goal-oriented categories ('things to pack in a suitcase': Barsalou 1991). While most research has focused on categories designated by nominals, prototype effects have also been reported for verbal (Pulman 1983) and adjectival (Dirven & Taylor 1988) categories. Most spectacularly, they show up even with categories which arguably do have a classical definition, such as 'odd number' (Armstrong, Gleitman & Gleitman 1983).

One might, of course, counter that the goodness-of-example ratings reported by Rosch and others are simply artifacts of the experimental situation and of the specific instructions that the subjects received. This view must be tempered by the fact that the goodness-of-example ratings turn out to be relevant on a number of other tasks. These are reported in Rosch et al. (1976) and include list effects, verification times, and priming effects. Thus, when asked to list members of a category, subjects tend to name good examples first. When asked to evaluate as true or false a sentence of the form *X is a Y*, subjects respond faster if X is a good example of Y (or not at all an example of Y) than when it is a not-so-good or marginal example. In addition, performance on a lexical decision task (in which subjects are required to decide, as quickly as possible, whether a string of letters constitutes a word or not) is enhanced if the target word is a good example of a category for which subjects have been primed by prior exposure to the category name. Thus, exposure to the word *fruit* facilitates recognition of APPLE as a word, as compared to recognition of OLIVE as a word.

The converging evidence from these different experimental paradigms – some, it will be noted, like priming, involving on-line tasks – strongly suggests that the goodness-of-example ratings cannot be dismissed as artifacts of the rating technique. On the contrary, there is reason to suppose that the various paradigms are tapping into a common representational format for the categories in question.

Mention should also be made of a specifically linguistic manifestation of goodness-of-example effects, namely, the use of hedges (Lakoff 1972). The hedges in question are adverb-like expressions which speakers can use in order to comment on the appropriateness of an entity's categorization. While penguins are undoubtedly birds, it would be odd (perhaps, even false) to say that penguins are birds *par excellence*. *Par excellence* picks out prototypical members of a category. And while bats are not birds – at least, *strictly speaking* they are not birds – it may nevertheless be true (or not obviously false) to claim that *loosely speaking* they are birds. Certain syntactic constructions may also have a hedging effect. *I am not much of a cook* conveys that the speaker regards herself as only a very marginal member of the category 'cook'.

3 Prototypes and the basic level

An important topic in Rosch's work was the relation between prototype effects and levels of categorization (Rosch 1978). As an illustration of what is meant by 'levels of categorization', consider an example from Brown (1958). The thing on the lawn may be named in various ways; it could be called a dog, a boxer, a quadruped, or an animate being. These categories stand in a taxonomic relation: a boxer is a kind of dog, a dog is a kind of quadruped, and a quadruped is a kind of animate creature. Each of the designations for the thing on the lawn may be equally correct. Yet they are not equally likely to be used. If a foreigner were to ask what the thing is called in English, you would probably say that it was a dog, possibly that it was a boxer, but hardly that it was a quadruped.

The basic level is the level in a taxonomy at which things are normally named, in the absence of reasons to the contrary. 'Dog' is a basic level category, 'boxer' a subordinate category, 'quadruped' a superordinate category.

To investigate the taxonomic relation between categories, Rosch & Mervis (1975) asked subjects to list the properties of basic, superordinate, and subordinate level terms. The general finding was that superordinate terms, such as *vehicle*, *clothing*, and *fruit*, elicited relatively few and rather general properties. Names at an intermediate level of categorization, e.g. *apple*, were associated with a much richer set of properties; moreover, the properties tended to be distinctive to that term and not to apply to other members of the superordinate category. Importantly, these features often had to do with the overall appearance of the entity, its constitution, its parts and their arrangement, as well as interactional properties, that is, how the thing is handled and how one would behave with respect to it. Subordinate terms (e.g. *Granny Smith*) also elicited a rich set of properties. These, however, tended to overlap with those of the basic level, and also with those of neighbouring terms (that is, names for other kinds of apple).

These findings shed light on a number of issues. First, they are able to provide a functional explanation for the salience of the basic level. Superordinate categories tend to be rather uninformative in comparison with basic and subordinate terms. To learn that something is a 'piece of fruit' does not tell you very much about it. Basic level and subordinate terms are much richer in information. However, in comparison to subordinate terms, basic level terms tend to be contrastive. Apples, oranges, and bananas contrast on many dimensions, particularly their appearance and how we go about eating them, whereas different kinds of apple contrast only minimally in these respects. The basic level thus turns out to be the most informative and efficient of the taxonomic levels. It is the level which packs the most information, both in terms of what something is, also with respect to what it is not. It is not surprising, therefore, that basic level terms tend to be of high frequency, they are short, and are learned early in first language acquisition.

The findings also make possible a more sophisticated understanding of prototypes. As noted, basic level categories tend to be contrastive. It is possible, then, to view the prototype as a category member which exhibits the maximum number of features which are typical of the category and which are not shared by members of neighbouring categories.

Rosch et al. (1976) in this connection speak of the cue validity of features. A feature has high cue validity to the extent that presence of the feature is a (fairly) reliable predictor of category membership. For example, [having a liver] has almost zero cue validity with respect to the category 'bird'. Although all birds do have a liver, so also do countless other kinds of creature. On the other hand, [having feathers] has very high cue validity, since being feathered is a distinctive characteristic of most, if not all birds, and birds alone. [Being able to fly] has a somewhat lower, but still quite high cue validity, since there are some other creatures (butterflies, wasps, bats) which also fly. [Not being able to fly] would have very low cue validity, not only because it applies to only a few kinds of birds, but because there are countless other kinds of things which do not fly. It is for these reasons that being able to fly, and having feathers, feature in the bird prototype.

Other researchers (e.g. Murphy 2002: 215) have drawn attention to the converse of cue validity, namely, category validity. If cue validity can be defined as the probability of membership in category C, given feature f, i.e. P(C|f), category validity can be defined as the probability that an entity will exhibit feature f, given its membership in C, i.e. P(f|C). The interaction of cue and category validity offers an interesting perspective on inferencing strategies, mentioned in section 1 in connection with the classical theory. (See also article 12 [Semantics: Typology, Diachrony and Processing] (Kelter & Kaup) *Conceptual knowledge, categorization and meaning.*) A person observes that entity e exhibits feature f. If the feature has high cue validity with respect to category C, the person may infer, with some degree of confidence, that e is a member of C. One may then make inferences about e, based on category validity. For example, an entity with feathers is highly likely to be a bird. If it is a bird, it is likely to be able to fly, and much more besides.

The hypothetical category mentioned in section 1 – the category defined by the features [is red], [was manufactured before 1980], and [weighs 8 kg] – exhibits extremely low cue and category validity, and this could be one reason why such a category would never be lexicalized in a human language. The fact that something is red scarcely predicts membership in the category, since there are countless other red things in the universe; likewise for the two other features. The only way to assign membership in the category would be to check off each of the three features. Having done this, one can make no predictions about further properties of the entity. To all intents and purposes, the hypothetical category would be quite useless.

A functional account of prototypes, outlined above, may be contrasted with an account in terms of frequency of occurrence. In response to the question 'Where does prototypicality come from?' (Geeraerts 1988), many people are inclined to say that prototypes (or prototypical instances) are encountered more frequently than more marginal examples and that that is what makes them prototypical. Although frequency of occurrence certainly may be a factor (our prototypical vehicles are now somewhat different from those of 100 years ago, in consequence of changing methods of transportation) it cannot be the whole story. Sofas and chairs are prototypical pieces of furniture, clocks and bookcases are not. But this is not due to the fact (if it is a fact) that we encounter sofas and chairs more frequently than clocks and bookcases. The intuition that prototypes occur more frequently could well be a consequence of prototype structure, not its cause.

4 The cultural context of categories

Rosch's work on categorization appealed extensively to features, attributes, and properties. This manner of speaking is liable to suggest that the attributes have some kind of priority vis-à-vis the categories. Rosch (1978: 42) came to question this assumption. She noted that a typical attribute of chairs is that they 'have a seat'. However, the very notion of something 'having a seat' is based on prior knowledge of how one interacts with chairs and chair-like objects. It is as if the attribute derives from knowledge of the category, rather than the category being a function of its attributes.

This observation has led to several interesting developments. The first is that objects – especially, basic level objects – may be apprehended holistically and experientially, in terms of what they look like, how they are put together, how we behave with respect to the them, and the roles they play in our interaction with the environment. Features, in turn, come to be seen, not as pre-existing building blocks out of which categories are constructed, but as commonalities which speakers perceive in an array of category instances (Langacker 1987: 22).

The second issue concerns the cultural embeddedness of categories. The categories that we recognize in the world are not objectively 'there', but are mediated by human concerns, interests, and values. As Rosch came to recognize, it would be an error to suppose that the categories that we identify in the world merely reflect "the natural correlation of attributes" (Rosch 1975: 197). This kind of objectivist view would predict (incorrectly) that all languages would identify the same categories in the world, and that categories would change only if the environment changed.

The theme of the cultural embeddedness of categories was pursued by Murphy & Medin (1985), who argued that a category is coherent and useful to its users to the extent that it plays a role in wider scenarios, in causal relations, or in deeply held beliefs. The theme was also addressed by Lakoff (1987) in terms of his notion of the Idealized Cognitive Model (ICM). The notion can be illustrated on the example of 'bachelor', introduced at the beginning of this article.

Intuitively, the definition of *bachelor* in terms of the four features [+human], [+adult], [+male], and [−married] seems reasonable enough. However, even this parade example of a classical category raises a number of issues. Consider, for example, the feature [+adult]. This feature itself defines a category, namely the category of adults. But how do we define this category? Bureaucrats may, of course, give the category a precise classical definition, namely in terms a person's age (18 years or older, or whatever). But in everyday usage, the word surely appeals to a number of aspects in addition to age, such as emotional and physical maturity, independence from parents, assumption of responsibilities, and so on. The category will inevitably have fuzzy boundaries and this fuzziness will be inherited by *bachelor* (would one confidently apply the term to an immature 18-year-old?) Consider, also, the feature [−married]. Marriage is a cultural institution par excellence, and such a feature can in no way be regarded as an 'objective' feature of the environment.

Although often cited as an example of a classical category, 'bachelor' is arguably subject to prototype effects. There are good examples of the category, less good, and marginal examples. Do Catholic priests count as bachelors? Is the Pope a bachelor? Tarzan? Men in long-term unmarried relationships? Gay men? Men in polygamous societies, who have only one wife but who are eligible to have another? Is it totally excluded to apply the word to women? Is *bachelor girl* a contradiction, and therefore meaningless?

One approach to this issue was suggested by Fillmore (1982) and developed by Lakoff (1987). The proposal is that the concept 'bachelor' needs to be understood against an Idealized Cognitive Model of society. According to the ICM, everyone is heterosexual and there is a certain age range at which everyone is expected to marry. Men who pass this age do so out of choice; they do not want the 'commitments' of marriage. Women who pass the age do so out of necessity; they cannot find a willing mate. (From these aspects of the ICM follow the generally positive connotations of *bachelor* and the negative associations of *spinster*.) In terms of the ICM, *bachelor* can indeed be defined, quite simply, as an (as yet) unmarried man, as per the classical theory. Prototype effects arise because the model does not always fit the social reality. The ICM makes no allowance for Catholic priests, gay people, or people in unmarried relationships.

Another example is provided by the notion of telling a lie. In a well-known article, Coleman & Kay (1981) promoted the notion of prototype category on the example of 'lie'. They surmised that there might be three features relevant to the categorization of a statement as a lie: its factual incorrectness, the speaker's belief in its factual incorrectness, and the speaker's intention to deceive the hearer. Coleman and Kay constructed eight little stories, one exhibiting all three of the features, the others exemplifying either two or only one of the features. Subjects were asked to evaluate the stories in terms of how good an example they were of lying. Predictably, the story with all three features was considered the best example, those with only one feature the poorest examples. Coleman and Kay were also able to show that the three features were differentially weighted with respect to category membership. The speaker's belief that the statement is factually incorrect was the most important, factual incorrectness was the least important.

Sweetser (1987) returned to Coleman and Kay's data and argued that lying should be understood against an ICM of verbal communication. According to ICM, people communicate in good faith, they state only that for which they have evidence, and, if they have evidence, they are justified in believing that their statements are true. In addition, the imparting of true information is deemed to be beneficial to hearers, and speakers strive to benefit hearers by providing true information. In terms of the ICM, lying can be defined, quite simply, as the making of a statement which is not true. Moreover, making a statement which is not true can only be with the intention of harming the hearer.

Once again, however, there are many circumstances in which the ICM does not apply, and in these cases we may be less confident to speak of lying. The ICM does not apply when language is being used to entertain, as when telling stories or making jokes. (No one, presumably, would accuse a joke-teller of lying, on the grounds that the events described never happened). It does not apply when the main purpose of linguistic activity is to establish and maintain social relations. Telling your host that you have had a delightful evening, when you haven't, would not normally be considered a lie, certainly not a prototypical one. The ICM also ignores cases where speakers might be genuinely ignorant of the facts, where they are simplifying information for pedagogical reasons, where 'the truth' might be distressing to the hearer, or where information is considered to be confidential and not at all public property. The status of information as public or private property can be expected to vary according to circumstances and cultural conventions.

5 Prototypes and categories

There are several ways of understanding the notion of prototype and of the relation between a prototype and a category (Taylor 2008). Some of these have been hinted at in the preceding discussion. In this section we examine them in more detail.

5.1 Categories are defined with respect to a 'best example'

On this approach, a category is understood and mentally represented simply in terms of a good example. One understands 'red' in terms of a mental image of a good red, other hues being assimilated to the category in virtue of their similarity to the prototype.

Some of Rosch's statements may be taken in support of this view. For example, Heider (1971: 455) surmises that "much actual learning of semantic reference, particularly in perceptual domains, may occur through generalization from focal exemplars". Elsewhere she writes of "conceiving of each category in terms of its clear cases rather than its boundaries" (Rosch 1978: 35–36).

An immediate problem arises with this approach. Any colour can be said to be similar to red in some respect (if only in virtue of its being a colour) and is therefore eligible to be described as red 'to some degree'. In order to avoid this manifestly false prediction we might suppose that the outer limits of category membership will be set by the existence of neighbouring, contrasting categories. As a colour becomes more distant from focal red and approaches focal orange, there comes a point at which it will no longer be possible to categorize it as red, not even to a small degree. The colour is, quite simply, not red.

Observe that this account presupposes a structuralist view of lexical semantics, whereby word meanings divide up conceptual space in a mosaic-like manner, such that the denotational range of one term is restricted by the presence of neighbouring terms (Lyons 1977: 260). It predicts (correctly in the case of colours, or at least, basic level colours) that membership will be graded, in that an entity may be judged to be a member of a category only to a certain degree depending on its distance from the prototype. The category, as a consequence, will have fuzzy boundaries, and degree of membership in one category will inversely correlate with degree of membership in a neighbouring category. The 'redder' a shade of orange, the less it is orange and the more it is red.

There are a small number of categories for which the above account may well be valid, including the household receptacles studied by Labov: as a vessel morphs from a prototypical cup into a prototypical bowl, categorization as cup gradually decreases, offset by increased categorization as bowl. The account may also be valid for scalar concepts such as *hot, warm, cool,* and *cold*, where the four terms exhaustively divide up the temperature dimension.

But for a good many categories it will not be possible to maintain that they are understood simply in terms of a prototype, with their boundaries set by neighbouring terms. In the first place, the mosaic metaphor of word meanings may not apply. This is the case with near synonyms, that is, words which arguably have distinct prototypes, but whose usage ranges overlap and which are not obviously contrastive. Take the pair *high* and *tall* (Taylor 2003b). *Tall* applies prototypically to humans (*tall man*), *high* to inanimates (*high mountain*). Yet the words do not mutually circumscribe each other at their boundaries. Many entities can be described equally well as *tall* or *high*; use of one term does not exclude use of the other. It would be bizarre to say of a mountain that it is high but not tall, or vice versa.

The approach is also problematic in the case of categories which cannot be reduced to values on a continuously varying dimension or on set of such dimensions. Consider natural kind terms such as *bird, mammal*, and *reptile*, or *gold, silver*, and *platinum*. Natural kinds are presumed to have a characteristic 'essence', be it genetic, molecular, or whatever. (This said, the category of natural kind terms may not be clear-cut; see Keil 1989. As a rule of thumb, we can say that natural kinds are the kinds of things which scientists study. We can imagine scientists studying the nature of platinum, but not the nature of furniture.) While natural kind categories may well show goodness-of-example effects, they tend to have very precise boundaries. Birds, as we know them, do not morph gradually into mammals (egg-laying monotremes like the platypus notwithstanding), neither can we conceive of a metal which is half-way between gold and silver. And, indeed, it would be absurd to claim that knowledge of the bird prototype (e.g. a small songbird, such as a robin) is all there is to the bird concept, to claim, in other words, that the meaning of *bird is* 'robin', and that creatures are called birds simply on the basis of their similarity to the prototype. While a duck may be similar to a robin in many respects, we cannot appeal to the similarity as evidence that ducks should be called robins. In the case of categories like 'bird', the prototype is clearly insufficient as a category representation. We need to know what kinds of things are likely to be members of the category, how far we can generalize from the prototype, and where (if only approximately) the boundaries lie. We need an understanding of the category which somehow encompasses all its members.

5.2 The prototype as a set of weighted attributes

In subsequent work Rosch came to a more sophisticated understanding of prototype, proposing that

> categories tend to become defined in terms of prototypes or prototypical instances that *contain the attributes most representative of items inside and least representative of items outside the category.*
>
> (Rosch 1978: 30; italics added)

A category now comes to be understood as a set of attributes which are differentially weighted according to their cue validity, that is, their importance in diagnosing category membership, and an entity belongs in the category if the cumulative weightings of its attributes achieve a certain threshold level. On this approach, category members need not share the same attributes, nor is an attribute necessarily shared by all category members. Rather, the category hangs together in virtue of a 'family resemblance' (Rosch & Mervis 1975), in which attributes 'criss-cross', like the threads of a rope (Wittgenstein 1978: 32). The more similar an instance to all other category members (this being a measure of its family resemblance), the more prototypical it is of the category.

A major advantage of the weighted attribute view is that it makes possible a "summary representation" of a category, which, like the classical theory, "somehow encompass[es] an entire concept" (Murphy 2002: 49). As a matter of fact, a classical category would turn out to be a limiting case, where each of the features has an equal and maximal weighting, and without the presence of each of the features the threshold value would not be attained.

The weighted attribute view raises the interesting possibility that the prototype may not correspond to any actual category member; it is more in the nature of an idealized abstraction. Confirmation comes from work with artificial categories (patterns of dots which deviate to varying degrees from a pre-established prototype), where subjects have been able to identify the prototype of a category they have learned, even though they had not been previously exposed to it (Posner & Keele 1968).

5.3 Categories as exemplars

A radical alternative to feature-based approaches construes a category simply as a collection of instances. Knowledge of a category consists in a memory store of encountered exemplars (Smith & Medin 1981). Categorization of a new instance occurs in virtue of similarities to one or more of the stored exemplars, a prototypical example being one which exhibits the highest degree of similarity with the greatest number of instances. There are several variants of the exemplar view of categories. The exemplars might be individual instances encountered on specific occasions; especially for superordinate categories, on the other hand, the exemplars might be the basic categories which instantiate them (Storms, de Boeck & Ruts 2000). In its purest form, the exemplar theory denies that people make generalizations over category exemplars. Mixed representations might also be envisaged, however, whereby instances which closely resemble each other might coalesce into a generic image which preserves what is common to the instances and filters out the idiosyncratic details (Ross & Makin 1999).

On the face of it, the exemplar view, even in its mixed form, looks rather implausible. The idea that we retain specific memories of previously encountered instances would surely make intolerable demands on human memory. Several factors, however, suggest that we should not dismiss the exemplar theory out of hand, and indeed Storms, de Boeck & Ruts (2000) report that the exemplar theory outperforms the summary representation theory, at least with respect to membership in superordinate categories. First, computer simulations have shown that exemplar models are able to account for a surprising range of experimental findings on human categorization, including, importantly, prototype effects (Hintzman 1986). Second, there is evidence that human memory is indeed rich in episodic detail (Schacter 1987). Even such apparently irrelevant aspects of encountered language, such as the position on a page of a piece of text (Rothkopf 1971), or the voice with which a word is spoken (Goldinger 1996), may be retained over substantial periods of time. Moreover, humans are exquisitely sensitive to the frequency with which events, including linguistic events, have occurred (Ellis 2002). Bybee (2001) has argued that frequency should be recognized as a major determinant of linguistic performance, acceptability judgements, and language change.

A focus on exemplars would tie in with the trend towards usage-based models of grammar (Langacker 2000, Tomasello 2003). It is axiomatic, in a usage-based model, that linguistic knowledge is acquired on the basis of encounters with actual usage events. While generalizations may be made over encountered events, the particularities of the events need not thereby be erased from memory (Langacker 1987: 29). Indeed, it is now widely recognized that a great deal of linguistic knowledge must reside in rather particular facts about a language, such as its phraseologies, idioms, and collocations (Moon 1998). Moreover, the frequency with which linguistic phenomena have been encountered would itself form part of linguistic knowledge and be a crucial factor in future performance (Bybee 2001, Hoey 2005).

5.4 Prototypes as category defaults

Another approach to prototypes and categorization is the view that prototypes constitute the default value of a category, activated in the absence of more specific information (cf. the notion of 'default inheritance' in Word Grammar: Hudson 1990). Thus, on hearing mention of birds, one would assume that the creatures in question possess the typical attributes of the category, for example, that they fly, perch on trees, and so on. Rosch (1977) showed that a statement involving birds tends to make sense if it is changed to one referring to a prototypical member of the category, such as robins, but becomes ludicrous if reference is changed to a non-prototypical member, such as turkeys. Imagine a person who muses *I wish I were a bird*. They would probably feel somewhat cheated if their wish was granted and they were miraculously transformed into a turkey (especially before Christmas or Thanksgiving!).

The prototypes as defaults approach would be compatible with each of the above mentioned approaches. The default could be the best example, an instance which maximizes attribute weighting, or one which maximizes similarity to stored instances. If prototypes are defaults, we should expect that attributes of the prototype will be overridden as more specific information becomes available. The notion of 'wooden spoon' evokes its own prototype, whose properties (for example, its size) override the specifications of the spoon prototype (Hampton 1987). Moreover, the default might vary according to context, background expectations, and the specific task in hand. If asked to take a Chinese perspective, American subjects select swan and peacock as typical exemplars of the bird category, whereas robin and eagle are taken as typical from an American perspective (Barsalou 1987: 106–107). This does not, of course, mean that Chinese subjects *would* rate swans and peacocks over robins and eagles, only that American subjects are able to construct a Chinese perspective, based on their stereotypical views of Chinese culture.

6 Objections to prototypes

Although prototype effects are very well documented, their relevance to linguistic semantics is by no means without controversy. Some skeptical views are reviewed below.

6.1 Combining concepts: the problem of the pet fish

Osherson & Smith (1981) observed that complex expressions typically fail to inherit the prototypes of their constituents, a point taken up by Fodor in his sustained criticism of the role of prototypes in linguistic semantics (Fodor 1980, 1998; Fodor & Lepore 1996). We might consider a prototypical fish to be herring and a prototypical pet to be a poodle. However, we do not arrive at an understanding of 'pet fish' by combining the prototypes of the constituents and imagining some sort of hybrid between a herring and a poodle. On the contrary, a pet fish is a fish (any kind of fish) which happens also to be a pet, a prototypal example being, perhaps, a goldfish. The prototypical fish and the prototypical pet play no role in our understanding of 'pet fish'. Similarly, we may well have an image of a prototypical grandmother (say, as a kindly, frail old lady with grey hair), but the prototype plays no role in our understanding of the expressions *my grandmother* and *grandmothers most of whose grandchildren are married to dentists* (Fodor 1980: 197).

Fodor's criticism is based on the assumption that a category is to be represented solely by its prototype. As we have seen, there are other ways to understand categories and their prototypes. The cases mentioned above clearly need to make reference to 'summary representations' (Murphy 2002: 49) of the respective categories, e.g. in terms of a set of weighted features, not simply to a prototypical exemplar. And, as already noted, concept combination can result in the overriding of certain features and in the setting of particular values and weightings to the features (Hampton 1987, 1991), as in the example *wooden spoon*.

6.2 Core definitions and recognition procedures: The problem of odd numbers

Armstrong, Gleitman & Gleitman (1983) queried the linguistic significance of goodness-of-example ratings, not by challenging the empirical evidence for prototype effects, but by demonstrating the very ubiquity of these effects. Thus, they reported goodness-of-example ratings even for odd numbers, with subjects judging 3 to be a 'better' odd number than 91. 'Odd number' is a category which uncontroversially requires a classical definition, a definition, moreover, which the subjects in Armstrong et al.'s experiments were familiar with and fully endorsed. The existence of prototype effects cannot therefore be taken as evidence against the classical view of categories.

A first point to note in connection with Armstrong et al.'s seemingly very strange findings is that the presence of goodness-of-example ratings does not entail that a category will have fuzzy boundaries. The bird category is not fuzzy, even though some birds are more birdy than others. Even so, Armstrong et al.'s findings can be interpreted to mean that prototype effects might have to do primarily with the process of assigning an instance to a category, not with the mental representation of the category as such. We might therefore wish to distinguish between the 'core', or strictly linguistic meaning of an expression, and the 'recognition procedures' on whose basis people make rapid decisions on category membership, as proposed by Osherson & Smith (1981). The recognition procedures would appeal to typical, easily observable properties, which may nevertheless not be defining of the category. More generally, the distinction between core definitions and recognition procedures raises the possibility that prototype effects might simply be due to the imperfect fit between concepts and the things that we encounter in the world. Coseriu (2000) took this line in his spirited critique of prototype categories. Against this is the fact that in many cases it is the concept itself that is structured prototypically, a point argued by Taylor (1999) in his riposte to Coseriu.

The distinction between a core definition and recognition procedures may, however, have some force in the case of some natural kind categories. Natural kinds, such as water and gold, are presumed to have a defining essence. Most speakers act in ignorance of the defining essence and how they might access it; for this, they defer to the experts. In everyday usage they rely instead on what Putnam (1975) refers to as a stereotype – what the things look like, where they are found, and so on. However, the distinction between the real essence of a thing and its stereotype may not be applicable outside the domain of natural kind terms. As mentioned earlier, Labov queried the idea that the set of things called cups might possess a defining essence, distinct from the recognition features which allow a person to categorize something as a cup. In this case, the stereotype turns out to be nothing other than the prototype.

Not to be forgotten also is the fact that speakers may operate with more than one understanding of a category. The case of 'adult' was already mentioned, where an 'expert' bureaucratic definition might co-exist with a looser, multi-dimensional, and inherently fuzzy understanding of what constitutes an adult.

6.3 Prototypes save: An excuse for lazy lexicographers?

Wierzbicka (1990) maintained that appeal to prototypes is simply an excuse for lazy semanticists to avoid having to formulate rigorous word definitions. Underlying Wierzbicka's position is the view that words are indeed amenable to definitions which are able to predict their full usage range. She offers sample definitions of the *loci classici* of the prototype literature, including 'game', 'lie', and 'bird'.

However, as Geeraerts (1997: 13–16) has aptly remarked, Wierzbicka's definitions often sneak in prototype effects by the back door, as it were. For example, Wierzbicka (1990: 361–362) claims that ability to fly is part of the bird-concept, in spite of the fact that some birds are flightless. The discrepancy is expressed in terms of how a person would imagine a bird, namely, as a creature able to move in the air, with the proviso that 'some creatures of this kind cannot move in the air'. Far from discrediting prototype structure, Wierzbicka's definition simply incorporates them.

7 Words and the world

Rosch's work addressed the relation between words and the things in the world to which the words can refer.

The relation can be studied from two perspectives (Taylor 2007). We can ask, for this word, what are the things which it can be used to refer to? This is the semasiological, or referring perspective. Alternatively we can ask, for this thing, what are the words that we can use to refer to it? This is the onomasiological, or naming perspective (Blank 2003). The two perspectives roughly correspond to the way in which dictionaries and thesauri are organized. A dictionary lists words and gives their meanings. A thesaurus lists concepts and gives words which can refer to them.

The two perspectives underlie much research in colour terminology. Consider, for example, the data elicitation techniques employed by MacLaury (1995). Three procedures were involved. The first requires subjects to name a series of colour chips presented in random sequence. This procedure elicits the basic colour terms of the language. Next, for each of the colour terms proffered on the naming task, subjects are asked to identify its focal reference on a colour chart. This procedure elicits the prototypes of the colour terms. Third, for each colour term, subjects map the term on the colour chart, indicating which colours could be named by the word. This procedure shows the referential range of the term.

MacLaury's research, therefore, combined an onomasiological perspective (from world to word, i.e. "What do you call this?") with a semasiological perspective (from word to world, i.e. "What can this word refer to?"). Importantly, the elicitation procedures make it possible to operationalize the notions of basic level term (the term preferentially used to describe a state of affairs), as well the prototype (in the sense of focal reference). By including mapping data, it becomes possible also to identify various kinds of semantic relations between words, such as inclusion, synonymy, overlap (or partial synonymy), and contrast. The methodology also makes it possible to rigorously study between-language differences, as well as differences between speakers of the same language, and indeed, differences within a single speaker on different occasions.

The onomasiological and semasiological perspectives have been employed in several studies of semantic typology; these include Bowerman (1996) on spatial relations (see also article 13 [Semantics: Typology, Diachrony and Processing] (Landau) *Space in semantics and cognition*), Enfield, Majid & van Staden (2006) on body-part terms, and Majid et al. (2007) on verbs of cutting and breaking. Perhaps the most thorough application of the two perspectives outside the colour domain, however, is Geeraerts, Grondelaers & Bakema (1994), who studied terms for outer clothing garments as depicted, and named, in fashion magazines and mail-order catalogues. The data allowed the researchers to identify the features of the garments named by a particular clothing term. The prototype could then be characterized by a cluster of frequently co-occurring features. Conversely, the researchers were able to identify the terms which were most frequently used to refer to garments exhibiting a certain set of features. In this way, basic level terms could be identified.

One of the many findings of this study was that the basic level does not constitute a fixed and stable level in a taxonomy. For example, there are good reasons to regard 'trousers' as a basic level term, in contrast to 'skirt', 'shirt', 'jacket', and 'coat'. 'Jeans' would be a subcategory of trousers. Yet jeans, and jeans-like garments, are typically referred to as such, not as trousers. What is from one point of view a subordinate term has acquired something of basic level status.

8 Prototypes and polysemy

The prototype concept was eagerly taken up by a number of linguists in the late 1980's and early 1990's (Lakoff 1982, 1987; Taylor 1989/2003a; Langacker 1987), especially for its relevance to lexical semantics and meaning change (Geeraerts 1997; see also article 7 [Semantics: Typology, Diachrony and Processing] (Geeraerts) *Cognitive approaches to diachronic semantics*). Since then, it has found applications in areas of linguistic description outside of semantics, including syntax, morphology, and phonology (Taylor 2002; 2008).

A particularly fruitful application has been in the study of lexical polysemy. The idea is that the different senses of a word are structured similar to how the different members of a category are structured, namely in terms of a central, or prototypical sense, to which less central senses are related. The word *over* provides a parade example. Lakoff (1987), based on Brugman (1981), proposed that the basic sense of the preposition involves movement of a trajector (or fig. object) 'above and across' a landmark (or ground) entity, as in *The plane flew over the city*. Other senses introduce modifications of some feature or features of the prototypical sense. Thus, *The plane flew over the hill* requires a concave landmark. *Sam walked over the hill* is similar, except that the trajector (Sam) is in contact with the landmark. *Sam climbed over the wall* involves an up-down movement, from one side of the landmark to the other. *Sam lives over the hill* locates Sam at the end-point of a path which goes 'over the hill'. Other senses involve a covering relation. In *I walked all over the hill*, the trajector traces a random path which 'covers' the hill. In *The board is over the hole*, the board completely obscures the hole. In this usage, the verticality of the trajector vis-à-vis the landmark is no longer obligatory: the board could be positioned vertically against the hole.

The examples give the flavour of what came to be known, for obvious reasons, as a radial category. The various senses radiate out from the central, prototypical sense, like spokes in a wheel.

This approach to polysemy has proved extremely attractive to many researchers, not least because it lends itself to the visual display of central and derived senses. For a particularly well worked-out example, see Fillmore & Atkins' (2000) account of English *crawl* in comparison to French *ramper*. The approach has been seen as a convenient way to handle the fact that the various senses of a word may not share a common definitional core. Just as the various things we call 'furniture' may not exhibit a set of necessary and sufficient features, so also the various senses of a word may resist a definition in terms of a invariant semantic core.

The approach has also been taken up with respect to the semantics of constructions (Goldberg 1995, 2006). Take, for example, the ditransitive [V NP_1 NP_2] construction in English. Its presumed prototype, illustrated by *give the dog a bone*, involves the transfer of one entity, NP_2, to another, NP_1, such that NP_1 ends up having NP_2. But in *throw the dog a bone* there is only the intention that NP_1 should have NP_2, there is no entailment that NP_1 does end up having NP_2. More distant from the prototypical sense are examples such as *deny someone access*, where the intention is that NP_2 should be withheld from NP_1.

In applying the notion of a prototype category to cases of polysemy (whether lexical or constructional), we must be aware of the differences between the two phenomena. On the one hand, we can use the word *fruit* to refer, firstly, to apples and oranges, but also to olives. Although the word can refer to different kinds of things, the word presumably has a single sense and designates a single category of objects (albeit, a prototypically structured category). But when we use the word to refer to the outcome of a person's efforts, as in *the fruit of my labours* or *The project bore fruit*, we are using the word in a different sense. The outcome of a person's efforts cannot be regarded as just another marginal example of fruit, akin to an olive or a coconut. Rather, the metaphorical sense has to be regarded as an extension from the botanical sense. Even so, to speak of the two senses as forming a category, and to claim that one of the senses is the prototype, is to use the terms 'category' and 'prototype' also in an extended sense.

In the case of *fruit*, it is reasonably clear which of the senses is to be taken as basic and which are extensions therefrom. But in other cases a decision may not be so easy. As noted above, for Lakoff and Brugman the central sense of *over* was movement 'above and across' (*The plane flew over the city*). For Tyler & Evans (2001), on the other hand, the 'protoscene' of the preposition is exemplified by *The bee is hovering over the flower*, which lacks the notion of movement 'across'.

The question now arises, on what basis is the central sense identified as such? Whereas Rosch substantiated the prototype notion by a variety of experimental techniques, linguists applying the prototype model to polysemous items appeal (implicitly or explicitly) to a variety of principles, which may sometimes be in conflict. One is descriptive elegance, whereby the prototype is identified as that sense to which the others can most reasonably, or most economically, be related. However, as the example of *over* demonstrates, different linguists are liable to come up with different proposals as to what is the central sense. Another principle appeals to the organic growth of the polysemous category, with a historically older sense being taken as more central than senses which have developed later. Relevant here are certain assumptions concerning metaphorical extension (see article 11 [Semantics: Lexical Structures and Adjectives] (Tyler & Takahashi) *Metaphors and metonymies*). Thus, Lakoff (1987: 416–417) claims that the spatial sense of *long* (as in *a long stick*) is 'more central' than the temporal sense (*a long time*), on the basis of what is supposed to be a very general conceptual metaphor which maps spatial notions onto non-spatial domains.

A controversial question concerns the psychological reality of radial categories. Experimental evidence, such as it is, would suggest that radial categories might actually have very little psychological reality for speakers of the language (Sandra & Rice: 1995). One might, for example, suppose that the radial structure represents the outcome of the acquisition process. Data from acquisition studies, however, do not always corroborate the radial analysis. Amongst the earliest uses of *over* which are acquired by children are uses such as *fall over*, *over here*, and *all over* (i.e. 'finished') (Hallan 2001). These would probably be regarded as marginal senses on just about any radial analysis. It is also legitimate to ask, what it would mean, in terms of a speaker's linguistic knowledge, for a particular sense of a word to be 'marginal' or 'non-prototypical'. Both the temporal and the spatial uses of *long* are frequent and both have to be mastered by any competent speaker of the language.

In the case of a prototype category (as studied by Rosch) we are dealing with a single sense (with its prototype structure) of a word. In the case of a radial category (as proposed by Lakoff) we are dealing with several senses (each of which will also no doubt have a prototype structure). The distinction is based on whether we are dealing with a single sense of a word or multiple (related) senses. However, the allocation of the various uses of a word to a single sense or to two different senses can be fraught with difficulty, and various tests for diagnosing the matter can give conflicting results (Geeraerts 1993, Tuggy 1993). For example, do *paint a portrait*, *paint the kitchen*, and *paint white stripes on the road* exemplify a single sense of *paint*, or two (or perhaps even three) closely related senses? There are arguments for each of these positions. Recently, a number of scholars have queried whether it is legitimate in principle to try to identify *the* senses of a word (Allwood 2003, Zlatev 2003).

Perhaps the most reasonable conclusion to draw from the above is that knowing a word involves learning a set (possibly, a very large and open-ended set) of established uses and usage patterns (Taylor 2006). Such an account would be reminiscent of the exemplar theory of categorization, in that a speaker retains memories, not of category members, but of word uses. Whether, or how, a speaker of the language perceives these uses to be related may not have all that much bearing on the speaker's proficiency in the language. The notion of prototype in the Roschean sense might not therefore be all that relevant. The notion of prototype, and extensions therefrom, might, however, be important in the case of novel, or creative uses. In this connection, Langacker (1987: 381) speaks of 'local' prototypes. Langacker (1987: 57) characterizes a language as an inventory of conventionalized symbolic resources. Often, the conceptualization that a speaker wishes to symbolize on a particular occasion will not correspond exactly with any of the available resources. Inevitably, some extension of an existing resource will be indicated. The existing resource constitutes the local prototype and the actual usage is an extension from it. If the extension is used on future occasions, it may become entrenched and will itself acquire the status of an established unit in the language and become available as a local prototype for further extensions.

9 References

Allwood, Jens 2003. Meaning potential and context. Some consequences for the analysis of variation in meaning. In: H. Cuyckens, R. Dirven & J. Taylor (eds.). *Cognitive Approaches to Lexical Semantics*. Berlin: Mouton de Gruyter, 29–65.
Armstrong, Sharon L., Lila R. Gleitman & Henry Gleitman 1983. What some concepts might not be. *Cognition* 13, 263–308.
Barsalou, Laurence 1983. Ad hoc categories. *Memory & Cognition* 11, 211–227.
Barsalou, Laurence 1987. The instability of graded structure. Implications for the nature of concepts. In: U. Neisser (ed.). *Concepts and Conceptual Development. Ecological and Intellectual Factors in Categorization*. Cambridge: Cambridge University Press, 101–140.
Barsalou, Laurence 1991. Deriving categories to achieve goals. In: G. H. Bower (ed.). *The Psychology of Learning and Motivation*, vol. 27. New York: Academic Press, 1–64.
Berlin, Brent & Paul Kay 1969. *Basic Color Terms. Their Universality and Evolution*. Berkeley, CA: University of California Press.
Blank, Andreas 2003. Words and concepts in time. Towards diachronic cognitive onomasiology. In: R. Eckardt, K. von Heusinger & Ch. Schwarze (eds.). *Words in Time. Diachronic Semantics from Different Points of View*. Berlin: Mouton de Gruyter, 37–65.
Bowerman, Melissa 1996. Learning how to structure space for language. A crosslinguistic perspective. In: P. Bloom et al. (eds.). *Language and Space*. Cambridge, MA: The MIT Press, 385–436.
Brown, Roger 1958. How shall a thing be called? *Psychological Review* 65, 14–21. Reprinted in: R. C. Oldfield & J. C. Marshall (eds.). *Language. Selected Readings*. Harmondsworth: Penguin, 1968, 81–91.
Brugman, Claudia 1981. *The Story of 'Over'*. MA thesis. University of California, Berkeley, CA.
Bybee, Joan L. 2001. *Phonology and Language Use*. Cambridge: Cambridge University Press.
Coleman, Linda & Paul Kay 1981. Prototype semantics. The English word 'lie'. *Language* 57, 26–44.
Coseriu, Eugenio 2002. Structural semantics and 'cognitive' semantics. *Logos and Language* 1, 19–42.

Dirven, René & John R. Taylor 1988. The conceptualization of vertical space in English. The case of tall. In: B. Rudzka-Ostyn (ed.). *Topics in Cognitive Linguistics*. Amsterdam: Benjamins, 379–402.
Ellis, Nick 2002. Frequency effects in language processing. A review with implications for theories of implicit and explicit language acquisition. *Studies in Second Language Acquisition* 24, 143–188.
Enfield, Nick, Asifa Majid & Miriam van Staden 2006. Parts of the body. Cross-linguistic categorisation. *Language Sciences* 28, special issue, 137–147.
Fehr, Beverly & James A. Russel 1984. Concept of emotion viewed from a prototype perspective. *Journal of Experimental Psychology: General* 113, 464–486.
Fillmore, Charles 1982. Towards a descriptive framework for spatial deixis. In: R. J. Jarvella & W. Klein (eds.). *Speech, Place, and Action. Studies in Deixis and Related Topics*. Chichester: Wiley, 31–59.
Fillmore, Charles & Beryl Atkins 2000. Describing polysemy. The case of 'crawl'. In: Y. Ravin & C. Leacock (eds.). *Polysemy. Theoretical and Computational Approaches*. Oxford: Oxford University Press, 91–110.
Fodor, Jerry 1980. The present status of the innateness controversy. In: J. Fodor. *Representations. Philosophical Essays on the Foundations of Cognitive Science*. Cambridge, MA: The MIT Press, 257–316.
Fodor, Jerry 1998. *Concepts. Where Cognitive Science Went Wrong*. Oxford: Oxford University Press.
Fodor, Jerry & Ernest Lepore 1996. The red herring and the pet fish. Why concepts still can't be prototypes. *Cognition* 58, 253–270.
Geeraerts, Dirk 1988. Where does prototypicality come from? In: B. Rudzka-Ostyn (ed.). *Topics in Cognitive Linguistics*. Amsterdam: Benjamins, 207–229.
Geeraerts, Dirk 1989. Prospects and problems of prototype theory. *Linguistics* 27, 587–612.
Geeraerts, Dirk 1993. Vagueness's puzzles, polysemy's vagaries. *Cognitive Linguistics* 4, 223–272.
Geeraerts, Dirk 1997. *Diachronic Prototype Semantics. A Contribution to Historical Lexicology*. Oxford: Oxford University Press.
Geeraerts, Dirk, Stefan Grondelaers & Peter Bakema 1994. *The Structure of Lexical Variation. Meaning, Naming, and Context*. Berlin: Mouton de Gruyter.
Gleason, Henry A. 1955. *An Introduction to Descriptive Linguistics*. New York: Holt, Rinehart & Winston.
Goldberg, Adele 1995. *Constructions. A Construction Grammar Approach to Argument Structure*. Chicago, IL: The University of Chicago Press.
Goldberg, Adele 2006. *Constructions at Work. The Nature of Generalization in Language*. Oxford: Oxford University Press.
Goldinger, Stephen D. 1996. Words and voices. Episodic traces in spoken word identification and recognition memory. *Journal of Experimental Psychology: Learning, Memory, and Cognition* 22, 1166–1183.
Hallan, Naomi 2001. Paths to prepositions? A corpus-based study of the acquisition of a lexico-grammatical category. In: J. Bybee & P. Hopper (eds.). *Frequency and the Emergence of Linguistic Structure*. Amsterdam: Benjamins, 91–120.
Hampton, James 1987. Inheritance of attributes in natural concept conjunctions. *Memory & Cognition* 15, 55–71.
Hampton, James 1991. The combination of prototype concepts. In: P. Schwanenflugel (ed.). *The Psychology of Word Meanings*. Hillsdale, NJ: Erlbaum, 91–116.

Heider, Eleanor 1971. 'Focal' color areas and the development of color names. *Developmental Psychology* 4, 447–455.
Heider, Eleanor 1972. Universals in color naming and memory. *Journal of Experimental Psychology* 93, 10–20.
Hintzman, Douglas 1986. 'Schema abstraction' in a multiple-trace memory model. *Psychological Review* 93, 411–428.
Hoey, Michael 2005. *Lexical Priming*. London: Routledge.
Hudson, Richard 1990. *English Word Grammar*. Oxford: Blackwell.
Keil, Frank C. 1989. *Concepts, Kinds, and Cognitive Development*. Cambridge, MA: The MIT Press.
Kleiber, Georges 1990. *La sémantique du prototype. Catégories et sens lexical*. Paris: PUF.
Labov, William 1973. The boundaries of words and their meanings. In: C.-J. Bailey & R. W. Shuy (eds.). *New Ways of Analyzing Variation in English*. Washington, DC: Georgetown University Press, 340–373. Reprinted in: B. Aarts et al. (eds.). *Fuzzy Grammar. A Reader*. Oxford: Oxford University Press, 2004, 67–89.
Lakoff, George 1972. Hedges. A study in meaning criteria and the logic of fuzzy concepts. In: P. M. Peranteau, J. N. Levi & G. C. Phares (eds.). *Papers from the Eighth Regional Meeting of the Chicago Linguistic Society (= CLS)*. Chicago, IL: Chicago Linguistic Society, 183–228.
Lakoff, George 1982. Categories. An essay in cognitive linguistics. In: The Linguistic Society of Korea (ed.). *Linguistics in the Morning Calm. Selected Papers from SICOL-1981*. Seoul: Hanshin, 139–193.
Lakoff, George 1987. *Women, Fire, and Dangerous Things. What Categories Reveal about the Mind*. Chicago, IL: The University of Chicago Press.
Langacker, Ronald 1987. *Foundations of Cognitive Grammar, vol. 1. Theoretical Prerequisites*. Stanford, CA: Stanford University Press.
Langacker, Ronald 2000. A dynamic usage-based model. In: M. Barlow & S. Kemmer (eds.). *Usage-Based Models of Language*. Stanford, CA: CSLI Publications, 1–63.
Lewandowska-Tomaszczyk, Barbara 2007. Polysemy, prototypes, and radial categories. In: D. Geeraerts & H. Cuyckens (eds.). *The Oxford Handbook of Cognitive Linguistics*. Oxford: Oxford University Press, 139–169.
Lyons, John 1977. *Semantics*. Cambridge: Cambridge University Press.
MacLaury, Robert 1991. Prototypes revisited. *Annual Review of Anthropology* 20, 55–74.
MacLaury, Robert 1995. Vantage theory. In: J. Taylor & R. MacLaury (eds.). *Language and the Cognitive Construal of the World*. Berlin: Mouton de Gruyter, 231–276.
Majid, Asifa, Melissa Bowerman, Miriam van Staden & James S. Boster 2007. The semantic categories of cutting and breaking events. A crosslinguistic perspective. *Cognitive Linguistics* 18, special issue, 133–152.
Moon, Rosamund 1998. *Fixed Expressions and Idioms in English. A Corpus-Based Approach*. Oxford: Clarendon Press.
Murphy, Gregory 2002. *The Big Book of Concepts*. Cambridge, MA: The MIT Press.
Murphy, Gregory & Douglas Medin 1985. The role of theories in conceptual coherence. *Psychological Review* 92, 289–316.
Osherson, Daniel & Edward E. Smith 1981. On the adequacy of prototype theory as a theory of concepts. *Cognition* 9, 35–58.
Posner, Michael & Steven Keele 1968. On the genesis of abstract ideas. *Journal of Experimental Psychology* 77, 353–363.
Pulman, Stephen G. 1983. *Word Meaning and Belief*. London: Croom Helm.

Putnam, Hilary 1975. *Philosophical Papers, vol. 2. Mind, Language and Reality*. Cambridge: Cambridge University Press.
Rosch, Eleanor 1975. Cognitive representations of semantic categories. *Journal of Experimental Psychology. General* 104, 192–233.
Rosch, Eleanor 1977. Human categorization. In: N. Warren (ed.). *Studies in Cross-Cultural Psychology, vol. 1*. London: Academic Press, 3–49.
Rosch, Eleanor 1978. Principles of categorization. In: E. Rosch & B. Lloyd (eds.). *Cognition and Categorization*. Hillsdale, NJ: Erlbaum, 27–48. Reprinted in: B. Aarts et al. (eds.). *Fuzzy Grammar. A Reader*. Oxford: Oxford University Press, 2004, 91–108.
Rosch, Eleanor & Carolyn B. Mervis 1975. Family resemblances. Studies in the internal structure of categories. *Cognitive Psychology* 7, 573–605.
Rosch, Eleanor, Carolyn Mervis, Wayne Grey, David Johnson & Penny Boyes-Braem 1976. Basic objects in natural categories. *Cognitive Psychology* 8, 382–439.
Ross, Brian H. & Valerie S. Makin 1999. Prototype versus exemplar models. In: R. J. Sternberg (ed.). *The Nature of Cognition*. Cambridge, MA: The MIT Press, 205–241.
Rothkopf, Ernst Z. 1971. Incidental memory for location of information in text. *Journal of Verbal Learning and Verbal Behavior* 10, 608–613.
Sandra, Dominiek & Sally Rice 1995. Network analysis of prepositional meaning. Mirroring whose mind – the linguist's or the language user's? *Cognitive Linguistics* 6, 89–130.
Schacter, Daniel 1987. Implicit memory. History and current status. *Journal of Experimental Psychology. Learning, Memory, and Cognition* 13, 501–518.
Smith, Edward E. & Douglas L. Medin 1981. *Categories and Concepts*. Cambridge, MA: Harvard University Press.
Storms, Gert, Paul de Boeck & Wim Ruts 2000. Prototype and exemplar-based information in natural language categories. *Journal of Memory and Language* 42, 51–73.
Sweetser, Eve 1987. The definition of lie. An examination of the folk models underlying a semantic prototype. In: D. Holland & N. Quinn (eds.). *Cultural Models in Language and Thought*. Cambridge: Cambridge University Press, 43–66.
Taylor, John R. 1999. Cognitive semantics and structural semantics. In: A. Blank & P. Koch (eds.). *Historical Semantics and Cognition*. Berlin: Mouton de Gruyter, 17–48.
Taylor, John R. 2003a. *Linguistic Categorization*. 3rd edn. Oxford: Oxford University Press. 1st edn. 1989.
Taylor, John R. 2003b. Near synonyms as co-extensive categories. 'High' and 'tall' revisited. *Language Sciences* 25, 263–284.
Taylor, John R. 2006. Polysemy and the lexicon. In: G. Kristiansen et al. (eds.). *Cognitive Linguistics. Current Applications and Future Perspectives*. Berlin: Mouton de Gruyter, 51–80.
Taylor, John R. 2007. Semantic categories of cutting and breaking. Some final thoughts. *Cognitive Linguistics* 18, 331–337.
Taylor, John. R. 2008. Prototypes in cognitive linguistics. In: P. Robinson & N. Ellis (eds.). *Handbook of Cognitive Linguistics and Second Language Acquisition*. New York: Routledge, 39–65.
Tomasello, Michael 2003. *Constructing a Language. A Usage-Based Theory of Language Acquisition*. Cambridge, MA: Harvard University Press.
Tuggy, David 1993. Ambiguity, polysemy, and vagueness. *Cognitive Linguistics* 4, 273–290.
Tyler, Andrea & Vyvyan Evans 2001. Reconsidering prepositional polysemy networks. The case of over. *Language* 77, 724–765.

Violi, Patrizia 1997. *Significato ed esperienza*. Milan: Bompiani. English Translation in: P. Violi. *Meaning and Experience*. Bloomington, IN: Indiana University Press, 2001.
Wierzbicka, Anna 1990. 'Prototypes save'. On the uses and abuses of the notion of 'prototype' in linguistics and related fields. In: S. Tsohatzidis (ed.). *Meanings and Prototypes. Studies in Linguistic Categorization*. London: Routledge, 347–367. Reprinted in B. Aarts et al. (eds.). *Fuzzy Grammar. A Reader*. Oxford: Oxford University Press, 2000, 461–478.
Wierzbicka, Anna 1996. *Semantics. Primes and Universals*. Oxford: Oxford University Press.
Wittgenstein, Ludwig 1978. *Philosophical Investigations*. Translated by G. E. M. Anscombe. Oxford: Blackwell.
Zlatev, Jordan 2003. Polysemy or generality? Mu. In: H. Cuyckens, R. Dirven & J. Taylor (eds.). *Cognitive Approaches to Lexical Semantics*. Berlin: Mouton de Gruyter, 447–494.

Jean-Mark Gawron
3 Frame Semantics

1 Introduction —— 57
2 Fillmorean frames —— 59
3 Related conceptions —— 68
4 Events, profiling, and perspectivalization —— 73
5 Lexicography —— 80
6 Discourse understanding —— 81
7 Conclusion —— 82
8 References —— 83

Abstract: Frames are conceptual structures that provide context for elements of interpretation; their primary role in an account of text understanding is to explain how our text interpretations can leap far beyond what the text literally says. The present article explores the role of frames in providing a principled account of the openness and richness of word-meanings, distinguishing a frame-based account from classical approaches, such as accounts based on conceptual primitives, lexical fields, and connotation, and showing how they can play a role in the account of how word meaning interacts with syntactic valence.

> For there exists a great chasm between those, on the one side, who relate everything to a single central vision, one system more or less coherent or articulate, in terms of which they understand, think and feel – a single, universal, organizing principle in terms of which alone all that they are and say has significance – and, on the other side, those who pursue many ends, often unrelated and even contradictory, connected, if at all, only in some de facto way, for some psychological or physiological cause, related by no moral or aesthetic principle.
>
> Berlin (1957: 1), cited by Minsky (1975)

1 Introduction

Two properties of word meanings contribute mightily to the difficulty of providing a systematic account.

One is the *openness* of word meanings. The variety of word meanings is the variety of human experience. Consider defining words such as *Tuesday, barber, alimony, seminal, amputate,* and *brittle.* One needs to make reference to diverse

---

Jean-Mark Gawron, San Diego, CA, USA

https://doi.org/10.1515/9783110589245-003

practices, processes, and objects in the social and physical world: repeatable calendar events, grooming and hair, marriage and divorce, discourse about concepts and theories, and events of breaking. Before this seemingly endless diversity, semanticists have in the past stopped short, excluding it from the semantic enterprise, and attempting to draw a line between a small linguistically significant set of primitive concepts and the openness of the lexicon.

The other problem is the closely related problem of the *richness* of word meanings. Words are hard to define, not so much because they invoke fine content specific distinctions, but because they invoke vast amounts of background information. The concept of buying presupposes the complex social fact of a commercial transaction. The concept of alimony presupposes the complex social fact of divorce, which in turn presupposes the complex social fact of marriage. Richness, too, has inspired semanticists simply to stop, to draw a line, saying exact definitions of concepts do not matter for theoretical purposes.

This boundary-drawing strategy, providing a response if not an answer to the problems of richness and openness, deserves some comment. As linguistic semanticists, the story goes, our job is to account for systematic, structurally significant properties of meaning. This includes:

(1) a. the kinds of syntactic constructions lexical meanings are compatible with.
  i. the kinds of participants that become subjects and objects
  ii. regular semantic patterns of oblique markings and valence alternations

 b. Regular patterns of inference licensed by category, syntactic construction or closed class lexical item.

The idea is to carve off that part of semantics necessary for knowing and using the syntactic patterns of the language. To do this sort of work, we do not need to pay attention to every conceptually possible distinction. Instead we need a small set of semantic primitives that make the distinctions that linguistically matter; what is left over can be dealt with using some open class of predicates or features whose internal details are not of concern. Jackendoff (1990) is a good example of this kind of approach. The generative semantics program, especially as outlined in Lakoff (1972), is another. Dowty (1979) has many of the same features, but in places expresses doubts that the program can be completely carried out. The kind of analysis I have in mind can be exemplified through Dowty's generative--semantics-like analysis of causatives like *break.tr* (transitive *break*):

(2) a. John broke the glass.
 b. DO(John, CAUSE(BECOME(*broken*(*glass*))))

Here the predicates in capitals (DO, CAUSE, BECOME) are from the inventory of linguistically significant primitives, and the lower case predicates *(broken, glass)* are from the open class predicates whose internal structure does not matter. At most we need to know that one expresses a state *(broken)* and the other a kind *(glass)*. The details beyond that are linguistically insignificant. Of course there are differences in truth-conditions between states like *broken* and *dead*, but these have only minor selectional effects on the causative inchoatives created from them *(break.tr* = DO ... CAUSE BECOME broken' and *kill* = DO ... CAUSE BECOME dead'). I will refer to this view of lexical semantics as the *classical view*.

In this paper I wish to consider a view of semantics in general and lexical semantics in particular that is quite at odds with this classical picture: *Frame Semantics* (Fillmore 1975, 1977b, 1978, 1982, 1985). Someone wishing to contest the classical picture has two options: first, contend that the wrong kinds of questions are being asked; second, argue that the program as outlined is not very well-suited to attaining its goals. As we shall see, both kinds of objection motivate Frame Semantics.

2 Fillmorean frames

2.1 Motivations

The version of Frame Semantics I will present here is largely the brainchild of Charles J. Fillmore. Although Frame Semantics has sprouted off in a number of directions and been applied to a number of problems, I will limit the present discussion in two ways: First I will confine myself largely to fleshing out the Fillmorean picture; second, I will confine myself mostly to questions of the lexicon, lexicography, and the lexicon-syntax interface, leaving for other work questions of discourse and text understanding to which frames are also relevant. I will briefly consider the different roles frames play in the account of sign meaning and discourse interpretation.

Although Fillmore has had many interesting things to say about the kinds of problems listed in (1) in early and late works on Case Grammar, the primary motivations given in Fillmore (1982, 1985) focus on Frame Semantics as a contribution to a theory of *text understanding*. Consider for example, the very different scenes evoked by the following pair of sentences, discussed in Fillmore (1985):

(3) a. I can't wait to be on the ground again.
    b. I can't wait to be on land again.

Sentence (3a) evokes a speaker who is in the air (on a plane), sentence (3b) a speaker who is at sea (on a ship). This contrast is tied to some difference between the words *land* and *ground*, yet, on the face of it, *land* and *ground* denote very similar things. Fillmore would say *land* is understood within a conceptual frame of sea travel, and within that frame it is opposed to *sea*, while *ground* is understood within a conceptual frame of air travel, and within that frame, it is opposed to *air*. Thus we can explain something that is very difficult to explain in terms what the words in the sentence denote by investigating the conceptual background against which the relevant word senses are defined. That conceptual background is what Fillmore calls a frame.

Frames are conceptual structures that provide context for elements of interpretation; their primary role in an account of text understanding is to explain how our text interpretations can (validly) leap far beyond what the text literally says. Frames can be introduced into interpretation in a variety of ways. They may be directly tied to word senses as in the example of *land* and *ground* or they may be introduced by patterns among the facts the text establishes. To use another example of Fillmore's (1985: 232):

(4) We never open our presents until morning.

This sentence *evokes* the Christmas frame by describing a situation that matches salient facts of Christmas practice, even though no word in it is specific to Christmas. If in fact the Christmas frame is the right one, that evocation makes a significant contribution to the understanding of the surrounding text.

Frames are motivated not just by words, then, but by stereotypes about customs, practices, institutions, and games. Moreover, the kinds of cognitive structures Fillmore has in mind have been proposed by a variety of researchers for a variety of purposes. Fillmore has adopted the terminology of AI researcher Minsky (1975) in calling them frames, but *schemata* in psychology (Bartlett 1932, Rumelhart 1980) are getting at something very similar, as are *scripts* (Schank & Abelson 1977), *cognitive models* (Lakoff 1983), *experiential gestalts* (Lakoff & Johnson 1980), *the base* (as opposed to the profile) (Langacker 1984), and Fillmore's own notion of *scene* (Fillmore 1976, 1977a). More recently, in articulating a *simulation view* of conceptual processing, Barsalou (1992, 1999) has proposed that object conceptualization is processed through simulators of objects linked to components of a variety of situation memories; one consequence is that objects may activate components from different situations in different perceptual contexts. In this theory, too, then, conceptualization is framed against a background with components that help provide an interpretation for scenes or objects. For more discussion, see article 12 [Semantics: Typology, Diachrony and Processing] (Kelter & Kaup) *Conceptual knowledge, categorization, and meaning.*

As an approach to word meanings specifically, the starting point for Frame Semantics is that the lexical semantics "problems" of openness and richness are connected. Openness depends on richness. Openness does not mean lack of structure. In fact, it presupposes structure. Most concepts are interpretable or understandable or definable only against the background of other concepts. Many backgrounds are rich enough to define a cluster of concepts, in particular, a cluster of words. These backgrounds are the frames. Thus because words are networked together through their shared backgrounds, frames can provide an organizing principle for the openness of the lexicon.

Consider one of the examples already discussed, discussed in Fillmore (1982). The concept of alimony depends on the concept of divorce. The concept of divorce in turn depends on the concept of marriage. The dependency is definitional. Unless you define what a marriage is, you can't define what a divorce is. Unless you define what a divorce is, you can't define what alimony is. Thus there is a very real sense in which the dependencies we are describing move us toward *simpler* concepts. Notice, however, that the dependency is leading in a different direction than an analysis that decomposes meanings into a small set of primitives like CAUSE and BECOME. Instead of leading to concepts of increasing generality and abstractness, we are being led to define the situations or circumstances which provide the necessary *background* for the concepts we are describing. The concepts of marriage and divorce are equally specific, but the institution of marriage provides the necessary background for the institution of divorce.

Or consider the complex subject of Tuesdays (Fillmore 1985). We live in a world of cyclic events. Seasons come and go and then return. This leads to a cyclic calendar which divides time up into repeating intervals, which are divided up further. Years are divided into months, which are divided into weeks, which are divided into days, which have cyclic names. Each week has a Sunday, a Monday, a Tuesday, and so on. Defining Tuesday entails defining the notion of a cyclic calendar. Knowing the word *Tuesday* may not entail knowing the word *Sunday*, but it does entail understanding at least the concept of a week and a day and their relation, and that each week has exactly one Tuesday.

We thus have words and background concepts. We will call the background concept the *frame*. Now the idea of a frame begins to have some lexical semantic bite with the observation that a single concept may provide the background for a set of words. Thus the concept of MARRIAGE provides the background for words/suffixes/phrases such as *bride, groom, marriage, wedding, divorce, -in-law, elope, fiancee, best man, maid-of-honor, honeymoon, husband,* and *wife,* as well as a variety of basic kinship terms omitted here for reasons of space. The concept of CALENDAR CYCLE provides the frame for lexical items such as *week, month, year, season, Sunday, ..., Saturday, January, ..., December, day, night, morning,* and *afternoon*.

Notice that a concept once defined may provide the background frame for further concepts. Thus, DIVORCE itself provides the background frame for lexical items such as *alimony, divorce, divorce court, divorce attorney, ex-husband*, and *ex-wife*.

In sum, a frame may organize a vocabulary domain:

> Borrowing from the language of gestalt psychology we could say that the assumed background of knowledge and practices – the complex frame behind this vocabulary domain – stands as a common ground to the figure representable by any of the individual words.
>
> [Words belonging to a frame] are lexical representatives of some single coherent schematization of experience or knowledge.
>
> Fillmore (1985: 223)

Now a premise of Frame Semantics is that the relation between lexical items and frames is open ended. Thus one way in which the openness of the lexicon manifests itself is in building concepts in unpredictable ways against the backdrop of other concepts. The concept of marriage seems to be universal or near-universal in human culture. The concept of alimony is not. No doubt concepts sometimes pop into the lexicon along with their defining frames (perhaps *satellite* is an example), but the usual case is to try to build them up out of some existing frame (Thus *horseless carriage* leading to *car* is the more usual model).

Summing up: openness does not mean structurelessness. Concepts and their related words have certain unidirectional backgrounding relations that frames capture.

(5)	Words	Frames
	bride, groom, marriage, wedding, divorce, -in-law, elope, fiancee, best man, maid-of-honor, honeymoon, husband, wife	MARRIAGE
	alimony, divorce court, divorce attorney, ex-husband, and *ex-wife*	DIVORCE
	week, month, year, Sunday, ..., Saturday, January, ..., December, morning, afternoon	CALENDAR CYCLE
	freezing, cold, cool, tepid, lukewarm, warm, hot, temperature, thermometer	TEMPERATURE

All of this obviously points in exactly the opposite direction from the classical view, a few salient primitives, a hard distinction between linguistic and encyclopedic, and a large uninvestigated class of open class predicates.

But from the other direction, support for the classical view has been eroding even among those whose concerns have primarily departed from the problems in

(1) such as Levin (1993) or from classic lexical semantic problems like polysemy (Pustejovsky 1995).

Consider the kind of problem Levin (1993) discusses in her seminal study of English verb classes. A theory that does not posit a systematic difference between the *broken* state of the verb *break* in (2) and the *dead* state in the decomposition of *kill* cannot account for the following contrast:

(6) a. John broke the glass against the wall.
    b. #John killed the cockroach against the wall.

Nor can it account for the fact that verbs in some sense close in meaning to *break* (*shatter, smash, crack, flatten*) will follow pattern (a), while verbs in some sense close to *kill* will follow pattern (b) (*strangle, murder, smother,* and *drown*). The generalization at issue is (roughly) that state change or directed action verbs whose effect is commonly achieved by moving one object against another will allow pattern (a) when the object whose state is changed or potentially changed is direct object. Other examples are *hit, knock, rap, bang,* and *slam*. None of the kill-type verbs fit the bill.

Thus if valence patterns are part of what is to be explained, then a language like English, with its rich inventory of prepositions and situationally specific constructions (see for example the pattern lists in Levin 1993), will require reference to a large inventory of concepts. It is difficult to see how a principled line between open class and closed class concepts can be drawn in carrying out this program. It is clear for example, that Levin's verbs of contact, which include the verbs like *hit* and *slap* discussed above, overlap signicantly with the verbs list for the IMPACT frame in FrameNet, a large computational instantiation of the ideas of Frame Semantics (Fillmore & Atkins 1994; Baker, Fillmore & Lowe 1998; Fillmore & Atkins 1998; Baker & Fillmore 2001; Boas 2001, 2005; Chang, Narayanan & Petruck 2002a, 2002b). At last count the NSF FrameNet project (Fillmore & Baker 2000) which is building a frame lexicon for English had over 800 frames for about 4500 words. Thus the problems of openness and richness arise whether one starts from text understanding or from syntax/semantics interface.

2.2 Basic tools

We have thus far focused on the role of frames in a theory of word meanings. Note that nothing in particular hangs on the notion *word*. Frames may also have a conventional connection to a simple syntactic constructions or idiom; *give someone the slip* probably belongs to the same frame as *elude*. Or they may be tied to more complex constructions such as the Comparative Correlative (cf. article 9 [Semantics: Interfaces] (Kay & Michaelis) *Constructional meaning*).

(7) The more I drink the better you look.

This construction has two "slots" requiring properties of quantity or degree. The same issues of background situation and profiled participants arise whether the linguistic exponent is a word or construction. The term *sign*, used in exactly the same sense as it is used by construction grammarians, will serve here as well.

As a theory of the conventional association of schematized situations and linguistic exponents, then, Frame Semantics makes the assumption that there is always some background knowledge relative to which linguistic elements do some profiling, and relative to which they are defined. Two ideas are central:

1. a background concept
2. a set of *signs* including all the words and constructions that utilize this conceptual background.

Two other important frame theoretic concepts are *frame elements* and *profiling*.

Thus far in introducing frames I have emphasized what might be called the modularity of knowledge. Our knowledge of the the world can usefully be divided up into concrete chunks. Equally important to the Fillmorian conception of frames is the integrating function of frames. That is, frames provide us with the means to integrate with other frames in context to produce coherent wholes. For this function, the crucial concept is the notion of a *frame element* (Fillmore & Baker 2000). A frame element is simply a regular participant, feature, or attribute of the kind of situation described by a frame. Thus, frame elements of the wedding frame will include the husband, wife, wedding ceremony, wedding date, best man and maid of honor, for example. Frame elements need not be obligatory; one may have a wedding without a best man; but they need to be regular recurring features.

Thus, frames have slots, replaceable elements. This means that frames can be linked to to other frames by sharing participants or even by being participants in other frames. They can be components of an interpretation.

In Frame Semantics, all word meanings are relativized to frames. But different words select different aspects of the background to *profile* (we use the terminology in Langacker 1984). Sometimes aspects profiled by different words are mutually exclusive parts of the circumstances, such as the husband and wife in the marriage frame, but sometimes word meanings differ not in what they profile, but in how they profile it. In such cases, I will say words differ in *perspective*

(Fillmore 1977a). I will use Fillmore's much-discussed commercial event example (Fillmore 1976) to illustrate:

(8) a. John sold the book to Mary for $100.
　　b. Mary bought the book from John for $100.
　　c. Mary paid John $100 for the book.

Verbs like *buy, sell, pay* have as background the concept of a commercial transaction, an event in which a *buyer* gives *money* to a *seller* in exchange for some *goods*. Now because the transaction is an exchange it can be thought of as containing what Fillmore calls two *subscenes: a goods_transfer,* in which the goods is transferred from the seller to the buyer, and *a money_transfer,* in which the money is transferred from the buyer to the seller. Here it is natural to say that English has as a valence realization option for transfers of possession one in which the object being transferred from one possessor to another is realized as direct object. Thus verbs profiling the money transfer will make the money the direct object *(pay* and *collect)* and verbs profiling the goods transfer will make the goods the direct object *(buy* and *sell).* Then the difference between these verb pairs can be chalked up to what is profiled.

But what about the difference between *buy* and *sell*? By hypothesis, both verbs profile a goods transfer, but in one case the buyer is subject and in another the seller is. Perhaps this is just an arbitrary choice. This is in some sense what the thematic role theory of Dowty (1991) says: Since (8a) and (8b) are mutually entailing, there can be no semantic account of the choice of subject.

In Frame Semantics, however, we may attempt to describe the facts as follows: in the case of *buy* the buyer is viewed as *(perspectivalized* as) agent, in the case of *sell*, the seller is. There are two advantages to this description. First, it allows us to preserve a principle assumed by a number of linguists, that cross-linguistically agents must be subjects. Second, it allows us to interpret certain adjuncts that enter into special relations with agents: instrumentals, benefactives, and purpose clauses.

(9) a. John bought the book from Mary with/for his last pay check. [Both *with* and *for* allow the reading on which the pay check provides the funds for the purchase.]
　　b. Mary sold the book to John ?with/for his last paycheck. [Only *for* allows the reading on which the pay check provides the funds.]
　　c. John bought the house from Sue for Mary. [allows reading on which Mary is ultimate owner, disallows the reading on which Mary is seller and Sue is seller's agent.]

d. Sue sold the house to John for Mary. [allows reading on which Mary is seller and Sue is seller's agent; disallows reading on which Mary is ultimate owner.]
e. John bought the house from Sue to evade taxes/as a tax dodge. [tax benefit is John's]
f. Sue sold the house to John to evade taxes/as a tax dodge. [tax benefit is Sue's]

But what does it mean to say that a verb takes a perspective which "views" a particular participant as an agent? The facts are, after all, that both the buyer and the seller are agents; they have all the entailment properties that characterize what we typically call agents; and this, Dowty's theory of thematic roles tells us, is why verbs like *buy* and *sell* can co-exist. I will have more to say on this point in section 4; for the moment I will confine myself to the following general observation on what Frame Semantics allows: What is profiled and what is left out is not determined by the entailment facts of its frame. Complex variations are possible. For example, as Fillmore observes, the COMMERCIAL TRANSACTION frame is associated with verbs that have no natural way of realizing the seller:

(10) John spent $100 on that book.

Nothing in the valence marking of the verb *spend* suggests that what is being profiled here is a possession transfer; neither the double object construction, nor *from* nor *to* is possible for marking a core COMMERCIAL TRANSACTION participant. Rather the pattern seems to be the one available for what one might call *resource consumption* verbs like *waste, lose, use (up),* and *blow*. In this profiling, there is no room for a seller. Given that such variation in what is profiled is allowed, the idea that the agenthood of a participant might be part of what's included or left out does not seem so far-fetched. As I will argue in section 4, the inclusion of events into the semantics can help us make semantic sense of what abstractions like this might mean.

These considerations argue that there can be more than one frame backgrounding a single word meaning; for example, concepts of commercial event, possession transfer, and agentivity simultaneously define *buy*. A somewhat different but related issue is the issue of event structure. There is strong evidence cross-linguistically at least in the form of productive word-formation processes that some verbs – for example, causatives – represent complex events that can only be expressed through a combination of two frames with a very specific semantics. So it appears that a word meaning can simultaneously invoke a configuration of frames, with particulars of the configuration sometimes spelled out morphologically.

The idea that any word meaning exploits a background is of use in the account of polysemy. Different senses will in general involve relativization to different frames. As a very simple example, consider the use of *spend* in the following sentence:

(11) John spent 10 minutes fixing his watch.

How are we to describe the relationship of the use of *spend* in this example, which basically describes a watch fixing event, with that in (10), which describes a COMMERCIAL TRANSACTION? One way is to say that one sense involves the COMMERCIAL TRANSACTION, and another involves a frame we might call ACTION DURATION which relates actions to their duration, a frame that would also be invoked by durative uses of *for*. A counter-proposal is that there is one sense here, which involves an actor using up a resource. But such a proposal runs up against the problem that *spend* really has rather odd disjunctive selection restrictions:

(12) John spent 30 packs of cigarettes that afternoon.

Sentence (12) is odd except perhaps in a context (such as a prison or boarding school) where cigarette packs have become a fungible medium of exchange; what it cannot mean is that John simply used up the cigarettes (by smoking them, for example). The point is that a single general resource consumption meaning ought to freely allow resources other than time and money, so a single resource consumption sense does not correctly describe the readings available for (12); however, a sense invoking a COMMERCIAL TRANSACTION frame constrained to very specific circumstances does. Note also, that the fact that 30 packs of cigarettes can be the *money* participant in the right context is naturally accommodated. The right constraint on the money participant is not that it be cash (for which Visa and Mastercard can be thankful), but that it be a fungible medium of exchange.

Summarizing:
1. Frames are motivated primarily by issues of understanding and converge with various schema-like conceptions advanced by cognitive psychologists, AI researchers, and cognitive linguists. They are experientially coherent backgrounds with variable components that allow us to organize families of concepts.
2. The concept of frames has far reaching consequences when applied to lexical semantics, because a single frame can provide the organizing background for

a set of words. Thus frames can provide an organizing principle for a rich open lexicon. FrameNet is an embodiment of these ideas.
3. In proposing an account of lexical semantics rich enough for a theory of understanding, Frame Semantics converges with other lexical semantic research which has been bringing to bear a richer set of concepts on problems of the syntax semantics interface.

Having sketched the basic idea, I want in the next two sections to briefly contrast the notion frame with two other ideas that have played a major role in semantics, the idea of a relation, as incorporated via set theory and predicate logic into semantics, and the idea of a lexical field.

3 Related conceptions

In this section I compare the idea of frames with two other concepts of major importance in theories of lexical semantics, relations and lexical fields. The comparison offers the opportunity to develop some other key ideas of Frame Semantics, including profiling and saliency.

3.1 Frames versus relations: profiling and saliency

Words (most verbs, some nouns, arguably all degreeable adjectives) describe relations in the world. Love and hate are relations between animate experiencers and objects. The verb *believe* describes a relation between an animate experiencer and a pro-position. These are commonplace views among philsophers of language, semanticists, and syntacticians, and they have provided the basis for much fruitful work. Where do frames fit in?

For Fillmore, frames describe the factual basis for relations. In this sense they are "pre-"relational. To illustrate, Fillmore (1985) cites Mill's (1847) discussion of the words *father* and *son*. Although there is a single history of events which establishes both the father- and the son- relation, the words *father* and *son* pick out different entities in the world. In Mill's terminology, the words *denote* different things, but *connote* a single thing, the shared history. This history, which Mill calls the *fundamentum relationis* (the foundation of the relation), determines that the two relations bear a fixed structural relation to each other. It is the idea of a determinate structure for a set of relations that Fillmore likens to the idea of a frame.

Thus, a frame defines not a single relation but, minimally, a structured set of relations.

This conception allows for a natural description not just of pairs of words like *father* and *son*, but also of single words which do not in fact settle on a particular relation. Consider the verb *risk*, discussed in Fillmore & Atkins (1998), which seems to allow a range of participants into a single grammatical "slot". For example,

(13) Joan risked
 a. censure.
 b. her car.
 c. a trip down the advanced ski slope.

The RISK frame has at least 3 distinct participants, (a) the bad thing that may happen, (b) the valued thing that may be lost, and (c) the activity that may cause the bad thing to happen. All can be realized in the direct object position, as (13) shows. Since there are three distinct relations here, a theory that identifies lexical meanings with relations needs to say there are 3 meanings as well. Frame Semantics would describe this as one frame allowing 3 distinct profilings. It is the structure of the frame together with the profiling options the language makes available which makes the 3 alternatives possible.

Other verbs with a similar indeterminacy of participant are *copy, collide,* and *mix*:

(14) a. Sue copied her costume (from a film poster).
 b. Sue copied the film poster.
 c. The truck and the car collided.
 d. The truck collided with the car.
 e. John mixed the soup.
 f. John mixed the paste into the soup.
 g. John mixed the paste and the flour.

In each of these cases the natural Frame Semantics account would be to say the frame remains constant while the profilings or perspective changes. Thus, under a Frame Semantics approach, verbal valence alternations are to be expected, and the possibility of such alternations provides motivation for the idea of a background frame with a range of participants and a range of profiling options.

Now on a theory in which senses are relations, all the verbs in (14) must have different senses. This is, for example, because the arguments in (14a) and (14b) fill different roles. Frame Semantics allows another option. We can say the same verb sense is used in both cases. The differences in interpretation arise because of differences in profiling and perspectivalization.

3.2 Frames versus lexical fields

Because frames define lexical sets, it is useful to contrast the concept of frames with an earlier body of lexical semantic work which takes as central the identification of lexical sets. This work develops the idea of *lexical fields* (Weisgerber 1962; Coseriu 1967; Trier 1971; Geckeler 1971; Lehrer & Kittay 1992). Lexical fields define sets of lexical items in mutually defining relations, in other words, lexical semantic paradigms. The classic example of a lexical field is the set of German labels used for evaluating student performance (Weisgerber 1962: 99):

(15) *sehr gut, gut, genügend* and *mangelhaft*

The terms are mutually defining because the significance of a single evaluation obviously depends on knowing the entire set and the relations of the terms in the set. Thus *gut* means one thing in a school system with the 4 possibilities in (15) and quite another if the possibilities are:

(16) *sehr gut, gut, befriedigend, ausreichend, mangelhaft* and *ungenügend*

Fillmore also cites the example of the tourist industry use of the term *first class* in their categorization of hotels; to many travelers, *first class* sounds pretty good; in fact, the top ranked class of hotels is *luxury* and *first class* is fourth from the top. The misunderstanding here seems exactly like a case of applying the wrong frame in the process of understanding.

Domains in which lexical fields have provided fruitful analyses include color, temperature, furniture and artifacts, kinship relations, intelligence, livestock, and terrain features (Fillmore 1985: 227).

The general hypothesis of lexical field theory is that the lexicon can be carved up into a number of (sometimes overlapping) lexical sets, each of which functions as a closed system. To this extent, there is agreement with the conception of frames, and in fact, the lexical sets associated with frames can include lexemes in paradigmatic, mutually defining relations. For example, we identified the TEMPERATURE frame in section 2, and this includes the lexical field of temperature words like *cold, cool, lukewarm, warm,* and *hot*.

However, the idea of a frame is distinct from the idea of a lexical field. To start with, the idea of a one-word lexical field is incoherent: How can a word have a function in a field in which there is nothing for it to be opposed to? However, there is no inherent difficulty with the idea of a one-word frame. Fillmore (1985) cites the example of *hypotenuse*, which requires for its background the concept of a right triangle. There appear to be no other English lexical items specific to right triangles (the term *leg* in the relevant sense seems to apply to triangle sides in general); and that is neither surprising nor problematic. The notion mutually defining is not necessary for lexical frame sets because words in frames are defined in contrast to or in terms of the frame alone. The frame, not its lexical instantiations, provides the background necessary to identify a semantic function. The primitive notion is not *defined in opposition to* but *profiled from the background of*.

A second way in which frames differ from lexical fields is that, even when there is more than one word, there is no requirement that words in the set function in paradigmatic opposition to one another. Thus the TEMPERATURE frame cited above also contains the noun *temperature*, just as the HEIGHT frame containing polar adjectives like *tall* and *short* will contain the noun *height*.

Thirdly, because of the notion of mutual definition, lexical fields come with strict criteria of individuation. In contrast, as we saw in section 2, frames of arbitrary specificity make sense. Thus, we have very general frames of TEMPERATURE and HEIGHT. But we also have a set of specific frames that recover the traditional mutually defining sets that preoccupied lexical field theorists, a specialization of HEIGHT that includes just the polar adjectives, a specialization of TEMPERATURE that includes just the set *cold, cool, warm, hot,* and so on. This level of specificity in fact roughly describes the granularity of FrameNet.

3.3 Minskian frames

As described in Fillmore (1982), the term *frame* is borrowed from Marvin Minsky. It will be useful before tackling the question of how profiling and perspectivalization work to take a closer look at this precursor.

In Minsky's original frames paper (Minsky 1975), frames were put forth as a solution to the problem of *scene interpretation* in vision. Minsky's proposal was in reaction to those who, like the Gestalt theorists (Koffka 1963), viewed scene perception as a single holistic process governed by principles similar to those at work in electric fields. Minsky thought scenes were assembled in independent chunks, constituent by constituent, in a series of steps involving interpretation and integration. To describe this process, a model factoring the visual field into a number of discrete chunks, each with its own model of change with its own discrete phases, was needed.

A frame was thus a dynamic model of some specific kind of object with specific participants and parameters. The model had built-in expectations about ways in which the object could change, either in time or as a viewer's perspective on it changed, formalized as operations mapping old frame states to new frame states. A frame also included a set of *participants* whose status changed under these operations; those moving into certain distinguished slots are *foregrounded*. Thus, for example, in the simplified version of Minsky's *cube frame*, shown before and after a rotation in Figs. 3.1. and 3.2, a frame state encodes a particular view of a cube and the participants are cube faces. One possible operation is a rotation of the cube, defined to place new faces in certain view-slots, and move old faces out and possibly out of view. The faces that end up in view are the foregrounded participants of the resulting frame state. Thus the cube frame offers the tools for representing particular views or *perspectives* on a cube, together with the operations that may connect them in time.

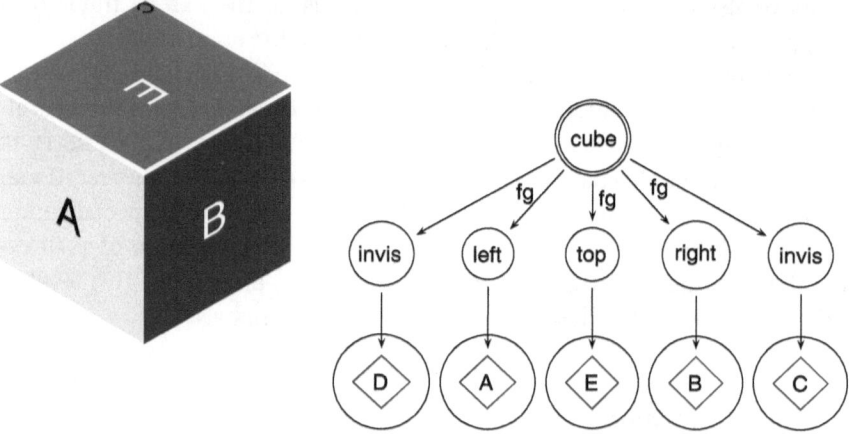

Fig. 3.1: View of cube together with simplified cube frame representing that view. Links marked "fg" lead to foregrounded slots; slots marked "invis" are backgrounded. Faces D and C are out of view.

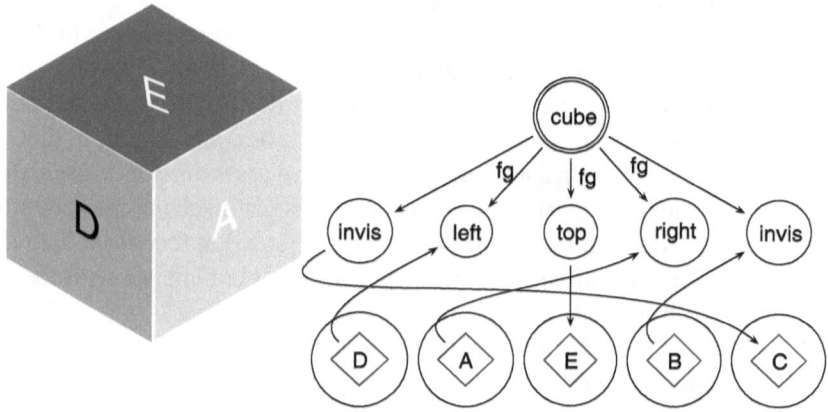

Fig. 3.2: Cube frame after counterclockwise rotation. Faces D and A are now foregrounded, B has moved out of view.

Fillmore's innovation, then, was to apply this Minskian idea in the domain of word meaning, importing not only the idea of chunked modular knowledge units, but also the idea of operations that take perspectives on such chunks. I used the terms profiling and perspectivalization to describe such operations in section 2. Although Fillmore himself does not attempt a formalization of these operations, I believe it is possible to clearly describe what is at issue using some ideas from event semantics (Davidson 1967, 1980, Parsons 1990), building on the event-based approach to frames in Gawron (1983).

4 Events, profiling, and perspectivalization

To spell out a bit better how word senses might invoke multiple frames, let us return to the case of the COMMERCIAL TRANSACTION frame discussed in section 2. The following development takes up and extends the ideas of Gawron (1983).

A rather natural account of the interface between frames and compositional semantics becomes available if we make use of neo-Davidsonian event-semantics (Davidson 1967, 1980; Parsons 1990). On a neo-Davidsonian account, we have, as the schematic semantics for *John bought the book on sale:*

$$\exists e[\text{buy'}(e) \land agent(e) = j \land patient(e) = b \land \text{on-sale}(e, b)]$$

We call *e* in the above representation the *lexical event*.

I assume that Fillmorean frames classify events. That is, there is such a thing as a COMMERCIAL TRANSACTION event. Further, I assume that lexical predicates like *give* and *buy* are predicates true of events. These lexical events cannot be directly identified with Fillmorean frame events. Rather the lexical events are perspectivalizations of Fillmorean frame events. Thus, for example, buying will be associated with three events, one *perspectivalizing* event that is directly related to syntactic realization, a second *profiling* event that is a profiling of a third COMMERCIAL TRANSACTION (or Filmorean frame event). I will call this latter the *circumstance* event. Perspectivalizing, profiling, and circumstance events will be related by functions.

Borrowing the machinery of sorted logic (Carpenter 1992; Smolka 1992; Rounds 1997), I will assume that all predicates are *sorted*; that is, it is a property of predicates and relations that in all models, for any given argument position, there is a sort of individuals for which that argument position is *defined*. I will write sorts in boldface and predicates in roman.

(17)   AGENT PATIENT : **agent_patient → truth-values**
       agent: **agent_patient → animate**
       patient: **agent_patient → entity**
       source : **agent_patient → (entity)**
       goal: **agent_patient → (entity)**

These declarations just say, in roughly standard mathematical notation that agent and patient are functions from one set to another. For example, the first declaration says that AGENT PATIENT is a function from the set (sort) to truth-values; the second says *agent* is a function from the set (sort) of AGENT PATIENT events to animates; *patient* from the set of AGENT PATIENT events to the set of things (the domain of entities). The parentheses in the source and goal role definitions may be taken to mean that the role is optional (or the function is *partial*). Not every AGENT PATIENT event has a source or a goal, but some do.

I assume the declarations (or axioms) in (17) are sufficient to define a very simple kind of frame. The first axiom defines a predicate AGENT PATIENT that is true of events of that sort; the rest define a set of roles for that sort of event. Thus a minimal frame is just an event sort defined for a set of roles. I will call AGENT PATIENT an *argument frame* because syntactic arguments of a verb will need to directly link to the roles of argument frames (such as *agent* and *patient*). We can represent this set of axioms as an attribute-value matrix (AVM):

(18) $\begin{bmatrix} \text{AGENT} & \text{PATIENT} \\ \text{agent} & \textbf{animate} \\ \text{source} & \textbf{entity} \\ \text{goal} & \textbf{entity} \\ \text{patient} & \textbf{entity} \end{bmatrix}$

Henceforth I use AVM notation for readability, but the reader should bear in mind that it is merely a shorthand for a set of axioms like those in (17), constraining partial functions and relations on sorts.

I will call AGENT PATIENT an *argument frame* because syntactic arguments of a verb will need to directly link to the roles of argument frames (such as *agent* and *patient*). The AGENT PATIENT frame is very general, too general to be of much semantic use. In order to use it a lexical item must specify some circumstance frame in which participant roles are further specified with further constraints.

The connection between an argument frame like AGENT PATIENT and simple circumstance frames can be illustrated through the example of the POSSESSION TRANSFER frame (related to verbs like *give, get, take, receive, acquire, bequeath, loan,* and so on). Represented as an AVM, this is:

(19) $\begin{bmatrix} \text{POSSESSION TRANSFER} \\ \text{donor} \quad \textbf{animate} \\ \text{possession} \; \textbf{entity} \\ \text{recipient} \; \textbf{animate} \end{bmatrix}$

Now both *give* and *acquire* will be defined in terms of the POSSESSION TRANSFER frame, but *give* and *acquire* differ in that with *give* the *donor* becomes subject and with *acquire* the *recipient* does. (Compare the difference between *buy* and *sell* discussed in section 2.2.)

We will account for this difference by saying that *give* and *acquire* have different mappings from the AGENT PATIENT frame to their shared circumstance frame (POSSESSION TRANSFER). This works as follows.

We define the relation between a circumstance and argument frame via a *perspectivalizing function*. Here are the axioms for what we will call the *acquisition* function, on which the recipient is agent:

(20) a. *acquisition* : **possession_transfer** → **agent_patient**
 b. *agent o acquisition = recipient*
 c. *patient o acquisition = possession*
 d. *source o acquisition = donor*

The first line defines *acquisition* as a mapping from the sort **possession_transfer** to the sort **agent_patient,** that is as a mapping from POSSESSION TRANSFER eventualities to AGENT PATIENT eventualities. The mapping is total; that is, each POSSESSION TRANSFER is guaranteed to have an AGENT PATIENT eventuality associated with it. In the second line, the symbol *o* stands for *function composition;* the composition of the *agent* function with the *acquisition* function (written *agent o acquisition*) is the same function (extensionally) as the *recipient* relation. Thus the filler of the *recipient* role in a possession transfer must be the same as the filler of the *agent* role in the associated AGENT PATIENT eventuality. And so on, for the other axioms. Summing up AVM style:

(21)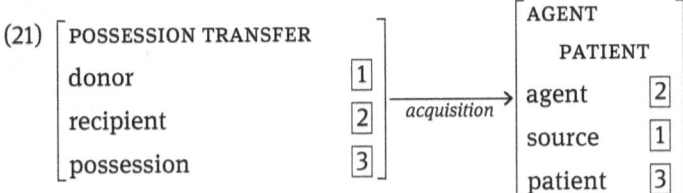

I will call the mapping that makes the *donor* agent *donation*.

(22)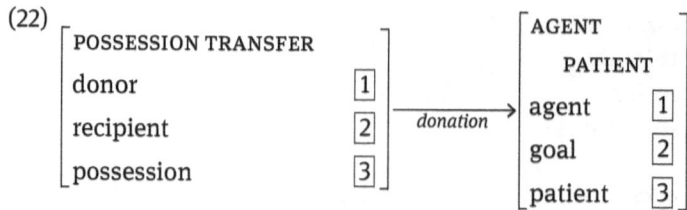

With the *acquisition* and *donation* mappings defined, the predicates *give* and *acquire* can be defined as compositions with *donation* and *acquisition*:

$$\text{give} = \text{POSSESSION TRANSFER} \circ donation^{-1}$$
$$\text{acquire} = \text{POSSESSION TRANSFER} \circ acquisition^{-1}$$

$donation^{-1}$ is an inverse of *donation*, a function from AGENT PATIENT eventualities to POSSESSION TRANSFERS defined only for those AGENT PATIENT events related to POSSESSION TRANSFERS. Composing this with the POSSESSION TRANSFER predicate makes *give* a predicate true of those AGENT PATIENT events related to possession transfers, whose agents are donors and whose patients are possessions. The treatment of *acquire* is parallel but uses the *acquisition* mappings. For more extensive discussion, see Gawron (2008).

Summarizing:
a. an argument frame AGENT PATIENT, with direct consequences for syntactic valence (agents become subject, patients direct object, and so on).
b. a circumstance frame POSSESSION TRANSFER, which captures the circumstances of possession transfer.
c. *perspectivalizing* functions *acquisition* and *donation* which map participants in the circumstances to argument structure.

This is the basic picture of perspectivalization. The picture becomes more interesting with a richer example.

In the discussion that follows, I assume a commercial transaction frame with at least the following frame elements:

(23) $\begin{bmatrix} \text{COMMERCIAL} \\ \quad \text{TRANSACTION} \\ \text{buyer} \quad \textbf{animate} \\ \text{seller} \quad \textbf{animate} \\ \text{money} \quad \textbf{fungible} \\ \text{goods} \quad \textbf{entity} \end{bmatrix}$

This is a declaration that various functions from event sorts to truth values and entity sorts exist, a rather austere model for the sort of rich backgrounding function we have assumed for frames. We will see how this model is enriched below.

Our picture of profiling and perspectivalization can be extended to the more complex cases of commercial transaction predicates with one more composition. For example, we may define buy' as follows:

(24) buy = COMMERCIAL TRANSACTION O (*acquisition* O *goods-transfer*)⁻¹

What this says is that the relation buy' is built in a series of steps, out of 3 functions:
1. *acquisition*: the function from possession transfer events to AGENT_PATIENT events already introduced.
2. *goods-transfer*: a new function from commercial events to possession transfers in which the goods is transferred:

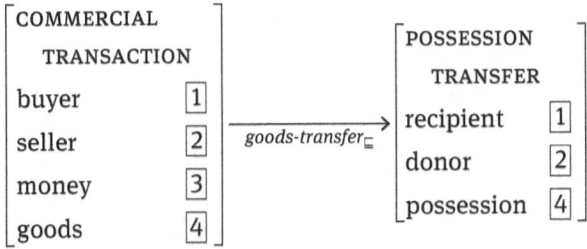

3. The inverse of the composition of *goods-transfer* with *acquisition*

(*acquisition* O *goods-transfer*)⁻¹

is a function from agent patient events to commercial transactions.
4. COMMERCIAL TRANSACTION: a sortal predicate true of commercial transactions.
5. The predicate *buy* is therefore true of AGENT PATIENT events that are related in certain fixed ways to a POSSESSION TRANSFER and a COMMERCIAL TRANSACTION.

The novelty in the definition above is the *goods_transfer* function. We will call this the *profiling function* because it selects the parts of the COMMERCIAL TRANSACTION event which the verb highlights. We will call *acquisition* – the function which determines subject and object – the perspectivalizing function. The role of the the perspectivalizing function is to select a syntactic realization.

A profiling function like *goods_transfer* has two independent motivations:
a. It enriches our rather impoverished model of COMMERCIAL TRANSACTION. We started out in (23) with little more than the assumption that there were 4

sorted participants we were calling buyer, seller, money, and goods. Now with the assumption of the *goods_transfer* function, a possession transfer *p* is entailed (because the function is total) in which the possession is the goods. Thus *goods_transfer* can be viewed as part of an enriched definition of the COMMERCIAL TRANSACTION frame. There will be other total functions enriching the definition further, for example, a *money_transfer* function of use in defining verbs like *pay* and *collect*, in which the money is transferred.

b. Both MONEY_TRANSFER and GOODS-TRANSFER are projections from commercial events to possession transfers; and possession transfer is a frame for which we have a pre-defined perspectivalization, independently motivated for other verbs like *acquire* and *get*. By composing a commercial event subscene projection with a possession transfer argument projection we derive an argument projection for commercial transactions.

Thus the *good transfer* function simultaneously serves knowledge representation needs (a) and valence theory needs (b).

There is an analogy between how profiling and perspectivalization work and the way the original Minskyan frames work. A Minskyan frame enables the integration of scene components in view with underlying objects by specifying, for example, how the faces of the cube in view relate to the cube as a whole. A Fillmorian perspective enables the integration of the realized elements of a text with an underlying text interpretation by specifying how syntactically realized frame components relate to frames as a whole. In both cases there are operations that mediate between rich representations and a constrained (perspectivalized) representation that belongs to an external representational system. Minskyan rotation operations mediate between 3D representations and the 2D representations of a scene, ultimately necessary because the human retina is a screen. Fillmorian profilings and perspectivalizations mediate between unlinearized representations in which there is no fixed individuation of participants and linearizable argument structure, ultimately necessary because the syntax of human language forces us to linearize participants.

Now consider a profiling which leaves things out. This is the case of spend.

(25)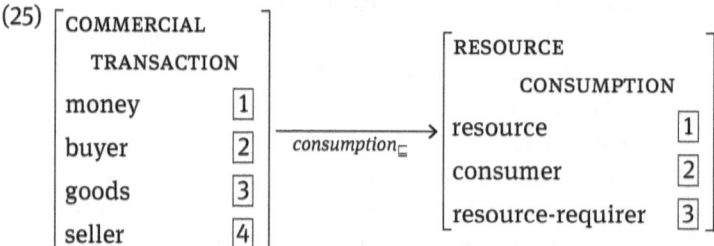

As discussed in section 2, the verb *spend* views a commercial transaction as a RESOURCE CONSUMPTION, where RESOURCE CONSUMPTION is the frame used by verbs like *waste, lose, use (up),* and *blow*. The profiling of the verb *spend* includes the seller and goods but leaves the seller out. The profiling of the verb *sell* includes the buyer and the goods, as well as the seller. The two subscenes overlap in participants but choose distinct, incompatible event types, which lead to distinct realization possibilities in the syntactic frame.

The frame-based picture of commercial transactions is schematized in Fig. 3.3.

The picture on the left shows what we might call the *commercial transaction neighborhood* as discussed here. The picture on the right shows that portion of the neighborhood that is activated by *buy*; the functions used in its definitions are linked by solid lines; the functions left out are in dashes; the boxed regions contains those frames that are used in the definition. If as is suggested in article 12 [Semantics: Typology, Diachrony and Processing] (Kelter & Kaup) *Conceptual knowledge, categorization and meaning*, concepts and word meanings need to be different knowledge structures, the picture in Fig. 3.3 may provide one way of thinking about how they might be related, with the frame nodes playing the role of concepts and a configuration of links between them the role of a word meaning.

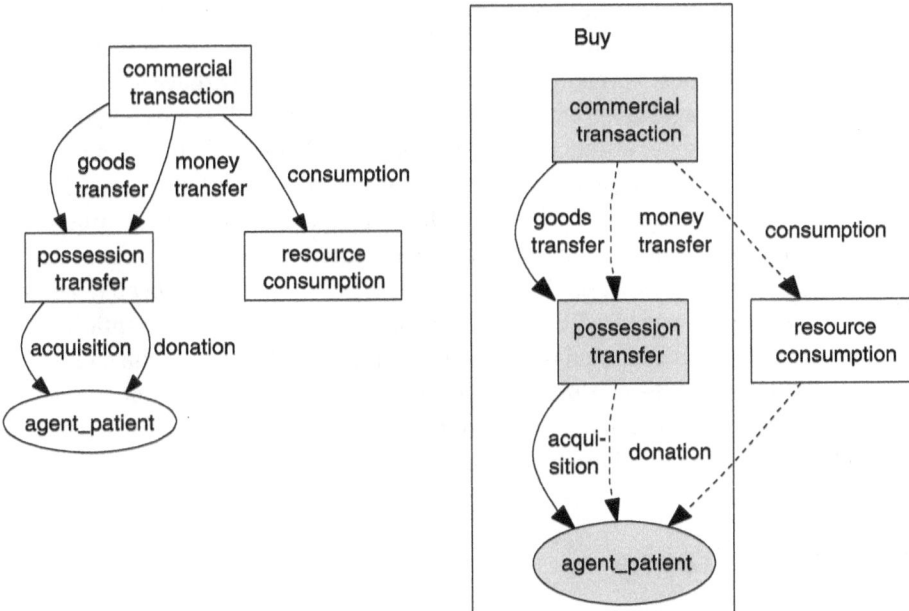

Fig. 3.3: Left: Lexical network for commercial transaction. Right: Same network with the perspectivalization chosen by *buy* in the boxed area.

We have called *goods-transfer* and *consumption* profiling functions. We might equally well have called them *subscene roles,* because they are functions from events to entities. Note that subscene roles don't attribute a fixed hierarchical structure to a frame the way DO ... CAUSE BECOME ... in Dowty's system attributes a fixed structure to causatives of inchoatives. As these examples show, a frame may have subscene roles which carve up its constituents in incompatible ways. Now this may seem peculiar. Shouldn't the roles of a frame define a fixed relation between disjoint entities? I submit that the answer is no. The roles associated with each sort of event are regularities that help us classify an event as of that sort. But such functions are not guaranteed to carve up each event into non-overlapping, hierarchically structured parts. Sometimes distinct roles may select overlapping constituents of events, particularly when independent individuation criteria are not decisive, as when the constituents are collectives, or shapeless globs of stuff, or abstract things such as events or event types. Thus we get the cases discussed above like *collide, mix,* and *risk,* where different ways of profiling the frames give us distinct, incompatible sets of roles. We may choose to view the colliders as a single collective entity (X and Y collided), or as two (X collided with Y). We may choose to separate a figure from a ground in the mixing event (14f), or lump them together (mix X and Y), or just view the mixed substance as one (14f). Finally, risks involve an action (13c) and a potential bad consequence (13a), and for a restricted set of cases in which that bad consequence is a loss, a lost thing (13b).

What of relations? Formally, in this frame-based picture, we have replaced relations with event predicates, each of which is defined through some composed set of mappings to a set of events that will be defined only for some fixed set of roles. Clearly, for every lexical predicate, there is a corresponding relation, namely one defined for exactly the same set of roles as the predicate. Thus in the end the description of the kind of lexical semantic entity which interfaces with the combinatorial semantics is not very different. However the problem has, I believe, been redefined in an interesting way. Traditionally, discussion of the lexical-semantic/syntax interface starts with a relation with a predefined set of roles. This is the picture for example, that motivates the formulation of Chomsky's (1981) Θ-Criterion. However, a major point of Frame Semantics is that, for many purposes, it is useful to look at a set of relations structured in a particular way. This is the domain of frames.

5 Lexicography

A word about the application of frames to lexicography is in order. Any set of frames imposes a certain classificational scheme on the lexicon. Other examples of such a classificational scheme are Roget's Thesaurus, Longman's valence classes, and Wordnet (Fellbaum 1998). Frames differ from all three in that they are not primarily oriented either to the task of synonym-classes or syntactic frame classes. One expects to find synonyms and antonyms in the same frame, of course, and many examples of valence similarity, but neither trend will be a rule. As we saw in section 2, near synonyms like *land* and *ground* may belong to different frames, and understanding those frames is critical to proper usage. As we saw in our investigations of profiling and perspective, differences of both kinds may result in very different valence options for verbs from the same frame. The value of the frame idea for lexicography is that it seems the most promising idea if the goal is to organize words according to usage. This of course is a hypothesis. FrameNet (Fillmore & Baker 2000) is a test of that hypothesis. Accordingly, frame entries are connected with rich sets of examples gleaned from the British National Corpus illustrating frame element realizations in a variety of syntactic contexts. Interested readers will find a tour of the web site far more persuasive than any discussion here.

6 Discourse understanding

In this section I propose to raise the issue of frames in discourse understanding, not to try to give the subject an adequate treatment, for which there is no space, but to talk a bit about how the role of frames in discourse understanding is related to their role in interpreting signs.

Let us return to the example of verbs conventionally connected with effects caused by movement:

(26) a. John broke the glass against the wall.
 b. # John killed the cockroach against the wall.

It is at least arguably the case that this contrast can be made without the help of a lexical stipulation. If movement can be a default or at least a highly prototypical way of breaking something, and not a highly prototypical way of killing something, then something like the default logic of Asher & Lascarides (1995) or abduction as in Hobbs et al. (1993), both of which have been applied successfully to a number of problems of discourse interpretation, could infer causality in (a) and not in (b). However, this still falls somewhat short of predicting the genuine oddity of (b). Notice, too, that when discourse coherence alone is at issue, both causality inferences go through:

(27) a. The glass was hurled against the wall and broke.
 b. The cockroach was hurled against the wall and died.

Thus the defaults at play in determining matters of "valence" differ from those in discourse. We can at least describe the contrasts in (26) – not explain it – by saying movement is an optional component of the breaking frame through which the denotation of the verb *break* is defined, and not a component of the killing frame; or in terms of the formal picture of section 4: Within the conventional lexical network linking frames in English there is a partial function from breaking events to movement subscenes; there is no such function for killing events.

In contrast Fillmore's (1985: 232) discussed in section 2.1:

(28) We never open our presents until morning.

The point of this example was that it evoked Christmas without containing a single word specific to Christmas. How might an automatic interpretation system simulate what is going on for human understanders? Presumably by a kind of application of Occam's razor. There is one and only one frame that explains both the presence of presents and the custom of waiting until morning, and that is the Christmas frame. Thus the assumption that gets us the most narrative bang for the buck is Christmas. In this case the frame has to be evoked by dynamically assembling pieces of information activated in this piece of discourse.

These two examples show that frames will function differently in a theory of discourse understanding than they will in a theory of sign-meanings in at least two ways. They will require a different notion of default, and they will need to resort to different inferencing strategies, such as inference to the most economical explanation.

7 Conclusion

The logical notion of a relation, which preserves certain aspects of the linearization syntax forces on us, has at times appeared to offer an attractive account of what we grasp when we grasp sign meanings. But the data we have been looking at in this brief excursion into Frame Semantics has pointed another way. Lexical senses seem to be tied to the same kind schemata that organize our perceptions and interpretations of the social and physical world. In these schemata participants are neither linearized nor uniquely individuated, and the mapping into the linearized regime of syntax is constrained but underdetermined. We see words with options in what their exact participants are and how they are realized. Frames offer a model that is both specific enough and flexible enough to accommodate these facts, while offering the promise of a firm grounding for lexicographic description and an account of text understanding.

8 References

Asher, Nicholas & Alex Lascarides 1995. Lexical disambiguation in a discourse context. *Journal of Semantics* 12, 69–108.

Baker, Collin & Charles J. Fillmore 2001. Frame Semantics for text understanding. In: *Proceedings of WordNet and Other Lexical Resources Workshop*. Pittsburgh, PA: North American Association of Computational Linguistics, 3–4.

Baker, Collin, Charles J. Fillmore & John B. Lowe 1998. The Berkeley FrameNet project. In: B.T.S. Atkins & A. Zampolli (eds.). *Proceedings of the Joint Conference of the International Committee on Computational Linguistics and the Association for Computational Linguistics, vol. 1*. Montreal: Association for Computational Linguistics, 86–90.

Barsalou, Lawrence 1992. Frames, concepts, and conceptual fields. In: A. Lehrer & E. Kittay (eds.). *Frames, Fields, and Contrasts. New Essays in Semantic and Lexical Organization*. Hillsdale, NJ: Lawrence Erlbaum, 21–74.

Barsalou, Lawrence 1999. Perceptual symbol systems. *Behavioral and Brain Sciences* 22, 577–660.

Bartlett, Frederick C. 1932. *Remembering. A Study in Experimental and Social Psychology*. Cambridge: Cambridge University Press.

Berlin, Isaiah 1957. *The Hedgehog and the Fox*. New York: New American Library. Reprinted in: I. Berlin. *The Proper Study of Mankind*. New York: Farrar, Straus, and Giroux, 1997.

Boas, Hans C. 2001. Frame Semantics as a framework for describing polysemy and syntactic structures of English and German motion verbs in contrastive computational lexicography. In: P. Rayson et al. (eds.). *Proceedings of the Corpus Linguistics 2001 Conference*. Lancaster: University Centre for Computer Corpus Research on Language, 64–73.

Boas, Hans C. 2005. Semantic frames as interlingual representations for multilingual databases. *International Journal of Lexicography* 18, 445–478.

Carpenter, Bob 1992. *The Logic of Typed Feature Structures. With Applications to Unification Grammars, Logic Programs and Constraint Resolution*. Cambridge: Cambridge University Press.

Chang, Nancy, Srini Narayanan & Miriam R.L. Petruck 2002a. From frames to inference. In: *Proceedings of the First International Workshop on Scalable Natural Language Understanding*. Heidelberg: International Committee on Computational Linguistics, 478–484.

Chang, Nancy, Srini Narayanan & Miriam R.L. Petruck 2002b. Putting frames in perspective. In: *Proceedings of the Nineteenth International Conference on Computational Linguistics*. Taipei, Taiwan: International Committee on Computational Linguistics, 231–237.

Chomsky, Noam 1981. *Lectures on Government and Binding*. Dordrecht: Foris.

Coseriu, Eugenio 1967. Lexikalische Solidaritäten. *Poetica* 1, 293–303.

Davidson, Donald 1967. The logical form of action sentences. In: N. Rescher (ed.). *The Logic of Decision and Action*. Pittsburgh, PA: University of Pittsburgh Press, 81–94. Reprinted in: D. Davidson (ed.). *Essays on Action and Events*. Oxford: Clarendon Press, 1980, 105–148.

Dowty, David R. 1979. *Word Meaning and Montague Grammar*. Dordrecht: Reidel.

Dowty, David R. 1991. Thematic proto roles and argument selection. *Language* 67, 547–619.

Fellbaum, Christiane (ed.) 1998. *WordNet. An Electronic Lexical Database*. Cambridge, MA: The MIT Press.

Fillmore, Charles J. 1975. An alternative to checklist theories of meaning. In: C. Cogen et al. (eds.). *Proceedings of the First Annual Meeting of the Berkeley Linguistics Society*. Berkeley, CA: Berkeley Linguistics Society, 123–131.

Fillmore, Charles J. 1976. Topics in lexical semantics. In: R. Cole (ed.). *Current Issues in Linguistic Theory.* Bloomington, IN: Indiana University Press, 76–138.
Fillmore, Charles J. 1977a. The case for case reopened. In: P. Cole & J. Sadock (eds.). *Syntax and Semantics 8: Grammatical Relations.* New York: Academic Press, 59–81.
Fillmore, Charles J. 1977b. Scenes-and-frames Semantics. Linguistic structures processing. In: A. Zampolli (ed.). *Linguistic Structures Processing.* Amsterdam: North-holland, 55–81.
Fillmore, Charles J. 1978. On the organization of semantic information in the lexicon. In: D. Farkas et al. (eds). *Papers from the Parasession on the Lexicon.* Chicago, IL: Chicago Linguistics Society, 148–173.
Fillmore, Charles J. 1982. Frame Semantics. In: Linguistic Society of Korea (ed.). *Linguistics in the Morning Calm.* Seoul: Hanshin, 111–137.
Fillmore, Charles J. 1985. Frames and the semantics of understanding. *Quaderni di Semantica* 6, 222–254.
Fillmore, Charles J. & B.T.S Atkins 1994. Starting where the dictionaries stop. The challenge for computational lexicography. In: B.T.S Atkins & A. Zampolli (eds.). *Computational Approaches to the Lexicon.* Oxford: Clarendon Press.
Fillmore, Charles J. & B.T.S Atkins 1998. FrameNet and lexicographic relevance. In: *Proceedings of the First International Conference on Language Resources and Evaluation.* Granada: International Committee on Computational Linguistics, 28–30.
Fillmore, Charles J. & Collin Baker 2000. *FrameNet,* http://www.icsi.berkeley.edu/~framenet, October 13, 2008.
Gawron, Jean Mark 1983. *Lexical Representations and the Semantics of Complementation.* New York: Garland.
Gawron, Jean Mark 2008. *Circumstances and Perspective. The Logic of Argument Structure.* http://repositories.cdlib.org/ucsdling/sdlp3/l, October 13, 2008.
Geckeler, Horst 1971. *Strukturelle Semantik und Wortfeldtheorie.* München: Fink.
Hobbs, Jerry R., Mark Stickel, Douglas Appelt & Paul Martin 1993. Interpretation as abduction. *Artificial Intelligence* 63, 69–142.
Jackendoff, Ray S. 1990. *Semantic Structures.* Cambridge, MA: The MIT Press.
Koffka, Kurt 1963. *Principles of Gestalt Psychology.* New York: Harcourt, Brace, and World.
Lakoff, George 1972. Linguistics and natural logic. In: D. Davidson & G. Harman (eds.). *Semantics of Natural Language.* Dordrecht: Reidel, 545–665.
Lakoff, George 1983. Category. An essay in cognitive linguistics. In: Linguistic Society of Korea (ed.). *Linguistics in the Morning Calm.* Seoul: Hanshin, 139–194.
Lakoff, George & Mark Johnson 1980. *Metaphors We Live By.* Chicago, IL: The University of Chicago Press.
Langacker, Ronald 1984. Active zones. In: C. Brugman et al. (eds.). *Proceedings of the Tenth Annual Meeting of the Berkeley Linguistics Society.* Berkeley, CA: Berkeley Linguistics Society, 172–188.
Lehrer, Adrienne & Eva Kittay (eds.) 1992. *Frames, Fields, and Contrasts. New Essays in Semantic and Lexical Organization.* Hillsdale, NJ: Lawrence Erlbaum.
Levin, Beth 1993. *English Verb Classes and Alternations.* Chicago, IL: The University of Chicago Press.
Mill, John Stuart 1847. *A System of Logic.* New York: Harper and Brothers.
Minsky, Marvin 1975. A framework for representing knowledge. In: P. Winston (ed.). *The Psychology of Computer Vision.* New York: McGraw-Hill, 211–277. http://web.media.mit.edu/~minsky/papers/Frames/frames.html, October 13, 2008.

Parsons, Terence 1990. *Events in the Semantics of English*. Cambridge, MA: The MIT Press.
Pustejovsky, James 1995. *The Generative Lexicon*. Cambridge, MA: The MIT Press.
Rounds, William C. 1997. Feature logics. In: J. van Benthem & A. ter Meulen (eds.). *Handbook of Logic and Language*. Amsterdam: Elsevier, 475–533.
Rumelhart, Donald 1980. Schemata. The building blocks of cognition. In: R.J. Spiro, B.C. Bruce & W.F. Brewer (eds.). *Theoretical Issues in Reading Comprehension*. Hillsdale, NJ: Lawrence Erlbaum, 33–58.
Schank, Roger C. & R.P. Abelson 1977. *Scripts, Plans, Goals, and Understanding*. Hillsdale, NJ: Lawrence Erlbaum.
Smolka, Gert 1992. Feature constraint logics for unification grammars. *Journal of Logic Programming* 12, 51–87.
Trier, Jost 1971. *Aufsätze und Vorträge zur Wortfeldtheorie*. The Hague: Mouton.
Weisgerber, J. Leo 1962. *Grundzüge der inhaltsbezogenen Grammatik*. Düsseldorf: Schwann.

Ray Jackendoff
4 Conceptual Semantics

1 Overall framework —— 86
2 Major features of Conceptual Structure —— 95
3 Compositionality —— 105
4 References —— 110

Abstract: Conceptual Semantics takes the meanings of words and sentences to be structures in the minds of language users, and it takes phrases to refer not to the world per se, but rather to the world as conceptualized by language users. It therefore takes seriously constraints on a theory of meaning coming from the cognitive structure of human concepts, from the need to learn words, and from the connection between meaning, perception, action, and nonlinguistic thought. The theory treats meanings, like phonological structures, as articulated into substructures or tiers: a division into an algebraic Conceptual Structure and a geometric/topological Spatial Structure; a division of the former into Propositional Structure and Information Structure; and possibly a division of Propositional Structure into a descriptive tier and a referential tier. All of these structures contribute to word, phrase, and sentence meanings. The ontology of Conceptual Semantics is richer than in most approaches, including not only individuals and events but also locations, trajectories, manners, distances, and other basic categories. Word meanings are decomposed into functions and features, but some of the features and connectives among them do not lend themselves to standard definitions in terms of necessary and sufficient conditions. Phrase and sentence meanings are compositional, but not in the strict Fregean sense: many aspects of meaning are conveyed through coercion, ellipsis, and constructional meaning.

1 Overall framework

Conceptual Semantics is a formal approach to natural language meaning developed by Jackendoff (1983, 1987, 1990, 2002, 2007) and Pinker (1989, 2007); Pustejovsky (1995) has also been influential in its development.

The approach can be characterized at two somewhat independent levels. The first is the overall framework for the theory of meaning, and how this framework is integrated into linguistics, philosophy of language, and cognitive science (section 1). The second is the formal machinery that has been developed to achieve the goals of this framework (sections 2 and 3). These two are somewhat independent: the general framework might be realized in terms of other formal approaches, and many aspects of the formal machinery can be deployed within other frameworks for studying meaning.

The fundamental goal of Conceptual Semantics is to describe how humans express their understanding of the world by means of linguistic utterances. From this goal flow two theoretical commitments. First, linguistic meaning is to be described in mentalistic/psychological terms – and eventually in neuroscientific terms. The theory of meaning, like the theories of generative syntax and phonology, is taken to be about what is going on in people's heads when they use language. Second, the theory aspires to describe the messages that speakers intend their utterances to convey. Thus it potentially includes everything that traditionally falls under the labels of 'pragmatics' and 'world knowledge' as well as 'semantics.' It does not specifically seek a level of representation that might be characterized as 'pure/literal linguistic meaning' or 'meaning that is relevant to grammar.' If there is such a level, it will emerge in the course of empirical investigation (see remarks in section 1.2). We take these two commitments up in turn.

1.1 Mentalism: reference and truth

The mentalist commitment of the theory sets it apart from traditions of formal semantics growing out of logic (e.g. Frege 1892, Russell 1905, Carnap 1939, Tarski 1956, Montague 1973, Lewis 1972; see article 3 [Semantics: Foundations, History an Methods] (Textor) *Sense and reference*; article 4 [Semantics: Foundations, History and Methods] (Abbott) *Reference*) which aspire to study the relation of sentences to "the world" or to "possible worlds" (where a "the/a world" is often specified in set-theoretic terms, see article 7 [this volume] (Zimmermann) *Model-theoretic semantics*. In generative grammar, a sentence is not regarded as a free-standing object that can be related to the world: it is a combinatorial structure in a speaker's mind that can be shared with other speakers via acoustic or visual signals. Similarly, an entire language is not a free-standing object (or set of sentences) in the world. Rather, a speaker's "knowledge of a language" is instantiated as a set of stored mental structures and stored relations among structures, plus the ability to combine these stored structures and relations into an unlimited number of meaningful expressions. The notion of "the English language" is thus regarded as an idealization over the systems of linguistic knowledge in the minds of a community of mutually intelligible speakers. We typically presume that these systems are homogeneous, but we readily drop this assumption as soon as we need to take into account dialect differences, vocabulary differences, and stages in children's acquisition of language.

This treatment of linguistic expressions extends to the meanings they convey. The meaning of a word or a sentence is not a free-standing object in the world either. Rather, the meaning of a word is to be regarded as a mental structure stored in a speaker's mind, linked in long-term memory to the structures that encode the word's pronunciation and its syntactic properties. The meaning of a sentence is likewise to be regarded as a mental structure, constructed in a speaker's mind in some systematic way from the meanings of its components. Under this conception, then, meaning must always be relativized to the language user. It makes no sense to say, with Putnam (1975), that speakers don't really *know* the meanings of words, or that the "true meaning" of, say, natural kind terms awaits a more mature science. There is no place other than in speaker's heads to localize meaning. Even if no speakers in 1500 knew the molecular structure of water or the DNA profile of tigers, it seems quixotic to maintain that no one was in possession of "the" meaning of *water* and *tiger*. People were managing to communicate with each other quite adequately, in terms of their understanding of these concepts at the time. Similarly, if speakers have different meanings for words (such as when experts have more highly articulated meanings for words in their area of expertise), mutual intelligibility is accomplished through tolerance of differences or, more rarely, through negotiation (as when people appeal to an expert for adjudication). And this seems a realistic assessment of how people use language.

The mentalist approach also leads to theoretical notions of reference and truth different from canonical formal semantics and philosophy of language. Reference is standardly regarded as a relation between linguistic expressions (typically noun phrases) and things in the world. For convenience, let us call this *realist reference* (or *r-reference*). However, the goal of Conceptual Semantics is not an account of free-standing sentences, but rather an account of human understanding. Thus the relation that plays the role of reference in the theory is between the mental structure encoding the linguistic expression and the language user's *conceptualization* of the world – all inside the mind. Let us call this relation *mentalist reference* (or *m-reference*).

For example, in sincerely uttering *The cat is on the mat*, a speaker is committed to there being a situation in the world in which an entity identifiable as a cat is in contact with the upper surface of another entity identifiable as a mat. A theory of meaning must account for these m-referential commitments. Now note that the speaker has not arrived at these commitments by somehow being in direct contact with reality. Rather, the speaker has arrived at these commitments through either hearsay, memory, inference, or perception. The first three of these require no direct contact with the cat or the mat. This leaves only perception as a potential means of direct contact with the world.

However, if we are to take the mentalist approach seriously, we must recognize that perception is far from direct. Visual perception, for example, is a hugely complex computation based on fragmentary information detected by the retina. It is far from well understood how the brain comes up with a unified perception of stable objects situated in a spatial environment, such as a cat on a mat (Neisser 1967, Marr 1982, Koch 2004). Nevertheless, it is this unified perception, computationally far removed from the objects in the world per se, that leads the speaker to making referential commitments about cats and mats.

This treatment of reference is an important respect in which Conceptual Semantics differs from the mentalistic theory of Fodor (1975, 1998). Although Fodor wishes to situate meaning in the mind, encoded in a combinatorial "language of thought," he insists that linguistic expressions are connected to the world by the relation of *intentionality* or *aboutness* (see article 2 [Semantics: Foundations, History and Methods] (Jacob) *Meaning, intentionality and communication*). For Fodor, the expression *the cat* is *about* some cat in the world, and a semantic theory must explicate this relation. In Conceptual Semantics, there is no such direct relation: the speaker's intention to refer to something in the world is mediated by conceptualization, which may or may not be related to the world through perception. For cases in which conceptualization is not based on perception, consider mortgages and dollars. We speak of them as though they exist in the world, but, unlike cats, these are entities that exist only by virtue of social convention, i.e. shared conceptualization. Nevertheless, *for us* they are just as real as cats. (And for cats, they are not!)

Similar remarks pertain to the notion of truth. For the purposes of a mentalist theory, what is of interest is not the conditions in the world that must be satisfied in order for a sentence to be true, but rather the conditions in *speakers' conceptualizations* of the world under which they *judge* a sentence to be true. That is, the theory is concerned with m-truth rather than r-truth.

On a tolerant construal of Conceptual Semantics, the investigation of m-reference and m-truth might be taken to be complementary to a classical approach in terms of r-reference and r-truth. To explain how speakers *grasp* r-truth, a theory of m-truth will play a necessary part. On a more confrontational construal, Conceptual Semantics might be taken to claim that only the mentalistic approach leads to a theory of meaning that integrates gracefully with a mentalistic theory of language and with cognitive psychology. Either construal is possible; both result in the same empirical questions for research.

It might be added that Conceptual Semantics, as part of its theory of word meaning, must of course describe the ordinary language or "folk" meanings of the words *refer* and *true*. These appear to correspond closely to the notion of r-reference and r-truth, that is, they express what people conceptualize as objective relations between linguistic expressions and the world. But note that Conceptual Semantics is also responsible for the meanings of nonscientific words such as *karma*, *ghost*, *tooth fairy*, and *phlogiston*. These too express possible human concepts, widely subscribed to in various cultures at various times. So including the "folk" meanings of *refer* and *true* among human concepts doesn't seem like a terrible stretch. But again, this does not entail that r-reference and r-truth should be the overall objectives of the theory, as they are in classical semantics.

1.2 Boundary conditions and comparison to other frameworks

A theory that seeks to describe the range of human thoughts that can be conveyed in language must meet a large collection of boundary conditions. The first two are shared with classical formal semantics.

> C1 (Compositionality): The meaning of an utterance must be composed systematically in a way that incorporates the meaning of its words and the contribution of its syntax. (However, this does not require that *all* parts of utterance meaning are expressed by particular words of the utterance, as in classical Fregean composition; see section 3.)
>
> C2 (Inference): Utterance meanings must serve as a formal basis for inference.

However, there are also boundary conditions that derive from the mentalist basis of the theory. Classical semantics speaks to none of these concerns.

> C3 (Categorization): The meanings of words must conform to what is known about human categorization (cf. Murphy 2002, Jackendoff 1983, Lakoff 1987; see article 12 [Semantics: Typology, Diachrony and Processing] (Kelter & Kaup) *Conceptual knowledge, categorization and meaning*).
>
> C4 (Learnability): The meanings of words must be learnable on the basis of the acquirer's experience with language and the world, preferably in conformance with empirical evidence on word learning (e.g. Macnamara 1982, Pinker 1989, Bloom 2000).
>
> C5 (Connection to perception and action): Phrase and utterance meanings that deal with physical objects and physical actions must be connected to mental representations appropriate to perception and action, so that one can, for instance, talk about what one sees and carry out actions based on imperative sentences (Landau & Jackendoff 1993, Bloom et al. 1996; see article 13 [Semantics: Typology, Diachrony and Processing] (Landau) *Space in semantics and cognition*).

A final tenet of Conceptual Semantics connects it with questions of the evolution of language, again an issue on which classical semantics is silent:

> C6 (Nonlinguistic thought): The mental structures that serve as utterance meanings are present to some degree in nonlinguistic organisms such as babies and apes, and play a role

in their understanding of the world. It is in service of expressing such prelinguistic thought that the language faculty evolved (Jackendoff 2002, chapter 8).

These conditions together serve to differentiate Conceptual Semantics from other major semantic frameworks. It differs from formal semantics not only in its commitment to mentalism, but in the corollary conditions C3–C6. A word meaning must be a mental structure, not a set of instances in possible worlds. Furthermore, human categorization does not operate strictly in terms of necessary and sufficient conditions, but rather in part in terms of default conditions, preference conditions, and distance from central exemplars (see section 2.5). Hence word meanings do not delimit classical categories and cannot be treated in terms of traditional definitions.

The learnability of an unlimited variety of word meanings argues that word meanings are composite, built up in terms of a generative system from a finite stock of primitives and principles of combination. By contrast, in classical semantics, word meanings (except for words with logical properties) are typically taken to be atomic. Fodor (1975, 1998) argues that all word meanings are atomic, and seeks to account for learnability by claiming that they are all innate. Beyond this position's inherent implausibility, it calls for a commitment to (a) only a finite number of possible word meanings in all the languages of the world, since they must all be coded in a finite brain; (b) a reliable triggering mechanism that accounts for concept learning; and eventually (c) a source in evolution for such "innate" concepts as *telephone*. Fodor's arguments for this position are based on the assumption that word meanings, if composite, must be statable in terms of definitions, which is denied by Conceptual Semantics and other cognitively rooted theories of meaning (section 2.5; Jackendoff 1983: 122–127; 1990: 37–41; 2002: 334–337; Lakoff 1987; see article 2 [this volume] (Taylor) *Prototype theory* and article 3 [this volume] (Gawron) *Frame Semantics*).

A different framework coming out of computational linguistics and cognitive psychology is Latent Semantic Analysis (Landauer et al. 2007). It characterizes the meanings of words in terms of their cooccurrence with other words in texts (i.e. linguistic use alone). Thus word meanings consist of a collection of linguistic contexts with associated probabilities. There is no account of compositionality or inference; word learning consists of only collating contexts and calculating their probabilities; and there is no relationship to nonlinguistic categorization and cognition. Similar considerations apply to WordNet (Fellbaum 1998).

Another framework, Natural Semantic Metalanguage (Wierzbicka 1996) is concerned primarily with decomposition of word meanings. Decompositions are carried out in terms of a small vocabulary of English words that are taken to represent semantic primitives. This approach does not aspire to account for any of the boundary conditions on Conceptual Semantics above.

Various other approaches to semantics are concerned primarily with the impact of semantics on grammatical form, for instance the Lexical Conceptual Structures of Levin and Rappaport Hovav (see article 4 [Semantics: Lexical Structures and Adjectives] (Levin & Rappaport Hovav) *Lexical Conceptual Structure*), Distributed Morphology (article 5 [Semantics: Interfaces] (Harley) *Semantics in Distributed Morphology*), and Lieber's approach to morphological meaning (article 3 [Semantics: Interfaces] (Lieber) *Semantics of derivational morphology*). Again there is little concern with a full account of meaning, nor with inference, word learning, or connection to perception, action, and nonlinguistic thought.

The major framework closest in spirit to Conceptual Semantics is Cognitive Grammar (Langacker 1987, Lakoff 1987, Talmy 2000, Fauconnier 1985; article 1 [this volume] (Talmy) *Cognitive Semantics*). This tradition takes seriously the cognitively-based rather than logically-based nature of meaning, and it stresses the nonclassical character of word meanings and sentence meanings. Besides differences in the phenomena that it focuses on, Cognitive Grammar differs from Conceptual Semantics in four respects. First, the style of its formalization is different and arguably less rigorous. Second, it tends to connect to nonlinguistic phenomena through theories of embodied cognition rather than through more standard cognitive neuroscience. Third (and related), many practitioners of Cognitive Grammar take a rather empiricist (or Lockean) view of learning, whereas Conceptual Semantics admits a considerable structured innate (or Kantian) basis to concept formation. Fourth, Conceptual Semantics is committed to syntax having a certain degree of independence from semantics, whereas Cognitive Grammar seeks to explain all aspects of syntactic form in terms of the meaning(s) expressed (see article 9 [Semantics: Interfaces] (Kay & Michaelis) *Constructional meaning*).

1.3 Conceptual Structure and Spatial Structure; interfaces with syntax and phonology

The central hypothesis of Conceptual Semantics is that there is a level of mental representation, *Conceptual Structure*, which instantiates sentence meanings and serves as the formal basis for inference and for connection with world knowledge and perception. The overall architecture of the mind in which this embedded is shown in Fig. 4.1.

Each of the levels in Fig. 4.1 is a generative system with its own primitives and principles of combination. The arrows indicate interfaces among representations: sets of principles that provide systematic mappings from one level to the other. On the left-hand side are the familiar linguistic levels and their interfaces to hearing and speaking. On the right-hand side are nonlinguistic connections to the world

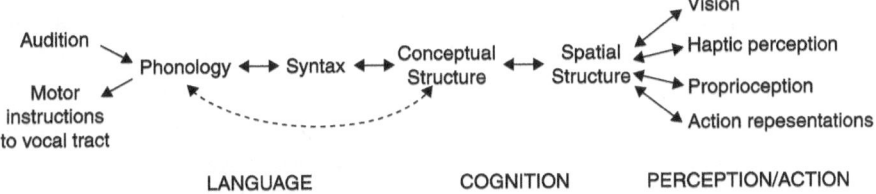

Fig. 4.1: Architecture of the mind

through visual, haptic, and proprioceptive perception, and through the formulation of action. (One could add general-purpose audition, smell, and taste as well.)

In the middle lies cognition, here instantiated as the levels of Conceptual Structure and Spatial Structure. Spatial Structure is hypothesized (Jackendoff 1987, 1996a; Landau & Jackendoff 1993) as a geometric/topological encoding of 3-dimensional object shape, spatial layout, motion, and possibly force. It is not a strictly visual representation, because these features of the conceptualized physical world can also be derived by touch (the haptic sense), by proprioception (the spatial position of one's own body), and to some degree by auditory localization. Spatial Structure is the medium in which these disparate perceptual modalities are integrated. It also serves as input for formulating one's own physical actions. It is moreover the form in which memory for the shape of familiar objects and object categories is stored. This level must be generative, since one encounters, remembers, and acts in relation to an indefinitely large number of objects and spatial configurations in the course of life (see article 13 [Semantics: Typology, Diachrony and Processing] (Landau) *Space in semantics and cognition*).

However, it is impossible to encode all aspects of cognition in geometric/topological terms. A memory for a shape must also encode the standard type/token distinction, i.e. whether this is the shape of a particular object or of an object category. Moreover, the taxonomy of categories is not necessarily a taxonomy of shapes. For instance, forks and chairs are not at all similar in shape, but both are artifacts; there is no general characterization of artifacts in terms of shape or the spatial character of the actions one performs with them. Likewise, the distinction between familiar and unfamiliar objects and actions cannot be characterized in terms of shape. Finally, social relations such as kinship, alliance, enmity, dominance, possession, and reciprocation cannot be formulated in geometric terms. All of these aspects of cognition instead lend themselves to an algebraic encoding in terms of features (binary or multi-valued, e.g. TYPE vs. TOKEN) and functions of one or more arguments (e.g. x INSTANCE-OF y, x SUBCATEGORY-OF y, x KIN-OF y). This system of algebraic features and functions constitutes Conceptual Structure. Note that at least some of the distinctions just listed, in particular the social relations, are also made by nonhuman primates. Thus a description of primate nonlinguistic cognition requires some form of Conceptual Structure, though doubtless far less rich than in the human case.

Conceptual Structure too has its limitations. Attempts to formalize meaning and reasoning have always had to confront the impossibility of coding perceptual characteristics such as color, shape, texture, and manner of motion in purely algebraic terms. The architecture in Fig. 4.1 proposes to overcome this difficulty by sharing the work of encoding meaning between the geometric format of Spatial Structure and the algebraic format of Conceptual Structure: spatial concepts have complementary representations in both domains. (In a sense, this is a more sophisticated version of Paivio's 1971 dual-coding hypothesis and the view of mental imagery espoused by Kosslyn 1980.)

Turning now to the interfaces between meaning and language, a standard assumption in both standard logic and mainstream generative grammar is that semantics interfaces exclusively with syntax, and in fact that the function of the syntax-semantics interface is to *determine* meaning in one-to-one fashion from syntactic structure (this is made explicit in article 5 [Semantics: Interfaces] (Harley) *Semantics in Distributed Morphology*). The assumption, rarely made explicit (but going back at least to Descartes), is that combinatorial thought is possible only through the use of combinatorial language. This comports with the view, common well into the 20th century, that animals are incapable of thought. Modern cognitive ethology (Hauser 2000; Cheney & Seyfarth 2007) decisively refutes this view, and with it the assumption that syntax is the source of combinatorial thought. Conceptual Semantics is rooted instead in the intuition that language is combinatorial because it evolved to express a pre-existing combinatorial faculty of thought (condition C6).

Under this approach, it is quite natural to expect Conceptual Structure to be far richer than syntactic structure – as indeed it is. Culicover & Jackendoff (2005) argue that the increasing complexity and abstraction of the structures posited by mainstream generative syntax up to and including the Minimalist Program (Chomsky 1995) have been motivated above all by the desire to encode all semantic relations overtly or covertly in syntactic structure. Ultimately the attempt fails because semantic relations are too rich and multidimensional to be encoded in terms of purely syntactic mechanisms.

In Conceptual Semantics, a word is regarded as a part of the language/thought interface: it is a longterm memory association of a piece of phonological structure (e.g./kæt/), some syntactic features (singular count noun), and a piece of Conceptual Structure (FELINE ANIMAL, PET, etc.). If it is a word for a concept involving physical space, it also includes a piece of Spatial Structure (what cats look like). Other interface principles establish correspondences between semantic argument structure (e.g. what characters an action involves) and syntactic argument structure (e.g. transitivity), between scope of quantification in semantics and position of quantifiers in syntax, and between topic and focus in semantics (information structure, see article 10 [Semantics: Sentence and Information Structure] (Hinterwimmer) *Information structure*) and affixation and/or position in syntax. In order to deal with situations where topic and focus are coded only in terms of stress and intonation (e.g. *The dog CHASED the mailman*), the theory offers the possibility of a further interface that establishes a correspondence directly between semantics and phonology, bypassing syntax altogether.

If it proves necessary to posit an additional level of "linguistic semantic structure" that is devoted specifically to features relevant for grammatical expression (as posited in article 5 [this volume] (Lang & Maienborn) *Two-level Semantics*, article 4 [Semantics: Lexical Structures and Adjectives] (Levin & Rappaport Hovav) *Lexical Conceptual Structure* and article 5 [Semantics: Interfaces] (Harley) *Semantics in Distributed Morphology*), such a level would be inserted between Conceptual Structure and syntax, with interfaces to both. Of course, in order for language to be understood and to play a role in inference, it is still necessary for words to bridge all the way from phonology to Conceptual Structure and Spatial Structure – they cannot stop at the putative level of linguistic semantic structure. Hence the addition of such an extra component would not at all change the content of Conceptual Structure, which is necessary to drive inference and the connection to perception. (Jackendoff 2002, section 9.7, argues that in fact such an extra component is unnecessary.)

2 Major features of Conceptual Structure

This section sketches some of the important features of Conceptual Structure (henceforth CS). There is no space here to spell out formal details; the reader is referred to Jackendoff (1983; 2002, chapters 11–12).

2.1 Tiers in CS

A major advance in phonological theory was the realization that phonological structure is not a single formal object, but rather a collection of *tiers*, each with its own formal organization, which divide up the work of phonology into a number of independent but correlated domains. These include at least segmental and syllabic structure; the amalgamation of syllables into larger domains such as feet, phonological words, and intonational phrases; the metrical grid that assigns stress; and the structure of intonation contours correlated with prosodic domains.

A parallel innovation is proposed within Conceptual Semantics. The first division, already described, is into Spatial Structure and Conceptual Structure. Within CS, the clearest division is into *Propositional Structure*, a function-argument encoding of who did what to whom, how, where, and when (arguments and modifiers), versus *Information Structure*, the encoding of Topic, Focus, and Common Ground. These two aspects of meaning are orthogonal, in that virtually any constituent of a clause, with any thematic or modifying role, can function as Topic or Focus or part of Common Ground. Languages typically use different grammatical machinery for expressing these two aspects of meaning. For instance, roles in Propositional Structure are typically expressed (morpho-)syntactically in terms of position and/or case with respect to a head. Roles in Information Structure are typically expressed by special focusing constructions, by special focusing affixes, by special topic and focus positions that override propositional roles, and above all by stress and intonation – which is never used to mark propositional roles. Both the syntactic and the semantic phenomena suggest that Propositional and Information Structure are orthogonal but linked organizations of the semantic material in a sentence.

More controversially, Jackendoff (2002) proposes segregating Propositional Structure into two tiers, a *descriptive tier* and a *referential tier*. The former expresses the hierarchical arrangement of functions, arguments, and modifiers. The latter expresses the sentence's referential commitments to each of the characters and events, and the binding relations among them; it is a dependency graph along the lines of Discourse Representation Theory (see article 11 [this volume] (Kamp & Reyle) *Discourse Representation Theory*). The idea behind this extra tier is that such issues as anaphora, quantification, specificity, and referential opacity are in many respects orthogonal to who is performing the action and who the action is being performed on. The canonical grammatical structures of language typically mirror the latter rather closely: the relative embedding of syntactic constituents reflects the relative embedding of arguments and modifiers. On the other hand, scope of quantification, specificity, and opacity are not at all canonically expressed in the surface of natural languages; this is why theories of quantification typically invoke something like "quantifier raising" to relate surface position to scope. The result is a semantic structure in which the referential commitments are on the outside of the expression, and the thematic structure remains deeply embedded inside, its arguments bound to quantifiers outside. Dividing the expressive work into descriptive and referential tiers helps clarify the resulting notational logjam.

The division into descriptive and referential tiers also permits an insightful account of two kinds of anaphora. Standard definite anaphora, as in (1a), is anaphoric on the referential tier and indicates coreference. *One*-anaphora, as in (1b), however, is anaphoric on the descriptive tier and indicates a different individual with the same description.

(1) a. Bill saw a balloon and I saw it too.
    b. Bill saw a balloon and I saw one too.

2.2 Ontological categories and aspectual features

Reference is typically discussed in terms of NPs that refer to objects. Conceptual Semantics takes the position that there is a far wider range of ontological types to which reference can be made (m-reference, of course). The deictic *that* is used in (2a) to (m-)refer to an object that the hearer is invited to locate in (his or her conceptualization of) the visual environment. Similarly, the underlined deictics in (2b-g) are used to refer to other sorts of entities.

(2) a. Would you pick that [*pointing*] up, please?   [reference to object]
    b. Would you put your hat there [*pointing*], please?   [reference to location]
    c. They went that away [*pointing*]!   [reference to direction]
    d. Can you do this [*demonstrating*]?   [reference to action]
    e. That [*pointing*] had better never happen in MY house!   [reference to event]
    f. The fish that got away was this [*demonstrating*] long.   [reference to distance]
    g. You may start ... right ... now [*clapping*]!   [reference to time]

This enriched ontology leads to a proliferation of referential expressions in the semantic structure of sentences. For instance, *John went to Boston* refers not only to John and Boston, but also to the event of John going to Boston and to the trajectory 'to Boston', which terminates at Boston. The event corresponds to the Davidsonian event variable (see article 8 [this volume] (Maienborn) *Event semantics*) and the events of Situation Semantics (see articles 9 [this volume] (Ginzburg) *Situation Semantics and NL ontology* and 10 [this volume] (Ginzburg) *Situation Semantics*. Event and Situation Semanticists have taken this innovation to be a major advance in the ontology over classical formal semantics. Yet the expressions in (2) clearly show a far more differentiated ontology; events are just a small part of the full story. At the same time, it should be recalled that the 'existence' of trajectories, distances, and so forth is a matter not of how the world *is*, but of how speakers *conceptualize* the world.

Incidentally, trajectories such as *to Boston* are often thought to intrinsically involve motion. A more careful analysis suggests that this is not the case. Motion along the trajectory is a product of composing the motion verb *went* with *to Boston*. But the very same trajectory is referred to in *the road leads to Boston* – a stative sentence expressing the extent of the road – and in *the sign points to Boston* – a stative sentence expressing the orientation of the sign. The difference among these examples comes from the semantics of the verb and the subject, not from the prepositional phrase.

The semantics of expressions of location and trajectory – including their crosslinguistic differences and relationships to Spatial Structure – has become a major preoccupation in areas of semantics related to Conceptual Semantics (e.g. Bloom et al. 1996, Talmy 2000, Levinson 2003, van der Zee & Slack 2003; see article 5 [Semantics: Typology, Diachrony and Processing] (Pederson) *The expression of space*; article 13 [Semantics: Typology, Diachrony and Processing] (Landau) *Space in semantics and cognition*).

Orthogonal to the ontological category features are *aspectual* features. It has long been known (Declerck 1979, Hinrichs 1985, Bach 1986, and many others) that the distinction between objects and substances (expressed by count and mass NPs respectively) parallels the distinction between events and processes (telic and atelic sentences) (see article 7 [Semantics: Noun Phrases and Verb Phrases] (Lasersohn) *Mass nouns and plurals*; article 9 [Semantics: Noun Phrases and Verb Phrases] (Filip) *Aspectual class and Aktionsart*). Conceptual Semantics expresses this parallelism (Jackendoff 1991) through a feature [±bounded]. Another feature, [±internal structure], deals with aggregation, including plurality. (3) shows how these features apply to materials and situations. (The situations in (3) are expressed as NPs but could just as easily be sentences.)

(3)

	Material	Situation
[+bounded, −internal structure]	object (*a dog*)	single telic event (*a sneeze*)
[−bounded, −internal structure]	substance (*dirt*)	atelic process (*sleeping*)
[+bounded, +internal structure]	group (*a herd*)	multiple telic event (*some sneezes*)
[−bounded, +internal structure]	aggregate (*dogs*)	iterated events (*sneezing repeatedly*)

Trajectories or paths also partake of this feature system: a path such as *into the forest*, with an inherent endpoint, is [+bounded]; *along the road*, with no inherent endpoint, is [−bounded].

Because these features cut across ontological categories, they can be used to calculate the telicity and iterativity of a sentence based on the contributions of all its parts (Jackendoff 1996b). For instance, (4a) is telic because its subject and path are bounded, and its verb is a motion verb. (4b) is atelic because its path is unbounded and its verb is a motion verb. (4c) is atelic and iterative because its subject is an unbounded aggregate of individuals and its verb is a motion verb. (4d) is stative, hence atelic, because the verb is stative – even though its path is bounded. (Jackendoff 1996b shows formally how these results follow.)

(4) a. John walked into the forest.
    b. John walked along the road.
    c. People walked into the forest.
    d. The road leads into the forest.

2.3 Feature analysis in word meanings

Within Conceptual Semantics, word meanings are regarded as composite, but not necessarily built up in a fashion that lends itself to definitions in terms of other words. This subsection and the next three lay out five sorts of evidence for this view, and five different innovations that therefore must be introduced into lexical decomposition.

The first case is when a particular semantic feature spans a number of semantic fields. Conceptual Semantics grew out of the fundamental observations of Gruber (1965), who showed that the notions of location, change, and causation extend over the semantic fields of space, possession, and predication. For example, the sentences in (5) express change in three different semantic fields, in each case using the verb *go* and expressing the endpoint of change as the object of *to*.

(5) a. John went to New York.   [space]
    b. The inheritance went to John.   [possession]
    c. The light went from green to red. [predication]

Depending on the language, sometimes these fields share vocabulary and sometimes they don't. Nevertheless, the semantic generalizations ring true crosslinguistically. The best way to capture this crosscutting is by analyzing motion, change of possession, and change of predication in terms of a common primitive function GO (alternating with BE and STAY) plus a "field feature" that localizes it to a particular semantic field (space vs. possession vs. predication). Neither the function nor the field feature is lexicalized by itself: GO is not on its own the meaning of *go*. Rather, these two elements are like features in phonology, where for example *voiced* is not on its own a phonological segment but when combined with other features serves to distinguish one segment from another. Thus these meaning components cannot be expressed as word-like primes.

An extension of this approach involves force-dynamic predicates (Talmy 1988, Jackendoff 1990: chapter 7), where for instance *force, entail, be obligated*, and the various senses of *must* share a feature, and *permit, be consistent with, have a right*, and the various senses of *may* share another value of the same feature. At the same time, these predicates differ in whether they are in the semantic field of physical force, social constraint, logical relation, or prediction.

Another such case was mentioned in section 2.2: the strong semantic parallel between the mass-count distinction in material substances and the process-event distinction in situations. Despite the parallel, only a few words cut across these domains. One happens to be the word *end*, which can be applied to speeches, to periods of time, and to tables of certain shapes (e.g. long ones but not circular ones). On the Conceptual Semantics analysis (Jackendoff 1991), *end* encodes a boundary of an entity that can be idealized as one-dimensional, whatever its ontological type. And because only certain table shapes can be construed as elaborations of a one-dimensional skeleton, only such tables have ends. (Note that an approach to *end* in terms of metaphor only restates the problem. Why do these metaphors exist? Answer: Because conceptualization has this feature structure.)

The upshot of cases like these is that word meanings cannot be expressed in terms of word-like definitions, because the primitive features are not on their own expressible as words.

2.4 Spatial structure in word meanings

One of the motivations for concluding that linguistic meaning must be segregated from "world knowledge" (as in Two-level Semantics and Lexical Conceptual Structure) is that there are many words with parallel grammatical behavior but clearly different semantics. For instance, verbs of manner of locomotion such as *jog, sprint, amble, strut*, and *swagger* have identical grammatical behavior but clearly differ in meaning. Yet there is no evident way to decompose them into believable algebraic features. These actions differ in how they look and how they feel. Similarly, a definition of *chair* in terms of "[+has-a-seat]" and "[+has-a-back]" is obviously artificial. Rather, our knowledge of the shape of chairs seems to have to do with what they look like and what it is like to sit in them – where sitting is ultimately understood in terms of performing the action. Likewise, our knowledge of *dog* at some level involves knowing that dogs bark. But to encode this purely in terms of a feature like "[+barks]" misses the point. It is what barking *sounds like* that is important – and of course this sound also must be involved in the meaning of the verb *bark*.

In each of these cases, what is needed to specify the word meaning is not an algebraic feature structure, but whatever cognitive structures encode categories of shapes, actions, and sounds. Among these structures are Spatial Structures of the sort discussed in section 1.3, which encode conceptualizations of shape, color, texture, decomposition into parts, and physical motion. As suggested there, it is not that these structures *alone* constitute the word meanings in question. Rather, it is the combination of Conceptual Structure with these structures that fills out the meanings.

Jackendoff (1996a) hypothesizes that these more perceptual elements of meaning do not interface directly with syntactic structure; that is, only Conceptual Structure makes a difference in syntactic behavior. For example, the differences in manner of motion among the verbs mentioned above are coded in Spatial Structure and therefore make no difference in their grammatical behavior. If correct, this would account for the fact that such factors are not usually considered part of "linguistic semantics", even though they play a crucial role in understanding. Furthermore, since these factors are not encoded in a format amenable to linguistic expression, they cannot be decomposed into definitions composed of words. The best one can do by way of definition is ostension, relying on the hearer to pick out the relevant factors of the environment.

2.5 Centrality conditions and preference rules

It is well known that many words do not have a sharply delimited denotation. An ancient case is *bald*: the central case is total absence of hair, but there is no particular amount of hair that serves as dividing point between bald and non-bald. Another case is color terms: for instance, there are focal values of *red* and *orange* and a smooth transition of hues between them; but there is no sharp dividing line, one side of which is definitely red and the other side is definitely orange. To reinforce a point made in section 1.1, it is not our ignorance of the true facts about baldness and redness that leads to this conclusion. Rather, there simply is no fact of the matter. When judgments of such categories are tested experimentally, the intermediate cases lead to slower, more variable, and more context-dependent judgments. The character of these judgments has to do more with the conceptualization of the categories in question than with the nature of the real world (see article 2 [this volume] (Taylor) *Prototype theory*; article 12 [Semantics: Typology, Diachrony and Processing] (Kelter & Kaup) *Conceptual knowledge, categorization and meaning*).

In Conceptual Semantics, such words involve *centrality conditions*. They are coded in terms of a focal or central case (such as completely bald or focally red), which serves as prototype. Cases that deviate from the prototype (as in baldness) – or for which another candidate prototype competes (as in color words) – result in the observed slowness and variability of judgments. Such behavior is in fact what would be expected from a neural implementation – sharp categorical behavior is actually much harder to explain in neural terms.

A more complex case that results in noncategorical judgments involves so-called cluster concepts. The satisfaction conditions for such concepts are combined by a non-Boolean connective (let's call it "*smor*") for which there is no English word. If a concept C is characterized by [condition A *smor* condition B], then stereotypical instances of C satisfy both condition A and condition B, and more marginal cases satisfy either A or B. For instance, the verb *climb* stereotypically involves (A) moving upward by (B) clambering along a vertically aligned surface, as in (6a). However, (6b) violates condition A while observing condition B, and (6c,d) are the opposite. (6e,f), which violate both conditions, are unacceptable. This shows that neither condition is necessary, yet either is sufficient.

(6) a. The bear climbed the tree. [upward clambering]

    b. The bear climbed down the tree/ across the cliff. [clambering only]

    c. The airplane climbed to 30,000 feet. [upward only]

    d. The snake climbed the tree. [upward only]

    e. *The airplane climbed down to 10,000 feet. [neither upward nor clambering]

    f. *The snake climbed down the tree. [neither upward nor clambering]

The connective between the conditions is not simple logical disjunction, because if we hear simply *The bear climbed*, we assume it was going upward by clambering. That is, both conditions are default conditions, and either is violable (Fillmore 1982). Jackendoff (1983) calls conditions linked by this connective *preference rules*.

This connective is involved in the analysis of Wittgenstein's (1953) famous example *game*, in the verb *see* (Jackendoff 1983: chapter 8), in the preposition *in* (Jackendoff 2002: chapter 11), and countless other cases. It is also pervasive elsewhere in cognition, for example gestalt principles of perceptual grouping

(Wertheimer 1923, Jackendoff 1983: chapter 8) and even music and phonetic perception (Lerdahl & Jackendoff 1983). Because this connective is not lexicalized, word meanings involving it cannot be expressed as standard definitions.

2.6 Dot-objects

An important aspect of Conceptual Semantics stemming from the work of Pustejovsky (1995) is the notion of *dot-objects* – entities that subsist simultaneously in multiple semantic domains. A clear example is a *book*, a physical object that has a size and weight, but that also is a bearer of information. Like other cluster concepts, either aspect of this concept can be absent: a blank notebook bears no information, and the book whose plot I am currently developing in my head is not (yet) a physical object. But a stereotypical book partakes of both domains. The information component can be linked to other instantiations besides books, such as speech, thoughts in people's heads, computer chips, and so on. Pustejovsky notates the semantic category of objects like books with a dot between the two domains: [PHYSICAL OBJECT • INFORMATION], hence the nomenclature "dot-object."

Note that this treatment of *book* is different from considering the word polysemous. It accounts for the fact that properties from both domains can be applied to the same object at once: *The book that fell off the shelf* [physical] *discusses the war* [information].

Corresponding to this sort of dot-object there are dot-actions. *Reading* is at once a physical activity – moving one's glance over a page – and an informational one – taking in the information encoded on the page. *Writing* is creating physical marks that instantiate information, as opposed to, say, *scribbling*, which need not instantiate information.

Implied in this analysis is that spoken language also is conceptualized as a dot-object: sounds dotted with information (or meaning). The same information can be conveyed by different sounds (e.g. by speaking in a different language), and the same sounds can convey different information (e.g. different readings of an ambiguous sentence, or different pragmatic construals of the same sentence in different contexts). Then *speaking* involves emitting sounds dotted with information; by constrast, *groaning* is pure sound emission.

Another clear case of a dot-object is a university, which consists at once of a collection of buildings and an academic organization: *Walden College covers 25 acres of hillside and specializes in teaching children of the rich*. Still another such domain (pointed out by Searle 1995) is actions in a game. For example, hitting a ball to a certain location is a physical action whose significance in terms of the game may be a home run, which adds runs, or a foul ball, which adds strikes. For such a case, the physical domain is "dotted" with a special "game domain," in terms of which one carries out the calculation of points or the like to determine who wins in the end.

Symbolic uses of objects, say in religious or patriotic contexts, can also be analyzed in terms of dot-objects and dot-actions with significance in the symbolized domain. Similarly with money, where coins, bills, checks, and so on – and the exchange thereof – are both physical objects and monetary values (Searle calls the latter *institutional facts*, in contrast with physical *brute facts*).

Perhaps the most far-reaching application of dot-objects is to the domain of *persons* (Jackendoff 2007). On one hand, a person is a physical object that occupies a position in space, has weight, can fall, has blue eyes, and so forth. On the other hand, a person has a personal identity in terms of which social roles are understood: one's kinship or clan relations, one's social and contractual obligations, one's moral responsibility, and so forth. The distinction between these two domains is recognized crossculturally as the difference between body on one hand and soul or spirit on the other. Cultures are full of beliefs about spirits such as ghosts and gods, with personal identity and social significance but no bodies. We quite readily conceptualize attaching personal identity to different bodies, as in beliefs in life after death and reincarnation, films like *Freaky Friday* (in which mother and daughter involuntarily exchange bodies), and Gregor Samsa's metamorphosis into a giant cockroach. A different sort of such dissociation is Capgras Syndrome (McKay, Langdon & Coltheart 2005), in which a stroke victim claims his wife has been replaced by an impostor who looks exactly the same. Thus persons, like books and universities, are dot-objects.

Social actions partake of this duality between physical and social/personal as well. For example, shaking hands is a physical action whose social significance is to express mutual respect between persons. The same social significance can be attached to other actions, say to bowing, high-fiving, or a man kissing a lady's hand. And the same physical action can have different social significance; for instance hissing is evidently considered an expression of approval in some cultures, rather than an expression of disapproval as in ours.

Note that this social/personal domain is not the same as Theory of Mind, although they overlap a great deal. On one hand, we attribute intentions and goals not just to persons but also to animals, who do not have social roles (with the possible exception of pets, who are treated as "honorary" persons). On the other hand, social characteristics such as one's clan and one's rights and obligations are not a consequence of what one believes or intends: they are just bare social facts. The consequence is that we likely conceptualize people in three domains "dotted" together: the physical domain, the personal/social domain, and the domain of sentient/animate entities.

A formal consequence of this approach is that the meaning of an expression containing dot-objects and dot-actions is best treated in terms of two or more linked "planes" of meaning operating in parallel. Some inferences are carried out on the physical plane, others on the associated informational, symbolic, or social plane. Particularly through the importance of social predicates to our thought and action, such a formal treatment is fundamental to understanding human conceptualization and linguistic meaning.

3 Compositionality

A central idealization behind most theories of semantics, including those of mainstream generative grammar and much of formal logic, is classical Fregean compositionality, which can be stated roughly as (7) (see article 6 [Semantics: Foundations, History and Methods] (Pagin & Westerståhl) *Compositionality*).

(7) (Fregean compositionality)
The meaning of a compound expression is a function of the meanings of its parts and of the syntactic rules by which they are combined. (A similar phrasing appears in article 4 [Semantics: Foundations, History and Methods] (Abbott) *Reference*)

(7) is usually interpreted in the strongest possible way: the meaning of a phrase is a function *only* of the meanings of its constituent words, assembled in simple fashion in accordance with the syntax. This is often supplemented with two further assumptions. The first, mentioned in section 1, is that semantics is *derived* from syntax (perhaps proof-theoretically); the second is that the principles of semantic composition mirror those of syntactic composition rule for rule (for instance in Montague Grammar).

Early work in Conceptual Semantics (Jackendoff 1983) adopted a position close to (7): heads of syntactic phrases correspond to semantic functions of one or more arguments; syntactic subjects and complements correspond to semantic constituents that instantiate these arguments. Syntactic adjuncts, which are attached differently from complements, correspond to semantic modifiers, which compose with semantic heads differently than arguments do.

However, subsequent work has revealed a host of cases where such simple relations between syntactic and semantic structure cannot obtain. One class of cases involves semantic information for which there is no evidence in the words or the syntax. (8) illustrates one variety, *aspectual coercion* (Talmy 1978, Verkuyl

1993, Pustejovsky 1995, Jackendoff 1997a; see also article 10 [Semantics: Lexical Structures and Adjectives] (de Swart) *Mismatches and coercion*). (8a) and (8b) are syntactically identical; however, (8a) implies repeated acts of jumping but (8b) does not imply repeated acts of sleeping.

(8) a. Jack jumped on the couch until the bell rang.
    b. Jack slept on the couch until the bell rang.

Strong Fregean composition would therefore require that *jump* (along with every other telic verb) is ambiguous between single and repeated jumping; repetition would come from the latter meaning of the word. (Note: if *jump* is semantically underspecified, then telicity comes from some nonlexical source, violating Fregean composition.) The problem is that telicity depends not just on the verb but on the entire verb phrase. For example, (9a) implies repeated (masochistic) action and (9b) does not. The difference is that 'run into the wall' is telic and 'run alongside the wall' is atelic, because of the paths implied by the two prepositions.

(9) a. Jack ran into the wall until the bell rang.
    b. Jack ran alongside the wall until the bell rang.

The solution proposed in the references above is that *until* places a temporal bound on an otherwise unbounded activity. In case the verb phrase is telic, i.e. it designates a temporally bounded event, semantic composition is licensed to reinterpret the verb phrase iteratively (i.e. it "coerces" the interpretation of the VP), so that the iterations constitute an unbounded activity. However, there is no reflex of this extra step of composition in syntactic structure. This view is confirmed by psycholinguistic experimentation (Piñango, Zurif & Jackendoff 1999); additional processing load is found in sentences like (8a), taking place at a time and in a brain location consistent with semantic rather than syntactic processing.

Another such case is *reference transfer* (Nunberg 1979), in which an NP is used to refer to something related such as 'picture of NP', 'statue of NP', 'actor portraying NP' and so on:

(10) a. There's Chomsky up on the top shelf,   [statue of or book by
        next to Plato.   Chomsky]

    b. [One waitress to another:]

        The ham sandwich in the corner wants   [person who ordered
        some more coffee.   sandwich]

c. I'm parked out back. I got smashed up   [my car]
   on the way here.

Jackendoff (1992) (also Culicover & Jackendoff 2005) shows that these shifts cannot be disregarded as "merely pragmatic," for two reasons. First, a theory that is responsible for how speakers understand sentences must account for these interpretations. Second, some of these types of reference transfer have interactions with anaphoric binding, which is taken to be a hallmark of grammar. Suppose Richard Nixon went to see the opera *Nixon in China*. It might have happened that ...

(11) Nixon was horrified to watch himself sing a foolish aria to Chou En-lai.

Here *Nixon* stands for the real person and *himself* stands for the portrayed Nixon on stage. However, such a connection is not always possible:

(12) *After singing his aria to Chou En-lai, Nixon was horrified to see himself get up and leave the opera house.

(11) and (12) are syntactically identical in the relevant respects. Yet the computation of anaphora is sensitive to which NP's reference has been shifted. This shows that reference transfer must be part of semantic composition. Jackendoff (1992) demonstrates that the meaning of reference transfer cannot be built into syntactic structure in order to derive it by Fregean composition.

Another sort of challenge to Fregean composition comes from *constructional meaning*, where ordinary syntax is paired with nonstandard semantic composition (see article 9 [Semantics: Interfaces] (Kay & Michaelis) *Constructional meaning*). Examples appear in (13): the verb is syntactically the head of the VP, but it does not select its complements. Rather, the verb functions semantically as a means or manner expression.

(13) a. Bill belched his way out of the restaurant.   ['Bill went out of the restaurant belching']

   b. Laura laughed the afternoon away.   ['Laura spent the afternoon laughing']

   c. The car squealed around the corner.   ['The car went around the corner squealing']

Jackendoff (1990, 1997b) and Goldberg (1995) analyze these examples as instances of distinct meaningful constructions in English. The *way*-construction in (13a) is an idiom of the form *V Pro's way PP*, meaning 'go PP by/while V-ing'; the *time-away* construction in (13b) has the form *V-NP[time period] away*, meaning 'spend NP V-ing'; the sound-motion construction in (13c) has the form *V PP*, meaning 'go PP while emitting sound of type V.' It is shown that there is no way to derive these meanings from standard syntactic structures; rather there are stipulated nonstandard ways to compose a VP in English (though by no means crosslinguistically).

Constructional meaning is also found in expressions with nonstandard syntax such as (14).

(14) a. The more I read, the less I understand.
 b. Into the cellar with you!
 c. One more beer and I'm leaving.
 d. rule for rule; day after day; student by student

In these cases one might be able to maintain a sort of Fregean composition, in that the special syntax directly denotes a particular sort of meaning composition. But the principles of composition here are (a) completely idiosyncratic and (b) introduce their own elements of meaning rather than just assembling the meanings of the words. This is not the spirit in which Fregean composition is usually intended.

A final set of cases that cast doubt on Fregean compositionality are those where syntactic composition vastly underdetermines semantic composition. An example is *Bare Argument Ellipsis*: in (15), the meaning of B's reply to A is not determined by the syntax of the reply, which is just *yeah* plus a bare NP. Rather, it has to do with a best pragmatic fit to A's utterance.

(15) A: I hear Ozzie's been drinking again.
 B: Yeah, scotch. ['Yeah, Ozzie's been drinking scotch.' – *not* 'Yeah, I/you hear Ozzie's been drinking scotch']

Mainstream generative theory (e.g. recently Merchant 2001) has maintained that B's reply is derived by deletion from an underlying structure which expresses the way the reply is understood and which therefore can undergo Fregean composition. However, Culicover & Jackendoff (2005) (along with a host of others, including among philosophers Stainton 2006) argue that in general it is impossible to state a canonical rule of ellipsis based on syntactic identity, and that the proper generalization must be stated over meaning relations between A's and B's utterances. This means that there is no syntactic structure from which the understood meaning of B's reply can be derived; hence Fregean composition again is violated (see article 9 [Semantics: Sentence and Information Structure] (Reich) *Ellipsis*).

A more radical example is pidgin languages, where there is arguably no syntactic structure (or at least very little), and yet structured meanings are conveyed (Givón 1995). In these cases, as in (15), it is up to the listener to use heuristics and world knowledge to surmise the overall semantic configuration intended by the speaker. However, such rudimentary syntax is not confined to pidgins. It also appears in standard language in noun-noun compounds, where the semantic relation between the two nouns is quite varied despite the very same uninformative syntactic configuration:

(16)   wheat flour = 'flour made from wheat'
        cake flour = 'flour of which cakes are made'
        dog house = 'house in which a dog characteristically lives'
        house dog = 'dog that lives in a house' (and not a doghouse!)
        garbage man = 'man who handles garbage'
        snow man = 'simulated man made of snow'
        sun hat = 'hat that protects one from the sun/that one wears in the sun'
        bike helmet = 'helmet that one wears while riding a bike'
        rocket fuel = 'fuel that powers a rocket' etc.

The range of semantic possibilities, though not unlimited, is quite broad; yet these examples show no syntactic contrast. Therefore the meaning cannot be derived simply by arranging the meanings of the words (see Jackendoff 2010: chapter 13 and article 4 [Semantics: Interfaces] (Olsen) *Semantics of compounds*).

These examples (see Jackendoff 1997a, Jackendoff 2002, and Culicover & Jackendoff 2005 for a more extensive enumeration and discussion) show that the relation between syntax and semantics is more flexible than Fregean compositionality. This might be stated as (17).

(17)   (Enriched composition)
        Phrase and sentence meanings are composed from the meanings of the words plus independent principles for constructing meanings, only some of which correlate with syntactic structure. Moreover, some syntactic structures express elements of meaning (not just arrangements of elements) that are not conveyed by individual words.

Fregean composition is the simplest case of (17), in which all elements of meaning come from the words, and syntactic structure expresses only the arrangement of word meanings, not content. This works for simple examples like *Pat kissed Frankie*, but not for the sorts of phenomena presented above. Such phenomena are pervasive in language; they involve both pieces of meaning expressed through meaningful syntactic constructions and pieces of meaning that are expressed neither lexically nor syntactically.

There are two important consequences of adopting this view of the syntax-semantics relation. First, it is possible to recognize that much of the complexity of mainstream syntax has arisen from trying to make covert syntax (D-structure or Logical Form) rich enough to achieve Fregean compositionality. Once one acknowledges the richer possibilities for composition argued for here, it becomes possible to strip away much of this complexity from syntax. The result is a far leaner theory of syntax, partly compensated for by a richer theory of the mapping between syntax and semantics (Culicover & Jackendoff 2005). The tradeoff, however is not even, because no defensible version of Fregean compositionality, no matter how complex the syntax, can account for any the phenomena adduced in this section.

A second consequence of Enriched Composition is that one can now come to view language not as a system that *derives* meanings from sounds (say proof-theoretically), but rather as a system that *expresses* meanings, where meanings constitute an independent mental domain – the system of thought. This is consistent with the view of Conceptual Semantics laid out in section 1 above, in which Conceptual Structure and Spatial Structure are the domains of thought and are related to linguistic expression through the interfaces with syntax and phonology. Thus the empirical phenomena studied within Conceptual Semantics provide arguments for the theory's overall worldview, one that is consistent with the constraints of the mentalistic framework.

4 References

Bach, Emmon 1986. The algebra of events. *Linguistics & Philosophy* 9, 5–16.
Bloom, Paul 2000. *How Children Learn the Meanings of Words*. Cambridge, MA: The MIT Press.
Bloom, Paul et al. (eds.) 1996. *Language and Space*. Cambridge, MA: The MIT Press.
Carnap, Rudolf 1939. *Foundations of Logic and Mathematics*. Chicago, IL: The University of Chicago Press.
Cheney, Dorothy L. & Robert M. Seyfarth 2007. *Baboon Metaphysics. The Evolution of a Social Mind*. Chicago, IL: The University of Chicago Press.
Chomsky, Noam 1995. *The Minimalist Program*. Cambridge, MA: The MIT Press.
Culicover, Peter W. & Ray Jackendoff 2005. *Simpler Syntax*. Oxford: Oxford University Press.
Declerck, Renaat 1979. Aspect and the bounded/unbounded (telic/atelic) distinction. *Linguistics* 17, 761–794.
Fauconnier, Gilles 1985. *Mental Spaces. Aspects of Meaning Construction in Natural Language*. Cambridge, MA: The MIT Press.

Fellbaum, Christiane (ed.) 1998. *WordNet. An Electronic Lexical Database*. Cambridge, MA: The MIT Press.
Fillmore, Charles 1982. Towards a descriptive framework for deixis. In: R. Jarvella & W. Klein (eds.). *Speech, Place, and Action*. New York: Wiley, 31–59.
Fodor, Jerry A. 1975. *The Language of Thought*. Cambridge, MA: Harvard University Press.
Fodor, Jerry A. 1998. *Concepts. Where Cognitive Science Went Wrong*. Oxford: Oxford University Press.
Frege, Gottlob 1892/1952. Über Sinn und Bedeutung. *Zeitschrift für Philosophie und philosophische Kritik* 100, 25–50. English translation in: P. Geach & M. Black (eds.). *Translations from the Philosophical Writings of Gottlob Frege*. Oxford: Blackwell, 1952, 56–78.
Givón, Talmy 1995. *Functionalism and Grammar*. Amsterdam: Benjamins.
Goldberg, Adele E. 1995. *Constructions. A Construction Grammar Approach to Argument Structure*. Chicago, IL: The University of Chicago Press.
Gruber, Jeffrey S. 1965. *Studies in Lexical Relations*. Ph.D. dissertation. MIT, Cambridge, MA. Reprinted in: J. S. Gruber. *Lexical Structures in Syntax and Semantics*. Amsterdam: North-Holland, 1976, 1–210.
Hauser, Marc D. 2000. *Wild Minds. What Animals Really Think*. New York: Henry Holt.
Hinrichs, Erhard W. 1985. *A Compositional Semantics for Aktionsarten and NP Reference in English*. Ph.D. dissertation. Ohio State University, Columbus, OH.
Jackendoff, Ray 1983. *Semantics and Cognition*. Cambridge, MA: The MIT Press.
Jackendoff, Ray 1987. *Consciousness and the Computational Mind*. Cambridge, MA: The MIT Press.
Jackendoff, Ray 1990. *Semantic Structures*. Cambridge, MA: The MIT Press.
Jackendoff, Ray 1991. Parts and boundaries. *Cognition* 41, 9–45. Reprinted in: R. Jackendoff, *Meaning and the Lexicon. The Parallel Architecture 1975–2000*. Oxford: Oxford University Press, 138–173.
Jackendoff, Ray 1992. Mme. Tussaud meets the binding theory. *Natural Language and Linguistic Theory* 10, 1–31.
Jackendoff, Ray 1996a. The architecture of the linguistic-spatial interface. In: P. Bloom et al. (eds.). *Language and Space*. Cambridge, MA: The MIT Press, 1–30. Reprinted in: R. Jackendoff, *Meaning and the Lexicon. The Parallel Architecture 1975–2010*. Oxford: Oxford University Press, 112–134.
Jackendoff, Ray 1996b. The proper treatment of measuring out, telicity, and possibly even quantification in English. *Natural Language and Linguistic Theory* 14, 305–354. Reprinted in: R. Jackendoff, *Meaning and the Lexicon. The Parallel Architecture 1975–2010*. Oxford: Oxford University Press, 175–221.
Jackendoff, Ray 1997a. *The Architecture of the Language Faculty*. Cambridge, MA: The MIT Press.
Jackendoff, Ray 1997b. Twistin' the night away. *Language* 73, 534–559. Reprinted in: R. Jackendoff, *Meaning and the Lexicon. The Parallel Architecture 1975–2010*. Oxford: Oxford University Press, 250–277.
Jackendoff, Ray 2002. *Foundations of Language. Brain, Meaning, Grammar, Evolution*. Oxford: Oxford University Press.
Jackendoff, Ray 2007. *Language, Consciousness, Culture. Essays on Mental Structure*. Cambridge, MA: The MIT Press.
Koch, Christof 2004. *The Quest for Consciousness. A Neurobiological Approach*. Englewood, CO: Roberts.

Kosslyn, Stephen M. 1980. *Image and Mind*. Cambridge, MA: Harvard University Press.
Lakoff, George 1987. *Women, Fire, and Dangerous Things. What Categories Reveal about the Mind*. Chicago, IL: The University of Chicago Press.
Landau, Barbara & Ray Jackendoff 1993. 'What' and 'where' in spatial language and spatial cognition. *Behavioral and Brain Sciences* 16, 217–238.
Landauer, Thomas et al. (eds.) 2007. *Handbook of Latent Semantic Analysis*. Mahwah, NJ: Erlbaum.
Langacker, Ronald 1987. *Foundations of Cognitive Grammar, vol. 1. Theoretical Prerequisites*. Stanford, CA: Stanford University Press.
Lerdahl, Fred & Ray Jackendoff 1983. *A Generative Theory of Tonal Music*. Cambridge, MA: The MIT Press.
Levinson, Stephen C. 2003. *Space in Language and Cognition. Explorations in Cognitive Diversity*. Cambridge: Cambridge University Press.
Lewis, David 1972. General semantics. In: D. Davidson & G. Harman (eds.). *Semantics of Natural Language*. Dordrecht: Reidel, 169–218.
Macnamara, John 1982. *Names for Things. A Study of Human Learning*. Cambridge, MA: The MIT Press.
Marr, David 1982. *Vision. A Computational Investigation into the Human Representation and Processing of Visual Information*. San Francisco, CA: Freeman.
McKay, Ryan, Robyn Langdon & Max Coltheart 2005. 'Sleights of mind'. Delusions, defenses, and self-deception. *Cognitive Neuropsychiatry* 10, 305–326.
Merchant, Jason 2001. *The Syntax of Silence. Sluicing, Islands, and the Theory of Ellipsis*. Oxford: Oxford University Press.
Montague, Richard 1973. The proper treatment of quantification in ordinary English. In: J. Hintikka, J. Moravcsik & P. Suppes (eds.). *Approaches to Natural Language*. Dordrecht: Reidel, 221–242.
Murphy, Gregory L. 2002. *The Big Book of Concepts*. Cambridge, MA: The MIT Press.
Neisser, Ulric 1967. *Cognitive Psychology*. Englewood Cliffs, NJ: Prentice Hall.
Nunberg, Geoffrey 1979. The non-uniqueness of semantic solutions. Polysemy. *Linguistics & Philosophy* 3, 143–184.
Paivio, Allan 1971. *Imagery and Verbal Processes*. New York: Holt, Rinehart & Winston.
Piñango, Maria M., Edgar Zurif & Ray Jackendoff 1999. Real-time processing implications of enriched composition at the syntax-semantics interface. *Journal of Psycholinguistic Research* 28, 395–414.
Pinker, Steven 1989. *Learnability and Cognition. The Acquisition of Argument Structure*. Cambridge, MA: The MIT Press.
Pinker, Steven 2007. *The Stuff of Thought. Language as a Window into Human Nature*. New York: Viking.
Pustejovsky, James 1995. *The Generative Lexicon*. Cambridge, MA: The MIT Press.
Putnam, Hilary 1975. The meaning of 'meaning'. In: K. Gunderson (ed.). *Language, Mind, and Knowledge*. Minneapolis, MN: University of Minnesota Press, 131–193.
Russell, Bertrand 1905. On denoting. *Mind* 14, 479–493.
Searle, John R. 1995. *The Construction of Social Reality*. New York: Free Press.
Stainton, Robert J. 2006. *Words and Thoughts. Subsentences, Ellipsis, and the Philosophy of Language*. Oxford: Oxford University Press.
Talmy, Leonard 1978. The relation of grammar to cognition. A synopsis. In: D. Waltz (ed.). *Theoretical Issues in Natural Language Processing*. New York: ACM, 14–24. Revised and

enlarged version in: L. Talmy. *Toward a Cognitive Semantics, vol. 1. Concept Structuring Systems*. Cambridge, MA: The MIT Press, 2000, 21–96.

Talmy, Leonard 1988. Force-dynamics in language and cognition. *Cognitive Science* 12, 49–100.

Talmy, Leonard 2000. *Toward a Cognitive Semantics*. Cambridge, MA: The MIT Press.

Tarski, Alfred 1956. The concept of truth in formalized languages. In: A. Tarski. *Logic, Semantics, Metamathematics*. Translated by J. H. Woodger. 2nd edn., ed. J. Corcoran. London: Oxford University Press, 152–197.

van der Zee & Jon Slack (eds.) 2003. *Representing Direction in Language and Space*. Oxford: Oxford University Press.

Verkuyl, Henk 1993. *A Theory of Aspectuality. The Interaction between Temporal and Atemporal Structure*. Cambridge: Cambridge University Press.

Wertheimer, Max 1923. Laws of organization in perceptual forms. Reprinted in: W. D. Ellis (ed.). *A Source Book of Gestalt Psychology*. London: Routledge & Kegan Paul, 1938, 71–88.

Wierzbicka, Anna 1996. *Semantics. Primes and Universals*. Oxford: Oxford University Press.

Wittgenstein, Ludwig 1953. *Philosophical Investigations*. Translated by G.E.M. Ascombe. Oxford: Blackwell.

Ewald Lang and Claudia Maienborn
5 Two-level Semantics: Semantic Form and Conceptual Structure

1 Introduction —— 114
2 Polysemy problems —— 125
3 Compositionality and beyond: Semantic underspecification and coercion —— 131
4 More on SF variables and their instantiation at the CS level —— 140
5 Summary and outlook —— 148
6 References —— 150

Abstract: Semantic research of the last decades has been shaped by an increasing interest in conceptuality, that is, in emphasizing the conceptual nature of the meanings conveyed by natural language expressions. Among the multifaceted approaches emerging from this tendency, the article focuses on discussing a framework that has become known as »Two-level Semantics«. The central idea it pursues is to assume and justify two basically distinct, but closely interacting, levels of representation that spell out the meaning of linguistic expressions: Semantic Form (SF) and Conceptual Structure (CS). The distinction of SF vs. CS representations is substantiated by its role in accounting for related parallel distinctions including 'lexical vs. contextually specified meaning', 'grammar-based vs. concept-based restrictions', 'storage vs. processing' etc. The SF vs. CS distinction is discussed on the basis of semantic problems regarding polysemy, underspecification, coercion, and inferences.

1 Introduction

1.1 The turn to conceptuality

Looking back at the major trends of linguistic research in the 80's and 90's, we observe a remarkable inclination to tackle semantic issues by emphasizing the conceptual nature of the meanings conveyed by linguistic expressions. Several models

Ewald Lang, Berlin, Germany
Claudia Maienborn, Tübingen, Germany

and frameworks of linguistic semantics developed at that time marked off their specific view on meaning by programmatically labeling the structure they focus on as *conceptual* (cf. article 4 [Semantics: Lexical Structures and Adjectives] (Levin & Rappaport Hovav) *Lexical Conceptual Structure*; article 4 [this volume] (Jackendoff) *Conceptual Semantics*; article 1 [this volume] (Talmy) *Cognitive Semantics*) and by elevating *concepts, conceptualization,* and *Conceptual System* to key words of semantic theorizing. The approach presented in this article is another outcome of these efforts, which implies that it shows commonalities with as well as differences from the approaches mentioned above.

The semantic issues which have been under debate since that time are summarized in (1) by listing the major topics and the crucial questions they have given rise to:

(1) a. compositionality: How far do we get by holding to the Frege Principle?
b. lexicalism: What can provide a better account of the internal meaning structure of lexical items – semantic decomposition or meaning postulates?
c. meaning variation: How do we account for polysemy and underspecification?
d. cognitivism: How can we avoid "uninterpreted markerese" by drawing on semantic primes which are (i) compatible with our linguistic intuition, (ii) reconstructible elements of our conceptual knowledge, and which (iii) can be traced back to our perceptual abilities?
e. modularity: How can we spell out and test the claim that our linguistic behavior results from the interaction of largely autonomous mental systems and subsystems?
f. interpretations: What are the respective roles of word knowledge and world knowledge in specifying what is commonly dubbed "sentence meaning" vs. "utterance meaning" vs. "communicative sense"?

The answers to (1a–f) as provided by various frameworks differ to a certain extent, though on closer inspection they will presumably turn out not to be strictly incompatible. However, typical features of theoretical innovations in linguistics such as terminological rank growth, lack of concern in dealing with equivocations, and confinement to selections of data and/or problems that are supportive of a given approach have impeded detailed comparisons between the competing approaches so far, but see Taylor (1994, 1995), Geeraerts (2010). Space limitations prevent us from delving into this endeavor here. Instead, the article attempts to convey some of the motives and tenets of what has become known as *Two-level Semantics* (which, incidentally, is not a registered trademark created by the adherents of the approach, but a label it received from reviewers) and restricts reference to kindred views to that of *Conceptual Semantics* expounded in Jackendoff (1996, 2002; article 4 of this volume).

1.2 Basic assumptions

Two-level Semantics is not at variance with the other frameworks in recognizing the conceptual nature of, and in pursuing a mentalistic approach to, linguistic meaning. The major difference between the former and the latter is hinted at in the subtitle, which presents the distinction of two levels of representation, i.e. *Semantic Form* (SF) vs. *Conceptual Structure* (CS), as the central issue this approach claims to deal with. The relations assumed to hold between SF and CS have in common that they induce certain asymmetries but they differ in the viewpoints that give rise to these distinctions. In the following, we briefly discuss a selection of features that have been proposed to distinguish SF representations from CS representations. To clarify the significance of these rather general claims, the goals and the problems connected with the assumptions will be commented on in more concrete terms.

(2) SF ⊂ CS

In substance, SF representations may be conceived of as those subsets of CS representations that are systematically connected to, and hence covered by, lexical items and their combinatorial potential to form more complex expressions.

Strictly speaking, SF and CS here stand for two sets of elements (inventories) which make up the respective representations. Due to the conditions specified in (3) and (4) below, SF representations and CS representations do not qualify as members of the same set – the former represent linguistic knowledge, the latter non-linguistic knowledge. The relationship expressed in (2) comprises two aspects. The uncontroversial one is the subset – set relation SF ⊂ CS which follows from the widely held view that for every linguistic expression e in language L there is a CS representation c assignable to it via SF(e), but not vice versa. It is obviously not the case that for every actual or latent CS item c there is an expression e in L with an SF(e) which makes c communicable to other speakers of L. Thus, (2) presupposes the existence of non-lexicalized concepts.

The problematic aspect of (2) is this: The view that CS representations are mental structures that mediate between language and the world as construed by the human mind implies that the Conceptual System provides representations whose contents originate in heterogeneous cognitive subsystems and which therefore have to be homogenized to yield knowledge structures that can be accessed and processed on the conceptual level. The conditions based on which, say, perceptual features stemming from vision, touch, proprioception etc. are conceptualized to figure in CS representations are far from clear. We will call this the "homogenization problem" posed by CS representations.

(3) grammar-based vs. concept-based
SF representations account for the fact that the meanings of linguistic expressions come with grammatically determined kinds of packaging in terms of morphosyntactic categories and semantic types, while the elements of CS representations, due to their mental source and intermodal homogeneity, lack grammar-based wrappings.

The distinction in (3) is not challenged in principle but it is under debate whether or not the types of grammatical packaging in which the meanings of linguistic expressions are conveyed yield a sufficient condition to postulate SF as a representation level of its own. So, e.g., Ray Jackendoff (article 4) does not absolutely exclude such a level in conceding "If it proves necessary to posit an additional level of »linguistic semantic structure« that is devoted specifically to features relevant for grammatical expression [...], the addition of such an extra component would not at all change the content of Conceptual Structure, which is necessary to drive inference and the connection to perception". Basically, however, he sticks to the view "that in fact such an extra component is unnecessary" (4 [this volume]). Let's call this the "justification problem" posed by the assumption of SF representations.

(4) linguistic vs. non-linguistic origin
SF representations form an integral part of the information cluster represented by the lexical entries of a given language L, whereas CS representations are taken to belong to, or at least to be rooted in, the non-linguistic mental systems based on which linguistic expressions are interpreted and related to their denotations.

The distinction referred to in (4) by locating the roots of SF and CS representations in different though mutually accessible mental subsystems is the view taken by adherents of Two-level Semantics, cf. Bierwisch (1983, 1996, 1997, 2007); Bierwisch & Lang (1989a); Bierwisch & Schreuder (1992) for earlier works.

Article 1 [Semantics: Lexical Structures and Adjectives] (Bierwisch) *Semantic features and primes* focuses on defining SF as an interface level whose basic elements, combinatorial rules, and well-formedness constraints directly reflect the conditions on which lexicon-based meanings of morpho-syntactically categorized, regularly combined linguistic expressions are composed and interpreted. While article 1 [Semantics: Lexical Structures and Adjectives] may well be taken as a state-of-the-art report on arguments in favor of assuming SF as a level of representation, much less attention is paid to CS representations that are supposed to connect the former with "the full range of mental structures representing the content to be expressed" (1 [Semantics: Lexical Structures and Adjectives]).

So we face problems connected with the intermodal validity and the crossmodal origin of CS representations: (i) how to relate linguistically designated SF representations with conceptually homogenized CS representations? (ii) how to trace the latter back to their respective cognitive sources that are determined by crucially differing sensory modalities?

(5) storage vs. processing
   SF representations are linguistic knowledge structures that are accessibly stored in long-term memory, whereas CS representations are activated and compiled in working memory, cf. article 12 [Semantics: Typology, Diachrony and Processing] (Kelter & Kaup) *Conceptual knowledge, categorization, and meaning*.

The distinction that (5) establishes by locating SF and CS representations in long-term memory and working memory, respectively, marks out what experimental psycholinguistics may contribute to clarifying the theoretically controversial interrelationship of SF and CS representations by drawing on evidence from language processing. The effects of taking (5) seriously can be expected to pay off in confirming or disconfirming the distinction of SF vs. CS but also in providing criteria for deciding what requirements the representations at issue have to meet.

The methodologically most relevant conclusion drawn by Kelter and Kaup (article 12 [Semantics: Typology, Diachrony and Processing]) reads as follows: "researchers should acknowledge the fact that concepts and word meaning are different knowledge structures." The claim in (5) suggests that if it is the SF of lexical items that is stored in long-term memory, the entries should be confined to representing what may be called "context-free lexical meanings", whereas CS representations compiled and processed in working memory should take charge of what may be called "contextually specified (parts of) utterance meanings". The difference between the two types of meaning representations indicates the virtual semantic underspecification of the former and the possible semantic enrichment of the latter. There is a series of recent experimental studies designed and carried out along these lines which – in combination with evidence from corpus data, linguistic diagnostics etc. – are highly relevant for the theoretical issues raised by SF vs. CS representations. Experiments reported by Stolterfoht, Gese & Maienborn (2010) and Kaup, Lüdtke & Maienborn (2010) succeeded in providing processing evidence that supports the distinction of, e.g., primary adjectives vs. adjectivized participles vs. verbal participles, that is, evidence for packaging categories relevant to SF representations. In addition, these studies reveal the processing costs of contextualizing semantically underspecified items, a result that supports the view that contextualizing the interpretation of a given linguistic expression *e* is realized by building up an enriched CS representation on the basis of SF (*e*).

1.3 SF vs. CS – an illustration from everyday life

To round off the picture outlined so far, we illustrate the features listed in (2)–(5) in favor of the SF vs. CS distinction by an example we are well acquainted with, *viz.* the representations involved in handling numbers, number symbols, and numerals in everyday life. Note that each of the semiotic objects in (6)–(8) below represents in some way the numerical concept »18«. However, how numerical concepts between »10« and »20« are stored, activated, and operated on in our memory is poorly understood as yet, so the details regarding the claim in (5) must be left open. Suffice it to agree that »18« stands for the concept we make use of, say, in trying to mentally add up the sum to be paid for our purchases in the shopping trolley. With this proviso in mind, we now look at the representations of the concept »18« in (6)–(8) to find out their interrelations.

(6) a. |||| |||| |||| |||
    b. :::   :::   :::

(7) a. *XVIII*   a'.   *IIXX*   (rarely occurring alternative)
    b. *18*

(8) a. *eighteen, achtzehn*   (8 + 10)   English, German
    b. *dix-huit, shi ba*   (10 + 8)   French, Mandarin
    c. *okto-kai-deka*   ((8)-and-(10))   Greek
    d. *diez y ocho*   ((10)-and-(8))   Spanish
    e. *vosem-na-dcat'*   ((8)-on-(10))   Russian
    f. *duo-de-viginti*   ((2)-of-(20))   Latin
    g. *ocht-deec*   (8 + (2 × 5))   Irish
    h. *deu-naw*   (2 × 9)   Welsh

(6) shows two iconic non-verbal representations of a quantity whose correlation with the concept »18« and/or with the numerals in (8) rests on the ability to count and the availability of numerals. The tallying systems in (6) are simple but inefficient for doing arithmetic and hence hardly suitable to serve as semantic representations of the numerals in (8).

(7) shows two symbolic non-verbal representations of »18«, generated by distinct writing systems for numbers. The Roman number symbols are partially iconic in that they encode addition by iterating up to three special symbols for *one*, *ten*, *hundred*, or *thousand*, partially symbolic due to placing the symbol of a small number in front of the symbol of a larger number, thus indicating subtraction, cf. (7a, a'). The lack of a symbol for *null* prevented the creation of a positional system, the lack of means to indicate multiplication or division impeded calculation. Both were obstacles to progress in mathematics. Thus, Roman number symbols may roughly render the lexical meaning of (8a–f) but not those of (8g–h) and all other variants involving multiplication or division.

The Indo-Arabic system of number symbols exemplified by *18* in (7b) is a positional system without labels based on exponents of *ten* ($10^0, 10^1, 10^2, \ldots, 10^n$). As a representational system for numbers it is recursive and potentially infinite in yielding unambiguous and well-distinguished chains of symbols as output. Thus, knowing the system implies knowing that *18* ≠ *81* or that *17* and *19* are the direct predecessor and successor of *18*, respectively, even if we do not have pertinent number words at our disposal to name them. Moreover, it is this representation of numbers that we use when we do arithmetic with paper and pencil or by pressing the keys of an electronic calculator. Enriched with auxiliary symbols for arithmetical operations and for marking their scope of application, as well as furnished with conventions for writing equations etc., this notational system is a well-defined means to reduce the use of mathematical expressions to representations of their Conceptual Structures, that is, to the CS representations they denote, independent of any natural language in which these expressions may be read aloud or dictated. Let's call this enriched system of Indo-Arabic number symbols the "CS system of mathematical expressions". Now, what about the SF representations of numerals?

Though all number words in (8) denote the concept »18«, it is obvious that their lexical meanings differ in the way they are composed, cf. the second column in (8). As regards their combinatorial category, the number words in (8) are neither determinative nor copulative compounds, nor are they conjoined phrases. They are perhaps best categorized as juxtapositions with or without connectives, cf. (8c–f) and (8a–b, g–h), respectively. The unique feature of complex number words is that the relations between their numeral constituents are nothing but encoded fundamental arithmetic operations (addition and multiplication are preferred; division and subtraction are less frequent). Thus, the second column in (8) shows SF representations of the number words in the first column couched in terms of the CS system of mathematical expressions. The latter are construable as functor-argument structures with arithmetic operators ('+', '−', '×' etc.) as functors, quantity constants for digits as arguments, and parentheses (...) as boundaries marking lexical building blocks. Now let's see what all this tells us about the distinctions in (2)–(5) above.

The subset – set relation SF ⊂ CS mentioned in connection with (2) also holds for the number symbols in (7b). The CS system of mathematical expressions is capable of representing all partitions of *18* that draw on fundamental arithmetic operations. Based on this, the CS system at stake covers the internal structures of complex number words, cf. (8), as well as those of equations at the sentence level like *18 = 3 × 6; 18 = 2 × 9; 18 = 72 : 4* etc.

By contrast, the subset of SF representations for numerals is restricted in two respects. First, not all admissible partitions of a complex number like *18* are designated as SF of a complex numeral lexicalized to denote »18«. The grammar of number words in *L* is interspersed with (certain types of) *L*-specific packing strategies, cf. Hurford (1975), Greenberg (1978). Second, since the ideal relationship between systems of number symbols and systems of numerals is a one-to-one correspondence, the non-ambiguity required of the output of numeral systems practically forbids creation or use of synonymous number names (except for the distinct numerals used for e.g. *1995* when speaking of years or of prices in €).

There is still another conclusion to be drawn from (6)–(8) in connection with (2). The CS system of mathematical expressions is a purposeful artifact created and developed to solve the "homogenization problem" raised by CS representations for the well-defined field of numbers and arithmetic operations on them. First, the mental operations of counting, adding, multiplying etc., which the system is designed to represent, have been abstracted from practical actions, *viz.* from lining up things, bundling up things, bundling up bundles of things etc. Second, the CS representations of mathematical expressions provided by the system are unambiguous, complete (that is, fully specified and containing neither gaps nor variables to be instantiated by elements from outside the system), and independent of the particular languages in which they may be verbalized.

The lexicon-based packaging and contents of the components of SF representations claimed in (3) and (4) are also corroborated by (6)–(8). The first point to note is the *L*-specific ways in which (i) numerals are categorized in morpho-syntactic terms and (ii) their lexical meanings are composed. The second point is this: Complex numerals differ from regular (determinative or copulative) compounds in that the relations between their constituents are construed as encodings of fundamental arithmetical operations, cf. (8a–h). This unique feature of the subgrammar of number words also yields a strong argument wrt. the "justification problem" posed by the assumption of lexicon-based SF representations.

The claims in (3) and (4) concerning the non-linguistic nature of CS representations are supported by the fact that e.g. *18* is an intermodally valid representation of the concept »18« as it covers both the perception-based iconic representations of »18« in (6) and the lexicon-based linguistic expressions denoting »18« in (8). Thus, the unique advantage of the CS system of mathematical expressions is founded on the representational intermodality and the conceptual homogeneity it has achieved in the history of mathematical thinking. No other science is more dependent on the representations of its subject than mathematics.

Revealing as this illustration may be, the insights it yields cannot simply be extended to the lexicon and grammar of a natural language L beyond the subgrammar of number words. The correlations between systems of number names and their SF representations in terms of the CS system of mathematical expressions form a special case which results from the creation of a non-linguistic semiotic artifact, *viz.* a system to represent number concepts under controlled laboratory conditions. The meanings, the combinatorial potential and hence the SF representations of lexical items outside the domain of numeric tools are far less strictly codified than those of numerals. Otherwise, the controversial issues listed in (1) would not emerge. The overwhelming majority of SF representations of lexical items have to account for ambiguity, polysemy, underspecification, context-dependency etc., that is, for phenomena which require the use of appropriate variables at the SF level to be instantiated by pieces of information available at the CS level.

1.4 Aims and limitations

Having outlined some perspectives and problems connected with the assumption of two separate but interacting levels of semantic representation, we conclude this introductory survey by some remarks on the weight one may attach to the pros and cons discussed so far.

First, regarding the justification problem raised by (3) there is a truism: the representations assigned to linguistic meaning depend on the meaning attributed to linguistic representations. In other words, in view of our limited knowledge of the principles based on which linguistic expressions and semantic interpretations are mutually assigned, we cannot get along without auxiliary terminology such as *tier, layer, plane, domain* etc. Thus, the term *level of representation* is just a heuristic aid that serves as a gathering place for distinctions considered to be necessary and worth systematizing. Any further assessment is premature.

Second, the crucial point is not the number of levels of linguistic structure formation we postulate but the validity of the arguments based on which such levels are substantiated. It is above all this guideline that characterizes the efforts subsumable under the label *Two-level Semantics*. There have been proposals to increase the number of levels, cf. Dölling (2001, 2003, 2005a); Schwarz (1992), as well as criticisms regarding the mapping operations assumed to apply between SF and CS, cf. Blutner (1995, 1998, 2004), Meyer (1994), Taylor (1994, 1995). Given the situation defined by the questions in (1), Two-level Semantics may be considered a series of attempts along the lines of (2)–(5) to achieve a more fine-grained picture of what we are used to calling "semantic interpretation". These attempts were, and still are, driven and guided by the following leitmotif:

(9) The semantic interpretation of a sentence *s* in isolation as well as of its utterance in use require to differentiate and interrelate those portions of its meaning that are lexicon-based and those possibly available portions of meaning that are context-based such that the latter may serve as specifications of the former.

Third, in view of the fact that lexical SF representations are discussed in detail by Manfred Bierwisch (article 1 [Semantics: Lexical Structures and Adjectives]), we will pay more attention to compositionality issues (§3) and CS representations and the way they account both for the semantic issues pointed out in (1) and for the various problems raised in connection with the distinctions in (2)–(5) above (§4).

Fourth, Two-level Semantics shares several objectives with the framework presented in article 4 [this volume] (Jackendoff) *Conceptual Semantics* but prefers different solutions. There is agreement on the guiding role of compositionality and the need for decomposition. Jackendoff's requirement that "Utterance meanings must serve as a formal basis for inference" (4 [this volume]) is accepted as contextualized inferencing at the CS level but in addition there are built-in inferences at the SF level. The two-level framework acknowledges the import of categorization and contextualization but places emphasis on the grammatical nature of SF as indicated in (3) and (4) above. On this view, the principles governing SF representations concern not only the internal meaning structure and the grammatical packaging of lexical items but also general conditions on the lexical system of *L*, e.g. grammatical categories, lexicalization patterns, options to be chosen as the basis of agreement etc. By way of illustration, note the following.

The English collective noun (i) *married couple* has two equivalents in German: (ii) *Ehepaar*, which is also a collective noun, and (iii) *Eheleute*, which, though based on a plural only noun, behaves like a regular individual plural and has no direct counterpart in English; cf. Dölling (1994), Lang (1994). Now, while all three are absolutely alike at the CS level in denoting a set of two individuals as HUSBAND AND WIFE, they differ at the SF level in the way they are sensitive to number agreement and selectional restrictions, cf. (10–13):

(10) a. Die Eheleute hassen [3P.Pl] einander/sich gegenseitig.
 b. Das Ehepaar hasst [3P.Sg] *einander/*sich gegenseitig.
 c. Das Ehepaar *ist/*sind [3P.Sg/Pl] beide Linkshänder.
 d. Die Eheleute sind [3P.Pl] beide Linkshänder.

(11) a. The married couple hate [3P.Pl] each other/are [3P.Pl] both left-handers.
 b. Each one of the married couple hates [3P.Sg] the other.

(12) a. The married couple is [3P.Sg] waiting for their visa.
 b. The married couple are [3P.Pl] waiting for their visas.

(13) a. Das Ehepaar$_i$ wartet [3P.Sg] auf sein$_i$/*ihr$_i$ Visum.
 b. Die Eheleute$_i$ warten [3P.Pl] auf ihre$_i$ Visa.

The antecedent of reciprocals like *einander* or *each other* must denote a set of two (or more) elements. In both languages, the antecedent is usually a plural NP or an *and*-coordination of NPs; with collective nouns, however, there are language-particular constraints. In German, agreement features for person, number, and gender are assigned on the basis of some morpho-syntactic correspondence between antecedent and target. A singular collective noun as subject requires a verb in the singular and excludes reciprocals like *einander* as complement, cf. (10b,c; 13a), whereas plural NPs or *and*-coordinated NPs as subjects usually come with plural verbs and allow for reciprocals as complements, cf. (10a,d; 13b). In British English, however, *committee*-type singular nouns as subjects may spread agreement features on a morpho-syntactic or on a semantic basis, cf. (11a,b; 12a,b). Cases of singular agreement like (12a) are conceptualized as referring to a single entity, cases of plural override like (12b) are conceptualized as referring to the individual members of the set. What is an option in English is an obligatory lexical choice in German. As lexical items, English singular collective nouns are unspecified for inducing morpho-syntactic or semantic agreement and for co-occurring with reciprocals, German singular collective nouns, however, are basically unavailable for plural agreement and/or reciprocals since number agreement in German strictly operates on morpho-syntactic matching. In sum, although having the same SF, the collective nouns *married couple* and *Ehepaar* differ in their impact on sentence formation.

Moreover, since SF forms a constitutive part of L as a natural language, it is subject to a series of pragmatic-based felicity conditions on communication. None of these aspects of SF as a linguistic level applies to CS representations.

The article attempts to show that the distinction of SF vs. CS representations may turn out to be a useful heuristic means in dealing with the issues listed in (1) as well as a promising research strategy to connect semantic theorizing with empirical methods of analyzing semantic processing along the lines of (5). Guided by the leitmotif in (9), §2 deals with some unsolved problems of polysemy. §3 explores the SF vs. CS distinction from the angle of compositionality, and in §4 we turn to contextualization by discussing case studies of variables in SF representations and their instantiation at the CS level. In doing so, we also examine how inferences are accounted for by SF and CS representations, respectively.

2 Polysemy problems

2.1 Institution nouns

Meaning multiplicity on the lexical level comprises three basic types: homonymy, polysemy, and indeterminacy (or vagueness). Bierwisch (1983), in a way the birth certificate of the SF vs. CS distinction, draws on institution nouns such as *school, university, museum, parliament* etc. to illustrate systematic polysemy, that is, a lexical item with one meaning representation acquiring further representations that differ from the first in predictable ways based on conceptual relations. (14a–d) below shows some of the readings that *school* may assume. The readings are numbered and the concepts they represent are added in ITALICIZED CAPS. NORMAL CAPS in (15) show the invariant SF representation for the lexeme *school*, which may be contextually specified at the CS level by applying certain functions to (15) that eventually yield the utterance meanings of (14a–d) as represented in (16a–d).

(14)   a. The school made a major donation. $school_1 \subset INSTITUTION$
        b. The school has a flat roof. $school_2 \subset BUILDING$
        c. He enjoys school very much. $school_3 \subset PROCESS$
        d. The school took a staff outing. $school_4 \subset PERSONNEL$

(15)   SF(*school*) = λX [PURPOSE X W]
       with W = PROCESSES_OF_LEARNING_AND_TEACHING

(16) a. λX [INSTITUTION X   & SF (*school*)]
     b. λX [BUILDING X   & SF (*school*)]
     c. λX [PROCESS X   & SF (*school*)]
     d. λX [PERSONNEL X   & SF (*school*)]

Taken together, (14)–(16) show a way of (i) keeping the lexical meaning of the lexeme *school* constant and avoiding problematic ambiguity assumptions and (ii) still accounting for the range of semantic variation the lexeme *school* may cover at the CS level. The conceptual interpretations of *school* in (16) are determined by selectional restrictions, cf. (14a–d), and come with distinctive grammatical features: so e.g. *school* in the PROCESS reading has no regular plural and in German the prepositions in *Max geht auf die/in die/zur Goethe-Schule* clearly select the INSTITUTION, BUILDING and PROCESS reading, respectively. So far, so good. Methodologically, however, the analysis of these institution nouns poses some problems.

First of all, we do not have reliable principles yet to find the SF of a polysemous lexeme, which makes it difficult to motivate a collection of templates that would account for the specifications in (16). Moreover, it is unclear (i) whether the members of the concept family associated with the noun *school* all draw on the abstract SF the same way (as suggested by (15–16)) or (ii) whether some of the concepts are more closely interconnected than others. Finally, it is unclear what conceptual (sub-)system is taken to serve as the source for the specifications in (16). To show the importance of these issues and their impact on the SF vs. CS distinction some brief comments might be in order.

The SF proposed in (15) takes *school* as a sort of artifact by drawing on the feature PURPOSE X W, which is not implausible as it inheres in all artifact-denoting nouns. However, (15) ignores the social relevance attributed to the purpose W = PROCESSES_OF_LEARNING_ AND_TEACHING or to the purposes W', W" of other institution nouns. Actually, what makes a created X into an INSTITUTION is its social importance evidenced by the fact that some PURPOSE W^i has been institutionalized by founding or keeping X. Therefore, instead of reducing the role of this feature common to all institution nouns to that of yielding a concept at the CS level, cf. INSTITUTION in (16a), the lexical semantics of these nouns should make use of it as an invariant component at the SF level. Heuristically, the starting point for construing the SF of *school* and the CS specifications in (16) might be the lexical meaning of *institution*, which is something like 'a legal entity that organizes purposeful events to be performed and/or received by authorized groups of persons in specific locations' such that it (i) also covers abstract instances like *the institution of marriage* and (ii) provides the basis for (16a–d) as metonymy-based conceptual shifts. The learned word *institution*, no doubt an element of the adult lexicon, has a lexical meaning that is sufficiently abstract to allow for each and every of the conceptual specifications of *school* in (16); its conceptual basis is a sort of world knowledge that rests on what may be called "created advanced level concepts", which in turn define a widely unexplored domain of the conceptual system.

In contrast, the conceptual subsystem of spatial orientation is a domain we know a bit more about, as it crucially draws on human perception and thus on "natural basic level concepts". So it is not a surprise that a number of pioneering works in the realm of conceptual structure deal with spatial issues. Since these studies provide better illustrations of the SF vs. CS distinction, we will focus on them in the next sections.

Another problem with this approach to systematic polysemy is the fact that, despite their ontological and/or categorial differences, the conceptual specifications of the SF (*school*) in (16a–d) are not absolutely incompatible but may occur in certain combinations, cf. the gradual acceptability of the examples in (17):

(17) a. The school which has a flat roof made a major donation.
b. ?? The school, which has a flat roof, made a major donation.
c. ?? The school, which has a flat roof, went out for a staff outing.
d. The school has a flat roof and *it/the school went out for a staff outing.

Whereas the INSTITUTION and the BUILDING readings are somewhat compatible, the BUILDING and the PERSONNEL readings are not; as regards the (type of) reading of the antecedent, anaphoric pronouns are less tolerant than relative pronouns or repeated DPs. The data in (17) show that the conceptual specifications of SF (*school*) differ in ways that are poorly understood as yet; cf. Asher (2011) for some discussion. The semantics of institution nouns, for a while the signature tune of Two-level Semantics, elicited a certain amount of discussion and criticism, cf. Herzog & Rollinger (1991), Bierwisch & Bosch (1995). The problems expounded in these volumes are still unsolved but they sharpened our view of the intricacies of the SF vs. CS distinction.

2.2 Locative prepositions

In many languages the core inventory of adpositions encode spatial relations to localize some x (called *theme*, *figure* or *located object*) wrt. the place occupied by some y (called *relatum*, *ground* or *reference object*), where x and y may pairwise range over objects, substances, and events. Regarding the conceptual basis of these relations, locative prepositions in English and related languages are usually subdivided into topological (*in, at, on*), directional (*into, onto*), dimensional (*above, under, behind*), and path-defining (*along, around*) prepositions. The semantic problems posed by these lexical items can be best illustrated with *in*, which supposedly draws on spatial containment, pure and simple, and which is therefore taken to be the prime example of a topological preposition.

To illustrate how SF (*in*) is integrated into a lexical entry with information on Phonetic Form (PF), Grammatical Features (GF), Argument Structure (AS) etc., we take German *in* as a telling example: It renders English *in* vs. *into* with distinct cases which in turn correspond to the values of the feature [± Dir(ectional)] subcategorizing the internal argument y, and to further syntactic distinctions. The entry in (18) is taken from Bierwisch (1988: 37), examples are added in (19). The interdependence of the values for the case feature [± Obl(ique)] and for the category feature [± Dir] is indicated by means of the meta-variable $\alpha \in \{+, -\}$ and by the conventions (i) – α inverts the value of α and (ii) (αW) means that W is present if α = + and absent if α = –.

(18) Lexical entry of the German preposition *in*:

PF	GF	AS	SF
/in/;	[–V,–N, α Dir];	λy λ<u>x</u> | [– α Obl]	[($_\alpha$FIN) [LOC x] ⊂ [LOC y]]

(19) a. Die Straße/Fahrt führt in die Stadt. [+ Dir, – Obl] = Acc, "x is a path
 The street/journey leads into the city. ending in y"

  /in/; [–V,–N, +Dir]; λy λ<u>x</u> [(FIN) [LOC x] ⊂ [LOC y]]
       |
       [– Obl]

 b. Die Straße/Fahrt ist in der Stadt. [– Dir, + Obl] = Dat, "x is located in y"
 The street/journey is in the city.

  /in/; [–V,–N, –Dir]; λy λ<u>x</u> [[LOC x] ⊂ [LOC y]]
       |
       [+ Obl]

Now let's take a closer look at the components of SF. The variables x and y represent entities ranging over the domains of objects, substances, or events. LOC is a SF functor-constant of category N/N such that LOC x assigns x the place it occupies in the domain it is an element of. The SF constant FIN yields the final part of [LOC x], thereby transforming the external argument of *in* into a path. The SF-constant ⊂ "specifies a particular relation between places, in the case of *in* simply (improper) inclusion" (Bierwisch 1988: 34). Confining our review to objects, the SF of *in* assigned to (19b) might thus be paraphrased as "the place occupied by the street x is (improperly) included in the place occupied by the city y" (op. cit.).

While it is widely accepted that the semantics of locative *in* should be based on spatial inclusion, the relativizing attribute "(improper)" in the explication of the SF-constant ⊂ quoted above is indicative of a hidden controversial issue. In fact, much ink has been spilled on the problem of how to determine the lexical meaning of *in* by keeping to the spatial inclusion approach. The discussion was ignited by groups of data that seem to challenge the [[LOC x] ⊂ [LOC y]] analysis of the preposition *in* in some way.

(20) a. The amount of *oxygen in the air* is diminishing.
b. The *balloons in the air* quickly escaped.
c. The *air in the balloons* quickly escaped.

(21) a. The *water in the vase* should be replaced.
b. The *flowers in the vase* are wilted.
c. The *cracks in the vase* cannot be repaired.
d. I did not notice the *splinter in his hand*.

Whereas the approach under review might capture the examples in (20) by letting x and y range over substances (a) or objects and substances (b, c), the differences of (20a vs. b) and of (20b vs. c) in the interpretation of LOC and ⊂ remain out of its reach. Obviously, (20a–c) differ in the way the place is assigned to x and to y by LOC, but are alike in clearly requiring that ⊂ has to be interpreted as proper inclusion. The examples in (21) show that the place assigned to the relatum by the functor LOC is not confined to the material boundaries of the object y but may vary to some extent. In (21a–c) the interpretation of *in the vase* involves function-based enrichment, e.g. by means of gestalt-psychological laws of closure, to account for the containment relation between x and y, which is proper in (21a), partial in (21b), and privative in (21c). The PP in (21d) is ambiguous, i.e. unspecified wrt. "x being materially included in y (as a foreign body)" or "x being functionally included in a cupped y (to prevent x from getting lost)".

The discussion of such data produced a series of theoretical revisions of the semantic analysis of topological prepositions. Wunderlich & Herweg (1991) propose (22) as a general schema for the SF of locative prepositions thereby abandoning the problematic functor ⊂ and revising the functor LOC:

(22) λy λx (LOC (x, PREP*(y))),
where LOC localizes the object x in the region determined by the preposition p and PREP* is a variable ranging over p-based regions.

Bierwisch (1996: 69) replaces SF (*in*) in (18) with λy λx [x [LOC [INT y]]] commenting "x LOC p identifies the condition that the location of x be (improperly) included in p" and "INT y identifies a location determined by the boundaries of y, that is, the interior of y". Although this proposal avoids some of the problems with the functor ⊂, the puzzling effect of "(improperly) included" remains and so does the definition of INT y as yielding "the interior of x".

Herweg (1989) advocates an abstract SF (*in*) which draws on proper spatial inclusion such that the examples in (21) are semantically marked due to violating the "Presupposition of Argument Homogeneity". The resulting truth value gap triggers certain function-based accommodations at the CS level that account for the interpretations of (21a–d).

Hottenroth (1991), in a detailed analysis of French *dans*, rejects the idea that SF (*dans*) might draw on imprecise region-creating constants like INT y. Instead, SF (*dans*) should encode the conditions on the relatum in prototypical uses of *dans*. The standard reference region of *dans* is a three-dimensional empty closed container (bottle, bag, box etc.). If the relatum of *dans* does not meet one or more of these characteristics, the reference region is conceptually adapted by means of certain processing principles (laws of closure, mental demarcation of unbounded y, conceptual switching from 3D to 2D etc.).

In view of data like those in (21), Carstensen (2001) proposes to do away with the region account altogether and to replace it with a perception-based account of prepositions that draws on the conceptual representation of changes of focused spatial attention.

To sum up, the brief survey of developments in the semantic analysis of prepositions may also be taken as proof of the heuristic productivity emanating from the SF vs. CS distinction. Among polysemous verbs, the verb *to open* has gained much attention, cf. Bierwisch (article 1 [Semantics: Lexical Structures and Adjectives]). Based on a French-German comparison, Schwarze & Schepping (1995) discuss what type of polysemy is to be accounted for at which of the two levels. Functional categories (determiners, complementizers, connectives etc.), whose lexical meanings lack any support in perception and are hence purely operative, have seldom been analyzed in terms of the SF vs. CS distinction so far; but cf. Lang (2004) for an analysis that accounts for the abstract meanings of *and*, *but* etc. and their contextual specification by inferences drawn from the structural context, the discourse context, and/or from world knowledge. Clearly, the 'poorer' the lexical meaning of such a synsemantic lexical item, the more will its semantic contribution need to be enriched by means of contextualization.

3 Compositionality and beyond: Semantic underspecification and coercion

Two-level Semantics was first mainly concerned with polysemy problems of the kind illustrated in the previous section. Emphasis was laid on developing an adequate theory of lexical semantics that would be able to deal properly and on systematic grounds with the distinction of *word* knowledge and *world* knowledge. A major tenet of Two-level Semantics as a lexicon-based theory of natural language meaning is that the *internal* decompositional structure of lexical items determines their *external* combinatorial properties, that is, their external syntactic behavior. This is why compositionality issues are of eminent interest to Two-level Semantics; cf. (1a).

There is wide agreement among semanticists that, given the combinatorial nature of linguistic meaning, some version of the principle of compositionality – as formulated, e.g., in (23) – must certainly hold. But in view of the complexity and richness of natural language meaning, there is also consensus that compositional semantics is faced with a series of challenges and problems; see article 6 [Semantics: Foundations, History and Methods] (Pagin & Westerståhl) *Compositionality*.

(23) Principle of compositionality:
 The meaning of a complex expression is a function of the meanings of its parts and the way they are syntactically combined.

Rather than weakening the principle of compositionality or abandoning it altogether, Two-level Semantics seeks to cope with the compositionality challenge by confining compositionality to the level of Semantic Form. That is, SF is understood as comprising exactly those parts of natural language meaning that are (i) context-independent and (ii) compositional, in the sense that they are built in parallel with syntactic structure. This leaves space to integrate non-compositional aspects of meaning constitution at the level of Conceptual Structure. In particular, the mapping of SF-representations onto CS-representations may include non-local contextual information and thereby qualify as non-compositional. Of course, the operations at the CS level as well as the SF – CS mapping operations are also combinatorial and can therefore be said to be compositional in a broader sense. Yet their combinatorics is not bound to mirror the syntactic structure of the given linguistic expression and thus does not qualify as compositional in a strict sense. This substantiates the assumption of two distinct levels of meaning representation as discussed in §1. Thus, Two-level Semantics' account of the richness and flexibility of natural language meaning constitution consists in assuming a division of labor between a rather abstract, context-independent and strictly compositionally determined SF and a contextually enriched CS that also includes non-compositionally derived meaning components. Various solutions have been proposed for implementing this general view of the SF vs. CS distinction. These differ mainly in (a) the syntactic fine-tuning of the compositional operations and the abstractness of the corresponding SF-representations, and in (b) the way of handling non-compositional meaning aspects in terms of, e.g., coercion operations. These issues will be discussed in turn.

3.1 Combinatory meaning variation

Assumptions concerning the spell-out of the specific mechanisms of compositionality are generally guided by parsimony. That is, the fewer semantic operations warranting compositionality are postulated, the better. On this view, it would be attractive to have a single semantic operation, presumably functional application, figuring as the semantic counterpart to syntactic binary branching. An illustration is given in (24): Given the lexical entries for the locative preposition *in* and the proper noun *Berlin* in (24a) and (24b) respectively, functional application of the preposition to its internal argument yields (24c) as the compositional result corresponding to the semantics of the PP.

(24) a. in: $\lambda y \, \lambda x \, (\text{LOC}(x, \text{IN}^*(y)))$
 b. Berlin: berlin
 c. [$_{PP}$ in [$_{DP}$ Berlin]]: $\lambda y \, \lambda x \, (\text{LOC}(x, \text{IN}^*(y)))\,(\text{berlin})$
 $\equiv \lambda x \, (\text{LOC}(x, \text{IN}^*(\text{berlin})))$

Functional application is suitable for syntactic head-complement relationships as it reveals a correspondence between the syntactic head-non-head relationship and the semantic functor-argument relationship. In (24c), for instance, the preposition *in* is both the syntactic head of the PP and the semantic functor, which takes the DP as its argument. Syntactic adjuncts, on the other hand, cannot be properly accounted for by functional application as they lack a comparable syntax-semantics correspondence. In syntactic head-adjunct configurations the semantic functor, if any, is not the syntactic head but the non-head; for an overview of the different solutions that have been put forth to cope with this syntax-semantics imbalance see article 14 [Semantics: Lexical Structures and Adjectives] (Maienborn & Schäfer) *Adverbs and adverbials*. Different scholars working in different formal frameworks have suggested remarkably convergent solutions, according to which the relevant semantic operation applying to syntactic head-adjunct configurations is predicate conjunction. This might be formulated, for instance, in terms of a modification template MOD as given in (25); cf., e.g. Higginbotham's (1985) notion of *θ-identification*, Bierwisch's (1997) *adjunction schema*, Wunderlich's (1997b) *argument sharing*, or the composition rule of *predicate modification* in Heim & Kratzer (1998).

(25) Modification template MOD:
 MOD: λQ λP λx (P(x) & Q(x))

The template MOD takes a modifier and an expression to be modified (= modifyee) and turns it into a conjunction of predicates. More specifically, an (intersective) modifier adds a predicate that is linked up to the referential argument of the expression to be modified. In (26) and (27) illustrations are given for nominal modification and verbal modification, respectively. In (26), the semantic contribution of the modifier is added as an additional predicate of the noun's referential argument. In (27), the modifier provides an additional predicate of the verb's eventuality argument.

(26) a. house: λz (HOUSE (z))
 b. [$_{PP}$ in Berlin]: λu (LOC (u, IN*(berlin)))
 c. [$_{NP}$ [$_{NP}$ house] [$_{PP}$ in Berlin]]:
  λQ λP λx (P(x) & Q(x)) (λz (HOUSE (z))) (λu (LOC (u, IN*(berlin))))
  ≡ λx (HOUSE (x) & LOC (x, IN*(berlin)))

(27) a. sleep: λz λe (SLEEP (e) & AGENT (e, z))
 b. [$_{PP}$ in Berlin]: λu (LOC (u, IN*(berlin)))
 c. [$_{VP}$ [$_{VP}$ sleep] [$_{PP}$ in Berlin]]:
  λQ λP λx (P(x) & Q(x))(λz λe (SLEEP (e) & AGENT (e, z)))
  (λu (LOC (u, IN*(berlin))))
  ≡ λz λe (SLEEP (e) & AGENT (e, z) & LOC (e, IN*(berlin)))

The semantic template MOD thus provides the compositional semantic counterpart to syntactic head-adjunct configurations. There are good reasons to assume that, besides functional application, some version of MOD is required when it comes to spelling out the basic mechanisms of compositionality.

The template MOD in (25) captures a very fundamental insight about the compositional contribution of intersective modifiers. Nevertheless, scholars working within the Two-level Semantics paradigm have emphasized that a modification analysis along the lines of MOD fails to cover the whole range of intersective modification; cf., e.g., Maienborn (2001, 2003) for locative adverbials, Dölling (2003) for adverbial modifiers in general, Bücking (2009, 2010) for nominal modifiers. Modifiers appear to be more flexible in choosing their compositional target, both in the verbal domain and in the nominal domain. Besides supplying an additional predicate of the modifyee's referential argument, as in (26) and (27), modifiers may also relate less directly to their host argument. Some illustrations are given in (28)–(30). (For the sake of simplicity the data are presented in English.)

(28) a. The cook prepared the chicken in a Marihuana sauce.
                                                                         (cf. Maienborn 2003)
    b. The bank robbers escaped on bicycles.
    c. Paul tickled Maria on her neck.

(29) a. Anna dressed Max's hair unobtrusively.   (cf. Dölling 2003: 530)
    b. Ede reached the summit in two days.   (cf. Dölling 2003: 516)

(30) a. the fast processing of the data   (cf. Bücking 2009: 94)
    b. the preparation of the chicken in a pepper sauce (cf. Bücking 2009: 102)
    c. Georg's querying of the men   (cf. Bücking 2010: 51)

The locative modifiers in (28) differ from the general MOD pattern as illustrated in (27) in that they do not locate the whole event but only one of its integral parts. For instance, in (28b) it's not the escape that is located on bicycles but – according to the preferred reading – the agent of this event, viz. the bank robbers. In the case of (28c), the linguistic structure does not even tell us what is located on Maria's neck. It could be Paul's hand but also, e.g., a feather he used for tickling Maria. Maienborn (2001, 2003) calls these modifiers "event internal modifiers" and sets them apart from "event external modifiers" such as in (27), which serve to holistically locate the verb's eventuality argument.

Similar observations are made by Dölling (2003) wrt. cases like (29). Sentence (29a) is ambiguous. It might be interpreted as expressing that Anna performed the event of dressing Max's hair in an unobtrusive manner. This is what the application of MOD would result in. But (29a) has another reading, according to which it is not the event of hair dressing that is unobtrusive but Max's resulting hairstyle. Once again, the modifier's contribution does not apply directly to the verb's eventuality argument but to some referent related to it. The same holds true for (29b), where the temporal adverbial cannot relate to the punctual event of Ede reaching the summit but only to its preparatory phase.

Finally, Bücking (2009, 2010) discusses a series of cases in the nominal domain which also show a less direct relationship between the modifier and its host argument than the one established by MOD; cf. (25). The modifier *fast* in (30a), for instance, may be interpreted event-externally, expressing that the overall duration of the processing was short. But (30a) also has an event-internal interpretation, according to which the subevents of processing the data were performed in a fast manner (whereas the whole processing might have taken a long time). In a similar vein, Georg need not necessarily be the agent of the querying in (30c). Bücking argues that the prenominal genitive establishes a more indirect relationship to the nominal referent, such that a more abstract control relation between Georg and the query would suffice; cf. the one provided by the context in (31).

(31) Georg wanted to know how mens' buying behavior is influenced by the weather. He therefore instructed his research assistants to interview men under varying weather conditions. Georg's querying of the men is still considered a milestone in consumer research.

(cf. Bücking 2010: 51)

The conclusion to be drawn from these and similar studies is that modifiers show a remarkable flexibility in relating to their compositionally determined host argument, thus giving rise to a wide spectrum of meaning variations.

Is there a way to treat this observation compositionally? The proposals developed by Bücking, Dölling and Maienborn basically amount to liberalizing MOD such that it may license the particular kind of semantic underspecification observed above. That is, besides linking the semantic contribution of the modifier directly to the verb's or noun's referential argument, as in (25), there should be a less direct variant that could be spelled out as in (32).

(32) Modification template MOD':
MOD': $\lambda Q\, \lambda P\, \lambda x\, (P(x)\, \&\, R(x, v)\, \&\, Q(v))$

MOD' introduces a free variable v that is linked to the modifyee's referential argument x by means of a relational variable R. Both v and R are so-called

SF-parameters, i.e. free variables that remain underspecified at the level of SF and will only be instantiated at the level of CS. Applying MOD' to a sentence such as (28c), repeated as (33), yields the following SF:

(33) Paul tickled Maria on her neck.
 SF: ∃e (TICKLE (e) & AGENT (e, paul) & PATIENT (e, maria) & R (e, v) & LOC (v, ON*(maria's neck))

According to the SF in (33), an entity v which is involved in the tickling event is located on Maria's neck. This is as far as the compositional semantics of event-internal modifiers takes us. The identification of v and its exact role in e can only be spelled out at the CS level by taking into account contextually available world knowledge. This would include, e.g., knowledge about the spatial configuration required for tickling, viz. contact, as well as knowledge about suitable and/or plausible instruments employed for tickling. A potential conceptual spell-out is given in (34); cf. Maienborn (2003: 490ff) for details.

(34) Paul tickled Maria on her neck.
 SF: ∃e (TICKLE (e) & AGENT (e, paul) & PATIENT (e, maria) & R (e, v) & LOC (v, ON*(maria's neck))
 CS: ∃ex (TICKLE (e) & AGENT (e, paul) & PATIENT (e, maria) & INSTR (e, x) & FEATHER (x) & LOC (x, ON*(maria's neck))

This conceptual spell-out provides a plausible utterance meaning for sentence (34). It goes beyond the compositionally determined meaning by exploiting our conceptual knowledge that tickling is performed with some instrument which needs to have spatial contact to the object being tickled. Consequently, the SF-parameter R can be identified as the instrument relation, and the parameter v may be instantiated, e.g., by a feather. Although not manifest at the linguistic surface, such conceptually inferred units are plausible potential instantiations of the compositionally introduced SF-parameter v. (Dölling and Maienborn use abduction as a formal means of deriving a contextually specified CS from a semantically underspecified SF; cf. Hobbs et al. (1993). We will come back to the SF-CS mapping in §4.)

Different proposals have been developed for implementing the notion of a more liberal and flexible combinatorics, such as MOD', into the compositional machinery. Maienborn (2001, 2003) argues that MOD' is only licensed in particular structural environments: Event-internal modifiers have a base adjunction site in close proximity to the verb, whereas event-external adjuncts adjoin at VP-level. These distinct structural positions provide the key to a compositional account.

Maienborn thus formulates a more fine-tuned syntax-semantics interface condition that subsumes MOD and MOD' under a single compositional rule MOD*.

(35) Modification template MOD*:
MOD*: $\lambda Q\, \lambda P\, \lambda x\, (P(x)\, \&\, R(x, v)\, \&\, Q(v))$
Condition on the application of MOD*: If MOD* is applied in a structural environment of categorial type X, then R = PART-OF, otherwise (i.e. in an XP-environment) R is the identity function.

If MOD* is applied in an XP-environment, then R is instantiated as identity, i.e. v is identified with the referential argument of the modified expression, thus yielding the standard variant MOD. If applied in an X-environment, R is instantiated as the PART-OF relation, which pairs entities with their integral constituents. Thus, in Maienborn's account the observed meaning variability is traced back to a grammatically constrained semantic indeterminacy that is characteristic of modification.

Dölling (2003) takes a different track by assuming that the SF-parameter R is not rooted in modification but is of a more general nature. Specifically, he suggests that R is introduced compositionally whenever a one-place predicate enters the composition. By this move, the SF of a complex expression is systematically extended by a series of SF-parameters, which guarantee that the application of any one-place predicate to its argument is systematically shifted to the conceptual level. On Dölling's account, the SF of a complex linguistic expression is maximally abstract and underspecified, with SF-parameters delineating possible (though not necessarily actual) sites of meaning variation.

Differences aside, the studies of Dölling, Maienborn and other scholars working in the Two-level Semantics paradigm emphasize that potential sources for semantic indeterminacy are not only to be found in the lexicon but may also emerge in the course of composition, and they strive to model this combinatory meaning variation in terms of a rigid account of lexical and compositional semantics.

A key role in linking linguistic and extra-linguistic knowledge is taken by so-called *SF-parameters*. These are free variables that are installed under well-defined conditions at SF and are designed to be instantiated at the level of CS. SF-parameters are a means of triggering and controlling the conceptual enrichment of a grammatically determined meaning representation. They delineate precisely those gaps within the Semantic Form that call for conceptual specification and they impose sortal restrictions on possible conceptual fillers. SF-parameters can thus be seen as well-defined windows through which compositional semantics allows linguistic expressions to access and constrain conceptual structures.

3.2 Non-compositional meaning adjustments

Conceptual specification of a compositionally determined, underspecified, abstract meaning skeleton, as illustrated in the previous section, is the core notion that characterizes the Two-level Semantics perspective on the semantics-pragmatics interface. Its focus is on the conceptual exploitation of a linguistic expression's *regular* meaning potential. A second focus typically pursued within Two-level Semantics concerns the possibilities of a conceptual solution of combinatory conflicts arising in the course of composition. These are combinatory adjustment operations by which a strictly speaking ill-formed linguistic expression gets an admissible yet *irregular* interpretation. In the literature such non-compositional rescue operations are generally discussed under the label of "coercion". An example is given in (36).

(36) The alarm clock stood intentionally on the table.

The sentence in (36) does not offer a regular integration for the subject-oriented adverbial *intentionally*, i.e, the subject NP *the alarm clock* does not fulfill the adverbial's selectional restriction for an intentional subject. Hence, a compositional clash results, and the sentence is ungrammatical. Nevertheless, although deviant, there seems to be a way to rescue the sentence so that it becomes acceptable and interpretable. In the case of (36), a possible repair strategy would be to introduce an actor who is responsible for the fact that the alarm clock stands on the table. This move would provide a suitable anchor for the adverbial's semantic contribution. Thus, we understand (36) as saying that someone put the alarm clock on the table on purpose. That is, in case of a combinatorial clash, there seems to be a certain leeway for non-compositional adjustments of the compositionally derived meaning. The defective part is "coerced" into the right format.

Coercion phenomena are a topic of intensive research in current semantics. Up to now the primary focus has been on the widely ramified notion of aspectual coercion (e.g. Moens & Steedman 1988; Pulman 1997; de Swart 1998; Dölling 2003, 2014; Egg 2005) and on cases of so-called "complement coercion" as in *Peter began the book* (e.g. Pustejovsky 1995; Egg 2003; Asher 2011); see article 10 [Semantics: Lexical Structures and Adjectives] (de Swart) *Mismatches and coercion* for an overview. The framework of Two-level Semantics is particularly suited to investigate these borderline cases at the semantics-pragmatics interface because of its comparatively strong assumptions and predictions about this interface in terms of SF- and CS-representations, and about the kind of knowledge available at each level. To give an example, one issue emphasized by Dölling (2014) is that it is not only grammatical conflicts that trigger coercion operations (as predominantly assumed in the literature), but that such operations may also be employed for solving conflicts or expectations that arise from world knowledge. If we take for instance a variant of sentence (36) such as (37), there is no immediate need for a non-compositional rescue operation anymore. The subject NP *the children* fulfills the adverbial's selectional restriction for an intentional subject, hence, the sentence can be interpreted strictly compositionally with the children as intentional subjects. Nevertheless sentence (37) still has a second reading – viz. the only possible reading for (36) – according to which someone else, e.g. their teacher, put the children on the table on purpose.

(37)   The children stood intentionally on the table.   (2 readings)

Dölling (2014) draws the conclusion that rather than being borderline cases with somehow irregular interpretations, so-called coercion phenomena are just another instance of semantic underspecification; cf. §3.1. Thus, he would propose to derive an abstract, underspecified SF for both (36) and (37), and to defer its specification to the level of CS. On the other hand, the following data are problematic for a radical underspecification account such as Dölling's.

(38)   *The alarm clock stood voluntarily on the table.

(39)   The children stood voluntarily on the table.   (1 reading)

Sentence (38) is ungrammatical. There is no way of rescuing it along the lines of (36). Although from a conceptual perspective it would make equally good sense to interpret (38) as expressing that someone put the alarm clock voluntarily on the table, there is no such rescue option available. Apparently the linguistic system prevents such a resort. In the same vein, sentence (39) only has one reading, according to which it is the children's will to stand on the table but not that of another person. These observations suggest that the additional readings available for (36) and (37) are not fully regular interpretations but coerced ones. They show the need for scrutinizing on a much broader empirical basis the conspiracy of grammatical, conceptual and pragmatic factors that license and constrain the coercion phenomena; see also the different viewpoints on this issue put forward by Dölling (2005b), Rothstein (2005) and Maienborn (2005a,b). A comparatively new kind of evidence that might help clarify matters is provided by psycholinguistic studies; see Pylkkänen & McElree (2006) for a state of the art report on coercion.

The short discussion of (36)–(39) gives a slight impression of the wide range of options currently tested in sharpening our understanding of the semantics-pragmatics interface and the implications they have for our assumptions about compositionality. The matter of how much grammar gets into meaning constitution and what else may join it to establish a full-fledged utterance meaning of natural language expressions is still far from being settled.

4 More on SF variables and their instantiation at the CS level

As pointed out in section 2.1, it was mainly the conceptual subsystem of spatial cognition that has stimulated pioneering investigations within Two-level Semantics. Therefore, it may be appropriate to report some of the analyses proposed in the realm of dimensional designation of spatial objects, cf. Bierwisch & Lang (1989a); Bierwisch (1996, 1997); Bierwisch & Schreuder (1992); Lang (1990, 1994, 2001); Lang, Carstensen & Simmons (1991). It is the complex interaction of two major grammatical modules, *viz.* gradation/comparison and dimension assignment, which make facts and insights in this field especially rewarding to semanticists. In order to discover the full range of relevant data, the basic assumption of Two-level Semantics (quoted at the outset of section 3), i.e. that the internal componential structure of lexical items determines their external combinatorial properties, has been converted into a heuristic guideline: Eliciting the combinatorics of dimension assignment (DA) terms for spatial objects by means of tasks like naming object extents or guessing objects by their dimensions etc. will reveal both the lexical meaning of each DA term and the structural pattern determining the lexical field which the DA term is an element of.

4.1 Variables in SF representations of spatial dimension terms

In Bierwisch & Lang (1989a), SF representations of German and English dimensional adjectives are taken to be complex 3-place predicates. Their general format is shown in (40); the variables in (40) are distinguished by the type of operators that bind them.

(40) λc λx [QUANT [DIM x] = [v ± c]]

First, there are variables in argument places that are subject to λ-abstraction, λ-conversion and other binding operations: (i) an object x that is assigned a dimension d, with d ∈ {DIM} and DIM being a metavariable on dimension assignment parameters, cf. (42) below; (ii) a difference value c which is added to (+), or subtracted from (−), the comparison value v.

Second, the variable v is a free variable which – depending on the respective structural context within the clause – may assume one of the following values: (iii) "0" if c contains a Measure Phrase or "norm of the class which x belongs to" if DIM is an AP in the positive without complement or "content of the comparative phrase" if DIM is part of a comparative construction. The admissible specifications of the comparison value v are subject to some general conditions which are motivated by CS but have been formulated as conditions on well-formed SF representations; for details justifying that solution, cf. Bierwisch & Lang (1989b).

The operator QUANT is an SF functor constant which selects the type of scale induced by DIM and triggers existential quantification of the value c in accordance with the Unspecified Argument Rule, (cf. Lang 1985; Bierwisch 1989: 76) such that the SF of, e.g., *The pole is long* comes out as in (41), where DEF.pole' abbreviates the meaning of the subject *the pole*:

(41) ∃c [[QUANT MAX DEF.pole'] = [Norm$_{pole}$ + c]]

This much on SF variables coming with dimension terms and on their instantiation in structural contexts that are provided by the morphosyntax of the sentence at issue. After a brief look at the elements instantiating the metavariable DIM, we will discuss a type of SF variable that is rooted in the lexical field structure of DA terms.

Conceived as a basic module of cognition, dimension assignment to spatial objects involves entities and operations at three levels. The perceptual level provides the sensory input from vision and other senses; the conceptual level serves as a filter system reducing perceptual distinctions to the level that our everyday knowledge of space needs, and the semantic level accounts for the ways in which conceptually approved features are encoded in categorized lexemes and arranged in lexical fields.

DA basically draws on Dimension Assignment Parameters (DAP) that are provided by two frames of reference, which determine the dimensional designation of spatial objects:

(42) a. The *Inherent Proportion Schema* (IPS) yields proportion-based gestalt features by identifying the object's extents as MAXimal, MINimal, and ACROSS axis, respectively.
b. The *Primary Perceptual Space* (PPS) yields contextually determined position features of spatial objects by identifying the object's extents as aligned with the VERTical axis, with the OBServer axis, and/or with an ACROSS axis in between.

The DAP in SMALL CAPS listed in (42) occur in two representational formats that reflect the SF vs. CS distinction. In SF representations, the DAP figure as functor constants of category N/N in the SF of L-particular dimension terms that instantiate {DIM} within the general schema in (40). In CS representations, elements of the DAP inventory figure as conceptual features in so-called *Object Schemata* (cf. 4.2 below) that contain the conceptually defining as well as the contextually specified spatial features of the object at issue.

Lang (2001) shows that the lexical field of spatial dimension terms in a language L is determined by the share it has in IPS and PPS, respectively. While reference to the vertical is ubiquitous, the lexical coverage of DA terms amounts to the following typology: *proportion-based languages* (Mandarin, Russian) adhere to IPS, *observer-based ones* (Korean, Japanese) adhere to PPS, and *mixed-type ones* (English, German) draw on an overlap between IPS and PPS. The semantic effects of this typology are *inter alia* reflected by the respective ACROSS terms: In P-based and in O-based languages, they are lexically distinct and referentially unambiguous, in mixed-type languages like English they lack both of these properties.

Note the referential ambiguity of the English ACROSS term *wide* in (44.1) and its contextualized interpretations in (44.2 – 4) when referring to a board sized 100 × 30 × 3 cm in the spatial settings I–III shown in (43):

(43)

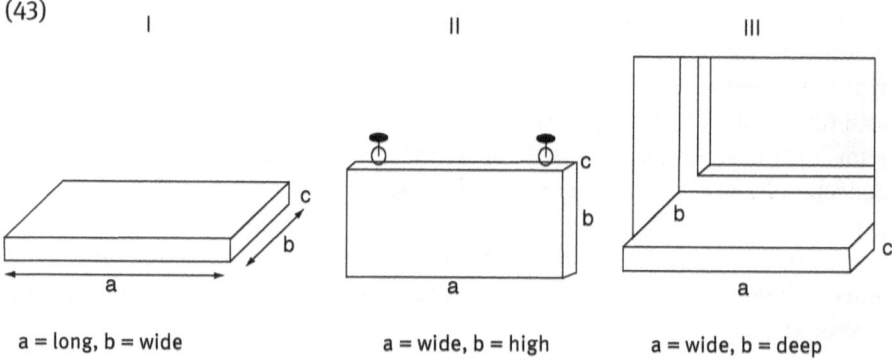

(44) 1. The board is *wide* enough, but too thin. [I: *wide* = b; II & III: *wide* = a]
2. The board is *long* and *wide* enough, but too thin. [*wide* = b as in setting I]
3. The board is *high* and *wide* enough, but too thin. [*wide* = a as in setting II]
4. The board is *deep* and *wide* enough, but too thin. [*wide* = a as in setting III]

As regards the manner of DA, note the following pairwise differences: (43 I) and (44.2) refer to the board as such by confining its DA to P-based gestalt properties, whereas (43 II, III) and (44.2, 3) account for the board's increasing integration into the surrounding spatial context. This in turn entails that (44.2) can be applied to setting II or III as well, but (44.4 and 3) may not be applied to setting II and I, respectively. Now let us look at the relationship between object extents and DA terms.

Whereas the coupling of extent c and the term *thin* (or its antonym *thick*) is constant in I–III, the ACROSS term *wide* can refer to a or to b. The choice is determined by the situational context, cf. (43 I–III), and/or the linguistic context available, cf. (44.1–4). In short, the English ACROSS term *wide* selects an object extent d that is orthogonal to an object extent d', with d' ∈ {max, vert, obs}. The set includes those dimensions from IPS (max) and from PPS (vert, obs) that are independently assignable to object extents. The inherent relativity of *wide* requires its SF to contain – in addition to the schema in (4) – an ∃-bound variable d' to be instantiated in the situational and/or the linguistic context:

(45) λc [λx [∃d' [[QUANT ACROSS ⊥ d' x] = [v ± c]]]],
with d' ∈ {max, vert, obs}

Without contextual clues about d', *wide* is ambiguous or unspecified between referring to extent a or to extent b, cf. (44.1). In the spatial settings in (43 I–III), the relevant extent d' is visible, in the sentences (44.2–4) d' is linguistically accessible. The intermodal equivalence of visual and verbal contexts wrt. selecting the constant that replaces d' provides a strong argument for the view that the specification of the object extent which *wide* refers to takes place at the CS level. It is CS representations that provide the visual and/or linguistic information based on which the selectional restriction "d' ∈ {max, vert, obs}" in (45) can be operative, cf. (43) and (44). However, the restriction on d' is not just an idiosyncratic feature of the lexical item *wide/small* but a condition on DA terms in L following from its typological make-up as a P/O-mixed-type language.

Correspondingly, P-based languages restrict ACROSS terms to IPS requiring "d' ∈ {max}", and O-based languages to PPS by requiring "d' ∈ {obs}", cf. Lang (2001) for details.

Now, having located the source of the referential ambiguity of *wide – small* at the SF level and identified CS as the level where the ambiguity is resolved, provided that suitable context information is available, we want to know how the spatial settings shown in (43) and verbally described in (44) can be homogenized at the level of CS representations.

4.2 Object Schemata as CS representations

A suitable way of representing concepts of spatial objects is by means of a matrix with 3 rows and up to 3 columns, called *Object Schema* (OS), cf. Lang (1989, 1990); Lang, Carstensen & Simmons (1991). An OS contains entries which represent spatial properties of objects in three tiers.

The 1st row represents an object's (i) dimensionality by variables for object axes, i.e. a, a b, or a b c, ordered by their relative salience such that within the general OS for buildings the entry vert in a vs. b vs. c differentiates the OS of a sky-scraper from that of an apartment house or of a bungalow; (ii) boundedness by <...> to set apart undimensionable objects (sky, weather) or objects named by mass nouns (air, water); (iii) integration of axes by (...) to distinguish a disk < (a b) c > from a pole < a (b c) > and a ball < (a b c) >.

The 2nd row lists the object's gestalt and position properties by *primary entries* like max, min, vert, obs, which stand either for (i) axial concepts induced by DA terms whose SF contains MAX, MIN, VERT, OBS or for (ii) concepts activated by non-linguistic, i.e. visual or tactile, input on the object at issue. Empty cells with Ø in the 2nd row mark object extents that may be designated by several distinct DAP depending on the position properties attributed to the object at hand.

The 3rd row (separated by a horizontal line) displays the results of contextualizing the entries in the 2nd row and hence the contextually specified DA of the object at issue. The mapping between DAP as SF functor constants in SMALL CAPS and their counterparts in OS as CS entries in lower case letters involves two operations defined as follows:

(46) a. Identification: P ⇒ p,
      with P ∈ { MAX, MIN, ACROSS, VERT, OBS ...},
            p ∈ { max, min, across, vert, obs ...} and p is a 3rd row entry in OS

b. Specification: Q ⇒ p,
    with   Q ∈ { VERT, OBS, ACROSS, ... },
           p ∈ { max, Ø, vert, ...} and p is licensed as a landing site for Q in OS

(47) below shows the distinct OS serving as CS representations of the board in the settings in (43) as well as of the utterance meanings of the sentences in (44). To elucidate (i) the intermodal equivalence of the context information available from (43) or (44) and (ii) how it is reflected in the corresponding OS, the setting numbers and the pertinent DA terms for a and b have been added in (47). The respective extent chosen as d' to anchor across in the OS at issue and/or to interpret *wide* in (44.2–4) is in boldface.

(47)

	I			II			III		
	< a	b	c >	< a	b	c >	< a	b	c >
	max	Ø	min	max	Ø	min	max	Ø	min
	max	across	min	across	**vert**	min	across	**obs**	min
	a = **long**, b = wide			a = wide, b = **high**			a = wide, b = **deep**		

The OS in (47) as CS representations of (43) and (44) capture all semantic aspects of DA discussed so far but they deserve some further remarks. First, (47-I) results from **primary identification** à la (46a) indicated by matching entries in the 2nd and 3rd row, while (47-II and III) are instances of **contextual specification** as defined in (46b). Second, the typological characteristics of a P/O-mixed-type language are met as d' for *wide* may be taken from IPS as in (47 I) or from PPS as in (47 II and III). Third, the rows of an OS, which contain the defining spatial properties and possibly also some contextual specifications, can be taken as a heuristic cue for designing the SF representations of object names that lexically reflect the varying degree of integration into spatial contexts we observe in (43–44), e.g. *board* (freely movable) < *notice-board* (hanging) < *windowsill* (bottom part of a window) – in this respect OS may be seen as an attempt to capture what Bierwisch (article 1 [Semantics: Lexical Structures and Adjectives]) calls "dossiers". Fourth, Lang, Carstensen & Simmons (1991) presents a Prolog system of DA using OS enriched by sidedness features, and Lang (2001) proposes a detailed catalogue of types of spatial objects with their OS accounting for primary entries and for contextually induced orientation or perspectivization. Fifth, despite their close interaction by means of the operations in (46), DAP as elements of SF representations and OS entries as CS elements are subject to different constraints, which is another reason to keep them distinct. The entries in an OS are subject to *conditions of conceptual compatibility* that inter alia define the set of admissible complex OS entries listed as vertically arranged pairs in (48):

(48) | max | max | max | Ø | Ø | Ø |
| --- | --- | --- | --- | --- | --- |
| across | vert | obs | across | vert | obs |

An important generalization is that (48) holds independently of the way in which the complex entry happens to come about. So, the combination of max and vert in the same column may result from primary identification in the 2nd row, cf. *The pole is 2m tall*, where the SF of *tall* contains MAX & VERT x as a conjunction of DAP, or from contextual specification, cf. *The pole is 2m high*, where vert is added in the 3rd row. The semantic structure of DA terms is therefore constrained by compatibility conditions at the CS level but within this scope it is cross-linguistically open to different lexicalization patterns and to variation of what is covered by the SF of single DA terms.

Finally, whereas OS may contain one or more Ø or entries that have a share in both IPS and PPS (as does e.g. across), the DA of spatial objects by linguistic means is subject to the following **uniqueness constraint**:

(49) In an instance of naming distinct axial extents a, b, c of some object x by enumerating DA terms, each DAP and each extent may occur only once.

Reminiscent of the Θ-criterion, (49) excludes e.g. (i) *The board is long and wide enough, but too small* or (ii) *The pole is 2m long and 2m high/tall* as ill-formed. Though disguised by distinct lexical labels, *wide* and *small* in (i) are conflicting occurrences of the DAP ACROSS, whereas *long* and *high/tall* in (ii) compete for one and the same extent a. The uniqueness constraint in (49) exemplifies one of the pragmatic felicity conditions on linguistic communication; cf. §1.4 above. Structurally, (49) follows from the homogeneity condition on the conjuncts in coordinate structures; theoretically, (49) is an outcome of the Gricean Maxim of Manner, especially of the sub-maxim "Avoid ambiguity!".

4.3 Inferences

The distinction of SF vs. CS representations, hitherto exemplified by DAP as SF constants for dimension terms and by OS as a CS format for spatial objects, respectively, is also relevant to the way inferences in the realm of spatial cognition are semantically accounted for. The SF vs. CS distinction outlined by (2)–(5) in §1.2 reappears in a division of labor between (i) inferences that draw on permanent lexical knowledge made available in SF format and (ii) inferences that are performed on contextually specified CS representations. We will illustrate this correlation by means of three groups of data.

4.3.1 Lexical antonymy

While hyponymy and synonymy are non-typical lexical relations among DA terms, various facets of antonymy seem to be indispensable to them; cf. Lang 1995. The SF of DA terms, cf. (40) and (45), is componential as it results from decomposing the meaning of lexical items into suitable building blocks, that is, into SF components which are interrelated by meaning postulates and which therefore allow for purely lexicon-based inferences. There are two sorts: (i) schema-forming SF components (e.g. become and cause, cf. Bierwisch 2005, 2010; Wunderlich 1997a); and (ii) schema-filling SF components (e.g. the elements of {dim} in (42) and (46) or operative elements like '$\exists$', '$\pm$' or '=' in (45)).

Two DA terms are *lexical antonyms* if (i) they share the same DAP in forming polar opposites, (ii) assign contrary values to d, (iii) allow for converse comparatives etc. Inferences that draw on lexical antonymy show up in entailments between sentences, cf. (50), and are codified as lexical knowledge postulates at the SF level, cf. (51). We neglect details concerning '=', abbreviate SF (*the board*) by B, and take N(orm value) and K(ey value) to instantiate the comparison value v in (50a) and (50b), respectively. For the whole range of entailments and SF postulates based on DA terms see Bierwisch (1989).

(50) a. The board is short → The board is not long.
 b. The board is not long enough ↔ The board is too short

(51) a. $\exists c\,[[\text{QUANT MAX B}] = [N - c]] \Rightarrow \sim [\exists c\,[[\exists c\,[[\text{QUANT MAX B}] = [N + c]]]]$
 b. $\sim [\exists c\,[[\text{QUANT MAX B}] = [K + c]]] \Leftrightarrow \exists c\,[[\text{QUANT MAX B}] = [K - c]]$

4.3.2 Contextually induced dimensional designation

Valid inferences like those in (52) are accounted for, and invalid ones like those in (53) are avoided, by drawing on the information provided by, or else lacking in, contextually specified OS.

(52) a. The board is 1m wide and → The board is 1m long and
   0.3 m high.   0.3m wide.
 b. The pole is 2m tall/2m high. → The pole is 2m long.

(53) a. The wall is wide and high enough. ↛ The wall is long and wide enough.
 b. The tower is 10 m tall/high. ↛ *The tower is 10 m long.

The valid inferences result from the operation of *de-specification*, which is simply the reverse of the operation of contextual specification defined in (46b):

(54) *De-specification:*
    a. For any OS for x with a vertical entry < p, q >, there is an OS' with < p, p >.
    b. For any OS for x with a vertical entry < Ø, q >, there is an OS' with < Ø, across >.

The inferences in (53a, b) are ruled out as invalid because the OS under review do not contain the type of entries needed for (54) to apply.

4.3.3 Commensurability of object extents

Note that the DA terms *long*, *wide* and/or *thick* are not hyponyms to *big* despite the fact that *big* may refer to the [v + c] of one, two or all three extents of a 3D object, depending on the OS of the objects at issue. When objects differing in dimensionality are compared by using the DA term *big*, the dimensions it covers are determined by the common share of the OS involved, cf. (55):

(55)   a. My car is too big for the parking space.   (too long and/or too wide)
       b. My car is too big for the garage door.   (too wide and/or too high)

So it is above all the two mapping operations between SF and CS representations as defined in (46a, b) and exemplified by DAP and OS that account for the whole range of seemingly complicated facts about DA to spatial objects.

5 Summary and outlook

In this article we have reported on some pros and cons related to distinguishing SF and CS representations and illustrated them by data and facts from a selection of semantic phenomena. Now we briefly outline the state of the art in more general terms and take a look at the desiderata that define the agenda for future research.

    The current situation can be summarized in three statements: (i) the SF vs. CS distinction brings in clear-cut advantages as shown by the examples in §§ 2–4;

(ii) we still lack reliable heuristic strategies for identifying the appropriate SF of a lexical item; (iii) it is difficult to define the scope of variation a given SF can cover at CS level.

What we urgently need is independent evidence for the basic assumption underlying the distinction: SF representations and CS representations differ in nature as they are subject to completely different principles of organization. By correlating the SF vs. CS distinction with distinctions relevant to other levels of linguistic structure formation, cf. (2)–(5) in section 1, the article has taken some steps in that direction. One of them is to clarify the differences between SF and CS that derive from their linguistic vs. non-linguistic origin; cf. (4).

The *linguistic basis of the SF-representations* of DA terms, for instance, is manifested (i) in the DAP constants' interrelation by postulates underlying lexical relations, (ii) in participating in certain lexicalization patterns (e.g. proportion-based vs. observer-based), (iii) in being subject to the uniqueness constraint in (49), which is indicative of the semioticity of the system it applies to, whereas the Conceptual System CS is not a semiotic one. Pursuing this line of research, phenomena specific to natural languages like idiosyncracies, designation gaps, collocations, connotations, folk etymologies etc. should be scrutinized for their possible impact on establishing SF as a linguistically determined level of representation.

The *non-linguistic basis of CS-representations*, e.g. OS involved in DA, is manifested (i) in the fact that OS entries are exclusively subject to perception-based compatibility conditions; (ii) in their function to integrate input from the spatial environment regardless of the channel it comes in; (iii) in their property to allow for valid inferences to be drawn on entries that are induced as contextual specifications. To deepen our understanding of CS-representations, presumptions like the following deserve to be investigated on a broader spectrum and in more detail: (i) CS representations may be underspecified in certain respects, cf. the role of 'Ø' in OS, but as they are not semiotic entities they are not ambiguous; (ii) the compatibility conditions defining admissible OS suggest that the following relation may hold wrt. the well-formedness of representations: sortal restrictions ⊂ selectional restrictions; (iii) CS representations have to be contingent since contradictory entries cause the system of inferences to break down; contradictions at SF level trigger accommodation activities.

As the agenda above suggests, a better understanding of the interplay of linguistic and non-linguistic aspects of meaning constitution along the lines developed here is particularly to be expected from interdisciplinary research combining methods and insights from linguistics, psycholinguistics, neurolinguistics and cognitive psychology.

6 References

Asher, Nicholas 2011. *Lexical Meaning in Context. A Web of Words.* Cambridge: Cambridge University Press.
Bierwisch, Manfred 1983. Semantische und konzeptuelle Interpretation lexikalischer Einheiten. In: R. Růžička & W. Motsch (eds.). *Untersuchungen zur Semantik.* Berlin: Akademie Verlag, 61–99.
Bierwisch, Manfred 1988. On the grammar of local prepositions. In: M. Bierwisch, W. Motsch & I. Zimmermann (eds.). *Syntax, Semantik und Lexikon.* Berlin: Akademie Verlag, 1–65.
Bierwisch, Manfred 1989. The semantics of gradation. In: M. Bierwisch & E. Lang (eds.). *Dimensional Adjectives: Grammatical Structure and Conceptual Interpretation.* Berlin: Springer, 71–261.
Bierwisch, Manfred 1996. How much space gets into language? In: P. Bloom et al. (eds.). *Language and Space.* Cambridge, MA: The MIT Press, 31–76.
Bierwisch, Manfred 1997. Lexical information from a minimalist point of view. In: Ch. Wilder, H.-M. Gärtner & M. Bierwisch (eds.). *The Role of Economy Principles in Linguistic Theory.* Berlin: Akademie Verlag, 227–266.
Bierwisch, Manfred 2005. The event structure of CAUSE and BECOME. In: C. Maienborn & A. Wöllstein (eds.). *Event Arguments: Foundations and Applications.* Tübingen: Niemeyer, 11–44.
Bierwisch, Manfred 2007. Semantic Form as interface. In: A. Späth (ed.). *Interfaces and Interface Conditions.* Berlin: de Gruyter, 1–32.
Bierwisch, Manfred 2010. BECOME and its presuppositions. In: R. Bäuerle, U. Reyle & T. E. Zimmermann (eds.). *Presupposition and Discourse.* Bingley: Emerald, 189–234.
Bierwisch, Manfred & Peter Bosch (eds.) 1995. *Semantic and Conceptual Knowledge* (Arbeitspapiere des SFB 340 Nr. 71). Heidelberg: IBM Deutschland.
Bierwisch, Manfred & Ewald Lang (eds.) 1989a. *Dimensional Adjectives: Grammatical Structure and Conceptual Interpretation.* Berlin: Springer.
Bierwisch, Manfred & Ewald Lang 1989b. Somewhat longer – much deeper – further and further. Epilogue to the Dimensional Adjective Project. In: M. Bierwisch & E. Lang (eds.). *Dimensional Adjectives: Grammatical Structure and Conceptual Interpretation.* Berlin: Springer, 471–514.
Bierwisch, Manfred & Rob Schreuder 1992. From concepts to lexical items. *Cognition* 42, 23–60.
Blutner, Reinhard 1995. Systematische Polysemie: Ansätze zur Erzeugung und Beschränkung von Interpretationsvarianten. In: M. Bierwisch & P. Bosch (eds.). *Semantic and Conceptual Knowledge* (Arbeitspapiere des SFB 340 Nr. 71). Heidelberg: IBM Deutschland, 33–67.
Blutner, Reinhard 1998. Lexical pragmatics. *Journal of Semantics* 15, 115–162.
Blutner, Reinhard 2004. Pragmatics and the lexicon. In: L. R. Horn & G. Ward (eds.). *The Handbook of Pragmatics.* Malden, MA: Blackwell, 488–514.
Bücking, Sebastian 2009. Modifying event nominals: Syntactic surface meets semantic transparency. In: A. Riester & T. Solstad (eds.). *Proceedings of Sinn und Bedeutung (= SuB) 13.* Stuttgart: University of Stuttgart, 93–107.
Bücking, Sebastian 2010. Zur Interpretation adnominaler Genitive bei nominalisierten Infinitiven im Deutschen. *Zeitschrift für Sprachwissenschaft* 29, 39–77.
Carstensen, Kai-Uwe 2001. *Sprache, Raum und Aufmerksamkeit.* Tübingen: Niemeyer.
Dölling, Johannes 1994. Sortale Selektionsbeschränkungen und systematische Bedeutungsvariabilität. In: M. Schwarz (ed.). *Kognitive Semantik – Cognitive Semantics.* Tübingen: Narr, 41–60.

Dölling, Johannes 2001. *Systematische Bedeutungsvariationen: Semantische Form und kontextuelle Interpretation* (Linguistische Arbeitsberichte 78). Leipzig: University of Leipzig.

Dölling, Johannes 2003. Flexibility in adverbal modification: Reinterpretation as contextual enrichment. In: E. Lang, C. Maienborn & C. Fabricius-Hansen (eds.). *Modifying Adjuncts*. Berlin: de Gruyter, 511–552.

Dölling, Johannes 2005a. Semantische Form und pragmatische Anreicherung: Situationsausdrücke in der Äußerungsinterpretation. *Zeitschrift für Sprachwissenschaft* 24, 159–225.

Dölling, Johannes 2005b. Copula sentences and entailment relations. *Theoretical Linguistics* 31, 317–329.

Dölling, Johannes 2014. Aspectual coercion and eventuality structure. In: K. Robering (ed.). *Aspects, Phases, and Arguments: Topics in the Semantics of Verbs*. Amsterdam: John Benjamins, 189–226.

Egg, Markus 2003. Beginning novels and finishing hamburgers. Remarks on the semantics of 'to begin'. *Journal of Semantics* 20, 163–191.

Egg, Markus 2005. *Flexible Semantics for Reinterpretation Phenomena*. Stanford, CA: CSLI Publications.

Geeraerts, Dirk 2010. *Theories of Lexical Semantics*. Oxford: Oxford University Press.

Greenberg, Joseph H. 1978. Generalizations about numerical systems. In: J. H. Greenberg (ed.). *Universals of Human Language, vol. 3: Word Structure*. Stanford, CA: Stanford University Press, 249–295.

Heim, Irene & Angelika Kratzer 1998. *Semantics in Generative Grammar*. Oxford: Blackwell.

Herweg, Michael 1989. Ansätze zu einer semantischen Beschreibung topologischer Präpositionen. In: Chr. Habel, M. Herweg, K. Rehkämper (eds.). *Raumkonzepte in Verstehensprozessen. Interdisziplinäre Beiträge zu Sprache und Raum*. Tübingen: Niemeyer, 99–127.

Herzog, Otthein & Claus-Rainer Rollinger (eds.) 1991. *Text Understanding in LILOG: Integrating Computational Linguistics and Artificial Intelligence* (Lecture Notes in Artificial Intelligence 546). Berlin: Springer.

Higginbotham, James 1985. On semantics. *Linguistic Inquiry* 16, 547–593.

Hobbs, Jerry R., Mark Stickel, Douglas Appelt & Paul Martin 1993. Interpretation as abduction. *Artificial Intelligence* 63, 69–142.

Hottenroth, Monika-Priska 1991. Präpositionen und Objektkonzepte. Ein kognitiv orientiertes, zweistufiges Modell für die Semantik lokaler Präpositionen. In: G. Rauh (ed.). *Approaches to Prepositions*. Tübingen: Narr, 77–107.

Hurford, James R. 1975. *The Linguistic Theory of Numerals*. Cambridge: Cambridge University Press.

Jackendoff, Ray 1996. The architecture of the linguistic-spatial interface. In: P. Bloom et al. (eds.). *Language and Space*. Cambridge, MA: The MIT Press, 1–30.

Jackendoff, Ray 2002. *Foundations of Language. Brain, Meaning, Grammar, Evolution*. Oxford: Oxford University Press.

Kaup, Barbara, Jana Lüdtke & Claudia Maienborn 2010. 'The drawer is still closed': Simulating past and future actions when processing sentences that describe a state. *Brain & Language* 112, 159–166.

Lang, Ewald 1985. Symmetrische Prädikate: Lexikoneintrag und Interpretationsspielraum. Eine Fallstudie zur Semantik der Personenstandslexik. *Linguistische Studien des ZISW, Reihe A* 127, 75–113.

Lang, Ewald 1989. The semantics of dimensional designation of spatial objects. In: M. Bierwisch & E. Lang (eds.). *Dimensional Adjectives: Grammatical Structure and Conceptual Interpretation*. Berlin: Springer, 263–417.

Lang, Ewald 1990. Primary perceptual space and inherent proportion schema. *Journal of Semantics* 7, 121–141.

Lang, Ewald 1994. Semantische vs. konzeptuelle Struktur: Unterscheidung und Überschneidung. In: M. Schwarz (ed.). *Kognitive Semantik – Cognitive Semantics*. Tübingen: Narr, 25–40.

Lang, Ewald 1995. Das Spektrum der Antonymie. In: G. Harras (ed.). *Die Ordnung der Wörter. Kognitive und lexikalische Strukturen*. Berlin: de Gruyter, 30–98.

Lang, Ewald 2001. Spatial dimension terms. In: M. Haspelmath et al. (eds.). *Language Typology and Universals. An International Handbook*. Vol. 2. Berlin: Walter de Gruyter, 1251–1275.

Lang, Ewald 2004. Schnittstellen bei der Konnektoren-Beschreibung. In: H. Blühdorn, E. Breindl & U. H. Waßner (eds.). *Brücken schlagen. Grundlagen der Konnektorensemantik*. Berlin: de Gruyter, 45–92.

Lang, Ewald, Kai-Uwe Carstensen & Geoff Simmons 1991. *Modelling Spatial Knowledge on a Linguistic Basis. Theory – Prototype – Integration*. Berlin: Springer.

Maienborn, Claudia 2001. On the position and interpretation of locative modifiers. *Natural Language Semantics* 9, 191–240.

Maienborn, Claudia 2003. Event-internal modifiers: Semantic underspecification and conceptual interpretation. In: E. Lang, C. Maienborn & C. Fabricius-Hansen (eds.). *Modifying Adjuncts*. Berlin: de Gruyter, 475–509.

Maienborn, Claudia 2005a. On the limits of the Davidsonian approach: The case of copula sentences. *Theoretical Linguistics* 31, 275–316.

Maienborn, Claudia 2005b. Eventualities and different things: A reply. *Theoretical Linguistics* 31, 383–396.

Meyer, Ralf 1994. Probleme von Zwei-Ebenen-Semantiken. *Kognitionswissenschaft* 4, 32–46.

Moens, Mark & Marc Steedman 1988. Temporal ontology and temporal reference. *Computational Linguistics* 14, 15–28.

Pulman, Stephen G. 1997. Aspectual shift as type coercion. *Transactions of the Philological Society* 95, 279–317.

Pustejovsky, James 1995. *The Generative Lexicon*. Cambridge, MA: The MIT Press.

Pylkkänen, Liina & Brian McElree 2006. The syntax-semantics interface: On-line composition of meaning. In: M. A. Gernsbacher & M. Traxler (eds.). *Handbook of Psycholinguistics*. 2nd edn. Amsterdam: Elsevier, 537–577.

Rothstein, Susan 2005. Response to 'On the limits of the Davidsonian approach: The case of copula sentences' by Claudia Maienborn. *Theoretical Linguistics* 31, 375–381.

Schwarz, Monika 1992. *Kognitive Semantiktheorie und neuropsychologische Realität. Repräsentationale und prozedurale Aspekte der semantischen Kompetenz*. Tübingen: Niemeyer.

Schwarze, Christoph & Marie-Theres Schepping 1995. Polysemy in a two-level semantics. In: U. Egli et al. (eds.). *Lexical Knowledge in the Organization of Language*. Amsterdam: Benjamins, 283–300.

Stolterfoht, Britta, Helga Gese & Claudia Maienborn 2010. Word category conversion causes processing costs: Evidence from adjectival passives. *Psychonomic Bulletin & Review* 17, 651–656.

de Swart, Henriëtte 1998. Aspect shift and coercion. *Natural Language and Linguistic Theory* 16, 347–385.
Taylor, John A. 1994. The two-level approach to meaning. *Linguistische Berichte* 149, 3–26.
Taylor, John A. 1995. Models for word meaning: The network model (Langacker) and the two-level model (Bierwisch) in comparison. In: R. Dirven & J. Vanparys (eds.). *Current Approaches to the Lexicon*. Frankfurt/M.: Lang, 3–26.
Wunderlich, Dieter 1997a. CAUSE and the structure of verbs. *Linguistic Inquiry* 28, 27–68.
Wunderlich, Dieter 1997b. Argument extension by lexical adjunction. *Journal of Semantics* 14, 95–142.
Wunderlich, Dieter & Michael Herweg 1991. Lokale und Direktionale. In: A. von Stechow & D. Wunderlich (eds.). *Semantik – Semantics. Ein internationales Handbuch der zeitgenössischen Forschung – An International Handbook of Contemporary Research* (HSK 6). Berlin: de Gruyter, 758–785.

Jerry R. Hobbs

6 Word meaning and world knowledge

1   Introduction —— 154
2   Core abstract theories —— 160
3   Linking word meaning with the theories —— 167
4   Distinguishing lexical and world knowledge —— 173
5   References —— 179

Abstract: Lexical semantics should be in part about linking the meanings of words with underlying theories of the world. But for this to be even remotely possible, the theories need to be informed by the insights of cognitive and other linguists about the conceptual structure on which language is based. They have to be axiomatizations of a kind of abstract topology that, for example, includes the domains of composite entities (things made of other things), scalar notions, change of state, and causality. Theories of each of these domains are sketched briefly, and it is shown how three very common polysemous words can be defined or characterized in terms of these theories. Finally, there is a discussion of what sort of boundary one can hope to draw between lexical knowledge and other world knowledge.

1 Introduction

We use words to talk about the world. Therefore, to understand what words mean, we should have a prior explication of how we view the world.

Suppose we have a formal logical theory of some domain, or some aspect of the world, that is, a set of predicates intended to capture the concepts in that domain and a set of axioms or rules that constrain the possible meanings of those predicates. Then a formal theory of lexical semantics in that domain would be a matter of writing axioms to relate predicates corresponding to the words in the domain to the predicates in the underlying theory of the domain. For example, the word "until" might be anchored in a formal theory of time that provides an axiomatization of intervals and a *before* relation. (See article 3 [this volume] (Gawron) *Frame Semantics* for a similar view, where frames correspond to the domain theory.)

Jerry R. Hobbs, Marina del Rey, CA, USA

https://doi.org/10.1515/9783110589245-006

For the last forty years researchers in artificial intelligence have made efforts to encode various aspects of world knowledge formally. These efforts have primarily been in commonsense physics in the areas of space, time, and qualitative physics, and, in commonsense psychology, in concepts related to belief and intention. A good review of this work that is old but has not lost its relevance is Davis (1990). Most of this work has focused on narrow areas of commonsense knowledge. But there have been several large-scale efforts to encode knowledge of many domains, most notably, Cyc (Lenat & Guha 1990; Cycorp 2008). One might think that this work could form the basis of an effort toward a formal theory of lexical semantics anchored in world knowledge. However, these theories for the most part were not designed with language in mind, and in particular what is missing is precisely some of the linguists' insights described in the previous several articles of this volume. All of this seriously undercuts the utility for lexical semantics of Cyc and similar large ontologies, and indeed of most of the small-scale theories as well.

In trying to link words and world, there are a number of bad ways to go about it. For example, we could take our theory of the world to be quantum mechanics and attempt to define, say, verbs of motion in terms of the primitives provided by that theory. A less obviously wrong approach, and one that has sometimes been tried, is to adopt Euclidean 3-space as the underlying model of space and attempt to define, say, spatial prepositions in terms of that. More common is a serious misstep, with respect to language, that many large-scale ontologies take at the start. Cyc begins by enforcing a rigid distinction between tangible and intangible entities, and in other hierarchical ontologies, the top-level split is between physical and abstract entities. Yet this distinction plays very little role in language. We can be in a room, in a social group, in the midst of an activity, in trouble, and in politics. We can move a chair from the desk to the table, move money from one bank account to another, move a discussion from religion to politics, and move an audience to tears. A fundamental distinction between tangibles and intangibles rules out the possibility of understanding the sense of "in" or "move" common to all these uses.

Our effort, by contrast, has sought to exploit the insights of linguists such as Gruber (1965), the generative semanticists, Johnson (1987), Lakoff (1987), Jackendoff (see article 4 [this volume] (Jackendoff) *Conceptual Semantics*), and Talmy (see article 1 [this volume] (Talmy) *Cognitive Semantics: An overview*). Johnson, Lakoff, Talmy and others have used the term "image schemas" to refer to a conceptual framework that includes topological relations but excludes, for example, Euclidean notions of magnitude and shape. We have been developing core theories that formalize something like the image schemas, and we have been using these to define or characterize words. Among the theories we have developed are theories of composite entities, or things made of other things, the figure-ground relation, scalar notions, change of state, and causality. The idea behind these abstract core theories is that they capture a wide range of phenomena that share certain features. The theory of composite entities, for example, is intended to accommodate natural physical objects like volcanos, artifacts like automobiles, complex events and processes like concerts and photosynthesis, and complex informational objects like mathematical proofs. The theory of scales captures commonalities shared by distance, time, numbers, money, and degrees of risk, severity, and happiness. The most common words in English (and other languages) can be defined or characterized in terms of these abstract core theories. Specific kinds of composite entities and scales, for example, are then defined as instances of these abstract concepts, and we thereby gain access to the rich vocabulary the abstract theories provide.

We can illustrate the link between word meaning and core theories with the rather complex verb "range". A core theory of scales provides axioms involving predicates such as *scale*, <, *subscale*, *top*, *bottom*, and *at*. Then we are able to define "range" by the following axiom:

$$(\forall x, y, z) range(x, y, z) \equiv$$
$$(\exists s, s_1, u_1, u_2) scale(s) \wedge subscale(s_1, s) \wedge bottom(y, s_1)$$
$$\wedge top(z, s_1) \wedge u_1 \in x \wedge at(u_1, y) \wedge u_2 \in x \wedge at(u_2, z)$$
$$\wedge (\forall u \in x)(\exists v \in s_1) at(u, v)$$

That is, x ranges from y to z if and only if there is a scale s with a subscale s_1 whose bottom is y and whose top is z, such that some member u_1 of x is at y, some member u_2 of x is at z, and every member u of x is at some point v in s_1. Then by choosing different scales and instantiating the *at* relation in different ways, we can get such uses as

The buffalo ranged from northern Texas to southern Saskatchewan.

The students' SAT scores range from 1100 to 1550.

The hepatitis cases range from moderate to severe.

His behavior ranges from sullen to vicious.

Many things can be conceptualized as scales, and when this is done, a large vocabulary, including the word "range", becomes available.

It may seem strange for one to embrace logic and the image-schema insight in the same framework, because the two are often taken by cognitive linguists to be contradictory. But the use of logic amounts to less than one might at first think. It can be viewed simply as a well-understood way of representing complex information. To use the notation of first-order logic is to adopt a style of representation that provides for predicate-argument relations (so we know the difference between "Dog bites man" and "Man bites dog"), conjunction (so we have the additive effect of two propositions), implication and modus ponens (so we can derive one proposition from others), and universal instantiation (so we can derive specific instances from general principles). Any adequate representation scheme for knowledge and information must give us at least these features.

The use of logic is also often taken to mean that words have strict definitions, and we know strict definitions are usually not possible. This is why I have used the phrase "define or characterize" rather than "define". In general, we cannot hope to find definitions for words. That is, for very few words p will we find necessary and sufficient conditions, giving us axioms of the form

$$(\forall x)p(x) \equiv \ldots$$

Rather, we will find many necessary conditions and many sufficient conditions.

$$(\forall x)p(x) \supset \ldots$$

$$(\forall x) \ldots \supset p(x)$$

However, the accumulation of enough such axioms will tightly constrain the possible interpretations of the predicate, and hence the meaning of the word.

This, by the way, gives us a different perspective on the notion of semantic primitives. Our theories should be as elegant as possible, and thus they will have as few "central" predicates as possible. These will give the semblance of a small set of semantic primitives; they in fact are similar to those usually proposed. But in our approach we do not attempt to reduce all concepts to undefinable primitive predicates. Rather, strictly speaking, every predicate is primitive, but its set of possible interpretations is more or less tightly constrained by the axioms it participates in (see article 2 [Semantics: Lexical Structures and Adjectives] (Engelberg) *Lexical decomposition*; 4 [Semantics: Lexical Structures and Adjectives] (Levin & Rappaport Hovav) *Lexical Conceptual Structure*; 6 [Semantics: Lexical Structures and Adjectives] (Cann) *Sense relations*).

A further feature required of our logic breaks down the rigidity of formal logic that cognitive linguists sometimes react against. There must be some mechanism for defeasibility; we have to be able to state inferences that are normally true but can be defeated in particular contexts. There are many such logics (e.g., McCarthy 1980; Ginsberg 1987; Shoham 1987). In Hobbs et al. (1993) and Hobbs (2004) it is argued that interpretation of discourse is a matter of coming up with the best proof of the content of an utterance and the fact of its occurrence, using a method of defeasible inference known as abduction. This provides a means of evaluating possibly contradictory "proofs" to determine the best proof, or interpretation. Thus there may be a large number of possible inferences that one may draw in any given context, but only some of them will be a part of the best interpretation. The mystery of how words acquire their manifold shades of meaning in different contexts thereby translates into the problem of how we choose the best interpretation, or, in a sense, how we select the right set of inferences to draw from the use of a word in context. This is far from a solved problem, but recasting meaning and interpretation in this way gives us a formal, computational way of approaching the problem.

Defeasibility in the logic gives us an approach to prototypes (see article 2 [this volume] (Taylor) *Prototype theory*; Rosch 1975). Categories correspond to predicates and are characterized by a set of possibly defeasible inferences, expressed as axioms, among which are their traditional defining features. For example, bachelors are unmarried and birds fly.

$$(\forall x) bachelor(x) \supset unmarried(x)$$

$$(\forall x) bird(x) \wedge etc_1(x) \supset fly(x)$$

where $etc_1(x)$ indicates the defeasibility of the axiom. Each instance of a category has a subset of the defeasible inferences that hold in its particular case. The more prototypical, the more inferences. In the case of the penguin, which is not a prototypical bird, the defeasible inference about flying is defeated. In this view, the basic level category is the predicate with the richest set of associated axioms. For example, there is more gain in useful knowledge from learning an animal is a dog than from learning a dog is a boxer.

Similarly, defeasible inference lends itself to a treatment of novel metaphor. In metaphor, some properties are transferred from a source to a target, and some are not. When we say Pat is a pig, we draw inferences about manner and quantity of eating from "pig", but not about four-leggedness or species membership. The latter inferences are defeated by the other things we know. Hobbs (1992) develops this idea.

Taking abstract core theories as basic may seem to run counter to a central tenet of cognitive linguistics, namely, that our understanding of many abstract domains is founded on spatial metaphor. It is certainly true that the field of spatial relationships, along with social relationships, is one of the domains babies have to figure out first. But I think that to say we figure out space first and then transfer that knowledge to other domains is to seriously underestimate the difficulty of figuring out space. There are many ways one could conceptualize space, e.g., via Euclidean geometry. But in fact it is the topological concepts which predominate in a baby's spatial understanding. A one-year-old baby fascinated by "in" might put a necklace into a trash can and a Cheerio into a shoe, despite their very different sizes and shapes. In spatial metaphor it is generally the topological properties that get transferred from the source to the target. In taking the abstract core theories as basic, we are isolating precisely the topological properties of space that are most likely to be the basis for understanding metaphorical domains.

If one were inclined to make innateness arguments, one position would be that we are born with a instinctive ability to operate in spatial environments. We begin to use this immediately when we are born, and when we encounter abstract domains, we tap into its rich models. The alternative, more in line with our development here, is that we are born with at least a predisposition towards instinctive abstract patterns – composite entities, scales, change, and so on – which we first apply in making sense of our spatial environment, and then apply to other, more abstract domains as we encounter them. This has the advantage over the first position that it is specific about exactly what properties of space might be in our innate repertoire. For example, the scalar notions of "closer" and "farther" are in it; exact measures of distance are not. A nicely paradoxical coda for summing up this position is that we understand space by means of a spatial metaphor. I take Talmy's critique of the "concreteness as basic" idea as making a similar point (see article 1 [this volume] (Talmy) *Cognitive Semantics: An overview*).

Many of the preceding articles have proposed frameworks for linking words to an underlying conceptual structure. These can all be viewed as initial forays into the problem of connecting lexical meaning with world knowledge. The content of this work survives translation among the various frameworks that have been used for examining it, and survives recasting it as a problem of explicitly encoding world knowledge, specifically, a theory of image schemas explicating such concepts as composite entities, figure-ground, scales, change of state, causality, aggregation, and granularity shifts – an abstract theory that can be instantiated in many different, more specialized domains. The core theories we are developing are not so much theories about *particular* aspects of the world, but rather abstract frameworks that are useful in making sense of a number of different kinds of phenomena. Levin and Rappaport Hovav (see article 4 [Semantics: Lexical Structures and Adjectives] (Levin & Rappaport Hovav) *Lexical Conceptual Structure*) say, "All theories of event structure, either implicitly or explicitly, recognize a distinction between the primitive predicates which define the range of event types available and a component which represents what is idiosyncratic in a verb's meaning." The abstract theories presented here are an explication of the former of these.

This work can be seen as an attempt at a kind of deep lexical semantics. Not only are the words "decomposed" into what were once called primitives, but also the primitives are explicated in axiomatic theories, enabling one to reason deeply about the concepts conveyed by the text.

2 Core abstract theories

2.1 Composite entities

Composite entities are things made of other things. A composite entity is characterized by a set of components, a set of properties of these components, and a set of relations among the components and between the components and the whole. The concept of composite entity captures the minimal complexity something must have in order for it to have structure. It is hard to imagine something that cannot be conceptualized as a composite entity. For this reason, a vocabulary for talking about composite entities will be broadly applicable.

The elements of a composite entity can themselves be viewed as composite entities, and this gives us a very common example of shifting granularities. It allows us to distinguish between the *structure* and the *function* of an entity. The function of an entity as a component of a larger composite entity is its relations to the other elements of the larger composite entity, its environment, while the entity itself is viewed as indecomposable. The structure of the entity is revealed when we decompose it and view it as a composite entity itself. We look at it at a finer granularity.

An important question any time we can view an entity both functionally and structurally is how the functions of the entity are implemented in its structure. We need to spell out the structure-function articulations.

For example, a librarian might view a book as an indecomposable entity and be interested in its location in the library, its relationship to other books, to the bookshelves, and to the people who check the book out. This is a functional view of the book with respect to the library. We can also view it structurally by inquiring as to its parts, its content, its binding, and so on. In spelling out the structure-function articulations, we might say something about how its content, its size, and the material used in its cover determines its proper location in the library.

A composite entity can serve as the *ground* against which some external *figure* can be located or can move (see article 1 [this volume] (Talmy) *Cognitive semantics: An overview*). A primitive predicate *at* expresses this relation. In

$$at(x, y, s)$$

s is a composite entity, y is one of its elements, and x is an external entity. The relation says that the figure x is at a point y in the composite entity s, which is the ground.

The *at* relation plays primarily two roles in the knowledge base. First, it is involved in the "decompositions" of many lexical items. We saw this above in the definition of "range". There is a very rich vocabulary of terms for talking about the figure-ground relation. This means that whenever a relation in some domain can be viewed as an instance of the figure-ground relation, we acquire at a stroke a rich vocabulary for talking about that domain.

This gives rise to the second role the *at* predicate plays in the knowledge base. A great many specific domains have relations that are stipulated to be instances of the *at* relation. There are a large number of axioms of the form

$$(\forall\, x, y, s) r(x, y, s) \supset at(x, y, s)$$

It is in this way that many of the metaphorical usages that pervade natural language discourse are accommodated. Once we characterize some piece of the world as a composite entity, and some relation as an *at* relation, we have acquired the whole locational way of talking about it. Once this is enriched with a theory of time and change, we can import the whole vocabulary of motion. For example, in computer science, a data structure can be viewed as a composite entity, and we can stipulate that if a pointer points to a node in a data structure, then the pointer is *at* that node. We have then acquired a spatial metaphor, and we can subsequently talk about, for example, the pointer *moving around* the data structure. Space, of course, is itself a composite entity and can be talked about using a locational vocabulary.

Other examples of *at* relations are

> A person at an object in a system of objects:
>> John is at his desk.
>
> An object at a location in a coordinate system:
>> The post office is at the corner of 34th Street and Eighth Avenue.
>
> A person's salary at a particular point on the money scale:
>> John's salary reached $75,000 this year.
>
> An event at a point on the time line:
>> The meeting is at three o'clock.

2.2 Scales

The theory of scales was mentioned in the introduction. It provides the basic vocabulary for talking about partial orderings, including *scale*, <, *subscale*, total ordering, *top*, *bottom*, *reverse*, and intervals. The theory also explicates monotone-increasing scale-to-scale functions ("the more *X*, the more *Y*"), the construction of composite scales, and the characterization of qualitatively high and low regions of a scale.

A scale is a composite entity, so we can talk about an entity being *at* a point on the scale. An obvious example of a scale is the scale of nonnegative integers. The cardinality of a set can be defined in the standard way:

$$card(\phi) = 0$$

$$(\forall\, x, s)\, x \notin s \supset card(\{x\} \cup s) = card(s) + 1$$

We can then define cardinality to be an *at* relation, where *N* is the scale of nonnegative integers:

$$(\forall\, s, n)\, card(s) = n \supset at(s, n, N)$$

This gives us access to the rich vocabulary of spatial relationships when talking about cardinality, allowing us to say things like

> The population of Cairo *reached* 15 million this year.

Many scales are composite. A scale *s* is a composite of scales s_1 and s_2 if its elements are the ordered pairs <*x*, *y*> where *x* is in s_1 and *y* is in s_2. The ordering in *s* has to be consistent with the orderings in s_1 and s_2; if x_1 is less than x_2 in s_1, and y_1 is less than y_2 in s_2, then <x_1, y_1> is less than <x_2, y_2> in *s*. The converse is not necessarily true; the composite scale may have more structure than that inherited from its component scales. We need composite scales to deal with complex scalar predicates, such as *damage*. When something is damaged, it no longer fulfills its function in a goal-directed system. It needs to be repaired, and repairs cost. Thus, there are (at least) two ways in which damage can be serious, first in the degradation of its function, second in the cost of its repair. These are independent scales. Damage that causes a car not to run may cost next to nothing to fix, and damage that only causes the car to run a little unevenly may be very expensive.

It is very useful to be able to isolate the high and low regions of a scale. We can do this with operators called *Hi* and *Lo*. The *Hi* region of a scale includes its top; the *Lo* region includes its bottom. The points in the *Hi* region are all greater than any of the points in the *Lo* region. Otherwise, there are no general topological constraints on the *Hi* and *Lo* regions. In particular, the bottom of the *Hi* region and the top of the *Lo* region may be indeterminate with respect to the elements of the scale. The *Hi* and *Lo* operators provide us with a coarse-grained structure on scales, useful when greater precision is not necessary or not possible.

The absolute form of adjectives frequently isolate *Hi* and *Lo* regions of scales. A totally ordered Height Scale can be defined precisely, but frequently we are only interested in qualitative judgments of height. The word "tall" isolates the *Hi* region of the Height Scale; the word "short" isolates the *Lo* region. A Happiness Scale cannot be defined precisely. We cannot get much more structure for a Happiness Scale than what is given to us by the *Hi* and *Lo* operators. The *Hi* and *Lo* operators can be iterated, to give us the concepts "happy", "very happy", and so on.

In any given context, the *Hi* and *Lo* operators will identify different regions of the scale. That is, the inferences we can draw from the fact that something is in the *Hi* region of a scale are context-dependent; indeed, inferences are always context-dependent. But two important constraints on the *Hi* and *Lo* regions relate them to distributions and functionality. The *Hi* and *Lo* regions must be related to common distributions of objects on the scale in an as-yet nonexistent qualitative theory of distributions. If something is significantly above average for the relevant set, then it is in the *Hi* region. The regions must also be related to goal-directed behavior; often something is in the *Hi* region of a scale precisely because that property aids or defeats the achievement of some goal in a plan. For example, saying that a talk is long often means that it is longer than the audience's attention span, and thus the goal of conveying information is defeated. Often when we call someone tall, we mean tall enough or too tall for some purpose.

2.3 Change of state

A predicate of central importance is the predicate *change*. This is a relation between situations, or conditions, or predications, and indicates a change of state. A change from *p* being true of *x* to *q* being true of *x*, using an ontologically promiscuous notation that reifies states and events (see Hobbs 1985; article 8 [this volume] (Maienborn) *Event semantics*), can be represented

$$change(e_1, e_2) \wedge p'(e_1, x) \wedge q'(e_2, x)$$

This says that there is a change from the situation e_1 of *p* being true of *x* to the situation e_2 of *q* being true of *x*. A very common pattern involves a change of location:

$$change(e_1, e_2) \wedge at'(e_1, x, y, s) \wedge at'(e_2, x, z, s)$$

That is, there is a change from the situation e_1 of x being at y in s to the situation e_2 of x being at z in s.

When there is a change, generally there is some entity involved in both the start and end states; there is something that is changing—x in the above formulas.

The predicate *change* possesses a limited transitivity. There was a change from Bill Clinton being a law student to Bill Clinton being President, because they are two parts of the same ongoing process, even though he was governor in between. There was a change from Bill Clinton being President to George W. Bush being President. But we probably do not want to say there was a change from Bill Clinton being a law student to George W. Bush being President. They are not part of the same process.

A state cannot change into the same state without going through an intermediate different state.

The concept of *change* is linked with time in the obvious way. If state e_1 changes into state e_2, then e_2 cannot be before e_1. My view is that the relation between change and time is much deeper, cognitively. The theory of change of state suggests a view of the world as consisting of a large number of more or less independent, occasionally interacting processes, or histories, or sequences of events. x goes through a series of changes, and y goes through a series of changes, and occasionally there is a state that involves a relation between the two. We can then view the time line as an artificial construct, a regular sequence of imagined abstract events – think of them as ticks of a clock in the National Institute of Science and Technology – to which other events can be related by chains of copresence. Thus, I know I went home at six o'clock because I looked at my watch, and I had previously set my watch by going to the NIST Web site. In any case, there is no need to choose between such a view of time and one that takes time as basic. They are inter-definable in a straightforward fashion (Hobbs et al. 1987).

For convenience, we define one-argument predicates changeFrom and changeTo, suppressing one or the other argument of *change*.

2.4 Cause

Our treatment of causality (Hobbs 2005) rests on a distinction between causal complexes and the predicate *cause*. When we flip a switch and the light comes on, we say that flipping the switch caused the light to come on. But many other factors were involved. The wiring and the light bulb had to be intact, the power had to be on in the city, and so forth. We say that all these other states and events constitute the causal complex for the effect. A causal complex for an effect is the set of all the eventualities that must happen or hold in order for the effect to occur. The two principal properties of causal complexes are that when all the eventualities happen, the effect happens, and that every eventuality in the causal complex is required for the effect to happen. These are strictly true, and the notion of causal complex is not a defeasible one.

The "cause" of an effect, by contrast, is a distinguished element within the causal complex, one that cannot normally be assumed to hold. It is often the action that is under the agent's immediate control. It is only defeasibly true that when a cause occurs the effect also occurs. This inference can be defeated because some of the other states and events in the causal complex that normally hold do not hold in this particular case. The notion of *cause* is much more useful in commonsense reasoning because we can rarely if ever enumerate all the eventualities in a causal complex. Most of our commonsense causal knowledge is expressed in terms of the predicate *cause*.

The concept *cause* has the expected properties, such as defeasible transitivity and consistency with temporal ordering. But we should not expect to have a highly developed theory of causality *per se*. Rather we should expect to see causal information distributed throughout our knowledge base. For example, there is no axiom of the form

$$(\forall e_1, e_2) cause(e_1, e_2) \equiv \ldots$$

defining *cause*. But there will be many axioms of the forms

$$p'(e_1, x) \supset q'(e_2, x) \wedge cause(e_1, e_2)$$
$$r'(e_3, x) \supset p'(e_1, x) \wedge cause(e_1, e_3)$$

expressing causal connections among specific states and events; e.g., *p*-like events cause *q*-like events or *r*-like events are caused by *p*-like events. We don't know precisely what causality is, but we know lots and lots of examples of things that cause other things.

Some would urge that causes and effects can only be events, but it seems to me that we want to allow states as well, since in

> The slipperiness of the ice caused John to fall.

the cause is a state. Moreover, intentional agents are sometimes taken to be the unanalyzed causes of events. In

> John lifted his arm.

John is the cause of the change of position of his arm, and we probably don't want to have to coerce this argument into some imagined event taking place inside John. Physical forces may also act as causes, as in

> Gravity causes the moon to circle the earth.

The world is laced with threads of causal connection. In general, two entities x and y are causally connected with respect to some behavior p of x, if whenever p happens to x, there is some corresponding behavior q that happens to y. Attachment of physical objects is one variety of causal connection. In this case, p and q are both *move*. If x and y are attached, moving x causes y to move. Containment is similar.

A particularly common variety of causal connection between two entities is one mediated by the motion of a third entity from one to the other. This might be called, somewhat facetiously, a "vector boson" connection. In particle physics, a vector boson is an elementary particle that transfers energy from one point to another. Photons, which really are vector bosons, mediate the causal connection between the sun and our eyes. Other examples of such causal connections are rain drops connecting a state of the clouds with the wetness of our skin and clothes, a virus transmitting disease from one person to another, and utterances passing information between people.

Containment, barriers, openings, and penetration are all with respect to paths of causal connection. Force is causality with a scalar structure (see article 1 [this volume] (Talmy) *Cognitive Semantics: An overview*).

The event structure underlying many verbs exhibits causal chains. Instruments, for example, are usually vector bosons. In the sentence,

> John pounded the nail with a hammer for Bill.

the underlying causal structure is that the agent John causes a change in location of the instrument, the hammer, which causes a change in location of the object or theme, the nail, which causes or should cause a change in the mental or emotional state of the beneficiary, Bill.

> Agent $-cause->$ $change(at(Instr, x, s), at(Instr, Object, s))$
> $-cause->$ $change(at(Object, y_1, s), at(Object, y_2, s))$
> $-cause->$ $change(p_1(Beneficiary), p_2(Beneficiary))$

Much of case grammar and work on thematic roles can be seen as a matter of identifying where the arguments of verbs fit into this kind of causal chain when we view the verbs as instantiating this abstract frame (see Jackendoff 1972; article 3 [Semantics: Lexical Structures and Adjectives] (Davies) *Thematic roles*; article 4 [Semantics: Lexical Structures and Adjectives] (Levin & Rappaport Hovav) *Lexical Conceptual Structure*).

In addition, in this theory we define such concepts as *enable*, *prevent*, *help*, and *obstruct*. There are also treatments of attempts, success, failure, ability, and difficulty.

With this vocabulary, we are in a position to characterize more precisely the intuitive notions of state, event, action, and process. A state is a static property that does not involve a change (at the relevant granularity), such as an *at* relationship, $at(x, y, s)$. To be up, for example, is a state. An event is a change of state, a common variety of which is a change of location:

$$change(e_1, e_2) \wedge at'(e_1, x, y, s) \wedge at'(e_2, x, z, s)$$

For example, the verb "rise" denotes a change of location of something to a higher point. An action is the causing of an event by an intentional agent:

$$cause(a, e) \wedge change'(e, e_1, e_2) \wedge at'(e_1, x, y, s) \wedge at'(e_2, x, z, s)$$

The verb "raise" denotes an action by someone of effecting a change of location of something to a higher point. A process is a sequence of events or actions. For example, to fluctuate is to undergo a sequence of risings and fallings, and to pump is to engage in a sequence of raisings and lowerings. We can coarsen the granularity on processes so that the individual changes of state become invisible, and the result is a state. This is a transformation of perspective that is effected by the progressive aspect in English. Thus, fluctuating can be viewed as a state.

Detailed expositions of all the core theories can be found in Part II of Gordon & Hobbs (2017) and at

   http://www.isi.edu/hobbs/csk.html

3 Linking word meaning with the theories

Once we have in place the core theories that capture world knowledge at a sufficiently abstract level, we can begin to construct the axioms that link word meaning to the theories. We illustrate here how that would go, using the words "have", "remove", and "remain". Words have senses, and for each sense the linkage will be different. Here we examine the word senses in WordNet (Miller 1995) and

FrameNet (Baker, Fillmore & Cronin 2003), since they are the most heavily used lexical resources in computational linguistics. The word sense numbers correspond to their order in the Web interfaces to the two resources:

> http://wordnet.princeton.edu/
> http://framenet.icsi.berkeley.edu

3.1 "Have"

In WordNet the verb "have" has 19 senses. But they can be grouped into three broad "supersenses". In its first supersense, X has Y means that X is in some relation to Y. The WordNet senses this covers are as follows:

1. a broad sense, including have a son, having a condition hold and having a college degree
2. having a feature or property, i.e., the property holding of the entity
3. a sentient being having a feeling or internal property
4. a person owning a possession
7. have a person related in some way: have an assistant
9. have left: have three more chapters to write
12. have a disease: have influenza
17. have a score in a game: have three touchdowns

The supersense can be characterized by the axiom

$$\text{have-s1}(x, y) \supset \text{relatedTo}(x, y)$$

In these axioms, supersenses are indexed with s, WordNet senses with w, and FrameNet senses with f. Unindexed predicates are from core theories.

The individual senses are then specializations of the supersense where more domain-specific predicates are explicated in more specialized domains. For example, sense 4 relates to the supersense as follows:

$$\text{have-w4}(x, y) \equiv \text{possess}(x, y)$$

$$\text{have-w4}(x, y) \supset \text{have-s1}(x, y)$$

where the predicate *possess* would be explicated in a commonsense theory of economics, relating it to the priveleged use of the object. Similarly, *have-w3(x, y)* links with the supersense but has the restrictions that x is sentient and that the "relatedTo" property is the predicate-argument relation between the feeling and its subject.

The second supersense of "have" is "come to be in a relation to". This is our *changeTo* predicate. Thus, the definition of this supersense is

$$\text{have-s2}(x, y) \equiv \text{changeTo}(e) \wedge \text{have-s1}'(e, x, y)$$

The WordNet senses this covers are as follows:

10. be confronted with: we have a fine mess
11. experience: the stocks had a fast run-up
14. receive something offered: have this present
15. come into possession of: he had a gift from her
16. undergo, e.g., an injury: he had his arm broken in the fight
18. have a baby

In these senses the new relation is initiated but the subject does not necessarily play a causal or agentive role. The particular change involved is specialized in the WordNet senses to a confronting, a receiving, a giving birth, and so on.

The third supersense of "have" is "cause to come to be in a relation to". The axiom defining this is

$$\text{have-s3}(x, y) \equiv \text{cause}(x, e) \wedge \text{have-s2}'(e, x, y)$$

The WordNet senses this covers are

5. cause to move or be in a certain position or condition: have your car ready
6. consume: have a cup of coffee
8. organize: have a party
13. cause to do: she had him see a doctor
19. have sex with

In all these cases the subject initiates the change of state that occurs.

FrameNet has five simple transitive senses for "have". Their associated frames are

1. Have associated
2. Possession
3. Ingestion
4. Inclusion
5. Birth

The first sense corresponds to the first WordNet supersense:

$$\text{have-f1}(x, y) \equiv \text{have-s1}(x, y)$$

The second sense is WordNet sense 4.

$$\text{have-f2}(x, y) \equiv \text{have-w4}(x, y)$$

The third sense is WordNet sense 6. The fourth sense is a *partOf* relation. It is a specialization of WordNet sense 2.

$$\text{have-f4}(x, y) \equiv \text{partOf}(x, y)$$

$$\text{have-f4}(x, y) \supset \text{have-w2}(x, y)$$

The fifth sense is WordNet sense 18.

3.2 "Remove"

If x removes y from z, then x causes a change from the state in which y is at z.

$$\text{remove}(x, y, z) \supset \text{cause}(x, e_1) \wedge \text{changeFrom}'(e_1, e_2) \wedge \text{at}'(e_2, y, z, s)$$

This is the "supersense" covering all of the WordNet and FrameNet senses of "remove".

WordNet lists 8 senses of "remove". In WordNet sense 1, *at* is instantiated as physical location. In sense 2, *at* is instantiated as position in an organization, as in "The board removed the VP of operations." In sense 3, y is somehow dysfunctional, as in removing trash. In sense 4, *at* is instantiated as the membership relation in a set; y is removed from set z. In sense 5, the change is functional or strategic, as in a general removing his troops from a vulnerable position. In sense 6, x and y are identical, as in "He removed himself from the contest." In sense 7, *at* is instantiated as "alive", as in "The Mafia don removed his enemy." In sense 8, y is abstract and dysfunctional, as in removing an obstacle.

FrameNet has two senses of the word. The first is the general meaning, our supersense. In the second sense, x is a person, y is clothes, and z is a body.

Note that the supersense gives the topological structure of the meaning of the verb. The various senses are then generated from that by instantiating the *at* relation to something more specific, or by adding domain constraints to the arguments x, y and z.

3.3 "Remain"

There are four WordNet senses of the verb "remain":

1. Not change out of an existing state: He remained calm.
2. Not change out of being at a location: He remained at his post.
3. Entities in a set remaining after others are removed: Three problems remain.
4. A condition remains in a location: Some smoke remained after the fire was put out.

The first sense is the most general and subsumes the other three. We can characterize it by the axiom

$$remain\text{-}w1(x, e) \supset arg(x, e) \land \neg changeFrom(e)$$

That is, if x remains in condition e, then e is a property of x (or x is an argument of e), and there is no change from state e holding. By the properties of *changeFrom* it follows that x is in state e, as is presupposed.

In the second sense, the property e of x is being in a location.

$$remain\text{-}w2(x, e) \equiv remain\text{-}w1(x, e) \land at'(e, x, y)$$

The fourth sense is a specialization of the second sense in which the entity x that remains is a state or condition.

$$remain\text{-}w4(x, e) \equiv remain\text{-}w2(x, e) \land state(x)$$

The third sense is the most interesting to characterize. As in the fourth WordNet sense of "remove", there is a process that removes elements from a set, and what remains is the set difference between the original and the set of elements that are removed. In this axiom x remains after process e.

$$remain\text{-}w3(x, e) \equiv remove\text{-}w4'(e, y, s_2, s_1) \land setdiff(s_3, s_1, s_2) \land member(x, s_3)$$

That is, x remains after e if and only if e is a removal event by some agent y of a subset s_2 from s_1, s_3 is the set difference between s_1 and s_2, and x is a member of s_3.

There are four FrameNet senses of "remain". The first is the same as WordNet sense 1. The second is the same as WordNet sense 3. The third and fourth are two specializations of WordNet sense 3, one in which the removal process is destructive and one in which it is not.

There are two nominalizations of the verb "remain"—"remainder" and "remains". All of their senses are related to WordNet sense 3. The first WordNet noun sense is the most general.

$$remainder\text{-}w1(x, e) \equiv remain\text{-}w3(x, e)$$

That is, x is the remainder after process e if and only if x remains after e. The other three senses result from specialization of the removal process to arithmetic division, arithmetic subtraction, and the purposeful cutting of a piece of cloth. The noun "remains" refers to what remains ($w3$) after a process of consumption or degradation.

3.4 The nature of word senses

The most common words in a language are typically the most polysemous. They often have a central meaning indicating their general topological structure. Each new sense introduces inferences that cannot be reliably determined just from a core meaning plus contextual factors. They tend to build up along what Brugman (1981), Lakoff (1987) and others have called a radial category structure (see article 2 [this volume] (Taylor) *Prototype theory*). Sense 2 may be a slight modification of sense 1, and senses 3 and 4 different slight modifications of sense 2. It is easy to describe the links that take us from one sense to an adjacent one in the framework presented here. Each sense corresponds to a predicate which is characterized by one or more axioms involving that predicate. A move to an adjacent sense happens when incremental changes are made to the axioms. As we have seen in the examples of this section, the changes are generally additions to the antecedents or consequents of the axioms. The principal kinds of additions are embedding in *change* and *cause*, as we saw in the supersenses of "have"; the instantiation of general predicates like *relatedTo* and *at* to more specific predicates in particular domains, as we saw in all three cases; and the addition of domain-specific constraints on arguments, as in restricting y to be clothes in *remove-f*2.

A good account of the lexical semantics of a word should not just catalog various word senses. It should detail the radial category structure of the word senses, and for each link, it should say what incremental addition or modification resulted in the new sense. Note that radial categories provide us with a logical structure for the lexicon, and also no doubt a historical one, but not a developmental one. Children often learn word senses independently and only later if ever realize the relation among the senses. See article 2 [this volume] (Taylor) *Prototype theory* for further discussion of issues with respect to radial categories.

4 Distinguishing lexical and world knowledge

It is perhaps natural to ask whether a principled boundary can be drawn between linguistic knowledge and knowledge of the world. To make this issue more concrete, consider the following seven statements:

(1) If a string w_1 is a noun phrase and a string w_2 is a verb phrase, then the concatenation $w_1 w_2$ is a clause.
(2) The transitive verb "moves" corresponds to the predication $move_2(x, y)$, providing a string describing x occurs as its subject and a string describing y occurs as its direct object.
(3) If an entity x moves (in sense $move_2$) an entity y, then x causes a change of state or location of y.
(4) If an entity y changes to a new state or location, it is no longer in its old state or location.
(5) If a physical object x moves a physical object y through a fluid medium, then x must apply force to y against the resistance of the medium.
(6) The function of a barge is to move freight across water.
(7) A barge moved the wreckage of Flight 1549 to New Jersey.

Syntax consists in part of rules like (1), or generalizations of them. One could view the lexicon as consisting of axioms expressing information like (2), specifying for each word sense and argument realization pattern what predication is conveyed, perhaps together with some generalizations of such statements. (Lexical knowledge of other languages would be encoded as similar axioms, sometimes linking to the same underlying predicates, sometimes different.) Axioms expressing information like (3) link the lexical predicates with underlying domain theories, in this case, theories of the abstract domains of causality and change of state. Axioms expressing facts like (4) are internal to domain theories, in this case, the theory of the abstract domain of change of state. Axioms expressing general facts like (5) are part of a commonsense or scientific theory of physics, which can be viewed as a specialization and elaboration of the abstract theories. Axioms expressing facts like (6) encode telic information about artifacts. Statement (7) is a specific, accidental fact about the world.

Many have felt that the viability of lexical semantics as a research enterprise requires a principled distinction between lexical knowledge and world knowledge, presumably somewhere below axioms like (2) and above facts like (7). Many of those who have believed that no such distinction is possible have concluded that lexical semantics is impossible, or at least can only be very limited in its scope.

For example, in his discussion of meaning, Bloomfield (1933, 139–140) rules out the possibility of giving definitions of most words.

> In order to give a scientifically accurate definition of meaning of every form of a language, we should have to have a scientifically accurate knowledge of everything in the speakers' world. While this may be possible for certain scientifically well-understood terms like "salt", we have no precise way of defining words like "love" or "hate" which concern situations that have not been accurately classified – and these latter are in the great majority.

He concludes that

> The statement of meanings is therefore a weak point in language-study, and will remain so until human knowledge advances very far beyond its present state.

Lexical semantics is impossible because we would need a theory of the world. Bloomfield goes on to talk about such phenomena as synonymy and antonymy, and leaves issues of meaning at that.

More recently, Fodor (1980) similarly argued that lexical semantics would need a complete and correct scientific theory of the world to proceed, and is consequently impossible in the foreseeable future.

A counterargument is that we don't need a scientifically correct theory of the world, because people don't have that as they use language to convey meaning. We rather need to capture people's commonsense theories of the world. In fact, there are a number of interesting engineering efforts to encode commonsense and scientific knowledge needed in specific applications or more broadly. Large ontologies of various domains, such as biomedicine and geography, are being developed for the Semantic Web and other computational uses. Cyc (Lenat & Guha 1990) has been a large-scale effort to encode commonsense knowledge manually since the middle 1980s; it now contains millions of rules. The Open Mind Common Sense project (Singh 2002) aims at accumulating huge amounts of knowledge rapidly by marshaling millions of "netizens" to make contributions; for example, a participant might be asked to complete the sentence "Water can …" and reply with "Water can put out fires." Many of these projects, including Cyc, involve a parallel effort in natural language processing to relate their knowledge of the world to the way we talk about the world. Might we do lexical semantics by explicating the meanings of words in terms of such theories?

Fodor (1983) can be read as responding to this possibility. He argues that peripheral processes like speech recognition and syntactic processing are encapsulated in the sense that they require only limited types of information. Central processes like fixation of belief, by contrast, can require any knowledge from any domain. He gives the example of the power of analogical reasoning in fixation of belief. The body of knowledge that can be appealed to in analogies can not be circumscribed; analogies might involve mappings from anything to anything else. Scientific study of modular processes is feasible, but scientific study of global processes is not. No scientific account of commonsense reasoning is currently available or likely to be in the foreseeable future; by implication reasoning about commonsense world knowledge is not currently amenable to scientific inquiry, nor is a lexical semantics that depends on it. Syntax *is* amenable to scientific study, but only, according to Fodor, because it is informationally encapsulated.

Thus, the debate on this issue often centers on the modularity of syntax. Do people do syntactic analysis of utterances in isolation from world knowledge? Certainly at time scales at which awareness functions, there is no distinction in the processing of linguistic and world knowledge. We rarely if ever catch ourselves understanding the syntax of a sentence we hear without understanding much about its semantics. For example, in Chomsky's famous grammatical sentence, "Colorless green ideas sleep furiously," there is no stage in comprehension at which we are aware that "colorless" and "green" are adjectives, but haven't yet realized they are contradictory.

Moreover, psychological studies seem to indicate that syntactic processing and the use of world knowledge are intricately intertwined. Much of this work has focused on the use of world knowledge to resolve references and disambiguate ambiguous prepositional phrase attachments. Tanenhaus & Brown-Schmidt (2008) review some of this research that makes use of methods of monitoring eye movements to track comprehension. For example, they present evidence that subjects access the current physical context while they are processing syntactically ambiguous instructions and integrate it with the language immediately. In terms of our examples, they are using facts like (1) and facts like (7) together. The authors contend that their results "are incompatible with the claim that the language processing includes subsystems (modules) that are informationally encapsulated, and thus isolated from high-level expectations."

Often the line between linguistic and world knowledge is drawn to include selectional constraints within language. Hagoort et al. (2004) used electroencephalogram and functional magnetic resonance imaging data to investigate whether there was any difference between the temporal course of processing true sentences like "Dutch trains are yellow and very crowded", factually false but sensible sentences like "Dutch trains are white and very crowded", and sentences that violate selectional constraints like "Dutch trains are sour and very crowded." The false sentences and the selectionally anomalous sentences showed a virtually identical peak of activity in the left inferior prefrontal cortex. The authors observed that there is "strong empirical evidence that lexical semantic knowledge and general world knowledge are both integrated in the same time frame during sentence interpretation, starting at ~300ms after word onset." However, there is a difference in frequency profile between the two conditions, consisting of a measurable increase in activity in the 30–70 Hz range (gamma frequency) for the false sentences, and an increase in the 4–7Hz range (theta frequency) in the anomalous condition. The authors conclude that "semantic interpretation is not separate from its integration with nonlinguistic elements of meaning," but that nevertheless "the brain keeps a record of what makes a sentence hard to interpret, whether this is word meaning or world knowledge."

Thus, if the brain makes a distinction between linguistic and world knowledge, it does not appear to be reflected in the temporal course of processing language.

The most common argument in linguistics and related fields for drawing a strict boundary between lexicon and world is a kind of despair that a scientific study of world knowledge is possible. Others have felt it is possible to identify lexically relevant domains of world knowledge that are accessible to scientific study.

Linguists investigating "lexical conceptual structure" (e.g., see article 4 [Semantics: Lexical Structures and Adjectives] (Levin & Rappaport Hovav) *Lexical Conceptual Structure*) are attempting to discover generalizations in how the way an entity occurs in the underlying description of a situation or event in terms of abstract topological predicates influences the way it is realized in the argument structure in syntax. For example, do verbs that undergo dative alternation all have a similar underlying abstract structure? Does the causative always involve embedding an event as the effect in a causal relation, where the cause is the agent or an action performed by the agent? The hypothesis of this work is that facts like (2), which are linguistic, depend crucially on facts like (3), which have a more world-like flavor. However, this does not mean that we have identified a principled boundary between linguistic and world knowledge. One could just as well view this as a strategic decision about how to carve out a tractable research problem.

Pustejovsky (1995) pushes the line between lanaguage and world farther into the world. He advocates representing what he calls the "qualia structure" of words, which includes facts about the constituent parts of an entity (Constitutive), its place in a larger domain (Formal), its purpose and function (Telic), and the factors involved in its origin (Agentive). One can then, for example, use the Telic information to resolve a metonymy like "She began a cigarette" into its normal reading of "She began smoking a cigarette," rather than any one of the many other things one could do with a cigarette – eating it, rolling it, tearing it apart, and so on. His framework is an attempt to relate facts like (2) about what arguments can appear with what predicates with facts like (6) about the functions and other properties of things. Several places in his book, Pustejovsky suggests that it is important to see his qualia structures as part of lexical semantics, and hence linguistics, as opposed to general commonsense knowledge that is not linguistic. But he never makes a compelling argument to this effect. All of his qualia structures and coercion mechanisms are straightforward to express in a logical framework, so there are no formal reasons for the distinction. I think it is best to see this particular carving out of knowledge and interpretation processes, as with the study of lexical conceptual stuctures, as a strategic decision to identify a fruitful and tractable research problem.

Pustejovsky's work is an attempt to specify the knowledge that is required for interpreting at least the majority of nonstandard uses of words. Kilgarriff (2001) tests this hypothesis by examining the uses of nine particular words in a 20-million word corpus. 41 of 2276 instances were judged to be nonstandard since they did not correspond to any of the entries for the word in a standard dictionary. Of these, only two nonstandard uses were derivable from Pustejovsky's qualia structures. The others required deeper commonsense knowledge or previous acquaintance with collocations. Kilgarriff's conclusion is that "Any theory that relies on a distinction between general and lexical knowledge will founder." (Kilgariff 2001: 325)

Some researchers in natural language processing have argued that lexical knowledge should be distinguished from other knowledge because it results in more efficient computation or more efficient comprehension and production. One example concerns hyperonymy relations, such as that $car(x)$ implies $vehicle(x)$. It is true that some kinds of inferences lend themselves more to efficient computation than others, and inferences involving only monadic predicates are one example. But where this is true, it is a result not of their content but of structural properties of the inferences, and these cut across the lexical-world distinction. Any efficiency realized in inferring $vehicle(x)$ can be realized in inferring $expensive(x)$ as well.

All of statements (1)–(7) are facts about the world, because sentences and their structure and words and their roles in sentences are things in the world, as much as barges, planes, and New Jersey. There is certainly knowledge we have that is knowledge about words, including how to pronounce and spell words, predicate-argument realization patterns, alternation rules, subcategorization patterns, grammatical gender, and so on. But words are part of the world, and one might ask why this sort of knowledge should have any special cognitive status. Is it any different in principle from the kind of knowledge one has about friendship, cars, or the properties of materials? In all these cases, we have entities, properties of entities, and relations among them. Lexical knowledge is just ordinary knowledge where the entities in question are words. There are no representational reasons for treating linguistic knowledge as special, providing we are willing to treat the entities in our subject matter as first-class individuals in our logic (cf. Hobbs 1985). There are no procedural reasons for treating linguistic knowledge as special, since parsing, argument realization, lexical decomposition, the coercion of metonymies, and so on can all be implemented straightforwardly as inference. The argument that parsing and lexical decomposition, for example, can be done efficiently on present-day computers, whereas commonsense reasoning cannot, does not seem to apply to the human brain; psycho-linguistic studies show that the influence of world knowledge kicks in as early as syntactic and lexical knowledge, and yields the necessary results just as quickly.

We are led to the conclusion that any drawing of lines is for the strategic purpose of identifying a coherent, tractable and fruitful area of research. Statements (1)–(6) are examples from six such areas. Once we have identified and explicated such areas, the next question is what connections or articulations there are among them; Pustejovsky's research and work on lexical conceptual structures are good examples of people addressing this question.

However, all of this does not mean that linguistic insights can be ignored. The world can be conceptualized in many ways. Some of them lend themselves to a deep treatment of lexical semantics, and some of them impede it. Put the other way around, looking closely at language leads us to a particular conceptualization of the world that has proved broadly useful in everyday life. It provides us with topological relations rather than with the precision of Euclidean 3-space. It focuses on changes of state rather than on correspondences with an *a priori* time line. A defeasible notion of causality is central in it. It provides means for aggregation and shifting granularities. It encompasses those properties of space that are typically transferred to new target domains when what looks like a spatial metaphor is invoked.

More specific domains can then be seen as instantiations of these abstract theories. Indeed, Euclidean 3-space itself is such a specialization. Language provides us with a rich vocabulary for talking about the abstract domains. The core meanings of many of the most common words in language can be defined or characterized in these core theories. When the core theory is instantiated in a specific domain, the vocabulary associated with the abstract domain is also instantiated, giving us a rich vocabulary for talking about and thinking about the specific domain. Conversely, when we encounter general words in the contexts of specific domains, understanding how the specific domains instantiate the abstract domains allows us to determine the specific meanings of the general words in their current context.

We understand language so well because we know so much. Therefore, we will not have a good account of how language works until we have a good account of what we know about the world and how we use that knowledge. In this article I have sketched a formalization of one very abstract way of conceptualizing the world, one that arises from an investigation of lexical semantics and is closely related to the lexical decompositions and image schemas that have been argued for by other lexical semanticists. It enables us to capture formally the core meanings of many of the most common words in English and other languages, and it links smoothly with more precise theories of specific domains.

I have profited from discussions of this work with Gully Burns, Peter Clark, Tim Clausner, Christiane Fellbaum, and Rutu Mulkar-Mehta. This work was performed in part under the IARPA (DTO) AQUAINT program, contract N61339-06-C-0160.

5 References

Baker, Colin F., Charles J. Fillmore & Beau Cronin 2003. The structure of the Framenet database. *International Journal of Lexicography* 16, 281–296.
Bloomfield, Leonard 1933. *Language*. New York: Holt, Rinehart & Winston.
Brugman, Claudia 1981. *The Story of 'Over'*. MA thesis. University of California, Berkeley, CA.
Cycorp 2008. http://www.cyc.com/. December 9, 2010.
Davis, Ernest 1990. *Representations of Commonsense Knowledge*. San Mateo, CA: Morgan Kaufmann.
Fodor, Jerry A. 1980. Methodological solipsism considered as a research strategy in cognitive science. *Behavioral and Brain Sciences* 3, 63–109.
Fodor, Jerry A. 1983. *The Modularity of Mind. An Essay on Faculty Psychology*. Cambridge, MA: The MIT Press.
Ginsberg, Matthew L. (ed.) 1987. *Readings in Nonmonotonic Reasoning*. San Mateo, CA: Morgan Kaufmann.
Gordon, Andrew S., and Jerry R. Hobbs 2017. *A Formal Theory of Commonsense Psychology: How People Think People Think*. Cambridge, United Kingdom: Cambridge University Press.
Gruber, Jefirey C. 1965/1976. *Studies in Lexical Relations*. Ph.D. dissertation. MIT, Cambridge, MA. Reprinted in: J. S. Gruber. *Lexical Structures in Syntax and Semantics*. Amsterdam: North-Holland, 1976, 1–210.
Hagoort, Peter, Lea Hald, Marcel Bastiaansen & Karl Magnus Petersson 2004. Integration of word meaning and world knowledge in language comprehension. *Science* 304(5669), 438–441.
Hobbs, Jerry R. 1985. Ontological promiscuity. In: *Proceedings of the 23rd Annual Meeting of the Association for Computational Linguistics (=ACL)*. Chicago, IL: ACL, 61–69.
Hobbs, Jerry R. 1992. Metaphor and abduction. In: A. Ortony, J. Slack & O. Stock (eds.). *Communication from an Artificial Intelligence Perspective. Theoretical and Applied Issues*. Berlin: Springer, 35–58.
Hobbs, Jerry R. 2004. Abduction in natural language understanding. In: L. Horn & G. Ward (eds.). *Handbook of Pragmatics*. Malden, MA: Blackwell, 724–741.
Hobbs, Jerry R. 2005. Toward a useful notion of causality for lexical semantics. *Journal of Semantics* 22, 181–209.
Hobbs, Jerry R., William Croft, Todd Davies, Douglas Edwards & Kenneth Laws 1987. Commonsense metaphysics and lexical semantics. *Computational Linguistics* 13, 241–250.

Hobbs, Jerry R., Mark Stickel, Douglas Appelt & Paul Martin 1993. Interpretation as abduction. *Artificial Intelligence* 63, 69–142.
Jackendoff, Ray 1972. *Semantic Interpretation in Generative Grammar*. Cambridge, MA: The MIT Press.
Johnson, Mark 1987. *The Body in the Mind. The Bodily Basis of Meaning, Imagination, and Reason*. Chicago, IL: The University of Chicago Press.
Kilgariff, Adam 2001. Generative lexicon meets corpus data. The case of nonstandard word uses. In: P. Bouillion & F. Busa (eds.). *The Language of Word Meaning*. Cambridge: Cambridge University Press, 312–328.
Lakoff, George 1987. *Women, Fire, and Dangerous Things. What Categories Reveal About the Mind*. Chicago, IL: The University of Chicago Press.
Lenat, Douglas B. & Ramanathan V. Guha 1990. *Building Large Knowledge-based Systems. Representation and Inference in the Cyc Project*. Reading, MA: Addison-Wesley.
McCarthy, John 1980. Circumscription. A form of non-monotonic reasoning. *Artificial Intelligence* 13, 27–39.
Miller, George 1995. WordNet. A lexical database for English. *Communications of the ACM* 38, 39–41.
Pustejovsky, James 1995. *The Generative Lexicon*. Cambridge, MA: The MIT Press.
Rosch, Eleanor 1975. Cognitive representations of semantic categories. *Journal of Experimental Psychology* 104, 192–233.
Shoham, Yoav 1987. Nonmonotonic logics. Meaning and utility. In: J. MacDermott (ed.). *Proceedings of the International Joint Conference on Artificial Intelligence (= IJCAI)* 10. San Mateo, CA: Morgan Kaufmann, 388–393.
Singh, Push 2002. The public acquisition of commonsense knowledge. In: *Proceedings of AAAI Spring Symposium on Acquiring (and Using) Linguistic (and World) Knowledge for Information Access*. Palo Alto, CA: AAAI. http://web.media.mit.edu/~push/AAAI2002-Spring.pdf. December 15, 2010.
Tanenhaus, Michael K. & Sarah Brown-Schmidt 2008. Language processing in the natural world. *Philosophical Transactions of the Royal Society of London, Series B, Biological Sciences* 363, 1105–1122.

Thomas Ede Zimmermann
7 Model-theoretic semantics

1   Truth-conditional semantics —— 182
2   Possible worlds semantics —— 189
3   Model-theoretic semantics —— 209
4   References —— 229

Abstract: *Model-theoretic semantics* is a special form of *truth-conditional semantics*. According to it, the truth-values of sentences depend on certain abstract objects called *models*. Understood in this way, models are mathematical structures that provide the interpretations of the (non-logical) lexical expressions of a language and determine the truth-values of its (declarative) sentences. Originally designed for the semantic analysis of mathematical logic, model-theoretic semantics has become a standard tool in linguistic semantics, mostly through the impact of Richard Montague's seminal work on the analogy between formal and natural languages. As such, it is frequently (and loosely) identified with *possible worlds semantics*, which rests on an identification of sentence meanings with regions in Logical Space, the class of all possible worlds. In fact, the two approaches have much in common and are not always easy to keep apart. In a sense, (i) model-theoretic semantics can be thought of as a restricted form of possible worlds semantics, where models represent possible worlds; in another sense, (ii) model-theoretic semantics can be seen as a wild generalization of possible worlds semantics, treating Logical Space as variable rather than given. Consequently, the present introductory exposition of model-theoretic semantics also covers possible worlds semantics – hopefully helping to disentangle the relationship between the two approaches. It starts with a general discussion of truth-conditional semantics (section 1), the main purpose of which is to provide some motivation and background. Model-theoretic semantics is then approached from the possible worlds point of view (section 2), highlighting the similarities between the two approaches that give rise to perspective (i). The final section 3 turns to model theory as providing a mathematical reconstruction of possible worlds semantics, ultimately arriving at the more abstract perspective (ii).

Thomas Ede Zimmermann, Frankfurt/Main, Germany

https://doi.org/10.1515/9783110589245-007

1 Truth-conditional semantics

The starting point for the truth-conditional approach to semantics is the tight connection between meaning and truth. From a pre-theoretic point of view, linguistic meaning may appear a multi-faceted blend of phenomena, partly subjective and private, partly social and inter-subjective, mostly vague, slippery, and apparently hard to define in precise terms. Nevertheless, there are a few unshakable, yet substantial (non-tautological) insights into meaning. Among these is the contention that differences in truth-value necessitate differences in meaning:

> *Most Certain Principle [MCP]* cf. Cresswell (1982: 69)
>
> If S_1 and S_2 are declarative sentences such that, under given circumstances, S_1 is true whereas S_2 is not, then S_1 and S_2 differ in meaning.

The *MCP* certainly has the flavour of an *a priori* truth. If it is one, an adequate analysis of meaning ought to take care of it by making a conceptual connection with truth; in fact, this connection might lie at the heart of any adequate theoretical reconstruction of meaning. If so, meaning is primarily sentence meaning; for sentences are the bearers of truth, i.e. the only expressions that can be true (or false).

We will say that the *truth value* of a (declarative) sentence *S* is 1 [under given circumstances] if *S* is true [under these circumstances]; and that its truth value […] is 0 otherwise. Then the lesson to be learnt from the *MCP* is that, given arbitrary circumstances, the meaning of a sentence *S* determines its truth value under these circumstances: nothing, i.e. no sentence *S'*, could have that meaning without having the same truth value. Whatever the meanings of (declarative) sentences may be, then, they must somehow determine their *truth conditions*, i.e. the circumstances under which the sentences are true. According to truth-conditional semantics, anything beyond this most marked trait of sentence meanings ought to be left out of consideration (or to pragmatics), thus paving the way for the following 'minimalist' semantic axiom:

> *Basic Principle of Truth-Conditional Semantics [BP]* cf. Wittgenstein (1922: 4.431)
>
> Any two declarative sentences agree in meaning just in case they agree in their truth conditions.

Since by (our) definition, truth conditions are circumstances of truth, the *BP* implies that sentences that differ in meaning, also differ in truth value under at least some circumstances. Truth-conditional semantics owes much of its flavour, as well as some of its problems, to this immediate consequence of the *BP*, to which we will return in section 2.

According to the *BP*, the meanings of sentences *covary* with their truth conditions. It is important to realize (and easy to overlook) that a statement of covariance is not an equation. The – common – *identification* of sentence meanings with truth conditions requires further justification. Some motivation for it may be sought in functionalist considerations, according to which truth conditions suffice to explain the extralinguistic rôles attributed to sentence meaning in social interaction and cognitive processes. Though we cannot go into these matters here, we will later see examples of covarying entities – the *material models* introduced in Section 2.3 – that are less likely to be identified with sentence meanings than truth conditions in the sense envisaged here. Bearing this in mind, we will still read the *BP* as suggesting that the meanings of sentences may as well be taken to be their truth conditions.

In its most radical form, truth-conditional semantics seeks to derive the meanings of non-sentential expressions from sentence meanings, as the *contributions* these expressions make to the truth conditions of the sentences in which they occur; cf. Frege (1884: 71). Without any further specification and constraints, this characterisation of non-sentential meaning is bound to be incomplete. To begin with, the contribution an expression makes to the truth conditions of a sentence in which it occurs, obviously depends on the *position* in which it occurs: the contribution of an expression A occupying position p in a sentence S to the meaning of S must be understood as the contribution of A *as occurring in p*; for the sake of definiteness, positions p can be identified with (certain) partial, injective functions on the domain of expressions, inserting occupants into hosts, so that an (occupant) expression A *occurs in* position p of a (host) expression B just in case $p(A) = B$. Positions in sentences are *structural* positions that need not coincide with positions in surface strings; in particular, the contributions made by the parts of structurally ambiguous (surface) sentences depend on the latters' readings, which have different structures, hosting their parts in different structural positions.

Given their sensitivity to syntactic structure, the truth-conditional contributions of its parts can hardly be determined by looking at one sentence in isolation. Otherwise minimal pairs like the following, taken from Abbott & Hauser (1995: 6, fn. 10), would create problems when it comes to the truth-conditional contributions of their parts:

(1) Someone is <u>buying</u> a car.
(2) Someone is <u>selling</u> a car.

(3) and (4) have the same truth conditions and the same overall structure, in which the underlined verbs occupy the same position. Since the two sentences

are otherwise identical, it would seem that the two alternatives make the same contribution. If so, this contribution cannot be their meaning – after all, the two underlined verb forms are not synonymous and generally do differ in their truth-conditional contributions, as in:

(3) Mary is buying a car.
(4) Mary is selling a car.

Hence, lest the two verbs come out as synonymous, their meanings can only be identified with their truth-conditional contributions if the latter are construed *globally*, taking into account all positions in which the verbs may occur. Generalising from this example, it emerges that sameness of meaning among any non-sentential expressions **A** and **B** (of the same category) requires sameness of truth-conditional contribution throughout the structural positions of all sentences. Since **A** and **B** occupy the same structural position in two sentences S_A and S_B if S_B derives from S_A by putting **B** in place of **A**, this condition on synonymy may be cast in terms of a:

Substitution Principle [Subst]

If two non-sentential expressions *of the same category* have the same meaning, either may replace the other in all positions within any sentence without thereby affecting the truth conditions of that sentence.

The italicized restriction is made so as to not rule out the possibility that two expressions make the same truth-conditional contribution without being grammatically equivalent. As argued in Gazdar et al. (1985: 32), *likely* and *probable* may be cases in point – given the grammatical contrast between *likely to leave* vs. **probable to leave*.

Taken together, the *BP* and *Subst* form the backbone of truth-conditional semantics: the meanings of sentences coincide with their truth conditions; and synonymy among non-sentential expression is restricted by the synonymies among the sentences in which they occur. *Subst* leaves open what kinds of entities the meanings of non-sentential expressions are. Keeping the 'minimalist' spirit behind the passage from the *MCP* to the *BP*, it is tempting to identify them by strengthening *Subst* to a bi-conditional, thereby arriving at a *synonymy criterion*, according to which two (non-sentential) expressions have the same meaning if they may always replace each other within a sentence without affecting the truth conditions of that sentence. Ontologically speaking, this synonymy criterion has meaning *supervene* on truth conditions; cf. Kupffer (2007). However, we will depart from radical truth-conditional semantics and not take it for granted that this criterion always applies; possible counterexamples will be addressed in due course.

The above considerations also support a more general version of *Subst* according to which various synonymous (non-sentential) expressions may be replaced simultaneously. As a result, the meaning of any complex expression can be construed as only depending of the meanings of its immediate parts – thus giving rise to a famous principle, which we note here for future reference:

Principle of Compositionality [Compo]

The meaning of a complex expression functionally depends on the meanings of its immediate parts and the way in which they are combined.

Like *Subst*, *Compo* does not say what kinds of objects non-sentential meanings are. In fact, a *permutation argument* has it that they are hopelessly underdetermined: if a truth-conditional account specified some objects x and y as the meanings of some (non-sentential) expressions A and B, then an alternative account could be given that would also be in line with *Subst*, but according to which x and y have changed their places. We will take a closer look at this argument in section 3.

Even though *Compo* and *Subst* are not committed to a particular concept of non-sentential meaning, some choices might be more natural than others. Indeed, *Subst* falls out immediately if truth-conditional contributions and thus meanings (of non-sentential expressions) are constructed by abstraction, as classes of expressions that make the same truth-conditional contributions in all positions in which they occur: if the meaning of an expressions A is identified with the set of all expressions with which A can be replaced without any change in truth conditions, then *Subst* trivially holds. However, there is a serious problem with this strategy: if (non-sentential) meanings were classes of intersubstitutable expressions, they would be essentially language-dependent. But if meanings were just substitution classes, then meaning-preserving translation between distinct languages would be impossible; and even more absurdly, all expressions of a language would have to change their meanings each time a new word is added to it! This certainly speaks against a construal of meanings in terms of abstraction, even though synonymy classes have proved useful as representatives of meanings in the algebraic study of compositionality; cf. Hodges (2001).

If contributing to truth conditions and conforming to *Subst* were all there is to non-sentential meanings, then there would be no fact of the matter as to what kinds of objects they are; moreover, there would be no obvious criteria for deciding whether two expressions of different languages have the same meaning.

Hence a substantial theory of non-sentential meaning cannot live on *Subst* alone. One way to arrive at such a theory is by finding a natural analogue to the *MCP* that goes beyond the realm of sentences. The most prominent candidate is what may be dubbed the:

Rather Plausible Principle [RPP]

If T_1 and T_2 are terms such that, under given circumstances, T_1 refers to something to which T_2 does not refer, then T_1 and T_2 differ in meaning.

A *term* in the sense of the *RPP* is an expression that may be said to refer to something. Proper names, definite descriptions, and pronouns are cases in point. Thus, in one of its usages, (i) the name *Manfred* refers to a certain person; under the current actual circumstances, (ii) the description *Regine's husband* refers to the same person; and in an email to Manfred Kupffer, I can use (iii) the pronoun *you* to refer to him. Of course, in different contexts, (iii) can also refer to another person; hence the two terms mentioned in the *RPP* must be understood as being used in the same context. Under different (past or counterfactual) circumstances, (ii) may refer to another person, or to no one at all; the *RPP* only mentions the reference of terms under the same circumstances, and in the latter case thus applies vacuously. For the purpose of this survey we will also assume that names with more than one bearer, like (i), are lexically ambiguous; the terms quantified over in the *RPP* must therefore be taken as disambiguated expressions rather than surface forms.

Why should the *RPP* be less certain than the *MCP*? One possible reason comes from ontology, the study of what there is: the exact subject matter of sentences containing referring terms is not necessarily clearly defined, let alone obvious. The reader is referred to the relevant literature on the *inscrutability of reference*; Williams (2005) contains a good, if biased, survey.

Putting ontological qualms aside, we may conclude from the *RPP* that whatever the meanings of terms may be, they must somehow determine their *reference conditions*, i.e. the referents as depending on the circumstances. According to a certain brand of truth-conditional semantics, anything beyond this most marked trait of term meanings ought to be left out of consideration (or to pragmatics), thus giving rise to a stronger version of our 'minimalist' semantic axiom:

Extended Basic Principle of Truth-Conditional Semantics [EBP]

Any two declarative sentences agree in meaning just in case they agree in their truth conditions; and any two terms agree in meaning just in case they agree in their reference conditions.

Like the *BP*, the *EBP* is merely a statement of covariance, not an equation. The – common – identification of term meanings with reference conditions, also requires further 'external' evidence. However, as in the case of the *BP*, we will read the *EBP* as suggesting that term meanings be reference conditions. Following this suggestion, and given *Subst*, the *EBP* may then be used to determine the meanings of at least some non-sentential expressions in a non-arbitrary and at the same time language-independent way, employing a heuristics based on:

Frege's Functional Principle [FFP]

If not specified by the *EBP*, the meaning of an expression **A** is the meaning of (certain) expressions in which **A** occurs as functionally depending on **A**'s occurrence.

Since the functional meanings of parts can be thought of as contributions to host meanings, *FFP* can be seen as a version of Frege's (1884: x) *Context Principle* that is not committed to the radical form of truth-conditional semantics: 'nach der Bedeutung der Wörter muss im Satzzusammenhange, nicht in ihrer Vereinzelung gefragt werden' '[≈'one must ask for the meanings of words in their sentential context, not in isolation']. Obviously, *FFP* is more specific; it also deviates from the original in having term extensions determined directly, in accordance with the *EBP* – and Frege's (1892) later policy.

According to *FFP*, the meaning of an expression **A** that is not a sentence or a term, turns out to be a function assigning meanings of host expressions (in which **A** occurs) to meanings of positions (in which **A** occurs) – where the latter can be made out in case the positions coincide with adjacent expressions whose meanings have been independently identified – either by the *EBP*, or by previous applications of the same strategy. As a case in point, the meanings of *(coordinating) conjunctions* **C** (like *and* and *or*) may be determined from their occurrences in unembedded coordinations of sentences **A** and **B**, i.e. sentences of the form **A C B**; these occurrences are completely determined by the two coordinated sentences and may thus be identified with the ordered pairs (**A**,**B**). Hence, following, the meaning of a conjunction comes out as a function from pairs of sentence meanings to sentence meanings, i.e. a function assigning truth conditions to pairs of truth conditions. In particular, the meaning of *and* assigns the truth conditions of any sentence **A** *and* **B** to the pair consisting of the truth conditions of **A** and the truth conditions of **B**. In a similar vein, by looking at simple predications of the form **T P** (where **T** is a term), the meanings of *predicates* **P** come out as functions assigning sentence meanings to term meanings. Since the latter are determined by the *EBP*, predicate meanings are thus construed as functions from reference conditions to truth conditions. This result may in turn be used to obtain the meanings of *transitive verbs V*, which may take terms *T* as objects to form predicates, the meanings of which have already been identified; hence, by another application of *FFP*, the meaning of a transitive verb comes out as a function assigning predicate meanings to reference conditions (= the meanings of terms in object position).

In one form or another, the heuristics just sketched has been applied widely, and rather successfully, in linguistic semantics. Following it, a large variety of expressions can be assigned meanings whose primary function is to contribute to truth and reference conditions without depending on any particular language. Nevertheless, for a variety of reasons, following *FFP* (in the way indicated here) does not settle the issue of determining meaning in a fully principled, non-arbitrary way:

- As the above examples show, the meanings of expressions depend on a choice of *primary occurrences*, i.e. positions in which they can be read off the immediate context. However, in general there is no way of telling which of a given number of grammatical constructions ought to serve this purpose; and the choice may influence the meanings obtained by applying *FFP*. *Quantifier phrases* – expressions like *nobody*; *most linguists*; *every atom in the universe*; etc. – are cases in point. Customarily they are analyzed by putting them in subject position and thus interpret them as functions from predicate meanings (determined in the way above) to sentence meanings (determined by the *EBP*). However, they also occur in a host of other environments, e.g. as direct objects. If the latter were chosen as their primary occurrences, their meanings would come out as functions from transitive verb meanings (determined in the way above) to predicate meanings (determined in the way above); and if both environments were taken together, they would be functions defined on both predicate and verb meanings, etc. Although there are one-one correspondences between these different construals of quantifier phrases, it would seem that none of them can lay claim to being more natural than the others.
- Once determined via *FFP* (in the way indicated here), there is no guarantee that the meaning of an expression will behave compositionally beyond the primary occurrences chosen. For instance, it is well known that the meaning of *and* determined along the above lines, can be put to work in predicate coordinations such as *sing and dance* – basically due to the existence of corresponding clausal paraphrases of the form *x sings and x dances*; but is not (or not so easily) adapted to cover 'collective' readings of coordinate proper names as in *John and Mary are performing a duet*.
- Due to limits of expressiveness of the language under scrutiny, the range of meanings covered by the primary occurrences of a given expression may

be restricted in various ways, sometimes by merely accidental gaps in the lexicon. For instance, if constructed strictly along the above lines, the predicate meanings will depend on what terms there are, and what they mean (i.e. their reference conditions, according to the *EBP*). However, in order to make the meanings thus determined general enough, their construction often crucially involves a certain amount of *idealisation*. Thus, in order to have two predicates from different languages come out as synonymous, their meanings would have to have the same domains; but then the meanings of the terms of the two languages need not be precisely the same: maybe one of them contains a name for some peculiar object that is hard to describe – a certain grain of sand, say – in which case it is not obvious that, in the other language, there is a corresponding term with the same reference conditions. In fact the idealisations made in model-theoretic semantics frequently go far beyond the inclusion of hard-to-describe objects as referents. As a result, the synonymy criterion mentioned above cannot always be upheld. We will return to this point.

These limitations notwithstanding, there can be no doubt that *FFP* has led to considerable advances in natural language semantics. Earlier approaches, trying to proceed in a bottom-up fashion, had encountered serious difficulties when it came to distinguishing the various modes of composing phrasal from lexical meanings. By changing the direction of analysis, *FFP* solves these problems and at the same time offers a much more differentiated picture of the varieties of meaning: combination mostly proceeds by functional application, and while earlier approaches were confined to (combinations of) content words, *FFP* strives to make all expressions amenable to semantic analysis, including functional ones such as determiners and conjunctions.

2 Possible worlds semantics

2.1 Logical space

According to the *EBP*, the meanings of sentences and terms are of a conditional nature: given the circumstances, they determine a truth value or a referent. Following semantic tradition, we will call the object that the meaning of an expression determines (for given circumstances), as the *extension* of the expression (for these circumstances); cf. Carnap (1947). In other words, the extension of a sentence is its truth value; and the extension of a term is its referent. It is a remarkable fact that the above strategy for determining meanings may be used to generalize the notion of extension to a wide range of expressions far beyond sentences and terms. In order to do so, *FFP* needs to be adapted so as to describe the extension of an expression *A* as a function assigning extensions of host expressions to extensions of positions in which *A* occurs. We thus have what may be called the:

Extensional Version of Frege's Functional Principle

If not specified by the *EBP*, the extension of an expression **A** is the contribution **A** makes to the extensions of (certain) expressions in which **A** (immediately) occurs.

As a case in point, the extensions of coordinating conjunctions may be determined from their occurrences in coordinations of sentences **A** and **B**; as we have seen, these occurrences are completely determined by the two sentences coordinated and may thus be identified with the ordered pairs (**A**,**B**). Hence, following (the extensional version of *FFP*), the extension of a conjunction comes out as a (*binary*) *truth table*, i.e. a function assigning truth values (= extensions of coordinated sentences) to pairs of truth values (= extensions of coordinations). In particular, the extension of *and* assigns the truth value of any sentence of the form *A and B* to the pair consisting of the truth value of **A** and the truth value of **B**, i.e. it assigns 1 to the pair (1,1) and 0 to the other three pairs of truth values. In a similar vein, setting out with simple predications, the extensions of predicates come out as functions assigning truth values (= sentence extensions) to individuals (= term extensions). Similarly, predicate extensions turn out to be characteristic functions of sets of individuals, i.e. functions from individuals to truth values. This result may in turn be used to obtain the extensions of transitive verbs, which come out as curried binary relations, i.e. functions assigning characteristic functions (= predicate extensions) to individuals (= the extensions of terms in object position).

[NB: The *characteristic function* of a set *M* of individuals is that function *f* that assigns 1 to any member of *M* and 0 to all other individuals:

$$f = \{(u, 1) \mid u \in M\} \cup \{(u, 0) \mid u \in U \setminus M\}$$

where *U* is the set of all individuals. Given a binary relation *R* among individuals, i.e. a set of ordered pairs of individuals, the *curried version of R* is the function that assigns the characteristic function of $\{y \in U \mid (y, x) \in R\}$ to any individual $x \in U$. It is not hard to see that sets of individuals and their characteristic functions stand in a one-one correspondence; similarly, binary relations among individuals correspond to their curried versions. Given this connection, we will not always distinguish between the extensions of predicates and transitives and the corresponding sets and binary relations].

In a similar vein, the extensions of quantifier phrases can be identified as (characteristic functions of) sets of predicate extensions; and once nouns are regarded as synonymous with predicates, the extensions of determiners turn out to be (curried) relations among predicate extensions. In particular, the members of the extension of *everybody* are precisely the supersets of the set of all persons; the extension of *no* is the relation of disjointness among sets of individuals; etc. Since the truth value of a sentence with a quantifier in subject position may depend on the value of the predicate extension for nameless individuals, the aforementioned idealised generalisation of predicate extensions to functions operating on arbitrary individuals turns out to be crucial for this step.

The above extensional adaptation is much more limited in its application than *FFP* in general: it only works as long as extensions behave compositionally; otherwise it is bound to fail; and there are a number of environments that cannot be analyzed by compositionally combining extensions. Still, a considerable portion of the grammatical constructions of English is *extensional* in that the extensional version of *FFP* may be applied to them, thus extending the notion of extension to ever more kinds of expressions. In the present and the following section we will be exclusively concerned with extensional constructions and, for convenience, pretend that all constructions are extensional.

The generalisation of extensions to expressions of (almost) arbitrary categories leads to a natural theoretical construction of meanings in terms of extensions and circumstances. The key to this construction lies in a generalisation of the *EBP*, which comes for free for those expressions whose extensions have been constructed in the way indicated, i.e. using the extensional version of *FFP*. To see this, we have to be more specific about truth conditions and reference conditions (in the sense intended here): since they are truth values and referents as depending on circumstances, we will henceforth take them to be functions assigning the former to the latter. This identification obviously presupposes that, whatever circumstances may be, they collectively form a set that may serve as the domain of these functions. Though we will not be entirely specific as to the nature of this set, we assume that it is vast, and that its members do not miss a detail:

Vastness: *Circumstances may be as hypothetical as can be.*
Detail: *Circumstances are as specific as can be.*

Vastness reflects the *raison d'être* of circumstances in semantic theory: according to the *EBP*, they serve to differentiate the meanings of non-synonymous sentences and terms by providing them with distinct truth values and referents, respectively. In order to fulfill this task in an adequate way, actual circumstances – those met in the actual world – obviously do not suffice, as a random example shows:

(5) The physicist who discovered the X-rays died in Munich.
(6) The first Nobel laureate in physics died in Munich.

As the educated reader knows, it so happens that the German physicist Wilhelm Conrad Röntgen discovered a phenomenon known as *X-rays* in 1895, was subsequently awarded the first Nobel prize in physics in 1901, and died in Munich in 1923. Hence the sentences (5) and (6) are both true; and their subjects refer to the same person. In fact, (5) and (6) are true under any actual circumstances; likewise, their subjects share their referent under any actual circumstances. Nevertheless, (5) and (6) are far from being synonymous, and neither are the definite descriptions in their subject position. In order to reflect these semantic differences in their truth and reference conditions, respectively, circumstances are called for under which (5) and (6) differ in truth value and, consequently, their subjects do not corefer. Such circumstances are not hard to imagine; the inventive reader is invited to concoct his or her pertinent favourite scenario. Since it is hardly foreseeable what kinds of differences are needed in order to separate two non-synonymous sentences or terms by circumstances under which their extensions do not coincide, we will assume that any conceivable circumstances count as evidence for non-synonymy, however far-fetched or bizarre they may be. The following pair, inspired by Macbeath (1982), is a case in point:

(7) Dr Who ate himself.
(8) Dr Who is his own father.

Lest both (7) and (8) come out as false for all circumstances and thus as synonymous, there better be circumstances that contradict current science, thereby reflecting the meaning difference between the two sentences.

Detail is an assumption made mostly for convenience and definiteness; but once made, it cannot be ignored. It captures the idea that circumstances are chosen in such a way as to determine the truth values of any sentence whatsoever. As far as actual circumstances are concerned, this is a rather natural assumption. My present circumstances are such that I am sitting in a train traveling through northern regions of Germany at a fairly high speed. I have no idea what precisely the speed is, nor do I know where exactly the train is right now, how many passengers are on it, how old the engineer is, etc. But all of these details, and innumerable others, are resolved by these circumstances, which are as specific as can be. The point of *Detail* is that counterfactual (= non-actual) circumstances are just as specific. Hence if I had been on a space shuttle instead of riding a train, the circumstances that I would have been in would have included a specific velocity, a specific number of co-passengers, etc. To be sure, these details could be filled in in different ways, all of which correspond to different counterfactual circumstances. Given *Detail*, then, counterfactual circumstances are unlike the ordinary conception of worlds of imagination or fiction: stories and novels usually, nay always, leave open a lot of details – like the exact number of hairs on the protagonist's head, etc. If anything, worlds of fiction correspond to *sets* of circumstances; for instance, 'the world of Sherlock Holmes' corresponds to the set of (counterfactual) circumstances that are in accordance with whatever Conan Doyle's stories say, and disagree on all kinds of unsettled details.

As was said above, we assume that the totality of all actual and counterfactual circumstances forms a rather large set which is called *Logical Space*; cf. Wittgenstein (1922: 3.4 & *passim*). We will follow logical and semantic tradition and refer to the elements of Logical Space as *possible worlds* rather than circumstances, even though the term is slightly misleading in that it not only suggests lack of detail (as was just noted) but also a certain grandeur, which the members of Logical Space need not have; it will be left open here whether possible worlds are all-inclusive agglomerations of facts, or whether they could also correspond to more mundane (!), medium-sized situations. What is important is that Logical Space is sufficiently rich to differentiate the meanings of arbitrary non-synonymous sentences and terms. Yet even the macroscopic *Vastness* of Logical Space and microscopic *Details* of its worlds cannot guarantee that any two sentences that appear to differ in meaning also differ in their truth conditions. Thus, e.g., (9)–(10) are true of precisely the same possible worlds, but arguably differ in meaning:

(9) General Beauregard Lee is a woodchuck.
(10) General Beauregard Lee is a groundhog, and either he lives in Georgia, or he does not live in Georgia.

(9) and (10) are *logically equivalent*, i.e. their truth values coincide in all possible worlds. By definition, logical equivalence marks the limit of truth-conditional analysis of (sentence) meaning: the relation holds between two sentences if no possible worlds, however remote and however detailed they may be, can distinguish them. Consequently, whatever the felt differences between logically equivalent sentences like (9) and (10), they cannot be accounted for by truth-conditional semantics alone, because they are not reflected in Logical Space.

We define the *intension* of an expression ***A*** as the function that assigns to each possible world the extension of ***A*** at (i.e.: for) that world. Since the intensions of sentences are functions characterising sets of possible worlds, they may be construed as forming a part of the power set of Logical Space. Using standard terminology, we will refer to the members of this power set, i.e. the subsets of Logical Space, as *propositions* and say that a sentence *S* *expresses* a proposition *p* just in case *p* is (or, more precisely: characterises) the intension of *S*. Like all power sets, the set of propositions has a straightforward algebraic structure induced by the familiar Boolean operations (union, intersection, and complement) and the concomitant subset relation; this is why the power set of Logical Space is also known as the *algebra of propositions*.

As far as sentences and terms are concerned, the *EBP* says that synonymy may be equated with sameness of intension. A straightforward, though tedious, inductive argument shows that this equation generalises to arbitrary expressions *A* with extensions that have been constructed by applying (the extensional version of) *FFP*; for reasons of space we leave this for the reader to verify.

We will end this section with a typical analysis of a simple example within the framework of possible worlds semantics:

(11) Every boy fancies Mary and Jane pouts.

The truth conditions of (11) will be specified by spelling out what it takes to make (11) true at an arbitrary world *w* (which we will now keep fixed). The lexical starting points should be clear from the above remarks and observations: the extension of the conjunction is a truth table; the extensions of the proper names are their bearers; those of the noun and the intransitive verb are (characteristic functions of) sets of individuals; the transitive verb has a (curried) binary relation as its extension; and the extension of the quantificational determiner is a (curried) relation between (characteristic functions of) sets of individuals – to wit, the relation of subsethood. Writing '$\|A\|^w$' for the extension of an expression *A* at world *w*, we thus have:

(12) a. $\|\textbf{every}\|^w = \lambda P. \lambda Q. \ulcorner P \subseteq Q \urcorner$
     b. $\|\textbf{boy}\|^w = \lambda x. \ulcorner x \text{ is a boy in } w \urcorner$
     c. $\|\textbf{fancies}\|^w = \lambda x. \lambda y. \ulcorner y \text{ fancies } x \text{ in } w \urcorner$
     d. $\|\textbf{Mary}\|^w = \text{Mary}$; $\|\textbf{Jane}\|^w = \text{Jane}$
     e. $\|\textbf{and}\|^w = \lambda u. \lambda v. u \times v$
     f. $\|\textbf{pouts}\|^w = \lambda x. \ulcorner x \text{ pouts in } w \urcorner$

A few words on the notation used in the equations (12) are in order:
– As usual in formal semantics, '$\lambda x. \ldots x \ldots$' denotes the function assigning to *x* whatever '$\ldots x \ldots$' denotes.

- If '...' is a statement, then '⊦...⊣' is its truth value, i.e. '⊦...⊣' is short for 'the truth value that is identical to 1 just in case ...'.
- In (12a), relations are identified with characteristic functions and, moreover, the succession order of arguments follows the surface bracketing of quantifier phrases, according to which the outermost argument ('*P*') corresponds to the extension of the noun.
- (12e) exploits the fact that truth values are numbers that can be subjected to arithmetical operations – in this case multiplication.
- For simplicity, the obvious temporal dependence of the right-hand sides of the equations (12b) and (12c) have been suppressed and may be thought of as being supplied by the utterance context.

Since the constituents of (11) all constitute primary occurrences of one of their parts, their extensions can be derived by functional application:

(13) a. ||**every boy fancies Mary**||^w
    = ||**every**||^w (||**boy**||)^w (||**fancies**||^w (||**Mary**||^w))
    = ⊦{x. ⊦x is a boy in w} ⊆ {y | y fancies Mary in w}⊣
  b. ||**Jane pouts**||^w
    = ||**pouts**||^w (||**Jane**||)^w
    = ⊦Jane pouts in w⊣
  c. ||**every boy fancies Mary and Jane pouts**||^w
    = ||**and**||^w (||**Jane pouts**||^w) (||**every boy fancies Mary**||^w)
    = ⊦Jane pouts in w⊣ × ⊦{x | x is a boy in w} ⊆ {y | y fancies Mary in w}⊣

– i.e. the product of the two truth values determined in (13a) and (13b), which is 1 just in case Jane pouts in w and the boys all fancy Mary in w. This appears to be a correct characterisation of the truth conditions (literally) expressed by (11).

2.2 Material models

As long as they can be derived compositionally from the extensions of their immediate parts, the extensions of complex expressions are fully determined by the extensions of their ultimate parts and the way the latter are combined. So in order to specify the extensions of arbitrary (extensional) expressions, it suffices to specify *(a)* the extensions of all (extensional) lexical expressions and *(b)* the way the (extensional) grammatical constructions combine them. If these constructions constitute the primary contexts of expressions analyzed in terms of (the extensional version of *FFP*), *(b)* is always a matter of functional application. For instance, since the primary occurrences of predicates P are simple predications $T\,P$, the extensions of the latter come out as the result of applying the extensions of the former to those of the subjects T:

(14) $\|T\,P\|^w = \|P\|^w (\|T\|^w)$

Other (extensional) constructions may require some ingenuity on the semanticist's part in order to determine the precise way in which extensions combine. Quantified objects are an infamous case in point. As the reader may verify, for any possible world w, the extension of a predicate of the form $V\,Q$, where V is transitive verb and Q is a quantifier phrase (in direct object position), can be given by the following equation:

(15) $\|V\,Q\|^w = \lambda x.\, \|Q\|^w (\lambda y.\, \|V\|^w (y)(x))$

Like (14), equation (15) completely specifies the extension of a certain kind of complex expression in terms of the extensions of its immediate parts; and it does so in a perfectly general manner, for arbitrary worlds w. By definition, this is so for all extensional constructions, which are extensional precisely in that the extensions of the expressions they combine determine the extensions of the resulting phrases, thus giving rise to general equations like (14) or (15). In particular, then, the combinatorial part *(b)* of the specification of extensions does not depend on the particular circumstances envisaged. It thus turns out that the world dependence of extensions is entirely a matter of lexical specification *(a)*. Hence the rôle worlds play in the determination of extensions can be seen as being restricted to the extensions of lexical expressions – the rest is compositionality, captured by general equations like (14) and (15). To the extent that the determination of extensions is the only rôle possible worlds w play in (compositional extensional) semantics, they could be identified with functions assigning extensions to lexical expressions. If A is a lexical expression, we would thus have:

(16) $\|A\|^w = F_w(A)$

In (16) F_w is a function assigning to any expression in its domain the extension of that expression at world w. What precisely is the domain of F_w? It has just been noted that it only contains lexical expressions – but does it include all of them? A brief reflection shows that this need not even be so; for some of the equations of the form (16) do not depend on a particular choice of w. For instance, as noted above, under any circumstances w the extension of a (sentence-) coordinating conjunction *and* is a binary function on truth values; the same goes for other 'logical' particles:

(17) a. $\|\textbf{and}\|^w = \lambda u.\, \lambda v.\, u \times v$ [= (12e)]
 b. $\|\textbf{or}\|^w = \lambda u.\, \lambda v.\, (u + v) - (u \times v)$
 c. $\|\textbf{not}\|^w = \lambda u.\, 1 - u$

The equations in (17) imply that, in any worlds w and w', the extensions of *and*, *or*, and *not* remain stable: $\|\textbf{and}\|^w = \|\textbf{and}\|^{w'}$, $\|\textbf{or}\|^w = \|\textbf{or}\|^{w'}$, and $\|\textbf{not}\|^w = \|\textbf{not}\|^{w'}$. This being so, the specifications of the world-dependent extensions of lexical expressions may safely skip such logical words. A similar case can be made for quantificational determiners and the *is* of identity:

(18) a. $\|\textbf{every}\|^w = \lambda P.\, \lambda Q.\, \vdash P \subseteq Q \dashv$ [= (12a)]
 b. $\|\textbf{no}\|^w = \lambda P.\, \lambda Q.\, \vdash P \cap Q = \varnothing \dashv$
 c. $\|\textbf{is}\|^w = \lambda x.\, \lambda y.\, \vdash x = y \dashv$

Again, the extensions specified in (18) do not seem to depend on the particular world w. However, there is a subtle difference to the equations in (17), which comes out by closer inspection of the ranges of the λ-bound variables: whereas 'u' and 'v' in (17) always stand for the truth values 0 and 1, in (18) 'x' and 'y' stand for individuals and 'P' and 'Q' for sets of them – but which, and how many, individuals there are, depends on the particular world w. As a consequence, the equations in (18) do depend on w, a fact which is obscured by our loose notation. On the other hand, the latter three equations *only* depend on what the set of all individuals in the world w is. In other words, their truth does not depend on the particularities of the world but (at most) on the domain of individuals. In this respect, logical words as analyzed in (17) and (18) are atypical: the extensions of the vast majority of lexical expressions do vary across Logical Space and also depend on more than what the domain of individuals is. As far as their extensions concerned, lexical equations like (19) represent the more typical cases than (17) and (18):

(19) $\|\textbf{boy}\|^w = \lambda x.\, \vdash x \text{ is a boy in } w \dashv$ [= (12b)]

One may thus distinguish three kinds of lexical expressions: *(i) truth-functional* ones, whose extension remains the very same across Logical Space; *(ii) combinatorial* ones, whose extension depends only on what the domain of individuals is; and *(iii) non-logical* ones, whose extensions may depend on all sorts of worldly facts. It has become customary to reflect this distinction in the assignments of world-dependent extensions to lexical expressions:

Definition

Given a possible world w and a language L, the *material model (for L based on w)* is the pair $\mathcal{M}_w = (U_w, F_w)$ consisting of the *domain* of individuals U_w in w and the lexical interpretation function F_w which assigns to every non-logical lexical expression **A** of L the extension of **A** at w.

The above definition is to be understood as presupposing a prior and independent specification of the non-logical vocabulary N_L of the language L under scrutiny – and thus implies that the interpretation functions of any two material models share their domain, which is precisely the set N_L. It should then be clear how the extensions of arbitrary expressions **A** of a language L can be characterised in terms of, and as depending on, material models $\mathcal{M}_w = (U_w, F_w)$. This characterisation can be given in the form of an inductive definition, which starts out with the lexical material and then moves on step by step, following the grammatical construction principles of L, which derive (analysed and disambiguated) complex expressions from their (immediate) parts, thereby creating an increase in syntactic complexity. The following sample clauses offer a glimpse of the overall structure and content of such a definition for an extensional fragment E of English:

(20) For any expression **A** of E and any material model $\mathcal{M}_w = (U_w, F_w)$ for E, the extension of **A** relative to $\mathcal{M}_w$ – $|A|^{\mathcal{M}_w}$ – is determined by the following induction (on the grammatical complexity of **A**):

(i-a) $|\textbf{and}|^{\mathcal{M}_w} = \lambda u.\, \lambda v.\, u \times v$ ... where $u \in \{0, 1\}$ and $v \in \{0, 1\}$

...   ...

(ii-a) $|\textbf{every}|^{\mathcal{M}_w} = \lambda P.\, \lambda Q.\, \vdash P \subseteq Q \dashv$ where $P \subseteq U_w$ and $Q \subseteq U_w$

...   ...

(iii) $|A|^{\mathcal{M}_w} = F_w(A)$, if $A \in N_E$

(iv-a) $|D\,N|^{\mathcal{M}_w} = |D|^{\mathcal{M}_w}(|N|^{\mathcal{M}_w})$

if **D N** is a quantifier phrase, where **D** is a quantificational determiner and **N** is a count noun;

...   ...

In order to complete (29), clauses *(i)* and *(ii)* would have to take care of all *logical words* of E. We will now give a semantic characterisation of logical words that helps to draw the line between the non-logical part N_E – or N_L in general – and the rest of the lexicon. We have already seen that one characteristic feature of logical words is that their extension is largely world-independent: it may depend on which individuals there are in the world but it does not depend on any particular worldly facts. However, having a world-independent intension (even *stricto sensu*) is not sufficient for being a logical word. Indeed, thereare good reasons for taking the intensions of proper names as constant functions over Logical Space.; cf. Kripke (1972), where terms with constant intensions are called *rigid designators*. Still, a name like *Jesus* can hardly be called logical even if its bearer turned out to be present in every possible world. What, then, makes a word, or an expression in general, *logical*? The (rather standard) answer given here rests on the intuition that the extension of a logical word can be described in purely structural terms. As a case in point, the determiner *no* is logical because its extension may be described as *the relation that holds between two sets of individuals just in case they do not overlap* – or, in terms of characteristic functions: *that function which, successively applied to two characteristic functions (of sets of individuals), yields (the truth value) 1 just in case these functions do not both assign 1 to any individual*. If one thinks of functions as configurations of arrows leading from arguments to values, then the extension of *no* – and that of a logical word in general – can be described solely in terms of the abstract arrangement of these arrows, without mentioning any particular individuals or other extensions – apart from the truth values. In other words, the descriptions do not depend on the identity of the individuals, which may be anything – or replaced by any other individuals. The idea, then, is to characterise logical words as having extensions that are *stable under any replacement of individuals*. In order to make this intuition precise, a bit of notation should come in handy.

It is customary to classify the extensions of expressions according to whether they derive (i) from the *EBP*, or (ii) by application of *FFP*: (i) the extensions of sentences are said to be of *type t*, those of terms are of type *e*; (ii) if the extension of an expression operates on extensions of some type *a* resulting in extensions of some type *b*, it is said to be of type (a,b). In other words, (i) *t* is the type of truth values; *e* is the type of individuals (or entities); (ii) (a,b) is the type of (total) functions from *a* to *b*. More precisely, *t* is a canonical label of the set of truth values, etc.; '*t*' is mnemonic for *truth value*, '*e*' abbreviates *entity*. In this notation, the extensions of sentences, terms, coordinating conjunctions, predicates, transitives, quantificational phrases, and determiners are of types t; e; $(t,(t,t))$; (e,t); $(e,(e,t))$; $((e,t),t)$; and $((e,t),((e,t),t))$, respectively. It should be noted that, unlike the extensions of the expressions, their types remain the same throughout Logical Space (and thus across all material models). The function τ_L assigning to each expression of a language *L* the unique type of its extensions is called the *type assignment* of *L*; we take τ_L to be part of the specification of the language *L* (and will usually suppress the subscript).

Now for the characterisation of logicality. Given (not necessarily distinct) possible worlds w and w', a *replacement* (of w by w') is a bijective function from the domain of individuals of w to the domain of individuals of w' (which must therefore have the same cardinality). Replacements may then be generalized from individuals (of type e) to all types of extensions: given a replacement ρ (from w to w'), the following recursive equations define corresponding functions ρ_a, for each type a:

- $\rho_e = \rho$;
- $\rho_t = \{(0,0),(1,1)\}$ [$= \lambda x.\, x$, where 'x' ranges over truth values];
- $\rho_{(a,b)} = \lambda f.\, \{(\rho_a(x), \rho_b(y)) \mid f(x) = y\}$ [where 'f' ranges over functions of type (a,b)].

In other words, the generalised replacement leaves truth values untouched – because they define the structure of extensions like characteristic functions – and maps functional extensions to corresponding functions, replacing arrows from x to y by arrows between substitutes; it is readily seen that, for any type a, ρ_a is the identical mapping on the extensions of type a if (and only if) ρ is the identical mapping on the domain of individuals. Given the above generalisation of replacements from individuals to objects of arbitrary types, a logical word **A** can be defined as one whose extensions cannot be affected by replacements. More precisely, if f is an intension of type a (i.e. a function from W to extensions of type a), then f is *(replacement-) invariant* just in case for any replacements ρ and ρ' of w by some world w', it holds that $\rho_a(f(w)) = \rho'_a(f(w))$; and *logical words* may then be characterised as lexical expressions **A** with invariant intensions: $\rho_{\tau(A)}(\|A\|^w) = \rho'_{\tau(A)}(\|A\|^w)$, for any worlds w and replacements ρ and ρ' of w by some world w'.

The definition implies that $\rho_{\tau(A)}(\|A\|^w) = \|A\|^w$, whenever **A** is a logical word and ρ is a replacement from a world w to itself (or any world with the same domain of individuals) –which is a classical criterion of logicality, going back to Lindenbaum & Tarski (1935), and rediscovered by a number of scholars since; cf. MacFarlane (2008: Section 5) for a survey. Extensive treatments of replacements in (models of) Logical Space can be found in Fine (1977) and Rabinowicz (1979).

Derivatively, we will also call extensions of types a invariant if they happen to be the values of invariant intensions of type a. Invariant extensions are always of a peculiar, combinatorial kind. In particular, and ignoring all too small universes (of cardinalities 1 and 2), extensions of type e are never invariant; there are only two invariant extensions of type (e,t), viz. the empty one and the universe; and four of type $(e,(e,t))$, viz. identity, distinctness, and the two trivial (empty and universal) binary relations; extensions of type $((e,t),t)$ are invariant just in case they classify sets of individuals according to their cardinalities; etc. As a consequence, the extensions of logical words are severely limited by the invariance criterion. Still, it takes more for an intension to be invariant than just having invariant extensions; in particular, a function that assigns different invariant extensions to worlds with the same domain cannot be invariant. More generally, if the domains U and U' of two material models $\mathcal{M}$ and $\mathcal{M}'$ have the same cardinality, the invariance condition on logical words of the second kind *(ii)* ensure that, intuitively speaking, they have analogous extensions. Thus, e.g., a determiner whose extension relative to $\mathcal{M}$ is the subset-relation on U will denote the subset on U' in $\mathcal{M}'$.

However, if U and U' have different cardinalities, logicality does not exclude that the extension varies between, say, subsethood on U and disjointness on U'. Analogous observations can be made in connection with the logical operations associated with syntactic constructions. Unfortunately, there seems to be no generally agreed identification procedure of extensions across varying domains to exclude such cardinality-sensitive shifts; cf. Machover (1994: 1081ff); Casanovas (2007). We will briefly return to this point in *Section 3.1*.

The reader may now verify for him- or herself that all extensions specified in clauses *(i)* and *(ii)* of (20) are indeed invariant. It may also be noted that the combinations specified in clause *(iv)* are invariant once they are themselves construed as extensions: the compositional combination of extensions generally proceeds by way of purely structural operations, corresponding to invariant functional extensions. The reader is reminded that we restrict attention to extensional constructions; non-extensional compositionality will be addressed in the following section.

The gaps in (20), then, are meant to be filled in as follows. The extensions of *truth-functional* logical words, i.e. those whose type consists of *t*s, commas, and brackets only, are specified in clause *(i)*; and this specification is entirely independent of any particular world. The extensions of all other logical words (which, for lack of a better term, we continue to call *combinatorial*) are specified in clause *(ii)*; their intensions are invariant, and their extensions in general depend on the domain of individuals. Finally, the ways in which the extensions of complex expressions depend on the extensions of their immediate parts, correspond to invariant (and generally domain-dependent) functional extensions and are specified in clause *(iv)*, according to the syntactic constructions involved. This ends our general characterisation of how extensions are determined according to material models.

Using the obvious correspondence with (12), (20) may then be completed to recapitulate the above analysis of (11), replacing possible worlds w with corresponding material models $\mathcal{M}_w$ and arriving at the following equation:

(21) $|\text{every boy fancies Mary and Jane pouts}|^{\mathcal{M}_w}$
= ⊢Jane pouts in w⊣ × ⊢{x | x is a boy in w} ⊆ {y | y fancies Mary in w}⊣

(21) easily follows from [a completion of] (20). In fact, once the relevant inductive clauses are adapted in the fashion illustrated above, equation (22a) holds quite generally, for any expression A of a language L and any world w and material model $\mathcal{M}_w$; and since (22a) holds for *all* expressions A (of a given language L), then (22b) is true of all expressions A and B (of the same language):

(22) a. $|A|^{\mathcal{M}_w} = \|A\|^w$
 b. $\|A\|^w = \|B\|^w$ iff $|A|^{\mathcal{M}_w} = |B|^{\mathcal{M}_w}$

In other words, two expressions are synonymous just in case their extensions coincide across all material models. As a consequence, material models can also be used to characterise sense relations in quite the same way as possible worlds were above. For instance, a sentence S implies a sentence S' in the sense of the above definition just in case the intension of the former is a subset of the latter, i.e. $\{w \mid \|S\|^w = 1\} \subseteq \{w \mid \|S'\|^w = 1\}$, which by (22a) is the case iff $\{w \mid |S|^{\mathcal{M}_w} = 1\} \subseteq \{w \mid |S'|^{\mathcal{M}_w} = 1\}$. Similar arguments apply to the other sense relations defined above.

Let us define the *L-intension* $|A|$ of an expression A (of a language L) as the function that assigns A's extension (according to $\mathcal{M}_w$) to each material model: $|A|(\mathcal{M}_w) = |A|^{\mathcal{M}_w}$, i.e. $|A| = \lambda \mathcal{M}_w. |A|^{\mathcal{M}_w}$. Observation (22) shows that L-intensions are as good as intensions when it comes to determining extensions; and we have seen that they may also be used to reconstruct sense relations defined via intensions, basically on account of (22b). Moreover, the Boolean structure of the set of propositions *expressible* in L (= those that happen to be the intensions of a sentence of L) turns out to be isomorphic to the Boolean structure of L-propositions (= the L-intensions of the sentences of L): as the patient reader may want to verify, the mapping from $\|S\|^w$ to $|S|^{\mathcal{M}_w}$ is one-one (injective) and preserves algebraic (Boolean) structure in that $\|S\|^w \subseteq \|S'\|^w$ iff $|S|^{\mathcal{M}_w} \subseteq |S'|^{\mathcal{M}_w}$, $\|S\|^w \cap \|S'\|^w = |S|^{\mathcal{M}_w} \cap |S'|^{\mathcal{M}_w}$, etc. The tight relation between Logical Space and the set of material models can also be gleaned from considering worlds that cannot be distinguished by the expressions of a given language L:

Definition

If w and w' are possible worlds and L is a language, then w is *L-indistinguishable* from w' – in symbols: $w \equiv_L w'$ – iff $\|A\|^w = \|A\|^{w'}$, for any expression A of L.

In general, L-indistinguishability will not collapse into identity. The special case in which it does, will be marked for future reference:

Definition

A language L is *discriminative* iff no two distinct possible worlds w and w' are L-indistinguishable.

Hence, in a discriminative language L any two distinct possible worlds w and w', can be distinguished by some expression A: $\|A\|^w \neq \|A\|^{w'}$; it is not hard to see that in this case the material models stand in a one-one correspondence with Logical Space. In particular, if L contains a term the referent of which at a given world is that world itself, L will certainly be discriminative; arguably, the definite description *the world* is such a term, thus rendering English discriminative. In any case, for almost all languages L, any two L-indistinguishable worlds give rise to the same material model:

(23) If $w \equiv_L w'$, then $\mathcal{M}_w = \mathcal{M}_{w'}$.

As a consequence, material models stand in a one-one correspondence to the equivalence classes induced by L-indistinguishability (which is obviously an equivalence relation).

Since L-intensions and material models are suited to playing the role of worlds in determining extensions and to characterising Boolean structure, one may wonder whether they could replace worlds and intensions in general. In other words, is it possible to do (extensional) semantics without Logical Space altogether? In particular, could meaning be defined in terms of material models instead of possible worlds? Ontological thrift seems to support this option: on the face of it, material models are rather down-to-earth mathematical structures as compared to the dubious figments of imagination thatpossible worlds may appear to the semantic layman. However, this impression is mistaken: though material models are mathematical structures, they consist of precisely the stuff that possible worlds are made of, viz. fictional individuals under fictional circumstances. Still, replacing intensions with L-intensions may turn out to be, if not ontologically less extravagant, at least theoretically more parsimonious, sparing us a baroque theory of Logical Space and its structure. However, this is not obvious either:
- So far material models have been defined in terms of Logical Space, since the extension a material model assigns to an expression A depends on details about w. If material models are to replace worlds altogether,

an independent characterisation for them would have to be given. For instance, we have seen that no possible world separates (9) from (10), particularly because there is no intensional difference between *woodchuck* and *groundhog*. Hence these two nouns have the same L-intension: this is a consequence of the above definition of a material model, relating it to the world w on which it is based; it is reflected in the general equation (20*iii*). Now, if the very notion of a material model is going to be defined independently of Logical Space, then the coincidence of |**woodchuck**|$^{\mathcal{M}_w}$ and |**groundhog**|$^{\mathcal{M}_w}$ in all material models $\mathcal{M}_w$ would have to be guaranteed in some other way, without reference to the worlds these models are based on. Hence some restriction to the effect that no model can assign different extensions to the nouns under consideration would have to be formulated. And even if in this particular case the restriction should appear unwelcome, there are other cases in which similar restrictions are certainly needed – like the infamous inclusion relation between the extensions of *bachelor* and *unmarried*. Arguably, at the end of the day the restrictions to be imposed on the material models amount to a theory of Logical Space; cf. Etchemendy (1990: 23f) for a similar point.

– Whereas Logical Space is absolute, material models are language-dependent. In particular (and disregarding neurotic cases), for any two distinct languages L and L', the sets of material models of L and of L' will not overlap. Hence if material models were to replace worlds in semantic theory, expressions from different languages would always have different intensions. In particular, sentences would never be true under the same circumstances, if circumstances corresponded to models. To make up for this obvious inadequacy, some procedure for translating material models across languages would be called for. For instance, a material model for English assigning a certain set of individuals to the noun *groundhog* would have to be translated into a material model for German assigning the same set to the noun *Murmeltier*. In general, then, circumstances would correspond to equivalence classes of material models of different languages. Obviously, at the end of the day the construction of these equivalence classes again recapitulates the construction of Logical Space; presumably, a one-one correspondence between material models and possible worlds requires an ideal 'language' of Logical Space, as envisaged by Wittgenstein (1922).

It thus appears that Logical Space can only be eliminated from (extensional) semantics at the price of a theory of something very much like Logical Space. The upshot is that neither ontological objectionability nor theoretical economy are sufficient motives for reversing the conceptual priority of Logical Space over the set of material models. On the other hand, this does not mean that material models ought to be dispensed with. On the contrary, they may be seen as compressions of possible worlds, reducing them to the barest necessities of semantic analysis.

2.3 Intensionality

The adaptation of *FFP* to derive extensions for expressions other than sentences and terms only works in so-called *extensional contexts*, i.e. (syntactic) constructions in which extensionally equivalent parts may replace each other without affecting the extension of the host expression. However, a number of environments prove to be non-extensional. Clausal complements to attitude verbs like *think* and *know* are classical cases in point: their contribution to the extension of the predicate cannot be their own extension which is merely a truth value; if it were, *materially equivalent* clausal complements (= those with identical truth values) would be substitutable *salva veritate* (= preserving the truth [value] of the host sentence) – which they are not. E.g., (24) and (25) may differ in truth value even if the the underlined clauses do not.

(24) John thinks <u>Mary is home</u>.
(25) John thinks <u>Ann is pregnant</u>.

This failure of substitutivity obviously blocks the derivation of the extension of *think* via the extensional version of *FFP*: if it were a function f assigning the predicate extension to the extension of the complement clause, then, as soon as the complement clauses have the same truth value (and are thus co-extensional), f would have to assign the same extension to the predicates:

(26) If: $\|\textbf{Mary is home}\|^w = \|\textbf{Ann is pregnant}\|^w$,
then: $f(\|\textbf{Mary is home}\|^w) = f(\|\textbf{Ann is pregnant}\|^w)$.

The argument (26) shows that an attitude verb like *think* cannot have an extension f that operates on the extension (= truth value) of its complement clause. It does not show that attitude verbs do not have extensions, nor that *FFP* cannot be used to determine them. Rather, since *FFP* seeks to derive the extension of an expression in terms of the contribution made by its natural environment (or primary context), the lesson from (26) ought to be that this contribution must consist in more than a truth value. On the other hand, given *Subst*, it is safe to assume that it is the intension of the complement clause; cf. Frege (1892). After all, by the *BP*, any two intensionally equivalent sentences are synonymous and may thus replace each other in any (sentential) position – including non-extensional ones – without affecting the truth conditions of the host sentence. In particular, any two sentences of the forms *T thinks S* and *T thinks S′* (where *T* is a term) will be synonymous if the sentences *S* and *S′* have the same intension. But then at any possible world, the extensions of the predicates *thinks S* and *thinks S′* coincide, and thus so do their intensions. In other words, there can be no difference in the extensions of the predicates without a difference in the intensions of the complement clauses, which is to say that the former functionally depend on the latter. Following the spirit of *FFP*, then, one can think of the intensions of the embedded clauses as the contributions they make to the extension of the predicate and thus take the extension of the attitude verb to be the function that assigns the extension of the host predicate to this contribution. Hence, at any world *w*, the extension of *thinks* comes out as a function that assigns sets of individuals to sets of possible worlds such that the following equation holds:

(27) $\|\mathbf{thinks}\|^w(\|S\|)(\|T\|^w) = \|T \text{ thinks } S\|^w$

(27) illustrates a common strategy of assigning extensions to expressions that create *non-extensional* contexts (= those in which extensional substitution fails): given compositionality, they are taken to denote functions operating on the intensions of the expressions in these contexts. This is why non-extensional contexts are usually referred to as *intensional*.

The above strategy of assigning extensions to expressions that create non-extensional contexts requires a richer system of types than the one introduced in the previous section (to which we will from now on refer to as *extensional types*). More specifically, the extensions of expressions are classified according to whether they derive (i) from the *EBP*, or (ii) by application of *FFP*: (i) the extensions of sentences of type *t*, those of terms are of type *e*; (ii) if the extensions of an expression operates on extensions of some type *a* resulting in extensions of some type *b*, it is of type (*a*,*b*); and it is of type ((*s*,*a*), *b*) if it operates on intensions of expressions whose extensions are of type *a*, resulting in extensions of type *b*. Hence (i) *t* is the type of truth values; *e* is the type of individuals (or entities); (ii) (*a*,*b*) is the type of (total) functions from *a* to *b*; and (*s*,*a*) is the type of (total) functions from Logical Space to *a*. The notation goes back to R. Montague (1970); '*s*' is reminiscent of *sense*, Frege's (1892) term for (something close to) *intension*. In this notation, the extension of an attitude verb like *think* is of type ((*s*,*t*),(*e*,*t*)).

Once the type of attitude verbs has been determined, the compositional derivation of the truth values of attitude reports is straightforward:

(28) ‖Jane doubts that every boy fancies Mary‖^w
    = ‖doubts that every boy fancies Mary‖^w (‖Jane‖^w)
    = ‖doubts‖^w (‖every boy fancies Mary‖)(‖Jane‖^w)

... which is the truth value 1 just in case in world w, Jane stands in a certain relation D_w – the extension of *doubt* at w – to the set of worlds in which the boys form a subset of the individuals fancied by Mary. An adequate lexical analysis of attitude verbs should imply that standing in D_w to any set p of worlds is incompatible with standing in B_w to it, where B_w is the extension of *believe*:

(29) [λp. λx. ‖**doubt**‖^w $(p)(x)$ ∩ ‖**believe**‖^w $(p)(x)$] = ∅

Compositional derivations like (28) suggest that they can again be simulated with material models in *lieu* of worlds, as in the case of extensional constructions. In fact, this only requires models to also assign extensions of *intensional types* containing 's' to certain lexical expressions (like attitude verbs) and to allow the extensions of complex operations to be obtained by combining the extensions and/or intensions of their immediate parts. In other words, the general definition of the notion of a material model can be kept as is, under the assumption that the reference to types is adapted so as to include the intensional ones; and on top of the clauses in (20), the recursive procedure for determining extensions relative to material models of $\hat{E}$ may also contain clauses like the following, where $\hat{E}$ is a more inclusive fragment of English than E:

(iv-c) $|VS|^{\mathcal{M}_w} = |V|^{\mathcal{M}_w} (\lambda w'. |S|^{\mathcal{M}_{w'}})$
    if *V S* is a predicate, where *V* is an attitude verb and *S* is a clausal complement.

Equations like *(iv-c)* show that the programme of eliminating Logical Space in favour of the set of material models cannot be upheld beyond the realm of extensional constructions. For, unlike the intension of the embedded clause, $\lambda w'.|S|^{\mathcal{M}_{w'}}$, the corresponding *L*-intension, $\lambda \mathcal{M}_{w'}.|S|^{\mathcal{M}_{w'}}$, cannot serve as an argument to the extension $|V|^{\mathcal{M}_w}$ of the attitude verb: the latter is the value of a lexical extension assignment F_w, which itself is a component of $M_{w'}$ which in turn is a member of the domain of $\lambda \mathcal{M}_{w'}. |S|^{\mathcal{M}_{w'}}$ – which cannot be, for set-theoretic reasons.

It should be noted that the intension of the embedded clause is defined in terms of its extensions relative to all other material models. While this does not present any technical problem, it does make the material models less self-contained than their extensional counterparts, which contain all the information needed to determine the extensions of all expressions. If need be, this seeming defect can be remedied by tucking in all of Logical Space and its inhabitants as components of material models:

Definition

Given a possible world w^* and a language L, the *intensional material model* (*for L based on w^**) is the quadruple $\hat{\mathcal{M}}_{w^*} = (W, \hat{U}, w^*, \hat{F})$ consisting of the set W of all possible worlds; the *domain* function $\hat{U}$ assigning to each possible world w the domain of individuals U_w; the world w^* itself; and the lexical interpretation function $\hat{F}$ which assigns to every non-logical lexical expression A of L the intension of A at w.

Two complications arising from this definition are worth noting:
- Universal and existential quantification over possible worlds are prime candidates for logical operations of type $((s,t),t)$, the former yielding the truth value 1 only if applied to Logical Space itself, whereas the latter is true of all but the empty set of possible worlds. Since the extensions of lexical expressions need not be of extensional types, the logicality border needs some adjustment. For the time being we will leave this matter open, returning to it in Section 3.2 with a natural extension of the replacement approach to logicality.
- Lest clauses like *(iv-c)* should make reference to anything outside the intensional model, the lexical interpretation function is defined for all worlds w. As a consequence, two distinct intensional material models only differ in their 3rd component, and each determines the extensions of all expressions at all possible worlds. Hence the procedure for determining the extensions is more general than expected; its precise format will also be given in Section 3.2.

Intensional material models are rather redundant objects, which is why they are not used in real-life semantics; we have mainly defined them here for future reference. Once again, it is obvious that set theory precludes Logical Space as it appears in them, from being replaced by the set of all intensional material models. On the other hand, its rôle might be played by the set of *extensional material models*, i.e. those that only cover the *extensional part* of L – containing only its lexical expressions with extensions of extensional types, and its extensional syntactic constructions.

3 Model-theoretic semantics

3.1 Extensional model space

One rather obvious strategy for constructing (extensional) models within set theory is to start with material models and replace their individuals by (arbitrary) set-theoretic objects; as it turns out, this can be done by a straightforward generalisation of the replacements used in the above characterisation of logical words (cf. Section 2.2). However, since the individuals to be replaced also function as the building blocks of extensions, the latter will have to be generalised first. Given any non-empty set U, the *U-extensions* of type e are the elements of U; the *U-extensions* of type t are the truth values; and if a and b are extensional types, then the *U-extensions* of type (a,b) are the (total) functions from *U-extensions* of type a to *U-extensions* of type b. Hence, *U-extensions* (of extensional types) are to the elements of U what ordinary extensions are to the individuals of a given possible world; and clearly, ordinary extensions come out as U_w-extensions, where U_w happens to be the domain of individuals in w.

Definition

Given a language L, a *formal model* (*for L*) is a pair $\mathcal{M} = (U, F)$ consisting of a non-empty set U (= the *universe of* $\mathcal{M}$) and a function F which assigns to every non-logical lexical expression **A** of L a *U-extension* of type $\tau_L(\mathbf{A})$.

Using the recursive procedure applied earlier, we can extend any bijection ρ between any (not necessarily distinct) non-empty sets U and $\tilde{U}$ of the same cardinality, to a family of functions ρ_a taking *U-extensions* to corresponding $\tilde{U}$-extensions (where a is an extensional type): $\rho_e = \rho$; $\rho_t(x) = x$, if x is a truth value; and $\rho_b(f(x)) = \rho_{(a,b)}(f)(\rho_a(x))$, whenever f and x are *U-extensions* of types (a,b) and a, respectively. It is readily verified that replacements assign structural analogues to the *U-extensions* they are applied to. For instance, if f is a *U-extension* of some type a, then $\rho_{(a,t)}(f)$ is (i.e., characterises) the set of all $\tilde{U}$-extensions of the form $\rho_a(x)$, where x is a *U-extension* of type a; in particular, andgiven that ρ_a is a bijection, f and $\rho_{(a,t)}(f)$ are of the same cardinality. It is also worth noticingthat the values of invariant extensions are themselves invariant, in an obvious sense:

Observations

Let U_w be the domain of individuals of some world w, X an invariant U_w-extension of some type a, and ρ a bijection from U_w to a set U of the same cardinality. Then:

(*) $\rho'_a(X) = \rho''_a(\rho_a(X))$, for any bijections ρ' and ρ'' from U_w and U to some set U' of the same cardinality, respectively;

(**) $\rho_a(X) = \rho'_a(X)$, for any bijection ρ' from U_w to U.

The proofs of (*) and (**) are rather straightforward and thus left to the readers.

Generalised replacements may now be put to use to substitute material models by structurally identical set-theoretic objects. If $\mathcal{M} = (U, F)$ and $\tilde{\mathcal{M}} = \tilde{U}, \tilde{F}$ are formal models, a bijection ρ from U to $\tilde{U}$ is called a *model-isomorphism (from $\mathcal{M}$ to $\tilde{\mathcal{M}}$)* just in case $\tilde{F}(A) = \rho_{\tau(A)}(F(A))$, whenever $A \in N_L$. If there exists a model-isomorphism from $\mathcal{M}$ to $\tilde{\mathcal{M}}$, $\mathcal{M}$ is said to be *isomorphic to $\tilde{\mathcal{M}}$* – in symbols: $\mathcal{M} \cong \tilde{\mathcal{M}}$. Obviously this relational concept is reflexive as well as symmetric and transitive. Clearly, even if two models are isomorphic, not every bijection between their domains is an isomorphism; but in general there exists more than one isomorphism between them.

Given a formal model $\mathcal{M} = (U,F)$ and any bijection ρ from U to a set U^* of the same cardinality, there exists a formal model $\mathcal{M}^* = (U^*, F^*)$ such that ρ is a model-isomorphism from $\mathcal{M}$ to $\mathcal{M}^*$ (and thus $\mathcal{M} \cong \mathcal{M}^*$): $\mathcal{M}^*$ can be constructed by putting: $F^*(A) := \rho_{\tau(A)}(F(A))$, whenever $A \in N_L$. Hence given a material model $\mathcal{M}_w = (U_w, F_w)$, an isomorphic formal model $\mathcal{M} = (U, F)$ can be constructed from any set U of the same cardinality as U_w, by choosing an arbitrary bijection ρ from U_w to U. In this case $\mathcal{M}$ is said to *represent* $\mathcal{M}_w$. It should be noted that, if $U = U_w$, the resulting formal model need not be a material model, because the structure imposed on its individuals may go against their very nature. For example, if U happens to contain the world w itself, then replacing it with Tom, Dick or Harry could put w in the extension of *bachelor*, which may be not be a genuine possibility for a world to be.

If a material model for a language L is represented by a formal model, the recursive procedure for determining extensions of arbitrary expressions relative to the former carries over to the latter:

(30) If ρ is a model-isomorphism from the material model $\mathcal{M}_w = (U_w, F_w)$ (of a language L) to the formal model $\mathcal{M} = (U, F)$, then the *extension* $[\![A]\!]^{\mathcal{M}}$ *of* an expression A is determined by the following induction on A's complexity:

(i) $[\![A]\!]^{\mathcal{M}} = |A|^{\mathcal{M}_w} [= ||A||^w]$, if A is a truth-functional lexical item;
(ii) $[\![A]\!]^{\mathcal{M}} = \rho_{\tau(A)}(|A|)^{\mathcal{M}_w})$, if A is a combinatorial lexical item;
(iii) $[\![A]\!]^{\mathcal{M}} = F(A) [= \rho_{\tau(A)}(F_w(A))]$, if $A \in N_L$;
(iv) $[\![A]\!]^{\mathcal{M}} = \rho_{\tau(A)}(G(\rho^{-1}_{\tau(B_1)}([\![B_1]\!]^{\mathcal{M}}),..., \rho^{-1}_{\tau(B_n)}([\![B_n]\!]^{\mathcal{M}})))$, if A is a complex expression with immediate constituents $B_1,..., B_n$ such that $|A|^{\mathcal{M}_w} = G(|B_1|^{\mathcal{M}_w},...,|B_n|^{\mathcal{M}_w})$.

The final clause relates to the compositional interpretation of L in terms of invariant functions that combine the extensions of the parts of complex expressions. In general, these semantic operations cannot be gleaned from the material models $\mathcal{M}_w$ or the extensions $|A|^{\mathcal{M}_w}$ determined relative to them; rather, they must be specified independently, as was done above for an extensional fragment of English. Given such a specification, the extensions defined in (30) turn out to be independent of ρ; the verification of this fact – which essentially turns on the above observation (**) on invariance – is left to the reader.

The following observation about isomorphic formal models $\mathcal{M}$ and $\tilde{\mathcal{M}}$ (for any language L) is fundamental to model-theoretic semantics:

(31) Let ρ be a model isomorphism from $\mathcal{M}$ to $\tilde{\mathcal{M}}$. Then
for all expressions A of L, $\rho_{\tau(A)}(\llbracket A \rrbracket^{\mathcal{M}}) = \llbracket A \rrbracket^{\tilde{\mathcal{M}}}$.

(31) follows from (30) by a straightforward inductive argument; clause *(iv)* makes use of the above observation (**) on invariance. The special case of (31) where $\mathcal{M} = \tilde{\mathcal{M}} = \mathcal{M}_w$ (for some world w) and ρ is the identical mapping on U_w, reveals that, as far as material models are concerned, the extensions defined in (30) are the familiar ones (and still independent of ρ):

(32) If $\mathcal{M}_w$ is a material model for a language L and A is an expression of L, then

$$\llbracket A \rrbracket^{\mathcal{M}_w} = |A|^{\mathcal{M}_w} = ||A||^w. \qquad \text{cf. Section 2.2, (22a)}$$

Another immediate consequence of (31) concerns (declarative) sentences S (of a given language L), for which $\tau_L(S) = t$ and hence $\rho_{\tau(S)}(\llbracket S \rrbracket^{\mathcal{M}}) = \llbracket S \rrbracket^{\mathcal{M}}$:

(33) If the formal model $\mathcal{M}$ (for a language L) represents the material model $\mathcal{M}_w$, then

$$\llbracket S \rrbracket^{\mathcal{M}} = \llbracket S \rrbracket^{\mathcal{M}_w},$$

for all sentences S of L.

This observation becomes important in the set-theoretic reconstruction of Logical Space, to which we now turn. As usual in set theory, we will refer to those objects that may occur as elements of sets without being sets themselves, as *urelements*; and to sets that can be constructed without the aid of urelements (and whose existence is thus guaranteed by set-theoretic principles alone) as *pure sets*. In view of ontological reservations against possible worlds, such pure sets ought to replace the universes of models:

Definition

If L is a language, then (L's) *Ersatz Space* is the class of all formal models $\mathcal{M} = (U, F)$ of L such that U is a pure set and $\mathcal{M}$ represents a material model.

We will henceforth refer to the elements of L's Ersatz Space as *ersatz models* (for L). Since the inventory of Logical Space consists of urelements, no material model is an ersatz model. On the other hand, every material model is represented by some ersatz model and thus makes a vicarious appearance in Ersatz Space, which is why the latter as a whole may be seen as a representation of Logical Space. It should also be noted that, according to our definitions, the material models and the ersatz models do not exhaust the class of all formal models for a language; and that merely having a pure set as its universe does not make a formal model an ersatz model.

Clearly, Ersatz Space is far too big to form a set and therefore calls for a background theory that includes proper classes alongside ordinary sets; cf. Mendelson (1997: 225ff) for a survey of a pertinent set-theoretical framework. Since we have been assuming that Logical Space (as we characterised it) is a set, one cannot expect the ersatz models (for a given language L) to stand in a one-one correspondence with possible worlds or material models. However, the very construction of Ersatz Space via representation suggests that the objects corresponding to worlds or material models are not the ersatz models themselves, but their *isomorphicity-classes*, i.e. the (proper) classes of the form:

(34) $|\mathcal{M}_0|_\cong := \{\mathcal{M} \mid \mathcal{M}$ is an ersatz model for L & $\mathcal{M} \cong \mathcal{M}_0\}$,

where $\mathcal{M}_0$ is an ersatz model for L. It is therefore natural to inquire into the relation between the classes characterised in (34) and the members of Logical Space. We have already seen that the latter may themselves be represented by material models, and that this representation is a perfect match if the language L is discriminative. However, even if the material models correspond to the possible worlds in a one-one fashion, there is no guarantee that so do the classes of ersatz models in (34). More precisely, even if (35) holds of any worlds w and w' and the corresponding material models $\mathcal{M}_w$ and $\mathcal{M}_{w'}$, the analogous implication (36) about the latter and their representations in Ersatz Space need not be true:

(35) If $w \neq w'$, then $\mathcal{M}_w \neq \mathcal{M}_{w'}$
(36) If $\mathcal{M}_w \neq \mathcal{M}_{w'}$, then $|\mathcal{M}_w|_\cong \neq |\mathcal{M}_{w'}|_\cong$

In other words, distinct material models may be represented by the same ersatz models – which will be the case precisely if L allows for distinct, but isomorphic material models in the first place. Discriminativity does not exclude this possibility: it only implies some extensional differences between any two material models; but these differences could be made up for by the replacements used in representing material models in Ersatz Space. In order to guarantee a perfect match between Logical Space and Ersatz Space, a stronger condition on L is needed than discriminativity. The natural candidate is *completeness*, which is defined like discriminativity, except that it is not based on indistinguishability but the weaker notion of equivalence:

Definitions

If w and w' are possible worlds and L is a language, then w is *L-equivalent* to w' – in symbols: $w \approx_L w'$ – iff $\|S\|^w = \|S\|^{w'}$, for any declarative sentence S of L.

A language L is *complete* iff no two distinct possible worlds w and w' are L-equivalent.

Unlike L-indistinguishability, L-equivalence is not affected by replacements in that it only concerns the truth values of sentences rather than the extensions of arbitrary expressions.

The following observations about arbitrary worlds w and w' and languages L are not hard to establish:

(37) a. If $w \equiv_L w'$, then $w \approx_L w'$.
 b. If L is complete, then L is discriminative.
 c. If L is complete and $w \neq w'$, then $|\mathcal{M}_w|_\cong \neq |\mathcal{M}_{w'}|_\cong$

In effect, (37c) says that, via the isomorphicity classes, the Ersatz Space of a completelanguage matches Logical Space. Thus, completeness plays a similar rôle for the adequacy of ersatz models as does discriminativity in the case of material models. However, whereas discriminative languages are easy to find, completeness seems a much rarer property. Of course, if a language is incomplete, its ersatz models could still match Logical Space in the sense of (37a), but then again their isomorphicity classes may equally well contain, and thus conflate, representations of distinct worlds. However, since the differences between distinct worlds that correspond to the same ersatz models are – by definition – inexpressible in the language under investigation, this imperfect match between Logical Space and Ersatz Space does not necessarily conflict with the general programme of replacing possible worlds with formal models. As far as its potential in descriptive semantics goes, then, Ersatz Space does seem to earn its name. However, as the reader will have noticed, its very definition still appears to be of no avail when it comes to soothing ontological worries: by employing the concept of representation, it depends on material models – and thus presupposes Logical Space. To overcome this embarrassment, a definition of Ersatz Space is needed that does not rely on Logical Space. The usual strategy is one of approximation, starting out from a maximally wide model space and gradually restricting it by eliminating those formal models that do not represent any material counterparts; the crucial point is that these restrictions be formulated without reference to Logical Space, i.e. in the language of pure set theory, or with reference only to urelements that are less dubious than the inhabitants of Logical Space. We will refer to the natural starting point of this enterprise as *L*'s *Model Space*, and identify it with the class of all pure models (for a given language *L*), i.e. all formal models whose universe is a pure set. It should be noted that the concept of a pure model only depends on *L*'s syntax and type assignment, both of which in principle may be given in terms of pure set theory.

In order to exploit Model Space for semantic purposes, the procedure for determining the extensions of expressions must be generalised from ersatz models to arbitrary pure models. Hence, for any pure model $\mathcal{M} = (U, F)$, the extensions of logical expressions need to be specified, as well as the combinations of extensions corresponding to the syntactic constructions. As in the case of Logical Space and Ersatz Space, this should not pose any particular problems. In fact, these extensions and combinations are invariant and should only depend on the universe U. Thus, for those U that happen to be of the same cardinality as the universe U_w of some material model $\mathcal{M}_w = (U_w, F_w)$, their specifications may be taken over from Ersatz Space that is bound to contain at least some pure model with universe U (and isomorphic to $\mathcal{M}_w$). For all other models they would have to be suitably generalised. Thus, e.g., it is natural to define the extension of the English determiner *every* as characterising the subset relation on a given universe U, even if the latter is larger than any of the universes U_w encountered in Logical Space; similarly, the extension of a quantifier phrase *D N*, where *D* is a determiner and *N* a count noun, can be determined by functional application – which, suitably restricted, is an invariant U-extension of type $((e,t),t),(e,t)$; etc.

At the end of the day, then, the formal models resemble their material and ersatz counterparts. In particular, the specification of extensions is strikingly similar:

(38) For any expression **A** of *E* and any formal model $\mathcal{M} = (U, F)$ for *E*, the *extension of A relative to* $\mathcal{M}$ – $[\mathbf{A}]^{\mathcal{M}}$ – is determined by the following induction (on the grammatical complexity of **A**):

(i-a) $[\![\textbf{and}]\!]^{\mathcal{M}} = \lambda u.\ \lambda v.\ u \times v$ ... where $u \in \{0, 1\}$ and $v \in \{0, 1\}$
...   ...
(ii-a) $[\![\textbf{every}]\!]^{\mathcal{M}} = \lambda P.\ \lambda Q.\ \vdash P \subseteq Q \dashv$ where $P \subseteq U$ and $Q \subseteq U$
...   ...
(iii) $[\![\textbf{A}]\!]^{\mathcal{M}} = F_w(\textbf{A})$, if $\textbf{A} \in N_E$
(iv-a) $[\![\textbf{D N}]\!]^{\mathcal{M}} = [\![\textbf{D}]\!]^{\mathcal{M}}([\![\textbf{N}]\!]^{\mathcal{M}})$
        if *D N* is a quantifier phrase, where *D* is a quantificational determiner and *N* is a count noun;
...   ...

Given specifications of extensions in the style (38), one may start approximating the Ersatz Space of a language *L* by restricting its Model Space. A common strategy to this end is to eliminate models that have certain sentences come out false, viz. *analytic* sentences that owe their truth to their very meaning. As a case in point, one may require of *appropriate* models for English that the extension of (39) be the truth value 1. For the sake of the example it may be assumed that the extension of a predicative adjective is a set of individuals and that it is passed on to the predicate (*Copula + Adjective*); cf. Heim & Kratzer (1998: 61ff).

(39) No bachelor is married.

More generally, a set Σ of sentences of *L* may be used to characterise the class of all pure models $\mathcal{M}$ (for *L*) such that $[\![\textbf{S}]\!]^{\mathcal{M}} = 1$, for all $\textbf{S} \in \Sigma$. Ever since Carnap (1952), sentences of a language *L* that are used to characterise the appropriateness of formal models *L* are called *meaning postulates*; and we will refer to a set of sentences used for this purpose as a *postulate system*.

Obviously, the truth of a meaning postulate like (39) may guarantee the truth or falsity of certain other sentences:

(40) Every bachelor is not married.
(41) Some bachelor is married.

Once (39) is adopted as a meaning postulate, there is no need to also take on (40), or to rule out (41) separately, because the truth values of these two sentences come out as intended in any formal model for English relative to which (39) is true. Alternatively, if (40) is taken as a meaning postulate, (39) and (41) come out as desired. As this example suggests, when it comes to approximating Ersatz Space by meaning postulates, there need not be a general criterion for preferring one postulate system over another. And it is equally obvious that the effect of a meaning postulate, or a postulate system, may be achieved by other means. Thus, e.g., the effect of adopting (39) as a meaning postulate may also be obtained by the following *constraint* on appropriate formal models $\mathcal{M} = (U, F)$ for E:

(42) $F(\textbf{bachelor}) \cap F(\textbf{married}) = \varnothing$

In other words, the effect of adopting (39) or (40) as a meaning postulate is to establish a certain sense relation between the noun *bachelor* and the participle *married* (which we take to be a lexical item, if only for the sake of the example). The relation is known as *incompatibility* and holds between any two expressions just in case their extensions of some type (a,t) cannot overlap. For future reference, we also define the relation of *compatibility* as it holds between *box* and *wooden* – and in general between expressions ***A*** and ***B*** if their extensions may overlap. Interestingly, compatibilities do not have to be established by meaning postulates because they are guaranteed by the existence of any model attesting the overlaps; hence compatibility will hold as long as Model Space is not (erroneoulsy) narrowed down so as to exclude all of these models.

Obviously any meaning postulate ***S*** can be replaced by a corresponding constraint on formal models to the effect that ***S*** come out true; and given a procedure for determining the extensions of arbitrary expressions, this constraint can be given directly in terms of the extensions of the (non-logical) lexical expressions ***S*** contains. On the other hand, not every constraint on formal models needs to correspond to a meaning postulate, or even a postulate system; cf. Zimmermann (1985) for a concrete example.

On top of restrictions on the range of possible extensions of lexical expressions, more global constraints may rule out pure models that do not belong to Ersatz Space for cardinality reasons. In general, then, the set-theoretic reconstruction of Logical Space consists in formulating suitable constraints on the members of Model Space, i.e. the pure models. Taken together, these constraints define a class $\mathcal{K}$ of *appropriate* models (according to the constraints). Ideally, this class should coincide with Ersatz Space. The closer $\mathcal{K}$ gets to this ideal, and the more it coincides with Ersatz Space in semantically relevant aspects, the more descriptively adequate will $\mathcal{K}$ be. Thus, e.g., the set of $\mathcal{K}$-*valid* sentences – those that are true according to all $\mathcal{M} \in \mathcal{K}$ – should be the same as the set of sentences that are true throughout Logical Space.

If two formal models are isomorphic, both represent precisely the same material models, and hence there is no reason for ruling out (or counting in) one but not the other. Appropriateness constraints are thus subject to the following meta-constraint on classes $\mathcal{K}$ of appropriate models:

(43) If $\mathcal{M} \cong \mathcal{M}'$, then $\mathcal{M} \in \mathcal{K}$ iff $\mathcal{M}' \in \mathcal{K}$.

In mathematical jargon, (43) says that the class $\mathcal{K}$ of appropriate models is *closed under isomorphism*: if $\mathcal{M}$ and $\mathcal{M}'$ are isomorphic formal models (for some language L), then $\mathcal{M}$ is appropriate according to a given set of constraints just in case $\mathcal{M}'$ is appropriate according to the same constraints.

Two things about (43) are noteworthy. First, as a consequence of (31), constraints formulated in terms of meaning postulates (or postulate systems) always satisfy (43): any two isomorphic models make the same sentences true. Secondly, if the constraints are jointly satsifiable at all (which they should be), the appropriate models always form a proper class; this is so because for any formal model $\mathcal{M} = (U, F)$ and any set U' of the same cardinality as U, there is an isomorphic model of the form $\mathcal{M}' = (U', F')$ – and hence any pure set whatsoever will be a member of some universe of an appropriate formal model.

One interesting consequence of (43) is that, no matter how closely a given system of constraints and/or meaning postulates may approximate Logical Space, it will never be able to pin down a specific model, let alone specific extensions of all expressions. In fact, given any term **A** (of some language L) and any pure set x, there will be an appropriate model $\mathcal{M}_x = (U_x, F)$ (for L), according to which $[\![A]\!]^{\mathcal{M}_x} = x$; $\mathcal{M}_x$ may be constructed from any given appropriate model $\mathcal{M} = (U, F)$ by replacing $[\![A]\!]^{\mathcal{M}}$ with x (and simultaneously x with U, in case $x \in U$) – thereby preserving appropriateness, by (43). This only reflects the strategy of having inhabitants of Logical Space represented by *arbitrary* set-theoretic objects and is thus hardly surprising. However, a similar line of thought does give rise to interesting consequences for the relation between reference and truth. This is the gist of the following *permutation argument*, made famous by Putnam (1977, 1980) with predecessors including Newman (1928: 137ff), Jeffrey (1964: 82ff), Field (1975), and Wallace (1977); see Devitt (1983), Lewis (1984), Abbott (1997), Williams (2005: 89ff), and Button (2011) for critical discussion of its impact.

Given a model $\mathcal{M}$ for a language L, the extensions according to any isomorphic model $\mathcal{M}^*$ may be characterised directly by an inductive specification in terms of $\mathcal{M}$, without mention of $\mathcal{M}^*$. For the present purposes, it suffices to consider the special case in which $\mathcal{M} = (U, F)$ and $\mathcal{M}^* = (U^*, F^*)$ are models for our extensional fragment of English and share their universe $U = U^*$. More specifically, since any bijection π on U is a model-isomorphism from $\mathcal{M}$ to a model $\mathcal{M}^* = (U^*, F^*)$, the following induction characterises the extensions relative to $\mathcal{M}^*$ entirely in terms of $\mathcal{M}$:

(44) For any expression **A** of E and any formal model $\mathcal{M} = (U, F)$ for E, the *permuted extension of **A** relative to $\mathcal{M}$* – $\|A\|^{\mathcal{M}}$ – is determined by the following induction (on the grammatical complexity of **A**):

(i-a) $\|\textbf{and}\|^{\mathcal{M}} = \lambda u. \lambda v. u \times v$ ... where $u \in \{0,1\}$ and $v \in \{0,1\}$

...

(ii-a) $\|\textbf{every}\|^{\mathcal{M}} = \lambda P. \lambda Q. \vdash P \subseteq Q \dashv$ where $P \subseteq U$ and $Q \subseteq U$

...

(iii) $\|\textbf{A}\|^{\mathcal{M}} = \pi_{\tau(A)}(F_w(A))$, if $A \in N_E$

(iv-a) $\|\textbf{D N}\|^{\mathcal{M}} = \|\textbf{D}\|^{\mathcal{M}}(\|\textbf{A}\|^{\mathcal{M}})$
if **D N** is a quantifier phrase, where **D** is a quantificational determiner and **N** is a count noun;

...

Obviously, $\|\textbf{A}\|^{\mathcal{M}} = \pi_{\tau(A)}([\textbf{A}]^{\mathcal{M}}) = [\textbf{A}]^{\mathcal{M}*}$, for any expression **A** of E. Moreover, there is a striking similariy between (44) and the specification (38) of the extensions relative to $\mathcal{M}$. In fact, the only difference lies in clause *(iii)*: according to (44), non-logical words are assigned the π-image of the U-extension they are assigned according to (38). The formulation of (44*iii*) may suggest that the values $\|\textbf{A}\|^{\mathcal{M}}$ somehow depend on the permutation π when of course, they are perfectly independent U-extensions in their own right – just like the values $[\textbf{A}]^{\mathcal{M}}$: any instantiation of either (38*iii*) or (44*iii*) will assign some specific U-extension to some specific expression. In particular, then, (44) is no more complicated or roundabout than (38); it is just different. Yet, as far as the specification of the truth values of sentences **S** of L is concerned, the two agree, since $\|\textbf{S}\|^{\mathcal{M}} = \pi_\tau([\textbf{S}]^{\mathcal{M}}) = [\textbf{S}]^{\mathcal{M}}$.

The construction (44) can also be carried out if $\mathcal{M} = \mathcal{M}_w$ is a material model. Of course, in this case the permutation model $\mathcal{M}^*$ cannot be expected to be a material model too, but then again it is not needed for the definition of the $\|\textbf{A}\|^{\mathcal{M}}$-values anyway. All that is needed is a permutation π of the domain of w. (44) will then deliver exactly the same truth valuation of L as (38). The comparison between (44) and (38) thus illustrates that truth is independent of reference in that the latter is not determined by the former. In particular, then, although the extensions of terms help determining the truth values of the sentences in which they occur, this rôle hopelessly underdetermines them: if reference is merely contribution to truth, then reference is arbitrary; else, reference has to be grounded independently.

3.2 Intensional Model Space

Beyond the realm of extensionality the strategy of approximating Logical Space in terms of formal models is bound to reach its limits. Even when restricted to the extensional part of a language L and constrained by meaning postulates or otherwise, Model Space is a proper class and thus cannot serve as the domain of any function. As a consequence, the set-theoretic reconstruction of intensional semantics cannot have intensional models assign L-intensions to expressions. However, this does not mean that formal models cannot be adapted to intensional languages. Rather, they would each have to come with their own set-theoretic reconstruction of Logical Space, consisting of an arbitrary (non-empty) set W representing the worlds and a system $\hat{U}$ of arbitrary (non-empty) universes, i.e. one set per world (representation):

Definition

A *formal ontology* is a pair $(W, \hat{U})$, where W is a non-empty set (the *worlds according to* $(W, \hat{U})$ and $\hat{U}$ is a function with domain W such that $\hat{U}(w)$ is a non-empty set whenever $w \in W$ [= the individuals of w, according to $(W, \hat{U})$].

In the literature on modal logic, the requirement of non-emptiness is sometimes weaker, applying to the union of all domains rather than each individual domain; cf. Fine (1977: 144). Given a formal ontology $(W, \hat{U})$, one may generalise U-extensions from extensional to arbitrary types. Due to the world-dependence of individual domains, these generalised extensions also depend on which element w of W is chosen. More precisely, $(W, \hat{U}, w)$-*extensions* may be defined by induction on (the complexity of) their types: (i) $(W, \hat{U}, w)$-extensions of type t are truth values; (ii) $(W, \hat{U}, w)$-extensions of type e are members of $\hat{U}(w)$; (iii) whenever a and b are types, $(W, \hat{U}, w)$-extensions of type (a,b) are functions assigning $(W, \hat{U}, w)$-extensions of type b to all $(W, \hat{U}, w)$-extensions of type a; and (iv) $(W, \hat{U}, w)$-extensions of type (s,a) are functions f with domain W assigning to any $w' \in W$ a $(W, \hat{U}, w')$-extensions of type a (where, again, a is a type). At first glance, this definition may appear gruesome, but closer inspections shows that it merely mimics(a staightforward generalisation of) the replacements defined in the previous part; we invite the reader to check this for her- or himself.

$(W, \hat{U}, w)$-extensions give rise to $(W, \hat{U})$-*intensions* of any type a as functions assigning a $(W, \hat{U}, w)$-extension of type a to any $w \in W$. We thus arrive at the following:

Definition

Given a language L, an *intensional formal model* (*for* L) is a quadruple $\hat{\mathcal{M}} = (W, \hat{U}, w^*, \hat{F})$, where $(W, \hat{U})$ is a formal ontology; a member w^* of W (= the *actual* world according to $\hat{\mathcal{M}}$); and a function $\hat{F}$ which assigns to every non-logical lexical expression A of L a $(W, \hat{U})$-intension of type $\tau_L(A)$ (= the lexical interpretation function according to $\hat{\mathcal{M}}$).

Moreover we say that an intensional formal model $\hat{\mathcal{M}} = (W, \hat{U}, w^*, \hat{F})$ is *based on* the ontology $(W, \hat{U})$ and call the members of W and $\bigcup_{w \in W} \hat{U}(w)$, the *worlds* and *individuals according to* $\hat{\mathcal{M}}$, respectively. In an obvious sense, intensional formal models are to intensional material models what (extensional) formal models are to (extensional) material models, replacing any dubious entities by arbitrary set-theoretic constructions. And like the extensional ones, intensional formal models can be used to determine the extensions of arbitrary expressions. To see this, we may adapt procedure (38) to intensional formal models $\hat{\mathcal{M}}$ for a more inclusive English fragment $\hat{E}$ by adding pertinent conditions to determine extensions in the presence of non-extensional constructions. Since the latter make reference to the intensions of (at least some of) the expressions, the semantic recursion must specify the extensions of all expressions at all worlds (as already observed at the end of section 2):

(45) For any expression A of $\hat{E}$, any intensional formal model $\hat{\mathcal{M}} = (W, \hat{U}, w^*, \hat{F})$ for $\hat{E}$, and any world w (according to $\hat{\mathcal{M}}$), the *extension* $[\![A]\!]^{\hat{\mathcal{M}},w}$ *of A at w relative to* $\hat{\mathcal{M}}$ is determined by the following induction:

(i-a) $[\![\mathbf{and}]\!]^{\hat{\mathcal{M}},w} = \lambda u. \lambda v. u \times v$ ... where $u \in \{0,1\}$ and $v \in \{0,1\}$

... ...

(ii-a) $[\![\mathbf{every}]\!]^{\hat{\mathcal{M}},w} = \lambda P. \lambda Q. \vdash P \subseteq Q \dashv$ ... where $P \subseteq \hat{U}(w)$ and $Q \subseteq \hat{U}(w)$

... ...

(ii-c) $[\![\mathbf{necessarily}]\!]^{\hat{\mathcal{M}},w} = \lambda p. \vdash p = W \dashv$ ... where $p \subseteq W$

... ...

(iii) $[\![A]\!]^{\hat{\mathcal{M}},w} = \hat{F}(A)(w)$, if $A \in N_E$

(iv-a) $[\![\mathbf{D\ N}]\!]^{\hat{\mathcal{M}},w} = [\![\mathbf{D}]\!]^{\hat{\mathcal{M}},w}([\![\mathbf{N}]\!]^{\hat{\mathcal{M}},w})$
       if $\mathbf{D\ N}$ is a quantifier phrase, where $\mathbf{D}$ is a quantificational determiner and $\mathbf{N}$ is a count noun;

... ...

(iv-c) if $\mathbf{V\ S}$ is a predicate, where $\mathbf{V}$ is an attitude verb and $\mathbf{S}$ is a clausal complement,
       $[\![\mathbf{V\ S}]\!]^{\hat{\mathcal{M}},w} = [\![\mathbf{V}]\!]^{\hat{\mathcal{M}},w}(\lambda w'. [\![\mathbf{S}]\!]^{\hat{\mathcal{M}},w'})$;

(iv-d) if $\mathbf{A\ S}$ is a sentence, where $\mathbf{A}$ is a sentential adverb and $\mathbf{S}$ is a sentence,
       $[\![\mathbf{A\ S}]\!]^{\hat{\mathcal{M}},w} = [\![\mathbf{A}]\!]^{\hat{\mathcal{M}},w}(\lambda w'. [\![\mathbf{S}]\!]^{\hat{\mathcal{M}},w'})$;

... ...

According to (45), an intensional formal model $\hat{\mathcal{M}} = (W, \hat{U}, w^*, \hat{F})$ for a language L assigns to each expression A of L both an extension $[\![A]\!]^{\hat{\mathcal{M}},w^*}$ and an intension $\lambda w. [\![A]\!]^{\hat{\mathcal{M}},w}$, which we will write as '$[\![A]\!]^{\hat{\mathcal{M}},w}$' and '$\wedge [\![A]\!]^{\hat{\mathcal{M}},w}$', respectively. Routine calculations now show that the truth conditions of sentences relative to intensional models closely resemble their truth conditions in Logical Space. This may be illustrated by (46a–c), which give the truth conditions of the same attitude report with respect to a possible world w_0 of Logical Space $\mathcal{L}$, arbitrary worlds $w \in W$, and the actual world w^* of a model $\hat{\mathcal{M}} = (W, \hat{U}, w^*, \hat{F})$, respectively:

(46) (a) $\|\text{Jane doubts that every boy fancies Mary}\|^{w_0} = 1$ iff
$(\|\text{Jane}\|^{w_0}, \{w' \in \mathcal{L} | \|\text{boy}\|^{w'} \subseteq \{x \in U_{w'} | (x, \|\text{Mary}\|^{w'}) \in \|\text{fancies}\|^{w'}\}) \in \|\text{doubts}\|^{w_0}$

(b) $[\![\text{Jane doubts that every boy fancies Mary}]\!]^{\hat{\mathcal{M}}, w} = 1$ iff $([\![\text{Jane}]\!]^{\hat{\mathcal{M}}, w}, \{w' \in W | [\![\text{boy}]\!]^{\hat{\mathcal{M}}, w'} \subseteq \{x \in \hat{U}(w') | (x, [\![\text{Mary}]\!]^{\hat{\mathcal{M}}, w'}) \in [\![\text{fancies}]\!]^{\hat{\mathcal{M}}, w'}\}\})$
$\in [\![\text{doubts}]\!]^{\hat{\mathcal{M}}, w}$

(c) $[\![\text{Jane doubts that every boy fancies Mary}]\!]^{\hat{\mathcal{M}}} = 1$ iff
$([\![\text{Jane}]\!]^{\hat{\mathcal{M}}}, \{w' \in W | [\![\text{boy}]\!]^{\hat{\mathcal{M}}, w'} \subseteq \{x \in \hat{U}(w') | (x, [\![\text{Mary}]\!]^{\hat{\mathcal{M}}, w'}) \in [\![\text{fancies}]\!]^{\hat{\mathcal{M}}, w'}\}\})$
$\in [\![\text{doubts}]\!]^{\hat{\mathcal{M}}}$

(45ii-c) gives the interpretation of a rather restrictive reading of the modal sentence adverb **necessarily**, acccording to which it expresses universal quantification overpossible worlds. It is understood that $\tau_E(\textbf{necessarily}) = ((s,t),t)$ and that the modaladverb combines with sentences according to clause *(iv-d)*. The following calculation shows that the truth value of a sentence introduced by **necessarily** does not dependon the world:

(47) $[\textbf{Necessarily } S]^{\hat{\mathcal{M}}, w}$
$= [\textbf{necessarily}]^{\hat{\mathcal{M}}, w} (\lambda w'. [\![S]\!]^{\hat{\mathcal{M}}, w'})$
$= [\lambda p. \vdash p = W \dashv] (\lambda w'. [\![S]\!]^{\hat{\mathcal{M}}, w'})$
$= \vdash \lambda w'. [\![S]\!]^{\hat{\mathcal{M}}, w'} = W \dashv$

which is indeed independent of w. These truth conditions reflect the peculiar reading (45ii-c) of **necessarily** as an unrestricted universal quantifier, which arguably reconstructs a logical or metaphysical construal of modality. Despite its limited linguistic value, this interpretational clause illustrates that logical words may come with extensions of non-extensional types, thus calling for a generalisation of the notion of logicality (as already observed at the end of section 2). As in the extensional case, we can give a characterisation in terms of replacements. Since extensions of non-extensional types take all possible worlds into account, replacements also have to act simultaneously on all worlds and domains of a given model:

Definition

If $(W, \hat{U})$ is a formal ontology, then a $(W, \hat{U})$-*replacement* is a pair $\rho = (\rho^s, \rho^e)$ of functions with domain W such that:

ρ^s is a bijection on W;

$\rho^e(w)$ is a bijection on $\hat{U}(\rho^s(w))$, whenever $w \in W$.

It ought to be noted that the second condition requires $\hat{U}(w)$ and $\hat{U}(\rho^s(w))$ to have the same cardinality whenever $w \in W$. In parallel to replacements of U-extensions of extensional types, $(W, \hat{U})$-replacements $\rho = (\rho^s, \rho^e)$ may then be generalised to $(W, \hat{U}, w)$-extensions of arbitrary types (for any $w \in W$); as in the extensional case, a $(W, \hat{U})$-intension f of some type a is *invariant* iff $\rho_a(f(w)) = \rho'_a(f(w))$, for all $(W, \hat{U})$-replacements ρ and ρ' and worlds $w \in W$ such that $\rho^s(w) = \rho'^s(w)$ – and intensional formal models $\mathcal{M} = (W, \hat{U}, w^*, \hat{F})$ are required to assign invariant intensions to logical words: $\rho_{\tau(A)}(\llbracket A \rrbracket^{\mathcal{M},w}) = \rho'_{\tau(A)}(\llbracket A \rrbracket^{\mathcal{M},w})$, for any worlds $w \in W$ and $(W, \hat{U})$-replacements ρ and ρ' such that $\rho^s(w) = \rho'^s(w)$. While this requirement reconstructs and extends the earlier approach to logical words in terms of replacements, it does not guarantee any homogeneity of their intensions across models: the same lexical item may be interpreted as conjunction in one model and as disjunction in another one – and still count as logical according to this definition. To rule out this possibility, a global notion of logicality is needed, and can be defined in terms of *(intensional) model isomorphisms*.

Definition

If $\mathcal{M}_1 = (W_1, \hat{U}_1, w_1, \hat{F}_1)$ and $\mathcal{M}_2 = (W_2, \hat{U}_2, w_2, \hat{F}_2)$ are intensional formal models for a language L, then a *model isomorphism from* $\mathcal{M}_1$ *to* $\mathcal{M}_2$ is a pair $\rho = (\rho^s, \rho^e)$ of bijections from W_1 to W_2 and from $U\hat{U}_1$ to $U\hat{U}_2$, respectively, such that $\rho^s(w_1) = w_2$;

$\rho_{\tau(A)}(\hat{F}_1(A)(w)) = \hat{F}_2(A)(\rho^s(w))$, whenever $w \in W_1$ and $A \in N_L$.

The second equation in this definition generalises the functions $\rho = (\rho^s, \rho^e)$ to objects of arbitrary types. Omitting the obvious details, this is to be understood as parallel to the corresponding generalisation of replacements given further above. Aiming at a more global notion of logicality, the extensions of logical words A are required to be invariant across models: $\rho_{\tau(A)}(\llbracket A \rrbracket^{\mathcal{M}_1,w}) = \llbracket A \rrbracket^{\mathcal{M}_2,\rho^s(w)}$, for any intensional formal models $\mathcal{M}_1$, worlds w (of $\mathcal{M}_1$) and model-isomorphisms ρ to some (isomorphic) model $\mathcal{M}_2$. It is then readily seen that this global requirement implies that logical words are assigned invariant intensions in the earlier, local sense. The 'globalisation' of invariance is needed if the extensions of logical words are to be specified independently of the details of individual models. Readers may check for themselves that the extension specified in (45ii) are indeed stable under model-isomorphisms. The same goes for the syntactic operations interpreted in (45iv), which correspond to invariant intensions, combining the intensions of their parts. As a case in point, according to (45iv-c), embedding a *that*-clause under an attitude verb is interpreted as functional application, which itself corresponds to a function of type $((s,t),(e,t)),((s,t),(e,t))$ – the identical mapping, which is certainly (globally) invariant.

With the definition of (global) invariance and the ensuing characterisation of logicality, the specification (45) of extensions relative to intensional formal models is complete. The rest of the technical apparatus layed out in the previous section carries over rather smoothly to the intensional case. In particular, one may now define *pure intensional models* as those intensional formal models $\hat{\mathcal{M}} = (W, \hat{U}, w^*, \hat{F})$ that are based on pure sets W of worlds w associated with pure domains $\hat{U}(w)$ – and are thus pure sets themselves. Collecting them all, we obtain *Intensional Model Space*. It is readily verified that each pure intensional model interprets the extensional part of the language in exactly the same way as a corresponding extensional model. It would thus seem that, quite generally, the effect of a meaning postulate S on (extensional) Model Space may be achieved by restricting Intensional Model Space to those models $\hat{\mathcal{M}}$ for which $[\![S]\!]^{\hat{\mathcal{M}}} = 1$. However, this would not guarantee the general validity of S given that, apart from its actual world w^*, each such $\hat{\mathcal{M}}$ comes with its own logical space W of possible worlds. Hence even though a sentence S may be true at the latter (and thus according to $\hat{\mathcal{M}}$), it need not be true throughout the former. In other words, even if S is true, it may express a *contingent* proposition within $\hat{\mathcal{M}}$, i.e. one that is neither empty nor coincides with $\hat{\mathcal{M}}$'s logical space: $[\![S]\!]^{\hat{\mathcal{M}},w^*}=1$, but $\varnothing \neq \{w \in W \mid [\![S]\!]^{\hat{\mathcal{M}},w}=1\} \neq W$. As a consequence, in such models (for $\hat{E}$) sentences of the form **Necessarily** S would come out false. To avoid this absurdity, a meaning postulate S should not only rule out intensional models according to which S is *actually* true, but all those according to which S is true *at some world*. Though this may be achieved by prefixing S with the modal adverb **necessarily**, a more principled, language-independent way to guarantee the intended effect of meaning postulates is to adapt the definition of validity to non-extensional languages:

Definition

Let S be a sentence of a language L, and let $\hat{\mathcal{M}}$ and $\hat{\mathcal{K}}$ be a pure model with possible worlds W and a class of pure models for L, respectively.
- S is *valid in* $\hat{\mathcal{M}}$ – in symbols: $\hat{\mathcal{M}} \vDash S$ – iff $^{\wedge}[\![S]\!]^{\hat{\mathcal{M}}} = W$.
- S is $\hat{\mathcal{K}}$-*valid* – in symbols: $\vDash_{\hat{\mathcal{K}}} S$ – iff S is valid in every member of $\hat{\mathcal{K}}$.

Like (extensional) Model Space, Intensional Model Space can be taken as a starting point to the set-theoretic reconstruction of Logical Space, gradually reducing the abundance of models by suitable constraints. To this end, meaning postulates employed in extensional semantics may be adapted in the way indicated, but they would have no effect on the interpretation of expressions of non-extensional types, for which additional postulates may be formulated. Thus, e.g., it has been argued that, due to the intensionality of their subject positions, certain verbs of change have extensions of type $((s,e),t)$; cf. Montague (1973), Löbner (1979), Lasersohn (2005). The analyses try to explain *Partee's Paradox*, i.e. the failure of the inference from *The temperature is ninety* and *The temperature is rising* to *Ninety is rising*. The incompatibility of *rise* and *fall* may then be captured by adopting the following sentence as a meaning postulate – or by a corresponding meta-linguistic constraint:

(48) Nothing both rises and falls.

Typically, however, the semantic relations between non-extensional expressions are beyond the expressive power of the object language. Hence, as in the extensional case, meta-linguistic constraints may be added if need be. The cardinality of Logical Space is a case in point:

(49) W is infinite.

Constraints like (49), and other ones concerning the class of possible worlds as a whole, have no analogues to constraints on Model Space, because they do not rule out particular worlds, but entire constellations of possible worlds instead. In order to guarantee the infinity of Logical Space, the constraints on Model Space would have to conspire in some way, but no single constraint on appropriate pure extensional models could express (49).

Like those applying to Model Space, the constraints and meaning postulates narrowing down Intensional Model Space may be seen as a means to approximate Logical Space by classes of models defined by appropriateness constraints. In the previous section we met a natural meta-constraint on such classes of pure (extensional) models, viz. that they be *closed under isomorphism*: constraints should only rule out models that do not represent possible constellations of facts, i.e. worlds; and since any two isomorphic models represent the same worlds, they stand and fall together. Closure under isomorphism is solely motivated by the fact that for the adequacy of set-theoretic representations, only set-theoretic structure counts. Clearly, then, closure under isomorphism equally applies to constraints ruling out pure intensional models. However, there is another, straightforward meta-constraint on narrowing down Intensional Model Space that does not have a counterpart in extensional Model Space. It is readily seen, that the actual world of an intensional formal model $\hat{\mathcal{M}}$ never offers a reason for ruling out a particular model: a pure intensional model violates a meaning postulate just in case its variants do, i.e. those models that only differ from it in their actual world. This is so because meaning postulates only concern Logical Space as a whole and do not bear on actual facts. The same goes for meta-theoretic constraints like (49), which all preserve closure under variation: if an intensional formal model satisfies one of them, then so do all its variants. Clearly, this is no coincidence: two variants only differ in their actual world, and so ruling out one but not the other amounts to deciding between which one assigns more appropriate extensions, i.e. truth values, referents, etc., while all that matters in semantics are tuth conditions, reference conditions, etc. Hence, in addition to closure under isomorphism, classes $\hat{\mathcal{K}}$ of appropriate pure intensional models $\hat{\mathcal{M}}$ and $\hat{\mathcal{M}}'$ should also satisfy *closure under variation*:

(50) If $\hat{\mathcal{M}} \cong \hat{\mathcal{M}}'$, then $\hat{\mathcal{M}} \in \hat{\mathcal{K}}$ iff $\hat{\mathcal{M}}' \in \hat{\mathcal{K}}$.
(51) If $\hat{\mathcal{M}}$ is a variant of $\hat{\mathcal{M}}'$, then $\hat{\mathcal{M}} \in \hat{\mathcal{K}}$ iff $\hat{\mathcal{M}}' \in \hat{\mathcal{K}}$.

Meta-constraint (51) clearly brings out one difference between Intensional Model Space and extensional Model Space, where the very notion of a variant does not appear to make sense. However, though both may be construed as approximations to Logical Space, there is a more fundamental difference in approach. Each member of Ersatz Space – the goal of the approximation – is meant to represent some (i.e., at least one) member of Logical Space; so the constraints on Model Space serve solely to eliminate models that do not represent any genuine possibility in that they do not correspond to any member of the Logical Space. The approximation process has reached its limit once the remaining class of models contains precisely the representations of all the worlds in Logical Space. In a sense, this is also true of Intensional Model Space. However, since each of its members comes with its own representation of Logical Space (as well as a representation of its actual world), this representation too, must be appropriate. Hence in the case of Intensional Model Space, the approximation process only reaches its limit once the remaining, *intended* models are precisely those based on ontologies that represent Logical Space as a whole; obviously by (50), this will also guarantee that each possible world of Logical Space is represented by (at least) one of the remaining models. The difference between Ersatz Space and the space of intended models comes out particularly clear in discriminative languages. Though in both cases the goal of the approximation process is a mathematical structure that stands in a one-one relation to Logical Space, this structure manifests itself in totally different ways. In the extensional case, it is formed by bundling together pure extensional models into isomorphicity classes; at the end of approximation day, the class of all of them, *Ersatz Space*, stands in a one-one relation to Logical Space. In the intensional case, each model comes with a representation of Logical Space of its own; when all is said and done, each of these representations will be an isomorphic image of its archetype. Borrowing standard terminology from plural semantics, one may thus say that Ersatz Space approximates Logical Space collectively, as a whole, whereas the space of intended models does so distributively, in each of its members.

Meta-theoretic though it may seem, this difference between extensional and intensional model theory in the approach to Logical Space does have repercussions upon descriptive issues. To see this, let us follow Zimmermann (1999: 544ff) and consider the realm of sense relations. In many cases, it seems as if two given expressions do not stand in any interesting semantic relation, even though their extensions are of the same type. The following pairs are cases in point:

(52) a. teacher : smoker
 b. Mary is asleep : Jane pouts
 c. expensive : green

As a matter of fact, many teachers smoke and some don't, some smokers are teachers and many are not; but then one could certainly imagine that teachers never smoke, or that smokers cannot be teachers, or that only teachers smoke, or even that only smokers may become teachers. Similarly, Mary may be awake while Jane is pouting, but then again she may also sleep etc. In other words, the extensions of the respective expressions in (52) may relate to each other in any way possible – they are *logically independent* of each other. Certainly logical independence is a sense relation, holding between the expressions in virtue of their meaning. And even though it might not be particularly thrilling one, if semantic theory strives for completeness, it should not miss it. As it turns out, Ersatz Space takes care of it without further ado: extensions vary across pure (extensional) models in any possible way (within their type), and hence for any distribution of these extensions and any relation between them, there will be a pure model representing this relation. This even goes for pairs like *bachelor* and *married*, before unwelcome models are eliminated in which the two overlap. Yet as long as the corresponding models are not accidentally eliminated, the full range of the distribution of the extensions of the pairs in (52) will be preserved. In that sense logical independence is captured by extensional Model Space without further ado. Not so for Intensional Model Space where each member is equipped with its own version of Logical Space. To be sure, any conceivable relation between the extensions of the expressions under (52) will be represented by some pure intensional models extending corresponding pure extensional models. Unfortunately, though, Intensional Model Space also allows for the intensions of these expressions to vary as widely as possible. In particular, there are pure intensional models according to which *teacher* and *smoker* have all kinds of weird extensions at any possible worlds: disjoint, identical, empty,... Certainly these models would have to be eliminated by suitable constraints or postulates before Intensional Model Space can make any claim at approximating Logical Space. Given the extreme frequency of such 'unmarked' cases as the ones under (52), this is certainly not a trivial task.

From the latter point of view, the attempt is successful if Intensional Model Space has been narrowed down enough so that Logical Space may be conceived of as the common structure of the possible worlds across the class of remaining intended models; the more restrictive this class is, the closer this enterprise gets to a full reconstruction of Logical Space. From the realistic perspective, Intensional Model Space may be understood as a mathematical model of what is known about Logical Space, with (abridged) formal intensional models representing (epistemic) possibilities of what the structure of Logical Space may be. This assessment is based on Zimmermann (1999); cf. Lasersohn (2000: 87ff) for some criticism. A fuller account of reducing Logical Space to Intensional Model Space can be found in Menzel (1990).

3.3 Variants

We have seen that constraints on (extensional or intensional) model space may go well beyond what is expressible in the object-language. However, they may be expressible in other languages, and particularly in the ones used in *indirect interpretation*. This technique, which goes back to Montague (1970), proceeds by assigning meanings to natural language expressions by translating them into logical formulae, which are themselves interpreted model-theoretically. As it turns out, formal languages of *higher-order type logic* are particularly suited for this purpose, since they allow for step-by-step translation procedures covering all expressions and sub-expressions of natural language, thereby inducing compositional meaning assignments; cf. Janssen (1983) for technical details. At the same time, these languages tend to be more expressive than the natural language sources (cf. 3.4). Consequently, they may be used to formulate more powerful restrictions on model space than the directly expressible meaning postulates considered above. Ample illustration of this – rather popular – technique of *indirect meaning postulates*, may be found in Dowty (1979). As a case in point, the property of being a *referentially transparent* (or *first-order reducible*) transitive verb can be expressed in type logic but not in pertinent fragments of English; cf. Zimmermann (1985) for details.

Another respect in which traditional model-theoretic approaches to natural language semantics may diverge, concerns the location of logical material. In the above sketch, logicality crops up as a feature of (i) certain lexical items (*logical words*) and (ii) of the *logical operations* on meanings that correspond to the grammatical constructions combining syntactic material. The former are determined by the models, but the latter are assigned as part of a model-independent global compositional interpretation procedure. In principle, we could have made them part of the models too, though, thereby making more space for variations between models – as in the classical account of Montague (1970), where however, logicality restrictions are not made explicit. An even more radical assimilation between (i) logical words and (ii) logical operations is obtained when the latter are represented by underlying 'functional' morphemes, which opens the possibility of keeping the logical combinations proper to a minimum. This approach is taken in LF-based *type-driven interpretation*, as made popular by Heim & Kratzer (1998).

3.4 Mathematical Model Theory

Model-theoretic interpretation originated in mathematical logic, where it is not used to approximate Logical Space but rather accounts for semantic variation among various (fragments of) formal *languages*; cf. Etchemendy (1990) for more on this difference in perspective, which incidentally does not affect any mathematical technicalities and results. Though a large part of the latter concern certain varieties of first-order predicate logic, they may have repercussions on model-theoretic semantics of natural language, especially if they concern questions of expressiveness. The two most fundamental results of mathematical model theory – usually derived as corollaries to completeness of first-order logic – are cases in point:

- According to the *Compactness Theorem*, a set Σ of (closed) first order formulae can only imply a particular (closed first-order) formula if the latter already follows from a finite subset of Σ. As a consequence, no first-order formula can express that the universe is infinite (though it may imply this) – because such a formula would be implied by the set of (first-order expressible) sentences that say that there are at least n objects, but not by any of its finite subsets.

- According to the *Löwenheim-Skolem Theorem*, a set Σ of (closed) first order formulae that is true in a model with an infinite universe, is true in models with universes of arbitrary infinite cardinalities. In particular, no collection of first-order formulae can express that the universe has a particular infinite cardinality.

According to a fundamental result of abstract model theory due to Lindström (1969), the above two theorems characterise first-order logic in that any language exceeding its expressive power is bound to fail at least one of them; cf. Ebbinghaus *et al.* (1994) for the technical background. In any case, there is little doubt that natural languages have the resources to express infinity. The model-theoretical study of higher-order logics is comparatively less well investigated, a major theme being the distinction between standard and non-standard models, the latter being introduced to restore axiomatisability – at the price of losing the kinds of idealisations in the set-theoretic construction of denotations mentioned and motivated in Section 2; a survey of the most fundamental results of higher-order model theory can be found in van Benthem & Doets (1983).

4 References

Abbott, Barbara 1997. Models, truth and semantics. *Linguistics & Philosophy* 20, 117–138.
Abbott, Barbara & Larry Hauser 1995. *Realism, Model Theory, and Linguistic Semantics*. Paper presented at the *Annual Meeting of the Linguistic Society of America*. New Orleans, January 8, 1995. http://cogprints.org/256/1/realism.htm. December 9, 2010.
Benthem, Johan van & Kees Doets 1983. Higher-order logic. In: D. M. Gabbay & F. Guenthner (eds.). *Handbook of Philosophical Logic, vol. I*. Dordrecht: Reidel, 275–329.
Button, Tim 2011. The metamathematics of Putnam's model-theoretic arguments. *Erkenntnis* 74, 321–349.
Carnap, Rudolf 1947. *Meaning and Necessity*. Chicago, IL: The University of Chicago Press.
Carnap, Rudolf 1952. Meaning postulates. *Philosophical Studies* 3, 65–73.
Casanovas, Enrique 2007. Logical operations and invariance. *Journal of Philosophical Logic* 36, 33–60.
Cresswell, Maxwell J. 1982. The autonomy of semantics. In: S. Peters & E. Saarinen (eds.). *Processes, Beliefs, and Questions*. Dordrecht: Kluwer, 69–86.
Devitt, Michael 1983. Realism and the renegade Putnam: A critical study of meaning and the moral sciences. *Noûs* 17, 291–301.
Dowty, David 1979. *Word Meaning and Montague Grammar*. Dordrecht: Kluwer.
Ebbinghaus, Heinz-Dieter, Jörg Flum & Wolfgang Thomas 1994. *Mathematical Logic*. 2nd edn. Berlin: de Gruyter.
Etchemendy, John 1990. *The Concept of Logical Consequence*. Cambridge, MA: The MIT Press.
Field, Hartry 1975. Conventionalism and instrumentalism in semantics. *Noûs* 9, 375–405.

Fine, Kit 1977. Properties, propositions, and sets. *Journal of Philosophical Logic* 6, 135–191.
Frege, Gottlob 1884/1950. *Die Grundlagen der Arithmetik: eine logisch-mathematische Untersuchung über den Begriff der Zahl.* Breslau: W. Koebner 1884. English translation in J. Austin.*The Foundations of Arithmetic: A Logico-mathematical Enquiry into the Concept of Number*.1st edn. Oxford: Blackwell, 1950.
Frege, Gottlob 1892/1980. Über Sinn und Bedeutung. *Zeitschrift für Philosophie und philosophische Kritik* 100, 25–50. English translation in: P. Geach & M. Black (eds.). *Translations from the Philosophical Writings of Gottlob Frege*. Oxford: Blackwell, 1980, 56–78.
Gazdar, Gerald, Ewan Klein, Geoffrey Pullum & Ivan A. Sag 1985. *Generalized Phrase Structure Grammar*. Cambridge, MA: The MIT Press.
Heim, Irene & Angelika Kratzer 1998. *Semantics in Generative Grammar*. Oxford: Oxford University Press.
Hodges, Wilfried 2001. Formal features of compositionality. *Journal of Logic, Language and Information* 10, 7–28.
Janssen, Theo M.V. 1983. *Foundations and Applications of Montague Grammar*. Doctoral dissertation. University of Amsterdam.
Jeffrey, Richard J. 1964. Review of Sections IV–V of E. Nagel et al. (eds.). *Logic, Methodology, and Philosophy of Science* (Stanford, CA 1962). *Journal of Philosophy* 61, 79–88.
Kripke, Saul A. 1972. Naming and necessity. In: D. Davidson & G. Harman (eds.). *Semantics of Natural Language*. Dordrecht: Kluwer, 253–355.
Kupffer, Manfred 2007. Contextuality as supervenience. In: M. Aloni, P. Dekker & F. Roelofsen (eds.). *Proceedings of the Sixteenth Amsterdam Colloquium*. Amsterdam: ILLC, 139–144. http://www.illc.uva.nl/AC2007/uploaded_files/proceedings-AC07.pdf. December 9, 2010.
Lasersohn, Peter 2000. Same, models and representation. In: B. Jackson & T. Matthews (eds.). *Proceedings from Semantics and Linguistic Theory (=SALT) X*. Ithaca, NY: Cornell University, 83–97.
Lasersohn, Peter 2005. The temperature paradox as evidence for a presuppositional analysis of definite descriptions. *Linguistic Inquiry* 36, 127–134.
Lewis, David K. 1984. Putnam's paradox. *Australasian Journal of Philosophy* 62, 221–236.
Lindenbaum, Adolf & Alfred Tarski 1935/1983. Über die Beschränktheit der Ausdrucksmittel deduktiver Theorien. *Ergebnisse eines mathematischen Kolloquiums* 7, 15–22. English translation in: J. Corcoran (ed.). *Logic, Semantics, Metamathematics*. 2nd edn. Indianapolis, IN: Hackett Publishing Company, 1983, 384–392.
Lindström, Per 1969. On extensions of elementary logic. *Theoria* 35, 1–11.
Löbner, Sebastian 1979. *Intensionale Verben und Funktionalbegriffe*. Tübingen: Niemeyer.
Macbeath, Murray 1982. "Who was Dr Who's Father?". *Synthese* 51, 397–430.
MacFarlane, John 2008. Logical constants. In: E. Zalta (ed.). *The Stanford Encyclopedia of Philosophy (Fall 2008 Edition)*. Online Publication. *Stanford Encyclopedia of Philosophy*. http://plato.stanford.edu/entries/logical-constants. December 9, 2010.
Machover, Moshé 1994. Review of G. Sher. *The Bounds of Logic. A Generalized Viewpoint* (Cambridge, MA 1991). *British Journal for the Philosophy of Science* 45, 1078–1083.
Mendelson, Elliott 1997. *An Introduction to Mathematical Logic*. 4th edn. London: Chapman & Hall.
Menzel, Christopher 1990. Actualism, ontological commitment, and possible world semantics. *Synthese* 85, 355–389.
Montague, Richard 1970. Universal grammar. *Theoria* 36, 373–398.

Montague, Richard 1973. The proper treatment of quantification in ordinary English. In: J. Hintikka, J.M.E. Moravcsik & P. Suppes (eds.). *Approaches to Natural Language*. Dordrecht: Kluwer, 221–242.
Newman, Maxwell H. A. 1928. Mr. Russell's 'causal theory of perception'. *Mind* 37, 137–148.
Putnam, Hilary 1977. Realism and reason. *Proceedings of the American Philosophical Association* 50, 483–498.
Putnam, Hilary 1980. Models and reality. *Journal of Symbolic Logic* 45, 464–482.
Rabinowicz, Wlodek 1979. *Universalizability. A Study in Morals and Metaphysics*. Dordrecht: Reidel.
Wallace, John 1977. Only in the context of a sentence do words have any meaning. *Midwest Studies in Philosophy* 2, 144–164.
Williams, John R. G. 2005. *The Inscrutability of Reference*. Doctoral dissertation. University of St Andrews.
Wittgenstein, Ludwig 1922. *Tractatus logico-philosophicus. Logisch-philosophische Abhandlung*. London: Kegan Paul, Trench, Trubner & Co.
Zimmermann, Thomas E. 1985. A note on transparency postulates. *Journal of Semantics* 4, 67–77.
Zimmermann, Thomas E. 1999. Meaning postulates and the model-theoretic approach to natural language semantics. *Linguistics & Philosophy* 22, 529–561.

Claudia Maienborn
8 Event semantics

1. Introduction —— 232
2. Davidsonian event semantics —— 235
3. The Neo-Davidsonian turn —— 240
4. The stage-level/individual-level distinction —— 245
5. Reconsidering states —— 252
6. Psycholinguistic studies —— 257
7. Conclusion —— 260
8. References —— 261

Abstract: Since entering the linguistic stage in the late sixties, Davidsonian event semantics has taken on an important role in linguistic theorizing. Davidson's (1967) central claim is that events are spatiotemporal things, i.e., concrete particulars with a location in space and time. This enrichment of the underlying ontology has proven to be of great benefit in explaining numerous combinatorial and inferential properties of natural language expressions. This article will trace the motivation, development, and applications of event semantics during the past decades and provide a picture of current views on the role of events in natural language meaning. Besides introducing the classical Davidsonian paradigm and providing an ontological characterization of events, the article discusses the Neo-Davidsonian turn with its broader perspective on eventualities and the use of thematic roles and/or decompositional approaches. Further topics are the stage-level/individual-level distinction, the somewhat murky category of states and some results of recent psycholinguistic studies that have tested the insights of Davidsonian event semantics.

1 Introduction

Since entering the linguistic stage in the late sixties, Davidsonian event semantics has taken on an important role in linguistic theorizing. The central claim of Donald Davidson's seminal (1967) work "The logical form of action sentences" is that events are spatiotemporal *things*, i.e., concrete particulars with a location

Claudia Maienborn, Tübingen, Germany

https://doi.org/10.1515/9783110589245-008

in space and time. This enrichment of the underlying ontology has proven to be of great benefit in explaining numerous combinatorial and inferential properties of natural language expressions. Most prominent among the many remarkable advances achieved within the Davidsonian paradigm since then have been the progress made in the theoretical description of verb semantics, including tense and aspect, and the breakthrough in analyzing adverbial modification. Numerous monographs and collections attest to the extraordinary fruitfulness of the Davidsonian program; see, e.g., Rothstein (1998), Tenny & Pustejovsky (2000), Higginbotham, Pianesi & Varzi (2000), Lang, Maienborn & Fabricius-Hansen (2003), Austin, Engelberg & Rauh (2004), Maienborn & Wöllstein (2005), Dölling, Heyde-Zybatov & Schäfer (2008) to mention just a few collections from the last decade.

In the course of the evolution of the Davidsonian paradigm, two moves have turned out to be particularly influential in terms of expanding and giving new direction to this overall approach. These are, first, the "Neo-Davidsonian turn" initiated by Higginbotham (1985, 2000) and Parsons (1990, 2000), and, secondly, Kratzer's (1995) merger of event semantics with the stage-level/individual-level distinction.

The Neo-Davidsonian approach has lately developed into a kind of standard for event semantics. It is basically characterized by two largely independent assumptions. The first assumption concerns the arity of verbal predicates. While Davidson introduced event arguments as an *additional* argument of (some) verbs, Neo-Davidsonian accounts take the event argument of a verbal predicate to be its *only* argument. The relation between events and their participants is accounted for by the use of thematic roles. The second Neo-Davidsonian assumption concerns the distribution of event arguments: they are considered to be much more widespread than originally envisaged by Davidson. That is, Neo-Davidsonian approaches typically assume that it is not only (action) verbs that introduce Davidsonian event arguments, but also adjectives, nouns, and prepositions. Thus, event arguments are nowadays widely seen as a trademark for predicates in general. For this broader notion of events, which includes, besides events proper, i.e., accomplishments and achievements in Vendler's (1967) terms, also processes and states, Bach (1986) coined the term "eventuality".

The second milestone in the development of the Davidsonian program is Kratzer's (1995) event semantic treatment of the so-called stage-level/individual-level distinction, which goes back to Carlson (1977) and, as a precursor, Milsark (1974, 1977). Roughly speaking, stage-level predicates (SLPs) express temporary or accidental properties, whereas individual-level predicates (ILPs) express (more or less) permanent or inherent properties. On Kratzer's (1995) account, the SLP/ILP-distinction basically boils down to the presence or absence of an extra event argument. Stage-level predicates are taken to have such an additional event argument, while individual-level predicates lack it. This difference in argument structure is then exploited syntactically by the assumption, e.g., of different subject positions for SLPs and ILPs; see Diesing (1992). Since then interest has been directed towards the role of event arguments at the syntax/semantics interface.

These developments are accompanied by a newly found interest in the linguistic and ontological foundation of events. To the extent that more attention is paid to less typical events than the classical "Jones buttering a toast" or "Brutus stabbing Caesar", which always come to the Davidsonian semanticist's mind first, there is a growing awareness of the vagueness and incongruities lurking behind the notion of events and its use in linguistic theorizing. A particularly controversial case in point is the status of *states*. The question of whether state expressions can be given a Davidsonian treatment analogous to process and event expressions (in the narrow sense) is still open to debate.

All in all, Davidsonian event arguments have become a very familiar "all-purpose" linguistic instrument over the past decades, and recent years have seen a continual extension of possible applications far beyond the initial focus on verb semantics and adverbials also including a growing body of psycholinguistic studies that aim to investigate the role of events in natural language representation and processing.

This article will trace the motivation, development, and applications of event semantics during the past decades and provide a picture of current views on the role of events in natural language meaning. Section 2 introduces the classical Davidsonian paradigm, providing an overview of its motivation and some classical and current applications, as well as an ontological characterization of events and their linguistic diagnostics. Section 3 discusses the Neo-Davidsonian turn with its broader perspective on eventualities and the use of thematic roles. This section also includes some notes on decompositional approaches to event semantics. Section 4 turns to the stage-level/individual-level distinction, outlining the basic linguistic phenomena that are grouped together under this label and discussing the event semantic treatments that have been proposed as well as the criticism they have received. Section 5 returns to ontological matters by reconsidering the category of states and asking whether indeed all of them, in particular the referents introduced by so-called "statives", fulfill the criteria for Davidsonian eventualities. And, finally, section 6 presents some experimental results of recent psycholinguistic studies that have tested the insights of Davidsonian event semantics. The article concludes with some final remarks in section 7.

2 Davidsonian event semantics

2.1 Motivation and applications

On the standard view in Pre-Davidsonian times, a transitive verb such as *to butter* in (1a) would be conceived of as introducing a relation between the subject *Jones* and the direct object *the toast*, thus yielding the logical form (1b).

(1) a. Jones buttered the toast.
    b. BUTTER (jones, the toast)

The only individuals that sentence (1a) talks about according to (1b) are Jones and the toast. As Davidson (1967) points out such a representation does not allow us to refer explicitly to the action described by the sentence and specify it further by adding, e.g., that Jones did it slowly, deliberately, with a knife, in the bathroom, at midnight. What, asks Davidson, does *it* refer to in such a continuation? His answer is that action verbs introduce an additional hidden event argument that stands for the action proper. Under this perspective, a transitive verb introduces a three-place relation holding between the subject, the direct object and an event argument. Davidson's proposal thus amounts to replacing (1b) with the logical form in (1c).

(1) c. $\exists e$ [BUTTER (jones, the toast, e)]

This move paves the way for a straightforward analysis of adverbial modification. If verbs introduce a hidden event argument, then standard adverbial modifiers may be simply analyzed as first-order predicates that add information about this event; cf. article 14 [Semantics: Lexical Structures and Adjectives] (Maienborn & Schäfer) *Adverbs and adverbials* on the problems of alternative analyses and further details of the Davidsonian approach to adverbial modification. Thus, Davidson's classical sentence (2a) takes the logical form (2b).

(2) a. Jones buttered the toast in the bathroom with the knife at midnight.
    b. $\exists e$ [BUTTER (jones, the toast, e) & IN (e, the bathroom) & INSTR (e, the knife) & AT (e, midnight)]

According to (2b), sentence (2a) expresses that there was an event of Jones buttering the toast, and this event was located in the bathroom. In addition, it was performed by using a knife as an instrument, and it took place at midnight. Thus, the verb's hidden event argument provides a suitable target for adverbial modifiers.

As Davidson points out, this allows adverbial modifiers to be treated analogously to adnominal modifiers: Both target the referential argument of their verbal or nominal host.

> Adverbial modification is thus seen to be logically on a par with adjectival modification: what adverbial clauses modify is not verbs but the events that certain verbs introduce.
>
> Davidson (1969/1980: 167)

One of the major advances achieved through the analysis of adverbial modifiers as first-order predicates on the verb's event argument is its straightforward account of the characteristic entailment patterns of sentences with adverbial modifiers. For instance, we want to be able to infer from (2a) the truth of the sentences in (3). On a Davidsonian account this follows directly from the logical form (2b) by virtue of the logical rule of simplification; cf. (3'). See, e.g., Eckardt (1998, 2002) on the difficulties that these entailment patterns pose for a classical operator approach to adverbials such as advocated by Thomason & Stalnaker (1973), see also article 14 [Semantics: Lexical Structures and Adjectives] (Maienborn & Schäfer) *Adverbs and adverbials*.

(3) a. Jones buttered the toast in the bathroom at midnight.
    b. Jones buttered the toast in the bathroom.
    c. Jones buttered the toast at midnight.
    d. Jones butterd the toast with the knife.
    e. Jones buttered the toast.

(3') a. $\exists e\ [\text{BUTTER (jones, the toast, e)}\ \&\ \text{IN (e, the bathroom)}\ \&\ \text{AT (e, midnight)}]$
     b. $\exists e\ [\text{BUTTER (jones, the toast, e)}\ \&\ \text{IN (e, the bathroom)}]$
     c. $\exists e\ [\text{BUTTER (jones, the toast, e)}\ \&\ \text{AT (e, midnight)}]$
     d. $\exists e\ [\text{BUTTER (jones, the toast, e)}\ \&\ \text{INSTR (e, the knife)}]$
     e. $\exists e\ [\text{BUTTER (jones, the toast, e)}]$

Further evidence for the existence of hidden event arguments can be adduced from anaphoricity, quantification and definite descriptions among others: Having introduced event arguments, the anaphoric pronoun *it* in (4) may now straightforwardly be analyzed as referring back to a previously mentioned event, just like other anaphoric expressions take up object referents and the like.

(4) It happened silently and in complete darkness.

Hidden event arguments also provide suitable targets for numerals and frequency adverbs as in (5).

(5) a. Anna has read the letter three times/many times.
    b. Anna has often/seldom/never read the letter.

Krifka (1990) shows that nominal measure expressions may also be used as a means of measuring the event referent introduced by the verb. Krifka's example (6) has a reading which does not imply that there were necessarily 4000 ships that passed through the lock in the given time span but that there were 4000 passing events of maybe just one single ship. That is, what is counted by the nominal numeral in this reading are passing events rather than ships.

(6) 4000 ships passed through the lock last year.

Finally, events may also serve as referents for definite descriptions as in (7).

(7) a. the fall of the Berlin Wall
    b. the buttering of the toast
    c. the sunrise

See, e.g., Bierwisch (1989), Grimshaw (1990), Zucchi (1993), Ehrich & Rapp (2000), Rapp (2007) for event semantic treatments of nominalizations; cf. also article 12 [Semantics: Noun Phrases and Verb Phrases] (Grimshaw) *Deverbal nominalization*. Engelberg (2000: 100ff) offers an overview of the phenomena for which event-based analyses have been proposed since Davidson's insight was taken up and developed further in linguistics.

The overall conclusion that Davidson invites us to draw from all these linguistic data is that events are *things* in the real world like objects; they can be counted, they can be anaphorically referred to, they can be located in space and time, they can be ascribed further properties. All this indicates that the world, as we conceive of it and talk about it, is apparently populated by such things as events.

2.2 Ontological properties and linguistic diagnostics

Semantic research over the past decades has provided impressive confirmation of Davidson's (1969/1980: 137) claim that "there is a lot of language we can make systematic sense of if we suppose events exist". But, with Quine's dictum "No entity without identity!" in mind, we have to ask: What kind of things *are* events? What are their identity criteria? And how are their ontological properties reflected through linguistic structure?

None of these questions has received a definitive answer so far, and many versions of the Davidsonian approach have been proposed, with major and minor differences between them. Focussing on the commonalities behind these differences, it still seems safe to say that there is at least one core assumption in the Davidsonian approach that is shared more or less explicitly by most scholars working in this paradigm. This is that eventualities are, first and foremost, *particular spatiotemporal entities* in the world. As LePore (1985: 151) puts it, "[Davidson's] central claim is that events are concrete particulars – that is, unrepeatable entities with a location in space and time." As the past decades' discussion of this issue has shown (see, e.g., the overviews in Lombard 1998, Engelberg 2000, and Pianesi & Varzi 2000), it is nevertheless notoriously difficult to turn the above ontological outline into precise identity criteria for eventualities. For illustration, I will mention just two prominent attempts.

Lemmon (1967) suggests that two events are identical just in case they occupy the same portion of space and time. This notion of events seems much too coarse-grained, at least for linguistic purposes, since any two events that just happen to coincide in space and time would, on this account, be identical. To take Davidson's (1969/1980: 178) example, we wouldn't be able to distinguish the event of a metal ball rotating around its own axis during a certain time from an event of the metal ball becoming warmer during the very same time span. Note that we could say that the metal ball is slowly becoming warmer while it is rotating quickly, without expressing a contradiction. This indicates that we are dealing with two separate events that coincide in space and time.

Parsons (1990), on the other hand, attempts to establish genuinely linguistic identity criteria for events: "When a verb-modifier appears truly in one source and falsely in another, the events cannot be identical." (Parsons 1990: 157). This, by contrast, yields a notion of events that is too fine-grained; see, e.g., the criticism by Eckardt (1998: § 3.1) and Engelberg (2000: 221–225). What we are still missing, then, are ontological criteria of the appropriate grain for identifying events. This is the conclusion Pianesi & Varzi (2000) arrive at in their discussion of the ontological nature of events:

> [...] the idea that events are spatiotemporal particulars whose identity criteria are moderately thin [...] has found many advocates both in the philosophical and in the linguistic literature. [...] But they all share with Davidson's the hope for a 'middle ground' account of the number of particular events that may simultaneously occur in the same place.
>
> Pianesi & Varzi (2000: 555)

We can conclude, then, that the search for ontological criteria for identifying events will probably continue for some time. In the meantime, linguistic research will have to build on a working definition that is up to the demands of natural language analysis.

What might also be crucial for our notion of events (besides their spatial and temporal dimensions) is their inherently relational character. Authors like Parsons (1990), Carlson (1998), Eckardt (1998), and Asher (2000) have argued that events necessarily involve participants serving some function. In fact, the ability of Davidsonian analyses to make explicit the relationship between events and their participants, either via thematic roles or by some kind of decomposition (see sections 3.2 and 3.3 below), is certainly one of the major reasons among linguists for the continuing popularity of such analyses. This feature of Davidsonian analyses is captured by the statement in (8), which I will adopt as a working definition for the subsequent discussion; cf. Maienborn (2005a).

(8) *Davidsonian notion of events:*
Events are particular spatiotemporal entities with functionally integrated participants.

(8) may be taken to be the core assumption of the Davidsonian paradigm. Several ontological properties follow from it. As spatiotemporal entities in the world, events can be perceived, and they have a location in space and time. In addition, given the functional integration of participants, events can vary in the way that they are realized. These properties are summarized in (9):

(9) *Ontological properties of events:*
 a. Events are perceptible.
 b. Events can be located in space and time.
 c. Events can vary in the way that they are realized.

The properties in (9) can, in turn, be used to derive well-known linguistic event diagnostics:

(10) *Linguistic diagnostics for events:*
 a. Event expressions can serve as infinitival complements of perception verbs.
 b. Event expressions combine with locative and temporal modifiers.
 c. Event expressions combine with manner adverbials, comitatives, etc.

The diagnostics in (10) provide a way to detect hidden event arguments. As shown by Higginbotham (1983), perception verbs with infinitival complements are a means of expressing direct event perception and thus provide a suitable test context for event expressions; cf. also Eckardt (2002). A sentence such as (11a) expresses that Anna perceived the event of Heidi cutting the roses. This does not imply that Anna was necessarily aware of, e.g., who was performing the action; see the continuation in (11b). Sentence (11c), on the other hand, does not express direct event perception but rather fact perception. Whatever it was that Anna perceived, it made her conclude that Heidi was cutting the roses. A continuation along the lines of (11b) is not allowed here; cf. Bayer (1986) on what he calls the *epistemic neutrality* of event perception vs. the *epistemic load* of fact perception.

(11) a. Anna saw Heidi cut the roses.
 b. Anna saw Heidi cut the roses, but she didn't recognize that it was Heidi who cut the roses.
 c. Anna saw that Heidi was cutting the roses (*but she didn't recognize that it was Heidi who cut the roses).

On the basis of the ontological properties of events spelled-out in (9b) and (9c), we also expect event expressions to combine with locative and temporal modifiers as well as with manner adverbials, instrumentals, comitatives and the like – that is, modifiers that elaborate on the internal functional set-up of events. This was already illustrated by our sentence (2); see article 14 [Semantics: Lexical Structures and Adjectives] (Maienborn & Schäfer) *Adverbs and adverbials* for details on the contribution of manner adverbials and similar expressions that target the internal structure of events.

This is, in a nutshell, the Davidsonian view shared (explicitly or implicitly) by current event-based approaches. The diagnostics in (10) provide a suitable tool for detecting hidden event arguments and may therefore help us to assess the Neo-Davidsonian claim that event arguments are not confined to action verbs but have many further sources, to which we will turn next.

3 The Neo-Davidsonian turn

3.1 The notion of eventualities

Soon after they took the linguistic stage, it became clear that event arguments were not to be understood as confined to the class of action verbs, as Davidson originally proposed, but were likely to have a much wider distribution. A guiding assumption of what has been called the *Neo-Davidsonian paradigm*, developed particularly by Higginbotham (1985, 2000) and Parsons (1990, 2000), is that any verbal predicate may have such a hidden Davidsonian argument as illustrated by the following quotations from Higginbotham (1985) and Chierchia (1995).

> The position E corresponds to the 'hidden' argument place for events, originally suggested by Donald Davidson (1967). There seem to be strong arguments in favour of, and little to be said against, extending Davidson's idea to verbs other than verbs of change or action. Under this extension, statives will also have E-positions.
>
> Higginbotham (1985: 10)

> A basic assumption I am making is that every VP, whatever its internal structure and aspectual characteristics, has an extra argument position for eventualities, in the spirit of Davidson's proposal. [...] In a way, having this extra argument slot is part of what makes something a VP, whatever its inner structure.
>
> Chierchia (1995: 204)

Note that already some of the first commentators on Davidson's proposal took a similarly broad view on the possible sources for Davidson's extra argument. For instance, Kim (1969: 204) notes: "When we talk of explaining an event, we are not excluding what, in a narrower sense of the term, is not an event but rather a state or a process." So it was only natural to extend Davidson's original proposal and combine it with Vendler's (1967) classification of situation types into *states*, *activities*, *accomplishments* and *achievements*. In fact, the continuing strength and attractiveness of the overall Davidsonian enterprise for contemporary linguistics rests to a large extent on the combination of these two congenial insights: Davidson's introduction of an ontological category of events present in linguistic structure, and Vendler's subclassification of different situation types according to the temporal-aspectual properties of the respective verb phrases; cf., e.g., Piñón (1997), Engelberg (2002), Sæbø (2006) for some more recent event semantic studies on the lexical and/or aspectual properties of certain verb classes.

The definition and delineation of events (comprising Vendler's *accomplishments* and *achievements*), processes (*activities* in Vendler's terms) and states has been an extensively discussed and highly controversial topic of studies particularly on tense and aspect. The reader is referred to the articles 9 [Semantics: Noun Phrases and Verb Phrases] (Filip) *Aspectual class and Aktionsart* and 4 [Semantics: Typology, Diachrony and Processing (Smith) *Tense and aspect*. For our present purposes the following brief remarks shall suffice:

First, a terminological note: The notion "event" is often understood in a broad sense, i.e. as covering, besides events in a narrow sense, processes and states as well. Bach (1986) has introduced the term "eventuality" for this broader notion of events. In the remainder of this article I will stick to speaking of events in a broad sense unless explicitly indicated otherwise. Other labels for an additional Davidsonian event argument that can be found in the literature include "spatiotemporal location" (e.g. Kratzer 1995) and "Davidsonian argument" (e.g. Chierchia 1995).

Secondly, events (in a narrow sense), processes, and states may be characterized in terms of dynamicity and telicity. Events and processes are dynamic eventualities, states are static. Furthermore, events have an inherent culmination point, i.e., they are telic, whereas processes and states, being atelic, have no such inherent culmination point; see Krifka (1989, 1992, 1998) for a mereological characterization of events and cf. also Dowty (1979), Rothstein (2004).

Finally, accomplishments and achievements, the two subtypes of events in a narrow sense, differ wrt. their temporal extension. Whereas accomplishments such as expressed by *read the book, eat one pound of cherries, run the 100m final* have a temporal extension, achievements such as *reach the summit, find the solution, win the 100m final* are momentary changes of state with no temporal duration. See Kennedy & Levin (2008) on so-called *degree achievements* expressed by verbs like *to lengthen, to cool*, etc. The variable aspectual behavior of these verbs – atelic (permitting the combination with a *for*-PP) or telic (permitting the combination with an *in*-PP) – is explained in terms of the relation between the event structure and the scalar structure of the base adjective; cf. (12).

(12) a. The soup cooled for 10 minutes.   (atelic)
     b. The soup cooled in 10 minutes.   (telic)

Turning back to the potential sources for Davidsonian event arguments, in more recent times not only verbs, whether eventive or stative, have been taken to introduce an additional argument, but other lexical categories as well, such as adjectives, nouns and also prepositions. Motivation for this move comes from the observation that all predicative categories provide basically the same kind of empirical evidence that motivated Davidson's proposal and thus call for a broader application of the Davidsonian analysis. The following remarks from Higginbotham & Ramchand (1997) are typical of this view:

> Once we assume that predicates (or their verbal, etc. heads) have a position for events, taking the many consequences that stem therefrom, as outlined in publications originating with Donald Davidson (1967), and further applied in Higginbotham (1985, 1989), and Terence Parsons (1990), we are not in a position to deny an event-position to any predicate; for the evidence for, and applications of, the assumption are the same for all predicates.
>
> Higginbotham & Ramchand (1997: 54)

As these remarks indicate, nowadays Neo-Davidsonian approaches often take event arguments to be a trademark not only of verbs but of predicates in general. We will come back to this issue in section 5 when we reconsider the category of states.

3.2 Events and thematic roles

The second core assumption of Neo-Davidsonian accounts, besides assuming a broader distribution of event arguments, concerns the way of relating the event argument to the predicate and its regular arguments. While Davidson (1967) introduced the event argument as an additional argument to the verbal predicate thereby augmenting its arity, Neo-Davidsonian accounts use the notion of thematic roles for linking an event to its participants. Thus, the Neo-Davidsonian version of Davidson's logical form in (2b) for the classical sentence (2a), repeated here as (13a/b) takes the form in (13c).

(13) a. Jones buttered the toast in the bathroom with the knife at midnight.
   b. ∃e [BUTTER (jones, the toast, e) & IN (e, the bathroom) & INSTR (e, the knife) & AT (e, midnight)]
   c. ∃e [BUTTER (e) & AGENT (e, jones) & PATIENT (e, the toast) & IN (e, the bathroom) & INSTR (e, the knife) & AT (e, midnight)]

On a Neo-Davidsonian view, all verbs are uniformly one-place predicates ranging over events. The verb's regular arguments are introduced via thematic roles such as AGENT, PATIENT, EXPERIENCER, etc., which express binary relations holding between events and their participants; cf. article 3 [Semantics: Lexical Structures and Adjectives] (Davis) *Thematic roles* for details on the nature, inventory and hierarchy of thematic roles. Note that due to this move of separating the verbal predicate from its arguments and adding them as independent conjuncts, Neo-Davidsonian accounts give up to some extent the distinction between arguments and modifiers. At least it isn't possible anymore to read off the number of arguments a verb has from the logical representation. While Davidson's notation in (13b) conserves the argument/modifier distinction by reserving the use of thematic roles for the integration of circumstantial modifiers, the Neo-Davidsonian notation (13c) uses thematic roles both for arguments such as the agent *Jones* as well as for modifiers such as the instrumental *the knife*; see Parsons (1990: 96ff) for motivation and defense and Bierwisch (2005) for some criticism on this point.

3.3 Decompositional event semantics

The overall Neo-Davidsonian approach is also compatible with adopting a decompositional perspective on the semantics of lexical items, particularly of verbs; cf. articles 1 [Semantics: Lexical Structures and Adjectives] (Bierwisch) *Semantic features and primes* and 2 [Semantics: Lexical Structures and Adjectives] (Engelberg) *Frameworks of decomposition*. Besides a standard lexical entry for a transitive verb such as *to close* in (14a) that translates the verbal meaning into a one-place predicate CLOSE on events, one might also choose to decompose the verbal meaning into more basic semantic predicates like the classical CAUSE, BECOME etc; cf. Dowty (1979). A somewhat simplified version of Parsons' "subatomic" approach is given in (14b); cf. Parsons (1990: 120).

(14) a. *to close:* λy λx λe [CLOSE (e) & AGENT (e, x) & THEME (e, y)]
 b. *to close:* λy λx λe [AGENT (e, x) & THEME (e, y) & ∃e' [CAUSE (e, e') & THEME (e', y) & ∃s [BECOME (e', s) & CLOSED (s) & THEME (s, y)]]]

According to (14b) the transitive verb *to close* expresses an action e taken by an agent x on a theme y which causes an event e' of y changing into a state s of being closed. On this account a causative verb introduces not one hidden event argument but three. See also Pustejovsky (1991, 1995) for a somewhat different conception of a decompositional event structure.

Additional subevent or state arguments as introduced in (14b) might also be targeted by particular modifiers. For instance, the repetitive/restitutive ambiguity of *again* can be accounted for by letting *again*, roughly speaking, have scope over either the causing event e (= repetitive reading) or the resulting state s (= restitutive reading); cf., e.g., the discussion in von Stechow (1996, 2003), Jäger & Blutner (2003). Of course, assuming further implicit event and state arguments, as illustrated in (14b), raises several intricate questions concerning, e.g., whether, when, and how such subevent variables that depend upon the verb's main event argument are bound. No common practice has evolved so far on how these dependent event arguments are compositionally treated. See also Bierwisch (2005) for arguments against projecting more than the highest event argument onto the verb's argument structure.

This might be the right place to add a remark on a further tradition of decompositional event semantics that goes back to Reichenbach (1947). Davidson's core idea of introducing event arguments can already be found in Reichenbach (1947), who, instead of adding an extra argument to verbal predicates, assumed a more general "event function" [p]*, by which a proposition p is turned into a characteristic property of events; see Bierwisch (2005) for a comparison of the Davidsonian, Neo-Davidsonian and Reichenbachian approaches to events. (Note that Reichenbach used the two notions "event function" and "fact function" synonymously.)

Thus, Reichenbach's way of introducing an event variable for the verb *to butter* would lead to the representation in (15a). This in turn yields (15b) as Reichenbach's version of the logical form for the classical sentence (2a).

(15) a. [BUTTER (x, y)]*(e)
 b. ∃e [[BUTTER (jones, the toast)]*(e) & IN (e, the bathroom) & INSTR (e, the knife) & AT (e, midnight)]

As Bierwisch (2005: 20) points out, Reichenbach's and Davidson's event variables were intended to account for roughly the same range of phenomena, including an analysis of adverbial modification in terms of conjunctively added event predicates.

Note that Kamp & Reyle's (1993) use of the colon to characterize an event e by a proposition p in DRT is basically a variant of Reichenbach's event function; cf. also 11 [this volume] (Kamp & Reyle) *Discourse Representation Theory*. Further notational variants are Bierwisch's (1988, 1997) INST-operator e INST p, or the use of curly brackets {p}(e) in Wunderlich (1997). All these are different notational versions for expressing that an event e is partially characterized by a proposition p.

Reichenbach's event function offers a way to pursue a decompositional approach to event semantics without being committed to a Parsons-style proliferation of subevent variables (with their unclear binding conditions) as illustrated in (14b). Thus, a (somewhat simplified) Bierwisch-style decomposition for our sample transitive verb *to close* would look like (16).

(16) *to close:* $\lambda y\, \lambda x\, \lambda e\, [e: \text{CAUSE}\, (x, \text{BECOME}\, (\text{CLOSED}\, (y)))]$

As these remarks show, there is a considerable range of variation exploited by current event semantic approaches as to the extent to which event and subevent variables are used and combined with further semantic instruments such as decompositional and/or thematic role approaches.

4 The stage-level/individual-level distinction

4.1 Linguistic phenomena

A particularly prominent application field for contemporary event semantic research is provided by the so-called stage-level/individual-level distinction, which goes back to Carlson (1977) and, as a precursor, Milsark (1974, 1977). Roughly speaking, stage-level predicates (SLPs) express temporary or accidental properties, whereas individual-level predicates (ILPs) express (more or less) permanent or inherent properties; some examples are given in (17) vs. (18).

(17) *Stage-level predicates*
   a. adjectives: *tired, drunk, available, …*
   b. verbs: *speak, wait, arrive, …*

(18) *Individual-level predicates*
    a. adjectives: *intelligent, blond, altruistic, ...*
    b. verbs: *know, love, resemble, ...*

The stage-level/individual-level distinction is taken to be a conceptually founded distinction that is grammatically reflected. Lexical predicates are classified as being either SLPs or ILPs. In the last years, a growing list of quite diverse linguistic phenomena have been associated with this distinction. Some illustrative cases will be mentioned next; cf., e.g., Higginbotham & Ramchand (1997), Fernald (2000), Jäger (2001), Maienborn (2003: §2.3) for commented overviews of SLP/ILP diagnostics that have been discussed in the literature.

4.1.1 Subject effects

Bare plural subjects of SLPs have, besides a generic reading ('Firemen are usually available.'), also an existential reading ('There are firemen who are available.') whereas bare plural subjects of ILPs only have a generic reading ('Firemen are usually altruistic.'):

(19) a. Firemen are available.   (SLP: generic + existential reading)
     b. Firemen are altruistic.   (ILP: only generic reading)

4.1.2 *There*-coda

Only SLPs (20) but not ILPs (21) may appear in the coda of a *there*-construction:

(20) a. There were children sick.   (SLP)
     b. There was a door open.

(21) a. *There were children tall.   (ILP)
     b. *There was a door wooden.

4.1.3 Antecedents in *when*-conditionals

ILPs cannot appear as restrictors of *when*-conditionals (provided that all argument positions are filled with definites; cf. Kratzer 1995):

(22) a. When Mary speaks French, she speaks it well. (SLP)
     b. *When Mary knows French, she knows it well. (ILP)

4.1.4 Combination with locative modifiers

SLPs can be combined with locative modifiers (23a), while ILPs don't accept locatives (23b):

(23) a. Maria was tired/hungry/nervous in the car. (SLP)
     b. ??Maria was blond/intelligent/a linguist in the car. (ILP)

Adherents of the stage-level/individual-level distinction take data like (23) as strong support for the claim that there is a fundamental difference between SLPs and ILPs in the ability to be located in space; see, e.g., the following quote from Fernald (2000: 24): "It is clear that SLPs differ from ILPs in the ability to be located in space and time."

4.1.5 Complements of perception verbs

Only SLPs, not ILPs, are admissible as small clause complements of perception verbs:

(24) a. Johann saw the king naked. (SLP)
     b. *Johann saw the king tall. (ILP)

4.1.6 Depictives

SLPs, but not ILPs, may build depictive secondary predicates:

(25) a. Paul$_i$ stood tired$_i$ at the fence. (SLP)
     b. Paul has bought the books$_i$ used$_i$.

(26) a. *Paul$_i$ stood blond$_i$ at the fence. (ILP)
     b. *Paul has bought the books$_i$ interesting$_i$.

Further cross-linguistic evidence that has been taken as support for the stage-level/individual-level distinction includes the alternation of the two copula forms *ser* and *estar* in Spanish and Portuguese (see Maienborn 2005c for a critical discussion), two different subject positions for copular sentences in Scottish Gaelic (e.g. Ramchand 1996), or the Nominative/Instrumental case alternation of nominal copular predicates in Russian (e.g. Geist 2006).

In sum, the standard perspective under which all these contrasts concerning subject effects, *when*-conditionals, locative modifiers, and so on have been considered is that they are distinct surface manifestations of a common underlying contrast. The *stage-level/individual-level hypothesis* is that the distinction of SLPs and ILPs rests on a fundamental (although still not fully understood) conceptual opposition that is reflected in multiple ways in the grammatical system. The following quotation from Fernald (2000) is representative of this view:

> Many languages display grammatical effects due to the two kinds of predicates, suggesting that this distinction is fundamental to the way humans think about the universe.
>
> Fernald (2000: 4)

Given that the conceptual side of the coin is still rather mysterious (Fernald (2000: 4): "Whatever sense of permanence is crucial to this distinction, it must be a very weak notion"), most stage-level/individual-level advocates content themselves with investigating the grammatical side (Higginbotham & Ramchand (1997: 53): "Whatever the grounds for this distinction, there is no doubt of its force"). We will come back to this issue in section 4.3.

4.2 Event semantic treatments

A first semantic analysis of the stage-level/individual-level contrast was developed by Carlson (1977). Carlson introduces a new kind of entities, which he calls "stages". These are spatiotemporal partitions of individuals. SLPs and ILPs are then analyzed as predicates ranging over different kinds of entities: ILPs are predicates over individuals, and SLPs are predicates over stages. Thus, on Carlson's approach the stage-level/individual-level distinction amounts to a basic difference at the ontological level. Kratzer (1995) takes a different direction locating the relevant difference at the level of the argument structure of the corresponding predicates. Crucially, SLPs have an extra event argument on Kratzer's account, whereas ILPs lack such an extra argument. The lexical entries for a SLP like *tired* and an ILP like *blond* are given in (27).

(27) a. *tired:* $\lambda x \lambda e\, [\text{TIRED}\,(e, x)]$
     b. *blond:* $\lambda x\, [\text{BLOND}\,(x)]$

This difference in argument structure may now be exploited for selectional restrictions, for instance. Perception verbs, e.g., require an event denoting complement; see the discussion of (11) in section 2.2. This prerequisite is only fulfilled by SLPs, which explains the SLP/ILP difference observed in (24). Moreover, the ban of ILPs from depictive constructions (see (25) vs. (26)) can be traced back to the need of the secondary predicate to provide a state argument that includes temporally the main predicate's event referent.

A very influential syntactic explanation for the observed subject effects within Kratzer's framework has been proposed by Diesing (1992). She assumes different subject positions for SLPs and ILPs: Subjects of SLPs have a VP-internal base position; subjects of ILPs are base-generated VP-externally. In addition, Diesing formulates a so-called *Mapping Hypothesis*, which serves as a syntax/semantics interface condition on the derivation of a logical form. (Diesing assumes a Lewis-Kamp-Heim-style tripartite logical form consisting of a non-selective quantifier Q, a restrictive clause (RC), and a nuclear scope (NS).) Diesing's (1992) Mapping-Hypothesis states that VP-material is mapped into the nuclear scope, and VP-external material is mapped into the restrictive clause. Finally, Diesing takes the VP-boundary to be the place for the existential closure of the nuclear scope. The different readings for SLP and ILP bare plural subjects follow naturally from these assumptions: If SLP subjects stay in their VP-internal base position, they will be mapped into the nuclear scope and, consequently, fall under the scope of the existential quantifier. This leads to the existential reading; cf. (28a). Or they move to a higher, VP-external subject position, in which case they are mapped into the restrictive clause and fall under the scope of the generic operator. This leads to the generic reading; cf. (28b). ILP subjects, having a VP-external base position, may only exploit the latter option. Thus, they only have a generic reading; cf. (29).

(28)   a. $\exists e, x$ [$_{NS}$ FIREMEN (x) & AVAILABLE (e, x)]   (cf. Kratzer 1995: 141)
       b. Gen e, x [$_{RC}$ FIREMEN (x) & IN (x, e)] [$_{NS}$ AVAILABLE (e, x)]

(29)   Gen x [$_{RC}$ FIREMEN (x)] [$_{NS}$ ALTRUISTIC (x)]

Kratzer's account also offers a straightforward solution for the different behavior of SLPs and ILPs wrt. locative modification; cf. (23). Having a Davidsonian event argument, SLPs provide a suitable target for locative modifiers, hence, they can be located in space. ILPs, on the other hand, lack such an additional event argument, and therefore do not introduce any referent whose location could be further specified via adverbial modification. This is illustrated in (30)/(31). While combining a SLP with a locative modifier yields a semantic representation like (30b), any attempt to add a locative to an ILP must necessarily fail; cf. (31b).

(30) a. Maria was tired in the car.
 b. ∃e [TIRED (e, maria) & IN (e, the car)]

(31) a. */??Maria was blond in the car.
 b. [BLOND (maria) & IN (???, the car)]

Thus, on a Kratzerian analysis, SLPs and ILPs indeed differ in their ability to be located in space (see the above quote from Fernald), and this difference is traced back to the presence vs. absence of an event argument. Analogously, the event variable of SLPs provides a suitable target for *when*-conditionals to quantify over in (22a), whereas the ILP case (22b) lacks such a variable; cf. Kratzer's (1995) *Prohibition against Vacuous Quantification*.

A somewhat different event semantic solution for the incompatibility of ILPs with locative modifiers has been proposed by Chierchia (1995). He takes a Neo-Davidsonian perspective according to which *all* predicates introduce event arguments. Thus, SLPs and ILPs do not differ in this respect. In order to account for the SLP/ILP contrast in combination with locatives, Chierchia then introduces a distinction between two kinds of events: SLPs refer to *location dependent events* whereas ILPs refer to *location independent events;* see also McNally (1998). The observed behavior wrt. locatives follows on the assumption that only location dependent events can be located in space. As Chierchia (1995: 178) puts it: "Intuitively, it is as if ILP were, so to speak, unlocated. If one is intelligent, one is intelligent nowhere in particular. SLP, on the other hand, are located in space."

Despite all differences, Kratzer's and Chierchia's analyses have some important commonalities. Both consider the SLP/ILP contrast in (30)/(31) as a grammatical effect. That is, sentences like (31a) do not receive a compositional semantic representation; they are grammatically ill-formed. Kratzer and Chierchia furthermore share the general intuition that SLPs (and only those) can be located in space. This is what the difference in (30a) vs. (31a) is taken to show. And, finally, both analyses rely crucially on the idea that at least SLPs, and possibly all predicates, introduce Davidsonian event arguments.

All in all, Kratzer's (1995) synthesis of the stage-level/individual-level distinction with Davidsonian event semantics has been extremely influential, opening up a new field of research and stimulating the development of further theoretical variants and of alternative proposals.

4.3 Criticisms and further developments

In subsequent studies of the stage-level/individual-level distinction two tendencies can be observed. On the one hand, the SLP/ILP contrast has been increasingly conceived of in information structural terms. Roughly speaking, ILPs relate to categorial judgements, whereas SLPs may build either categorial or thetical judgements; cf., e.g., Ladusaw (1994), McNally (1998), Jäger (2001). On this move, the stage-level/individual-level distinction is usually no longer seen as a lexically codified contrast but rather as being structurally triggered.

On the other hand there is growing skepticism concerning the empirical adequacy of the stage-level/individual-level hypothesis. Authors such as Higginbotham & Ramchand (1997), Fernald (2000), and Jäger (2001) argue that the phenomena subsumed under this label are actually quite distinct and do not yield such a uniform contrast upon closer scrutiny as a first glance might suggest.

For instance, as already noted by Bäuerle (1994: 23), the group of SLPs that support an existential reading of bare plural subjects is actually quite small; cf. (19a). The majority of SLPs, such as *tired* or *hungry* in (32) behaves more like ILPs, i.e., they only yield a generic reading.

(32) Firemen are hungry/tired. (SLP: only generic reading)

In view of the sentence pair in (33) Higginbotham & Ramchand (1997: 66) suspect that some notion of *speaker proximity* might also be of relevance for the availability of existential readings.

(33) a. (Guess whether) firemen are nearby/at hand.
      b. ?(Guess whether) firemen are far away/a mile up the road.

There-constructions, on the other hand, also appear to tolerate ILPs, contrary to what one would expect; cf. the example (34) taken from Carlson (1977: 72).

(34) There were five men dead.

Furthermore, as Glasbey (1997) shows, the availability of existential readings for bare plural subjects – both for SLPs and ILPs – might also be evoked by the context; cf. the following examples taken from Glasbey (1997: 170ff).

(35) a. Children are sick. (SLP: no existential reading)
      b. We must get a doctor. Children are sick. (SLP: existential reading)

(36) a. Drinkers were under-age. (ILP: no existential reading)
      b. John was shocked by his visit to the Red Lion. Drinkers were under-age, drugs were on sale, and a number of fights broke out while he was there. (ILP: existential reading)

As these examples show, the picture of the stage-level/individual-level contrast as a clear-cut, grammatically reflected distinction becomes a lot less clear upon closer inspection. The actual contributions of the lexicon, grammar, conceptual knowledge, and context to the emergence of stage-level/individual-level effects still remain largely obscure. While the research focus of the stage-level/individual-level paradigm has been directed almost exclusively towards the apparent grammatical effects of the SLP/ILP contrast, no major efforts were made to uncover its conceptual foundation, although there has never been any doubt that a definition of SLPs and ILPs in terms of the dichotomy "temporary vs. permanent" or "accidental vs. essential" cannot be but a rough approximation. Rather than being a mere accident, this missing link to a solid conceptual foundation could be a hint that the overall perspective on the stage-level/individual-level distinction as a genuinely grammatical distinction that reflects an underlying conceptual opposition might be wrong after all. The studies of Glasbey (1997), Maienborn (2003, 2004, 2005c) and Magri (2008, 2009) point in this direction. They all argue against treating stage-level/individual-level effects as grammatical in nature and provide alternative, pragmatic analyses for the observed phenomena. In particular, Maienborn argues against an event-based explanation objecting that the use of Davidsonian event arguments does not receive any independent justification in terms of the event criteria discussed in section 2.2 in such stage-level/individual-level accounts. The crucial question is whether all state expressions, or at least those state expressions that express temporary/accidental properties, i.e. SLPs, can be shown to introduce a Davidsonian event argument. This takes us back to the ontological issue of a proper characterization of states.

5 Reconsidering states

As mentioned in section 3.1 above, one of the two central claims of the Neo-Davidsonian paradigm is that *all* predicates, including state expressions, have a hidden event argument. Despite its popularity this claim has seldom been defended explicitly. Parsons (1995, 2000) is among the few advocates of the Neo-Davidsonian approach who have subjected this assumption to some scrutiny. And the conclusion he reaches wrt. state expressions is rather sobering:

> Based on the considerations reviewed above, it would appear that the underlying state analysis is not compelling for any kind of the constructions reviewed here and is not even plausible for some (e.g., for nouns). There are a few outstanding problems that the underlying state analysis might solve, […] but for the most part the weight of evidence seems to go the other way.
>
> (Parsons 2000: 88)

Parsons (2000) puts forth his so-called *time travel argument* to make a strong case for a Neo-Davidsonian analysis of state expressions; but cf. the discussion in Maienborn (2007). In any case, if the Neo-Davidsonian assumption concerning state expressions is right, we should be able to confirm the existence of hidden state arguments by the event diagnostics mentioned in section 2.2; cf. (10). Maienborn (2003, 2005a) examines the behavior of state expressions wrt. these and further event diagnostics and shows that there is a fundamental split within the class of non-dynamic expressions: State verbs such as *sit, stand, lie, wait, gleam,* and *sleep* meet all of the criteria for Davidsonian eventualities. In contrast, stative verbs like *know, weigh, own,* and *resemble* do not meet any of them. Moreover, it turns out that copular constructions behave uniformly like stative verbs, regardless of whether the predicate denotes a temporary property (SLP) or a more or less permanent property (ILP).

The behavior of state verbs and statives with respect to perception reports is illustrated in (37). While state verbs can serve as infinitival complements of perception verbs (37a-c), statives, including copula constructions, are prohibited in these contexts (37d-e). (The argumentation in Maienborn (2003, 2005a) is based on data from German. For ease of presentation I will use English examples in the following.)

(37) *Perception reports:*
    a. I saw the child sit on the bench.
    b. I saw my colleague sleep through the lecture.
    c. I noticed the shoes gleam in the light.
    d. *I saw the child be on the bench.
    e. *I saw the tomatoes weigh 1 pound.
    f. *I saw my aunt resemble Romy Schneider.

Furthermore, as (38a-c) shows, state verbs combine with locative modifiers, whereas statives do not; see (38d-g).

(38) *Locative modifiers:*
    a. Hilda waited at the corner.
    b. Bardo slept in a hammock.
    c. The pearls gleamed in her hair.
    d. *The dress was wet on the clothesline.
    e. *Bardo was hungry in front of the fridge.
    f. *The tomatoes weighed 1 pound besides the carrots.
    g. *Bardo knew the answer over there.

Three remarks on locatives should be added here. First, when using locatives as event diagnostics we have to make sure to use true event-related adverbials, i.e., locative VP-modifiers. They should not be confounded with locative frame adverbials such as those in (39). These are sentential modifiers that do not add an additional predicate to a VP's event argument but instead provide a semantically underspecified domain restriction for the overall proposition. Locative frame adverbials often yield temporal or conditional interpretations (e.g. 'When he was in Italy, Maradona was married.' for (39c)) but might also be interpreted epistemically, for instance ('According to the belief of the people in Italy, Maradona was married.'); see Maienborn (2001) for details and cf. also article 14 [Semantics: Lexical Structures and Adjectives] (Maienborn & Schäfer) *Adverbs and adverbials*.

(39) *Locative frame adverbials:*
    a. By candlelight, Carolin resembled her brother.
    b. Maria was drunk in the car.
    c. In Italy, Maradona was married.

Secondly, we are now in a position to make more precise what is going on in sentence pairs like (23), repeated here as (40), which are often taken to demonstrate the different behavior of SLPs and ILPs wrt. location in space; cf. the discussion in section 4.

(40)   a. Maria was tired/hungry/nervous in the car.   (SLP)
       b. ??Maria was blond/intelligent/a linguist in the car.   (ILP)

Actually, this SLP/ILP contrast is not an issue of *grammaticality* but concerns the *acceptability* of these sentences under a temporal reading of the locative frame; cf. Maienborn (2004) for a pragmatic explanation of this *temporariness effect*.

Thirdly, sentences (38d/e) are well-formed under an alternative syntactic analysis that takes the locative as the main predicate and the adjective as a depictive secondary predicate. Under this syntactic analysis sentence (38d) would express that there was a state of the dress being on the clothesline, and this state is temporally included in an accompanying state of the dress being wet. This is not the kind of evidence needed to substantiate the Neo-Davidsonian claim that states can be located in space. If the locative were a true event-related modifier, sentence (38d) should have the interpretation: There was a state of wetness of the dress, and this state is located on the clothesline. (38d) has no such reading; cf. the discussion on this point between Rothstein (2005) and Maienborn (2005b).

Turning back to our event diagnostics, the same split within the group of state expressions that we observed in the previous cases also shows up with manner adverbials, comitatives and the like – that is, modifiers that elaborate on the internal functional structure of events. State verbs combine regularly with them, whereas statives do not, as (41) shows. Katz (2003) dubbed this the *Stative Adverb Gap*.

(41) *Manner adverbials etc.:*
 a. Bardo slept calmly/with his teddy/without a pacifier.
 b. Carolin sat motionless/stiff at the table.
 c. The pearls gleamed dully/reddishly/moistly.
 d. *Bardo was calmly/with his teddy/without a pacifier tired.
 e. *Carolin was restlessly/patiently thirsty.
 f. *Andrea resembled with her daughter Romy Schneider.
 g. *Bardo owned thriftily/generously much money.

There has been some discussion on apparent counterexamples to this Stative Adverb Gap such as (42). While, e.g., Jäger (2001), Mittwoch (2005), Dölling (2005) or Rothstein (2005) conclude that such cases provide convincing evidence for assuming a Davidsonian argument for statives as well, Katz (2000, 2003, 2008) and Maienborn (2003, 2005a,b, 2007) argue that these either involve degree modification as in (42a) or are instances of *event coercion*, i.e. a sentence such as (42b) is, strictly speaking, ungrammatical but can be "rescued" by inferring some event argument to which the manner adverbial may then apply regularly; see the discussion in section 6.2. For instance, what John is passionate about in (42b) is not the state of being a Catholic but the activities associated with this state (e.g. going to mass, praying, going to confession). If no related activities come to mind for some predicate such as *being a relative of Grit* in (42'b) then the pragmatic rescue fails and the sentence becomes odd. According to this view, understanding sentences such as (42b) requires a non-compositional reinterpretation of the stative expression that is triggered by the *lack* of a regular Davidsonian event argument.

(42) a. Lisa firmly believed that James was innocent.
 b. John was a Catholic with great passion in his youth.

(42') b. ??John was a relative of Grit with great passion in his youth.

See also Rothmayr (2009) for a recent analysis of the semantics of stative verbs including a decompositional account of stative/eventive ambiguities as illustrated in (43):

(43) a. Hair obstructed the drain. (stative reading)
 b. A plumber obstructed the drain. (preferred eventive reading)

A further case of stative/eventive ambiguities is discussed by Engelberg (2005) in his study of dispositional verbs such as German *helfen* (*help*), *gefährden* (*endanger*), *erleichtern* (*facilitate*). These verbs may have an eventive or a stative reading depending on whether the subject is nominal or sentential; cf. (44). Trying to account for these readings within the Davidsonian program turns out to be challenging in several respects. Engelberg advocates the philosophical concept of *supervenience* as a useful device to account for the evaluative rather than causal dependency of the effect state expressed by these verbs.

(44) a. Rebecca helped Jamaal in the kitchen. (eventive)
 b. That Rebecca had fixed the water pipes helped Jamaal in the kitchen.
 (stative)

In view of the evidence reviewed above, it seems justified to conclude that the class of statives, including all copular constructions, does not behave as one would expect if they had a hidden Davidsonian argument, regardless of whether they express a temporary or a permanent property. What conclusions should we draw from these linguistic observations concerning the ontological category of states? There are basically two lines of argumentation that have been pursued in the literature.

Maienborn takes the behavior wrt. the classical event diagnostics in (10) as a sufficiently strong linguistic indication of an underlying ontological difference and assumes that only state verbs denote true Davidsonian eventualities, i.e., *Davidsonian states*, whereas statives resist a Davidsonian analysis but refer instead to what Maienborn calls *Kimian states*, exploiting Kim's (1969, 1976) notion of temporally bound property exemplifications. Kimian states may be located in time and they allow for anaphoric reference, Yet, in lacking an inherent spatial dimension, they are ontologically "poorer", more abstract entities than Davidsonian eventualities; cf. Maienborn (2003, 2005a, b, 2007) for details.

Authors like Dölling (2005), Higginbotham (2005), Ramchand (2005) or Rothstein (2005) take a different track. On their perspective, the observed linguistic differences call for a more liberal definition of eventualities that includes the referents of stative expressions. In particular, they are willing to give up the assumption of eventualities having an inherent spatial dimension. Hence, Ramchand (2005: 372) proposes the following alternative to the definition offered in (8):

(45) Eventualities are abstract entities with constitutive participants and with a constitutive relation to the temporal dimension.

So the issue basically is whether we opt for a narrow or a broad definition of events. 40 years after Davidson's first plea for events we still don't know for sure what kind of *things* event(ualitie)s actually are.

6 Psycholinguistic studies

In recent years, a growing interest has emerged in testing hypotheses on theoretical linguistic assumptions about event structure by means of psycholinguistic experiments. Two research areas involving events have attracted major interest within the still developing field of semantic processing; cf. articles 15 [Semantics: Foundations, History and Methods] (Bott, Featherston, Radó & Stolterfoht) *Experimental methods*, 9 [Semantics: Typology, Diachrony and Processing] (Frazier) *Meaning in psycholinguistics*. These are the processing of underlying event structures and of event coercion.

6.1 The processing of underlying event structures

The first focus of interest concerns the issue of distinguishing different kinds of events in terms of the complexity of their internal structure. Gennari & Poeppel (2003) show that the processing of event sentences such as (46a) takes significantly longer than the processing of otherwise similar stative sentences such as (46b).

(46) a. The visiting scientist solved the intricate math problem.   (eventive)
      b. The visiting scientist lacked any knowledge of English.   (stative)

This processing difference is attributed to eventive verbs having a more complex decompositional structure than stative verbs; cf. the Bierwisch-style representations in (47).

(47) a. *to solve:* $\lambda y \lambda x \lambda e$ [e: CAUSE (x, BECOME (SOLVED (y)))]
      b. *to lack:* $\lambda y \lambda x \lambda s$ [s: LACK (x, y)]

Thus, the study of Gennari & Poeppel (2003) adduces empirical evidence for the event vs. state distinction and it provides experimental support for the psychological reality of structuring natural language meaning in terms of decompositional representations. This is, of course, a highly controversial issue; cf. the argumentation in Fodor, Fodor & Garrett (1975), de Almeida (1999) and Fodor & LePore

(1998) against decomposition, and see also the more differentiated perspective taken in Mobayyen & de Almeida (2005).

McKoon & Macfarland (2000, 2002), taking up a distinction made by Levin & Rappaport Hovav (1995) investigate two kinds of causative verbs, viz. verbs denoting an externally caused event (e.g. *break*) as opposed to verbs denoting an internally caused event (e.g. *bloom*). Whereas the former include a causing subevent as well as a change-of-state subevent, the latter only express a change of state; cf. McKoon & Macfarland (2000: 834). Thus, the two verb classes differ wrt. their decompositional complexity. McKoon and Macfarland describe a series of experiments that show that there are clear processing differences corresponding to this lexical distinction. Sentences with external causation verbs take significantly longer to process than sentences with internal causation verbs. In addition, this processing difference shows up with the transitive as well as the intransitive use of the respective verbs; cf. (48) vs. (49). McKoon and Macfarland conclude from this finding that the causing subevent remains implicitly present even if no explicit cause is mentioned in the *break*-case. That is, their experiments suggest that both transitive and intransitive uses of, e.g., *awake* in (49) are based on the same lexical semantic event structure consisting of two subevents. And conversely, if an internal causation verb is used transitively, as *wilt* in (48a), the sentence is still understood as denoting a single event with the subject referent being part of the change-of-state event.

(48) *Internal causation verbs:*
 a. The bright sun wilted the roses.
 b. The roses wilted.

(49) *External causation verbs:*
 a. The fire alarm awoke the residents.
 b. The residents awoke.

In sum, the comprehension of *break, awake* etc. requires understanding a more complex event conceptualization than that of *bloom, wilt* etc. This psycholinguistic finding corroborates theoretically motivated assumptions on the verbs' lexical semantic representations. See also Härtl (2008) on a more thorough and differentiated study on implicit event information. Härtl discusses whether, to what extent, and at which processing level implicit event participants and implicit event predicates are still accessible for interpretation purposes.

Most notably, the studies of McKoon & Macfarland (2000, 2002) and Gennari & Poeppel (2003) provide strong psycholinguistic support for the assumption that verb meanings are represented and processed in terms of an underlying event structure.

6.2 The processing of event coercion

The second focus of psycholinguistic research on events is devoted to the notion of *event coercion*. Coercion refers to the forcing of an alternative interpretation when the compositional machinery fails to derive a regular interpretation. In other words, event coercion is a kind of rescue operation which solves a grammatical conflict by using additional knowledge about the involved event type; cf. also article 10 [Semantics: Lexical Structures and Adjectives] (de Swart) *Mismatches and coercion*. There are two types of coercion that are prominently discussed in the literature. The first type, the so-called *complement coercion* is illustrated in (50). The verb *to begin* requires an event-denoting complement and forces the given object-denoting complement *the book* into a contextually appropriate event reading. Hence, sentence (50) is reinterpreted as expressing that John began, e.g., to read the book; cf., e.g., Pustejovsky (1995), Egg (2003).

(50) John began the book.

The second kind, the so-called *aspectual coercion* refers to a set of options for adjusting the aspectual type of a verb phrase according to the demands of a temporal modifier. For instance, the punctual verb *to sneeze* in (51a) is preferably interpreted iteratively in combination with the durative adverbial *for five minutes*, whereas the temporal adverbial *for years* forces a habitual reading of the verb phrase *to smoke a morning cigarette* in (51b), and the stative expression *to be in one's office* receives an ingressive reinterpretation due to the temporal adverbial *in 10 minutes* in (51c); cf., e.g., Moens & Steedman (1988), Pulman (1997), de Swart (1998), Dölling (2003), Egg (2005). See also the classification of aspectual coercions developed in Hamm & van Lambalgen (2005).

(51) a. John sneezed for five minutes.
    a. John smoked a morning cigarette for years.
    b. John was in his office in 10 minutes.

There are basically two kinds of theoretical accounts that have been developed for the linguistic phenomena subsumed under the label of event coercion: type-shifting accounts (e.g., Moens & Steedman 1988, de Swart 1998) and underspecification accounts (e.g., Pulman 1997, Egg 2005); cf. articles 9 [Semantics: Lexical Structure and Adjectives] (Egg) *Semantic underspecification* and 10 [Semantics: Lexical Structures and Adjectives] (de Swart) *Mismatches and coercion*. These accounts and the predictions they make for the processing of coerced expressions have been the subject of several psycholinguistic studies; cf., e.g., de Almeida (2004), Pickering, McElree & Traxler (2005) and Traxler et al. (2005) on complement coercion and Piñango, Zurif & Jackendoff (1999), Piñango, Mack & Jackendoff (2006), Pickering et al. (2006), Bott (2008a, b), Brennan & Pylkkänen (2008) on aspectual coercion. The crucial question is whether event coercion causes additional processing costs, and if so at which point in the course of meaning composition such additional processing takes place. The results obtained so far still don't yield a fully stable picture. Whether processing differences are detected or not seems to depend partly on the chosen experimental methods and tasks; cf. Pickering et al. (2006). Pylkkänen & McElree (2006) draw the following interim balance: Whereas complement coercion always raises additional processing costs (at least without contextual support), aspectual coercion does not appear to lead to significant processing difficulties. Pylkkänen & McElree (2006) propose the following interpretation of these results: Complement coercion involves an ontological type conflict between the verb's request for an event argument and a given object referent. This ontological type conflict requires an immediate and time-consuming repair; otherwise the compositional process would break down. Aspectual coercion, on the other hand, only involves sortal shifts within the category of events that do not seem to affect composition and should therefore best be taken as an instance of semantic underspecification. For a somewhat more differentiated picture on the processing of different types of aspectual coercion see Bott (2008a).

7 Conclusion

Although psycholinguistic research on event structure might be said to be still in its infancy, the above remarks on some pioneer studies already show that Davidsonian events are about to develop into a genuine subject of psychological research on natural language. Hidden event arguments, as introduced by Davidson (1967), have not only proven to be of great benefit in explaining numerous combinatorial and inferential properties of natural language expressions, such that they show up virtually everywhere in present-day assumptions about linguistic structure. In addition, there is growing evidence that they are also psychologically real. Admittedly, we still don't know for sure what kind of things events actually are. Nevertheless, 40 years after they appeared on the linguistic scene, Davidsonian events continue to be both an indispensable everyday linguistic instrument and a constant source of fresh insights into the constitution of natural language meaning.

8 References

de Almeida, Roberto G. 1999. What do category-specific semantic deficits tell us about the representation of lexical concepts? *Brain & Language* 68, 241–248.
de Almeida, Roberto G. 2004. The effect of context on the processing of type-shifting verbs. *Brain & Language* 90, 249–261.
Asher, Nicholas 2000. Events, facts, propositions, and evolutive anaphora. In: J. Higginbotham, F. Pianesi & A. Varzi (eds.). *Speaking of Events*. Cambridge, MA: The MIT Press, 123–150.
Austin, Jennifer, Stefan Engelberg & Gesa Rauh (eds.) 2004. *Adverbials. The Interplay between Meaning, Context, and Syntactic Structure*. Amsterdam: Benjamins.
Bach, Emmon 1986. The algebra of events. *Linguistics & Philosophy* 9, 5–16.
Bäuerle, Rainer 1994. Zustand – Prozess – Ereignis. Zur Kategorisierung von Verb(al)-phrasen. *Wuppertaler Arbeitspapiere zur Sprachwissenschaft* 10, 1–32.
Bayer, Josef 1986. The role of event expressions in grammar. *Studies in Language* 10, 1–52.
Bierwisch, Manfred 1988. On the grammar of local prepositions. In: M. Bierwisch, W. Motsch & I. Zimmermann (eds.). *Syntax, Semantik und Lexikon*. Berlin: Akademie Verlag, 1–65.
Bierwisch, Manfred 1989. Event nominalizations: Proposals and problems. In: W. Motsch (ed.). *Wortstruktur und Satzstruktur*. Berlin: Akademie Verlag, 1–73.
Bierwisch, Manfred 1997. Lexical information from a minimalist point of view. In: Ch. Wilder, H.-M. Gärtner & M. Bierwisch (eds.). *The Role of Economy Principles in Linguistic Theory*. Berlin: Akademie Verlag, 227–266.
Bierwisch, Manfred 2005. The event structure of CAUSE and BECOME. In: C. Maienborn & A. Wöllstein (eds.). *Event Arguments: Foundations and Applications*. Tübingen: Niemeyer, 11–44.
Bott, Oliver 2008a. *The Processing of Events*. Doctoral dissertation. University of Tübingen.
Bott, Oliver 2008b. Doing it again and again may be difficult, but it depends on what you are doing. In: N. Abner & J. Bishop (eds.). *Proceedings of the West Coast Conference on Formal Linguistics (= WCCFL) 27*. Somerville, MA: Cascadilla Proceedings Project, 63–71.
Brennan, Jonathan & Liina Pylkkänen 2008. Processing events: Behavioral and neuromagnetic correlates of aspectual coercion. *Brain & Language* 106, 132–143.
Carlson, Gregory N. 1977. *Reference to Kinds in English*. Ph.D. dissertation. University of California, Irvine, CA. Reprinted: New York: Garland, 1980.
Carlson, Gregory N. 1998. Thematic roles and the individuation of events. In: S. Rothstein (ed.). *Events and Grammar*. Dordrecht: Kluwer, 35–51.
Chierchia, Gennaro 1995. Individual-level predicates as inherent generics. In: G. N. Carlson & F. J. Pelletier (eds.). *The Generic Book*. Chicago, IL: The University of Chicago Press, 176–223.
Davidson, Donald 1967. The logical form of action sentences. In: N. Resher (ed.). *The Logic of Decision and Action*. Pittsburgh, PA: University of Pittsburgh Press, 81–95. Reprinted in: D. Davidson (ed.). *Essays on Actions and Events*. Oxford: Clarendon Press, 1980, 105–122.

Davidson, Donald 1969. The individuation of events. In: N. Resher (ed.). *Essays in Honor of Carl G. Hempel*. Dordrecht: Reidel, 216–234. Reprinted in: D. Davidson (ed.). *Essays on Actions and Events*. Oxford: Clarendon Press, 1980, 163–180.
Diesing, Molly 1992. *Indefinites*. Cambridge, MA: The MIT Press.
Dölling, Johannes 2003. Flexibility in adverbal modification: Reinterpretation as contextual enrichment. In: E. Lang, C. Maienborn & C. Fabricius-Hansen (eds.). *Modifying Adjuncts*. Berlin: Mouton de Gruyter, 511–552.
Dölling, Johannes 2005. Copula sentences and entailment relations. *Theoretical Linguistics* 31, 317–329.
Dölling, Johannes, Tatjana Heyde-Zybatow & Martin Schäfer (eds.) 2008. *Event Structures in Linguistic Form and Interpretation*. Berlin: de Gruyter.
Dowty, David R. 1979. *Word Meaning and Montague Grammar. The Semantics of Verbs and Times in Generative Semantics and in Montague's PTQ*. Dordrecht: Reidel.
Eckardt, Regine 1998. *Adverbs, Events and Other Things. Issues in the Semantics of Manner Adverbs*. Tübingen: Niemeyer.
Eckardt, Regine 2002. Event semantics. In: F. Hamm & T. E. Zimmermann (eds.). *Semantics* (Linguistische Berichte, Sonderheft 10). Hamburg: Buske, 91–128.
Egg, Markus 2003. Beginning novels and finishing hamburgers. Remarks on the semantics of 'to begin'. *Journal of Semantics* 20, 163–191.
Egg, Markus 2005. *Flexible Semantics for Reinterpretation Phenomena*. Stanford, CA: CSLI Publications.
Ehrich, Veronika & Irene Rapp 2000. Sortale Bedeutung und Argumentstruktur: *ung*-Nominalisierungen im Deutschen. *Zeitschrift für Sprachwissenschaft* 19, 245–303.
Engelberg, Stefan 2000. *Verben, Ereignisse und das Lexikon*. Tübingen: Niemeyer.
Engelberg, Stefan 2002. Intransitive accomplishments and the lexicon: The role of implicit arguments, definiteness, and reflexivity in aspectual composition. *Journal of Semantics* 19, 369–416.
Engelberg, Stefan 2005. Stativity, supervenience, and sentential subjects. In: C. Maienborn & A. Wöllstein (eds.). *Event Arguments: Foundations and Applications*. Tübingen: Niemeyer, 45–68.
Fernald, Theodore B. 2000. *Predicates and Temporal Arguments*. Oxford: Oxford University Press.
Fodor, Janet D., Jerry A. Fodor & Merrill Garrett 1975. The psychological unreality of semantic representations. *Linguistic Inquiry* 6, 515–532.
Fodor, Jerry A. & Ernest LePore 1998. The emptiness of the lexicon: Reflections on James Pustejovsky's "The Generative Lexicon". *Linguistic Inquiry* 29, 269–288.
Geist, Ljudmila 2006. *Die Kopula und ihre Komplemente. Zur Kompositionalität in Kopulasätzen*. Tübingen: Niemeyer.
Gennari, Silvia & David Poeppel 2003. Processing correlates of lexical semantic complexity. *Cognition* 89, 27–41.
Glasbey, Sheyla 1997. I-level predicates that allow existential readings for bare plurals. In: A. Lawson (ed.). *Proceedings of Semantics and Linguistic Theory (= SALT) VII*. Ithaca, NY: Cornell University, 169–179.
Grimshaw, Jane 1990. *Argument Structure*. Cambridge, MA: The MIT Press.
Hamm, Fritz & Michiel van Lambalgen 2005. *The Proper Treatment of Events*. Oxford: Blackwell.
Härtl, Holden 2008. *Implizite Informationen: Sprachliche Ökonomie und interpretative Komplexität bei Verben*. Berlin: Akademie Verlag.

Higginbotham, James 1983. The logic of perceptual reports: An extensional alternative to situation semantics. *Journal of Philosophy* 80, 100–127.
Higginbotham, James 1985. On semantics. *Linguistic Inquiry* 16, 547–593.
Higginbotham, James 1989. Elucidations of meaning. *Linguistics & Philosophy* 12, 465–517.
Higginbotham, James 2000. On events in linguistic semantics. In: J. Higginbotham, F. Pianesi & A. Varzi (eds.). *Speaking of Events*. Oxford: Oxford University Press, 49–79.
Higginbotham, James 2005. Event positions: Suppression and emergence. *Theoretical Linguistics* 31, 349–358.
Higginbotham, James & Gillian Ramchand 1997. The stage-level/individual-level distinction and the mapping hypothesis. *Oxford University Working Papers in Linguistics, Philology & Phonetics* 2, 53–83.
Higginbotham, James, Fabio Pianesi & Achille Varzi (eds.) 2000. *Speaking of Events*. Oxford: Oxford University Press.
Jäger, Gerhard 2001. Topic-comment structure and the contrast between stage-level and individual-level predicates. *Journal of Semantics* 18, 83–126.
Jäger, Gerhard & Reinhard Blutner 2003. Competition and interpretation: The German adverb *wieder* ('again'). In: E. Lang, C. Maienborn & C. Fabricius-Hansen (eds.). *Modifying Adjuncts*. Berlin: Mouton de Gruyter, 393–416.
Kamp, Hans & Uwe Reyle 1993. *From Discourse to Logic*. Dordrecht: Kluwer.
Katz, Graham 2000. Anti Neo-Davidsonianism: Against a Davidsonian semantics for state sentences. In: C. Tenny & J. Pustejovsky (eds.). *Events as Grammatical Objects. The Converging Perspectives of Lexical Semantics and Syntax*. Stanford, CA: CSLI Publications, 393–416.
Katz, Graham 2003. Event arguments, adverb selection, and the Stative Adverb Gap. In: E. Lang, C. Maienborn & C. Fabricius-Hansen (eds.). *Modifying Adjuncts*. Berlin: Mouton de Gruyter, 455–474.
Katz, Graham 2008. Manner modification of state verbs. In: L. McNally & Ch. Kennedy (eds.). *Adjec-tives and Adverbs. Syntax, Semantics, and Discourse*. Oxford: Oxford University Press, 220–248.
Kennedy, Christopher & Beth Levin 2008. Measure of change: The adjectival core of degree achievements. In: L. McNally & Ch. Kennedy (eds.). *Adjectives and Adverbs. Syntax, Semantics, and Discourse*. Oxford: Oxford University Press, 156–182.
Kim, Jaegwon 1969. Events and their descriptions: Some considerations. In: N. Rescher (ed.). *Essays in Honor of Carl G. Hempel*. Dordrecht: Reidel, 198–215.
Kim, Jaegwon 1976. Events as property exemplifications. In: M. Brand & D. Walton (eds.). *Action Theory. Proceedings of the Winnipeg Conference on Human Action*. Dordrecht: Reidel, 159–177.
Kratzer, Angelika 1995. Stage-level and individual-level predicates. In: G. N. Carlson & F. J. Pelletier (eds.). *The Generic Book*. Chicago, IL: The University of Chicago Press, 125–175.
Krifka, Manfred 1989. Nominal reference, temporal constitution and quantification in event semantics. In: R. Bartsch, J. van Benthem & P. van Emde Boas (eds.). *Semantics and Contextual Expression*. Dordrecht: Foris, 75–115.
Krifka, Manfred 1990. Four thousand ships passed through the lock: Object-induced measure functions on events. *Linguistics & Philosophy* 13, 487–520.
Krifka, Manfred 1992. Thematic relations as links between nominal reference and temporal constitution. In: I. Sag & A. Szabolcsi (eds.). *Lexical Matters*. Stanford, CA: CSLI Publications, 29–53.

Krifka, Manfred 1998. The origins of telicity. In: S. Rothstein (ed.). *Events and Grammar*. Dordrecht: Kluwer, 197–235.

Ladusaw, William 1994. Thetic and categorical, stage and individual, weak and strong. In: M. Harvey & L. Santelmann (eds.). *Proceedings of Semantics and Linguistic Theory (= SALT) IV*. Ithaca, NY: Cornell University, 220–229.

Lang, Ewald, Claudia Maienborn & Cathrine Fabricius-Hansen (eds.) 2003. *Modifying Adjuncts*. Berlin: Mouton de Gruyter.

Lemmon, Edward J. 1967. Comments on D. Davidson's "The Logical Form of Action Sentences". In: N. Resher (ed.). *The Logic of Decision and Action*. Pittsburgh, PA: University of Pittsburgh Press, 96–103.

LePore, Ernest 1985. The semantics of action, event, and singular causal sentences. In: E. LePore & B. McLaughlin (eds.). *Actions and Events: Perspectives on the Philosophy of Donald Davidson*. Oxford: Blackwell, 151–161.

Levin, Beth & Malka Rappaport Hovav 1995. *Unaccusativity: At the Syntax-Lexical Semantics Interface*. Cambridge, MA: The MIT Press.

Lombard, Lawrence B. 1998. Ontologies of events. In: S. Laurence & C. Macdonald (eds.). *Contemporary Readings in the Foundations of Metaphysics*. Oxford: Blackwell, 277–294.

Magri, Giorgio. 2008. *A Theory of Individual-level Predicates Based on Blind Scalar Implicatures* (Extended version). Ms. Cambridge, MA, MIT. http://web.mit.edu/gmagri/www/. December 11, 2010.

Magri, Giorgio 2009. A theory of individual-level predicates based on blind mandatory scalar implicatures. *Natural Language Semantics* 17, 245–297.

Maienborn, Claudia 2001. On the position and interpretation of locative modifiers. *Natural Language Semantics* 9, 191–240.

Maienborn, Claudia 2003. *Die logische Form von Kopula-Sätzen*. Berlin: Akademie Verlag.

Maienborn, Claudia 2004. A pragmatic explanation of the stage-level/individual-level contrast in combination with locatives. In: B. Agbayani, V. Samiian & B. Tucker (eds.). *Proceedings of the Western Conference on Linguistics (= WECOL) 15*. Fresno, CA: CSU, 158–170.

Maienborn, Claudia 2005a. On the limits of the Davidsonian approach: The case of copula sentences. *Theoretical Linguistics* 31, 275–316.

Maienborn, Claudia 2005b. Eventualities and different things: A reply. *Theoretical Linguistics* 31, 383–396.

Maienborn, Claudia 2005c. A discourse-based account of Spanish 'ser/estar'. *Linguistics* 43, 155–180.

Maienborn, Claudia 2007. On Davidsonian and Kimian states. In: I. Comorovski & K. von Heusinger (eds.). *Existence: Semantics and Syntax*. Dordrecht: Springer, 107–130.

Maienborn, Claudia & Angelika Wöllstein (eds.) 2005. *Event Arguments: Foundations and Applications*. Tübingen: Niemeyer.

McKoon, Gail & Talke Macfarland 2000. Externally and internally caused change of state verbs. *Language* 76, 833–858.

McKoon, Gail & Talke Macfarland 2002. Event templates in the lexical representations of verbs. *Cognitive Psychology* 45, 1–44.

McNally, Louise 1998. Stativity and theticity. In: S. Rothstein (ed.). *Events and Grammar*. Dordrecht: Kluwer, 293–307.

Milsark, Gary L. 1974. *Existential Sentences in English*. Ph.D. dissertation. MIT, Cambridge, MA. Reprinted: Bloomington, IN: Indiana University Linguistics Club, 1976.

Milsark, Gary L. 1977. Toward an explanation of certain peculiarities of the existential construction in English. *Linguistic Analysis* 3, 1–29.
Mittwoch, Anita 2005. Do states have Davidsonian arguments? Some empirical considerations. In: C. Maienborn & Angelika Wöllstein (eds.). *Event Arguments: Foundations and Applications.* Tübingen: Niemeyer, 69–88.
Mobayyen, Forouzan & Roberto G. de Almeida 2005. The influence of semantic and morphological complexity of verbs on sentence recall: Implications for the nature of conceptual representation and category-specific deficits. *Brain and Cognition* 57, 168–171.
Moens, Marc & Mark Steedman 1988. Temporal ontology and temporal reference. *Computational Linguistics* 14, 15–28.
Parsons, Terence 1990. *Events in the Semantics of English. A Study in Subatomic Semantics.* Cambridge, MA: The MIT Press.
Parsons, Terence 1995. Thematic relations and arguments. *Linguistic Inquiry* 26, 635–662.
Parsons, Terence 2000. Underlying states and time travel. In: J. Higginbotham, F. Pianesi & A. Varzi (eds.). *Speaking of Events.* Oxford: Oxford University Press, 81–93.
Pianesi, Fabio & Achille C. Varzi 2000. Events and event talk: An introduction. In: J. Higginbotham, F. Pianesi & A. Varzi (eds.). *Speaking of Events.* Oxford: Oxford University Press, 3–47.
Pickering, Martin J., Brian McElree & Matthew J. Traxler 2005. The difficulty of coercion: A response to de Almeida. *Brain & Language* 93, 1–9.
Pickering, Martin J., Brian McElree, Steven Frisson, Lillian Chen & Matthew J. Traxler 2006. Underspecification and aspectual coercion. *Discourse Processes* 42, 131–155.
Piñango, Maria M., Jennifer Mack & Ray Jackendoff 2006. Semantic combinatorial pro-cesses in argument structure: Evidence from light-verbs. In: *Proceedings of the Annual Meeting of the Berkeley Linguistics Society (= BLS)* 32, 573–583.
Piñango, Maria M., Edgar Zurif & Ray Jackendoff 1999. Real-time processing implications of enriched composition at the syntax-semantics interface. *Journal of Psycholinguistic Research* 28, 395–414.
Piñón, Christopher 1997. Achievements in an event semantics. In: A. Lawson & E. Cho (eds.). *Proceedings of Semantics and Linguistic Theory (= SALT) VII.* Ithaca, NY: Cornell University, 276–293.
Pulman, Stephen G. 1997. Aspectual shift as type coercion. *Transactions of the Philological Society* 95, 279–317.
Pustejovsky, James 1991. The syntax of event structure. *Cognition* 41, 47–81.
Pustejovsky, James 1995. *The Generative Lexicon.* Cambridge, MA: The MIT Press.
Pylkkänen, Liina & Brian McElree 2006. The syntax-semantics interface: On-line composition of meaning. In: M. A. Gernsbacher & M. Traxler (eds.). *Handbook of Psycholinguistics.* 2nd edn. New York: Elsevier, 537–577.
Ramchand, Gillian 1996. Two subject positions in Scottish Gaelic: The syntax-semantics interface. *Natural Language Semantics* 4, 165–191.
Ramchand, Gillian 2005. Post-Davidsonianism. *Theoretical Linguistics* 31, 359–373.
Rapp, Irene 2007. „Was den Besuch zum Ereignis macht" – eine outputorientierte Analyse für die Verb-Nomen-Konversion im Deutschen. *Linguistische Berichte* 208, 407–437.
Reichenbach, Hans 1947. *Elements of Symbolic Logic.* New York: Macmillan.
Rothmayr, Antonia 2009. *The Structure of Stative Verbs.* Amsterdam: Benjamins.
Rothstein, Susan (ed.) 1998. *Events and Grammar.* Dordrecht: Kluwer.

Rothstein, Susan 2004. *Structuring Events: A Study in the Semantics of Lexical Aspect*. Oxford: Blackwell.
Rothstein, Susan 2005. States and modification: A reply to Maienborn. *Theoretical Linguistics* 31, 375–381.
Sæbø, Kjell Johan 2008. The structure of criterion predicates. In: J. Dölling, T. Heyde-Zybatow & M. Schäfer (eds.). *Event Structures in Linguistic Form and Interpretation*. Berlin: de Gruyter, 127–147.
von Stechow, Arnim 1996. The different readings of *wieder* 'again': A structural account. *Journal of Semantics* 13, 87–138.
von Stechow, Arnim 2003. How are results represented and modified? Remarks on Jäger & Blutner's anti-decomposition. In: E. Lang, C. Maienborn & C. Fabricius-Hansen (eds.). *Modifying Adjuncts*. Berlin: Mouton de Gruyter, 417–451.
de Swart, Henriëtte 1998. Aspect shift and coercion. *Natural Language and Linguistic Theory* 16, 347–385.
Tenny, Carol & James Pustejovsky (eds.) 2000. *Events as Grammatical Objects. The Converging Perspectives of Lexical Semantics and Syntax*. Stanford, CA: CSLI Publications.
Thomason, Richmond H. & Robert C. Stalnaker 1973. A semantic theory of adverbs. *Linguistic Inquiry* 4, 195–220.
Traxler, Matthew J., Brian McElree, Rihana S. Williams & Martin J. Pickering 2005. Context effects in coercion: Evidence from eye movements. *Journal of Memory and Language* 53, 1–25.
Vendler, Zeno 1967. *Linguistics in Philosophy*. Ithaca, NY: Cornell University Press.
Wunderlich, Dieter 1997. CAUSE and the structure of verbs. *Linguistic Inquiry* 28, 27–68.
Zucchi, Alessandro 1993. *The Language of Propositions and Events*. Dordrecht: Kluwer.

Jonathan Ginzburg
9 Situation Semantics and the ontology of natural language

1 Introduction —— 267
2 Introducing situations into semantics: Empirical motivations —— 269
3 The Austinian picture —— 272
4 A wider ontological net —— 278
5 A type theoretic ontology for interaction —— 282
6 Conclusions —— 290
7 References —— 291

Abstract: Situation Semantics emerged in the 1980s with an ambitious program of reform for semantics, both in the domain of semantic ontology and with regard to the integration of context in meaning. This article takes as its initial focus the topic of a situation-based ontology, more generally discussing the approach to NL ontology that emerged from situation semantics. The latter part of the article will explain how recent work synthesizing situation semantics with type theory enables the original intuitions from situation semantics to be captured in a dynamic, computationally tractable framework.

1 Introduction

Situation Semantics emerged in the 1980s with an ambitious program of reform for semantics, both in the domain of semantic ontology and with regard to the integration of context in meaning. In their 1983 book *Situations and Attitudes* (Barwise & Perry 1983), Barwise and Perry argued for the preeminence of a situation-based ontology and took contexts of utterance to be situations, thereby offering the potential for a richer view of context. For situation semantics and utterance–oriented interpretation, see article 10 [this volume] (Ginzburg) *Situation Semantics*. This article takes as its initial focus the topic of a situation-based ontology, more generally discussing the approach to NL ontology that emerged from situation semantics. The latter part of the article will explain how recent

---

Jonathan Ginzburg, Paris, France

https://doi.org/10.1515/9783110589245-009

work synthesizing situation semantics with type theory enables the original intuitions from situation semantics to be captured in a dynamic, computationally tractable framework.

As a semantic framework, Barwise & Perry (1983) view Situation Semantics as following on – but also crucially breaking from – the tradition of Montogovian model theoretic semantics. The strategy this latter embodies they view as being Fregean: intensions providing a logically fruitful way of explicating "[Frege's] third realm, a realm neither of ideas nor of worldly events, but of senses." (Barwise & Perry 1983: 4) Given Barwise and Perry's ambitious program they reject aspects of the Frege-Montague programme as cognitively intractable, and argue that the ontology it postulates is unnecessarily coarse grained. For instance, the choice of truth values as the denotata of declarative sentences they view as resting on a bad argument ('The slingshot').

The desiderata for a semantic framework Barwise and Perry put forward include the following:

- The priority of information: language has *external significance*, as model theoretic semantics has always emphasized, but, as cognitive scientists of various stripes emphasize, it also has *mental significance*, yielding information about agents' internal states; in this respect see also article 11 [Semantics: Foundations, History and Methods] (Kempson) *Formal semantics and representationalism*. What is needed is a way of capturing the commonality between the external and the mental, a matter exacerbated when multimodal meaning (gesture, gaze, visual access) enters into the picture.
- Cognitive realizability: in common with all other biological organisms, language users are resource bounded agents. This requires that only relatively "small" entities feature in semantic accounts, hence the emphasis on situations and their characterization in a computable fashion.
- Structured objects: semantic objects such as propositions need to be treated in a way that treats their identity conditions very much on a par with 'ordinary' individuals. Such entities are *structured objects*:

(1) The primitives of our theory are all real things: individuals, properties, relations, and space-time locations. Out of these and objects available from the set theory we construct a universe of abstract objects. (Barwise & Perry 1983: 178)

That is, structured objects arrive on the scene with certain constraints that 'define them' in terms of other entities of the ontology in a manner that is inspired by proof theoretic approaches. This way of setting up the ontology has the potential of avoiding various foundational problems that beset classical theories of properties and propositions. For propositions, these problems typically center around doxastic puzzles such as logical omniscience and its variants.

An important component in fulfilling these desiderata, according to Barwise and Perry, is a theory by means of which external (and internal) reality can be represented – an ontology of some kind. The formalism that emerged came to be known as Situation Theory – its make up and motivation constitute the focus of sections 2, 3, and 4 of the paper. These proceed in an order that reflects the evolution of Situation Theory: initially as a theory of situations, then as a theory that includes both concrete entities such as situations and abstract ones such as propositions, finally as a more extended ontology, comprising in addition entities such as questions, outcomes, and possibilities. Section 5 of the paper concerns the emergence of a type theoretic version of the theory, within a formalism initiated by Robin Cooper. Section 6 provides some concluding remarks.

2 Introducing situations into semantics: Empirical motivations

Situation Semantics owes its initial prominence to its analysis of the naked infinitive (NI) construction, exemplified in (2). Here is a construction, argued Barwise (1989b), that intrinsically requires positing situations – spatio-temporally located *parts* of the world. One component of this argument goes as follows: the difference in meaning between (2a) and (2b) illustrates that "logically equivalent" NIs (relative to an evaluation by a *world*) are not *semantically* equivalent. And yet, the intuitive validity of the inference from (2b) to (2c) and the inference described in (2d) shows that NIs bring with them clear logical structure. This is a purely linguistic argument, to add to other more methodological ones, that the appropriate ontology for NL cannot be one based solely on worlds, but must include events and situations.

(2) a. Bo saw Millie enter.
 b. Bo saw Millie enter and Jan leave or not leave.
 c. Bo saw Jan leave or not leave.
 d. Bo saw Jan not leave. So, it's not the case that Bo saw Jan leave. In fact, Bo saw Jan engaged in something inconsistent with leaving.

The account of NI clauses is based on a theory of situations characterized in terms of *situation types*. Here a few words on nomenclature are due. Barwise and Perry used the term 'situation' as a cover term for what have often been called 'eventualities', including events, situations, states and so forth; for detailed discussion see also article 8 [this volume] (Maienborn) *Event semantics*. I will stick with this choice here, for historical reasons, but the wider intended extension should be noted throughout. Similar remarks apply *mutandis mutandi* to the term 'situation type'. Indeed this is Barwise and Perry's original name of such entities, which subsequently came to be known as states-of-affairs, infons, or SOAs. The return to the original term is intentional given the current type theoretic turn discussed in section 5.

Situation types are structured objects that function as 'potential properties' situations can possess: situation types are taken to be structured from two components, a relation R, and an assignment a, which assigns real world entities to the argument roles of R, as in (3a). The notation in (3b) indicates that the situation s is of the type given by the situation type $\langle\!\langle R; a \rangle\!\rangle$. If a situation fails to be correctly classified by a situation type σ, this is notated as in (3c); ':' was traditionally notated as $\models$.

(3) a. $\langle\!\langle CALM; loc = Jerusalem \rangle\!\rangle$
 b. $s : \langle\!\langle R; a \rangle\!\rangle$
 c. $s : / \langle\!\langle R; a \rangle\!\rangle$

Situation types are assumed to come in positive/negative pairs, i.e. every relation/assignment pair gives rise to a positive situation type and a negative situation type. We will assume the positive ones to be (notationally) unmarked and notate the corresponding negative with an 'overline', as in (4a). Because situations are partial, there is a difference between a situation failing to be correctly classified by σ and being correctly classified by $\bar{\sigma}$. For any situation s and situation type σ, (4b) holds, but (4c) generally fails. The intuition is that classifying s with $\bar{\sigma}$ means that s actually possesses information which rules out σ, rather than simply lacking concrete evidence for σ. So, e.g., a situation I perceive in London, s_{london}, would typically neither be of the type $\langle\!\langle CALM; loc = Jerusalem \rangle\!\rangle$, nor of the type $\overline{\langle\!\langle CALM; loc = Jerusalem \rangle\!\rangle}$. s_{london} is simply indeterminate about the issue of Jerusalem's calamity or calmness. Cooper (1998) has proposed a pair of axioms that attempt to capture this intuition. (4d) states that if a situation s supports the dual of σ, then s also supports positive information that precludes σ being the case. (4e) tells us that if a situation s supports the dual of σ, then s also supports information that defeasibly entails that σ is the case. I discuss some linguistic evidence relating to (4e) in section 4., in connection with negative polar interrogatives.

(4) a. $s : \overline{\langle\!\langle R; a \rangle\!\rangle}$
 b. Either $s : \sigma$ or $s : /\sigma$

c. Either $s : \sigma$ or $s : \bar{\sigma}$
d. $\forall s, \sigma [s : \bar{\sigma}$ implies $\exists(Pos) \psi [s : \psi$ and $\psi \Rightarrow \bar{\sigma}]]$
e. $\forall s, \sigma [s : \bar{\sigma}$ implies $\exists(Pos)\psi [s : \psi$ and $\psi > \sigma]]$

The treatment of NIs and its wider semantic implications opened various debates, debates in which one of the main issues was: does an account of NIs require a radical overhaul of the underlying semantic ontology? Muskens (1989) showed that a Montogovian framework could offer an account if it embraced 4-valued logic. Higginbotham (see Higginbotham 1983, 1994) argued that Davidsonian event theory was sufficient to explicate NIs. Neale (1988) and Cooper (1998) subsequently provided counter arguments to Higginbotham. Cooper claimed, *inter alia*, that the existence of negative situation types in Situation Theory allows it to explicate cases like (5a) in terms of the perceived scene satisfying (5b), which seem beyond Higgibotham's Davidsonian account, which is limited to something like (5c):

(5) a. Ralph saw Mary not serve Bill.
 b. $s : \overline{\langle\!\langle Serve; server : m, servee : b \rangle\!\rangle}$
 c. $s : /\langle\!\langle Serve; server : m, servee : b \rangle\!\rangle$

However one thinks these debates played out – the reckoning must be done relative to the range of phenomena and tractability each framework can ultimately accommodate – one apparently uncontroversial outcome is the recognition that situations are needed in the ontology. Nonetheless, the question that arises is this: how significant are situations for semantics? A syntactic analogy might be the following: there is incontrovertible evidence that NL is not context free, as demonstrated e.g. by Swiss German crossing dependencies. Are situations exotica like Swiss German Crossing Dependencies, or are they an absolutely pervasive feature like unbounded dependencies, inability to deal with which renders any grammar quite unviable? Barwise and Perry's claim was that the latter is the case. Their claim is that situations are at the heart of semantic use. As discussed in detail in article 10 [this volume] (Ginzburg) *Situation Semantics,* one of the early claims of situation semantics, following Austin, was that the meaning of declarative sentences is to be explicated as relating utterance situations to described situations. This intuition can be made concrete: anaphora shows that (described) situations enter into context as a consequence of the assertion of an episodic sentence, even if the assertion is not accepted, as in (6b):

(6) a. A: Jo and Mo got married yesterday. It was a wonderful occasion.
 b. A: Jo's arriving next week. B: No, that's happening in about a month.

Barwise and Perry also argued, and their arguments were sharpened by Robin Cooper (see Cooper 1993, 1996), that a given utterance can also concern an event/situation that is distinct from the described situation. Ever since Russell (1905), at least one influential school has sought to explain the meaning of singular definites using some notion of uniqueness; for detailed discussion see article 2 [Semantics: Noun Phrases and Verb Phrases] (Heim) *Definiteness and indefiniteness*. More generally, quantification presupposes a domain (cf. terms such as *the domain of discourse, the universe* etc). With some notable exceptions (e.g. McCawley 1979, Lewis 1979), until Barwise and Perry's proposal, the requisite relativization was not considered a matter to be handled in semantic theory. Barwise and Perry's essential idea is that in language use more than one situation comes into the picture: they make a distinction between the *described* situation, the situation which roughly speaking a declarative utterance picks out, and a *resource* situation, so called because it is used as a resource to fix the range/reference of an NP. Cooper's argument is based on data such as (7), modelled on an example from Lewis (1979), where two domains are in play, a local one and a New Zealand one. The former is exploited in the first two sentences, after which the New Zealand domain takes over. At the point marked || we are to imagine a sudden shift back to the local domain. By assuming that domains are situations we capture the fact that once a shift is made, it encompasses the entire situation, ensuring that the dog referred to is local:

(7) The dog is under the piano and the cat is in the carton. The cat will never meet our other cat because our other cat lives in New Zealand. Our New Zealand cat lives with the Cresswells and their dog. And there he'll stay because the dog would be sad if the cat went away. || The cat's going to pounce on you. And the dog's coming too.

For computational work using resource situations, integrated also with visual information see Poesio (1993). For experimental work on the resolution of definites in conversation taking a closely related perspective see Brown-Schmidt & Tanenhaus (2008).

3 The Austinian picture

The ontology we have discussed so far comprises situations and situation types (as well as of course the elements that make up these entities – individuals, role to individual assignments). Situations are the main ingredient in a treatment of bare perceptual reports and play a significant role in underpinning NP meaning and assertion. This is essentially the ontology of *Situations and Attitudes* in which there were no propositions. These were rejected as 'artifact(s) of the semantic endeavor' (Barwise & Perry 1983). As Barwise & Perry (1985) subsequently admitted, this was not a move they were required to make. Indeed propositional-like entities, more intensional than situations, are a necessary ingredient for accounts of attitude reports and illocutionary acts. *Sets* of situations, although somewhat more fine grained than sets of worlds, are vulnerable to sophisticated variants of logical omniscience (see e.g. Soames' puzzle in Soames 1985). Nonetheless, Angelika Kratzer has initiated an approach, somewhat confusingly also known as *Situation Semantics*, that does attempt to exploit sets of situations for precisely this role and develops accounts for a wide range of linguistic phenomena, including modality, donkey anaphora, exhaustivity, and factivity. See Kratzer (1989) for an early version of this approach, and Kratzer (2008) for a detailed, recent survey.

The next cheapest solution available within the *Situations and Attitudes* ontology would be to draft the situation types to serve as the propositional entities. Indeed, situation types *are* competitive in such a role: they can distinguish identity statements that involve distinct constituents (e.g. (8a) corresponds to the situation type in (8c), whereas (8b) corresponds to the situation type in (8d), while allowing substitutivity of co-referentials and cross-linguistic equivalents, as exemplified respectively by (8e) and (8f), the Hebrew analogue of (8b):

(8) a. Enesco is identical with himself.
 b. Poulenc is identical with himself.
 c. $\langle\langle Identical; enesco, enesco \rangle\rangle$
 d. $\langle\langle Identical; poulenc, poulenc \rangle\rangle$
 e. He is identical with himself.
 f. Poulank zehe leacmo.

Nonetheless, post 1985 situation theory did not go for the cheapest solution; as we will see in section 4., not succumbing to ontological stinginess pays off when scaling up the theory to deal with other abstract entities.

Building on a conception articulated 30 years earlier by Austin (1970), Barwise & Etchemendy (1987) developed a theory of propositions in which a proposition is a structured object $prop(s,\sigma)$, individuated in terms of a situation s and a situation type σ. Here the intuition is that s is the described situation (or the belief situation, in so far as it is used to describe an agent's belief, or utterance token, in the case of locutionary propositions discussed below), with the relationship between s and σ being the one introduced above in our discussion of NIs, leading to a straightforward notion of truth and falsity:

(9) a. prop(s, σ) is true iff $s : \sigma$ (s is of type σ).
    b. prop(s, σ) is false iff $s : /\sigma$ (s is not of type σ).

In saying that a proposition prop(s, σ) is individuated in terms of s and σ, the intention is to say that prop(s, σ) = prop(t, τ) if and only if $s = t$ and $\sigma = \tau$. Individuating propositions in terms of their "subject matter" (i.e. the situation type component) is familiar, but what is innovative and/or puzzling is the claim that two propositions can be distinct *despite* having the same subject matter.

I mention three examples from the literature of cases which motivate differentiating propositions on the basis of their situational component. The first is one we saw above in the case of definiteness resolution, where the possibility of using 'the dog' is underwritten by distinct presuppositions; the difference in the presuppositions resides in the different resource situations exploited:

(10) a. prop(s_{local}, ⟪*UNIQUE, Dog*⟫)
     b. prop($s_{newzealand}$, ⟪*UNIQUE, Dog*⟫)

A second case are the *locutionary propositions* introduced by Ginzburg (2012). Ginzburg argues that characterizing both the update potential and the range of utterances that can be used to seek clarification about a given utterance u_0 requires reference to the utterance token u_0, as well as to its grammatical type T_{u_0} (see article 10 [this volume] (Ginzburg) *Situation Semantics* for details). By defining propositions (*locutionary propositions*) individuated in terms of u_0 and T_{u_0} one can simultaneously define update and clarification potential for utterances. In this case, there are potentially many instances of distinct locutionary propositions, which need to be differentiated on the basis of the utterance token – minimally any two utterances classified as being of the same type by the grammar.

The original motivation for Austinian propositions was in the treatment of the Liar paradox by Barwise & Etchemendy (1987). This paradox concerns sentences like (11a,b) which, pretheoretically, are false if true and true if false. Although one approach to this issue involves banning self reference, this is an arbitrary prohibition that runs counter to the felicity of various self referential utterances such as (11c). Moreover, as Kripke (1975) showed, Liar paradox cases can arise in certain contexts from sentences that are normally perfectly felicitous.

(11) a. This claim is false.
     b. What I am saying now is false.
     c. This is the last announcement about flight 345.

9 Situation Semantics and the ontology of natural language — 275

Very briefly, Barwise and Etchemendy's diagnosis is that the apparent paradox is similar to ones involving other implicit parameters (time zones, spatial orientation,…), where "paradoxes" loom if perspectives are ignored:

(12) a. A (in Tashkent): It's 9pm, B (in Baghdad): No, it's 7pm; *Does not license*: It's 7pm and it's not 7pm.
b. (A and B facing each other) A: The cupboard is to our right. B: No it's to our left. *Does not license*: The cupboard is to our right and to our left.

Similarly, for the Liar, according to Barwise and Etchemendy: the phenomenon dissolves as a paradox once one adopts the Austinian conception of propositions, which recognizes the *situational relativity* of propositions. In their formalization, liar utterances like (11a) express propositions which satisfy the equation in (13):

(13) $f_s = prop(s, \overline{\langle\!\langle True, f_s \rangle\!\rangle})$

The *existence* of such circular propositions is ensured in Barwise and Etchemendy's account given their use of the non-well founded set theory developed by Aczel (1988), though the Austinian conception does not depend in any way on using such set theory. In Barwise and Etchemendy's model theory situations are modelled as sets of situation types. A situation s is of type σ iff $\sigma \in s$ and, moreover, for any actual situation s and proposition p: (a) $\langle\!\langle True, p \rangle\!\rangle \in s$ only if p is true, (b) $\overline{\langle\!\langle True, p \rangle\!\rangle} \in s$ only if p is false. Given this, a proposition such as (13) ends up being false – if f_s is true, then $\overline{\langle\!\langle True, f_s \rangle\!\rangle} \in s$. This entails that f_s is false. Once we accept the falsity of this proposition, there exist situations in which the situation type $\overline{\langle\!\langle True, f_s \rangle\!\rangle}$ is factual. The minimal such situation is $s1 = s \cup \{\overline{\langle\!\langle True, f_s \rangle\!\rangle}\}$ and, hence, prop($s1$, $\overline{\langle\!\langle True, f_s \rangle\!\rangle}$) *is* true. This account thereby captures an intuition that liar claims are double edged.

This solution crucially depends on a view of propositions as concerning situations and not worlds. As Barwise and Etchemendy explain in detail, in an alternative solution (which they label *Russellian*), where propositions are not relativized by a situational parameter, there is no way to accommodate the existence of propositions that are not true but whose falsehood is internal to the world.

Let us take stock: the Austinian conception builds up from an ontology with situations and situation types and adds to these propositions prop(s, σ) whose truth condition involves that s is of type σ. Some empirical pluses: it enables accounts of NP situational relativity, update/clarificational potential of utterances, and the Liar (though this latter also requires non-well-founded set theory). It also enables an account of situational anaphora (see e.g. the examples in (6)). As with any theory that employs non-concrete entities, a variety of issues arise – for critical discussion in context of the Liar, see Moss (1989) and McGee (1991). The most obvious ones center on the vagueness of situations. For instance, how can Austinian propositions be shared? How can we be clear about the identity of propositions? Aren't we populating the world with a flood of propositions?

Taking these in reverse order – technically, it is indeed true that the world is potentially populated with lots of propositions. However, like other contextual parameters, the situations which figure as possible described/belief/utterance situations are in most possible applications ones that are in some sense accessible to the relevant agent. As for sharing Austinian propositions, this is a trickier issue. The undoubted vagueness of situations means that there is a technical issue here, if one insists that successful communication presupposes agents resolving all aspects of content identically. However, this criterion is equally problematic for property terms, a difficulty that does not stop semanticists from postulating such entities as denotations of various expression types. The reason for this is that typically agents will agree on the central, defining characteristics of properties. By the same token, it is also the case that given two very similar situations s, s' by and large propositions of the form prop(s, σ), prop(s', σ) will have identical truth values. These highly sketchy comments are only intended as directions by means of which these issues can be addressed, theoretically – but of course a proper debate requires a detailed theory of situations. For such a theory see *inter alia* Barwise (1989a) and other papers in Barwise (1989c), and various papers in Cooper, Mukai & Perry (1990), Barwise et al. (1991) and Aczel et al. (1993). Worlds have a role to play in such a theory, typically viewed as maximal situations that resolve all issues. Whether one needs to admit *possible* situations is a more controversial issue. A treatment of modality, for instance, does not *require* this, as pointed out by e.g. Schulz (1993) and by Cooper & Poesio (1994) – the non-actuality can be encoded entirely in the situation types. Still, it is certainly possible to develop a version of situation theory that has possible situations, to the extent there are good linguistic or philosophical reasons for this, as argued by Vogel & Ginzburg (1999).

One might also wish to link discussion to more empirical investigations. Indeed, for whatever it is worth, arguably, this type of representation for utterances jives well with psychological work on memory (see e.g. Fletcher 1994 for a review), which argues that the two robust memory traces from an utterance are (a) the *situational model* and (b) the *propositional text base*. The former is a representation which integrates various modalities (e.g. visual and linguistic stimuli), whereas the latter differs from the surface form of an utterance for instance in that referents have been resolved. It is also worth pointing out that it would be quite consistent to develop an ontology which involved a mixed picture of propositions: as recognized already by Barwise & Perry (1985), one might wish to avoid positing a described situation with general sentences, such as *Two and two are four* or *Fish swim*. See Glasbey (1998) and Kim (1998) for proposals that some propositions are Austinian, whereas others (e.g. mathematical and individual-level statements) are Russellian i.e., do not make reference to a particular situation.

But wait, I have talked about situations and propositions and their use in reference, assertion or even metacommunicative interaction – what of the attitudes? While writing *Situations and Attitudes* Barwise and Perry's original hope was that replacing worlds with situations would yield an account of one of Montogovian semantics' bugbears, namely *attitude reports*, on which see also article 16 [Semantics: Noun Phrases and Verb Phrases] (Swanson) *Propositional attitudes*. However, this hope did not survive even past the penultimate chapter of the book. A solid result of philosophical work of the 1990s (e.g. Richard 1990 and Crimmins 1993) is that no viable theory of propositions can on its own deliver a viable theory of the attitudes. This is because attitudes have structure not perfectly mirrored by their external content, a realization of which prompted Barwise and Perry to abandon their initial essentially proposition-based account. The most striking illustration of this is in puzzles like Kripke's Pierre (Kripke 1979), who is unaware that the wonderful city of Londres about which he learnt as a child is the same place as the squalid London, where he currently resides. While his beliefs are perfectly rational, we can say of him that he believes that London is pretty and also does not believe that London is pretty.

One possible conclusion from this (see e.g. Crimmins 1993), a way out of paradox, is that attitude reports involve implicit reference to attitudinal states: relative to information acquired in France, Pierre believes London is pretty; relative to information acquired on the ground in London, he believes the opposite. Here is yet another important role for situations in linguistic description. One way to integrate this in an account of complementation was offered in Cooper & Ginzburg (1996) and Ginzburg (1995) for declarative and interrogative attitude reports, respectively. This constitutes a compositional reformulation of the philosophical accounts cited above.

The main idea is to assume that attitude predicates involve at least three arguments: an agent, an attitudinal state and a semantic entity. For instance with respect to belief, this relates an agent's belief in a proposition to facts about the agent's mental situation. This amounts to linking a positive belief attribution of proposition p relative to the mental situation ms with the existence of an *internal* belief state whose *content* is p. An example of such a mental situation is given in section 5.

4 A wider ontological net

The ontology of Situation Theory (ST) was originally designed on the basis of a rather restricted data set. One of the challenges of more recent work has been to extend this ontology in order to account for two related key domains for semantics: root clauses in conversational use and verb complementation. A large body of semantic work that has emerged since the late 1970s demonstrating that interrogative clauses possess denotations (*questions*) distinct in semantic type from declarative ones; imperative and subjunctive clauses possess denotations (dubbed *outcomes* by Ginzburg & Sag 2000) distinct in semantic type from declarative and interrogative ones; facts are distinct from true propositions; for detailed empirical evidence for these distinctions, see Vendler (1972), Asher (1993), Peterson (1997) and Ginzburg & Sag (2000); see also article 5 [Semantics: Sentence and Information Structure] (Krifka) *Questions* and article 6 [Semantics: Sentence and Information Structure] (Han) *Imperatives*.

The main challenge in developing an ontology which distinguishes the diverse menagerie of abstract entities including propositions, questions, outcomes and facts is characterizing the structure of these entities, indeed figuring out how the distinct entities *relate* to each other. As pointed out by Ginzburg & Sag (2000), quantified NPs and certain adverbs are possible in declarative, interrogative and imperative semantic environments. Hence, the ontology must provide a semantic unit which constitutes the input/output of such adverbial modifiers and of NP quantification. To make this concrete – the assumption that the denotation of imperatives is of a type distinct from t (however cashed out) is difficult to square with (a simplistic implementation) of the received wisdom that NPs such as 'everyone' are of type $<<e, t>, t>$. If the latter were the case, composing 'everyone' with 'vacate the building' in (14c) would yield a denotation of type t:

(14) a. Everyone vacated the building.
b. Did everyone vacate the building?
c. Everyone vacate the building!
d. Kim always wins.
e. Does Kim always win?
f. Always wear white!

As we will see subsequently, a good candidate for this role are situation types. These, as we observed in section 3., are not conflated with propositions in the situation theoretic universe.

Ginzburg & Sag (2000) set out to construct an ontology that appropriately distinguishes these entities and yet retains the features of the ST ontology discussed earlier. The ontology, dubbed a *Situational Universe with Abstract Entities* (SU+AE), was developed in line with the strategy of Barwise and Perry's (1). This was implemented on two levels, one within a universe of type-based feature structures (Carpenter 1992). This universe underpinned grammatical analysis, using Head Driven Phrase Structure Grammar (HPSG). A denotational semantics was also developed in the Axiom of Foundation with Atoms (AFA)–based set theoretic framework of Seligman & Moss (1997). In what follows, I restrict attention to the latter.

A semantic universe is identified with a relational structure S of the form $[A, S_1,..., S_m; R_1, ..., R_m]$. Here A – sometimes notated also as $|S|$ – is the universe of the structure. From the class of relations we single out the $S_1, ..., S_m$ which are called the *structural relations*, as they are to capture the structure of certain elements in the domain. Each S_i can be thought of as providing a condition that defines a single structured object in terms of a list of n objects $x_1, ..., x_n$.

Situations and situation types serve as the 'basic building blocks' from which the requisite abstract entities of the ontology are constructed:

- Propositions are structurally determined by a situation and a situation type. (See discussion in section 3.)
- Intuitively, each outcome is a specification of a situation which is futurate relative to some other given situation. Given this, outcomes are structurally determined by a situation and a situation type abstract whose temporal argument is abstracted away, thereby allowing specification of fulfilledness conditions.
- Possibilities, a subclass of which constitutes the universe's *facts*, are structurally determined by a proposition. This reflects the tight link between propositions and possibilities. As Ginzburg & Sag (2000) explain, there is no obvious priority between possibilities and propositions: one could develop an ontology where propositions are built out of possibilities.

An additional assumption made is that the semantic universe is closed under *simultaneous abstraction*. Simultaneous abstraction, originally defined by Aczel & Lunnon (1991), is a semantic operation akin to λ-abstraction with one significant extension: abstraction is over sets of elements, including the empty set. Moreover, abstraction (including over the empty set) is *potent* – the body out of which abstraction occurs is distinct from the abstract. The assumption about closure under simultaneous abstraction is akin to the common type theoretic assumption about closure under functional type formation.

Putting this together, and simplifying somewhat, an SU+AE is an extensional relational structure of the following kind:

(15) $[A, \textit{Possibility}, \textit{Proposition}, \textit{Outcome}, \textit{Fact}, \textit{True}, \textit{Fulfill}, \rightarrow_{prop}]$

Let me gloss the key notions involved here: A is a λ-situation structure (λ-SITSTR). That is, a situation structure closed under simultaneous abstraction. A situation structure (SITSTR) is a universe which supports a basic set theoretic structure. It contains among its entities a class of spatio-temporally located situations and a class of situation types. Proposition, Possibility, and Outcome are sorts whose elements represent, respectively, the propositions, possibilities, and outcomes of the universe. Those possibilities that are factual, as determined by the predicate *Fact*, will constitute the facts of the universe. Analogously, there will be properties *True* and *Fulfill*, which capture the notions of truth and fulfilledness for propositions and outcomes; $\rightarrow_{prop}$ is a notion of entailment defined for propositions.

What about questions? Their existence follows without further stipulation, once one adopts Ginzburg and Sag's assumption that they are propositional abstracts: the universe contains propositions, it is closed under simultaneous abstraction, hence it contains questions. Assuming the identification of questions with propositional abstracts is descriptively adequate, this is an instance of an explanatorily satisfying piece of ontological engineering. On the other hand, one would hope that the existing explication of facts within SU+AEs could be improved on, for instance by uncovering additional internal structure such entities possess.

To conclude this section, I point to two examples (from Ginzburg & Sag 2000) of linguistic phenomena whose explication relies strongly on properties of SU+AEs. The first concerns the distribution of *in situ wh*-phrases. In declarative clause-types, which in the absence of a *wh-phrase* denote propositions, the occurrence of such phrases leads to an ambiguity between two readings, as exemplified in (16a–c): a 'canonical' use which expresses a direct query and a use as a reprise query to request clarification of a preceding utterance. In all other clause types, ones which denote outcomes, (16d), questions, (16e), or facts, (16f) – Ginzburg & Sag (2000) argue that exclamative clauses denote facts – the ambiguity does not arise, only a reprise reading is available; *a priori* one might expect (16d), for instance, to have a reading as a direct question paraphrasable as *who should I give the book to?* if one could simply abstract over the *wh*-parameter within an 'open outcome':

(16) a. The bagels, you gave to who? (can be used to make a non-reprise query)
b. You gave the bagels to who? (can be used to make a non-reprise query)
c. Who talked to who? (can be used to make a non-reprise query)
d. Give who the book? (can be used ONLY to make a reprise query)
e. Do I like who? (can be used ONLY to make a reprise query)
f. What a winner who is? (can be used ONLY to make a reprise query)

(Ginzburg & Sag 2000: 282, example (72))

Given the assumption that questions are exclusively *propositional* abstracts, it follows without further stipulation what is the clause type out of which non-reprise in situ interrogatives are constructed, namely ones with a propositional denotation. Reprise clauses, in contrast, can be built from antecedents of any clause type – the antecedent provides an illocutionary proposition whose main relation is the illocutionary force associated with the given clause type.

The second phenomenon concerns the interaction of negation and interrogation: the fact that propositions are constructed from situations and situation types has a consequence that, in contrast to approaches where questions are characterized in terms of exhaustive answerhood conditions (see Groenendijk & Stokhof 1997), positive and negative polar interrogatives are assigned distinct denotations. For instance, (17a) and (17b), due to Hoepelmann (1983), would be assigned the 0-ary abstracts in (17c) and (17d) respectively:

(17) a. Is 2 an even number?
  b. Isn't 2 an even number?
  c. $\mapsto \lambda\{\}prop(s, \langle\langle EvenNumber, 2\rangle\rangle)$
  d. $\mapsto \lambda\{\}prop(s, \langle\langle \overline{EvenNumber, 2}\rangle\rangle)$

This means that the ontology can explicate the distinct presuppositional backgrounds associated with positive and negative polar interrogatives. For instance, Hoepelmann, in arguing for this distinction, suggests that the contexts appropriate for a question like (17a) is likely to be asked by a person recently introduced to the odd/even distinction, whereas (17b) is appropriate in a context where, say, the opaque remarks of a mathematician sow doubt on the previously well-established belief that *two is even*. The latter can be tied to the factuality conditions of negative situation types. As I mentioned in section 2., one axiom associated with negative situation types is the following: if a situation s supports the dual of σ, then s also supports information which *defeasibly* entails that σ is the case. Hence, wondering about $\lambda\{\}prop(s, \bar{\sigma})$ involves wondering about whether s has the characteristics that typically involve σ being the case, but which – nonetheless, in this case – fail to bring about σ. These contextual differences gives rise in some languages including French and Georgian to distinct words to affirm a positive polar question (*oui, xo*) and a negative polar question (*si, diax*). Nonetheless, given the definitions of answerhood available in this system, positive and negative interrogatives specify identical answerhood relations. Hence, the identity of truth conditions of sentences like (18) can be captured:

(18) a. Kim knows whether Bo left.
  b. Kim knows whether Bo did not leave.

5 A type theoretic ontology for interaction

In previous sections we have observed the gradual evolution of the situation theoretic ontology: from a theory of situations, through a theory of situations and Austinian propositions, to an SU+AE, which includes a variety of abstract entities and is closed under abstraction. This ontology has, as we saw, a wide range of linguistic applications, including perception and attitude complements, definite reference, the Liar, and a rudimentary theory of interaction (for the latter, see Ginzburg 1996).

However, as a new millenium dawned the theory was hamstrung by a number of foundational problems. The logical underpinnings for the theory in terms of non-well-founded set theory, originating in Barwise & Etchemendy (1987), extensively discussed in Barwise (1989c), and comprehensively developed in Seligman & Moss (1997), were rather complex. Concretely, simultaneous λ-abstraction with restrictions is a tool with a variety of uses, including quantification, questions, and the specification of attitudinal states and meanings (for the latter see article 10 [this volume] (Ginzburg) *Situation Semantics*). Its complex set theoretic characterization made it difficult to use. Concomitantly, the theory in this form required an auxiliary coding into a distinct formalism (e.g. typed feature structures) for grammatical and computational applications. Neither of these versions of the theory provides an adequate notion of role-dependency that has become standard in recent treatments of anaphora and quantification on which much semantic work has been invested in frameworks such as Discourse Representation Theory and Dynamic Semantics; see Gawron & Peters (1990) for a detailed theory of anaphora and quantification in situation semantics, though one that is not dynamic.

Motivated to a large extent by such concerns, the situation theoretic outlook has been redeveloped using tools from Type Theory with Records (TTR), a framework initiated by Robin Cooper. Ever since Sundholm and Ranta's pioneering work (Sundholm 1986; Ranta 1994), there has been interest in using constructive type theory (often referred to as *Martin-Löf Type Theory*) as a framework for semantics (see e.g. Fernando 2001 and Krahmer & Piwek 1999). TTR is a model theoretic outgrowth of constructive type theory. Its provision of entities at both levels of tokens and types allows one to combine aspects of the typed feature structures world and the set theoretic world, enabling its use as a computational grammatical formalism. As we will see, TTR provides the semanticist with a formalism that satisfies the desiderata I mentioned in section 1. Cooper (2006a) has shown that the lion's share of situation theoretic results can be recast in TTR – the main exception being those results that depend explicitly on the existence of a non-well-founded universe, for instance Barwise and Etchemendy's account of the Liar; the type theoretic universe is well founded. But one could, according to Cooper (p.c.), recreate non-well-foundedness at the level where witnessing of types occurs. In addition, TTR allows for DRT-oriented or Montogovian treatment of anaphora and quantification. For a computational implementation of TTR, see Cooper (2008); for a closely related framework, the Grammatical Framework see Ranta (2004).

The move to TTR is, however, not primarily a means of capturing and perhaps mildly refining past results, but crucially underpins a theory of conversational interaction on both illocutionary and metacommunicative levels. A side effect of this is, via a theory of generation, an account of attitude reports.

In the remaining space, I will briefly exposit the basics of TTR, show its ability to underpin SU+AEs and briefly sketch how this can be used to define basic information states in dialogue. One linguistic application will be provided, one that ties up situations, information states, and meaning: a specification of the meaning of a discourse-bound pronoun.

5.1 Generalizing the situation/situation type relation

The most fundamental notion of TTR is the typing *judgement* $a : T$ classifying an object a as being of type T. This can be seen as a generalization of the situation semantics judgement $s : \sigma$, generalization in that not only situations can figure as subjects of typing judgements. Note that the theory provides the objects and the types, but this form of judgement, as well as other forms are metatheoretical. Examples are given in (19). (19a–c) are typing judgements that presuppose the existence of types SIT(uation), IND(ividual), REL(ation), whose identity can be amplified. (19d) is the direct analogue of the situation semantics statement $s : \langle\!\langle RUN; b, t \rangle\!\rangle$; here run(b, t) is a *proof type*, about which more below; 'proof' can be equally glossed as 'observation' or even 'situation', as explained by Ranta (1994); the source of the 'proof-based' terminology is constructive type theory's original use as a foundation for mathematics.

(19) a. s   : SIT
    b. b   : IND
    c. run : REL
    d. s   : run(b, t)

A useful innovation TTR introduces relative to earlier version of type theory are records and record types. A record is an ordered tuple of the form (20), where crucially each successive field can depend on the values of the preceding fields:

(20) $$\begin{bmatrix} l_i = k_i \\ l_{i+1} = k_{i+1}(l_i) \ldots \\ l_{i+j} = k_{i+j}(l_i, \ldots, l_{i+j-1}) \end{bmatrix}$$

Together with records come record *types*. Technically, a record type is simply an ordered tuple of the form (21), where again each successive type can depend on its predecessor types within the record:

(21) $$\begin{bmatrix} l_i : T_i \\ l_{i+1} = T_{i+1}(l_i) \ldots \\ T_{i+j} = T_{i+j}(l_i, \ldots, l_{i+j-1}) \end{bmatrix}$$

Record types allow us to place constraints on records: the basic typing mechanism assumed is that a record r is of type RT if all the typing constraints imposed by RT are satisfied by r. More precisely,

(22) The record:

$$\begin{bmatrix} l_1 = a_1 \\ l_2 = a_2 \\ \ldots \\ l_n = a_n \end{bmatrix} \text{ is of type: } \begin{bmatrix} l_1 : T_1 \\ l_2 : T_2(l_1) \\ \ldots \\ l_n : T_n(l_1, l_2, \ldots, l_{n-1}) \end{bmatrix}$$

iff $a_1 : T_1, a_2 : T_2(a_1), \ldots, a_n : T_n(a_1, a_2, \ldots, a_{n-1})$

5.2 Recreating SU+AEs in TTR

Ginzburg (2005b) shows how to recreate SU+AEs within the type theoretic universe constructed in Cooper (2006a). As with SU+AEs, one can recognize here the sitsemian strategy Barwise and Perry allude to in (1). The universe is connected to the real world via a model which assigns witnesses to the basic types and sets of witnesses to the proof types depending on their r-ity. From these beginnings, arise structured objects via type construction which allows for a recursive building up of the type theoretic universe. Ranta (1994) and Cooper (2006a) list a dozen such constructors. Here, apart from the afore mentioned record typing construction, I will list only a small number that are necessary for the tasks to be performed here:

(23) a. Function types: if T_1 and T_2 are types, then so is $(T_1 \to T_2)$, the type of functions from elements of type T_1 to elements of type T_2.
  b. The type of lists: if T is a type, then [T], the type of lists each of whose members is of type T, is also a type. $[a_1, ..., a_n] : [T]$ iff for all i $a_i : T$
  c. The unique type: if T is a type and $x : T$, then T_x is a type. $a : T_x$ iff $a = x$.

5.2.1 Abstraction

Function types allow one to model abstraction. As Cooper points out, although abstraction in TTR works in a deceptively familiar 'type theoretic' way, the existence of record typing yields a rich notion of abstraction. It is simultaneous and restricted, i.e. it allows for multiple entities to be abstracted over simultaneously while encoding restrictions, and allows for vacuous abstraction. As an illustration of abstraction in TTR, consider a mental state that Pierre can be assumed to possess (see section 3. and Cooper 2006a, where this example is discussed in detail). (24a), a function mapping records into record types, represents the internal type, whereas (24b) represents a possible external setting for this type. The internal type is a perfectly consistent type, external incoherence is captured by the fact that applying the internal type to the setting yields a contradiction.

(24) (a) r: $\left(\begin{bmatrix} x : \text{Ind} \\ c1 : \text{Named}(x, \text{'Londres'}) \\ y : \text{Ind} \\ c2 : \text{Named}(y, \text{'London'}) \end{bmatrix} \right) \begin{bmatrix} c3 : \text{pretty}(r.x) \\ 4 : \neg \text{pretty}(r.x) \end{bmatrix}$

  (b) $\begin{bmatrix} x = \text{london} \\ c1 : s_{Named(london, \text{'Londres'})} \\ y : \text{london} \\ c2 : s_{Named(london, \text{'London'})} \end{bmatrix}$

See also article 10 [this volume] (Ginzburg) *Situation Semantics* for the use of this sort of abstraction in the specification of the meaning/content relationship.

5.2.2 Situations

Cooper (2006a) proposes that situations (in the sense of Situation Theory) be modelled as records. Situation types are then directly accommodated as record types. The type of a situation with a woman riding a bicycle would then be the one in (25a). A record of this type (a *witness* for this type) would be as in (25b), where the required corresponding typing judgements are given in (25c):

(25) (a) $\begin{bmatrix} x : \text{IND} \\ c_1 : \text{woman}(x) \\ y : \text{IND} \\ c_2 : \text{bicycle}(y) \\ \text{time} : \text{TIME} \\ \text{loc} : \text{LOC} \\ c_3 : \text{ride}(x, y, \text{time}, \text{loc}) \end{bmatrix}$ (b) $\begin{bmatrix} \dots \\ x = a \\ c_1 = p_1 \\ y = b \\ c_2 = p_2 \\ \text{time} = t_0 \\ \text{loc} = 10 \\ c_3 = p_3 \\ \dots \end{bmatrix}$

(c) a IND; p_1 : woman(a); b : IND; p_2 : bicycle(b); t_0 : TIME; 10 : LOC; p_3 : ride(a,b,t_0,10);

In particular, given an identification of utterances with speech events, this enables us to have simultaneous access to utterances *and* utterance types (or *signs*). These are important ingredients for a theory of metacommunicative interaction, as discussed in article 10 [this volume] (Ginzburg) *Situation Semantics*.

In a series of recent papers (e.g. Fernando 2007a, 2007b), Tim Fernando has provided a type theoretic account of the *internal* make up of situations. Events and situations are represented by strings of temporally ordered observations, on the basis of which the events and situations are recognized. This allows a number of important temporal constructions to be derived, including Allen's basic interval relations Allen (1983) and Kamp's event structures Kamp (1979). Observations are generalized to temporal propositions, leading to event-types that classify event-instances.

5.2.3 Propositions

There are two obvious ways to develop an account of propositions in TTR, implicitly Austinian or explicitly so. Cooper (2006a) develops the former in which a proposition *p* is taken to be a record type. A witness for this type is a situation as e.g. (25b). On this strategy, a witness is not directly included in the semantic representation. Ginzburg (2005b) develops an explicitly Austinian approach. The type of propositions is the record type (26a). The correspondence with the situation semantics conception is quite direct. We can define truth conditions as in (26b).

(26) a. $\text{Prop} =_{def} \begin{bmatrix} \text{sit} & : & \text{Record} \\ \text{sit-type} & : & \text{RecType} \end{bmatrix}$

b. A proposition $p = \begin{bmatrix} \text{sit} & = & s_0 \\ \text{sit-type} & = & ST_0 \end{bmatrix}$ is true iff $s_0 : ST_0$

TTR actually provides very fine-grained entities and so does not run into the problems that beset traditional semantic approaches with respect to logical omniscience and various other puzzles. In fact, as Cooper (2006a) discusses, this can be too much of a good thing, given that record types distinct only by their labelling are distinguished. Cooper goes on to offer a criterion of type individuation of record types using Σ-types, where the corresponding 'labels' function as bound variables.

Ginzburg (2005a) shows how to formulate a theory of questions as propositional abstracts in TTR, while using the standard TTR notion of abstraction. In this way, a possible criticism of the approach of Ginzburg & Sag (2000), that they use an *ad hoc* and complex notion of abstraction, can be circumvented. Similarly, Ginzburg (2005b) shows how to explicate outcomes within TTR.

5.3 Ontology in interaction

The most active area in the application of TTR to the description of NL is in the area of dialogue. Larsson (2002) and Cooper (2006b) showed how to decompose interaction protocols, such as those specified situation theoretically in Ginzburg (1996), by using TTR to describe update rules on the information states of dialogue participants. This was extended by Ginzburg (2012) to cover a variety of illocutionary moves, metacommunicative interaction (see article 10 [this volume] (Ginzburg) *Situation Semantics* for some discussion) and conversational genres. Fernández (2006) uses TTR to develop a wide coverage of the range of non-sentential utterances that occur in conversation.

In these works, information states are assumed to consist of a public and unpublicized part. For current purposes we restrict attention to the public part, also known as each participant's *dialogue gameboard* (DGB). Each DGB is a record of the type given in (27) – the *spkr, addr* fields allow one to track turn ownership, *Facts* represents conversationally shared assumptions, *Pending* and *Moves* represent respectively moves that are in the process of/have been grounded, *QUD* tracks the questions currently under discussion:

(27) ⎡ spkr : Ind ⎤
    ⎢ addr : Ind ⎥
    ⎢ c-utt : addressing(spkr,addr) ⎥
    ⎢ Facts : Set(Prop) ⎥
    ⎢ Pending : list(LocProp) ⎥
    ⎢ Moves : list(LocProp) ⎥
    ⎣ QUD : poset(Question) ⎦

We call a mapping that indicates how one DGB can be modified by conversationally related action a *conversational rule*, and the types specifying its domain and its range respectively the *preconditions* and the *effects*. Here I exemplify the use of TTR to give a partial characterization of the meaning of pronouns in dialogue, a task that links assertion acceptance, situations, and meaning.

The main challenge for a theory of meaning for pronouns is of course how to characterize their antecedency conditions; here I restrict attention to intersentential cases, see Ginzburg (2011) for an extension of this account to intra-sentential cases. Dialogue takes us away quite quickly from certain received ideas on this score: antecedents can arise from queries (28a), from partially understood or even disfluent utterances ((28b,c) respectively). Moreover, as (28d) illustrates, where 'he' cannot refer to 'Jake', the shelf life of an antecedent is potentially quite short. Although the data are subtle, a plausible assumption is that for non-referential NPs anaphora are not generally possible from within a query (polar or wh) (Groenendijk 1998), or from an assertion that has been rejected (e.g. (28e,f)).

(28) a. A: Did John phone? B: He's out of contact in Daghestan.
    b. A: Did John phone? B: Is he someone with a booming bass voice?
    c. Peter was, well he was fired.
    d. A: Jake hit Bill. / B: No, he patted him on the back. / A: Ah. Is Bill going to the party tomorrow? /B: No. / A: Is #he/Jake?
    e. A: Do you own an apartment? B: Yes. A: Where is it located?
    f. A: Do you own an apartment? B: No. A: #Where might you buy it?

This means, naturally enough, that witnesses to non-referential NPs can only emerge in a context where the corresponding assertion has been accepted. A natural move to make in light of this is to postulate a witnessing process as a side effect of assertion acceptance, a consequence of which will be the emergence of referents for non-referential NPs. For uniformity's sake, we can assume that these witnesses get incorporated into the contextual parameters (C-PARAMS) of that utterance, which in any case includes (witnesses for) the referential NPs. This means that c-params serves uniformly as the locus for witnesses of 'discourse anaphora'. The rule of incorporating non-referential witnesses in c-params is actually simply a minor add on to the rule that underwrites assertion acceptance (see Ginzburg 2011, chapter 4) – the rule underpinning the utterance of acceptances – it can be viewed as providing for a witness for situation/event anaphora since this is what gets directly introduced into c-params. In cases where the witness is a record (essentially when the proposition is positive), NP witnesses will emerge. In (29) the preconditions involve the fact that the speaker's latest move is an assertion of a proposition whose type is T1. The effects change the speaker/addressee roles (since the asserted to becomes the accepter) and adds a record w, including a witness for T1, to the contextual parameters.

(29) Accept move:

$$\begin{bmatrix} \text{preconds}: \begin{bmatrix} \text{spkr}: \text{Ind} \\ \text{addr}: \text{Ind} \\ p = \begin{bmatrix} \text{sit} = \text{sit1} \\ \text{sit-type} = \text{T1} \end{bmatrix} : \text{Prop} \\ \text{LatestMove}^{\text{content}} = \text{Assert}(\text{spkr}, \text{addr}, p) : \text{IllocProp} \end{bmatrix} \\ \text{effects} : \begin{bmatrix} \text{spkr} = \text{preconds.addr}: \text{Ind} \\ \text{addr} = \text{preconds.spkr}: \text{Ind} \\ w = \text{preconds.LatestMove.c-params} \cup [\text{sit} = \text{sit1}] : \text{Rec} \\ \text{Moves} = m1 \oplus \text{preconds.Moves} : \text{list(LocProp)} \\ m1^{\text{content}} = \text{Accept}(\text{spkr},\text{addr},p) : \text{LocProp} \\ m0.\text{c-param} = w : \text{Rec} \end{bmatrix} \end{bmatrix}$$

We can now state the meaning of a singular pronoun somewhat schematically as follows: it is a word whose contextual parameters include an antecedent, which is to be sought from among the constituents of an *active move*; the pronoun is identical in reference to this antecedent and agrees with it. Space precludes a careful characterization of what it means to be *active*, but given the data we saw above it is a composite property determined by QUD – essentially being specific to an element of QUD – and Pending. See article 10 [this volume] (Ginzburg) *Situation Semantics* for the justification for including reference to an utterance's constituents in grammatical representation. In (30), I provide a lexical entry in the style of HPSG that captures this specification: here m represents the *active move* and a the antecedent; the final condition on *c-params* requires that within m's contextual parameters is one whose index is identical to that of a's content:

(30) $\begin{bmatrix} \text{PHON} : \langle \text{she} \rangle \\ \text{c-params} : \begin{bmatrix} \text{m} : \text{LocProp} \\ \text{a} : \text{Sign} \\ \text{c1} : \text{member(a,m.constits)} \\ \text{c2} : \text{ActiveMove(m)} \\ \text{m.sit.c-params} : [\text{a.c-params.index} = \text{a.cont.index} : \text{Ind}] \end{bmatrix} \\ \text{cat} = \begin{bmatrix} \text{head} : \text{N} \\ \text{ana} : + \\ \text{agr} = \text{c-params.m.cat.agr} : \begin{bmatrix} \text{num} = \text{sg} : \text{Number} \\ \text{gen} = \text{fem} : \text{Gender} \\ \text{pers} = \text{third} : \text{Person} \end{bmatrix} \end{bmatrix} : \text{syncat} \\ \text{cont} : [\text{index} = \text{a.cont.index} : \text{Ind}] \end{bmatrix}$

6 Conclusions

Situation semantics initiated an ontology–oriented approach to semantics: the aim being to develop means of representing the external and internal reality of agents in a cognitively tractable way. The initial emphasis was on situations, based in part on evidence from the naked infinitival construction. Situations, parts of the world, have proved to be of significant importance to a variety of phenomena ranging from the domains associated with NP use to negation and, one way or the other, play a significant role in the very act of asserting. The theory of situations subsequently lead to a theory of propositions (*Austinian* propositions), structured objects constructed from situations and situation types: Austinian propositions are significantly more fine-grained than possible worlds propositions, but coarse grained enough to pass translation and paraphrase criteria. They also have a potential construal in terms of differingly coarse grained memory traces.

The technique of individuating abstract entities as structured objects enables the theory to scale up: by integrating questions, outcomes and facts into the ontology, Situation Theory was able to underpin a rudimentary theory of illocutionary interaction (entities such as questions, propositions and outcomes serve as the descriptive content of queries, assertions and requests) and a theory of complementation for attitudinal predicates.

A recent development has been to recast the theory in type theoretic terms, concretely using the formalism of Type Theory with Records. Type Theory with

Records has many similar characteristics to situation theory – an ontology – oriented approach, computational tractability, structured objects. This enables most of the results situation theory achieved to be maintained. On the other hand, Type Theory with Records brings with it a more transparent formalism and the existence of dependent types allows both dynamic semantic and unification grammar techniques to be utilized. Indeed, all these can be combined to construct a theory of illocutionary and metacommunicative interaction, one of the key areas of development for semantics in the early 21st century.

7 References

Aczel, Peter 1988. *Non Well Founded Sets*. Stanford, CA: CSLI Publications.
Aczel, Peter, David Israel, Stanley Peters & Yasuhiro Katagiri (eds.) 1993. *Situation Theory and Its Applications, III*. Stanford, CA: CSLI Publications.
Aczel, Peter & Rachel Lunnon 1991. Universes and parameters. In: J. Barwise et al. (eds.). *Situation Theory and its Applications, II*. Stanford, CA: CSLI Publications, 3–24.
Allen, James 1983. Maintaining knowledge about temporal intervals. *Communications of the ACM* 26, 832–843.
Asher, Nicholas 1993. *Reference to Abstract Objects in English: A Philosophical Semantics for Natural Language Metaphysics*. Dordrecht: Kluwer.
Austin, John L. 1970. Truth. In: J. Urmson & G. J. Warnock (eds.). *Philosophical Papers*. 2nd edn. Oxford: Oxford University Press, 117–133.
Barwise, Jon 1989a. Branch points in Situation Theory. In: J. Barwise. *The Situation in Logic*. Stanford, CA: CSLI Publications, 255–276.
Barwise, Jon 1989b. Scenes and other situations. In: J. Barwise. *The Situation in Logic*. Stanford, CA: CSLI Publications, 5–36.
Barwise, Jon 1989c. *The Situation in Logic*. Stanford, CA: CSLI Publications.
Barwise, Jon & John Etchemendy 1987. *The Liar: An Essay on Truth and Circularity*. Oxford: Oxford University Press.
Barwise, Jon et al. (eds.) 1991. *Situation Theory and Its Applications, II*. Stanford, CA: CSLI Publications.
Barwise, Jon & John Perry 1983. *Situations and Attitudes*. Cambridge, MA: The MIT Press.
Barwise, Jon & John Perry 1985. Shifting situations and shaken attitudes. *Linguistics & Philosophy* 8, 399–452.
Brown-Schmidt, S. & Michael K. Tanenhaus 2008. Real-time investigation of referential domains in unscripted conversation: A targeted language game approach. *Cognitive Science: A Multidisciplinary Journal* 32, 643–684.
Carpenter, Bob 1992. *The Logic of Typed Feature Structures: With Applications to Unification Grammars, Logic Programs, and Constraint Resolution*. Cambridge: Cambridge University Press.
Cooper, Robin 1993. Generalized quantifiers and resource situations. In: P. Aczel et al. (eds.). *Situation Theory and Its Applications, III*. Stanford, CA: CSLI Publications, 191–211.
Cooper, Robin 1996. The role of situations in Generalized Quantifiers. In: S. Lappin (ed.). *Handbook of Contemporary Semantic Theory*. Oxford: Blackwell, 65–86.

Cooper, Robin 1998. Austinian propositions, Davidsonian events and perception complements. In: J. Ginzburg et al. (eds.). *The Tbilisi Symposium on Logic, Language and Computation: Selected Papers*. Stanford, CA: CSLI Publications, 19–34.
Cooper, Robin 2006a. Austinian truth in Martin-Löf Type Theory. *Research on Language and Computation* 3, 333–362.
Cooper, Robin 2006b. A type theoretic approach to information state update in issue based dialogue management. In: L. Moss (ed.). *Jon Barwise Memorial Volume*. Bloomington, IN: Indiana University Press.
Cooper, Robin 2008. *Oz Implementation of Type Theory with Records*. http://www.ling.gu.se/~cooper/records/ttr0.zip. December 15, 2010.
Cooper, Robin & Jonathan Ginzburg 1996. A compositional Situation Semantics for attitude reports. In: J. Seligman & D. Westerståhl (eds.). *Logic, Language, and Computation*. Stanford, CA: CSLI Publications, 151–165.
Cooper, Robin, Kuniaki Mukai & John Perry (eds.) 1990. *Situation Theory and Its Applications, I*. Stanford, CA: CSLI Publications.
Cooper, Robin & Massimo Poesio 1994. Situation Theory. *Fracas Deliverable D8*. Centre for Cognitive Science, Edinburgh: The Fracas Consortium.
Crimmins, Mark 1993. *Talk about Beliefs*. Cambridge, MA: The MIT Press.
Fernández, Raquel 2006. *Non-Sentential Utterances in Dialogue: Classification, Resolution and Use*. Ph.D. dissertation. King's College, London.
Fernando, Tim 2001. Conservative generalized quantifiers and presupposition. In: R. Hastings, B. Jackson & Z. Zvolenszky (eds.). *Proceedings of Semantics and Linguistic Theory (= SALT) XI*. Ithaca, NY: Cornell University, 172–191.
Fernando, Tim 2007a. Observing events and situations in time. *Linguistics & Philosophy* 30, 527–550.
Fernando, Tim 2007b. Situations from events to proofs. In: K. Korta & J. Garmendia (eds.). *Meaning, Intentions, and Argumentation*. Stanford, CA: CSLI Publications, 113–129.
Fletcher, Charles 1994. Levels of representation in memory for discourse. In: M. A. Gernsbacher (ed.). *Handbook of Psycholinguistics*. San Diego, CA: Academic Press, 589–607.
Gawron, Mark & Stanley Peters 1990. *Anaphora and Quantification in Situation Semantics*. Stanford, CA: CSLI Publications.
Ginzburg, Jonathan 1995. Resolving questions, I. *Linguistics & Philosophy* 18, 459–527.
Ginzburg, Jonathan 1996. Interrogatives: Questions, facts, and dialogue. In: S. Lappin (ed.). *Handbook of Contemporary Semantic Theory*. Oxford: Blackwell, 359–423.
Ginzburg, Jonathan 2005a. Abstraction and ontology: Questions as propositional abstracts in constructive type theory. *Journal of Logic and Computation*, 113–130.
Ginzburg, Jonathan 2005b. Situation Semantics: The ontological balance sheet. *Research on Logic and Computation* 3, 363–389.
Ginzburg, Jonathan 2010. *The Interactive Stance: Meaning for Conversation*. Oxford: Oxford University Press.
Ginzburg, Jonathan & Ivan A. Sag 2000. *Interrogative Investigations: The Form, Meaning and Use of English Interrogatives*. Stanford, CA: CSLI Publications.
Glasbey, Sheila 1998. A situation theoretic interpretation of bare plurals. In: J. Ginzburg et al. (eds.). *The Tbilisi Symposium on Logic, Language and Computation: Selected Papers*. Stanford, CA: CSLI Publications, 35–54.
Groenendijk, Jeroen 1998. Questions in update semantics. In: J. Hulstijn & A. Nijholt (eds.). *Proceedings of TwenDial 98, 13th Twente Workshop on Language Technology*. Twente: Twente University, 125–137.

Groenendijk, Jeroen & Martin Stokhof 1997. Questions. In: J. van Benthem & A. ter Meulen (eds.). *Handbook of Logic and Linguistics*. Amsterdam: North-Holland, 1055–1124.
Higginbotham, James 1983. The logic of perceptual reports: An extensional alternative to Situation Semantics. *Journal of Philosophy* 80, 100–127.
Higginbotham, James 1994. *The Semantics and Syntax of Event Reference*. ESSLLI Course Notes. Copenhagen: Copenhagen Business School.
Hoepelmann, Jacob 1983. On questions. In: F. Kiefer (ed.). *Questions and Answers*. Dordrecht: Reidel, 191–227.
Kamp, H. 1979. Events, instants and temporal reference. In: R. Bäuerle, U. Egli & A. von Stechow (eds.). *Semantics from Different Points of View*. Berlin: Springer, 376–417.
Kim, Yookyung 1998. Information articulation and truth conditions of existential sentences. *Language and Information* 1, 67–105.
Krahmer, Emiel & Paul Piwek 1999. Presupposition projection as proof construction. In: H. Bunt & R. Muskens (eds.). *Computing Meaning: Current Issues in Computational Semantics*. Dordrecht: Kluwer, 281–300.
Kratzer, Angelika 1989. An investigation of the lumps of thought. *Linguistics & Philosophy* 12, 607–653.
Kratzer, Angelika 2008. Situations in natural language semantics. In: E. N. Zalta (ed.). *The Stanford Encyclopedia of Philosophy (Fall 2008 Edition)*. http://plato.stanford.edu/entries/situation-semantics/. December 15, 2010.
Kripke, Saul 1975. Outline of a theory of truth. *The Journal of Philosophy*, 690–716.
Kripke, Saul 1979. A puzzle about belief. In: A. Margalit (ed.). *Meaning and Use*. Dordrecht: Reidel, 239–283.
Larsson, Staffan 2002. *Issue based Dialogue Management*. Doctoral dissertation. University of Gothenburg.
Lewis, David K. 1979. Score keeping in a language game. In: R. Bäuerle, U. Egli & A. von Stechow (eds.). *Semantics from Different Points of View*. Berlin: Springer, 172–187.
McCawley, James D. 1979. Presupposition and discourse structure. In: C.-K. Oh & D. Dinneen (eds.). *Presupposition*. New York: Academic Press, 371–388.
McGee, Vann 1991. Review of J. Barwise & J. Etchemendy. *The Liar* (Oxford, 1987). *Philosophical Review* 100, 472–474.
Moss, Lawrence 1989. Review of J. Barwise & J. Etchemendy. *The Liar* (Oxford, 1987). *Bulletin of the American Mathematical Society* 20, 216–225.
Muskens, Reinhard 1989. *Meaning and Partiality*. Doctoral dissertation. University of Amsterdam. Reprinted: Stanford, CA: CSLI Publications, 1995.
Neale, Stephen 1988. Events and logical form. *Linguistics & Philosophy* 11, 303–321.
Peterson, Philip 1997. *Fact, Proposition, Event*. Dordrecht: Kluwer.
Poesio, Massimo 1993. A situation–theoretic formalization of definite description interpretation in plan elaboration dialogues. In: P. Aczel et al. (eds.). *Situation Theory and Its Applications, III*. Stanford, CA: CSLI Publications, 339–374.
Ranta, Aarne 1994. *Type Theoretical Grammar*. Oxford: Oxford University Press.
Ranta, Aarne 2004. Grammatical framework. *Journal of Functional Programming* 14, 145–189.
Richard, Mark 1990. *Propositional Attitudes: An Essay on Thoughts and How We Ascribe Them*. Cambridge, MA: The MIT Press.
Russell, Bertrand 1905. On denoting. *Mind* 14, 479–493.
Schulz, Stephen 1993. Modal Situation Theory. In: P. Aczel et al. (eds.). *Situation Theory and Its Applications, III*. Stanford, CA: CSLI Publications, 163–188.

Seligman, Jerry & Larry Moss 1997. Situation Theory. In: J. van Benthem & A. ter Meulen (eds.). *Handbook of Logic and Linguistics*. Amsterdam: North-Holland, 239–309.
Soames, Scott 1985. Lost innocence. *Linguistics & Philosophy* 8, 59–71.
Sundholm, Göran 1986. Proof Theory and meaning. In: D. Gabbay & F. Guenthner (eds.). *Handbook of Philosophical Logic*. Oxford: Oxford University Press, 471–506.
Vendler, Zeno 1972. *Res Cogitans*. Ithaca, NY: Cornell University Press.
Vogel, Carl & Jonathan Ginzburg 1999. A situated theory of modality. Paper presented at the *3rd Tbilisi Symposium on Logic, Language, and Computation,* Batumi, Republic of Georgia, September 1999.

Jonathan Ginzburg
10 Situation Semantics: From indexicality to metacommunicative interaction

1 Introduction —— 295
2 Desiderata for semantics —— 296
3 The Relational Theory of Meaning —— 298
4 Meaning, utterances, and dialogue —— 303
5 Closing remarks —— 317
6 References —— 317

Abstract: Situation Semantics emerged in the 1980s with an ambitious program of reform for semantics, both in the domain of semantic ontology and with regard to the integration of context in meaning. This article takes as its starting point the focus on utterance (as opposed to sentence) interpretation. The far reaching aims Barwise and Perry proposed for semantic theory are spelled out. Barwise and Perry's Relational Theory of Meaning is described, in particular its emphasis on utterance situations and on the reification of information. The final part of the article explains how conceptual apparatus from situation semantics has ultimately come to play an important role in a highly challenging enterprise, modelling dialogue interaction, in particular metacommunicative interaction.

1 Introduction

Situation Semantics emerged in the 1980s with an ambitious program of reform for semantics, both in the domain of semantic ontology and with regard to the integration of context in meaning. In their 1983 book *Situations and Attitudes* (Barwise & Perry 1983), as well as a host of other publications around that time collected in Barwise (1989) and Perry (2000), Barwise and Perry argued for the preeminence of a situation-based ontology and took contexts of utterance to be situations, thereby offering the potential for a richer view of context than was available previously. For situation semantics and ontology, see article 9 [this volume] (Ginzburg) *Situation Semantics and NL ontology*. This article takes as its starting point the focus on utterance (as opposed to sentence) interpretation.

Jonathan Ginzburg, Paris, France

https://doi.org/10.1515/9783110589245-010

In section 2 I spell out the far reaching aims Barwise and Perry proposed for semantic theory. In section 3 I sketch Barwise and Perry's *Relational Theory of Meaning*, in particular its emphasis on utterance situations and on the reification of information. I also point out some of the weaknesses of Barwise and Perry's enterprise, particularly the approach to context. One of these weaknesses, in my view, is that the theory is quite powerful, but it was, largely, applied to dealing with traditional, sentence-level semantics. The final section of this article, section 4, explains how conceptual apparatus from situation semantics has ultimately come to play an important role in a highly challenging enterprise, modelling dialogue interaction.

2 Desiderata for semantics

Barwise and Perry's starting point is model theoretic semantics, as developed in the classical Montague Semantics tradition (see e.g. Montague 1974; Dowty, Wall & Peters 1981; Gamut 1991 and article 7 [this volume] (Zimmermann) *Model-theoretic semantics*): a natural language is likened to a formal language (first order logic, intensional logic etc). On this approach, providing a semantics for such a language involves primarily assigning *interpretations* (or *denotations*) to the words of the language and rules that allow phrases to be interpreted in a compositional manner. This allows both the productivity of NL meaning and the potential for various kinds of ambiguity to be explicated. Contexts, on this view, are identified with *indices* – tuples consisting of a small and fixed number of dimensions, prototypically providing values for *speaker, addressee, time, location*. Interpretations of words/phrases are then all taken to be relative to contexts, thereby yielding two essential semantic entities: *characters/meanings* which involve abstracting away indices from *contents/interpretations*. These – supplemented by lexical meaning postulates – can be used to explicate logically valid inference.

Barwise and Perry view this picture of semantics as significantly too restrictive. The basic perspective they adopt is one in which linguistic understanding is assimilated to the extraction of information by resource bounded agents in their natural environment (inspired in part by the work of Gibson, e.g. Gibson 1979). This drives their emphasis on a number of unorthodox seeming fundamental desiderata for semantic theory, desiderata we will subsequently come to see find considerable resonance in the desiderata for a theory of meaning for conversational interaction.

The first class of desiderata are metatheoretical in nature and can be summed up as follows:

Desideratum 1: THE PRIORITY OF INFORMATION

Language has external significance, as model theoretic semantics has always emphasized, but, as cognitive scientists of various stripes emphasize, it also has mental significance, yielding information about agents' internal states. What is needed is a way of capturing the commonality between the external and the mental, the flow of information – the chain from fact to thought in one participant's mind to utterance to thought in another participant's mind, graphically exemplified in Fig. 10.1.

Fig. 10.1: The Flow of Information. (Barwise & Perry 1983: 17)

An important component in fulfilling this desideratum, according to Barwise and Perry, is a theory by means of which external (and internal) reality can be represented – an ontology of some kind. This is what developed into situation theory and type theory with records (see article 9 [this volume] (Ginzburg) *Situation Semantics and NL ontology*). A key ingredient in such a theory are some notion of *constraints,* a way of capturing necessary, natural, or conventional linkages between situations (e.g. smoke means fire, image being such and such means leg is broken etc.), along with a theory of how agents in a situation extract information using constraints. The other crucial component is the naturalization of linguistic meanings – their reduction to concepts from the physical world – in terms of *constraints.*

The other two pivotal desiderata put forward by Barwise and Perry are more directly aimed at repositioning the semantic fulcrum, from interpretation towards context.

Desideratum 2: INFORMATION CONTENT IS UNDERDETERMINED BY INTERPRETATION
We might provide news about the Argentinean elections using any of the following sentences in (1). All three sentences uttered in these circumstances intuitively have the same external significance – we would wish to identify their content and, on some accounts, their meaning as well. Nonetheless, different information can be acquired from each: for instance, (1b) allows one to infer that Kirchner is a woman, whereas Lavagna is a man.

(1) a. Kirchner beat Lavagna.
　　b. Señora Kirchner defeated Señor Lavagna.
　　c. Cristina's losing opponent was Lavagna.

Desideratum 3: LANGUAGE IS AN EFFICIENT MEDIUM
Barwise and Perry emphasize that the flip side of productivity gets less attention as a fundamental characteristic of NL: the possibility of reusing the same expression to say *different* things. Examples of the phenomena Barwise and Perry had in mind are in (2), which even in 2018 are tricky. By 'tricky' I don't mean we lack a diagnosis, I mean there is no single formal and/or implemented semantic/pragmatic theory that picks them all off with ease, interfacing along the way with *inter alia* theories of gesture, gaze, and visual access.

(2) a. A: I'm right, you're wrong. B: I'm right, you're wrong.
　　b. I want you, you, and you to stand here and I want you, you, and you to stand here. (based on examples in Levinson 1983; Pollard & Sag 1994)
　　c. A: John is irritating John no end. B: He can't be annoying him so badly.
　　d. In last week's FoLLI dissertation prize meeting sadly the linguist voted for the linguist, whereas the logician voted for the logician. (based on an example in Cooper 1996)

3 The Relational Theory of Meaning

At the heart of situation semantics is the *Relation Theory of Meaning*. There are two fundamentally innovative aspects underlying this theory, which bear significant importance to current semantic theory in the wider sense:

(3) a. Meaning Reification: the reification of meanings as entities on which humans reason (rather than as metatheoretical entities, as standard in logic).

b. Speech Events as Semantic Entities: recognition of speech events (incl speakers, addressees, the speech token) as fundamental semantic units; sentences are viewed as derivative: type-like entities that emerge from utterances, or, as Barwise and Perry put it, *uniformities over utterances.*

To get a feel for the theory, consider a simple example. (4b), taken to be the meaning of (4a), is a crude representation of an early version of the Relational Theory of Meaning: a (declarative) meaning relates all utterance events u in which there exists a speaker a, addressee b, spatiotemporal locations l, t, referents j, m (for the names 'Jacky' and 'Molly' respectively) to described events e in which j bites m at t. This relation is exemplified graphically in Fig. 10.2, which emphasizes the reality of the utterance situation. I have purposely used quasi-Davidsonian notation (see article 8 [this volume] (Maienborn) *Event semantics)* to indicate that the central insight there is independent of the various more and particularly less standard formalisms in which the Relational Theory of Meaning has been couched. As we will soon see, there are various ways which differ significantly to cash out the characterization of u, e and their interrelation.

(4) a. Jacky bit Molly.
 b. { u,e | ∃a,b,l,j,m,t [uttering(a,'Jacky is biting Molly',u) ∧ addressee(u,b) ∧ In(u,l) ∧ referring(a,j, 'Jacky') ∧ Named(j, 'Jacky') ∧ referring(a,m, 'Molly') ∧ Named(m, 'Molly') ∧ coincident(l,t) ∧ describing(a,e) ∧ bite (e,j,m,t)] }

Fig. 10.2: The meaning of 'Jacky is biting Molly' as a relation between situations in which this construction is uttered and events in which a Jacky bites a Molly. (Barwise & Perry 1983: 122)

Of the two assumptions, Speech Events as Semantic Entities was introduced by Barwise and Perry in a stronger form than (3), graphically exemplified in Fig. 10.2 – not only do they make reference to speech event, but Barwise and Perry actually posit a compositional aspect to speech events:

(5) a. If α is a phrase with sub-constituents X,Y, then uttering(a, α, u) entails the existence of two subevents of e e_1, e_2 such that
 b. $e_1 \prec e_2$ (e_1 temporally precedes e_2)
 c. uttering(a, X, u_1)
 d. uttering(a, Y, u_2)

This formulation raises a variety of issues concerning syntax, presupposing essentially a strongly surfacey and linearized approach. For obvious reasons of space I cannot enter into these, but they constitute an important backdrop. Speech Events as Semantic Entities underlay a number of grammar fragments subsequent to Barwise & Perry (1983) (e.g. Gawron & Peters 1990; Cooper & Poesio 1994), but on the whole was not the focus of much interest until Poesio realized its significance for conversational processing, as we discuss in section 4.2. In contrast, issues concerning Meaning Reification drove much research in the hey day of Situation Semantics. The relation exemplified in (4b) is certainly a relation with relevance to the semantics of utterances of 'Jacky is biting Molly': it relates events in which the speaker mouths a particular linguistic form while referring to a Jacky and a Molly with an event the speaker is describing in which that Jacky bit that Molly. Barwise and Perry view *attunement* – the awareness of similarities between situations and of relationships that obtain between such similar situations – to the constraint in (4) as being what underlies our competence to use and understand such utterances. Nonetheless, there are two aspects which the formulation above abstracts away from: contextual parameter instantiation and truth evaluation. (4) does not make explicit the fact that understanding such an utterance involves finding appropriate referents for the two NP sub-utterances, as indeed in certain circumstances – e.g. for an overhearer who cannot see the speech participants or hears a recording – for the speaker and the time. In fact, in the original formulation of the Relational Theory of Meaning Barwise and Perry made a point of not packaging all of context in one event/situation, but distinguished three components of context: (a) *the discourse situation*, comprising the public aspects of an utterance (including all the standard indexical parameters), (b) *the speaker connections*, comprising information pertaining to a speaker's referential intentions, and (c) *resource situations*, events/situations distinct from the described situation, used to serve as referential/quantificational domains. Although the discourse situation/speaker connection dichotomy does not seem to have survived – examples such as (2b) illustrate the importance of speaker intention even with 'simple indexicals', the ultimate insight to be drawn here, it seems, is the unbounded nature of contextual dependence. Resource situations are one of the important contributions of situation semantics (see particularly Cooper 1996), and are further discussed in article 9 [this volume] (Ginzburg) *Situation Semantics and NL ontology*.

Returning to (4), the formulation of the Relational Theory of Meaning as a relation between contextual situations (the discourse situation, speaker connections, zero or more resource situations) and described situations, is problematic. It means that the latter cannot serve as the denotations of declarative utterances (since they are not truth bearers), nor does it generalize to non-declarative meaning. This reflects the fact that in *Situations and Attitudes* Barwise and Perry attempt to stick to an avowedly "concrete" ontology, one which eschews abstract entities such as propositions, leading them into various foundational problems.

This stance was abandoned soon after – various notions of propositions emerged as situation theory developed. Hence, in works such as Gawron & Peters (1990), Cooper & Poesio (1994), works from a maturer version of situation semantics, (declarative) sentential meanings came to be formulated as relating utterance situations – from whence values for contextual parameters would be drawn – and propositions; meanings for sub-sentential constituents would analogously relate an utterance situation for that constituent with an associated *described object* (referent [NP], property [VP] etc). As an example of the Relational Theory of Meaning in a current formalism that fixes both problematic aspects discussed above, consider (6), which uses the formalism of Type Theory with Records (see Cooper 2006), discussed in more detail in article 9 [this volume] (Ginzburg) *Situation Semantics and NL ontology*. (6a) corresponds to an utterance type *(utterance type* in the sense of *sign* as in constraint-based grammars like Head Driven Phrase Structure Grammar or similar notions in Type Logical Grammar. A witness for the type (6a) is given in (6b) – it includes a phonetic token – distinguished here from its associated phonological type in terms of spelling, contextual parameters – a situation *sit0*, a time *time0*, a speaker *spkr0*, addressee *addr0*, utterance time *time1*, an individual named Jo *j0*, and situations grounding the truth of the addressing, precedence, and naming conditions $c10, c20, c30$ – and the Austinian prepositional entity $\begin{bmatrix} \text{sit} = \text{sit0} \\ \text{sit-type} = \text{Leave}(j0, time0) \end{bmatrix}$. C-PARAMS represents the type of entities need to instantiate a meaning:

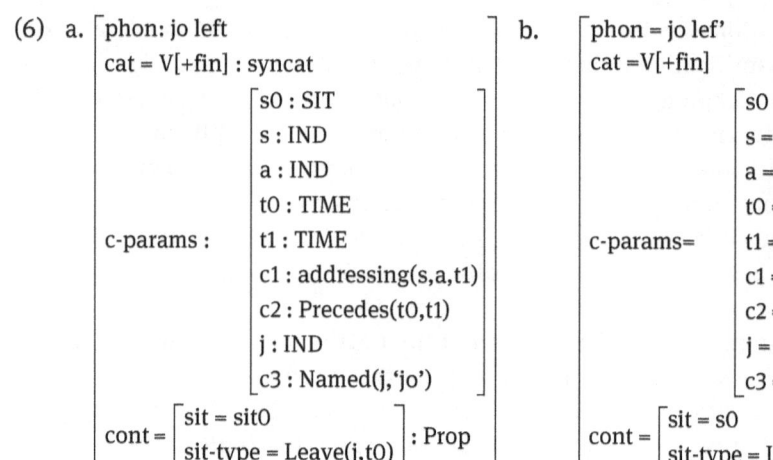

Reconstructing the meaning/content relationship in terms of two fields C-PARAMS and CONTENT, originating in HPSG, allows in the current setting for the possibility of partially instantiating a content and maintaining this as the semantic representation of an utterance until a more detailed instantiation is available, an important possibility in conversational interaction, as we discuss in section 4.3.

Situation Semantics is one of the harbingers of dynamic semantics: the relational theory of meaning can be straightforwardly reconstrued as a specification of input/output contexts associated with uttering a given sentence. Indeed the paper (Barwise 1987) was one of the first to spell out a dynamic semantics for NPs, though (in common with most other works in the dynamic semantics tradition) does not spell out how to interface with the discourse/utterance situation in the above sense. This ties in with a number of weaknesses which Barwise and Perry's conception of context exhibits:

- No dynamics of indexicality is worked out (e.g. interaction between turn taking and structure of context) to deal with cases like (2a,b).
- It ignores metacommunication (the focus of sections 4.2. and 4.3.).
- In common with traditional speech act theory, it ignores conversational structure: to take two simple examples, the interpretation of the second 'hi' as a *counter greeting* derives from its position following an initial greeting. Similarly, the resolution of 'No' picks up in some way on the adjacent assertion:

(7) a. A: Hi. B: Hi
    b. A: I'm right, you're wrong. B: No. I'm right, you're wrong.

– Due to lack of calculus of constraints, it is not easy to use the Relational Theory of Meaning as a logic which could allow an explicit account of which information can be derived from an utterance.

The utterance-based formulation of semantic theory pioneered by Situation Semantics was criticized as misguided by Kaplan (1989), Partee (1985); for a subsequent argument *contra*, along with a good review of Kaplan's and related approaches, see Israel & Perry (1996). Indeed the utterance-based formulation has until recently had relatively little impact. Why? Putting aside sociological explanations, one might say that although the theory was intended for conversational language, the methodology and setting were that of the traditional isolated sentence, for which the pay offs do not seem sufficiently significant given the apparent theoretical investment. When these tools *are* applied to a dialogue setting, significant pay offs for this perspective emerge.

4 Meaning, utterances, and dialogue

4.1 Phenomena from spoken language

There has been growing interest in recent years in developing notions of context that can be used to semantically analyze linguistic phenomena characteristic of conversational language and to model dialogue interaction (see Ginzburg 1996b; Poesio & Traum 1997; Larsson 2002; Asher & Lascarides 2003; Ginzburg 2012). The *efficiency of language*, in the sense discussed above, and concomitant importance of context becomes yet more urgent an issue given how pervasive non-sentential utterances are in conversational settings – one word utterances are estimated to constitute between 30–40% of all utterances, 25% of these are propositional or interrogative, and hence involve significant contextual resolution (see e.g. Fernández 2006). In the remainder of this article I will focus on a number of semantic phenomena that occur in conversational interaction, whose analysis builds on the conceptual apparatus brought into prominence by situation semantics, in particular, the reification of utterances as real world events and the view of meanings as first class citizens of the ontology, not metatheoretical entities. As it turns out, this apparatus provides powerful tools that also offer solutions to old linguistic problems, viz. how to integrate into context non-semantic parallelism conditions, characteristic of ellipsis constructions, and grammatical gender agreement in anaphora.

The phenomena I consider here revolve around metacommunicative acts, which are rare in texts, but pervasive in dialogue. There are two main types of metacommunicative interactions – acknowledgements of understanding and clarification requests.

An addressee can acknowledge speaker's utterance, either once the the utterance is completed, as in (8a), or concurrently with the utterance as in (8b):

(8) a. Tommy: So Dalmally I should safely say was my first schooling. Even though I was about eight and a half. Anon 1: Mm. Now your father was the the stocker at Tormore is that right? (British National Corpus (BNC), K7D)
b. A: Move the train . . .
B: Aha
A: . . . from Avon . . .
B: Right
A: . . . to Danville. (Adapted from the Trains corpus)

Concomitantly with an utterance's addressee acknowledging her understanding of an utterance, are a variety of facts about the utterance that potentially enter into the common ground. This is evinced, here for (9a), by the possibility of embedding them under a factive-presupposition predicate such as 'interesting'. (9) exemplifies two classes of facts about the utterance that become presupposable, facts about the content of sub-utterances (9b–d) and also facts that concern solely the phonology and word order of the utterance (9e).

(9) a. A: Did Mark send you a love letter?
b. B: No, though it's interesting THAT YOU REFER TO MARK/MY BROTHER/OUR FRIEND.
c. B: No, though it's interesting THAT YOU BRING UP THE SENDING OF LOVE LETTERS.
d. B: No, though it's interesting THAT YOU ASK ABOUT MARK'S EPISTOLARY HABITS.
e. B: No, though it's interesting THAT THE FINAL TWO WORDS YOU JUST UTTERED START WITH 'L'.

A recurring theme since the Russell/Strawson dispute over definites has been the notion of *presupposition failure* (see article 2 [Semantics: Noun Phrases and Verb Phrases] (Heim) *Definiteness and indefiniteness* and article 14 [Semantics: Interfaces] (Beaver & Geurts) *Presupposition*). However, in interaction there is rarely *failure* as such. Rather, conversationalists' mismatches lead to a CLARIFICATION

REQUEST (CR) – a query about an unclear aspect of a previous utterance – being posed. Natural Language allows for fine grained potential for CRs, using both sentential and non-sentential means. (10) illustrates a form-based taxonomy of CRs that covers virtually all of the CRs occurring in the BNC:

(10) a. A: Did Bo leave?
 b. WOT: B: Eh? / What? / Pardon?
 c. EXPLICIT: B: What did you say? / Did you say 'Bo' / What do you mean 'leave'?
 d. LITERAL REPRISE: B: Did BO leave? / Did Bo LEAVE?
 e. WH-SUBSTITUTED REPRISE (SUB): B: Did WHO leave? / Did Bo WHAT?
 f. REPRISE SLUICE (SLU): B: Who? / What? / Where?
 g. REPRISE FRAGMENTS (RF): B: Bo? / Leave?
 h. GAP: B: Did Bo ... ?
 i. FILLER: A: Did Bo ... B: Win? (Table I from Purver 2006)

In this taxonomy, four classes of contents were identified: they can be exemplified in the form of Explicit CRs:

(11) a. REPETITION: What did you say? Did you say 'Bo'?
 b. CLAUSAL CONFIRMATION: Are you asking if Bo left? You're asking if who left?
 c. INTENDED CONTENT: What do you mean ()? Who is 'Bo'?
 d. CORRECTION: Did you mean to say 'Bro'?

In practice, though most CRs are not of the Explicit category. Many CR utterances are multiply ambiguous. The most extreme case are reprise fragments, which seems able to exhibit all four readings, though in practice 99% of cases found in the corpus study Purver, Ginzburg & Healey (2001) were either CLAUSAL CONFIRMATION or INTENDED CONTENT. Ginzburg & Cooper (2004) and Ginzburg (2012) demonstrate that reprise fragments display parallelism on a syntactic and phonological level with its source. Clausal confirmation readings, on the one hand, and intended content and repetition readings, on the other, involve distinct parallelism conditions, suggesting that different linguistic mechanisms underlie the distinct understandings. CLAUSAL CONFIRMATION readings do not require phonological identity between target and source, as shown in (12a,b). Nonetheless, as (12c–f) show, they require partial syntactic parallelism: an XP used to clarify an antecedent sub-utterance u_1 must match u_1 categorially:

(12) a. A: Did Bo leave? B: My cousin? (Are you asking if BO, my cousin, left?)
 b. A: Did she annoy Bo? B: Sue? (Are you asking if SUE annoyed Bo?)

c. A: I phoned him. B: him? / #he?
d. A: Did he phone you? B: he? / #him?
e. A: Did he adore the book. B: adore? / #adored?
f. A: Were you cycling yesterday? B: Cycling?/biking?/#biked?

That repetition readings of RF involve (segmental) phonological identity with their source follows from their very nature ('Did you say ...'). And this requirement also applies to intended content readings of RF:

(13) (i) A: Did Bo leave? B: Max? (cannot mean: intended content reading: WHO ARE YOU REFERRING TO? or WHO DO YOU MEAN?)

The existence of syntactic and phonological parallelism in CRs across utterances is further evidence to that provided above in (9) that the notion of context we need is one that tracks non-semantic information associated with utterances, not merely content, presuppositions and the like. I will show that one way to capture this requirement is by defining contextual updates in terms of *locutionary propositions*, propositions constructed from utterances and the types that classify them. This idea has antecedents in the Relational Theory of Meaning and in the Austinian conception of propositions, discussed in detail in article 9 [this volume] (Ginzburg) *Situation Semantics and NL ontology.*

It should be emphasized just how central a phenomenon metacommunicative interaction is in interaction: a rough idea of the frequency of acknowledgements can be gleaned from the word counts for 'yeah' and 'mmh' in the demographic part of the BNC: 'yeah' occurs 58,810 times (rank: 10; 10–15% of turns), whereas 'mmh' occurs 21,907 times (rank: 30; 5% of turns). Clarification Requests (CRs) constitute approximately 4–5% of all utterances (see e.g. Purver 2004; Rodriguez & Schlangen 2004). Moreover, there is suggestive evidence from artificial life simulation studies that the existence of CRs is not an incidental feature of interaction but a key component in the long-term viability of a language. Macura & Ginzburg (2006) and Macura (2007) show that when repair acts are a part of a linguistic interaction system, a stable language can be maintained over generations. Whereas, in a community endowed with a language that *lacks* CRification, as I refer to the interaction brought about by a CR, the emergent divergence among language users is so high that the language eventually dies out. Ignoring metacommunicative interaction, as has been the case for just about the entire tradition of formal semantics, means missing out one of the basic building blocks of linguistic interaction. Situation Semantics was itself complicit in this. However, the view of language it provides, with its reference to speech events as part of the semantic domain, and the reification of meanings provides important building blocks for a theory of metacommunicative interaction.

How then to integrate metacommunicative aspects into the semantic process? Such phenomena have been studied extensively by psycholinguists and conversational analysts in terms of notions such as *grounding* and *feedback* (in the sense of Clark 1996 and Allwood 1995, respectively) and of *repair* (in the sense of Schegloff 1987). The main claim that originates with Clark & Schaefer (1989) is that any dialogue move m_1 made by A must be grounded (viz acknowledged as understood) by the other conversational participant B before it enters the common ground; failing this *CRification* must ensue. While Clark and Schaefer's assumption about grounding is somewhat too strong, as Allwood argues, it provides a starting point, indicating the need to interleave the potential for grounding/CRification incrementally; the size of the increments being an important empirical issue. From a semantic theory, we might expect the ability to generate concrete predictions about forms/meanings of metacommunicative interaction utterances in context. Such a characterization needs to cover both the range of possibilities associated with successful communication (grounding), as well as with imperfect communication – indeed it has been argued that *mis*communication is the more general case (see e.g. Healey 2008). Thus, we can suggest that the adequacy of semantic theory involves *the ability to characterize for any utterance type the update that emerges in the aftermath of successful grounding and the full range of possible CRs otherwise*. This is, arguably, the early 21st century analogue of truth conditions. The update component of this criterion builds on earlier adequacy criteria that emerged from dynamic semantics' frameworks (see article 12 [this volume] (Dekker) *Dynamic semantics*). Nonetheless, these frameworks have abstracted away from metacommunication.

I now consider two general approaches that strive to develop semantic theories capable of delivering grounding conditions/CRification potential. The first approach, an extension of Discourse Representation Theory (DRT) (see article 11 [this volume] (Kamp & Reyle) *Discourse Representation Theory*), aims at explicating *inter alia* the potential for acknowledgements and utterance-oriented presuppositions; the second approach, constructed from the start as a theory of dialogue *per se*, shows how to characterize CRification potential.

A crucial assumption both approaches bear in common, one that distinguishes them from other dynamic semantic work (e.g. Roberts 1996; Groenendijk 1998; Dekker 2004; Asher & Lascarides 2003), but one that seems inescapable if metacommunicative interaction is to be tackled, is the need for *semantic distributivity*: given the fact that a single (public) input can lead to distinct outputs for each conversationalist, the effect of semantic operations can no longer be defined on a common ground *simpliciter*, but this needs in one way or another to be relativized across the conversational participants. This is exemplified in Turn Taking Puzzles (Ginzburg 1997) such as (14) and (15), where depending on who gets the turn, resolution possibilities for ellipsis vary:

(14) a. A: Who does Bo admire? B: Bo?
 b. Reading 1 (SHORT ANSWER): Does Bo admire Bo?
 c. Reading 2 (CLAUSAL CONFIRMATION): Are you asking who BO (of all people) admires?
 d. Reading 3 (INTENDED CONTENT CLARIFICATION): Who do you mean 'Bo'?

(15) a. A: Who does Bo admire? Bo?
 b. Reading 1: (SHORT ANSWER): Does Bo admire Bo?
 c. Reading 2: (SELF CORRECTION): Did I say 'Bo'?

The relativization of context is what enables an account of the contrast between (14) and (15), sketched in section 4.3.: the semantic material necessary for ellipsis resolution in cases like (14c,d) can only emerge once a clarification request has been introduced by the addressee.

4.2 Acknowledgements, grounding, and micro conversational events

Massimo Poesio and David Traum and collaborators (e.g. Poesio & Traum 1997; Matheson, Poesio & Traum 2000; Poesio & Rieser 2010) have developed a framework known as PTT (not an acronym), which integrates a dynamic semantic framework (a version of DRT, Kamp & Reyle 1993) with a framework for representing conversational interaction inspired by speech act theory. One of the starting points of PTT is the assumption Speech Events as Semantic Entities (see (3b) above). On the basis of this, they assimilate the treatment of speech acts to the treatment of other events in DRT. Thus, conversational events can serve as the antecedents of anaphoric expressions, just like normal events. The standard DRT construction algorithm would assign to the text in (16a) an interpretation along the lines of (16b) (using the syntax from Poesio & Muskens 1997) for Discourse Representation Structures (DRSs) – a single DRS containing the merged propositional content of both assertions.). In contrast, Poesio and Traum hypothesize that upon hearing an assertion of that sentence, the common ground in a conversation would be roughly in (16c):

(16) a. A: There is an engine at Avon. B: It is hooked to a boxcar.
b. [x,w,y,z,s,s'| engine(x), Avon(w), s: at(x,w), boxcar(y), s':hooked-to(z,y), z is x]
c. [ce1,ce2| ce1 : assert(A,B,[x,w,s| engine(x), Avon(w), s: at(x,w)])
ce2 : assert(B,A,[y,z,s'| boxcar(y), s':hooked-to(z,y), z is x])]

(16c) records the occurrence of two conversational events, ce1 and ce2, both of type ASSERT, whose propositional content are separate DRSs specifying the interpretation of the two utterances in (16a). The discourse entities ce1 and ce2 can serve as antecedents both of implicit anaphoric references, e.g. in the case of 'backward' acts like answers to questions, and of explicit ones. Consider (17): this may be viewed as performing at least two functions here: implicitly accepting the option proposed in ce1, and performing a query. Indeed *backward-looking acts* – (for the *backward/forward-looking dialogue act* dichotomy see Core & Allen 1997) such as ACCEPT are all implicitly anaphoric to a previous conversational event (ce1 in this case), hence the assumption that conversational events introduce discourse markers just like normal events do.

(17) a. A: We should send an engine to Avon. B: Shall we use engine E3?
b. [ce1,ce2,ce3| ce1: open-option(A,B,[x,w,e| engine(x), Avon(w), e: send (A,B,x,w)]), ce2: accept(B,ce1) ce3: ask(B,A,[y,e'| engine(y), E3(y), e':use (A,B,y)])]

In fact, as mentioned earlier, Poesio and Traum develop their theory on the basis of a strong and dynamicized version of Speech Events as Semantic Entities: an utterance is taken to be a sequence of *micro-conversational events* (MCEs). On this view, the discourse situation is updated not just when a complete sentence has been observed, but whenever a new event is observed. Psychological research suggests that such updates can take place every few milliseconds (Tanenhaus & Trueswell 1995), so that observing the utterance of a phoneme is sufficient to cause an update; but in practice PTT typically assumes that updates take place after every word. The incremental update hypothesis is not just motivated by psychological findings about incremental interpretation in sentential utterances, but by the fact that in dialogue many types of conversational acts are hardly, if ever, performed with full sentences. A class of non-sentential utterances that quite clearly lead to immediate updates of the discourse situation are those used to perform *dialogue control acts* such as TAKE-TURN, KEEP-TURN and RELEASE-TURN actions whose function is to synchronize the two participants in the conversation as to whom is holding the floor (Traum & Hinkelmann 1992) and ACKNOWLEDGEMENTS. These conversational actions are sometimes performed by sentential utterances that also generate a core speech act (e.g., the second utterance in (17a)), but more commonly they are generated by single-word discourse markers like 'mmh', 'okay', 'well', 'now'.

In PTT, lexicon and grammar are formulated as defeasible rules characterizing the update potential of *locutionary acts*. The motivation for defeasibility include psycholinguistic results about lexical access, e.g. work such as Onifer & Swinney (1981) demonstrating that conversationalists simultaneously access all meanings of ambiguous words. Lexical entries and syntactic rules link a precondition stated in terms of the phonological/syntactic characteristics of a micro-conversational event and a possible effect stated in terms of the possible meaning of that event. In particular, syntactic rules enable the construction of compound locutionary events, whose atomic constituents are the MCEs corresponding to utterances of individual words. Each locutionary act la_1 sets up the potential for a subsequent illocutionary act il_1 (one of whose) effects is to constitute an acknowledgement of la_1.

This provides the basis for a treatment of grounding and dialogue control particles. I illustrate this for 'okay' in its use as an acknowledgement particle; PTT assumes that locutionary acts *generate* – here in a causal sense introduced by Goldman (1970) – core speech acts. The lexical entry could be specified, roughly, as in (18), where *u* represents a locutionary and *ce* an illocutionary act resepctively:

(18) lexical entry for 'OK': [u,ce| u: utter (A,'okay'), ce: acknowledge(A,ce),
        generate (u,ce)]

(A highly simplified view of) the conversational score resulting from such an acknowledgement to an (ongoing) utterance by A in (19a) would be *roughly* as in (19b). This gives a schematic illustration of the emergence of utterance-related presuppositions – there are four micro-conversational events – each characterized in terms of its phonological syntactic, and semantic characteristics respectively – the events mce1, mce2 of uttering 'an' and 'engine' respectively, the compound event mce_3 of uttering 'an engine' and the event mce2 of uttering 'OK'; mce2 generates a core speech act, the acknowledgement of mce3:

(19) a. ... A: an engine B: OK ...
    b. [mce1,mce2,mce3,mce4,ce4|
        mce1: utter(A,"an"), cat(mce1) = det, mce1 $\mapsto \lambda P, Q[x]; P(x); Q(x)$
        mce2: utter(A,"engine"), cat(mce2) = N, mce2 $\mapsto \lambda x\ engine(x)$

mce1 ≺ mce2, Dtrs({*mce1, mce2*}, *mce3*), cat(mce3) = NP
mce3 ↦ λQ[x]; *engine*(x); Q(x), generate(mce3,ce3),
mce4: utter(B, 'okay'), cat(mce4) = intj,
ce4: acknowledge(B,mce3), generate(mce4,ce4)]

4.3 CRification and Meaning Reification

The ability to both process and generate clarification questions is vital in all areas of Human-Computer Interaction, ranging from web search to expert systems. This is one reason why interest in integrating CRification into the semantic process is an issue that has attracted significant interest in computational semantic work (see Schlangen 2004; Purver 2006, DeVault et al. 2005). Above and beyond this, developing a theory which can predict the clarification potential of utterances, the possible forms and contents available for their clarification, is an important theoretical challenge. It represents one of the fundamental aspects of interactivity. To date, the main attempts in this direction have been made within the KoS framework (not an acronym) (Ginzburg & Cooper 2004; Purver 2004; Purver 2006; Ginzburg 2012), where a detailed treatment of the phenomena discussed in this section can be found. KoS is formalized in Type Theory with Records. What is crucial for current purposes about this formalism, which takes situation semantics as one of its inspirations, is that it provides access to both types and tokens at the object level. Concretely, this enables simultaneous reference to both utterances and utterance types, a key desideratum for modelling metacommunicative interaction. This distinguishes Type Theory with Records from Discourse Representation Theory, for instance, where the witnesses are at a model theoretic level, distinct from the level of discourse representations.

On the view developed in KoS, there is actually no single context, for reasons explained previously – instead of a single context, analysis is formulated at a level of information states, one per conversational participant. The type of such information states is given in (20a). I leave the structure of the private part unanalyzed here, for details on this, see Larsson (2002). The dialogue gameboard represents information that arises from publicized interactions. Its structure is given in the type specified in (20b):

(20) a. TotalInformationState (TIS):
$$\begin{bmatrix} \text{Dialoguegameboard} : \text{DGB} \\ \text{private} : \text{Private} \end{bmatrix}$$

b. DGB =

$$\begin{bmatrix} \text{spkr : Ind} \\ \text{addr : Ind} \\ \text{c-utt : addressing(spkr,addr)} \\ \text{Facts : set(Proposition)} \\ \text{Pending : list(locutionary Proposition)} \\ \text{Moves : list (locutionary Proposition)} \\ \text{QUD : Poset(Question)} \end{bmatrix}$$

In this view of context:

- The speaker/addressee roles serve to keep track of turn ownership.
- FACTS represents the shared knowledge conversationalists utilize during a conversation. More operationally, this amounts to information that a conversationalist can use embedded under presuppositional operators.
- PENDING: represents information about utterances that are as yet un-grounded. Each element of Pending is a *locutionary proposition*, a proposition individuated by an utterance event and a grammatical type that classifies that event. The motivation for this crucial modelling decision, which concerns the input to grounding and CRification processes and which carries on to the Moves repository, is discussed below.
- MOVES: represents information about utterances that have been grounded. The main motivation is to segregate from the entire repository of presuppositions information on the basis of which coherent reactions to the latest conversational move can be computed. For various purposes (e.g. characterizing the preparatory conditions of moves such as greeting and parting) it is actually important to keep track of the entire repository of moves.
- QUD: (mnemonic for Questions Under Discussion) – questions that constitute a "live issue". That is, questions that have been *introduced for discussion* at a given point in the conversation and not yet been *downdated*. The role of questions in structuring context has been recognized in a variety of works, including Hamblin (1970), Carlson (1983), van Kuppevelt (1995), Ginzburg (1994), Ginzburg (1996a), Roberts (1996), Larsson (2002). There are additional ways for questions to get added into QUD, the most prominent of which is during metacommunicative interaction, as we will see shortly. Being maximal in QUD (MAX-QUD) corresponds to being the current 'discourse topic' and is a key component in the theory.

The Dialogue GameBoard, then, constitutes the publicized context in KoS – taking into account that conversationalists' DGBs need not be identical throughout.

Work in KoS (e.g. Fernández & Ginzburg 2002; Fernández 2006; Ginzburg 2012) has shown that virtually all types of non-sentential utterance, ranging from short answers, propositional lexemes (e.g. 'yes', 'no'), through reprise fragments, can be analyzed as *indexical* expressions relative to the DGB.

Context change is specified in terms of *conversational rules*, rules that specify the *effects* applicable to a DGB that satisfies certain *preconditions*. This allows both illocutionary effects to be modelled (preconditions for and effects of greeting, querying, assertion, parting etc), interleaved with *locutionary effects*, our focus here. In the immediate aftermath of the speech event u, PENDING gets updated with a record of the form $\begin{bmatrix} \text{sit} = u \\ \text{sit-type} = T_u \end{bmatrix}$ (of type LocProp (*locutionary proposition*)). Here T_u is a grammatical type that emerges during the process of parsing u, as already exemplified above in (6). The relationship between u and T_u – describable in terms of the Austinian proposition (see (6) and article 9 [this volume] (Ginzburg) *Situation Semantics and NL ontology*) $p_u = \begin{bmatrix} \text{sit} = u \\ \text{sit-type} = T_u \end{bmatrix}$ – can be utilized in providing an analysis of grounding/CRification conditions:

(21) a. Grounding: p_u is true: the utterance type fully classifies the utterance token.
b. CRification: T_u is weak (e.g. incomplete word recognition); u is incompletely specified (e.g. incomplete contextual resolution).

Thus, pending utterances are the locus off of which to read grounding/CR conditions.

Without saying much more, we can formulate a lexical entry for CR particles like 'eh?' (Purver 2004). Given a context that supplies speaker, addressee and a pending utterance the content expressed is a question querying the intended content of the utterance:

(22) $\begin{bmatrix} \text{phon}: \langle \text{eh} \rangle \\ \text{cat} = interjection: \text{syncat} \\ \text{c-params}: \begin{bmatrix} \text{spkr}: \text{IND} \\ \text{addr}: \text{IND} \\ \text{pending}: \text{utt} \\ c2: \text{address}(\text{addr.spkr}, \text{pending}) \end{bmatrix} \\ \text{cont} = \text{Ask}(\text{c-params.spkr}, \text{c-params.addr}, \\ \lambda x \ \text{Mean}(\text{c-params.addr}, \text{c-params.pending}, x)): \text{IllocProp} \end{bmatrix}$

(22) is straightforward apart from one point – what is the type *utt*. This actually is a fundamental semantic issue, one which, as we will see, responds to the *underdetermination of information by interpretation* desideratum raised in section 1: what is the semantic type of PENDING? In other words, what information needs to be associated with PENDING to enable the formulation of grounding conditions/ CR potential? The requisite information needs to be such that it enables the original speaker to interpret and recognize the coherence of the range of possible clarification queries that the original addressee might make.

Meanings – in the sense I discussed earlier of functions from contexts, which provide values for certain parameters (the *contextual parameters*), to contents – provide a useful notion for conceptualizing grounding/clarification potential (and were exploited for this purpose in Ginzburg 1996b). This is because the range of contextual parameters offers a possible characterization of the contextually variable and hence potentially problematic constituents of utterance content. Note though that if we conceive of meanings as entities which characterize potential sources of misunderstanding, the contextual parameters will need to include all open class sub-utterances of a given utterance type (i.e. including verb, common noun, and adjective, sub-utterances). This is a far cry from the 4 place indices of Montague and Kaplan, from the meanings envisaged by Barwise and Perry, and even from dynamicized meanings in dynamic semantics. (For experimental evidence about which lexical categories are viewed to be clarifiable see Purver 2004.)

Ginzburg & Cooper (2004) argue that, nonetheless, even radically context dependent meanings of this kind are not quite sufficient to characterize CR potential. One problem is the familiar one of grain. In terms of the concept or property that they represent, one would be hard pressed to distinguish the meanings of words such as *attorney* and *lawyer*. And yet, since knowledge of language is not uniform, it is clear that the clarification potential of the sentences in (23) is not identical. Which word was used initially makes a difference as to how the clarification can be formulated:

(23) a. Ariadne: Jo is a lawyer. Bora: A lawyer?/What do you mean a lawyer?/#What do you mean an advocate?/#What do you mean an attorney?
b. Ariadne: Jo is an advocate. Bora: #What do you mean a lawyer?/An advocate?/What do you mean an advocate?/#What do you mean an attorney?

Other arguments derive from syntactic and phonological parallelism exhibited by non-sentential CRs (exemplified by (10f,g)) to their antecedent sub-utterance, and the existence of CRs whose function is to request repetition of (parts of) an utterance. Such CRs can, in principle, arise from any sub-utterance and are specified in terms of the utterance's phonological type. Indeed the fact that any sub-utterance can, in principle, give rise to clarification motivates one one relatively minor enhancement to the standard grammatical representation. Instead of keeping track solely of immediate constituents, as is handled in formalisms such as HPSG the feature DTRS, we enhance the representation itself so it keeps track of *all* constituents. This is done by positing an additional, set valued field in the type definition of signs dubbed CONSTIT(UENT)s, illustrated below in Fig. 10.3. In Ginzburg (2012), it is shown that this enhancement plays a key role in capturing cross-utterance parallelism, agreement, and scopal and anaphoric antecedency, though here I will only hint at the role it plays in formulating rules that regulate grounding and CRification.

The arguments provided hitherto point to the fact that PENDING must incorporate the utterance *type* associated by the grammar with the clarification target. This would have independent utility since it would be the basis for an account of the various utterance presuppositions whose source can only derive from the utterance type (see example (9)). In fact, we encounter here evidence for the assumption Speech Events as Semantic Entities: CRs typically involve *utterance anaphoricity*. In (24a,b) the issue is not *what do you mean by leaving* or *who is Bo* IN GENERAL, but *what do you mean by leaving* or *who is Bo* IN THIS PARTICULAR SUB-UTTERANCE:

(24) a. A: Max is leaving. B: leaving?
      b. A: Did Bo leave? B: Who is Bo?

Taken together with the obvious need for PENDING to include values for the contextual parameters specified by the utterance type, Ginzburg (2012) argues that the type of PENDING combines tokens of the utterance, its parts, and of the constituents of the content with the utterance type associated with the utterance. An entity that fits this specification is the *locutionary proposition* defined by the utterance, as introduced before in (21).

With this in hand, I formulate in (25) a highly simplified utterance processing protocol, which interleaves illocutionary and metacommunicative interaction:

(25) UTTERANCE PROCESSING PROTOCOL
      For an agent A with DGB *DGB*0: if a locutionary proposition
      $$p_u = \begin{bmatrix} \text{sit} = u \\ \text{sit-type} = T_u \end{bmatrix}$$ is Maximal in PENDING:

      (a) If p_u is true, update Moves with p_u.
      (b) Otherwise: introduce a clarification issue derivable from p_u as the maximal element of QUD; use this context to formulate a clarification request.

There are a small number of schemas that specify the possible clarification issues derivable from a given locutionary proposition p_u. These include the issues 'What did A mean by u1' and 'What did A utter in u1', where A is the speaker provided in the contextual assignment represented in p_u and $u1$ is a sub-utterance of u. The hypothesis that the context has been incremented with such an issue is taken to be the explanation for how non-sentential CRs such as (10b,f,g) and (12) are interpretable domain independently.

To conclude, Fig. 10.3 offers a schematic illustration of how a single utterance – here of 'Did Bo leave?' – can lead to distinct updates among distinct participants at the 'public level' of context. In this case this arises due to differential ability to anchor the contextual parameters. The utterance u0 has three sub-utterances, u1, u2, u3, given in Fig. 10.3 with their approximate pronunciations. A can ground her own utterance since she knows the values of the contextual parameters, which I assume here for simplicity include the speaker and the referent of the sub-utterance 'Bo'. This means that the locutionary proposition associated with u0 – the proposition whose situational value is a record that arises by unioning u0 with the witnesses for the contextual parameters and whose type is given in Fig. 10.3 – is true. This enables the 'canonical' illocutionary update to be performed: the issue 'whether b left' becomes the maximal element of QUD. In contrast, let assume that B lacks a witness for the referent of 'Bo'. As a result, the locutionary proposition associated with u0 which B can construct is not true. Given this, B increments QUD with the issue 'who was meant by A as the referent of subutterance u2', and the locutionary proposition associated with u0 which B has constructed remains in Pending.

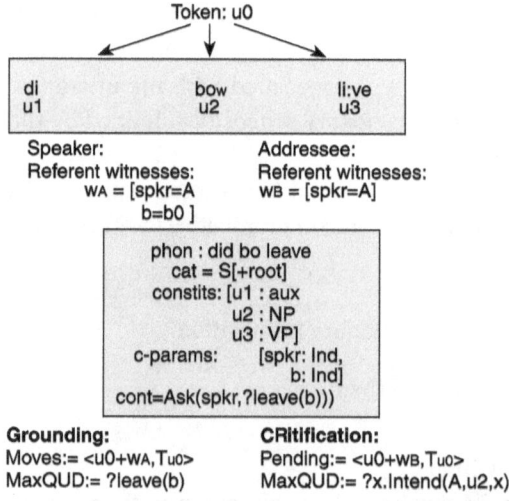

Fig. 10.3: A single utterance gives rise to distinct Updates of the DGB for distinct participants

5 Closing remarks

One of the innovative contributions of situation semantics has been the Relational Theory of Meaning, an utterance oriented approach to semantics, which naturalizes meanings as first class entities. The origins of this theory were somewhat philosophical, rooted in a desire for an ecologically realistic semantics, a semantics that takes seriously the resource bounded nature of situated agents. The tools that emerged in the wake of this stance have emerged in recent years as technically significant in the development of semantic analyses of actual conversational speech, specifically in the analysis of metacommunicative interaction, one of the constitutive features of conversation.

I would like to thank Robin Cooper and the Editors for many helpful comments on an earlier draft and Noor van Leusen for much helpful advice on finalizing this document.

6 References

Allwood, Jens 1995. An activity based approach of pragmatics. *Gothenburg Papers in Theoretical Linguistics* 76. Reprinted in: H. Bunt & W. Black (eds.). *Abduction, Belief and Context in Dialogue: Studies in Computational Pragmatics*. Amsterdam: Benjamins, 2000, 47–80.
Asher, Nicholas & Alex Lascarides 2003. *Logics of Conversation*. Cambridge: Cambridge University Press.
Barwise, Jon 1987. Noun phrases, generalized quantifiers, and anaphora. In: P. Gärdenfors (ed.). *Generalized Quantifiers: Linguistic and Logical Approaches*. Dordrecht: Reidel, 1–30.
Barwise, Jon 1989. *The Situation in Logic*. Stanford, CA: CSLI Publications.
Barwise, Jon & John Perry 1983. *Situations and Attitudes*. Cambridge, MA: The MIT Press.
Carlson, Lauri 1983. *Dialogue Games: An Approach to Discourse Analysis*. Dordrecht: Reidel.
Clark, Herbert 1996. *Using Language*. Cambridge: Cambridge University Press.
Clark, Herbert & Edward Schaefer 1989. Contributing to discourse. *Cognitive Science* 13, 259–294.
Cooper, Robin 1996. The role of situations in Generalized Quantifiers. In: S. Lappin (ed.). *Handbook of Contemporary Semantic Theory*. Oxford: Blackwell, 65–86.
Cooper, Robin 2006. Austinian truth in Martin-Löf Type Theory. *Research on Language and Computation* 3, 333–362.
Cooper, Robin & Massimo Poesio 1994. *Situation Theory*. Fracas Deliverable D8, Centre for Cognitive Science, Edinburgh: The Fracas Consortium.
Core, Mark & James Allen 1997. Coding Dialogs with the DAMSL annotation scheme. In: D. Traum (ed.). *Working notes of the AAAI Fall Symposium on Communicative Action in Humans and Machines*. Cambridge, MA: MIT, 28–35.
Dekker, Paul 2004. The pragmatic dimension of indefinites. *Research on Language and Computation* 2, 365–399.

DeVault, David, Natalia Kariaeva, Anubha Kothari, Iris Oved & Matthew Stone 2005. An information-state approach to collaborative reference. In: M. Nagata & T. Pedersen (ed.). *Proceedings of the ACL 2005 on Interactive Poster and Demonstration Sessions.* Morristown, NJ: Association for Computational Linguistics, 1–4.

Dowty, David, Robert Wall & Stanley Peters 1981. *Introduction to Montague Semantics.* Dordrecht: Reidel.

Fernández, Raquel 2006. *Non-Sentential Utterances in Dialogue: Classification, Resolution and Use.* Ph.D. dissertation. King's College, London.

Fernández, Raquel & Jonathan Ginzburg 2002. Non-sentential utterances: A corpus study. *Traitement automatique des languages. Dialogue* 43, 13–42.

Gamut, Louis 1991. *Logic, Language, and Meaning, vol. 2: Intensional Logic and Logical Grammar.* Chicago, IL: The University of Chicago Press.

Gawron, Mark & Stanley Peters 1990. *Anaphora and Quantification in Situation Semantics.* Stanford, CA: CSLI Publications.

Gibson, James 1979. *The Ecological Approach to Visual Perception.* Mahwah, NJ: Lawrence Erlbaum Associates.

Ginzburg, Jonathan 1994. An update semantics for dialogue. In: H. Bunt, R. Muskens & G. Rentier (eds.). *Proceedings of the 1st International Workshop on Computational Semantics.* Tilburg: ITK, Tilburg University.

Ginzburg, Jonathan 1996a. Dynamics and the semantics of dialogue. In: J. Seligman & D. Westerståhl (eds.). *Logic, Language, and Computation.* Stanford, CA: CSLI Publications, 221–237.

Ginzburg, Jonathan 1996b. Interrogatives: Questions, facts, and dialogue. In: S. Lappin (ed.). *Handbook of Contemporary Semantic Theory.* Oxford: Blackwell, 359–423.

Ginzburg, Jonathan 1997. On some semantic consequences of turn taking. In: P. Dekker, M. Stokhof & Y. Venema (eds.). *Proceedings of the 11th Amsterdam Colloquium.* Amsterdam: ILLC, 145–150.

Ginzburg, Jonathan 2012. *The Interactive Stance: Meaning for Conversation.* Oxford: Oxford University Press.

Ginzburg, Jonathan & Robin Cooper 2004. Clarification, ellipsis, and the nature of contextual updates. *Linguistics & Philosophy* 27, 297–366.

Goldman, Alvin I. 1970. *A Theory of Human Action.* Eaglewood Cliffs, NJ: Prentice Hall.

Groenendijk, Jeroen 1998. Questions in update semantics. In: J. Hulstijn & A. Nijholt (eds.). *Proceedings of TwenDial 98, 13th Twente workshop on Language Technology.* Twente: Twente University, 125–137.

Hamblin, Charles L. 1970. *Fallacies.* London: Methuen.

Healey, Patrick 2008. Interactive misalignment: The role of repair in the development of group sub-languages. In: R. Cooper & R. Kempson (eds.). *Language in Flux: Dialogue Coordination, Language Variation, Change and Evolution.* London: College Publications.

Israel, David & John Perry 1996. Where monsters dwell. In: J. Seligman & D. Westerståhl (eds.). *Logic, Language, and Computation.* Stanford, CA: CSLI Publications, 303–316.

Kamp, Hans & Uwe Reyle 1993. *From Discourse to Logic.* Dordrecht: Kluwer.

Kaplan, David 1989. Demonstratives. In: J. Almog, J. Perry & H. Wettstein (ed.). *Themes from Kaplan.* New York: Oxford University Press, 481–614.

van Kuppevelt, Jan 1995. Discourse structure, topicality and questioning. *Journal of Linguistics* 32, 109–147.

Larsson, Staffan 2002. *Issue based Dialogue Management.* Doctoral dissertation. University of Gothenburg.

Levinson, Stephen 1983. *Pragmatics*. Cambridge: Cambridge University Press.
Macura, Zoran 2007. *Metacommunication and Lexical Acquisition in a Primitive Foraging Environment*. Ph.D. dissertation. King's College, London.
Macura, Zoran & Jonathan Ginzburg 2006. Lexicon convergence in a population with and without metacommunication. In: P. Vogt (ed.). *Proceedings of EELC 2006*. Heidelberg: Springer, 100–112.
Matheson, Colin, Massimo Poesio & David Traum 2000. Modeling grounding and discourse obligations using update rules. In: *Proceedings of the 1st Annual Meeting of the North American Chapter of the ACL*. San Francisco, CA: Morgan Kaufmann, 1–8.
Montague, Richard 1974. The proper treatment of quantification in ordinary English. In: R. Thomason (ed.). *Formal Philosophy. Selected Papers of Richard Montague*. New Haven, CT: Yale University Press, 247–270.
Onifer, William & David A. Swinney 1981. Accessing lexical ambiguities during sentence comprehension: Effects of frequency of meaning and contextual bias. *Memory and Cognition* 9, 225–236.
Partee, Barbara 1985. Situations, worlds, and contexts. *Linguistics & Philosophy* 8, 53–58.
Perry, John 2000. *The Problem of the Essential Indexical, Enlarged Edition*. Stanford, CA: CSLI Publications.
Poesio, Massimo & Reinhard Muskens 1997. The dynamics of discourse situations. In: P. Dekker, M. Stokhof & Y. Venema (eds.). *Proceedings of the 11th Amsterdam Colloquium*. Amsterdam: ILLC, 247–252.
Poesio, Massimo & Hannes Rieser 2010. *(Prolegomena to a theory of) Completions, Continuations, and Coordination in Dialogue*. Dialogue and Discourse 1:1–89.
Poesio, Massimo & David Traum 1997. Conversational actions and discourse situations. *Computational Intelligence* 13, 309–347.
Pollard, Carl & Ivan A. Sag 1994. *Head Driven Phrase Structure Grammar*. Chicago, IL: The University of Chicago Press.
Purver, Matthew 2004. *The Theory and Use of Clarification in Dialogue*. Ph.D. dissertation. King's College, London.
Purver, Matthew 2006. CLARIE: Handling clarification requests in a dialogue system. *Research on Language & Computation* 4, 259–288.
Purver, Matthew, Jonathan Ginzburg & Patrick Healey 2001. On the means for clarification in dialogue. In: J. van Kuppevelt & R. Smith (eds.). *Current and New Directions in Discourse and Dialogue*. Dordrecht: Kluwer, 235–256.
Roberts, Craige 1996. Information structure: Towards an integrated formal theory of pragmatics. In: J.-H. Yoon & A. Kathol (eds.). *OSU Working Papers in Linguistics, vol. 49: Papers in Semantics*. Columbus, OH: The Ohio State University, 91–136.
Rodriguez, Kepa & David Schlangen 2004. Form, intonation and function of clarification requests in German task-oriented spoken dialogues. In: J. Ginzburg & E. Vallduvi (eds.). *Proceedings of Catalog'04. The 8th Workshop on the Semantics and Pragmatics of Dialogue*. Barcelona: Universitat Pompeu Fabra, 101–108.
Schegloff, Emanuel 1987. Some sources of misunderstanding in talk-in-interaction. *Linguistics* 25, 201–218.
Schlangen, David 2004. Causes and strategies for requesting clarification in dialogue. In: M. Strube & C. Sidner (eds.). *Proceedings of the 5th SIGdial Workshop on Discourse and Dialogue*. Stroudsburg, PA: Association for Computational Linguistics, 136–143.

Tanenhaus, Michael & John Trueswell 1995. Sentence comprehension. In: J. Miller & P. Eimas (eds.). *Handbook of Perception and Cognition, vol. 11: Speech, Language and Communication*. New York: Academic Press, 217–262.

Traum, David & Elizabeth Hinkelmann 1992. Conversation acts in task-oriented spoken dialogue. *Computational Intelligence* 8, 575–599.

Hans Kamp and Uwe Reyle
11 Discourse Representation Theory

1 Introduction —— 322
2 DRT at work —— 324
3 Presupposition and binding —— 341
4 Binding in DRT —— 348
5 Lexicon and inference —— 352
6 Extensions —— 362
7 Direct reference and anchors —— 374
8 Coverage, extensions of the framework, implementations —— 376
9 References —— 379

Abstract: Discourse Representation Theory (DRT) originated from the desire to account for aspects of linguistic meaning that have to do with the connections between sentences in a discourse or text (as opposed to the meanings that individual sentences have in isolation). The general framework it proposes is dynamic: the semantic contribution that a sentence makes to a discourse or text is analysed as its contribution to the semantic representation – Discourse Representation Structure or DRS – that has already been constructed for the sentences preceding it. Interpretation is thus described as a transformation process which turns DRSs into other (as a rule more informative) DRSs, and meaning is explicated in terms of the canons that govern the construction of DRSs. DRT's emphasis on semantic representations distinguishes it from other dynamic frameworks (such as the Dynamic Predicate Logic and Dynamic Montague Grammar developed by Groenendijk and Stokhof, and numerous variants of those). DRT is – both in its conception and in the details of its implementation – a theory of semantic representation, or logical form.

The selection of topics for this survey reflects our view of what are the most important contributions of DRT to natural language semantics (as opposed to philosophy or artificial intelligence).

Hans Kamp and Uwe Reyle, Stuttgart, Germany

https://doi.org/10.1515/9783110589245-011

1 Introduction

1.1 Origins

The origins of Discourse Representation Theory (DRT) had to do with the semantic connection between adjacent sentences in discourse. Starting point was the analysis of tense, and more specifically the question how to define the different roles of Imperfect (Imp) and Simple Past (PS) in French. The semantic effects these tenses produce are often visible through the links they establish between the sentences in which they occur and the sentences preceding them.

A telling example, which has become something of a prototype for the sentence linking role of tenses, is the following. (1) is the original example, in French; (2), its translation into English, establishes the same point.

(1) Quand Alain ouvrit (PS) les yeux, il vit (PS) sa femme qui était (Imp) debout près de son lit.
   a. Elle lui sourit. (PS)
   b. Elle lui souriait. (Imp)

(2) When Alain opened his eyes he saw his wife who was standing by his bed.
   a. She smiled.
   b. She was smiling.

The difference between (1a) and (1b) is striking: The PS-sentence in (1a) is understood as describing the reaction of Alain's wife to his waking up, the Imp-sentence in (1b) as describing a state of affairs that already holds at the time when Alain opens his eyes and sees her: the very first thing he sees is his smiling wife.

In the late seventies the study of the tenses in French and other languages led to the conviction that their discourse linking properties are an essential aspect of their meaning and an effort got under way to formulate interpretation rules for different tenses that make their linking roles explicit. In 1980 came the awareness that the mechanisms which account for the inter-sentential connections that are established by tenses can also be invoked to explain the inter- and intra-sentential links between pronouns and their anaphoric antecedents. (An analogy in the spirit of Partee 1973, but within the realm of anaphora rather than deixis.) DRT was the result of working out the details for a small fragment dealing with sentence-internal and -external anaphora. This first fragment (Kamp 1981a) dealt only with pronominal anaphora, but a treatment of temporal anaphora, which offered an analysis of, among others, the anaphoric properties of PS and Imp, followed in the same year (Kamp 1981b). The theory presented in Kamp (1981a) proved to be equivalent to the independently developed File Change Semantics of Heim, which became available to a general audience at roughly the same time (Heim 1982). However, DRT and FCS were inspired by different intentions from the start, a difference that became more pronounced with the advent of Groenendijk and Stokhof's Dynamic Semantics (Groenendijk & Stokhof 1991; Groenendijk & Stokhof 1990). Dynamic Semantics in the spirit of Groenendijk and Stokhof followed the lead of FCS, not DRT (Barwise & Perry 1983; Rooth 1987).

From the very beginning one of the strong motivations of DRT was the desire to capture certain features of the way in which interpretations of sentences, texts and discourses are represented in the mind of the interpreter, including features that cannot be recaptured from the truth conditions that the chosen interpretation determines. This representational aspect of DRT was at first seen by some as a draw-back, viz. as an unwelcome deviation from the emphatically anti-psychologistic methods and philosophy of Montague Grammar (Montague 1973; Montague 1970a; Groenendijk & Stokhof 1990); but with time this resistance appears to have lessened, largely because of the growing trend to see linguistics as a branch of cognitive science. (How good the representations of DRT are from a cognitive perspective, i.e. how much they tell us about the way in which humans represent information – or at least how they represent the information that is conveyed to them through language – is another matter, and one about which the last word has not been said.)

In the course of the 1980s the scope of DRT was extended to the full paradigm of tense forms in French and English, as well as to a range of temporal adverbials, to anaphoric plural pronouns and other plural NPs, the representation of propositional attitudes and attitude reports, i.e. sentences and bits of text that describe the propositional attitudes of an agent or agents (Kamp 1990; Asher 1986; Kamp 2003), and to ellipsis (Asher 1993; Lerner & Pinkal 1995; Hardt 1992.) The nineties saw, besides extension and consolidation of the applications mentioned, a theory of lexical meaning compatible with the general principles of DRT (Kamp & Roßdeutscher 1992; Kamp & Roßdeutscher 1994a), and an account of presupposition (van der Sandt 1992; Beaver 1992; Beaver 1997; Beaver 2004; Geurts 1994; Geurts 1999; Geurts & van der Sandt 1999; Kamp 2001a; Kamp 2001b; van Genabith, Kamp & Reyle 2010). The nineties also saw the beginnings of two important extensions of DRT that have become theories in their own right and with their own names, *U(nderspecified) DRT* (Reyle 1993) and *S(egmented) DRT* (Asher 1993; Lascarides & Asher 1993; Asher & Lascarides 2003). SDRT would require a chapter on its own and we will only say a very few words about it here; UDRT will be discussed (all too briefly) in Section 8.2. In the first decade of the present century DRT was extended to cover focus-background structure (Kamp 2004; Riester 2008;

Riester & Kamp 2010) and the treatment of various types of indefinites (Bende-Farkas & Kamp 2001; Farkas & de Swart 2003).

2 DRT at work

In this section we show in some detail how DRT deals with one of the examples that motivated its development.

2.1 Tense in texts

As noted in Section 1, the starting point for DRT was an attempt in the late seventies to come to grips with certain problems in the theory of tense and aspect. In the sixties and early seventies formal research into the ways in which natural languages express temporal information had been dominated by temporal logics of the kind that had been developed from the fifties onwards, starting with the work of Prior and others (Prior 1967; Kamp 1968; Vlach 1973). It became increasingly clear, however, that there were aspects to the way in which temporal information is handled in natural languages which neither the original Priorean logics nor later extensions of them could handle.

One of the challenges that tenses present to semantic theory is to determine how they combine temporal and aspectual information and how those two kinds of information interact in the links that tenses establish between their own sentences and the ones preceding them. (1) and (2) are striking examples of this challenge. Here we will look at a pair of slightly simplified discourses which illustrate the same point.

(3)   Alain woke up.
    a.   His wife smiled.
    b.   His wife was smiling.

We will assume that (3a) and (3b) are related to the first sentence of (3) in the same way as the second sentences of (1) and (2) are related to the first sentences there: in the case of (3b) Alain's wife was smiling when Alain opened his eyes, in (3a) she smiled as a reaction to that. These respective interpretations may not be as compelling as they are in the case of (2) or (1), but they are there and it is these readings for which we are now going to construct semantic representations.

We assume that the first sentence has the syntactic structure given in (4).

(4)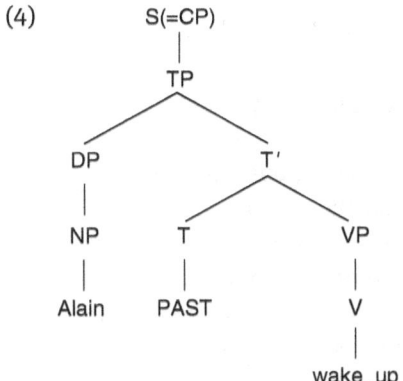

Note that this structure makes the assumption, familiar from syntactic theories based on the work of Chomsky, that the interpretation provided by tense is located at a node T high up in the sentence tree and above the one containing the verb. We will see presently what implications this has for the construction of a semantic representation. We assume that the construction is bottom up (unlike in the first explicit formulations of DRT (Kamp 1981a; Kamp & Reyle 1993) where it is top down, and which for many years were treated as a kind of standard in DRT). Before we describe the construction procedure, we show the resulting DRS in (5), so that the reader will have an idea of what we are working towards. We will then describe the procedure in more detail.

(5)
$$\boxed{\begin{array}{l} t \quad e \quad x \\[4pt] t < n \\ \text{Alain}(x) \\ e \subseteq t \\ e : \text{wake\_up}'(x) \end{array}}$$

Formally DRSs are pairs ⟨U,Con⟩ consisting of (i) a set U of discourse referents, and (ii) a set Con of conditions. (5) exemplifies the graphical convention in DRT to represent DRSs as 2-dimensional structures, with the universe displayed at the top and the condition set below it. We will keep to that convention throughout this article. Discourse referents play the role of representatives of entities. They behave much like the variables of predicate logic, but not quite. In fact, the behaviour of some discourse referents resembles more closely that of individual constants – details will become clear as we go along.

In general, discourse referents come with certain sortal restrictions built into them. For instance, (5) has discourse referents of three different sorts – x stands for an individual (by *individual* we understand any entity that can be the referent of a definite noun phrase), e stands for an event and t for a time. DRS-conditions are in essence formulas of predicate logic, built from predicates and discourse referents. The discourse referents play the part of argument terms. The predicates are either translations of predicate words from the represented natural language – such as e.g. the verb *wake up* in (5) or the proper name *Alain* – into the DRS representation formalism, or else they are *primes* of the representation formalism, to which no simple word of the represented natural language has a privileged connection. Examples of such primes are the relational predicates < and ⊆. (The condition t < n means that the point or interval of time t precedes the utterance time n. The condition e ⊆ t means that the event e is temporally included in the time point or interval t.)

Wake_up' is the predicate corresponding to the English verb *wake up*. The discourse referent e stands for the waking up event that is described by the sentence. The notation e:wake_up'(x) is to be read as "e is an event of the type x waking up". We could also have written wake_up'(e,x) – a notation one often sees elsewhere – but stick with the notation using ":" which was originally introduced to highlight the asymmetry between the referential argument e of *wake up* and its non-referential argument x.

A brief explanation may be needed here of the distinction between referential and non-referential arguments. We assume with Williams (1977) that all words which function semantically as predicates (names, prepositions, adjectives and adverbs) have one referential argument and in addition one or more non-referential arguments. The referential argument of a verb is always the event or state the verb is used to describe. (Whether this argument is an event or a state is determined by the lexical properties of the verb in question.) Verbs also always have at least one non-referential argument, which is realised as the grammatical subject when the verb is used in the active voice. Intransitive verbs have just this one non-referential argument, simple transitive verbs have two and so on. Most nouns, adjectives and adverbs just have a referential argument but no non-referential arguments. But there are also relational nouns, adjectives and adverbs, which have non-referential arguments as well. An example is the noun *wife*. In a DP such as *Alain's wife* the non-referential argument is the referent of the embedded DP *Alain*. The referential argument is not represented by a separate phrase but introduced by the predicate word *wife* itself;

it becomes the referent of the complete phrase of which the noun *wife* is the lexical head – here the DP *Alain's wife*.

The non-relational noun *woman* only has a referential argument, which for instance can be expressed by a containing DP like *the woman*. We write woman(y) and wife(y,z) rather than y:woman or y:wife-of(z), which might have been expected given what has just been said in connection with verbs. This arguably is a slight inconsistency of notation, but it is harmless and it has become standard practice within DRT, so we will stick to it here. Proper names like *Alain* are also treated as predicates, with a built-in *referential uniqueness*. For instance, Alain(x) means that the discourse referent x represents the individual referred to (in the represented utterance) by the name *Alain*.

This completes the informal description of the different parts of the DRS in (5). A formally precise description is provided by the model-theoretic semantics for DRSs. From a logical point of view DRSs are the formulas of DRT's semantic representation languages. These languages come – like other logical formalisms, such as the predicate calculus – with a syntax which defines the possible forms of expressions (here: the well-formed DRSs and DRS-conditions), and with a model theory which describes for each of the well-formed expressions its denotation in each of the models that it specifies for the given DRS-language. We won't go into the formal definition of the models for DRS languages that include DRSs like that in (5), but refer the reader to the literature (Kamp & Reyle 1993 or van Genabith, Kamp & Reyle 2010).

Since the DRSs of our formalism involve discourse referents for entities of various sorts, models must have a fairly complicated structure (much more so than the models for standard first order logic): they must have a time structure as well as temporal relations between times and eventualities (*eventuality* is used as a cover term for both events and states). For any model M the *denotation of* (5) in M will be the set of all functions of the universe of (5) into the universe of M such that: (i) f(t) is a time of M (i.e. an interval or point of the time structure of M), (ii) f(e) is an event of M, (iii) f(x) is an individual of M, (iv) the conditions of (5) are all satisfied in M by the f-values of their arguments: (a) f(t) temporally precedes the utterance time of the first sentence of (3); (b) f(e) is temporally included in f(t); (c) f(x) is Alain (i.e. the person referred to by the speaker in using *Alain* on the given occasion; it is assumed that Alain is one of the individuals of M); (d) f(e) is an event of f(x) waking up. Such functions, from the universe of a DRS into the universe of a model, are usually called *embedding functions* or, simply, *embeddings*. If an embedding function verifies all the conditions of the DRS in the model – in the case of (5) this means that it satisfies the requirements (a) - (d) – then it is called a *verifying embedding*.

With this definition of the denotation of (5) in a model comes a definition of truth: (5) is *true in* M if there exists a verifying embedding of (5) in M, i.e. if the denotation of (5) in M is non-empty. Note the existential form of this definition: (5) is true in M if *there exists* a way of associating entities from M with the universe of (5) such that the conditions of (5) are satisfied in M.

To construct (5) from (4) we proceed bottom up, associating semantic representations with the nodes of (4) as we traverse the tree from its leaves to its root, working our way up, roughly speaking, from bottom right to top left. We start by replacing the given occurrence of the verb, *wake up*, with the appropriate instantiation of its semantic representation. This representation is provided by the lexical entry for the verb, which we assume is given in the following form.

(6) *wake up*   verb   nom
                      e   **x**
   Selectional Restrictions: event   animal
   Semantic Representation: e:wake_up'(**x**)

This entry says that *wake up* is a verb, that its referential argument is an event (see the Selection Restrictions), that *wake up* has one non-referential argument, which must always be an animal (this is also part of the Selection Restrictions); and, finally, that the semantics of *wake up* is given by the condition e:wake_up'(**x**). (This condition doesn't tell us very much about what *wake up* really means. More about lexical entries in Section 5.) Note that the non-referential argument **x** is given in bold face. **x** is not a discourse referent (and in this it differs from the referential argument e, which *is* a discourse referent). Bold face letters do not play the part of discourse referents, but of *argument position markers*. When the semantic representation of a lexical entry is used in the construction of a DRS, its argument position markers must be replaced at some point by discourse referents. This requires information about how arguments of predicate words can be realised as argument phrases. In lexical entries like (6) this is indicated by the annotations above the argument position markers. For instance, "nom" above the position marker **x** indicates that when the intransitive verb *wake up* is used – strictly speaking: when this verb is used in the active voice; but for intransitive verbs that is the only way they can be used – , then the phrase realising **x** must be the grammatical subject. We assume that recognising such links between argument positions and argument phrases which realise them is the task of the parser that assigns the sentence its syntactic structure. (If the parser couldn't recognise these links, then it wouldn't be able to do its work properly.) Thus in the example at hand the parser will have linked the subject DP of the first sentence of (3) to the argument position marker **x**. In a partially interpreted syntactic structure in which the semantics of the verb has been inserted for its morphological form this information can be represented by co-indexation. This is what has been done in (7).

(7)
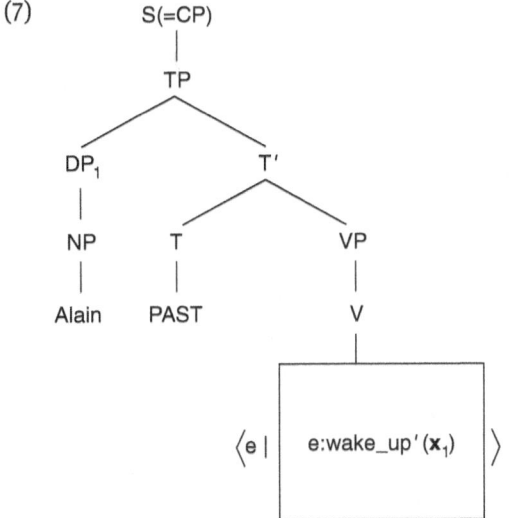

In the semantic representation of the VP we have put the discourse referent that is introduced by the verb in store, as a reminder that it still needs to be *bound*. A store is simply a sequence of discourse referents. Stores are always left-adjoined to some DRS. Binding will be discussed below.

The next step deals with the information contributed by tense, which the syntactic parse has located at T. Temporal location is implemented as follows: the time where the event e of VP is located is represented by a discourse referent t (introduced when the construction reaches T) and the location relation between e and t is given by the condition $e \subseteq t$. t itself is related to the speech time n by the information PAST at T. For occurrences of the past tense in simple sentences this relation is represented by the condition $t < n$. It is assumed that the operation which temporally locates the described event e also leads to existential binding of the discourse referent e that represents the event. Existential binding takes the form of transferring e from the store into the universe of the DRS to its right. The new discourse referent t still requires binding, and to this end it is placed in the store. (The discourse referent n, which represents the utterance time, is subject to a special indexical binding regime, which is reminiscent of the treatment of the word *now* as an indexical (Kaplan 1989). We follow the convention adopted in much DRT-based work that 'n' is not placed in any DRS-universe or -store, as a way of emphasising the special way in which n is bound.)

(8)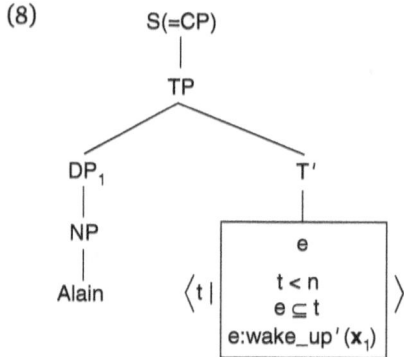

The next steps assign a semantic representation to the subject DP. The NP *Alain* of this DP has the form of a proper name. For now we will assume that names act as nominal predicates which introduce a discourse referent – x, in the present example – for the individual they are being used to refer to, together with a condition which expresses that the discourse referent stands for this individual. Here we use the condition Alain(x) to express this. With these assumptions the semantic representation for the NP can be given as ⟨ x | Alain(x)⟩. About the binding of x (as part of the interpretation of the DP *Alain*) more will be said in Section 3. At this point we will make do with the solution proposed in earlier versions of DRT, according to which x is existentially bound while the condition Alain(x) imposes the constraint that the only possible value for x is the individual that *Alain* refers to.

The coindexation of the subject DP with the argument position marker **x** in (7) and (8) will be instrumental in the next step, which combines DP and TP. This step inserts the representing discourse referent of the DP into the argument slot marked by **x** in the TP representation. Part of this insertion process is that the DRSs of TP and DP get merged. We will assume – but again this is a kind of stopgap measure; see Section 3 – that as part of this process the discourse referent x which represents the referent of the DP is existentially bound by being transferred from the DP store to the universe of the DRS that results from the merge. This leads to the representation in (9).

(9)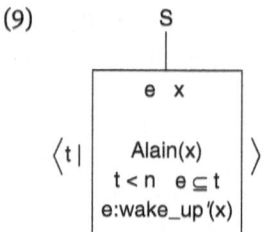

The one remaining task is the binding of t. In the present case, where the S node we are dealing with is the S node of a discourse-initial main clause, binding of the discourse referent t is existential, which once again amounts to transferring the discourse referent from its store to the universe of the DRS adjacent to it. The resulting representation is the one that was already shown as (5).

We now turn to the two second sentences (a) and (b) of (3). This is where the special features of DRT, which concern the semantic relations between successive sentences in a discourse, come into prominence. We start with sentence (3b). To avoid unhelpful complications we treat the form *be smiling* as a single verb, which serves to describe states: the condition s: be_smiling'(x) means that s is a state to the effect that x is smiling.

Construction of the semantic representation of (3b) proceeds in much the same way as that of the first sentence of (3). The only differences have to do with the temporal location of the state s, with the representation of the subject phrase *his wife* and with the binding of the temporally locating discourse referent t'. The first difference manifests itself in the transition from VP to TP. We assume that states are located at times in the sense that the time is one at or during which the state holds; that is, the location relation between t' and s is t' ⊆ s (rather than the converse relation which was assumed for events). So we get as representation at this construction stage:

(10)

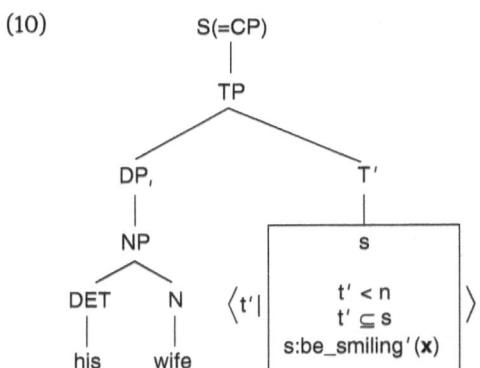

The representation of the subject phrase *his wife* differs from that of *Alain* in several respects. First, the discourse referent introduced as referential argument of wife' must be a fresh discourse referent (i.e. one that is distinct from the discourse referents that have been previously introduced into the representation of the discourse) so that no clashes can occur between the referential roles they are meant to play. In particular, the new discourse referent must be different from the discourse referent x that was introduced to represent the referent of *Alain*. As new discourse referent we choose x'.

The second difference has to do with the DET-constituent *his*. *His* is a pronoun and in this case it picks up the sentence-external antecedent *Alain*. We represent the need for the pronoun to find an antecedent provisionally by placing the discourse referent u that the pronoun introduces in the store while attaching a question mark to it.

His is a possessive pronoun, which expresses some kind of *possessive* relation. In the present case this relation is nothing but the thematic relation that the non-referential argument of the relational noun *wife* bears to its referential argument. Representing the word *wife* by the 2-place DRS predicate wife' (and assuming once more existential binding for the discourse referent x' that is introduced by the noun) we get as DP representation:

(11)
$$\langle u^?, x' \mid \begin{array}{|c|} \hline x' \\ \hline \text{wife}'(x', u) \\ \hline \end{array} \rangle$$

Combining this representation with that of the TP (and once again transferring the discourse referent representing the DP from the DP's store to the DRS universe) yields (12).

(12)
$$\langle t', u^? \mid \begin{array}{|c|} \hline s\ x' \\ \hline \text{wife}'(x', u) \\ t' < n \quad t' \subseteq s \\ s:\text{be\_smiling}'(x') \\ \hline \end{array} \rangle$$

(12) has two elements in its store which are still waiting to be bound. In the present case this involves linking (12) with the representation (5) of the first sentence of (3), which now functions as *discourse context* for the interpretation of (3b). The link to be established by u, the discourse referent for the pronoun *his*, was mentioned already: the pronoun is to be interpreted as co-referential with the subject DP *Alain* of the first sentence. We implement this by stipulating

equality between the discourse referent u introduced by the pronoun and the discourse referent x that was introduced by the intended antecedent, and we express this by means of the condition u = x. At the same time u is transferred from the store to the DRS universe. The temporal connection between (12) and (5), which was the main point of our discussion of the related discourse (1) in Section 1, should result in a representation according to which the event e from the first sentence is temporally included in the state s from the second sentence. We achieve this by identifying t' with t, and we implement this in the same way as the identification of u with x. In this manner (12) is turned into (13).

(13)
```
| t' s x' u                    |
|                              |
|        wife'(x', u)          |
| t' < n   t' ⊆ s   t' = t  u = x |
|        s:be_smiling'(x')     |
```

The identification of t' with t also amounts to a kind of anaphora resolution. In fact, past tenses in non-initial sentences of a discourse tend to be *anaphoric* in this sort of way. It is this anaphoric dimension which enables them to contribute to the temporal connectedness of texts and discourses, something that the present examples are meant to illustrate.

Note that (13) is not a *proper* DRS in the sense that some of the discourse referents occurring in its conditions (viz. x and t) do not occur in its universe. Such improper DRSs do not have well-defined denotations in the sense we specified earlier: embeddings of their universes do not determine the satisfaction of all of their conditions. The improperness of (13) disappears, however, when it is merged with the representation of the first sentence (by forming the union of their universes and the union of their condition sets). The result of the merge is given in (14).

(14)
```
| t e x t' s x' u              |
|                              |
|        Alain (x)             |
|     t < n    e ⊆ t           |
|       e:wake_up' (x)         |
|         wife'(x',u)          |
|   t' < n  t' ⊆ s  t' = t  u = x |
|        s:be_smiling'(x')     |
```

(14) is the joint representation of the two sentences of (3b). It is a proper DRS and thus has a denotation and a truth value in every model.

The representation construction for (3a) is in most respects like that for (3b). The only differences have to do with the fact that (3a) functions as an event description, and not, like (3b), as a state description. This difference shows up, first, in that the verb *smile* introduces an event discourse referent e' (and not a state discourse referent) and, second, in that the temporal relation established between e' and e is different from that between s and e in the case of (3b).

Intuitively, we saw, the relationship between e' and e is that e' follows e. But how does this relationship get established? Although this has been the subject of discussion for several decades, it continues to be a topic for ongoing research and debate. But this much is clear: How successions of event sentences are interpreted depends very much on the rhetorical relations between them, and these vary. For instance, the event described in the second of two connected sentences in a discourse is sometimes understood as a *reaction* to the event described in the first sentence – the natural interpretation in the case of (3a) – but in other cases it can also be understood as the *cause* of that event – the most salient interpretation for *John fell. Bill pushed him*; or it can be understood as an elaboration of the event of the first sentence – as in *John went to see his mother. He took the bus.* (And these are just some of the various possibilities.) The interactions between rhetorical relations and temporal relations have been a central issue in SDRT (*Segmented Discourse Representation Theory*; see Lascarides & Asher 1993; Asher & Lascarides 2003), and in fact, they were an important impetus to the development of that approach. They are a topic that we can do no more than mention here; the reader is referred to the just mentioned publications and to further work cited in Asher & Lascarides (2003).

The rhetorical relation between (3a) and the first sentence of (3) is called *Narration* in SDRT (as well as in some other accounts of discourse relations, cf. Mann & Thompson 1988, as well as article 13 [this volume] (Zeevat) *Rhetorical relations*). The Narration relation between two successive sentences is one of the relations which entail that the event of the second sentence temporally follows that of the first. We implement the implications of this for DRS construction by assuming that the same relation holds between the location times t and t' of these events and use for this the condition $t < t'$. This time the joint representation of the two sentences together has the form given in (15).

(15)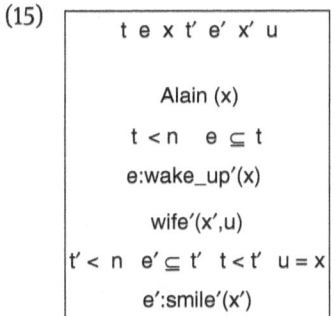

We have dealt with these two examples at a level of detail that some readers may have thought excessive, and inappropriate for a handbook. We have done so for two reasons. First, the DRS-construction principles we have discussed reflect some of the fundamental assumptions of DRT about the nature of verbal and nominal predication. These are intimately connected with the principles of sentence-external and -internal discourse connection for which DRT has long been primarily known and to which much that will be said in this article will be devoted. Without the details we have gone into in our discussion of (3) it would have been much more difficult to explain these more specifically dynamic aspects of DRT.

Through the work of van der Sandt and Geurts starting in the late eighties (van der Sandt 1992; van der Sandt & Geurts 1991; Geurts 1994; Geurts 1999), the basic architecture of DRT underwent a fundamental change. One part of that change is illustrated by the two-step procedure we have just used in dealing with the second sentences of (3): first a *preliminary* representation was constructed solely on the basis of the sentence itself, and then the issues that this construction had left unsettled were resolved on the basis of the context representation provided by the antecedent part of the discourse. (In our example this was just the representation of the first sentence of (3).)

What is still missing, though, is a precise articulation of the steps that provide the links between the two sentence representations. A more detailed proposal for how such links are established will be discussed below in Section 3.

2.2 Donkey sentences and complex DRS conditions

Before we get to that discussion we will first have a look at examples, given in (16) and (17), of the two types of *donkey sentences* which were used in Geach (1962) to illustrate the puzzle known as the *donkey sentence problem* or the *donkey pronoun problem*. The early development of DRT, and its initial reception, were closely connected with this problem.

(16) If Alain owns a donkey he beats it.

(17) Every farmer who owns a donkey beats it.

In both these sentences the pronoun *it* is understood as referring back to the indefinite DP *a donkey*. The methods that are suggested by classical predicate logic for constructing logical forms for these sentences, in which pronouns are treated as bound variables and indefinite DPs as existential quantifiers, have trouble with such sentences – their logical forms come out either as ill-formed or they give the wrong truth conditions. The two apparent options for (16) are shown in (18) and (19).

(18) $\exists y(donkey'(y) \wedge own'(a,y)) \rightarrow beat'(a,y)$

(19) $\exists y(donkey'(y) \wedge (own'(a,y) \rightarrow beat'(a,y))$

In (18) the final occurrence of y is not bound, so we have an open formula, which doesn't determine any definite truth conditions. This problem does not arise for (19), but the truth conditions of this formula are clearly not those of (16). The solution of DRT (Heim 1982; Kamp 1981a) was based on a conceptual parallel between the sentences in (16) and (17) and a two sentence discourse like (20).

(20) Alain owns a donkey. He beats it.

In (20) the pronouns *he* and *it* of the second sentence are anaphoric to *Alain* and *a donkey* in the first sentence in the same way that *his* is anaphoric to *Alain* in (1) and (3); and a DRT-based interpretation of (20) will establish these anaphoric links in the same way in which we assumed the link was established between *his* and *Alain* in the treatment we have presented of (3b). The point about (16) and (17) is that here too the same linking mechanism is involved. Let us focus first on (16). This sentence has the form of a conditional "if A then B". The DRT conception of a conditional is this: the antecedent A functions as the description of a certain type of situation, and the conditional as a whole has the function to express that if a situation is of this type then it is also of the type described by the consequent B. And since it is about situations of the type described by A that the claim is made that they also satisfy the description given by B, it is possible and permissible to phrase B in a way which presupposes the description provided by A.

In DRT this way of viewing conditionals is interpreted as follows: The description provided by A can be converted into a semantic representation in the form of a DRS, and this DRS can then be used as discourse context in the interpretation of B in the same way that, for instance, the first sentence of (3) can be used as discourse context for the interpretation of the second sentences (3a) and (3b). The only difference between (16) and (20) is that the DRS K_1 for the antecedent of (16), which is also the DRS for the first sentence of (20), and the DRS K_2 for the consequent of (16), which is also the DRS for the second sentence of (20), are differently connected in the final representation. The representation of (20) is, just as we saw when discussing the interpretation of (3b), the merge of K_1 and K_2. The representation of (16) takes the form of a conditional with K_1 as antecedent and K_2 as consequent. The DRSs K_1 and K_2 are given in (21a) and (21b) and the representations of (20) and (16) in (21c) and (21d).

(21) a.

K_1
| t s x y |
| t = n   t ⊆ s |
| Alain(x) donkey'(y) |
| s:own'(x,y) |

b.

K_2
| t' s' u v |
| t'= n   t' ⊆ s' |
| s:beat'(u,v) |
| u = x   v = y |

c. $K_1 \oplus K_2$ (⊕ means merge)

d.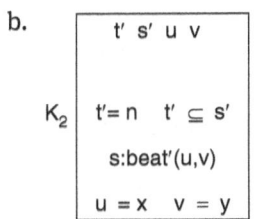

$K_1 \Rightarrow K_2$

Note that in (21b) we have treated *beat* as a stative verb. The intuition is that as it is used in (16) *beat* expresses a kind of disposition on the part of the subject.

(Treating *beat* as a stative verb is a similar simplification as the treatment of *is smiling* as a lexical verb in its own right that we assumed when dealing with (3b).)

The expression $K_1 \Rightarrow K_2$ in (21d) is a DRS condition which is true in a model M if every embedding f of K_1 in M which makes the conditions of K_1 true can be extended to an embedding of $K_1 \oplus K_2$ in M which also makes the conditions in K_2 true. It is easy to verify that this stipulation of when DRS conditions of the form $K \Rightarrow K'$ are true assigns the following truth conditions to the DRS condition in (21d): If at the utterance time n there is a donkey f(y) such that Alain owns f(y), then at n Alain beats f(y). These are the truth conditions that speakers associate with (17), or at least they come quite close to those. (Certainly much closer than the "logical form" in (18), which comes nowhere near.)

The expression in (21d) is a DRS condition, we said. But (16) is a sentence that can be asserted in its own right (i.e. without the benefit of a discourse context provided by preceding sentences). So we want a DRS to represent it, as a "one sentence discourse" so to speak, with well defined truth conditions (just as we wanted and had a DRS for the first sentence of (2)). We resolve this conflict by taking the DRS for (16) to be the one which has an empty universe and whose condition set contains just the condition $K_1 \Rightarrow K_2$. (What we have said here isn't entirely accurate. In the standard representation for this sentence (Kamp & Reyle 1993) the discourse referent x and the condition Alain(x) are part of the main DRS and not of the antecedent DRS K_1. As promised in connection with the treatment of (2) we will return to this matter when we come to discuss presupposition in Section 3.)

(21d) is our first example of a *complex* DRS condition. All conditions we encountered previously were *atomic* DRS conditions – they consist of a predicate of the given DRS language with discourse referents as arguments. The expressive power of DRSs that are built just from discourse referents and atomic conditions is quite limited – semantically speaking such DRSs are always existential quantifications over conjunctions of atomic predications. Negation, disjunction, implication and universal quantification – to mention just the operations familiar from standard first order logic – cannot be expressed with these means and require complex conditions of some form. To this end DRT employs a number of operators which form DRS conditions out of one or two DRSs: ¬ for negation, ⇒ for implication, ∨ for disjunction and

for universal quantification. The syntax of a DRS language which includes all or some of these operations requires a simultaneous recursion over DRSs and DRS conditions:

Definition 1 (Syntax for DRS languages with complex conditions)
(a) A *DRS* is a pair ⟨U,Con⟩, where U is a set of discourse referents and Con is a set of DRS conditions.
(b) (i) An *atomic DRS condition* is of the form $P_n(x_1,...,x_n)$, where P_n is an n-place predicate and $x_1,..., x_n$ are discourse referents.
  (ii) If K_1 and K_2 are DRSs and x is a discourse referent,

  then $\neg K_1$, $K_1 \Rightarrow K_2$, $K_1 \vee K_2$ and $K_1 \; \langle\!\!\!\begin{smallmatrix}\forall\\x\end{smallmatrix}\!\!\!\rangle \; K_2$ are *(complex) DRS conditions*.

For each of the complex DRS conditions in (b-ii) we need model-theoretic *verification conditions*. So far, we have given these only for $\Rightarrow$. The following definition restates these more formally and adds those for the other operators. We use the following notation: Where f and g are functions from sets of discourse referents into the universe of a model $\mathcal{M}$ and X is a set of discourse referents, $g \supseteq_x f$ means that Dom(g) = Dom(f) ∪ X. Moreover, when K is a DRS, then $g \supseteq_K f$ is short for $g \supseteq_X f$, where X = U_K.

Definition 2 (Verification of complex DRS conditions)
Let f be a function from discourse referents to elements of the model $\mathcal{M}$, and let K_1 and K_2 be DRSs.

(a) f *verifies* $\neg K_1$ *in* $\mathcal{M}$ if there is no extension $g \supseteq_{K_1} f$ which verifies all the conditions of K_1 in $\mathcal{M}$.
(b) f *verifies* $K_1 \Rightarrow K_2$ *in* $\mathcal{M}$ if every extension $g \supseteq_{K_1} f$ which verifies all the conditions of K_1 in $\mathcal{M}$ has an extension $h \supseteq_{K_2} g$ which verifies all the conditions of K_2 in $\mathcal{M}$.
(c) f *verifies* $K_1 \vee K_2$ *in* $\mathcal{M}$ if either there is an extension $g1 \supseteq_{K_1} f$ which verifies all the conditions of K_1 in $\mathcal{M}$ or there is an extension $g2 \supseteq_{K_2} g$ which verifies all the conditions of K_2 in $\mathcal{M}$.
(d) f *verifies* $K_1 \; \langle\!\!\!\begin{smallmatrix}\forall\\\alpha\end{smallmatrix}\!\!\!\rangle \; K_2$ *in* $\mathcal{M}$ if every extension $g \supseteq_U f$, where $U = U_{K_1} \cup \{\alpha\}$,

such that g verifies all the conditions of K_1 in $\mathcal{M}$ has an extension $h \supseteq_{K_2} g$ which verifies all the conditions of K_2 in $\mathcal{M}$.

DRS languages which include the operators mentioned in Def. 1 (with the semantics given for them in Def. 2) have at least the expressive power of first order predicate logic. As in standard formulations of first order logic the set of operators is redundant – some operators in the set can be expressed with the help of others. But for the given set of DRS operators the redundancy is more extreme. Since existential quantification and conjunction are built into the structure of DRSs, just adding ¬ already suffices to express all the remaining classical operators.

It should be stressed, however, that the operators of extensional logic cover only a small part of the operator-like constructions that are found in natural languages and that play a crucial part in making natural languages the powerful and flexible instruments of expression and communication they are. In order to cover more of these operations DRS languages have been extended repeatedly as time went on. Some such extensions will be discussed in Section 6.

We return to the discussion of the sentences in (16) and (17). The point of departure for that discussion was the analogy between those sentences and discourses like (20): The discourse context that the first sentence (20) provides for the second sentence of (20) is provided in the conditional sentence (16) by the conditional's antecedent for the conditional's consequent. A similar analogy applies to (17), where it is the restrictor of the quantifier that provides a discourse context for the nuclear scope. The DRS for (17) is given in (22).

(22)

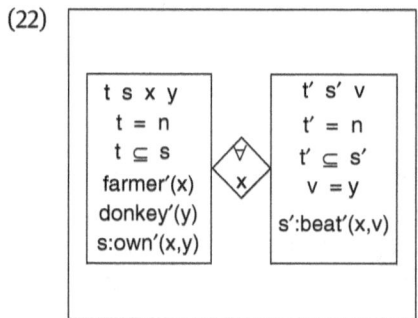

We omit details about the construction of (22), but see e.g. Kamp & Reyle (1993) or Reyle, Rossdeutscher & Kamp (2008).

The recursion in Def. 1 entails that DRSs can have arbitrarily complex structure – they can have complex conditions built from DRSs containing complex conditions built from DRSs containing … . With the nesting structure of DRSs within DRSs within DRSs … comes a notion that is central to the way in which DRT deals with anaphora and presupposition. This is (DRS-)*accessibility*. Accessibility is a relation between sub-DRSs of a given DRS K, with K itself also counting as an (improper) sub-DRS of K. A pronoun belonging to a sentence part that gives rise to a sub-DRS K′ of the DRS K for the sentence as a whole can be anaphoric to a DP elsewhere in the sentence only if the discourse referent introduced by this

DP occurs in the universe of K′ itself or else in a universe of a sub-DRS of K that is accessible from K′. We will see in Section 3 that a similar constraint holds for presupposition justification. A proper definition of accessibility must partake in the recursive definition of DRSs and DRS conditions. We refer to Kamp & Reyle (1993) for details. Here we just give some examples: (i) the antecedent K_1 of a DRS condition $K_1 \Rightarrow K_2$ is accessible from the consequent but not conversely; (ii) the restrictor DRS K_1 of a DRS condition $K_1 \langle\substack{\forall \\ \alpha}\rangle K_2$ is accessible from the nuclear scope DRS but not conversely; (iii) the DRS K_1 of a condition $\neg K_1$ is *not* accessible from any condition belonging to the same condition set as $\neg K_1$; (iv) neither of the two DRSs K_1 and K_2 of a condition $K_1 \vee K_2$ is accessible from the other.

3 Presupposition and binding

For a long time presupposition was a concern of logicians. Their concern mostly took the form of a worry – that failed presuppositions would cause lack of truth value and thereby compromise the validity of classical, bivalent logic. And their concern was exclusively with referential terms, all of which they tended to identify with definite descriptions: when such a term would fail to properly denote and thereby violate the presupposition that it does properly denote, then that would create a truth value gap for the sentence and this would lead to the failure of certain logical laws. It was only the late sixties that saw a shift both in our understanding of the nature and role of presuppositions and in the communities that preoccupied themselves with presuppositional phenomena. In fact, there were two new perspectives, each of them focussed more on the structure and use of natural language than on the properties of logical calculi. The first, best known through the writings of Stalnaker (Stalnaker 1972; Stalnaker 1974; Stalnaker 1979), is the view that presupposition is a pragmatic phenomenon, in the following sense. When we use language to communicate we always assume that there is much information we already share with those we are trying to communicate with; without such a supporting *Common Ground* it would be virtually impossible to convey any information concisely and clearly. So it is a natural and ubiquitous feature of verbal communication that much information is *presupposed* without which we couldn't express ourselves as concisely as we want to. The second perspective – sometimes somewhat unfortunately referred to as "semantic" – emphasises the conventional aspect of presupposition: Certain words and grammatical constructions come with presuppositions in the sense that no utterance in which these words or constructions occur can be considered felicitous unless the context in which the utterance is made verifies the presuppositions they introduce. A speaker who uses such words or constructions *cannot help but* make the corresponding presuppositions, the Common Ground of which she assumes that it obtains between her and her interlocutors must verify those presuppositions. Historically this second view, according to which linguistic presuppositions are conventionally associated with their triggers, is primarily connected with the names of Langendoen and Savin, Kiparsky, and Karttunen (Langendoen & Savin 1971; Kiparsky & Kiparski 1970; Karttunen 1973; Karttunen 1974). (See also article 14 [Semantics: Interfaces] (Beaver & Geurts) *Presupposition*.) It is this second perspective that motivates the treatment of presupposition within DRT.

With the semantic perspective came the awareness that presupposition is much more widespread than had previously been assumed. Presuppositions are not only triggered by definite descriptions and other singular terms, but also by many other words and constructions. Indeed, when investigations inspired by this new awareness got under way, a significant part of the work consisted in identifying the presupposition triggers that can be found in English and other natural languages; and even today that search is far from over.

The central challenge that this way of looking at presupposition was soon seen to present for the theoretical linguist, however, was the Projection Problem (Karttunen 1973). Karttunen noted that presuppositions carried by simple sentences often disappear when these sentences are embedded within more complex ones. Our intuitions about the truth and felicity conditions of simple sentences give us reliable information about which words and constructions are presupposition triggers, and about what presuppositions they trigger; but sometimes, when the triggers occur in logically complex sentences, these very presuppositions seem to be absent nonetheless. To give an example: the word *again* carries the presupposition that an event or state of the kind described by the clause containing it happened or obtained at some time preceding the event or state that is being described. Thus compare the utterances (23a) and (23b).

(23) a. He will come.
　　 b. He will come again.
　　 c. He won't come again.
　　 d. Will he come again?

(23b) is felicitous only in a context in which it is known or assumed that the person referred to by *he* has come also on some previous occasion. (23a) does not carry such a presupposition (and in fact it implies on the contrary that an earlier coming is not salient in the context). (23c) and (23d) provide evidence that the earlier coming implied by (23b) is a case of presupposition. (Preservation of an implication when the sentence is negated, or when it is turned into a question, are the principal tests for whether the implication is in fact a presupposition.)

But while the occurrence of an earlier coming event is presupposed by (23b)–(23d) it is not presupposed by (24a); a similar observation applies to (24b).

(24) a. If he came yesterday, he will come again.
 b. Everyone who came to last night's concert will come again to your next one.

(24a) and (24b) can be uttered felicitously in a context in which no earlier comings have been assumed or mentioned. The reason for this is not hard to see. The basic insight was first stated in Karttunen (1974). In a conditional like (24a), Karttunen observed, the presupposition generated in the consequent is entailed by the antecedent, and that is what explains why this presupposition does not manifest itself as a presupposition of the sentence (24a) as a whole. Similarly, in (24b) the presupposition is generated in the nuclear scope of the quantifier *everyone*, but entailed by the restrictor, with the same over-all effect.

The DRT-based account of presupposition of van der Sandt rests on the observation that the cases where a logically triggered presupposition disappears as presupposition of the sentence as a whole because it is entailed by some part of the sentence are precisely those where the part which entails the presupposition is *accessible* from the part in which the presupposition is triggered; or, put more accurately, the presupposition disappears in those cases where the DRS for the entire sentence contains a sub-DRS which entails the presupposition and which is accessible (in the technical sense of DRT accessibility mentioned above) from the DRS representing the part of the sentence in which the presupposition is triggered. It is worth noting that this also covers cases like the one in (24b) where the entailing sub-DRS (the quantifier restrictor) and the presupposition contain a free variable (the one that is bound on the outside by the quantifier *everyone*). Cases of this sort are not handled by the proposals of Karttunen (1974) or the dynamic version of this theory in Heim (1983).

The natural interpretation of the observations lying at the foundation of the presupposition accounts of Karttunen, Heim and van der Sandt is that the sentence part that prevents a presupposition from becoming a presupposition of the entire sentence acts as a *local context* for the part in which the presupposition was generated. In the case of van der Sandt these local contexts are sub-DRSs.

In order to implement a DRT version of this general idea it is necessary to first construct semantic representations of sentences in which presuppositions are explicitly represented. (25a) gives such a preliminary representation for (23b) and (25b) for (24a). The representation of the *again*-presupposition is always left-adjoined to the (sub-)DRS for the part of the sentence which contains its trigger. Two remarks are in order wrt. (25a,b): (1) In our discussion of temporal reference in Section 2.1 we did not deal with temporal adverbs like *yesterday*. Such temporal locating adverbs are treated as imposing additional constraints on the location times of described events and states. For instance, *yesterday* in (25b) expresses the constraint $t1 \subseteq t$ (with t the discourse referent representing the time denoted by *yesterday*). That the discourse referent t and the condition yesterday(t) appear in the universe of the main DRS (and not in the DRS representing the antecedent of the conditional) has to do with the fact that *yesterday* is a directly referential term. See Section 7. (2) In general the same sentence or sentence part can generate several different presuppositions at once; in such cases the representation will have a set of presupposition representations left-adjoined to the non-presuppositional part of the representation. Hence the curly brackets around the presuppositions in (25.a,b).

(25) a.

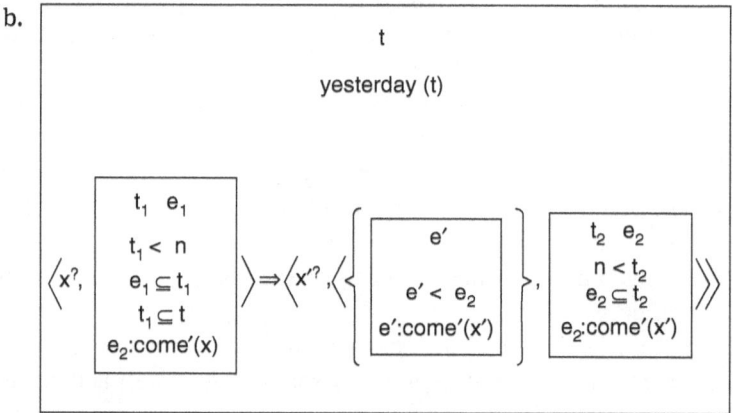

b.

In (25a) there is no local context that could entail the presupposition. So the presupposition "survives" and the represented sentence (23b) can be uttered felicitously only in a context that entails it. But in (25b) there is a local context, viz. the DRS representing the antecedent of the conditional, and this DRS does entail the presupposition adjoined to the DRS representing the consequent. So here the presupposition "disappears".

This last statement isn't quite correct as it stands; for the presupposition is about some individual represented as x', whereas the antecedent DRS speaks of an individual represented as x; and the entailment goes through only on the assumption that $x' = x$. This observation leads us to the next aspect of the treatment of presupposition within DRT. It was noted above that the (sub-)DRSs that can function as local contexts for the *justification* of presuppositions generated in other parts of the sentence are just those that can also supply antecedents for anaphoric pronouns. This suggests that presupposition and anaphora are closely related phenomena: both involve constraints on context – some part of the available context must contain the information that is needed to satisfy the requirements they impose. Van der Sandt took this idea further than anyone before him: presupposition and anaphora are but two sides of the same coin and his account does not really distinguish between them: the contextual constraint imposed by, say, an anaphoric pronoun is different in form from the presupposition imposed by a word like *again*, but that is as far as the difference goes. In van Genabith, Kamp & Reyle (2011) a distinction is made between *anaphoric* and *non-anaphoric* presuppositions. Anaphoric presuppositions always involve anaphoric discourse referents and impose on the context the constraint that it supplies discourse referents which can serve as antecedents for those. The anaphoric discourse referent is then interpreted as standing to its antecedent in a certain relation; often this relation is coreference, but not always (not e.g. in cases of temporal anaphora). Non-anaphoric presuppositions are presuppositions in the sense of presupposition theory "before DRT" and act as entailment requirements: they express presuppositions that the context is required to entail. (As a matter of fact, both these types of presuppositions can be seen as special cases of a more general form of *anaphora cum presupposition:* a constraint to the effect that the context provides one or more discourse referents for which it entails certain properties and/or relations; arguably van der Sandt's theory can be interpreted as advocating this generalised notion.)

Here we follow the version of presupposition theory presented in van Genabith, Kamp & Reyle (2011) In this version anaphoric pronouns are treated as triggers of presuppositions of the form: $<x^?, C1(x),..,Cn(x)>$, where x is the discourse referent representing the pronoun and $C1,..,Cn$ are conditions connected with the pronoun in question (e.g. a condition to the effect that the referent must be a person of the female sex) and as before the question mark behind the discourse referent x serves as indicator that the context must provide an antecedent discourse referent with which x is to be identified. With this new treatment of anaphoric pronouns the representation of (23b) will no longer require a store.

(However, we will see below that stores are still needed.) Instead the two pronoun occurrences now each contribute a presupposition. The new representation, which replaces (25b), is given in (26).

(26)
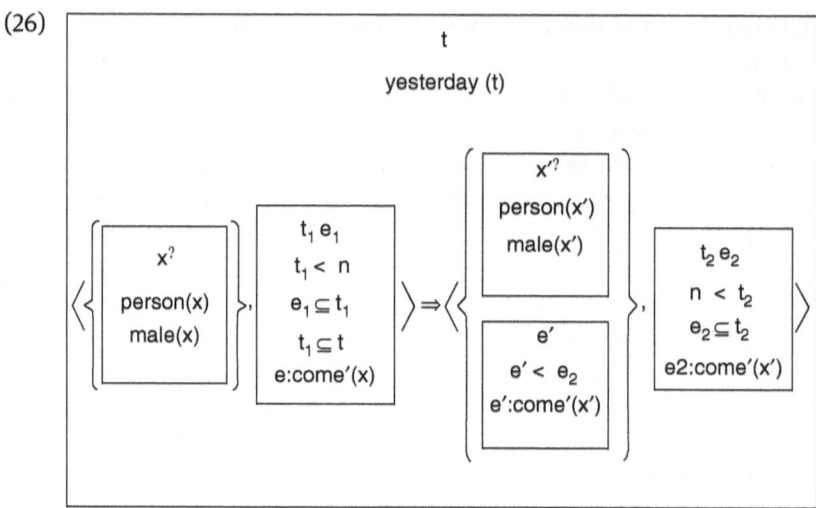

Resolution of the first pronoun presupposition is possible only if a suitable discourse referent is provided by the utterance context. In such a context the second pronoun presupposition can then also be resolved to that discourse referent. This will lead to identification of x' with x. And once this identification has been made, the antecedent DRS will entail the *again*-presupposition.

(26) is a typical example of a *preliminary sentence representation*, in which all anaphoric and presuppositional constraints that parts of the sentence impose on their respective contexts have been explicitly represented in the form of anaphoric and non-anaphoric presuppositions.

One of the unsolved issues in presupposition theory is *accommodation*. It often happens that a speaker utters a sentence which carries a presupposition that is neither entailed by some local context provided by the sentence itself nor by what the interpreter has reason to assume is the *global context* (or Common Ground; we do not make a distinction in this article between global context and Common Ground). In such cases the interpreter will normally accommodate the presupposition by adjusting the global context so that it satisfies the constraint that the presupposition imposes. Apparently, thus the implicit reasoning behind accommodation, the speaker is assuming a global context distinct from the one I was assuming myself, for otherwise she would not have used the sentence she did use (Beaver 1997; Beaver 2002). (A problem arises in those cases where the necessary adjustments conflict with some of the interpreter's beliefs: should he give these up or should he rather dismiss the speaker's utterance as infelicitous? How recipients resolve conflicts of this sort can depend on all sorts of factors. The presupposition theory of DRT has nothing to say about this.)

It should be stressed that accommodation of a presupposition need not take the form of simply adopting the presupposition itself as a new context constituent. Often the recepient will assume that the Common Ground contains additional information that exceeds what is needed to entail a presupposition, simply because that is the more plausible adjustment. And on the other hand it is often the case that the accommodated information need not entail the presupposition on its own but only in combination with information that is already present, say in the local context where the presupposition can be resolved. In such cases the accommodated information may be weaker than the presupposition (or the two may be logically independent). The first of these points has been emphasised by Beaver and the second in Kamp & Roßdeutscher (1994a), which proposes the term *presupposition justification* to cover all cases of (a) verification of the presupposition by the context as is, (b) wholesale accommodation and (c) satisfaction by a combination of old and new (that is, accommodated) contextual information. A further intriguing feature of presupposition justification is that the given discourse context often points to a particular accommodation that will guarantee presupposition verification; and the force of this pointing may be so powerful that it confers upon the indicated accommodation the apparent status of a valid inference (Kamp 2001b). One famous illustration of this last effect is an example due to Kripke (Kripke 2009), which once more involves the presupposition trigger *again*. Compare the sentences in (27).

(27) a. We won't have pizza on John's birthday if we are going to have pizza on Mary's birthday.
b. We won't have pizza again on John's birthday if we are going to have pizza on Mary's birthday.
c. We already had pizza on Billie's birthday last week. So we won't have pizza again on John's birthday if we are (also) going to have pizza on Mary's birthday.

Between (27a) and (27b) there is the following difference: (27b) seems to imply that Mary's birthday is before John's birthday, whereas (27a) does not carry this implication. Given what has been said above, the reason for this difference is not hard to find. In (27b) the occurrence of *again* in the main clause triggers the presupposition that there was a previous event of 'we' having pizza. If and only if it is assumed that Mary's birthday comes before John's, can the local context provided by the *if*-clause be used to justify this presupposition. Apparently the pressure to exploit the local context provided by the *if*-clause in this way is so strong that the interpreter is more or less forced to conclude that Mary has her birthday before John does.

That the inference is nevertheless due to the need to justify the *again*-presupposition is shown by the fact that if we embed (27b) within a discourse which provides some other earlier pizza eating event, as in (27c), then the "inferential effect" disappears. In such a context the *again*-presupposition is entailed by the first sentence, so that no accommodation is needed.

Much recent work on presupposition theory has concentrated on the problem of presupposition justification. There are many intriguing questions in this area. Among them: (i) What limitations exist on the accommodation of which presuppositions? (ii) What are the principles governing the simultaneous resolution of multiple presuppositions? (It is very common for a sentence to trigger not just one presupposition but several; cf. the discussion of (24a).) (iii) When does presupposition accommodation take on the character of an inference to the accommodated information (cf. (26))? Moreover, a systematic and explicit treatment of presupposition within a framework like DRT shows that the *computation* of presuppositions – in the present theory: the construction of the presupposition representations that are part of preliminary DRSs – can be a quite complicated matter as well. For discussion of some cases see Kamp (2001a).

4 Binding in DRT

The term *binding* has a range of different uses in logic and linguistics, a state of affairs that has been the source of a good deal of confusion. Fully clear is the notion of variable binding within formal logic: what it means for a variable to be bound by a quantifier or operator (such as the λ-operator of the λ-calculus) is made explicit both by the model theory of the relevant logical formalisms (such as the predicate calculus or the l-calculus) and also, in case a proof theory is available, by the rules of that proof theory. In some linguistic theories, such as, for instance, the Theory of Government and Binding (Chomsky 1981), the term binding is used with a quite different purport. There the semantic import of one expression being bound by another is rather something like coreference – something that can be made explicit by treating the bound expression and its binder as designators that refer to the same referent. DRT's account of anaphoric binding can be seen as a kind of compromise between these two notions of binding. It combines the features of logical binding as variable binding with those of linguistic binding as a coreference mechanism.

We begin by looking at the nominal domain. Full projections of nouns – DPs in the terminology we have been using – always introduce a discourse referent that represents their denotation. As we have seen, this discourse referent is typically inserted into an argument position (of a verb or other predicate word in relation to which the DP appears as argument phrase). But in addition to that the discourse referent must also be bound. In DRT, binding in the nominal domain (i.e. of the discourse referents representing DPs) can take three different forms: In all cases part of the binding operation is to place the discourse referent that is being bound in some DRS universe. But otherwise the operations differ. The three types of binding are:

(i) quantificational binding
(ii) presuppositional binding
(iii) structural binding

ad(i): Cases of quantificational binding are those in which the discourse referent α representing the DP is bound by the logical operator denoted by the DP's determiner. An example is the binding of x by the universal quantifier denoted by *everyone* in the DRS (22) for (17). In this case the bound discourse referent x appears in the universe of the restrictor of the duplex condition introduced by the quantificational DP as well as jointly with the operator in the central component of the condition.

ad(ii): A discourse referent α representing a definite DP is always bound via presuppositional resolution. In these cases the context must provide a discourse referent β with which α can be identified (or, sometimes, related in some other way). Resolution of the presupposition (with or without accommodation) implies that β belongs to some universe of the context representation; identification of α with β can be implemented either by replacing α everywhere by β or by inserting α into the universe of the DRS to which the presupposition representation was left-adjoined and adding the equation $\alpha = \beta$ to the condition set of that DRS.

ad(iii): Structural binding has often been seen as DRT's main claim to faim. In the original versions of DRT it applied just to indefinite DPs. This is still true as far as the nominal domain is concerned: of the different types of DP that are found in a language like English – quantificational, definite and indefinite – it is only the indefinites that give rise to this kind of binding.

The name 'structural' for the type of binding described under (iii) reflects the idea that it is simply by virtue of belonging to a certain DRS universe that the discourse referents representing indefinite DPs get their quantificational force. This force derives from the truth definition for DRSs, and it is because of the existential element in this definition – 'there exists an embedding function from the DRS universe into the universe of the model which verifies the conditions of the DRS' – that indefinites often have existential force. However, this isn't always so. See for instance the discussion of donkey sentences in Section 2.2.

In the examples we have considered so far each indefinite contributed its discourse referent to its local universe (i.e. to the universe of the most deeply embedded (sub-)DRS representing a part of the sentence in which the indefinite is contained). There are cases, however, where indefinites are not interpreted as having local scope. The earliest examples are due to Farkas (1981). A much discussed example, due to Farkas, is that in (28).

(28) Every student in the syntax class has to discuss three arguments why some claim of Chomsky is wrong.

(28) has an interpretation according to which for each student there was some claim of Chomsky's such that that student had to discuss three arguments why that claim was wrong – not three arguments each of which showed that some claim of Chomsky's was wrong but three arguments for one and the same claim. So this is a case where the indefinite *some claim by Chomsky* is assigned scope over the phrase *three arguments why some claim of Chomsky is wrong*, although it is syntactically embedded within that phrase. Since Farkas made her seminal observation, a substantial literature has accumulated in which various cases of such non-local scope interpretations of indefinites are discussed. We don't go into details, but only note that when DRSs are constructed bottom-up the discourse referent that is introduced by an indefinite that is given a non-local interpretation must be kept in store until the (sub-)DRS has been created. Such wide scope indefinites are among the constructs which make some type of store mechanism indispensable.

Binding of the referential arguments of nominal projections other than DPs
The binding options discussed above apply to the referential arguments of nouns that are the lexical heads of DPs. But that is not the only way in which nouns occur. Other occurrences are found in the NPs that act as predicates of copula constructions and small clauses. (Often these come in the company of an article – *John is the lover of Brenda, I consider myself a failure* – but in such cases the article does not appear to play the part of a genuine determiner, which acts as the functional head of a DP.) Another way for nouns to occur without

being part of a DP is as heads of *incorporating NPs* – argument phrases of verbs and other predicate words but with a semantics which suggests that what they contribute to the meaning of the verb-NP complex is a property rather than an individual that fills the argument position to which the phrase is syntactically linked. What mechanisms are involved in binding the referential arguments of such noun occurrences is still a matter of debate. For discussions of incorporation within a DRT-based framework see Farkas & de Swart (2003) and Bende-Farkas & Kamp (2001).

So far, the discussion has concentrated on count nouns (even if this wasn't stated explicitly). But mass nouns also have referential arguments, and these too must be bound in some way. There are some obvious and suggestive parallels between the binding of the referential arguments of mass nouns and incorporation phenonema involving count nouns, but exactly what that relation is (and more particularly whether it could be right to see the binding of the referential arguments of mass nouns as a form of incorporation) remains unclear. As things stand, there exists no explicit DRT-based treatment of mass nouns; this is a gap that ought to be filled.

Binding of temporal variables and of the referential arguments of verbs.
Binding in the verbal domain obeys the same general principles as binding in the nominal domain. For a language like English this is not so easy to see, since in the verbal domain the different binding types do not correlate with easily recognizable features of the expressions that introduce the relevant discourse referents.

In our construction of the DRS for (5) in Section 2.1 we saw that temporal reference is represented using discourse referents of two sorts - discourse referents for eventualities (events and states) and discourse referents for times. Binding of eventuality discourse referents is always structural and local. But the discourse referents that represent their location times can be bound in each of the three ways listed above for nominal discourse referents. In our examples so far we have only encountered structural binding of location times. But instances of the other two types are also found. Quantificational binding of location times occurs in the presence of temporal adverbs like *always* and *mostly*. These adverbs give rise to temporal duplex conditions and introduce location time discourse referents that are bound by the quantifiers which the adverbs introduce (see Reyle, Rossdeutscher & Kamp 2008 for details).

There are also cases where location times are bound presuppositionally. In (29a) the temporal relative clause *ten minutes after Bill called her* serves to locate the event described by the main clause *Mary left the house*. The relative clause introduces a location time for the calling event which serves to locate the event described by the main clause.

(29) a. Mary left the house ten minutes after Bill called her.
    b. Mary didn't leave the house ten minutes after Bill called her.

That both the *Bill called* event and its location time have a presuppositional status is shown by (29b), the negation of (29a). The most prominent interpretation of this sentence is one according to which Bill did call Mary at some time t and that ten minutes after t Mary did not leave the house. (An interpretation according to which the time at which Mary left the house wasn't ten minutes after the time when Bill called because Bill didn't call seems possible only in quite special contexts.) This indicates that both the event discourse referent of the relative clause and the discourse referent for its location time are bound presuppositionally.

5 Lexicon and inference

The meanings of the sentences we utter and the texts we write are a function of the meanings of the words from which they are built. So any account of linguistic meaning must start with the meanings of words. And that entails that any semantic theory must include a lexicon. In fact, the lexicon is arguably the most demanding part of semantics, on the one hand because languages have so many words, and on the other because capturing the meaning of even a single word – or crafting a satisfactory semantic entry for it – can be very hard.

How hard will depend on what purpose the entry is supposed to serve. But we have already hinted at what that purpose should be: the semantics of words that is specified by their entries must be such that the meanings of sentences and texts can be computed from these entries in a systematic, compositional fashion. From the start this has been the guiding principle for lexicon development within DRT (see in particular Kamp & Roßdeutscher 1994a). And here it takes the following form: The semantic specifications given in the lexical entries of words should be such that they can be imported into the semantic representations of the sentences and texts that can be constructed out of those words, and these representations should capture the meanings of the represented texts and sentences in the specific sense that they support the inferences that human interpreters are able to draw from those texts and sentences.

In DRT the problem of semantic lexical specification is thus tied directly to the problem of inference: Suppose that T is a text and that S is a sentence which an interpreter would naturally infer (or be able to infer) from T. Then the DRS for T should entail the DRS for S and our theory should allow us to show this. And whether the theory can do that will in almost all cases depend on what the lexical entries for the words that occur in T and S contribute to their representations.

Although the development of a DRT-based lexicon has been a concern for many years, there still is a long way to go. In particular, current DRT-based lexicons lack the broad coverage that is indispensable in automated natural language processing. Even so, existing results exceed by a wide margin what could be reported within the limits of this article. We have therefore decided to focus on some of the methodological problems of semantic lexicon design as they present themselves within DRT, instead of presenting an inevitably fragmentary overview of the proposals for the entries of particular words and word classes. (For more on lexical semantics within a DRT-based framework see Kamp & Roßdeutscher 1994a; Kamp & Roßdeutscher 1994b; Roßdeutscher 1994; Roßdeutscher 2000; Solstad 2007, and for a more recent perspective Lechler & Roßdeutscher 2009; Hamm & Kamp 2009.)

Our first encounter with the lexicon was in Section 2 when we looked at the DRS construction for the sentences in (3). DRS construction always starts with the insertion of semantic representations for the words of the sentence for which a DRS is being built. This presupposes that the lexical entries for those words provide the representations that are suited for this task. For verbs, we saw, this minimally involves two requirements: the entry must (i) provide a semantic representation with slots for the verb's arguments and (ii) contain information that is needed by the syntactic parser (which provides the input trees to the DRS construction algorithm) to link these slots to argument phrases in the sentence.

But these are just the minimal requirements. In addition we would also like lexical entries to provide semantic information that will make it possible to deduce from DRSs for sentences or bits of discourse those conclusions that are readily available to a human interpreter. On this point the one entry we have so far presented – that for the verb *wake up*, given in (6) and repeated here as (30) – seems to score pretty close to the bottom of the scale: To simply use a DRS predicate wake_up' as semantics for the verb *wake up* doesn't tell us very much about what *wake up* means, or what inferences it supports.

(30) *wake up*   (verb)   nom
                  e   x
   Sel. Restr.: event   animal
   Sem. Repr.: $\boxed{e:\text{wake\_up}'(\mathbf{x})}$

Of course there is little that can be predicted about the inferential power of an entire system from just one entry. Most of the inferences that we draw from what we hear or read have to do with the semantic connections between words and not *just* with the meanings of single words. To take one, very simple example: from the information that Alain woke up at t we can infer that he was awake immediately after t and that he was asleep or unconscious immediately before. It is conceivable that even with the simplistic entry in (30) these inferences could be computed as long as enough is said, in some part of the overall theory, about the connections between the predicate wake_up' and the meanings of *awake*, *asleep* and *unconscious*. But where would this information be stored if it isn't part of the entry for *wake up*?

This brief discussion shows that the lexicon builder is facing two connected questions: (i) What semantic information about individual words should the lexicon make available? and (ii) Where should which information go? There are no simple answers to these questions. Answers to the first depend on what inferences we want our system to be able to draw. But even when these answers are settled, that won't in general settle the second question. Since most of the information that needs to be coded is relational – it concerns the meanings of two or more lexical items, not of a single one – there are several suggestions that come to mind as to where it should be stored: as part of the entry for the first lexical item, as part of the entry for the second, ... ; as part of each of those entries (creating a good deal of redundancy); or in some other place altogether. The last option is in essence that of coding lexical semantic information in the form of *meaning postulates* in the sense in which this notion has come down to us from the work of Carnap and Montague (who however use meaning postulates primarily as ways of coding information about single lexical items). The use of meaning postulates as part of a DRT-based lexicon goes back to Kamp & Rossdeutscher (1994a), where they serve as the axioms of *Lexical Theory*, a formal axiomatic theory which supports inferencing from representations that contain the lexical predicates which its postulates are about. The core vocabulary of this theory consists of so-called *lexical primes*, predicates that are used to articulate fundamental ontological relationships such as those that determine the structure of time and space, motion and causation. (Thus Lexical Theory is assumed to include formal ontology as a part.)

Here we will give two examples of how connections between lexical predicates can be made explicit. That between *wake up* and *awake* is naturally captured by changing the semantics of the lexical entry for *wake up* so that it says that the events described by *wake up* are transitions from a state in which the subject is not awake to one in which it is. The new entry is given in (31).

(31) *wake up* (verb)   nom
              e   x
    Sel. Restr.: event   animal

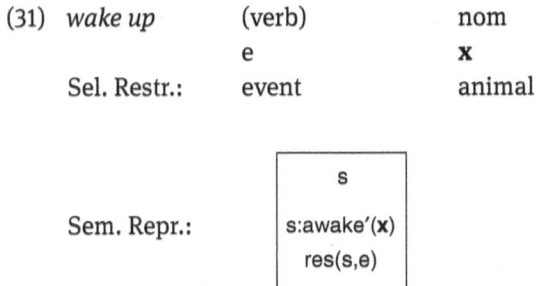

Sem. Repr.:

Here res(s,e) is to be read as "s is the state resulting from the event e". ("res" is one of the primes of the Lexical Theory.) The relation between *awake*, *asleep* and *unconscious* is one of those that are naturally cast in the form of meaning postulates, as in (32).

(32)
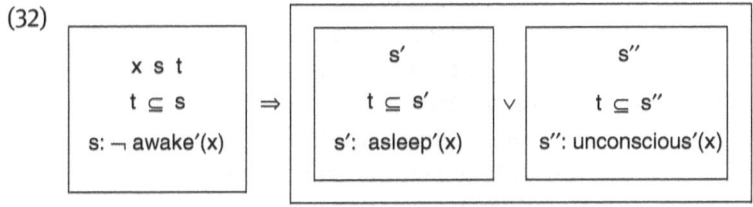

The modified entry (31) for *wake up* and the meaning postulate (32) should enable us to infer (33b) and (33c) from (33a).

(33) a. Alain woke up at 10.
     b. For some time after 10 Alain was awake.
     c. For some time just before 10 Alain was either asleep or unconsious.

These are not particularly interesting inferences, but when such inferences won't work, hardly anything will. To be able to draw them within the present framework we need DRSs for (33b) and (33c) as well as for (33a), and that will require, among other things, entries for the adjectives *awake*, *asleep* and *unconscious*. We focus on *awake*, but the discussion extends straightforwardly to the other two adjectives. What should the entry for *awake* be like? That is a question with a twist. Let us adopt as format for the entry of *awake* (and other adjectives) the one which we have been using already for the verb *wake up*. Such entries distinguish between the referential argument of a lexical item and its non-referential arguments (if any). For *awake* there seems only one option: the referential argument is the individual that is awake, and there are no other arguments. In other words, the entry for *awake* should be as in (34).

(34) *awake* adj

	x
Sel. Restr.:	animal
Sem. Repr.:	awake'(**x**)

Note, however, that the semantic component of this entry – the condition awake'(**x**) – is not in the form in which we need it in order to carry out the intended inferences. For instance, in (31) awake' occurs as part of the condition s:awake'(**x**) and that should therefore also be the form in which it occurs in the DRS for (33a). To achieve this we must assume that when an occurrence of *awake* in a sentence is replaced by its semantic representation, then the condition awake'(**x**) is converted into one of the form s:awake'(**x**). But of course this requires further rules for the temporal location of s. In cases where *awake* occurs as complement of the copula verb *to be*, this is straightforward. The copula, a stative verb, contributes a state s which gets temporally located by its tense (and, if present, by temporal adverbs) in the same way as the eventualities introduced by other verbs; and the complement of the copula provides the predication that serves as characterisation of s. In this way we obtain a DRS for (33b) of the following form.

(35)
$$\begin{array}{|l|} \hline x\ t\ s'\ t' \\ \hline \text{Alain}(x) \\ 10\ (t') \quad t < n \\ t' \supset\!\subset t \quad t \subseteq s' \\ s':\text{awake}'(x) \\ \hline \end{array}$$

We cannot go into the details of the construction of (35) here. But in any case, the copula construction is only one among many in which predication conditions like awake'(x) have to be transformed into conditions of the form s:awake'(x). In general, such conversions pose a non-trivial problem, not only for adjectives, but also for other non-verbal predicates, such as nouns and prepositions. If we cast the lexical entries of these words in the same mould as (34), with semantic components that take the form of simple predications – e.g. wife'(**x,y**) in the entry for the noun *wife* – then these predications too will often have to be converted into conditions like s: wife'(x,y) with one or more additional conditions to locate s. The occurrence of *wife* in (3) provides us with a glimpse of what the problems are that may arise in this connection. In 2.1 we represented the information about x' being the wife of u simple in the form wife'(x', u). But this is, strictly speaking, a way of prevaricating on a question that can be raised about (3), and that in certain contexts one might well want to raise: *When* is or was x' the wife of u – at the time of the event of which (3) speaks, or at the time when the sentences are uttered?

As this example suggests, there are no simple general rules for resolving such ambiguities. The problem, in other words, is not so much that of converting conditions of the form 'wife'(y,x)' into conditions of the form s: wife'(y,x), but to determine the intuitively correct temporal locating conditions for s. For discussion of this problem see Musan (1995), Tonhauser (2000) and Kamp (2001a).

The DRS for (33a) is much like the one we gave in 2.1 for the first sentence of (3), except that (i) there will now be an additional discourse referent t" representing 10 o'clock, together with the condition that it includes t (t ⊆ t"), and (ii) the new entry (31) for *wake up* imports into the DRS a result state, s' of the waking up event e, with the conditions s':awake'(x) and res(s',e). The DRS is given in (36).

(36)
```
         t t"  e  x  s
t < n  10-o-clock(t")  t ⊆ t"  e ⊆ t
res(s,e)   Alain(x)   s:awake'(x)
```

To infer (35) from (36) we need two more principles. The first has been implicit in what has already been said: if s is a result state of e, then s abuts e on the right. Formally:

(37)
```
  e  s
res(s,e)   ⇒   e ⊃⊂ s
```

The second principle has to do with the punctual character of the time specification *10 o'clock*. Intuitively such a time t cannot extend beyond the duration of an event e happening at that time. This entails that if e happens at t and s is a state that right-abuts e, then s must include some initial segment of the period that stretches from t into the future. Using "punct" to represent the notion of punctuality that is conveyed by expressions like *10 o'clock*, we can formalise this principle as in (38).

(38)
$$\boxed{\begin{array}{l} t\ e\ s \\ \text{punct}(t) \\ e \subseteq t \\ e \asymp s \end{array}} \Rightarrow \boxed{\begin{array}{l} t' \\ t \supset\!\subset t' \\ t' \subseteq s \end{array}}$$

With the help of (37) and (38), (36) can be modified into (39), from which (34) can be obtained by renaming discourse referents and thinning (i.e. throwing away discourse referents and conditions).

(39)
$$\boxed{\begin{array}{c} t\ t'\ e\ x\ s\ t'' \\ t < n\ \ 10\text{-o-clock}(t')\ \ t \subseteq t'\ \ e \subseteq t \\ \text{res}(s,e)\ \ e \asymp s \\ t \supset\!\subset t''\ \ t'' \subseteq s\ \ \text{Alain}(x)\ \ s{:}\text{awake}'(x) \end{array}}$$

To infer the DRS for (33c) from that of (33a) a little more is involved. We now need in addition: (i) entries for *asleep* and *unconscious* (which are like (34)) and the meaning postulate (32): (ii) a general principle to the effect that if a state s of a certain type is the result state of an event e, then immediately before e there was a state of the opposite type, i. e. a state s' which is characterised by the negation of the condition that characterises s. (Often s' and s are referred to as the *prestate* and *poststate* of e.)

The prestate of an event e will hold at the moment e begins. Sometimes it will last throughout e, but it may also cease before that, in which case the gap between it and the result state will be bridged by some transitional state. However, if we assume that for each state s and interval t included in the duration of s there is a state s' of the same time as s and with t as its duration, then the Prestate Principle can be formulated simply that there is a state which abuts e on the left and is of a type opposite to e's result state.

Note that the Prestate Principle has the status of making explicit a presupposition. Compare for instance the sentences *Bill left the room* and *Bill didn't leave the room*. For both of these the salient interpretation is that according to which, at the time in question, Bill is inside the room. For some reason the question is raised whether Bill left the room at that time, and the two sentences resolve that issue in opposite ways – the one says that Bill did leave the room and the other that he remained in it. (The negated sentence can be used in relation to a situation in which Bill is not in the room at t, as in *Bill didn't leave the room for the simple reason that he wasn't in the room to begin with at that time.* But such contexts are marked, and they typically involve information which denies that the pre-state held at the relevant time.)

The upshot of this is that the general principle according to which any combination of an event e and a result state s implies the existence of a corresponding prestate s' must take the form of adding to the representation of event e and result state s a presupposition saying that e is left-abutted by a state whose characterisation is the opposite of that of s. (40) gives the template for adding pre-state presuppositions to arbitrary representations of this kind (i.e. to arbitrary representations introduced by change-of-state verbs). K is a schematic letter for DRSs, K' for a DRS or a DRS-condition.

(40)
$$K \oplus \boxed{\begin{array}{c} s \\ \hline res(s,e) \\ s: K' \end{array}} \leadsto K \oplus \left\langle \boxed{\begin{array}{c} s_0 \\ \hline s_0: \neg K' \\ s_0 \supset\!\subset e \end{array}}, \boxed{\begin{array}{c} s \\ \hline res(s,e) \\ s: K' \end{array}} \right\rangle$$

To infer the DRS for (33c) from the DRS (36) for (33a) we first expand the latter by an application of (40) in which K' is instantiated by the conditon awake'(x). ((41) shows this instantiation of the second term in (40) of the second occurrence of ⊕.) The condition that the event of x waking up was immediately preceded by a sate to the effect that x was not awake, is incorporated into (36) as a presupposition (see (42)). After the presupposition of (42) has been justified (possibly through accommodation), it is available as non-presuppositional information and can be merged with the rest of (42), see (43). At this point we can apply (32) to replace the characterisation awake'(x) of the pre-state s_0 by asleep'(x) ∨ unconscious'(x). Moreover, we can also apply to the state s_0 a principle that is the mirror image of principle (38): if t" is punctual, e ⊆ t", and $s_0 \supset\!\subset e$, then s_0 includes some period of time t' " that left-abuts t". With this last application a DRS has been obtained from which the DRS for (33.c) can be derived by renaming and thinning.

(41)
$$\left\langle \boxed{\begin{array}{c} s_0 \\ \hline s_0: \neg \text{awake}'(x) \\ s_0 \supset\!\subset e \end{array}}, \boxed{\begin{array}{c} s \\ \hline s:\text{awake}'(x) \\ res(s,e) \end{array}} \right\rangle$$

(42)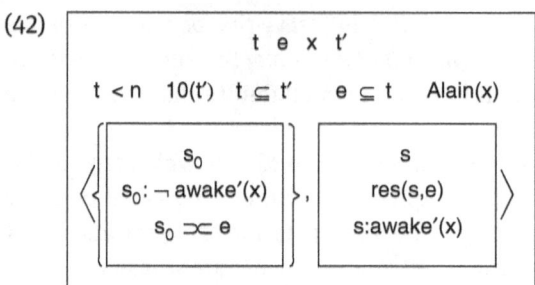

(43)
```
         t e x t' s₀ s
t < n  10(t')  t ⊆ t'  e ⊆ t  s₀ ⊃⊂ e  res(s,e)  Alain(x)
            s₀: ¬ awake'(x)   s:awake'(x)
```

The main point of this discussion has been to show how closely the design of the semantic components of lexical entries has to be tied to questions of inference if the inferential support role of the lexicon is taken as seriously as DRT claims it should. Moreover, it isn't just the semantic components of the lexical entries themselves that must be fine-tuned to inferential requirements; the same is true, and perhaps even more emphatically, for the meaning postulates that constitute the Lexical Theory without which the entries would not be able to discharge their inferential obligations. Inferences in the temporal domain provide good illustrations of this intimate connection between inference and the lexicon, but they are in no way alone in this. Therefore, inference always has to be foremost in the mind of the lexical semanticist, no matter what part of the lexicon he is dealing with.

The examples we have discussed bring to the fore two aspects of lexical semantics that DRT-based work has been at pains to do justice to: event structure and presupposition. Presupposition has played its part here only in the form of the pre-state presupposition associated with the change-of-state verb *wake up*. But since pre-state presuppositions are associated with all change-of-state verbs, we accounted for the case that arises in our example by means of the general schema (40) rather than adding the pre-state presupposition explicitly to the semantic part of the lexical entry for the verb *(wake up)* itself (though technically that could have been an alternative way to proceed). However, there are many lexical items which carry presuppositions as an idiosyncratic part of their individual meaning, and in such cases the only natural place for encoding those presuppositions is as part of the semantics of their own lexical entries. An example is the presupposition carrier *again*. (Reasons of space keep us from presenting and discussing its lexical entry explicitly.)

A third important aspect of lexical meaning is *intentionality*. Intentionality is a far more common aspect of lexical meaning than it tends to being given credit for. For instance, we find it in most action verbs, whose default interpretation is that the agent has a certain intention and that the action the verb describes is an attempt to make that intention come true. Representing these intention-related components of lexical meaning puts serious demands on the representation formalism one uses. This has been one reason for the special effort that has been made within DRT to put such a formalism in place. (See Section 6.3 on Propositional Attitudes.)

For the formal logician our discussion carries a different moral. The inferences of which we have offered reconstructions in this section have an appearance of almost embarrassing simplicity. This simplicity has been largely confirmed by the reconstructions we have offered. But these reconstructions also show that a certain amount of inference-like work is involved in these reconstructions nevertheless. That work consists largely in identifying the language-related principles that allow the premise DRS to be transformed or expanded to the point where the entailment relation between it and the conclusion DRS has become fully transparent. In our reconstructions above we coded these language-related principles in the form of meaning postulates; and it was only in the application of these postulates to the premise representation that the inference rules of classical formal logic came into play. In the examples we have looked at the uses we have made of such rules have been very elementary, and in this respect our examples have been good illustrations of what is involved in such inferences generally: The real action – or there is of it – in such inference processes is in selecting the postulates that make it possible to transform the premise DRS in the ways required. Since the number of meaning postulates that are part of knowing a language is very large, choosing the right ones for a given inferential task could well be a non-trivial problem. It seems however that this is something at which language users are remarkably adept. So, inasmuch as knowing meaning postulates and making the right choices from the set of meaning postulates one knows is arguably part of our *linguistic* competence, the conclusion would seem to be that our inferential abilities depend as much as on our knowledge of language as on a language-independent capacity for abstract formal reasoning.

We conclude this discussion with a word of caution. The inferences reconstructed above were strict, deductively valid inferences. But most of the inferences people draw in the day to day business of real life aren't like that; they are approximate and defeasible. Lexical entries should be such that they can support such inferences too. However, our understanding of how defeasible inferencing works is still fragmentary and tentative. And so long as our grasp of this part of the general problem of inference remains as feeble as it is today, there is no way of telling how well the lexical semantics we propose will stand up in the longer run.

6 Extensions

6.1 Plurals

Natural languages such as English mark the distinction between singular and plural. Plural nouns are as common as singular ones. This in itself would be reason enough to demand of a theory dealing with the semantics of such a language that it can handle plurals as well as singulars. But in the case of DRT there is a special reason for wanting to cover plurals and not only singulars, which has to do with the original motivations for the theory. As noted earlier, one of the main selling points of early DRT was the way it treats the anaphoric relation between pronouns and their indefinite antecedents. A crucial ingredient of that account is the assumption that the interpretation of an anaphoric pronoun always involves a discourse referent that is either made available by the DRS of the preceding discourse or by the DRS of the sentence itself. It is to this discourse referent that the pronoun is then related (often, though not invariably, in the sense of coreference). Plural pronouns, however, do not behave in strict accordance with this principle. They are often interpreted as referring back to elements of the discourse context that are not (yet) represented by discourse referents and that must first be constructed from material that is explicitly contained in the representation.

Our first task in this section will be to review the relevant observations about the behaviour of plural pronouns and DRT's account of them. But the extension of DRT to cover plurals also has another important aspect: By extending DRT so that plurals are covered as well as singulars we move from first to second order logic. This point is not as obvious as it might seem, and requires careful discussion. But it is methodologically important. We will discuss the two issues – plural anaphora and the expressive power of the extended DRS language – in that order.

Many plural DPs denote sets with two or more members. (Not invariably, see Kamp & Reyle (1993, Ch.4); but in this brief review we will confine ourselves to DPs for which this is the case.) This applies also to anaphoric plural pronouns. But often the sets that these pronouns refer to are not explicitly represented in the discourse representation that should supply the pronoun's antecedent – not, at least, when that representation has been constructed from the antecedent discourse along the lines sketched in Section 2. An example is (44).

(44) Alan took his wife out to dinner. They shared the hors d'oeuvre.

Here the pronoun *they* in the second sentence clearly refers to the pair consisting of Alan and his wife. But if the DRS for the first sentence is constructed according to the standard rules of DRS construction, then it will have no discourse referent representing this pair; it will only have discourse referents – x and y, say – that represent Alan and his wife separately. To obtain a discourse referent that can serve as antecedent for *they* we have to apply the operation of Summation. This application takes the form of introducing a new plural discourse referent Z and adding the condition $Z = x \oplus y$, which defines Z as the sum of x and y.

The possibility of constructing discourse referents that can serve as antecedents for plural pronouns is of methodological interest because it is subject to certain restrictions. This is illustrated by (45).

(45) Half of the shareholders were present at the meeting. They learned about what had been said and decided at the meeting only from the newspapers the next morning.

In this sentence *they* can only refer to the half of the shareholders that were at the meeting, even if that interpretation makes little sense in the given context. The interpretation that would make more sense – the one according to which *they* refers to the other half, who were not at the meeting – is blocked: subtraction of one set from another is not an operation that is available for creating pronominal antecedents. (It has been argued that subtraction is possible in certain circumstances, though speakers vary in their judgements about such cases. For extensive discussion of this issue see Nouwen 2003 and Kibble 1997.) Creation of pronoun antecedents is thus not just a matter of logical inference from the DRS representing the given discourse context. Only certain operations, such as the Summation operation that was used to synthesise the Z in constructing a representation for (44), are permitted. (For more details see Kamp & Reyle 1993). Moreover, the restrictions to which this process is subject, and which distinguish it from standard logical deduction, are specific to the interpretation of pronouns: There is no difficulty in referring to the half of the shareholders that were not at the meeting, provided we use a definite description. (In fact, we just did; and in (45) the phrase *the other half* would have done as well.)

The upshot of these considerations: There are a number of principles that can be used to construct antecedents for plural pronouns from material that is explicitly present in the given DRS, but these principles do not exhaust the full power of logical inference. Moreover, these principles, with their built-in restrictions, apply not only within the sentence but equally to cases of inter-sentential anaphora. And as we just saw, they are specific to pronouns; anaphoric definite descriptions, for instance, are not subject to them. The methodological interest of these observations is that what we are seeing here is a distinctive property of some particular linguistic category (plural pronouns), and which applies not just to what happens within single sentences, but equally to multi-sentential discourse. This is a case, in other words, where the grammatical properties of a certain type of expression exert their influence beyond the sentences in which they occur.

The restrictions on the construction of plural pronoun antecedents illustrated in (45) find a parallel in the famous "ball" example due to Partee:

(46) a. One of the ten balls is not in the bag. It/the missing ball is under the sofa.
b. Nine of the ten balls are in the bag. *It/the missing ball is under the sofa.

Getting the intended antecedent for *it* in (46b) by subtracting the mentioned set of nine balls (the balls in the bag) from the mentioned set of ten balls (the set of all balls) doesn't work, or at any rate not very well.

This gets us to a question that imposes itself once it has been accepted that the antecedents of plural pronouns may be constructed using a certain range of special purpose principles: How does this account for plural anaphoric pronouns relate to the one for singular pronouns that was outlined in Section 2? The simplest relationship would be that of subsumption: If we accept that singular pronouns must always refer to single individuals (or singleton sets, the distinction doesn't matter here), then the operations that permit antecedent construction will be otiose; they cannot create a discourse referent for a single individual, unless they start from a discourse referent that belongs to the representation already and which they then simply return. As it turns out, things are not quite that simple. One of the operations that can be used to construct antecedents for plural pronouns is *Abstraction*. It takes a nominal predication represented within the DRS as input and returns its extension as output. An example is (47), in which Abstraction can be applied to the predicate *friend that Alan had invited* and returns as output a discourse referent for the extension of this predicate which can then serve as antecedent for the pronoun *they* in the second sentence.

(47) No friend that Alan had invited came to his party. They were too busy.

If the same rules that can be used to produce antecedents for plural pronouns are available in principle for singular pronouns as well, couldn't Abstraction be used to yield antecedents for singular pronouns as well, in those cases where the predicate to which it is applied has a unique instance? As it turns out, the evidence suggests that this is indeed the case. A variant of an often quoted example is (48).

(48) It is not true that there is no rabbi officiating at this wedding. He is standing over there, right next to the buffet.

One way to account for the felicity of this discourse is to construe the antecedent of *he* as the result of applying Abstraction to the predicate *rabbi officiating at this wedding* together with the general assumption that the number of officiating rabbis at a wedding is ≤ 1. If this is right, then a uniform account of singular and plural anaphoric English pronouns is a live option, but the earlier principle that the antecedent of a singular pronoun must always be present in the DRS should be abandoned. However, there are also other proposals for dealing with examples like (48), so it is not easy to resolve this issue conclusively. We should mention in this connection in particular one way of dealing with pronominal anaphoricity that is known as the E-type approach. The central principle of this approach is reminiscent of Abstraction, but the over-all architecture is quite different. (See e.g. Heim 1990; Elbourne 2005 or article 2 [Semantics: Noun Phrases and Verb Phrases] (Heim) *Definiteness and indefiniteness*).

There are many more puzzles connected with plural DPs. For some of these, and for suggestions as to how they might be dealt within a setting provided by DRT, see Kamp & Reyle (1993, Ch.4).

The circumstance that many plural DPs refer to sets might be seen as leading directly to the conclusion that a formalism in which their denotations can be represented must be second order. But this would be too hasty. Many sentences with plural DPs have first order truth conditions. For just one example, consider (49a), which can be rendered by a first order formula just as (49b) can.

(49) a. All tourists bought tickets to the musical.
b. Every tourist bought a ticket to the musical.

In fact, plural DPs like *all tourists* function as first order quantifiers, on a par with singular DPs like *every tourist*. That DRS languages suitable for representing the content of sentences with plural DPs must nonetheless have the power of second order logic has to do with the quasi-quantificational role that can be played by plural indefinites. One way to see this is to observe that the Principle of Mathematical Induction can be stated (if somewhat awkwardly) using the plural indefinite *some numbers* and otherwise only a bare minimum of number-theoretic vocabulary (*zero* and *successor*).

(50a) gives an English sentence which expresses mathematical induction and (50b) the DRS representing it. (Capitals are used for discourse referents representing pluralities; for any nominal predicate N, N* denotes the predicate that is true not only of members of the extension of N but also of sets that are included in the extension of N; ϵ means "is among".)

(50) a. If zero is among some numbers and for any number that is among them its successor is also among them, then every number is among them.

b.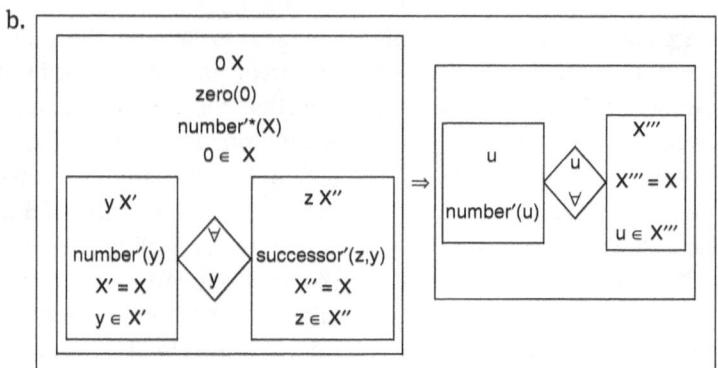

Both (50b) and the sentence (50a) are known to be essentially second order (meaning that their truth conditions cannot be captured by any first order statement) and to yield, when conjoined with (representations of) first order sentences that express the familiar properties of addition and multiplication, a non-axiomatisable theory. This establishes the non-axiomatisability of the logic expressible in a fragment of English with plurals, and likewise of a DRS-language which has plural discourse referents and just a handful of predicates (among which ∈ and the *-predicate that occurs in (50b)).

DRS languages which licence DRSs like (50b) (such as e.g. the DRS-language assumed in Ch. 4 of Kamp & Reyle 1993) thus have the power of second order logic. (Versions of the argument given here have been known for several decades. A seminal paper on the topic is Boolos 1984, in which a very similar method to the one used here is attributed to David Kaplan.) Attempts to find natural and independently motivated characterisations of sublanguages of such DRS languages which retain the ability of representing a significant portion of English sentences with plurals, but whose logic is axiomatisable (and which must therefore exclude DRSs like (50b)), have thus far been without success, and at this point it seems doubtful that such sublanguages can be found.

6.2 Intensionality

Only some natural language constructions that build clauses out of other clauses are extensional. The majority are intensional, in the sense that the denotation of the resulting clause is a function of the intensions of the clause or clauses from which it is constructed, and not from their truth values. Modifying DRT so that it can handle intensional constructions is straightforward in principle. All that is needed for this is that we replace the extensional models we have been considering up to now by intensional models. We can take these intensional models to be bundles of extensional models indexed by possible worlds. A simple formalisation of this notion is as a pair $\mathcal{M} = \langle W, M \rangle$, where W is a non-empty set of *possible worlds* and M is a function from W to extensional models. In relation to such intensional models $\mathcal{M}$ we can define the *denotation of* a DRS K *in* $\mathcal{M}$, $[\![K]\!]_{\mathcal{M}}$, to be the set of all pairs $\langle w, f \rangle$ where $w \in W$ and f is an embedding of K into the universe of $M(w)$ which verifies the conditions of K in $M(w)$; and the *proposition expressed by* K *in* $\mathcal{M}$ can be defined as the set $\{w \mid \exists f\ (\langle w, f \rangle \in [\![K]\!]_{\mathcal{M}})\}$. In analogous ways we can also define the intensions in a model $\mathcal{M}$ that are determined by expressions other than sentences. The details are straightforward.

For this to be of any practical use in linguistic analysis we of course also need linguistically motivated predicates and functors that take intensions as arguments. Here it is useful to distinguish between modal and attitudinal predicates and functors, even if it is not possible to draw a sharp line between these categories. As far as modal notions are concerned, there is (to our knowledge) not much work that has been done towards their analysis within a specifically DR-theoretical context. But any of the existing proposals for the analysis of modal words or constructions (including counterfactuals and other conditionals) can be incorporated into DRS-languages once intensional models have been adopted, since all further structure that might be needed (such as, for instance, various Kripkean accessibility relations between worlds) can be imposed on these models. The analysis of propositional attitudes is another matter. The account of propositional attitudes and of the operators (*believes*, *intends*, etc.) that are used in natural language to describe them differs significantly from the paradigm provided by modal logic, and, directly connected with this, from proposals that have been made within other semantic frameworks. This treatment of attitudinal contexts is the topic of the next section.

Not all intensional operators in natural language are sentence operators. Among those which operate on other categories than complete clauses are the *aspect operators*. Of two such operators we caught a passing glimpse in Section 2, when we had to deal with the progressive form *be smiling* and the dispositional reading of *beat*. We treated these as independent verbs, instead of representing their meanings as resulting from applying operators to the semantics of the event verbs *smile* and *beat*, but as we said, that was just a stopgap measure. We had to resort to this because the operators needed for a proper treatment are intensional, and at that point we had no way of handling intensionality.

That the *progressive operator* (which turns *smile* into *be smiling*) is intensional is a long and well-known fact that is connected with one of the classical problems from the theory of aspect, known as the *imperfective paradox* (Dowty 1979; Landman 1992): For some (but not all) VPs it is possible to make a past tense claim in the progressive even when the corresponding non-progressive claim is false. For instance, it can be true to say of someone that she was crossing the street, but false that she crossed the street (for while she was crossing the street she was hit by a truck and so she never made it to the other side). The existence of an event described by the non-progressive *cross the street* is thus not a necessary condition for the truth of the progressive *be crossing the street*; rather, whether the progressive *be crossing the street* applies to a given stretch of activity is a matter of what sorts of events street crossings are. In other words, it is a function of the *property* of being a crossing of the street.

Assuming that the progressive operator, which we represent as PROG, operates at the level of VP, these considerations suggest the following formal representation for the VP of sentence (3b):

(51)
```
         t' s

      t' < n  t' ⊆ s

                   ┌─────────────┐
                   │      e      │
      s: PROG (^e. │             │ )
                   │ e:smile'(x) │
                   └─────────────┘
```

Here the sign ∧ indicates property abstraction over discourse referents occurring in DRSs. Thus the expression

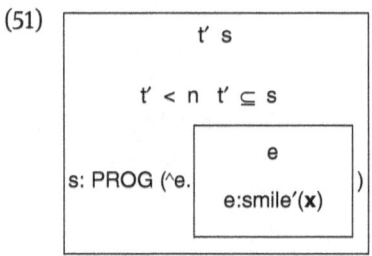

denotes in any intensional model $\mathcal{M}$, and given an individual d of $\mathcal{M}$ (to be thought of as potential value in $\mathcal{M}$ for the discourse referent x' that will eventually replace **x**), the property P which assigns to each w ∈W the set of all events E that satisfy the condition e: smile'(x') when d is assigned to x' (i.e. P(w) is the set of those events E from M(w) for which the function f with f(x') = d and f(e) ∈ E verifies e: smile'(x') in M(w)). The complete representation of sentence (3.b) can then be obtained by an analogous replacement in (13).

Of course, this way of representing progressive verb forms does not solve the classical puzzle connected with the progressive. (It doesn't tell us what must be the case in a model $M(w)$ at a given time t in order that a state s exists in $M(w)$ at t which satisfies the 'PROG'- condition in (51). What (51) illustrates is the general logical form of the progressive operator. This form makes it possible to address the questions surrounding the imperfective paradox within the present DRT-based framework, but that is a task that requires a separate effort.

Dispositional readings of event verbs such as *beat* raise similar issues. Whether the relation expressed by dispositional *beat* – the relation which consists in d beating d' on a regular basis and/or from a disposition of d to do so – obtains at or over a certain period of time isn't just a matter of the number of actual beatings to which d' is subjected by d. Under some circumstances, e.g. when it can be recognised as a manifestation of an already known or suspected mean streak of d's character, even one beating may suffice for describing the relation between d and d' as one of habitual beating. But in other cases that won't be so. (Suppose for instance that d is known as a basically gentle person and that the one beating of d' of which he has made himself guitly was provoked by d' steadfastly refusing to budge and then viciously kicking him the moment it was given the opportunity.)

Thus the dispositional and habitual uses of verbs depend, like the progressive, on more than just the extension of the verb in its basic (non-progressive, non-habitual, non-dispositional) use.

More closely connected with central ideas of DRT are extensions which adopt discourse referents for possible worlds (in addition to those mentioned in earlier sections). The first proposals in this direction go back to the discussions of modal subordination phenomena (Roberts 1986; Roberts 1996; Roberts 1989). Among the examples Roberts discusses are sentence pairs like the following.

(52) A wolf might come in. It would eat you first.

To see how such pairs could be analysed, first consider the slightly different (53).

(53) A wolf might come in. And it might eat you first.

We can analyse (53) by using a discourse referent to represent a possible world of the kind described in the first sentence. We represent the first sentence accordingly as in (54).

(54)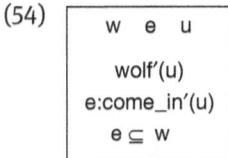

Note well, the evalution of DRS like (54) and the next two in intensional models is not covered by what was said at the begining of this section and requires a separate definition. However, the details of this are quite stright forward and hence are quitted.

We can extend this DRS with the contribution made by the second sentence of (53) by treating its modal operator *might* as anaphoric to the *might* of the first sentence. The world introduced by the second *might* is identified with the one introduced by the first *might*. This leads to the representation in (55).

(55)
$$\boxed{\begin{array}{c} w\ e\ u\ w'\ e'\ v\ a \\ \\ wolf'(u) \\ e{:}come\_in'(u) \\ e \subseteq w \\ w' = w \quad v = u \\ addressee(a) \\ e'{:}eat'(v,a) \\ e' \subseteq w' \end{array}}$$

(52) differs from (53) in that its second sentence seems to involve a universal quantification over worlds: Any world in which a wolf would come in would be one in which it would eat you first. As Roberts saw, an adequate semantic representation requires a new interpretation principle (characteristic of modal subordination phenomena) which treats the representation of the first sentence of (52) as the antecedent of a conditional that has the representation of the second sentence as its consequent. The representation is given in (56).

(56)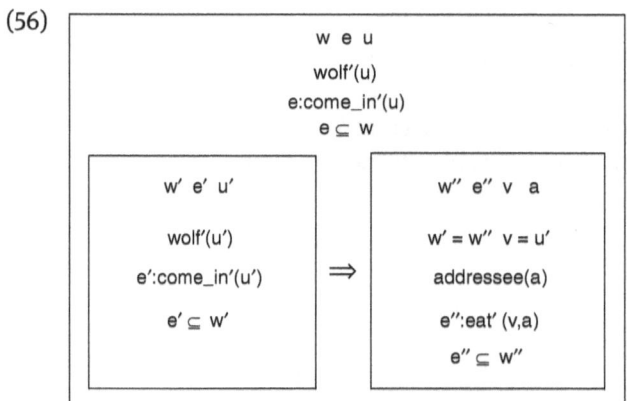

In more recent times the use of discourse referents for worlds has become more common, notably in the work of Bittner (Bittner 2005; Bittner 2007; Bittner 2008) and Brasoveanu (Brasoveanu 2007). (Just as in Montague Grammar the type-language of Gallin, cf. Gallin 1975, has been adopted by many as replacement of Montague's own Higher Order Intensional Logic, HOIL, see Montague 1970b.)

6.3 Propositional attitudes

The classical treatment of belief, knowledge and other propositional attitudes as it has come to us through the work of Carnap, Montague, Kaplan, Lewis and others treats the objects of the attitudes – that which is believed, known, etc. – to be intensions, as defined in the last subsection. There is one major objection to this kind of analysis, often referred to as the problem of logical omniscience: intensions do not allow for distinctions that are sufficiently fine-grained. In particular, any two sentences that are logically equivalent express the same proposition (i.e. propositional intension). An account that takes intensions to be the objects of belief cannot explain how a person could stand in a relation of belief to a sentence S while failing to stand in that relation to a sentence S' in cases where S and S' happen to be logically equivalent, but where this is not so easy to see and the person in question hasn't seen it. If the person professes belief in S but denies belief in S', then all the theory could say is that she must either be wrong about S or about S'. There is wide (if not universal) agreement that this conclusion is incompatible with the actual aetiology of belief.

To obtain an ontology of attitudinal objects that is immune to this objection Asher (Asher 1986; Asher 1993) offers a DRT-based account in which the objects of the attitudes are identified as equivalence classes of DRSs. The equivalence relation that generates these classes is defined in terms of the structural properties of DRSs and is substantially tighter than the relation of logical equivalence in classical logic. This approach has the merit of providing an explicit definition of intensional identity that escapes the problem of logical omniscience (at least in its most obvious and unacceptable manifestations). A potential drawback is that it is hard to see which relation of structural equivalence between DRSs gives us the intuitively correct notion of intensional identity. (The problem seems to be in part that intensional identity varies with context.)

A second DRT-based approach, related to Asher's, but different at certain points, was first outlined in Kamp (1990) and subsequently developed in explicit formal detail in Kamp (2003). (See also Kamp 2006 and van Genabith, Kamp & Reyle (2011)). Here the emphasis is on the development of a representation formalism that is capable of representing not just single propositional attitudes but also combinations of attitudes involving different attitudinal modes – e.g. the combination of a belief and a desire, or of a belief and a doubt. Moreover, it can represent such combinations of two or more attitudes not only for a single agent at a single time, but also combinations of attitudes that a person entertains at different times, or that are held by different persons at the same or at different times. The basic construct of this extension of DRT is a predicate 'Att' whose first argument slot is for the bearer of the represented attitudinal state, while the second slot is for a representation of the attitudinal state that is being ascribed to him. (There is also a third slot, which is reserved for connections between discourse referents occurring in the second slot and objects in the world to which these are anchored, so that these discourse referents function as directly referring terms. For ease of exposition we ignore this slot until further notice; but see the next subsection.) The representations that fill the second slot of 'Att' are sets of pairs consisting of an attitudinal mode indicator (such as BEL for belief, DES for desire, etc.) and a DRS specifying the propositional content of the attitude represented by the pair.

An important feature of this way of representing attitudinal states is that the representations which occur as second members of the pairs may share discourse referents between them. The meaning of a discourse referent x being shared between the content representation K_1 of one attitude (a belief, say) and the content representation K_2 of another attitude (say, a desire) is that the agent to whom this pair of attitudes is ascribed takes his two attitudes to be about one and the same thing 'x'; and this possibility of taking the two attitudes to be about the same x is independent of whether there exists an external object that can be construed as the common referential target of the two attitudes. An example is given in the DRS in (57).

(57)

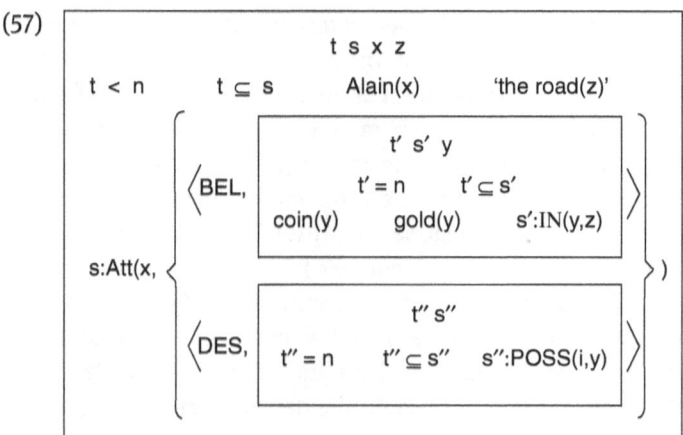

(57) represents the case of a person, Alain, who was, at some time t in the past of the current time n, in a mental state which included a pair of connected attitudes – the belief that there was a gold coin lying in the middle of the road and the desire to be in possesion of this coin. Belief and desire are about the same coin, even if both attitudes are based on a phantasy or a mistake and there is no real object (coin or otherwise) that they could be taken to be about. (The discourse referent i in the last DRS represents the self of the agent; this discourse referent is always used in the representation of properties that the agent attributes to himself – in other words, to represent his de se attitudes, see Lewis 1979.)

Enriching DRS-languages with Att opens up the possibility of representing information about attitudinal states of unlimited complexity. For 'Att' may occur in a DRS K that is part of a pair <MOD,K> occurring as an element of the second argument of another occurrence of 'Att' this makes it possible to represent attitudes of one person about the attitudes of another person (or, for that matter about her own attitudes). Such embeddings can be iterated at libitum.

In the model theory for predicational conditions involving 'Att' that is given in Kamp (2003) and van Genabith, Kamp & Reyle (2011) the possibility of improving on the notoriously problematic ontology of attitudinal objects in terms of classical intensions was given up, partly for the sake of transparency. There would be no difficulty in principle in changing this semantics in favour of one in the spirit of Asher, in which the objects of the attitudes are identified in terms of the syntax of the given DRS language; but other ontological alternatives are in principle possible as well, and a definitive choice should wait until our understanding of the identity conditions for attitudinal objects has improved beyond what it is today.

One important application of the DRT-extension that is obtained by adding the predicate 'Att' is in the semantics of attitude reports (i.e. of the sentences and bits of discourse that are used to ascribe attitudes and attitude complexes to other persons or to oneself). This application requires, in addition to the extension itself, lexical entries for attitudinal predicates - *believe, doubt, intend, learn, belief, intention, acquainted with* – as well as new DRS construction rules for the constituents of the clauses and sentences that serve as complements to such verbs, nouns and adjectives. It should be emphasised, however, that the account we have described is in the first instance an account of the attitudes themselves. More precisely: it is first and foremost an account of mental states that are composed of such attitudes – and only in the second instance of the linguistic forms that natural languages use to describe such mental states and their components.

7 Direct reference and anchors

According to some (we ourselves among them) certain phrases can be used to refer directly. When a phrase α refers directly to an entity d, the link between them guides all possible evaluations of the sentence S to which α belongs, in non-actual circumstances as well as in the actual circumstances in which S is uttered: in each case the evaluation is based on the assumption that α refers to d. In virtue of this direct reference link the proposition expressed by S is a *singular* proposition; it is, to be precise, the *singular* proposition *(expressed by* S *with respect to* α and d), which consists of those worlds w in which d satisfies S when assigned to the argument slot occupied by α.

In DRT terms this can be made explicit as follows. First, let K be a DRS, let x be a discourse referent occurring in the universe of K, $\mathcal{M}$ an intensional model for the DRS language to which K belongs and d an individual of $\mathcal{M}$. Then the *singular proposition expressed in* $\mathcal{M}$ *by* K *with respect to* x *and* d, $[\![K]\!]_{\mathcal{M},\langle x,d \rangle}$ is the set of those worlds w of $W_{\mathcal{M}}$ for which there is an embedding f of the universe of K into the universe of $M(w)$ such that (i) f(x) = d and (ii) f verifies the conditions of K in $M(w)$. (This definition can be generalised straightforwardly to several discourse referents and corresponding individuals in $\mathcal{M}$.)

Second, let K be a DRS for the sentence s and assume that the discourse referent x representing a occurs in the universe of K. Let K' be the DRS obtained from K by deleting from it all contributions that are due to a, except for the two occurrences of x in (i) the universe of K and (ii) the argument position corresponding to the argument position occupied by α in s. (What these deletions come to takes some spelling out and can be made explicit only given a detailed characterisation of the DRS construction algorithm and the language fragment to which it can be applied. But the operations are basically straightforward.) Then the *(singular) proposition expressed by* S *in* $\mathcal{M}$ *with respect to* α *and* d, *given* K is the proposition $[\![K']\!]_{\mathcal{M},\langle x,d \rangle}$.

This is in essence the standard definition of singular propositions expressed by sentences that contain directly referring expressions. But in DRT we are also concerned with the question how content is to be *represented*. So, how can we represent direct reference and its effect on propositional content? The positive answer that DRT offers to this question is connected with the representation of propositional attitudes via the predicate 'Att' that was described in the last section. As we noted there, 'Att' has a third argument slot, which we decided to ignore for the time being. This slot serves to capture the effects of direct reference. Let us return to example (57), and focus on the belief it attributes to Alain, while forgetting about the desire. Let z' and y' be discourse referents that we, as attributors of the belief, use to represent the road and the coin on which the belief we attribute is targeted. Then we can use the formalism of the last section to express that the attributed belief is (doubly) singular – with respect to z and the road and with respect to y and the coin – by inserting in the third argument position of 'Att' *external anchors* for y and z. These external anchors can be given the simple form of ordered pairs <z,z'> and <y,y'>, where z' and y' are again discourse referents, and for the term we insert into the third slot of 'Att' we can use the canonical way of denoting the set consisting of these two anchors, i.e. {<z,z'>, <y,y'>}. If we now also add z' and y' to the universe of the main DRS of (57), then we get a DRS which says that there are two entities (represented by z' and y') such that Alain has a belief that is singular with respect to these entities. The model-theoretic semantics for 'Att' guarantees that the contents of the attributed attitudes are singular propositions in the sense defined above.

We have assumed that in order to entertain a proposition that is singular with respect to an object an agent must (i) stand in some non-representational relation to d (representational relations are inherently descriptive, yielding general, not singular propositional content), and (ii) take himself to stand in such a relation to the object. Thus the discourse referent x he uses to represent the object must on the one hand stand in a non-representational relation to the object (parasitic on the non-representational relation between the object and the agent himself). And on the other hand x must have conditions associated with it at the level of internal representation which express that x is non-representationally connected with the object in the relevant way. A condition, or set of conditions, which expresses that a certain discourse referent is non-representationally connected to the object it represents is called an *internal anchor*.

Sometimes an agent will have an internally anchored discourse referent for which there is no corresponding external anchor. These are cases where the agent is under some kind of illusion, as when he thinks he is seeing a coin in the middle of the road, but, in reality there is nothing there, neither a coin nor some other object that he mistakes for a coin. Such representations are deficient; they presuppose the existence of an external anchor, but the presupposition fails to be true. Strictly speaking such representations have no well-defined propositional content – the content tries to be that of a singular proposition, but doesn't succeed. On the other hand an external anchor for a discourse referent of an internal representation for which there is no matching internal anchor will be irrelevant to propositional content; this content would be the same that it would be if the external anchor didn't exist.

These contributions of DRT to questions of direct reference depend essentially on extending its representation formalism with the predicate 'Att' discussed in the last section. What we said in the concluding paragraph of that section also applies to the contributions to the theory of direct reference discussed in this one: Direct reference, according to the view presented here, is in the first instance an aspect of *thought*; thoughts – beliefs, desires etc – can be directly referential by virtue of involving representations with anchored discourse referents. Utterances can be directly referential as well, but only by virtue of expressing directly referential thoughts.

8 Coverage, extensions of the framework, implementations

8.1 Coverage

The preceding sections have given some impression of the linguistic scope of DRT: Singular and plural DPs of various types; the behaviour of tenses and temporal adverbs, as well as certain aspect operators; presuppositions of any kind; certain modal and intensional operators (the aspect operators among them); propositional attitudes and direct reference. Among contributions to these topics that make a significant use of DRT but have not yet been mentioned are Stirling (1993) on switch reference, Farkas & de Swart (2003) on incorporation, de Swart (1991), Reyle, Rossdeutscher & Kamp (2008) on temporal quantification, and de Swart & Molendijk (1999) on the interaction between tense and negation.

There are also natural language phenomena that so far have not been mentioned at all, but where there is substantial DRT-based work. We mention two: (i) Ellipsis (Hardt 1992; Klein 1987; Asher, Hardt & Busquets 1997; Bos 1993) and (ii) Information Structure (Kamp 2004; Riester 2008).

8.2 Extensions: SDRT and UDRT

DRT has led to a number of extensions that differ from it substantially and that have come to be known by their own names. The best known of these are *S(egmented) DRT* and *U(nderspecified) DRT*. Each of these would need a separate contribution. Rather than compromising by attempting a presentation that would be far too brief to do them justice we limit ourselves here to a mere statement of their goals and a few references. a. SDRT (Asher & Lascarides 1993, 2003): SDRT extends DRT in that it uses DRSs as building blocks of more complex structures in which rhetorical and other discourse relations between the successive sentences that make up a discourse or text are analysed as relations between DRSs representing those sentences. This adds an additional level of discourse structure, with its own principles of structure and computation. SDRT has developed into what is arguably the most sophisticated current approach to some of the most challenging questions on the borderline between semantics and pragmatics. b. UDRT (Reyle 1993; Reyle 1996; Reyle, Rossdeutscher & Kamp 2008): The aims of UDRT are quite different from those of SDRT. UDRT was motivated by the problem of computing DRT's semantic representations – i.e. DRSs – from syntactic input. A major problem that affects the computation of semantic representations generally (whether DRSs or representations of some other form) is that natural language is full of ambiguity. Words are often ambiguous and of the ambiguous words many are multiply ambiguous, with three or more (often many more) different readings. Ambiguity arises also in connection with certain syntactic configurations (e.g. those that give rise to scope ambiguities). But in the practice of language use these ambiguities are much less of a problem than they might have been, for mostly they are resolved by context, provided either by the sentences in which they occur or by the circumstances in which these sentences are produced. For the theorist, however, disambiguation is a challenge; and it is an inexorable challenge for those who try to build effective, semantically sophisticated NLP systems.

Disambiguation is not only an issue that arises in connection with interpreting nearly every sentence we ever come across; it is also something that almost always requires inference. One of the premises for the inferences that are needed for resolving an ambiguity in a given sentence is always the still ambiguous representation of the sentence itself. It is important to structure this representation in such a way that the required inferences can be drawn efficiently. In particular it will as a rule be useful to avoid long sentence level disjunctions in which each disjunct represents a potential complete reading of the reading of the sentence as a whole.

This is the central concern of UDRT. UDRT offers ways of representing ambiguous premises that permit deductions which avoid many of the duplications that are typically involved in such 'proofs by cases'. At the same time the 'underspecified' representations proposed by UDRT (known as 'UDRSs') support the inferences that are typically needed for ambiguity resolution. Thus the inferential component of a UDRT-based system serves a double purpose: (i) assist in ambiguity resolution and (ii) draw inferences from premises for which complete disambiguation can't be achieved. (See also article 9 [Semantics: Lexical Structures and Adjectives] (Egg) *Semantic underspecification*. The advantages of underspecification have been challenged in Ebert 2005.)

8.3 DRT and Dynamic Semantics

DRT has often been compared with Dynamic Semantics as developed by Groenendijk and Stokhof and others (see in particular Groenendijk & Stokhof 1991; Groenendijk & Stokhof 1990; Dekker 1993, as well as article 12 [this volume] (Dekker)

Dynamic semantics). In Dynamic Semantics sentences are explicitly analysed as relations between information states: The meaning of a sentence S manifests itself in the way S changes the information state of one who receives it, interprets it and accepts it. So in Dynamic Semantics it is the concept of meaning itself that has become dynamic (meanings are transformers of information states into other information states), whereas in DRT the notion of meaning remains static. As in classical Montague Grammar meanings in DRT are relations between sentences or texts (or their semantic representations) on the one hand and models or possible worlds on the other hand. Here the dynamics doesn't concern the notion of meaning as such, but the process of interpretation.

Muskens (1994) showed how DRT can be formalised within a version of the λ-calculus (a modest extension of Montague's HOIL) and as part of that how DRSs can be given a compositional relational semantics of the kind proposed by Dynamic Semantics (see also Eijck & Kamp 1997; Muskens, van Benthem & Visser 1997). This is an elegant and insightful way of eating one's cake and having it. Since the mid-nineties this dynamic approach to the analysis of meaning in natural language has been developed further, especially during the past decade in the work of, among others, Bittner and Brasoveanu (Bittner 2005; Bittner 2007; Bittner 2008; Brasoveanu 2007).

8.4 Cognitive significance

From the very beginning one of the central motivations behind DRT has been the hope that it can tell us more about the processes of language interpretation and semantic representation in the human mind than Montague Semantics – the approach out of which DRT developed and which it shares most of its theoretical and methodological commitments – either can or wants to. The DRSs of DRT ought to tell us some things about the form in which we retain the contents that we extract from what we hear or read. One important aspect of this, it has been held, is that the very representations that are formed to represent the content of what has been heard or read so far can serve effectively as contexts for interpreting what comes next.

But can DRSs lay any further claim to being psychologically realistic. This continues to be a topic of debate. There have been some psychological experiments to test the roles of discourse referents in mental representations: for instance, how hard or easy is it for human interpreters to retrieve a discourse referent that is needed as antecedent of a given pronoun, depending on such factors as syntactic complexity, distance between pronoun and antecedent or depth of clausal embedding (Gordon & Hendrick 1998). Unfortunately, the predictions that

DRT could be seen to make about, for instance, the ease or difficulty of antecedent retrieval seem to be too crude to allow for testing by means of established experimental techniques (e.g. timing experiments). Some more refined models of mental processing of language have been made, however, in which DRT serves as general framework.

8.5 Implementation

From its earliest beginnings DRT was conceived not only as a theory of the representation of meaning but also – and inseparably – as a theoretical foundation for the computation of semantic representations by machine. But articulating the principles of DRS construction on paper is not the same thing as building actual systems that compute semantic representations by applying those principles (and that not only for the reasons to which we just drew attention in our remarks on UDRT).

Toy implementations of DRS construction for small, carefully chosen fragments go back almost as far as DRT itself. But developing systems that construct DRSs from unrestricted text (such as, say, a year's worth of the Wall Street Journal) is incomparably harder. Several efforts to build systems with such large scale capacities have been made over the years, some of them also going back to DRT's early days (e.g. the LILOG project, see Herzog & Rollinger 1991). To date the most successful work of this kind would appear to be that of Bos – see e.g. Bos (2008), Bos (2009) – whose implementations have proved serious contenders in recent text processing and semantic inferencing competitions sponsored by representative AI and Computing Consortia.

9 References

Asher, Nicholas 1986. Belief in Discourse Representation Theory. *Journal of Philosophical Logic* 15, 127–189.
Asher, Nicholas 1993. *Reference to Abstract Objects in Discourse.* Dordrecht: Kluwer.
Asher, Nicholas, Daniel Hardt & Joan Busquets 1997. Discourse parallelism, scope, and ellipsis. In: A. Lawson (ed.). *Proceedings of Semantics and Linguistic Theory (=SALT) VII.* Ithaca, NY: Cornell University, 42–62.
Asher, Nicholas & Alex Lascarides 2003. *Logics of Conversation.* Cambridge: Cambridge University Press.
Barwise, Jon & John Perry 1983. *Situations and Attitudes.* Cambridge, MA: The MIT Press.
Beaver, David 1992. The kinematics of presupposition. In: P. Dekker & M. Stokhof (eds.). *Proceedings of the Eighth Amsterdam Colloquium.* Amsterdam: ILLC, 17–36.

Beaver, David 1997. Presupposition. In: J. van Benthem & A. ter Meulen (eds.). *Handbook of Logic and Language*. Amsterdam: Elsevier, 939–1008.

Beaver, David 2002. Presupposition in DRT. In: D. Beaver et al. (eds.). *The Construction of Meaning*. Stanford, CA: CSLI Publications, 23–43.

Beaver, David 2004. Accomodating topics. In: H. Kamp & B. Partee (eds.). *Context-Dependence in the Analysis of Linguistic Meaning*. Amsterdam: Elsevier, 79–90.

Bende-Farkas, Agnes & Hans Kamp 2001. *ESSLLI 2001 Lecture Notes on Indefinites*. Ms. Stuttgart, University of Stuttgart.

Bittner, Maria 2005. Future discourse in a tenseless language. *Journal of Semantics* 22, 339–387.

Bittner, Maria 2007. Online update: Temporal, modal and de se anaphora in polysynthetic discourse. In: Ch. Barker & P. Jacobson (eds.). *Direct Compositionality*. Oxford: Oxford University Press, 363–404.

Bittner, Maria 2008. Aspectual universals of temporal anaphora. In: S. Rothstein (ed.). *Theoretical and Crosslinguistic Approaches to the Semantics of Aspect*. Amsterdam: Benjamins, 349–385.

Boolos, George 1984. To be is to be the value of a variable (or some values of some variables). *Journal of of Philosophy* 81, 430–450.

Bos, Johan 1993. *VP Ellipsis and Presupposition in an Implementation of Discourse Representation Theory*. MA thesis. University of Groningen.

Bos, Johan 2008. Wide-coverage semantic analysis with Boxer. In: J. Bos & R. Delmonte (eds.). *Semantics in Text Processing. STEP 2008 Conference Proceedings*. London: College Publications, 277–286.

Bos, Johan 2009. Towards a large-scale formal semantic lexicon for text processing. In: R. Eckart de Castilho, C. Chiarcos & M. Stede (eds.). *From Form to Meaning: Processing Texts Automatically. Proceedings of the Biennal GSCL Conference 2009*. Tübingen: Narr, 3–14.

Brasoveanu, Adrian 2007. *Structured Nominal and Modal Reference*. Ph.D. dissertation. Rutgers University, New Brunswick, NJ.

Dekker, Paul 1993. *Transsentential Meditations. Ups and Downs in Dynamic Semantics*. Ph.D. dissertation. University of Amsterdam. Reprinted: Amsterdam: ILLC Publications.

Dowty, David 1979. *Word Meaning and Montague Grammar*. Dordrecht: Reidel.

Ebert, Christian 2005. *Formal Investigations of Underspecified Representations*. Ph.D. dissertation. King's College London.

van Eijck, Jan & Hans Kamp 1997. Representing discourse in context. In: J. van Benthem & A. ter Meulen (eds.). *Handbook of Logic an Language*. Amsterdam: Elsevier, 179–237.

Elbourne, Paul D. 2005. *Situations and Individuals*. Cambridge, MA: The MIT Press.

Farkas, Donka F. & Henriëtte de Swart 2003. *The Semantics of Incorporation: From Argument Structure to Discourse Transparency*. Stanford, CA: CSLI Publications.

Gallin, Daniel 1975. *Intensional and Higher Order Logic; With Applications to Montague Semantics*. Amsterdam: North-Holland.

Geach, Peter T. 1962. *Reference and Generality: An Examination of Some Medieval and Modern Theories*. Ithaca, NY: Cornell University Press.

van Genabith, Josef, Hans Kamp & Uwe Reyle 2011. Discourse Representation Theory. In: D. Gabbay & F. Guenthner (eds.). *Handbook of Philosophical Logic*. 2nd edn. Dordrecht: Springer, 123–394.

Geurts, Bart 1994. *Presupposition*. Doctoral dissertation. University of Stuttgart.

Geurts, Bart 1999. *Presuppositions and Pronouns*. Amsterdam: Elsevier.

Geurts, Bart & Rob van der Sandt 1999. Presuppositions and backgrounds. In: P. Dekker, M. Stokhof & Y. Venema (eds.). *Proceedings of the 11th Amsterdam Colloquium*. Amsterdam: ILLC.
Gordon, Peter C. & Randall Hendrick 1998. The representation and processing of coreference in discourse. *Cognitive Science* 22, 389–424.
Groenendijk, Jeroen & Martin Stokhof 1990. Dynamic Montague Grammar. In: L. Kalman & L. Polos (eds.). *Papers from the Second Symposium on Logic and Language*. Budapest: Akademiai Kiadoo, 3–48.
Groenendijk, Jeroen & Martin Stokhof 1991. Dynamic Predicate Logic. *Linguistics & Philosophy* 14, 39–100.
Hamm, Fritz & Hans Kamp 2009. Ontology and inference: The case of German *ung*-nominals. In: A. Roßdeutscher (ed.). *Disambiguation and Reambiguation* (SinSpeC 06. Working Papers of the SFB 732 *Incremental Specification in Context*). Stuttgart: University of Stuttgart.
Hardt, Daniel 1992. An algorithm for VP ellipsis. In: D. Appelt (ed.). *Proceedings of the 30th Annual Meeting of the Association for Computational Linguistics (= ACL)*. Newark, DE: ACL, 9–14.
Heim, Irene 1982. *The Semantics of Definite and Indefinite Noun Phrases*. Ph.D. dissertation. University of Massachusetts, Amherst, MA. Reprinted: Ann Arbor, MI: University Microfilms.
Heim, Irene 1983. On the projection problem for presuppositions. In: D. Flickinger et al. (eds.). *Proceedings of the Second West Coast Conference on Formal Linguistics*. Stanford, CA: Stanford University Press, 114–125.
Heim, Irene 1990. E-type pronouns and donkey anaphora. *Linguistics & Philosophy* 13, 137–177.
Herzog, Otthein & Claus-Rainer Rollinger (eds.) 1991. *Text Understanding in LILOG*. Berlin: Springer.
Kamp, Hans 1968. *Tense Logic and the Theory of Order*. Ph.D. dissertation. University of California, Los Angeles, CA.
Kamp, Hans 1981a. A theory of truth and semantic representation. In: J. Groenendijk, T. Janssen & M. Stokhof (eds.). *Formal Methods in the Study of Language*. Amsterdam: Mathematical Centre, 277–322.
Kamp, Hans 1981b. Evénements, representation discursive et reference temporelle. *Langages* 64, 39–64.
Kamp, Hans 1990. Prolegomena to a structural account of belief and other attitudes. In: C. A. Anderson & J. Owens (eds.). *Propositional Attitudes – The Role of Content in Logic, Language, and Mind*. Stanford, CA: CSLI Publications, 27–90.
Kamp, Hans 2001a. The importance of presupposition. In: Ch. Rohrer, A. Roßdeutscher & H. Kamp (eds.). *Liguistic Form and its Computation*. Stanford, CA: CSLI Publications, 207–254.
Kamp, Hans 2001b. Presupposition computation and presupposition justification. In: M. Bras & L. Vieu (eds.). *Pragmatic and Semantic Issues in Discourse and Dialogue*. Amsterdam: Elsevier, 57–84.
Kamp, Hans 2003. Einstellungszustände und -zuschreibungen in der DRT. In: U. Haas-Spohn (ed.). *Intentionalität zwischen Subjektivität und Weltbezug*. Paderborn: mentis, 209–289.
Kamp, Hans 2004. Information structure in a dynamic theory of meaning. In: *Proceedings of the Linguistic Society of Korea Conference*, Seoul.
Kamp, Hans 2006. Temporal reference inside and outside propositional attitudes. In: K. von Heusinger & K. Turner (eds.). *Where Semantics Meets Pragmatics*. Amsterdam: Elsevier, 439–472.

Kamp, Hans & Uwe Reyle 1993. *From Discourse to Logic*. Dordrecht: Kluwer.
Kamp, Hans & Antje Roßdeutscher 1992. *Remarks on Lexical Structure, DRS-Construction and Lexically Driven Inferences* (Arbeitspapiere des Sonderforschungsbereichs 340, 21). Stuttgart: University of Stuttgart.
Kamp, Hans & Antje Roßdeutscher 1994a. DRS-construction and lexically driven inferences. *Theoretical Linguistics* 20, 165–235.
Kamp, Hans & Antje Roßdeutscher 1994b. Remarks on lexical structure and DRS-construction. *Theoretical Linguistics* 20, 97–164.
Kaplan, David 1989. Demonstratives. In: H. Wettstein, J. Almog & J. Perry (eds.). *Themes form Kaplan*. Oxford: Oxford University Press, 481–564.
Karttunen, Lauri 1973. Presuppositions of compound sentences. *Linguistic Inquiry* 4, 169–193.
Karttunen, Lauri 1974. Presupposition and linguistic context. *Theoretical Linguistics*, 181–194.
Kibble, Rodger 1997. Complement anaphora and dynamic binding. In: A. Lawson (ed.). *Proceedings of Semantics and Linguistic Theory (= SALT) VII*. Ithaca, NY: Cornell University, 258–275.
Kiparsky, Paul & Carol Kiparsky 1970. Fact. In: M. Bierwisch & K. Heidolph (eds.). *Progress in Linguistics*. The Hague: Mouton, 143–173.
Klein, Ewald 1987. VP ellipsis in DR theory. In: J. Groenendijk, D. de Jongh & M. Stokhof (eds.). *Studies in Discourse Representation Theory and the Theory of Generalized Quantifiers*. Dordrecht: Foris, 161–187.
Kripke, Saul 2009. Presuppositions and anaphora: Remarks on the formulation of the projection problem. *Journal of Philosophy* 40, 367–386.
Landman, Fred 1992. The progressive. *Natural Language Semantics* 1, 1–32.
Langendoen, Terrence & Harris Savin 1971. The projection problem for presuppositions. In: C. Filmore & T. Langendoen (eds.). *Studies in Linguistic Semantics*. New York: Holt, Rinehart & Winston, 55–62.
Lascarides, Alex & Nicholas Asher 1993. Temporal interpretation, discourse relations, and commonsense entailment. *Linguistics & Philosophy* 16, 437–449.
Lechler, Andrea & Antje Roßdeutscher 2009. German particle verbs with *auf*. Reconstructing their composition in a DRT-based framework. *Linguistische Berichte* 220, 439–478.
Lerner, Jean-Yves & Manfred Pinkal 1995. Comparative ellipsis and variable binding. In: M. Simons & T. Galloway (eds.). *Proceedings of Semantics and Linguistic Theory (= SALT) V*. Ithaca, NY: Cornell University, 222–236.
Lewis, David 1979. Attitudes de dicto and de se. *Philosophical Review* 88, 513–543.
Mann, William & Sandra Thompson 1988. Rhetorical Structure Theory: Toward a functional theory of text organization. *Text* 8, 243–281.
Montague, Richard 1970a. Universal Grammar. *Theoria* 36, 373–398.
Montague, Richard 1970b. Pragmatics and Intensional Logic. *Synthese* 22, 68–94.
Montague, Richard 1973. The proper treatment of quantification in ordinary English. In: J. Hintikka, J. Moravcsik & P. Suppes (eds.). *Approaches to Natural Language*. Dordrecht: Reidel, 221–242.
Musan, Renate 1995. *On the Temporal Interpretation of Noun Phrases*. Ph.D. dissertation. MIT, Cambridge, MA.
Muskens, Reinhard 1994. A Compositional Discourse Representation Theory. In: P. Dekker & M. Stokhof (eds.). *Proceedings of the 9th Amsterdam Colloquium*. Amsterdam: ILLC, 467–486.
Muskens, Reinhard, Johan van Benthem & Albert Visser 1997. Dynamics. In: J. van Benthem & A. ter Meulen (eds.). *Handbook of Logic and Language*. Amsterdam: Elsevier, 587–648.

Nouwen, Rick 2003. Complement anaphora and interpretation. *Journal of Semantics* 20, 73–113.
Partee, Barbara 1973. Some structural analogies between tenses and pronouns in English. *Journal of Philosophy* 70, 601–609.
Prior, Arthur 1967. *Past, Present and Future*. Oxford: Clarendon Press.
Reyle, Uwe 1993. Dealing with ambiguities by underspecification: Construction, representation and deduction. *Journal of Semantics* 10, 123–179.
Reyle, Uwe 1996. Co-indexing labeled DRSs to represent and reason with ambiguities. In: K. van Deemter & S. Peters (eds.). *Semantic Ambiguity and Underspecification*. Stanford, CA: CSLI Publications, 239–268.
Reyle, Uwe, Antje Roßdeutscher & Hans Kamp 2008. Ups and downs in the theory of temporal reference. *Linguistics & Philosophy* 30, 565–635.
Riester, Arndt 2008. A semantic explication of information status and the underspecification of the recipients' knowledge. In: A. Grønn (ed.). *Proceedings of Sinn und Bedeutung* 12. Oslo: University of Oslo, 508–522.
Riester, Arndt & Hans Kamp 2010. Squiggly issues: Alternative sets, complex DPs, and intensionality. In: M. Aloni & K. Schulz (eds.). *Proceedings of the 17th Amsterdam Colloquium*. Amsterdam: ILLC. http://www.ims-stuttgart.de/~arndt/doc/ riesterKampAC09.pdf. December 15, 2010.
Roberts, Craige 1986. *Modal Subordination, Anaphora, and Distributivity*. Ph.D. dissertation. University of Massaschusetts, Amherst, MA.
Roberts, Craige 1989. Modal subordination and pronominal anaphora in discourse. *Linguistics & Philosophy* 12, 683–721.
Roberts, Craige 1996. Anaphora in intensional contexts. In: S. Lappin (ed.). *The Handbook of Contemporary Semantic Theory*. Oxford: Blackwell, 215–246.
Rooth, Mats 1987. NP interpretation in Montague Grammar, File Change Semantics and Situation Semantics. In: P. Gärdenfors (ed.). *Generalized Quantifiers: Linguistic and Logical Approaches*. Dordrecht: Reidel, 237–269.
Roßdeutscher, Antje 1994. Fat child meets DRT. A semantic representation for the opening lines of Kaschnitz' "Das dicke Kind". *Theoretical Linguistics* 20, 237–305.
Roßdeutscher, Antje 2000. *Lexikalisch gestützte formale Textinterpretation* (Arbeitsberichte des Sonderforschungsbereichs 340, 157). Stuttgart: University of Stuttgart.
van der Sandt, Rob 1992. Presupposition projection as anaphora resolution. *Journal of Semantics* 9, 333–377.
van der Sandt, Rob & Bart Geurts 1991. *Presupposition, Anaphora, and Lexical Content*. Technical Report 185. Stuttgart, IWBS, IBM Germany.
Solstad, Torgrim 2007. Lexical pragmatics and unification: The semantics of German causal 'durch'. *Research on Language and Computation* 5, 481–502.
Stalnaker, Robert 1972. Pragmatics. In: D. Davidson & G. Harman (eds.). *Semantics of Natural Language*. Dordrecht: Reidel, 380–397.
Stalnaker, Robert 1974. Pragmatic presuppositions. In: M.K. Munitz & P.K. Unger (eds.). *Semantics and Philosophy*. New York: New York University Press, 197–213.
Stalnaker, Robert 1979. Assertion. In: P. Cole (ed.). *Syntax and Semantics 9: Pragmatics*. New York: Academic Press, 315–332.
Stirling, Lesley 1993. *Switch-reference and Discourse Representation*. Cambridge: Cambridge University Press.
de Swart, Henriëtte 1991. *Adverbs of Quantification: A Generalized Quantifier Approach*. Ph.D. dissertation. University of Groningen.

de Swart, Henriëtte & Arie Molendijk 1999. Negation and the temporal structure of narrative discourse. *Journal of Semantics* 16, 1–42.
Tonhauser, Judith 2000. *Dynamic Semantics and the Temporal Interpretation of Noun Phrases.* MA thesis. University of Stuttgart.
Vlach, Frank 1973. *'Now' and 'Then': A Formal Study in the Logic of Tense Anaphora.* Ph.D. dissertation. University of California, Los Angeles, CA.
Williams, Edwin 1977. Discourse and logical form. *Linguistic Inquiry* 8, 101–139.

Paul Dekker
12 Dynamic semantics

1   Introduction —— 385
2   Dynamic predicate logic —— 391
3   Pragmatic generalizations —— 399
4   Methodological issues —— 407
5   References —— 410

Abstract: In this article we give an introduction to the idea and workings of dynamic semantics. We start with an overview of its historical background and motivation. An in-depth description of a paradigm version of dynamic semantics, Dynamic Predicate Logic, is given in section 2. In section 3 we show how the dynamic paradigm can be used to account for a number of empirical phenomena, and we discuss some extensions of the basic paradigm, systematically incorporating previously deemed pragmatic aspects of meaning. We conclude with a discussion of some theoretical issues surrounding dynamic semantics in section 4.

1 Introduction

1.1 Theoretical background

What is dynamic semantics? Some people claim it embodies a radical new view of meaning, departing from the main logical paradigm as it has been prominent in most of the twentieth century. Meaning is not some abstract Platonic entity, but it is something that changes information states. "Natural languages are programming languages for minds", it has been said. A more modest way of putting the same point consists in acknowledging that natural language is not only devised to describe an independently given world. Natural languages have other points and there are lots of other functions of language than just a descriptive one. Eventually a theory of natural language meaning ought to extend the standardly given framework of a descriptive or referential semantics, and seek to incorporate arguably pragmatic aspects of interpretation. The term 'dynamic semantics' may serve as a generic label for this type of theorizing that does not deny its well-established philosophical, logical, and linguistic roots. Historically, dynamic semantics emerged as a focal point of developments in philosophy, psychology, artificial intelligence, and linguistics.

Paul Dekker, Amsterdam, The Netherlands

The interplay between language, meaning, knowledge and belief has become one of the major philosophical themes in the late 19th and the early 20th century in the writings of Frege, Peirce, Russell, Wittgenstein, Carnap and Tarski, all of them sharing the interest in a core notion of truth. From the very start, it has been acknowledged that the issues of truth and meaning are hard to separate from matters of context and use. In the second half of the 20th century Wittgenstein, and fellow philosophers like Strawson, Austin, and Grice have made the use of language a matter of focal concern. From there it is a relatively small step to a conception of meaning as something that is both context dependent, and capable of changing the very same context, a dynamic notion of meaning, that is.

In the second half of the 20th century, in the area of cognitive psychology, meaning has been located in the mind, and cognitively oriented approaches endorsed by Fodor, Lakoff, and Jackendoff, have taken recourse to mental languages, as the internalized carriers of meanings. No matter their misgivings, the view of the mind as a goal directed information processor has gained prominence, and it has inspired the study of language as a means for updating and processing information. The prominent framework of discourse representation theory has been put forward with the aim of reconciling the psychologically realistic models of interpretation with those of a logico-philosophical nature.

The later quarter of the 20th century witnessed the development of dynamic logics in the area of computer science. Dynamic logics give one the tools to reason about, e.g., correctness, and termination conditions of computer programs. Programs here are abstractly understood as certain transformations of computer states, induced, for instance, by runs of a program. Formally characterized these are relations on computer states, viz., the so-called input–output relation of runs of the program. This perspective on programming languages has been taken as a metaphor for natural language, so that the meanings of sentences can be conceived of as state transformers as well.

The three developments mentioned, in philosophy, psychology and artificial intelligence, have provided a breeding ground for the type of dynamic semantics discussed in this article. Its conception didn't come without a proper logico-linguistic motivation, though. There was motivation internal to linguistic theorizing as well.

1.2 The linguistic impetus

A variety of linguistic observations point to the need of a dynamic semantics for natural language or, at least, a dynamic account of interpretation. Consider the following simple examples.

(1) a. A dog enters the garden. It is barking.
    b. ?It is barking. A dog enters the garden.

(2) a. If a cat is hungry it usually meows.
    b. ?It usually meows if a cat is hungry.

In both (1a) and (2a), a pronoun appears well-behaved, since it is preceded by a noun phrase, an indefinite one here, which may serve as its antecedent. Turning things around, as in examples (1b) and (2b) produces an odd discourse though, or at least one in which the pronouns have to be resolved differently. This phenomenon is often explained by saying that the indefinite noun phrase may 'set up a discourse referent' which can be 'referred back to' by a subsequent pronoun.

Basically the same goes for definite descriptions.

(3) a. Mike has children. Mikes sons are blues and his daughters are soul.
    b. Mikes sons are blues and his daughters are soul. Mike has children.

Once we have 'introduced' Mike's children, we are entitled to talk about his sons and daughters, but if we already have talked about Mike's sons and daughters it doesn't make sense to say he has children. (Or the conclusion should be more pregnant, as with "Well, you know, that's what it means, 'having children'!")

The following pair of examples has to do with presuppositions.

(4) a. Rebecca married Thomas. She regrets that she married him.
    b. Rebecca regrets that she married Thomas. ?She married him.

Since one can regret only something which has happened, it is odd to state that Rebecca married Thomas after we already heard she did, when she was said to have regretted it. The next examples display specific discourse relations.

(5) a. Bob left. Conny started to cry.
    b. Conny started to cry. Bob left.

If the two reported events are ordered as they are presented in (5a), Bob's leaving seems by default to precede, and cause, Conny's crying; if they are reported as presented in (5b), Conny appears to have cried first, and then, and probably therefore, Bob left. Of course, it is possible to read the examples in a different way. The main point is that *some* relation between the reported events gets assumed, that the interpretation of the two sentences must allow for such a connection, and that the order of presentation matters.

Discourse acts are also intrinsically ordered. The following sentence may be true, when uttered, but a successful assertion of it cannot be successfully repeated.

(6) Phoebe is waiting at your door, and you don't know it!

Apparently, saying something may affect such a change in the context that what is said, which was true when uttered first, turns out false afterwards.

The final examples are conditionals, in which, arguably, the antecedent (or *if-*) clause 'sets the stage' for the consequent clause. The classical example is called a 'donkey sentence', in the folklore.

(7) If a farmer owns a donkey he (normally) beats it.

Of course one may ask "Who beats what?", and there seems to be no definite answer, other than a conditional one, viz., "The farmer who owns a donkey, and the donkey that that farmer owns, in situations in which a farmer owns a donkey." Clearly, such an answer can only be given relative to such possible situations as set up by the antecedent clause. Finally look at examples (8a) and (8b).

(8) a. If Isabel is in the bathroom, Petra might be there, too.
    b. If Isabel is in the bathroom and nobody else is, Petra might be there, too.

The first example is perfectly acceptable, whereas the second is up to inconsistent. From a standard logical perspective this is rather strange. For if Isabel is in the bathroom and nobody else is, then, logically speaking, Isabel is in the bathroom, so with example (8a) we might want to conclude that Petra might be there, too. But we should not conclude this, because if there is nobody else, then neither is Petra.

The above are only a limited number of examples which show the need of a dynamic notion of interpretation. They show that one cannot always swap two conjuncts, or reverse a conditional, or repeat a sentence. They show that language depends on context, and that it changes the context, in discourse, but also in sentences themselves.

1.3 Discourse representation theory

A dynamic perspective has been adopted in the seminal Kamp (1984), which was intended to bridge the apparent gap between formal logic oriented approaches to the semantics of natural language, and the cognitive models of reasoning from cognitive psychology. To this end, a version of the language of first order predicate logic gets employed as an indispensable ingredient in the interpretation of natural language. This representation language serves two main roles at the same time. On the one hand, it is used to state the contents, viz., truth conditions, of natural language utterances, or rather of that of whole discourses. On the other hand, it makes up an essential ingredient in the process of interpretation, since already established representations may be key to the understanding of parts which are to come. They mimick, so to speak, the models the cognitive agents make of the discourse as it has been interpreted till a certain point. The ensuing architecture is aptly called *Discourse Representation Theory (DRT)*. (See also article 11 [this volume] (Kamp & Reyle) *Discourse Representation Theory*.)

By way of illustration, the *DRS*s in (10) serve to represent the rudimentary contents of a small, fancy discourse like (9) at three stages in its interpretation.

(9) Once upon a time there was an old king, who didn't have a son. He did have a daughter, though. Whenever she saw a frog, she kissed it.

(10)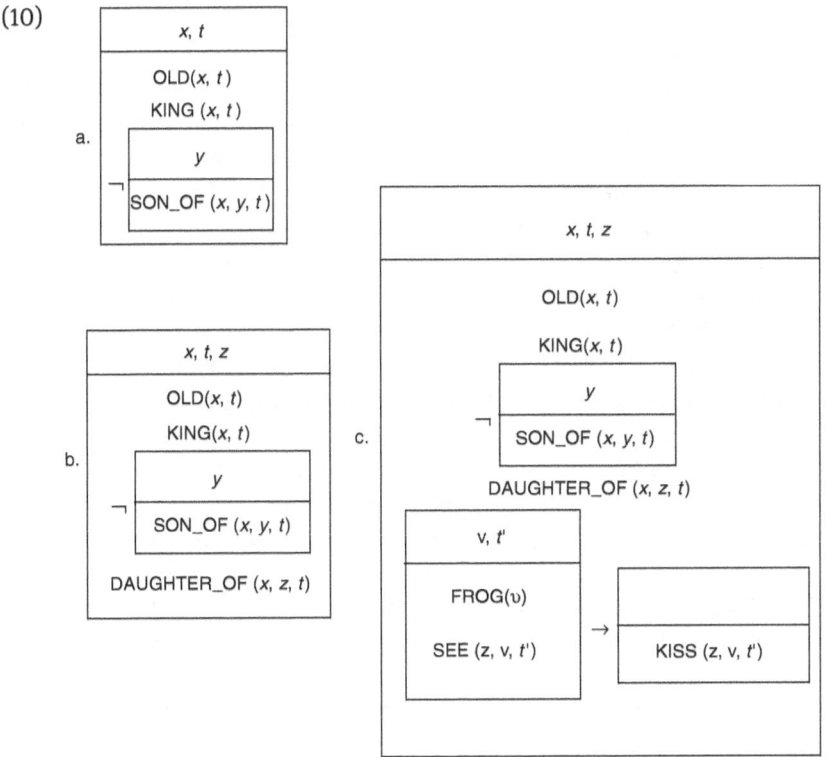

These three *DRS*s represent the contents of the discourse in (9) after processing the first sentence (10a), the first two sentences (10b), and after processing the whole (10c). Notice that the material contributed by the second and the third sentence gets added *in* the representations that result from processing the first and the first two sentences. In this way, the pronouns *he* and *she* are appropriately related to the established domain of discourse.

1.4 Historical remarks

We end this introductory section with some historical remarks on the treatment of indefinite anaphoric relationships in terms of discourse reference. The subject has gained prominence by, among many others, the logico-philosophical (Geach 1962), and the seminal but relatively informal work on discourse reference in Karttunen (1968). Kamp (1984) and Heim (1988) were the first, independently, to present a formal framework of interpretation for anaphoric phenomena, *DRT* and *File Change Semantics (FCS)* respectively. (Slightly misleadingly, both were classified as theories of discourse representation at the time. Heim's main concern was not the representation of discourse, but a compositional architecture of interpretation.)

After *DRT* had settled as one of the major semantic frameworks, the need for a more classical and arguably semantic approach developed, and this gave rise to the theories of interpretation of Staudacher, of Barwise and of Groenendijk and Stokhof, the last one of these gained most prominence. These systems, and their off-spring, have generally been labeled as 'non-representational', 'compositional', and 'dynamic'. Many alternatives, notational variants, and extensions gained their way in the nineties of the previous century. Some were almost indistinguishable from Heim's own 'non-representational' formulation of her File Change Semantics. Others were tailored for algebraic and computational applications (Zeevat 1989; Vermeulen & Visser 1996; van Eijck 2001). A detailed overview of the field of dynamic logics can be found in (Muskens, van Benthem & Visser 1997). Of course, discourse representation theory remained an attractive framework. Simultaneously so-called E-type approaches and epsilon- or choice function approaches, which already existed before the dynamic turn, established themselves as appealing non-dynamic treatments of indefinite anaphora. (See, for instance, Barker 1997 and Slater 2000; von Heusinger 2004.) However, although these approaches have established a lively tradition, they didn't gain the status of a rival *framework*, simply because they were tailored to giving a treatment of indefinites and pronouns in a standard framework of interpretation.

2 Dynamic predicate logic

Dynamic Predicate Logic (henceforth: *DPL*, Groenendijk & Stokhof 1991), has emerged as a reply to *DRT*'s representational treatment of anaphoric relationships. Implicit in *DRT*'s presentation and part of its appeal is the idea that a realistic account of interpretation should take into account the representations people make up of the contents of an ongoing discourse they are engaged in. Anaphora appears to be a strong case in point. The interpretation of pronouns consists in establishing a relation of coreference with a term, which is (part of) a representation of a referent.

One of the main philosophical or methodological points of *DPL* – as a matter of fact this is something that is presented as a demonstrative proof – is that at least the phenomenon of anaphora, after all, does not motivate a representational architecture of interpretation. It is submitted that, as many people have realized, the treatment is problematic in standard architectures, like that of, e.g., Montague grammar, but this only shows that *some* modification of such architectures is called for. In *DPL*, an arguably non-representational but dynamic account is presented of the data *DRT* was originally developed for.

2.1 Dynamic interpretation

In *DPL* the dynamics of interpretation is concerned with information about referents that may get introduced in a discourse, and which may serve as possible antecedents for subsequent anaphoric pronouns. This idea is fleshed out in a most immediate way. Noun phrases are associated with indices, or variables, so as to indicate cases of coreference and binding. The kind of information concerned is information about the possible values of these variables, and these possible values may get changed and updated in a discourse.

Consider the following little discourse, with indices (variables) on the relevant noun phrases, and some 'check-points ✓' for evaluation.

(11) ✓^{0} Mary borrowed (a copy of *Naming and Necessity*)$_x$ from (a professor in linguistics)$_y$. ✓^{1} (The)$_x$ pages were covered with comments and exclamation marks. ✓^{2} (He)$_y$ must have been studying (it)$_x$ intensively. ✓^{3}

At check-point 0 we have no information about the discourse, besides, possibly, some preliminary observations beyond the scope of *DPL*. At check-point 1 a copy of *Naming and Necessity* has been introduced, with label x, and a professor in linguistics, with label y, and these are dressed with the information that

Mary borrowed copy x from professor y. At check-point 2 copy x is qualified as worn-out, and at check-point 3, finally, the supposition is added that professor y studied the copy x intensively.

These informal observations have been implemented formally in the system of *DPL* in the following way. The language of (first order) predicate logic is taken as the representational medium. Information about the values of variables is encoded in variable assignments, and for any formula ϕ, the interpretation of ϕ relative to an ordinary model M, $[[\phi]]_M$, is a set of pairs of variable assignments $\langle g, h \rangle$. The idea is that such a pair $\langle g, h \rangle$ is in the interpretation of ϕ relative to M if, and only if, ϕ can be successfully interpreted upon input assignment g, and yield assignment h as a possible output. The meanings of formulas can be conceived of as tests upon, and changes in, the information about the possible values of variables.

A language L for *DPL* is an ordinary language for first order logic, based on a set of individual constants, sets of relational constants R of arity n, and a set of variables. Formulas are built up from atomic formulas using negation ($\neg$), existential and universal quantification ($\exists x$, $\forall y$), and conjunction ($\wedge$), disjunction ($\vee$), and (material) implication ($\rightarrow$). Interpretation is defined relative to the usual models $M = \langle D, I \rangle$, consisting of a domain of individuals D and an interpretation function I for the individual and relational constants of L. The interpretation function I assigns an individual $I(c) \in D$ to the individual constants c of L and a set of n-tuples of individuals $I(R) \subseteq D^n$ to its n-ary relational constants R.

In the interpretation of *DPL* we use variable assignments, g, h, k, l, ..., which assign individuals $g(x) \in D$ to the variables x of L. The interpretation $[t]_{M,g}$ of a term t in a model M, and relative to assignment g, is $I(t)$ if t is an individual constant and $g(t)$ if t is a variable. In what follows we use $g[x/d]$ for the variable assignment h that is like g except that it assigns d to x. We say $g[x]h$ iff assignment $h = g[x/d]$ for some individual d, and we say $g[X]h$ iff $X = \{x_1, ..., x_n\}$ and there are $k_1, ..., k_{n-1}$ such that $g[x_1]k_1, ...,$ and $k_{n-1}[x_n]h$. Armed with these notation devices we can state the semantics of *DPL* as follows.

Definition 1 (DPL Semantics)

$$[[Rt_1...t_n]]_M = \{\langle g, h \rangle \mid g = h \text{ and } \langle [t_1]_{M,g},...,[t_n]_{M,g} \rangle \in I(R)\}$$

$$[[t_i = t_j]]_M = \{\langle g, h \rangle \mid g = h \text{ and } [t_i]_{M,g} = [t_j]_{M,g}\}$$

$$[[\neg\phi]]_M = \{\langle g, h \rangle \mid g = h \text{ and for no } k: \langle g, k \rangle \in [[\phi]]_M\}$$

$$[[\exists x\phi]]_M = \{\langle g, h \rangle \mid \text{for some } k: g[x]k \text{ and } \langle k, h \rangle \in [[\phi]]_M\}$$

$[\![\phi \wedge \psi]\!]_M$ = $\{\langle g, h\rangle \mid$ for some k: $\langle g, k\rangle \in [\![\phi]\!]_M$ and $\langle k, h\rangle \in [\![\psi]\!]_M\}$

$[\![\forall x\phi]\!]_M$ = $\{\langle g, h\rangle \mid g = h$ and for all k: if $g[x]k$

then there is h: $\langle k, h\rangle \in [\![\phi]\!]_M\}$

$[\![\phi \vee \psi]\!]_M$ = $\{\langle g, h\rangle \mid g = h$ and for some k: $\langle g, k\rangle \in [\![\phi]\!]_M$

or for some k: $\langle g, k\rangle \in [\![\psi]\!]_M\}$

$[\![\phi \rightarrow \psi]\!]_M$ = $\{\langle g, h\rangle \mid g = h$ and for all k: if $\langle g, k\rangle \in [\![\phi]\!]_M$

then there is h: $\langle k, h\rangle \in [\![\psi]\!]_M\}$

Most clauses require the input assignment g and output assignment h to be the same, besides some standard predicate logical conditions. For instance, if an atomic formula like $Rt_1... t_n$ or $t_i = t_j$ is true relative to M and g then the input-output pair $\langle g, g\rangle$ is in the interpretation of such a formula. Intuitively this says that, if the standard test succeeds, g is accepted as possible input and the interpretation of the formula does not change anything in its output. If the test fails then g is not accepted as possible input and in that case there is no assignment h such that $\langle g, h\rangle$ is in the interpretation of that formula.

Exactly when this is the case, that is, when the conditions imposed by a formula ϕ upon M and g is not satisfied, then its negation *is* satisfied, and g is a possible input for $\neg\phi$ relative to M. In other words, if ϕ cannot be executed upon input g, then $\neg\phi$ can, and its interpretation will yield g again as output. Apart from the clauses for existentially quantified formulas and conjunctions, the other clauses in the definition are also static, in the sense that they do not allow input assignments to really change. The associated conditions are straightforward adjustments of the static interpretation of the embedded formulas to the dynamic (relational) interpretation. Only the interpretation of an implication is a bit more involved. An implication $(\phi \rightarrow \psi)$ is satisfied (relative to M and g) iff relative to all ways of satisfying ϕ on input g in M, ψ is true as well. Since ψ here gets evaluated relative to outputs (k) of interpreting ϕ, dynamic effects of ϕ may affect the interpretation of ψ.

Changes in assignment functions are due to the interpretation of existentially quantified formulas. According to the above definition, if we have some input assignment g, then the interpretation of $\exists x\phi$ requires us to try out any assignment k which differs from g only in its valuation of x, then see if it serves as an input for interpreting ϕ, and if it does and outputs h, then h is also a possible output for interpreting $\exists x\phi$ on input g. Notice that if x indeed, as in most examples, occurs free in ϕ, and ϕ imposes certain conditions on the valuation of x, then the output valuation of x will have to satisfy these conditions. Metaphorically speaking, a 'discourse referent' with the properties attributed to x is introduced by such a formula, and it is labeled with the variable x.

A conjunction does not change any context all by itself, but it does preserve, or rather compose, possible changes brought about by the combined conjuncts. That is to say, if ϕ accepts an input g and produce some possibly different output k, and if ψ accepts k as input and delivers h as possible output, then the conjunction $(\phi \wedge \psi)$ accepts g as possible input upon which h is a possible output. This implements the dynamic idea that the interpretation of $(\phi \wedge \psi)$ involves the interpretation of ϕ first and ψ next.

2.2 Dynamic binding

By way of illustration, let us first consider a simple example in detail, throughout neglecting reference to a model M.

(12) A farmer owned a donkey. It was unhappy. It didn't have a tail.
$\exists x(Fx \wedge \exists y(Dy \wedge Oxy)) \wedge Uy \wedge \neg\exists z(Tz \wedge Hyz)$

Relative to input assignment g this will have as output assignment h if we can find assignments k and l such that k is a possible output of interpreting $\exists x(Fx \wedge \exists y(Dy \wedge Oxy))$ relative to g, and l a possible output of interpreting Uy relative to k, and h a possible output of interpreting $\neg\exists z(Tz \wedge Hyz)$ relative to l. Since the second formula is atomic, and the third a negation, we know that in that case $k = l$ and $l = h$.

Assignment h (that is: k) is obtained from g by resetting the value of x so that $h(x) \in I(F)$, and by next resetting the value of y so that $h(y) \in I(D)$ and $\langle h(x), h(y)\rangle \in I(O)$. That is, $h(x)$ is a farmer who owns a donkey $h(y)$. Observe that for any farmer f and donkey d that f owns, there will be a corresponding assignment $h': g[\{x, y\}]h'$ and such that $h'(x) = f$ and $h'(y) = d$.

The second conjunct first tests whether y is unhappy, that is, whether $h(y) = l(y) \in I(U)$. The third conjunct, a negation, tests whether assignment h cannot serve as input to satisfy the embedded formula $\exists z(Tz \wedge Hyz)$. This is the case if we cannot change the valuation of z into anything that is a tail had by $h(y)$. Putting things together, $\langle g, h\rangle$ is in the interpretation of our example (12) if, and only if, $g[\{x, y\}]h$ and $h(x)$ is a farmer who owns a donkey $h(y)$ which is unhappy and does not have a tail. Observe that for any farmer f and unhappy tail-failing donkey d that f owns, there will be a corresponding assignment $h': g[\{x,y\}]h'$ and such that $h'(x) = f$ and $h'(y) = d$.

In the example discussed above we see that a free variable y, for instance in the second conjunct, gets semantically related to, or effectively bound by, a preceding existential quantifier which does not have the variable in its syntactic scope. This is an example of a much more general fact about interpretation in *DPL*, which goes under the folkloric name of a 'donkey equivalence'.

Observation 1 (Donkey Equivalences) For any formulas ϕ and ψ

$$(\exists x \phi \wedge \psi) \equiv \exists x (\phi \wedge \psi)$$

$$(\exists x \phi \rightarrow \psi) \equiv \forall x (\phi \rightarrow \psi)$$

These equivalences are classical, but for the fact that they do *not* come with the proviso that x not occur free in ψ. This is dynamic binding at work. In the first equivalence we see that a *syntactically free* variable x in ψ may get *semantically bound* by a previous existential quantifier. The second one shows that this semantic binding gains strong, universal, force in implications. The use of the second equivalence is exemplified by the following, canonical, examples.

(13) If a farmer owns a donkey, he beats it.
$(\exists x(Fx \wedge \exists y(Dy \wedge Oxy)) \rightarrow Bxy)$

(14) Every farmer beats every donkey he owns.
$\forall x(Fx \rightarrow \forall y((Dy \wedge Oxy) \rightarrow Bxy))$

These two sentences have generally been judged equivalent, and so are the naturally associated translations in *DPL*. (As a historical remark, back in 1979 Urs Egli has proposed the above equivalences, in order to account for the anaphoric puzzles that plagued the literature. One of the merits of *DPL* is that the equivalences show up as true theorems.)

The following, classical, equivalences are also valid in *DPL*.

Observation 2 (Equivalences that Hold)

$\neg\neg\neg\phi \equiv \neg\phi$ $\quad\quad\quad$ $\forall x \phi \equiv \neg \exists x \neg \phi$

$(\phi \vee \psi) \equiv \neg(\neg\phi \wedge \neg\psi)$ $\quad$ $(\phi \rightarrow \psi) \equiv \neg(\phi \wedge \neg\psi)$

As we have seen $\neg$ is an operator that introduces tests without any further dynamic impact, and $\forall$, $\vee$ and $\rightarrow$ do likewise. That is, if ϕ contains a quantifier with binding potential, this potential gets lost when it occurs in the scope of $\neg$, $\forall$, $\vee$ or $\rightarrow$. As a consequence other equivalences typically do not hold in *DPL*.

Observation 3 (Equivalences that do Not Hold)

$$\neg\neg\phi \not\equiv \phi \qquad \exists x\phi \not\equiv \neg\forall x\neg\phi$$
$$(\phi \wedge \psi) \not\equiv \neg(\neg\phi \vee \neg\psi) \qquad (\phi \wedge \psi) \not\equiv \neg(\phi \rightarrow \neg\psi)$$

These non-equivalences are motivated by the observation that the pronouns in the following examples do not seem to be resolved, or at least not bound by the indefinite which figures in the scope of one of the mentioned operators.

(15) Farley doesn't have car. It is red.

(16) Every man here owns a car. It is a mustang.

(17) Mary has a donkey or she doesn't have one. It brays.

The facts about (undoing) dynamic binding, which follow by the definition of the semantics, correspond one to one with the facts about (in-)accessibility of discourse referents in basic *DRT*, cf. article 14 [Semantics: Sentence and Information Structure] (Geurts) *Accessibility and anaphora*.

2.3 Dynamic consequences

DPL has been motivated by the desire to bring out the logic of a system of interpretation that accounts for anaphoric relationships, like *DRT*. It allows us to study the logical consequences in full formal detail. Before we can see this more clearly, we have to present the *DPL* notions of truth and dynamic entailment first.

Definition 2 (DPL Truth and Entailment)
- Formula ϕ is true relative to model M and assignment g (written as: $\models_{M,g} \phi$) iff there is an assignment h such that $\langle g, h \rangle \in [\![\phi]\!]_M$.
- A (possibly empty) sequence of formulas $\phi_1...\phi_n$ (in that order) entails ψ (written as: $\phi_1...\phi_n \models \psi$) iff relative to all models M and all assignments g_n, if there are assignments $g_0, ... g_{n-1}$ such that $\langle g_0, g_1 \rangle \in [\![\phi_1]\!]_M$, ..., and $\langle g_{n-1}, g_n \rangle \in [\![\phi_n]\!]_M$ then $\models_{M,g_n} \psi$.

Truth relative to a model M and assignment g is defined in a relatively standard way. It is required that ϕ can be satisfied, i.e., that there is some output assignment h in the interpretation of M relative to input assignment g. This notion of truth can be conceived of as a mere adaptation of a standard notion of truth to a slightly more involved notion of interpretation.

The notion of entailment is inherently dynamic though. It is required that whenever a whole sequence of premises, in that order, is satisfied, then the conclusion must be true as well, relative to the (or rather: any) result of interpreting the premises. This formulation allows for binding relations between existentials occurring in the premises and free variables in the conclusion. This actually can be taken to justify two lines of reasoning found in the literature. Consider the following examples, with corresponding, valid, translations.

(18) If a man is from Rhodes, he is not from Athens.
Here is a man from Rhodes.
So he is not from Athens. (Heim)
$\exists x(Mx \wedge Rx) \rightarrow \neg Ax, \exists y(My \wedge Ry) \models \neg Ay$

(19) A: A man has just drunk a pint of sulphuric acid.
B: Nobody who drinks a pint of sulphuric acid lives through the day.
A: Very well then, he wont live through the day. (Geach)
$\exists x(Mx \wedge DPSAx), \neg \exists y(DPSAy \wedge LDy) \models \neg LDx$

The following observation shows that the *DPL* notion of entailment properly corresponds to the *DPL* notion of implication.

Observation 4 (Deduction Theorem)

$$\phi_1, ..., \phi_n \models \psi \text{ iff } \phi_1, ..., \phi_{n-1} \models (\phi_n \rightarrow \psi) \text{ iff } \models (\phi_1 \rightarrow ... (\phi_n \rightarrow \psi) ...).$$

This observation may also serve to show that existentials in the premises of an entailment are also interpreted strongly, that is, as *any* individual that satisfies the things existentially quantified over. Schematically: $\exists x \phi \models \psi$ iff (deduction theorem) $\models (\exists x \phi \rightarrow \psi)$ iff (donkey equivalence) $\models \forall x(\phi \rightarrow \psi)$.

With the notions of truth and entailment in place, we can bring out what sets *DPL* apart from standard, static, predicate logic, and why. As a first step, it is expedient to define the notion of a normal binding form. In the normal binding form ϕ^* of a DPL-formula ϕ the semantic binding relations coincide with the syntactic scope relations. It is defined as follows.

Definition 3 (DPL Normal Binding Form)
- $(Rt_1...t_n)^*$ $\quad = Rt_1...t_n$
- $(\neg\phi)^*$ $\quad\quad = \neg(\phi)^*$
- $(\exists x\phi)^*$ $\quad\quad = \exists x(\phi)^*$
- $(Rt_1...t_n \wedge \psi)^* = (Rt_1...t_n)^* \wedge (\psi)^*$
- $(\neg\phi \wedge \psi)^* \quad = (\neg\phi)^* \wedge (\psi)^*$
- $((\exists x\phi) \wedge \psi)^* = (\exists x (\phi \wedge \psi))^*$
- $((\phi\wedge\psi) \wedge \chi)^* = (\phi\wedge(\psi \wedge \chi))^*$

(The normal binding forms of universally quantified formulas, disjunctions, and implications follow from this definition and observation 2 above.) The following two observations are crucial.

Observation 5 (DPL, Normal Bindings Forms, and PL)
- In all M, $[\![\phi]\!]_M = [\![\phi^*]\!]_M$.
- $\vDash_{M,g} \phi^*$ in DPL iff $\vDash_{M,g} \phi^*$ in PL.

The first clause tells us that ϕ and ϕ^* are fully equivalent in *DPL*. The second tells us that a normal binding form ϕ^* has standard, static truth conditions. It follows that the normal binding form ϕ^* gives a *static, i.e., standard* account of the truth conditions of ϕ under its *dynamic, i.e.,* DPL interpretation. So, the effects obtained by the dynamic interpretation of a formula ϕ have been captured or formulated in a static way in the normal binding form of ϕ.

Armed with this observation we can establish what the difference between static and dynamic predicate logic precisely consists in. For, from a classical perspective the only 'surprising' clause in the definition of the normal binding form of a formula is the one dealing with a conjunction with an existentially quantified first conjunct. These observations thus imply that the only difference between static predicate logic, and *DPL* (or *DRT*, for that matter) is that it allows us to present the truth conditions of $\exists x(\phi \wedge \psi)$ in a dynamic way by means of $(\exists x\phi \wedge \psi)$.

Now we have established that *DPL* has successfully modified static predicate logic in that it (just) allows for dynamic binding of variables, we may inspect on the consequences of this move for the ensuing logic. An immediate and obvious consequence of this dynamification is that conjunction is no longer commutative, that is, it is no longer in general the case that $(\phi \wedge \psi)$ and $(\psi \wedge \phi)$ are equivalent. Surely, if formulas are both context dependent and capable of changing the context, then it matters, of course, whether we first interpret ϕ and then ψ, or the other way around.

For basically the same reasons, formally and intuitively, the dynamic entailment relation is not monotone, not reflexive, and not transitive. An entailment may dynamically hold, because upon any way of satisfying the premises the conclusion holds. But then an additional premise may undo the required effects of the premises. Hence, the relation is not monotone. (In *DPL*, for instance, $\exists x Ex \models Ex$, but $\exists x Ex, \exists x Ox \not\models Ex$.) Entailment is not reflexive either: a formula may change a context in which it is satisfied into one in which it is not. (In *DPL*, $(Ex \wedge \exists x Ox) \not\models (Ex \wedge \exists x Ox)$.) Finally, cutting out the middle term of a two step entailment may involve cutting out an essential – entailed but not executed – change in the context. Consider the following type of reasoning, after an example from Johan van Benthem.

(20) If Jane has a house, she has a garden and if Jane has a garden, she sprinkles it. Now Jane actually has a house. So$_1$ she has a garden, and, so$_2$ she sprinkles it.

This type of reasoning is fine, intuitively, and it is valid in *DPL*. However, if we cut out the first conclusion, the one headed by "So$_1$ ...", the result is odd, and not valid in *DPL*. (($\exists x Hx \rightarrow \exists y Gy$), ($\exists y Gy \rightarrow Sy$), $\exists x Hx \not\models Sy$.) To conclude this section, it appears that, what seems to be a minimal change in the semantics of predicate logic, i.e., enabling a form of dynamic binding, has interesting consequences for the ensuing logic.

3 Pragmatic generalizations

DPL is only one of a family of interpretational architectures dealing with the dynamics of only one phenomenon, that of singular anaphoric relationships. Extensions of this system to other phenomena can be implemented in a straightforward manner, but these implementations also show that the dynamics of discourse interpretation is a fruitful subject of its own. A dynamic perspective on interpretation raises new questions, and discloses an area of semantic research which has not been fully exploited yet. This point is illustrated here by a concise overview of three typical subject areas, exemplifying the pay-off of adopting a dynamic outlook upon interpretation: plurals, updates, and presupposition.

3.1 Plurals and generalized quantifiers

The scope of a system of dynamic interpretation can be substantively broadened by extending the sorts of things dynamically talked about and quantified over, taking into account all kinds of things other than plain individuals, that tend to be introduced in discourses and dialogues. The variety of things is in principle unlimited, as it may concern plurals objects, groups, masses, events, times, intervals, facts, propositions, situations, worlds, and what have you. All of them can be handled, in principle, by the dynamic mechanism of setting up, and referring back to, discourse referents, as it has been fleshed out in *DPL* and *DRT*. (See also the articles 11 [this volume] (Kamp & Reyle) *Discourse Representation Theory* and 7 [Semantics: Noun Phrases and Verb Phrases] (Lasersohn) *Mass nouns and plurals*.) A *DPL*, or *DRT*, interpretation procedure can easily account for the semantic dependencies established in the following sentences.

(21) Five students came to the party. They had a splendid evening.

(22) Many liberals voted against the law. They were not convinced.

(23) None of the girls failed. They had studied hard.

The dynamics of discourse is much more involved than these simple examples suggest. It is not just the passing on of information exchanged, and not just the creation and utilization of discourse referents. This type of information comes by in a structured manner, as the following examples serve to show.

Notice, first, that plural pronouns may pick up plural entities which have not as such been introduced in the discourse.

(24) Bob and Carol went to play bridge with Ted and Alice. They had a wonderful evening.

Obviously the pronoun "they" should not be taken to refer to either Bob, or one of the others. The pronoun can, however, refer to the couple of Bob and Carol, and also to the whole group of four, Bob, Carol, Ted and Alice. However, this group of four has not been mentioned as such in the first line of example (24). Somehow this plural referent may have to be constructed from the four persons that have been explicitly introduced. (This process of forming plural discourse referents is called 'summation' in Kamp & Reyle 1993.)

Besides this type of summation of individual referents more is at stake. When we deal with plural anaphoric dependencies all questions about the distributive, collective or cumulative interpretation of plurals play up, in a dynamic fashion. Consider the following example.

(25) Seven pupils and four teachers wrote five ballads and some rhymes. They performed them at an evening during the spring holiday.

The first sentence here can be taken to introduce a group X of pupils and teachers, and a group Y of ballads and rhymes, such that X wrote Y and X performed Y at a certain evening. Of course, the writing of Y by X can be analyzed in more detail. Maybe the intended reading is that the pupils wrote the ballads and the teachers the rhymes. Also, the pronouns "they" and "them" can be taken to require further analysis, possibly depending on the particular kind of reading associated with the first sentence. The performers can be taken to have performed, individually or group-wise, the ballads and rhymes *they wrote* themselves. Upon this rather natural analysis, the truth conditions of the second sentence are dependent on the analysis chosen for the first, so that the dynamics of interpreting the first sentence must, not only deliver just two plural discourse referents, but some internal relation between these referents as well.

This point also shows in quantified constructions.

(26) Almost all students chose a book. Most of them wrote an essay about it.

The first sentence in this example can be taken to yield a referent set of students who chose a book, and this is the set of individuals which the pronoun "them" intuitively refers to. However, assuming not everyone of them chose the same book, there is no singular referent figuring as the chosen book, which the pronoun *it* could have referred to. A natural interpretation of the second sentence of (26) is that the students wrote an essay about a book that they individually chose. We witness again a close interaction between the specific interpretation of two noun phrases in one construction, and the dynamic interpretation of dependent pronouns in another.

The examples show that the dynamics of discourse does not just consist in the passing on of discourse referents, but in the construction and utilization of more involved entities, like relational structures (as in van den Berg 1996; Nouwen 2007), or parametrized or functional antecedents (as in Krifka 1996; Dekker 2008), or, of course, like representations thereof (as in Kamp & Reyle 1993).

Once adopting a dynamic perspective, further amendments are required in at least two more respects. When meaningful parts of speech get combined, a (dynamic) conjunction or composition of meanings is surely straightforward. It is not that straightforward to interpret other methods of combination dynamically. For instance, second order quantifiers, which combine set denoting terms, are not that easily handled. Consider the following donkey sentence.

(27) Most farmers who own a donkey beat it.

Upon the received analysis, the quantifier *MOST* is supposed to hold of two sets A and B, if and only if the number of A's that are B exceeds the number of A's that are not. Deciding the number of A's is fairly easy, also when A is dynamically interpreted, but it may be difficult to establish the number of B's, if 'B' contains a pronoun apparently anaphoric on material in A. This question has raised a whole theoretical tradition of discussion of its own. Kamp & Reyle (1993) and Chierchia (1992) propose that the general, schematic, analysis of sentences like (27) should really be $D(A)(A\&B)$, so that example (27) can be taken to say that most farmers who own a donkey, own a donkey and beat it. Several authors, have argued that for several determiners and in several contexts this delivers too weak truth conditions. Instead, one should take $D(A)(A \rightarrow B)$ as an analysis, thus raising the reading that most farmers who own a donkey beat every donkey they own. Intermediate solutions have been suggested as well, in Elbourne (2005) for instance. Theoretically, as well as empirically, the preferred dynamic treatment is still an open issue.

Another challenge to the dynamic implementation of discourse reference comes from the co- and subordination of tense and modalities. Consider the following examples, which can be multiplied at will.

(28) Conny opened the door. The room was pitch dark.

(29) Conny switched on the light. The room was pitch dark.

(30) A wolf might enter the house. It would eat Leo.

(31) Roseanne is sure that Mark doesn't have a car. She would have seen it.

In all of these examples, the tense or modality of the second sentence, as well as its content, is related to that of the first, which can be seen to have been set up as a temporal or modal discourse referent. However, there is no unique relation of coreference involved, because the temporal and modal connections come about in complicated structures. In order to deal with these kind of phenomena, then, the system has to allow, not only, for more involved temporal and modal structure, but also for more intricately structured contextual dependencies. See Roberts (1989), Frank (1997) and Geurts (1999) for empirical details and relevant theoretical discussion. See also Stone & Hardt (1999), Brasoveanu (2006), and Fernando (2007), and article 14 [Semantics: Sentence and Information Structure] (Geurts) *Accessibility and anaphora*. The main conclusion here is that structural semantic relationships get revealed if one pays due attention to the dynamics of discourse interpretation and that they would have gone unnoticed otherwise.

3.2 Updates in discourse

A dynamic outlook upon interpretation also provides the basis for investigating, detecting, and formalizing various systematic pragmatic aspects of interpretation. Stalnaker (1978) has pictured assertions, or the assertive use of indicative sentences, as a kind of acts whose contents depend on their contexts, and which are meant to change these contexts. Assertions can be seen to characterize 'the actual world' as being a certain way, by locating it among a set of possible ways the world might be. A common ground may figure here as a shared body of information which is established between a group of interlocutors engaged in a conversation. The point of an assertion then can be taken to be that its contents are *added* to such a common ground, yielding as a new common ground the intersection of the expressed contents with the old common ground.

These pragmatic observations can be combined with those of Grice (1975) about cooperative conversations. A rational and cooperative conversation should proceed according to a couple of gricean maxims, one of which requires speakers to convey information which they have evidence for. A speaker's own private information state, one might say, has to support the things she says, or at least, for the time being, the speaker has to pretend to have this kind of support. Conversely, a hearer can be expected to update his own private information with the contents of assertions which have not been rejected, or at least, for the time being, pretend to do so.

These insights about assertions and about cooperative behavior, can be formulated in a system of update semantics (Veltman 1996). In such a system the act of expressing a propositional content, and next incorporating it in a common ground, are fused into a dynamic notion of meaning which is a function from information states to (updated) information states. It is written so that if p is the proposition (set of possible worlds) expressed by ϕ, then the update of a state (ground, context, also a set of possible worlds) τ with ϕ, written as $(\tau)[\![\phi]\!]$, equals $(\tau \cap p)$. Such an update system has been taken as the basis for a study of epistemic modalities and presupposition (see the next subsection), but also as a starting point for the study of organized, rational information exchange.

A driving insight is that if speaker and hearer have correct information, as they can be taken to assume they have, then also the information is correct which they have after the hearer has updated her information state with the contents of an assertion, provided that it is supported by the information of the speaker. This point is well-motivated, and easily accounted for, but once it is made explicit it becomes obvious that it is not so trivial as it might appear at first glance. For one thing, such a principle need not hold once the interlocutors start making assertions about the conversation itself, or about each other's information (as in example (6) above). For another, it appears to be hard to formulate such a requirement in the framework of *DRT* or *DPL*, because these systems fail appropriate notions of support (Aloni 2000).

Informative types of discourse not only consist of assertions, but they are, typically, also guided by questions: interrogatives, topics which the interlocutors raise, and questions they themselves face. Already at the outset of formal semantic theorizing about questions their *dynamic* role, their role in discourse or dialogue, has been obvious. Adopting a dynamic theoretical perspective, discourses or dialogues can be described as games of stacking and answering 'questions under discussion' or as processes of 'raising and resolving issues'.

Such processes are not unstructured, but governed by structural linguistic rules, and highly pragmatic principles of reasonable or rational coordination (Ginzburg 1995; Roberts 1996; Hulstijn 1997). A quite minimal way to account for this proceeds by representing information as a set of possibilities, one of which is supposed to be actual. The possibilities are grouped in sorts. The sorting indicates that the current issue is, not which of the possibilities is the actual one, but which is the sort of the actual one, that is, in which sort of possibilities the actual world can be found. Information states then can be taken to be sets of sets of possibilities, which may get updated with further questions and more data in the development of a discourse.

Such a tentative sketch already provides the basics for characterizing certain basic discourse and dialogue notions like that of a coherent and felicitous dialogue. For a dialogue to proceed coherently and felicitously, one may require assertions to be consistent with the current information state, but also informative: logically speaking it is of no use to accept a state of inconsistent information or to assert what is already (commonly) known. Questions can be required to be non-superfluous as well, so that one doesn't *raise* an issue which is already there. Assertions can also be required to address issues at stake and not to provide unsolicited information. These observation and requirements, and many others, find a neat formulation in update style systems of interpretation. Asher & Lascarides (2003) gives an impression of the wealth of data to be covered in this direction, and Aloni, Butler & Dekker (2007) gives an overview of recent formalizations in a dynamic paradigm.

3.3 Modality and presupposition

Like we said, a pragmatic system of interpretation along the lines of Veltman's update semantics provides a ground for evaluating epistemic modals, assertions made with the auxiliaries *may* and *must* or adverbials like *maybe* and *evidently*. The sententials operators *may* and *must* neatly seem to fit in the dynamic paradigm, as the first can be used to express consistence with the *current* context of information, and *must* to express something that can be derived from this context. Thus, the effect of a modal MOD, which expresses contextual epistemic possibility, can be tentatively defined as follows.

(32) $(\tau)[\text{MOD}\phi] = \tau$, if $(\tau)[\![\phi]\!]$ is possible, and $(\tau)[\![\text{MOD}\phi]\!] = \bot$ otherwise.

Since the interpretation of the modality is stated in terms of the possible update of the current information state τ with the embedded sentence ϕ, the interpretation of these modal sentences may be variable. For instance, it may be the case at one point in an exchange that Nancy might be home, as far as we all know, while later in the discourse we may have collected information which rules out that she is home. Epistemically used modals *might* and *must* may change their truth, or acceptability, in the course of events. The dynamic logic of such epistemic operators is investigated in detail in various *dynamic epistemic logics*. Groenendijk, Stokhof & Veltman (1996) present a non-trivial combination of Veltman's update semantics with the dynamic interpretation of *DPL*. In a more philosophical setting von Fintel and Gillies have investigated the uses of epistemic modals. Of a more linguistic nature is recent work by Asher, McCready and Ogata.

Also the pragmatic behavior of presuppositions lends itself to a natural dynamic treatment. Presuppositions figure as preconditions for linguistic items (expressions) or acts (utterances) to make sense. They are preconditions for terms to be referring, for predicates to be applicable, or for sentences to be true or false. A presupposition of a sentence is typically preserved when the sentence is put under a negation. Thus, from both "Don stopped smoking cannabis" and "Don didn't stop smoking cannabis" one can draw the conclusion that Don used to smoke cannabis. Normally, presuppositions are also preserved when they occur under other operators, like modals and quantifiers. Presuppositions need not always be preserved though, and the dynamics of their so-called projection has been studied intensively. Consider one example.

(33) Sally believes that Harry didn't quit smoking cannabis.

The most deeply embedded sentence "Harry quit smoking cannabis" comes with the presupposition that Harry smoked cannabis. If we all know that Harry was a regular cannabis user, then the presupposition that he smoked cannabis is satisfied, and we may obtain a reading according to which Sally's belief concerns Harry's continuing smoking habit. If we are not sure about Harry's use of drugs, it may be that for all we know Sally believes he was a cannabis smoker, and that he didn't stop. It may be a bit awkward, but if Sally is already known to believe that Harry didn't ever smoke cannabis, then she can be taken to believe that he didn't quit doing so. In the cases mentioned, the triggering presupposition either gets cancelled or modified and a lot of the literature about presupposition has been devoted to a study of the cases in which presuppositions are not inherited by larger configurations, or in which they are modified, and how. The two main theories of presupposition in this area nowadays are the 'satisfaction theory' and the 'accommodation and binding theory' (the 'AB theory'). (See also article 14 [Semantics: Interfaces] (Beaver & Geurts) *Presupposition*.)

According to both theories, presuppositions are required to be contextually given, or 'satisfied', in the common ground. A satisfaction theory requires presuppositions to be semantically satisfied in the local context in which they are evaluated (Karttunen 1974; Heim 1991; Beaver 1995; van Rooij 2005). Since these contexts *change* in the process of updating information, and the information the interlocutors have may grow in the development of a discourse, their different demands on different contexts can be accounted for, or better, are predicted. A most appealing aspect of this theory is that it comes with an automated satisfaction test, because the underlying notion of support is independently argued for. No separate notion of grounding presuppositions is called for.

Consider again the examples (3a) and (3b) from above.

(3) a. Mike has children. Mikes sons are blues and his daughters are soul.
    b. Mikes sons are blues and his daughters are soul. Mike has children.

If we indicate that a formula χ presupposes that ϕ by means of a subscript as in χ_ϕ, then we can render example (3a) as $(\phi \wedge \chi_\phi)$. According to the update notion of conjunction as function composition, the second formula's presupposition that ϕ ("Mike has children") is automatically satisfied by the update of the context with the first conjunct ϕ. Not so according to the rendering of example (3b) as $(\chi_\phi \wedge \phi)$. This conjunction as a whole still presupposes that ϕ, while its second conjunct still needlessly and explicitly conveys what has already been presupposed by the first. An update semantics precisely accounts for this difference.

The AB theory of presupposition (van der Sandt 1992; Geurts 1999) is dynamic like the satisfaction theory, but it presents a different account of resolution. According to the AB theory, presuppositions appear in a preliminary phase of interpretation, and at some intermediary level, as distinguished information units which have to be 'resolved' for the interpretation process to be completed. Being resolved roughly means being semantically invisible, the AB counterpart of being satisfied. If they are resolved these information units as it were dissolve at the intermediary level of *DRT*'s discourse representation structures. If they are not resolved, they get 'accommodated', or, rather, they accommodate themselves, like true squatters. In such a case their contents are settled in a relevant part of a representation which resolves them in the slot where they originally appeared.

For a very sketchy illustration, consider again example (33).

(33) Sally believes that Harry didn't quit smoking cannabis.

Nowhere in example (33) it is literally said or communicated that Harry did smoke cannabis, or that Sally believes so. So if the preceding context of such an example does not supply a way of resolving this presupposition, it has to accommodate itself. Even though this may require some further contextual support, one way for this presupposition to accommodate itself is right there where it stands, thus bringing about a reading according to which Sally is taken to believe that it is not the case that Harry smoked cannabis and stopped, similar to the last reading above. It may be easier to obtain a reading by accommodating the presupposition in Sally beliefs. Sally would then be taken to believe that Harry did smoke cannabis and didn't stop doing so, as one gets from the second reading above. Probably the most straightforward interpretation is one where the presupposition accommodates itself at the main level of interpretation, so that example (33) is taken to say that Harry used to smoke cannabis, and that according to Sally he didn't stop doing so, basically the first reading again.

While the underlying ideas of the satisfaction and the binding theory on satisfaction and resolution are similar, and while both are dynamic, the specific treatments are quite different. The first is a logical approach, in that it predicts presuppositions as a type of entailments following from an independently specified semantics; according to the second presuppositions are typically computational constructions. The difference is vast, but not unbridgeable. A semantic variant of the AB theory, which fleshes out a logical notion of the meaning or interpretation of unresolved presuppositional structures, is presented in Dekker (2008).

4 Methodological issues

In this section we discuss two more theoretical issues. They are related to the classical Fregean themes of compositionality, representationalism, dynamicity and contextuality, which show to be very actual still in current debates.

4.1 Representationalism and dynamism

The dynamic remodeling of semantic theory has given rise to a revival of an old philosophical discussion around the representation and dynamics of meaning. The discussion has, largely inadvertently, been centered on the understanding of intersentential anaphoric relationships, but it can be taken to relate to all sorts of dynamic interpretation. See also articles 6 [Semantics: Foundations, History and Methods] (Pagin & Westerståhl) *Compositionality* and 11 [Semantics: Foundations, History and Methods] (Kempson) *Formal semantics and representationalism*.

It has been claimed, in particular by those who adhere to a *DRT*-style framework, that a principled account of certain semantic phenomena requires access to an independent level of representation. It has also been claimed, by advocates of a dynamic approach, that a compositional account of structural relations in discourse requires the adoption of a dynamic notion of meaning. It appears that the adoption of, at least some, dynamic aspects of interpretation are unavoidable also in a framework like *DRT*. The update of discourse representation structures proceeds in a typically dynamic fashion, and its embedding or satisfaction conditions are often stated in a dynamic way, most notably the satisfaction conditions of conditional structures.

But also a dynamic framework has to acknowledge, at least some, representational aspects of the way in which information is given. Already when only anaphoric relationships are at issue, both *DRT* and *DPL* need access to some notion of a 'discourse referent', and it seems discourse referents cannot but be taken to model the fact that in some ongoing discourse a noun phrase has been used in a specific way. It establishes "a fact about the conversation, and not about the subject matter," as Stalnaker (1998, 13) puts it, or, in the words of Groenendijk, Stokhof & Veltman (1996, 183): "(...) one (...) has to store *discourse information*. ....Discourse information (...) looks more like a book-keeping device, than like real information."

It appears, however, that the phenomena at issue do not motivate more radical conclusions. True representationalists might want to convince themselves that the data show that meaning is irreducibly representational, but such a conclusion seems unfounded. The dynamic semantic reformulations of *DRT*'s treatments of anaphora and presupposition show that a realist, or referentially based, theory of meaning can be maintained if the interpretational architecture allows access to some dynamic aspects of the presentation of information. Devote pragmatists may be tempted to believe that meaning is an inherently dynamic thing. Again, the data do not seem to support such a conclusion. Dynamic accounts of anaphora and presupposition have been given a static reformulation, or one based on traditional, algebraic and satisfaction based notions of meaning, with the addition of some suitable dynamic module of conjoining information (Zeevat 1989; Dekker 2008).

In either case, for a dynamic system of interpretation, a rather standard notion of meaning may remain as a basis for systematic extensions, extensions with the dynamic, or pragmatic, representational tools, which are required to establish meaningful relations in discourse. And even though this hasn't been done in a down to atomic level in basic *DRT* and *DPL,* it can be done in a fully compositional way. The basic adaptation required to this end consists in assigning sentences, not the basic type t of truth values, but a new type *ccp* of context change potentials, for instance, the *DRT* or *DPL* type of relations between variable assignments or some type of update functions. Needless to say that such a program can be carried out in many different ways, for there are various insights as to what kinds of entities live in the *ccp* domain, and the way in which they relate to the usual objects of the sentential type t. Some systems employ versions of Montague's own *intensional logic,* or multi-sorted type theory, or a constructive type theory, or a theory with simultaneous abstraction. Arguably the most perspicuous version has been given by Muskens (1996). Specific alternatives worth mentioning include Reyle's Underspecified DRT, Kohlhase and Kuschert's Λ-DRT, and Asher and Lascarides' Segmented DRT.

4.2 Pragmatics and contextuality

According to a well-established division of labour, the study of language divides up in syntax, semantics and pragmatics. It is the task of syntacticians to describe what are the well-formed expressions of some language, of the semanticists to characterize the meanings of these expressions, and that of the pragmaticians to determine what one can do with these expressions with their assigned meanings. As a result, arm-chair syntacticians and semanticists have happily and reflectively studied the structural aspects of language, under complete abstraction of its use. Apparent, dirty, counterexamples to aesthetically appealing theories could be hand-waived as being of a pragmatic origin. See also article 5 [Semantics: Foundations, History and Methods] (Green) *Meaning in language use.*

Under the influence of Wittgenstein and Strawson, and Austin and Searle later, more pragmatically oriented philosophers and linguists came to realize that, for a general understanding of the meaning of language, aspects of its use could or should not be neglected. With the advance of systems of dynamic semantics such a pragmatic development of natural language semantics seems to have found a solid formal ground. In most of the applications studied above arguably pragmatic aspects of the use of language make their way in a systematic account of meaning or interpretation. Typical examples of dynamic interpretation relate to matters of use, such as introducing discourse referents, updating discourse contexts, establishing discourse structure, etc. Such, however, raises the question what, then, can be said to properly belong to the area of semantics, and what to that of pragmatics, if any such distinction of fields remains eventually tenable at all.

A dynamic semantics typically takes account of matters of usage which are or were seen to be of a pragmatic nature. Next to truth conditions it takes usage conditions into account. The question is how far this may take us, and this, really, is an open question. Descriptions may be read in a variety of ways, referential, predicative, quantificational, or else; ascriptions of beliefs and desires to other people are highly context-sensitive as well, and so are the notoriously vague predicates like 'small' and 'bald' and 'generous'. It seems quite unfortunate to have to distinguish all of the different kinds of uses to which these predications can be put, and to make them multiply ambiguous. It is unclear, however, what would be the rationale to stop here, or somewhere else. Otherwise, if we don't stop here, it seems we get lost in something like a radical type of contextualism, viz., that whatever it is that we ideally end up with, it is so totally and deeply pragmatically infected ambiguous, that still calling it 'meaning' or 'semantics' would be quite a vacuous thing indeed.

This last mentioned subject relates to a very open question, a live issue in the 'contextualist debate' (see, e.g., Recanati 2004; Stanley 2005). For now, we have to stop here and conclude that this year, in 2011, dynamic semantics has grown beyond the age of 21, that it is grown up, quite successful, and alive. Its success may be attributed to the fact that it comes without a particular philosophical message but with a specific methodological advantage. It is a semantic system open to pragmatic intrusion and it easily escapes the straightjacket of standard truth-conditional semantics. Maybe too easily, but that has not been our concern here.

5 References

Aloni, Maria 2000. Conceptual covers in dynamic semantics. In: N. Braisby et al. (eds.). *Logic, Language and Computation, vol. III*. Stanford, CA: CSLI Publications, 23–48.
Aloni, Maria, Alastair Butler & Paul Dekker (eds.) 2007. *Questions in Dynamic Semantics*. Amsterdam: Elsevier.
Asher, Nicholas & Alex Lascarides 2003. *Logics of Conversation*. Cambridge: Cambridge University Press.
Barker, Stephen J. 1997. E-type pronouns, DRT, dynamic semantics and the quantifier/variable-binding model. *Linguistics & Philosophy* 20, 195–228.
Barwise, Jon 1987. Noun phrases, generalized quantifiers and anaphora. In: P. Gärdenfors (ed.). *Generalized Quantifiers: Linguistic and Logical Approaches*. Dordrecht: Reidel, 1–30.
Beaver, David 1995. *Presupposition and Assertion in Dynamic Semantics*. Ph.D. dissertation. University of Edinburgh. Reprinted: Stanford, CA: CSLI Publications, 2001.
van den Berg, Martin H. 1996. *The Internal Structure of Discourse*. Ph.D. dissertation. University of Amsterdam.

Brasoveanu, Adrian 2006. Structured discourse reference to propositions. In: B. Gyuris et al. (eds.). *Proceedings of the Ninth Symposium on Logic and Language*. Budapest: Eötvös Loránd University, 35–44.

Chierchia, Gennaro 1992. Anaphora and dynamic binding. *Linguistics & Philosophy* 15, 111–83.

Dekker, Paul 2008. A multi-dimensional treatment of quantification in extraordinary English. *Linguistics & Philosophy* 31, 101–127.

Egli, Urs 1979. The Stoic concept of anaphora. In: U. Egli, R. Bäuerle & A. von Stechow (eds.). *Semantics from Different Points of View*. Berlin: Springer, 266–283.

van Eijck, Jan 2001. Incremental dynamics. *Journal of Logic, Language and Information* 10, 319–351.

Elbourne, Paul 2005. *Situations and Individuals*. Cambridge, MA: The MIT Press.

Fernando, Tim 2007. Observing events and situations in time. *Linguistics & Philosophy* 30, 527–550.

Frank, Anette 1997. *Context Dependence in Modal Constructions*. Doctoral dissertation. University of Stuttgart.

Geach, Peter T. 1962. *Reference and Generality. An Examination of Some Medieval and Modern Theories*. Ithaca, NY: Cornell University Press.

Geurts, Bart 1999. *Presuppositions and Pronouns*. Amsterdam: Elsevier.

Ginzburg, Jonathan 1995. Resolving questions, I & II. *Linguistics & Philosophy* 18, 459–527 and 567–609.

Grice, Paul 1975. Logic and conversation. In: P. Cole & J. L. Morgan (eds.). *Syntax and Semantics 3: Speech Acts*. New York: Academic Press, 41–58.

Groenendijk, Jeroen & Martin Stokhof 1991. Dynamic predicate logic. *Linguistics & Philosophy* 14, 39–100.

Groenendijk, Jeroen, Martin Stokhof & Frank Veltman 1996. Coreference and modality. In: S. Lappin (ed.). *The Handbook of Contemporary Semantic Theory*. Oxford: Blackwell, 179–213.

Heim, Irene 1988. *The Semantics of Definite and Indefinite Noun Phrases*. New York: Garland.

Heim, Irene 1991. On the projection problem for presuppositions. In: S. Davis (ed.). *Pragmatics: A Reader*. Oxford: Oxford University Press, 397–405.

von Heusinger, Klaus 2004. Choice functions and the anaphoric semantics of definite NPs. *Research in Language and Computation* 2, 309–329.

Hulstijn, Joris 1997. Structured information states. Raising and resolving issues. In: A. Benz & G. Jäger (eds.). *Proceedings of MunDial97*. München: University of München, 99–117.

Kamp, Hans 1984. A theory of truth and semantic representation. In: J. Groenendijk, T. Janssen & M. Stokhof (eds.). *Truth, Interpretation and Information*. Dordrecht: Foris, 1–41.

Kamp, Hans & Uwe Reyle 1993. *From Discourse to Logic*. Dordrecht: Kluwer.

Karttunen, Lauri 1968. *What Do Referential Indices Refer To*. Santa Monica, CA: RAND Corporation. http://www.rand.org/pubs/papers/2008/P3854.pdf. December 9, 2010.

Karttunen, Lauri 1974. Presupposition and linguistic context. *Theoretical Linguistics* 1, 181–193.

Kohlhase, Michael & Susanna Kuschert 1997. Dynamic lambda calculus. In: T. Becker & H.-U. Krieger (eds.). *Proceedings of the 5th Meeting on Mathematics of Language (= MOL5)*. Saarbrücken: DFKI, 85-92.

Krifka, Manfred 1996. Parametrized sum individuals for plural reference and partitive quantification. *Linguistics & Philosophy* 19, 555–598.

Muskens, Reinhard 1996. Combining Montague semantics and discourse representation. *Linguistics & Philosophy* 19, 143–186.

Muskens, Reinhard, Johan van Benthem & Albert Visser 1997. Dynamics. In: J. van Benthem & A. ter Meulen (eds.). *Handbook of Logic and Language*. Amsterdam: Elsevier, 587–649.

Nouwen, Rick 2007. On dependent pronouns and dynamic semantics. *Journal of Philosophical Logic* 36, 123–154.

Recanati, Frannçois 2004. *Literal Meaning*. Cambridge: Cambridge University Press.

Roberts, Craige 1989. Modal subordination and pronominal anaphora in discourse. *Linguistics & Philosophy* 12, 683–722.

Roberts, Craige 1996. Information structure: Towards an integrated formal theory of pragmatics. In: J. H. Yoon & A. Kathol (eds.). *OSU Working Papers in Linguistics, vol. 49: Papers in Semantics*. Columbus, OH: The Ohio State University, 91–136.

van Rooij, Robert 2005. A modal analysis of presupposition and modal subordination. *Journal of Semantics* 22, 282–305.

van der Sandt, Rob A. 1992. Presupposition projection as anaphora resolution. *Journal of Semantics* 9, 333–377.

Slater, Hartley 2000. Quantifier/variable-binding. *Linguistics & Philosophy* 23, 309–321.

Stalnaker, Robert 1978. Assertion. In: P. Cole (ed.). *Syntax and Semantics 9: Pragmatics*. New York: Academic Press, 315–332.

Stalnaker, Robert 1998. On the representation of context. *Journal of Logic, Language and Information* 7, 3–19.

Stanley, Jason 2005. Semantics in context. In: G. Preyer & G. Peter (eds.). *Contextualism in Philosophy: Knowledge, Meaning, and Truth*. Oxford: Oxford University Press, 221–254.

Staudacher, Peter 1987. Zur Semantik indefiniter Nominalphrasen. In: B. Asbach-Schnitker & J. Roggenhofer (eds.). *Neuere Forschungen zur Wortbildung und Histographie der Linguistik. Festgabe für Herbert E. Brekle*. Tübingen: Narr, 239–258.

Stone, Matthew & Daniel Hardt 1999. Dynamic discourse referents for tense and modals. In: H. Bunt & R. Muskens (eds.). *Computing Meaning*. Dordrecht: Kluwer, 302–321.

Veltman, Frank 1996. Defaults in update semantics. *Journal of Philosophical Logic* 25, 221–261.

Vermeulen, Kees & Albert Visser 1996. Dynamic bracketing and discourse representation. *Notre Dame Journal of Formal Logic* 37, 321–365.

Zeevat, Henk 1989. A compositional approach to Discourse Representation Theory. *Linguistics & Philosophy* 12, 95–131.

Henk Zeevat
13 Rhetorical relations

1 Why study rhetorical relations? —— 413
2 Which rhetorical relations should be assumed? —— 415
3 What do rhetorical relations relate? —— 420
4 Where must rhetorical relations be assumed? —— 426
5 Applications —— 427
6 Outlook —— 436
7 References —— 438

Abstract: An overview is given of some main positions with respect to rhetorical relations with an emphasis on the open linguistic, philosophical and computational issues and the possibilities for progress. The first part tries to motivate the relations, after which applications to various phenomena and areas are considered. The paper tries to look at rhetorical relations as a single field to which the various models have made important contributions. In this view Rhetorical Structure Theory has discovered the relations, the Linguistic Discourse Model has made grammar out of them and Interpretation by Abduction and Structured Discourse Representation Theory are models of how to recognise them. The proponents of these models as well as many others have analysed the relation between rhetorical relations and phenomena like information structure, pronoun resolution, topic questions, presupposition and temporal reference, have analysed rhetorical relations from various perspectives and developed annotation schemata for them. There is no attempt to treat any approach comprehensively or to choose between approaches.

1 Why study rhetorical relations?

There are two observations that motivate rhetorical relations and rhetorical structure for text. The first is that everybody infers in examples like (1) that what happens in the second sentence is caused by what happens in the first.

(1) His assailants came closer and closer. Jones ducked away behind the couch.

In fact, somebody who failed to make the inference would fail in his understanding of the text. Something would be missing in his competence as an interpreter.

Henk Zeevat, Amsterdam, The Netherlands

https://doi.org/10.1515/9783110589245-013

But the causality is not expressed by a lexical item or a syntactic construction. Researchers in this area have assumed the following principle, often implicitly.

(2) Connection Principle

In a coherent text, each sentence except the first one is connected to an earlier sentence by a rhetorical relation.

The earlier sentence is very often the last sentence before it, but this is not necessary, witness (3). Here the sentence to which the last sentence has its discourse relation (its PIVOT) is the last but one.

(3) His assailants came closer and closer. There were four of them. Jones ducked away behind the couch.

Pivots can be arbitrarily far away, since the intervening material can be expanded at will.

The second motivating observation is that in texts (and conversations) the sentences come in a meaningful and non-arbitrary order. This contrasts with the notion of a sentence in logic (a formula without free variables) and the notion of a theory (a set of logical sentences). In a logical theory, the order of the sentences is unimportant. In natural languages on the other hand, the order of the sentences is of crucial importance and carries various dimensions of meaning. Rhetorical relations form one of these dimensions, others are anaphoric relations and information structure. It turns out that these dimensions are closely connected with each other, even though they are about very different things. There is little hope for a theory of any one dimension to achieve much in the way of explanation without proper accounts of the other. And little hope for a theory of the meaning of texts that does not bring in all three dimensions. This is the main reason why rhetorical relations are important: without them, a serious account of anaphora and information structure is not possible. It follows that without rhetorical relations, it is hard to even start developing an account of the meaning of natural language sentences, given that sentences are typically part of larger structures like texts and conversations and full of anaphoric elements.

The recipe in (4) (Singh 1970) brings the order out quite clearly. The instructions are meant to be carried out in the order of their occurrence and only make sense in that order. The one rhetorical relation involved is called *Narration* or *Sequence* and the pivot is invariably the immediately preceding sentence.

(4) Soak the rice in cold water for 1 hour. Prepare spices. Divide bird into 8 pieces. Drain rice and leave to dry. Brown the grated onions in butter until all

moisture has dried. Put in the chicken and fry over medium heat. Add ginger and cook a further 5 minutes. Add a few tablespoons of yoghourt. Season with salt. Cook on low heat.

The following permutation (5) has an entirely different meaning, to the extent that it can be understood at all.

(5) Add ginger and cook a further 5 minutes. Drain rice and leave to dry. Cook on low heat. Divide bird into 8 pieces. Put in the chicken and fry over medium heat. Soak the rice in cold water for 1 hour. Season with salt. Prepare spices. Add a few tablespoons of yoghourt. Brown the grated onions in butter until all moisture has dried.

What happens in the permutation – next to the temporal reordering – is that the anaphoric elements (add, further, rice, put in, etc.) cannot be resolved anymore to their original antecedents.

2 Which rhetorical relations should be assumed?

Consider (6). In addition to what the sentences mean, the combination also entails that John giving the speech was caused by Bill asking him. Here the extra entailment is marked by the causal marker "because" and the fact that it is the second sentence that gives the cause of the event referred to in the first sentence seems to come from the fact that the second sentence stands after the first.

(6) John gave the speech. Because Bill had asked him.

If one inserts an extra sentence in between the two as in (7) the causal relation is preferably interpreted as obtaining between the second and the third sentence (or between a combination of the first and the second sentence).

(7) John gave the speech. He gave all the credit to the committee. Because Bill had asked him to.

But also the first and second sentence are related. John's crediting the committee was part of his giving the speech, quite possibly a particular part of the speech. This relation –normally called an *Elaboration* – is mostly not indicated by a specific marker. In fact, nothing much seems to change either, if the causal marker is omitted as in (8). The past perfect seems to be sufficient in this case to infer that Bill asking John to credit the committee must be the cause of John doing so.

(8) a. John gave the speech.
  b. He gave all the credit to the committee.
  c. Bill had asked him to.

Relations between sentences like *Explanation* and *Elaboration* are known as rhetorical relations (also *discourse relations*) and they form the subject matter of this chapter. It is often assumed that all the sentences in a text (but things do not change much if one switches to dialogue, though it is less appropriate to call the relations "discourse relations" or "rhetorical relations" in that case) are related to other sentences by rhetorical relations. If this is so, marking the relations by labelled arrows and distinguishing between subordinating and coordinating relations gives texts a tree-like structure, referred to as the *rhetorical structure, rhetorical tree* or *discourse tree* of the text. For example, (8) leads to the tree in Fig. 13.1.

a
↓ *Elaboration*
b
↓ *Explanation*
c

Fig. 13.1: Tree for (8)

A slightly more complex example (Lascarides & Asher 1993) is (9).

(9) a. Guy had a lovely evening.
  b. He went to town.
  c. He had a good meal.
  d. He devoured lots of salmon.
  e. He won a dance competition.
  f. He caught the bus home at 12.

The tree is given in Fig. 13.2 (many other formats are in use).

a → *Elaboration* → f
↓ *Elaboration*
b
↓ *Elaboration*
c → *Narration* → e
↓ *Elaboration*
d

Fig. 13.2: Tree for (9)

The list of discourse relations in Tab. 13.1 is taken from the RST website (http://www.sfu.ca/rst/). RST is Rhetorical Structure Theory, the oldest systematic account of rhetorical relations.

Tab. 13.1: Rhetorical relations in RST

Presentational Relations
Antithesis, Background, Concession, Enablement, Evidence, Justify, Motivation, Preparation, Restatement, Summary
Subject Matter Relations
Circumstance, Condition, Elaboration (set : member, abstraction : instance, whole : part, process : step, object : attribute, generalization : specific), Evaluation, Interpretation, Means, Non-volitional Cause, Non-volitional Result, Otherwise, Purpose, Solutionhood, Unconditional, Unless, Volitional Cause, Volitional Result
Multinuclear Relations
Conjunction, Contrast, Disjunction, Joint, List, Multinuclear Restatement, Sequence

At the website, they each come with a definition and an example. For example, the following can be found for *Concession*. RST distinguishes nuclei and satellites in a relation (unless it is a multinuclear relation, like *Contrast* or *Disjunction*), where the nucleus expresses the point of the combination and the satellite has a supporting role.

(10) *Constraints on Nucleus and Satellite*:
on Nucleus: Writer has positive regard for Nucleus
on Satellite: Writer is not claiming that Satellite does not hold

Constraints on Nucleus+Satelite:
Writer acknowledges a potential or apparent incompatibility between Nucleus and Satelite; recognizing the compatibility between Nucleus and Satellite increases Reader's positive regard for Nucleus

Intention of Writer:
Reader's positive regard for Nucleus is increased

Example:
(Satellite) Tempting as it may be, (Nucleus) we shouldn't embrace every popular issue that comes along.

The definitions and examples should support the analysis of text structure, the construction of a diagram for the text and RST-based annotation of corpora.

It should be clear that they are not sufficient for a semantics of the text or for that part of it that is defined by rhetorical relations.

The division in three groups is motivated by the intuition that there are relations which relate the events and states referred to by the sentences or clauses that are related and ones that are not. The division into nucleus-satellite relations and multinuclear ones is based on the intuition that in the last case both relata have equal status.

The list is meant to be a classification scheme for the case that two clauses are rhetorically related: there should then be one relation from the list that characterises the relation.

While it cannot be disputed that the relations distinguished above can in fact be distinguished from each other and the many years in which they have been used to analyse texts give a guarantee that new ones will not be found lightly (the ones in other classification schemes are there, but sometimes have a different label, e.g. *Narration* is *Sequence*), there can be disputes about what should be in a list of discourse relations and what are the criteria for separating one relation up into special cases and for amalgamating others. It may also well be that a list of this kind is inappropriate and that a featural analysis is preferable, as proposed in the area of speech acts by Traum (2000).

In fact, there is quite a case for an analysis of discourse relations in terms of features and this has been pursued in Knott & Sanders (1998) who come up with a featural analysis. In this analysis, four primitives are considered: causal versus additive, semantic versus pragmatic, positive versus negative polarity and basic versus non basic order (for causal relations only, cause precedes effect) and a strong case is made for these giving a natural classification, in terms of a comparison of the overt marking systems of English and Dutch. Knott & Mellish (1996) add extra features: presuppositionality and modal status.

The four features used by Knott & Sanders (1998) give the following 12 combinations:

(11) causal semantic positive basic: Result
causal semantic positive non basic: Causal Explanation
causal semantic negative basic: Concession
causal semantic negative non basic: Inverted Concession
causal pragmatic positive basic: Conclusion
causal pragmatic positive non basic: Justification
causal pragmatic negative basic: Pragmatic Concession
causal pragmatic negative non basic: Inverted Pragmatic Concession

additive semantic positive: Additive Conjunction
additive semantic negative: Causal Explanation

additive pragmatic positive: Pragmatic Additive Conjunction
additive pragmatic negative: Contrast

It is clear that while this gives far fewer than the RST relations, it also splits a number of those relations into two.

Another way of being more principled is given by the Hume–Hobbs–Kehler analysis (Kehler 2002), cf. also article 13 [Semantics: Sentence and Information Structure] (Kehler) *Cohesion and coherence,* of rhetorical relations based on David Hume's classification of "association between ideas": Similarity, Contiguity in time and place and Cause/Effect. Similarity led Kehler to distinguish the *Resemblance* relations (*List, Formal Contrast, Elaboration*), from the *Causal Relations* (*Explanation, Effect, Justification*) and the *Contiguity Relations* (*Narration*). Kehler (2002) is able to show that the distinction between *Resemblance* and the other relations correlates with important differences in VP ellipsis, differences which correlate with differences in pronoun resolution and temporal anaphora. So it seems that from the perspective of sentence interpretation, this three-way distinction is all one needs. But there are semantic aspects to rhetorical relations that go beyond Hume's distinction and their functional aspects are of the first importance in choosing whether to realise them in a text generation system. These additional semantic and functional aspects cannot be captured without finer-grained distinctions like the distinction between *List, Elaboration* and *Formal Contrast.*

Determining the inventory of rhetorical relations once and for all requires an in depth analysis of all the purposes to which one would put them and the features that are required for those purposes. This does not seem a feasible enterprise at this moment and one has to live with the fact that there are various proposals available for an inventory. Next to the RST proposal, there is an SDRT one and the proposals for discourse annotation (Carlson & Marcu 2001; Webber 2004) have been forced into their own classification under the pressure of having to give precise guidelines to their annotators.

Dialogue brings a number of dialogue specific extra relations like *(Self)-Correction, Answer, Acknowledgement, Denial, Rebuttal* and others. These seem out of place in coherent monologue, but on closer inspection, some of them are there after all. One can answer one's own rhetorical questions, acknowledge and deny suggestions attributed to others, rebut similar suggestions and even correct oneself and others within the boundaries of a text. A reorientation of rhetorical structure research towards dialogue – the real product of the cultural-evolutionary process that created languages, texts, speeches, letters, newspapers and novels – would lead to an inventory of rhetorical relations that has a better claim of being representative of what is possible in interhuman communication.

The enterprise of answering what rhetorical relations there are does therefore not seem to have come to a conclusion. The proposal of Traum (2000) of speech act classification by features could perhaps be adopted for rhetorical relations as well. It would lead to full featural analyses of rhetorical relations and offer a common semantics for all of the current proposals. Another aspect is that making an assertion with a specific rhetorical relation to a pivot would seem a further subclassification of the assertion, i.e. a refinement of speech act análysis.

3 What do rhetorical relations relate?

Above, we let *Cause* and *Elaboration* relate proper sentences (in the typographical sense, a phonological definition is problematic). But in both cases it is quite possible to think of these relations as obtaining not so much between the linguistic expressions or even their meanings but as relations between the events and states that these expressions and their meanings are purporting to describe.

This can be maintained for quite a number of rhetorical relations, though it is not always as clear as for *Cause* or *Elaboration*. Some cases will be discussed below. The relation of *Restatement* is particularly relevant here. One formulation is that the event described in the pivot and the event described in the sentence under discussion must be identical. This view is problematic since on many people's view (e.g. Danlos & Gaiffe 2004) if the two verbs are not synonymous, they would describe the same event as having two different types. Can the same individual have two different types? Similar problems have been raised in the area of particulars, with famous cases being the identity between a vase and the clay it is made from. In Aristotelian metaphysics, these objects must be distinct with a relation of constituency holding between the vase and the clay at moments that the quantity of clay in fact forms a vase. Mutatis mutandis, the same would apply to events of two types: they can constitute each other, but not be identical.

A good example is the many levels that Austin (1962) distinguished in the simple request: "Please sit down". There is the phonetic act, the production of the sound, the uttering of the three words (the phatic act), the uttering of the words with a particular reference (the rhetic act), saying "Please sit down" (the locutionary act), asking you to sit down (the illocutonary act), and trying to get you to sit down (the perlocutionary act). It seems right to distinguish all the different acts, but here typically one act constitutes the other, and one can infer one act from the other, using common ground knowledge. One could try to redefine *Restatement* as not implying the identity of the events but as mutual constituency. The difference is that the hierarchy in Austin's actions will not be there: a *Restatement* does not need to give the evidential support for what is restated, or the other way around.

One way of describing what is going on is that many events happen, but that they are collected in one experience which allows of one overarching description and where the other events evidentially support the one overarching event. This allows one to count the overarching event as one and the other descriptions as (sufficient) evidential support for them. Evidential support is an important notion, because it connects a range of rhetorical relations: *Elaboration, Justify, Motivate, Cause, Background, Enablement, Preparation, Circumstance* (and perhaps even the relations of the *Condition* group: *Condition, Otherwise, Unless*). The non-conditional relations from this group imply strong relations between the eventualities: mutual constituency also implies overlaps in spatial and temporal location.

Elaboration is specifying subevents/states of a given event/state. For example: uttering the word "can" is a subevent of uttering "Can you pass me the salt"? *Background* specifies a state in which a given event occurs. The state can, but does not need to be part of the circumstances that brought the event about or allowed it to happen.

(12) John fell. It was a cold day.

Cause (or *Volitional Cause*) specifies why the pivot came to be the case. *Justify* how the speaker has come to know the truth of the pivot.

(13) a. John fell. Bill pushed him. (*Nonvolitional Cause*)
     b. John pushed Bill. He was angry. (*Volitional Cause*)
     c. John pushed Bill. I saw it myself. (*Justify*)

A special case are also elaborations that give extra information about participants or the location, for the purpose of identification or for motivating or explaining the pivot.

This whole group of relations can – with some charity – be described as relations between the state or event described by the current sentence and the state or event described by the pivot. All other relations are different. They are *Contrast, Concession, Narration* and *List* and seem primarily related to the strategic level: what is reported belongs together because it is relevant to the same issue, but the events and states that are reported are not necessarily related to each other. This does not mean that they cannot have causal, temporal or local relations to each other. *Contrast* and *Concession* often go together with temporal simultaneity and local overlap. The elements of *Lists* also often have non-accidental temporal and local relations to each other. But none of these relations seems to entail any particular temporal, local or causal relationship between the events and states involved. If they nonetheless have a relation of this kind it would be due to their shared relation with an overarching topic. *Narration* (*Sequence* in the list of relations above) is connected with moving through time and will imply temporal succession and that is a reason for distinguishing *Narration* from *List*.

In a *Narration,* a story is told. The pivot event is abandoned and the current sentence reports the next event that is relevant for the story. That is the definitional property for *Narration*: the new event happens after the pivot event. Hobbs (1985) adds another element: the new event is contingent on the pivot event. Contingency should be defined in terms of causality, but it is not obvious how this must be done. The idea is that the pivot event does not itself cause the utterance event, but establishes one of its preconditions. This can be expressed as a counterfactual (14) and an illustration is (15).

(14) If the pivot event had not happened, the current event would not have happened either.

(15) John stepped out of his car and walked up to the door.
contingency: John's stepping out of the car brings him in a state and at a place which makes it possible for him to walk to the door.
counterfactual: If John had not stepped out of his car, he would not have walked up to the door.

Stories are held together not just by temporal succession and contingency, but also by protagonists and locations (the aboutness topic). One can try to express the unity of stories by thinking of them as an *Elaboration* of a single event. Another way of defining the unity of a story tries to see the whole story as an answer to a single question (the story topic) that gets answered by the events that make it up. Unfortunately, clear ideas about the construction of this topic question from the story have not been forthcoming, except for simple constructed cases.

Narration cannot be reduced to a relation between the reported events, not even if with Hobbs one adopts *Contingency*. On the topic view, it is the relation to the event described by the whole story or the overarching topic question that makes the pivot and the current sentence stand in the *Narration* relation.

Topic questions (see article 11 [Semantics: Sentence and Information Structure] (Roberts) *Topics*) do a much better job with *Lists*. A *List* (a sequence of sentences connected by the *List* relation) can be seen as an answer in many parts to a single topic question, typically in a situation in which single sentence answers would not do the same job. Here there are algorithms, e.g. Prüst, Scha & van den Berg 1994 that compute the topic question (or a closely related object) for simple cases. *Lists* can also be seen as an answer to the problem that one cannot fully specify binary or ternary relations in a single sentence, unless one is very lucky.

For instance, let John love Mary and Sue, Bill Mary and Harriet and Tom only Sue, while there are other boys and girls. It is impossible to give a simple clause which specifies the whole relation, in response to a question: Which boy loves which girl? (16) is true but fails to give the details.

(16) John, Bill and Tom love Mary, Sue and Harriet.

But a *List* like (18) does. Full specification is possible by splitting up the given question into subquestions as in (17) and answering each in turn as in (18).

(17) Which girls does *x* love?

The *List* in (18) can be seen as a strategy to avoid the problem.

(18) John loves Mary and Sue. Bill Mary and Harriet. And Tom Sue.

Contrast is the topic of ongoing discussions. Umbach (2001) provides a definition for the case when the English "but" or rather the German "aber" does not express *Concession* but what is normally called *Formal Contrast*. The definition runs as follows:

> A positively addresses a topic question Q which B (directly or indirectly) addresses negatively. This is illustrated in (19).

(19) John is tall but Bill is small.
topic question: Are John and Bill tall?
background knowledge: Small implies not tall.

(19) should be contrasted with (20) which requires a different topic question.

(20) John is tall and Bill is small.
topic question: How tall are John and Bill?

The generality of this approach can be undermined however by looking at languages where *Concession* and *Formal Contrast* are expressed by different words. A case in point is Russian, where the expressions *a* and *no* both correspond to English *but* with *no* specialising in the *Concessive* readings (Malchukov 2004).

A is sometimes rendered by *but* in English. In many cases however, the correct translation is *and*. The problem is that the other Russian conjunction *i* is subject to strong restrictions which prevent it to be the uniform translation of *and*. One hypothesis (due to Jasinskaja & Zeevat 2008) is that *a* relates to double contrast: a doubly distinct answer to a double wh-question, as in example (21).

(21) John likes Susan "a" Bill likes Harriet.
topic question: Who like who?

No would not be adequate in this case, since *no* marks a special case of an answer to a double wh-question, namely the case where one wh-element is *why* and the other is *whether*. The polarity switch is then due to the fact that there are only two distinct polarities that can answer a whether-question.

Concession can be defined along the lines proposed by König (1991) as anticausative: Concession(A, B) iff A normally causes B to be false. This is however not fully general, as was already noted by Ducrot (1973). In an example like (22), the first conjunct argues for going to a restaurant, the second against going there. Typically, the speaker can be taken as committing herself to the drift of the second conjunct, i.e. as proposing not to go.

(22) The food is good but it is expensive.

This can be fitted into the scheme of double wh-questions by making the concessive case provide doubly distinct answers to a why-whether question. In (22), the first conjunct gives a reason for going to the restaurant, and the second conjunct a reason for not going there. The anticausal readings are then the ones where the second conjunct itself is the conclusion that is argued against (in the first conjunct) and argued for (by itself) in the second conjunct.

Concession has its origin in conversation. A *Concession* is typically partly acknowledgment of what the other said. Suppose the other said "A". Then one can concede any part of A or a consequence of A. It goes together with not accepting A in its entirety, normally with a rejection of A. In a conversational concession what is conceded is already accepted by the other speaker and so has common ground status. What is not conceded from A, lacks this status. This may explain why subordinate concessive clauses are presupposition triggers.

In English, it is necessary to mark *Concession*, by markers like *but*, *(al)though*, *however* and *nonetheless*. In languages like German and Dutch there are concessive markers like *zwar* and *weliswaar* inside the first clause that indicate that one is in a *Concession* and announce the *aber-* or *maar*-clause that will follow. So these languages have a coordinate structure that is unambiguously concessive, unlike the English construction with *but*.

All rhetorical relations allow asyndetic expression (expression without any overt marking) and there are often lexical markers. A curious fact is that while most relations can be expressed by specific grammaticalised markers and can be marked as a relation between constituent clauses in a syntactically integrated complex construction there are exceptions to this principle.

The analysis of many of the markers as listed in Tab. 13.2 is problematic. Good analyses would give an account of the rhetorical relation(s) they can mark. The growing body of research on the semantics and pragmatics of particles is therefore directly relevant for a better understanding of rhetorical relations (see also article 15 [Semantics: Sentence and Information Structure] (Zimmermann) *Discourse particles*).

Tab. 13.2: Grammaticalised cues for the RST relations

Label	GRAMMATICALISED MARKERS
Antithesis	*but*
Background	
Concession	*but, though*
Enablement	
Evidence	*because, since*
Justify	*because, since*
Motivation	*because, since*
Preparation	
Restatement	
Summary	*so*
Circumstance	*while*
Condition	*if*
Elaboration	*namely*
Evaluation	
Interpretation	*so*
Means	
Non-volitional Cause	*because, since*
Non-volitional Result	*so*
Otherwise	*otherwise, else*
Purpose	
Solutionhood	
Unconditional	*anyway*
Unless	*unless*
Volitional Cause	*so*
Volitional Result	*so*
Conjunction	*and*
Contrast	*but, and*
Disjunction	*or*
Joint	

(continued)

Tab. 13.2: (continued)

Label	GRAMMATICALISED MARKERS
List	*and, also*
Multinuclear Restatement	
Sequence	*then*

4 Where must rhetorical relations be assumed?

The table at the end of section 3. already can serve to make an important point: it is not just the sentences of a discourse that are related by rhetorical relations. Rhetorical relations must also must be assumed within a single sentence as obtaining between coordinated clauses and between main clauses and subordinated clauses. And between subordinate clauses as in the following example (23).

(23) Stepping out of his car and walking to the door John noticed a squirrel in the tree.

Stirling (1993) reports that this is in fact the favourite way of telling a story in switch-reference languages. In Latin – where the case system allows a far more reliable way of tracking the different participants in a sentence than the pronominal systems of many modern languages – multiple participial constructions with rhetorical relations holding between them are much favoured. (24) is from Caesar (1869: book 1,24).

(24) a. ipsi confertissima acie, reiecto nostro equitatu, phalange facta sub primam nostram aciem successerunt
 b. they themselves in very close order, after having repulsed our cavalry and formed a phalanx, advanced up to our front line.

In (24), the relation of *Narration* between throwing back the cavalry and forming a phalanx, both expressed by an absolute ablative is only expressed by the linear order.

This raises the question how deep one should go into syntactic structure for applying rhetorical relations. Very far it seems. Any subordinate predication can in principle be related by a rhetorical relation to another predication, although not to any other predication. Predications have to be related to other ones, since the speaker has put them there for a reason and the hearer needs to figure out why the material was deemed useful by the speaker. An exception is material that is used for the purpose of identification, but also such material can be simultaneously used to give *Causes* or *Justifications*.

(25) a. The angry farmers blocked the road. (*Volitional Cause*)
   b. Pushing the button, John blew up the wall. (*Means*)
   c. Holding the flowers in his arm, John crossed the road. (*Circumstance*)
   d. When he reached the crossing, he turned right, following Mary's instructions. (*Volitional Cause*)

One can even quite legitimately ask the opposite question. How much of the semantic connections expressed by lexical and syntactic means are in fact rhetorical relations? As it turns out many are. Typically all the connectors between sentences have a semantics that is reminiscent of a rhetorical relation. The thematic relations expressed by case and word order have to be analysed by the proto-thematic properties following the analysis of Dowty (1989). And those are suspiciously reminiscent of rhetorical relations: *Cause, Volition, Affected, Beneficiary, Result, Instrument*. Complement sentences can be related to *Elaborations*. On this perspective, one could say that there are fundamental semantic relations for natural language which should be recognised in interpretation and that the rhetorical relations are an important subset of them and not specific for relatingsentences or even clauses.

The possibility of asyndetic connection between sentences bearing a rhetorical relation seems a special property of rhetorical relations, but it is not. Natural languages get away with having syntactic connections that can mean many different things in particular contexts. The participial construction is a good example in English, and so are nonrestrictive nominal modifiers. The range of rhetorical relations that can be expressed is limited in these cases by the fact that the referent of the predication is fixed. In Latin, this restriction is removed in the ablativus absolutus participial construction. That can in fact mean the whole range of rhetorical relations.

So it seems that the conclusion must be that rhetorical relations connect semantic objects like states and events, as well as propositions and speech acts, but that there is not a syntactic definition of the objects they relate, other than that the syntactic expression (or sentence or combination of sentences) should be able to refer to a state or event, express a proposition or express a speech act.

5 Applications

5.1 Anaphora, tense and ellipsis

Anaphoric expressions are expressions that pick up some contextually given entity and use it to determine their own reference. An interesting case is the temporal modifier *soon* that picks up a salient moment of time in the context or (if there is no such moment) the moment of speech and returns an interval of moments: those that are soon after the given moment.

The rhetorical structure is all-important when it comes to determining if there is a suitable salient moment. This would be the moment given by the pivot if any and the discourse relation must support a shift forward. It does not in an example like (26) (an *Explanation*) so that anaphora to the time of release cannot be assumed and *soon* has to be evaluated with respect to speech time.

(26) You will be released in a couple of minutes. The pilot is going to press the button soon.

This contrasts with examples like (27) (a *Narration*)

(27) You will be released in a couple of minutes. Soon you will be quite far away from the plane.

The most important generalisation is here the Right Frontier Constraint (Polanyi 1988; Webber 1988).

(28) Right Frontier Constraint (RFC)
Non-local antecedents for third person pronouns in an utterance can only be in the pivot of the utterance. The pivot is always on the right frontier of the discourse tree.

The discourse tree comes into being by assuming that some relations are coordinating and others subordinating, an assumption that is as old as RST: multinuclear relations put their nuclei next to each other on the tree, satellites hang below the nucleus in a nucleus-satellite relation. In other frameworks, a number of relations can be classified as coordinating, while others are subordinating. In some cases, the decision is not simple, e.g. for *Restatements*. The RFC makes one strong prediction:

(29) Prediction
No third person pronoun can be bound in S_2 from S_0 if S_0 is coordinated with S_1 and S_1 is coordinated with S_2.

This still allows the possibility that antecedents in S_0 bind pronouns in S_2 by an intermediate reference to the antecedent in S_1, but it rules out many potential antecedent-anaphora bindings. The RFC makes a precise statement about when anaphora to antecedents that are further away than the last clause can be allowed to a pivot P: when the interrupting material is subordinated to P.

Importantly, the RFC can be generalised to other kinds of anaphora and ellipsis, to tense and even to bridging. The other kinds of anaphora include anaphoric expressions such as *so, one, such, other, there, thereby, then* and *meanwhile* in this way and many others. If they have antecedents that do not come from the current utterance, the pivot must refer to these antecedents as well.

Tense seems to constitute a problem but this is only on the popular view going back to Reichenbach (1947) that tense is a temporal anaphor, like *soon* or *meanwhile*. That view is hard to maintain when one is not like Hinrichs (1986), the first full development of the anaphoric view, looking exclusively at western novelettes for one's data. Contrastive pairs and lists form clear counterexamples to the claim that the past tense is a temporal anaphor: no temporal relation is inferred. If one wants to infer a relation, overt temporal anaphors are necessary and clearly none of the three possibilities listed in (30) is already implicated.

(30) Jones went to work. (Soon/meanwhile/then) Smith started off towards the city center.

On Kehler's view (Kehler 2002), derived from Comrie (1999), tense just marks the relationship to speech time while other temporal relations between the events in the connected sentences, if any, depend on the inferred rhetorical relation. Here *Narration* and *Result* entail $e_1 < e_2$, and *Explanation* $e_2 < e_1$. The *Similarity* cases do not impose temporal constraints. This implies that tense itself is not subject to the RFC. In Kehler's view (presumably also the view of Lascarides & Asher 1993) the real temporal anaphors are the discourse relations themselves and they trivially obey the RFC.

There is a second generalisation with the same domain as the RFC: parallelism. It is here formulated without restriction and it will soon be clear why it must be restricted.

(31) Parallelism Constraint
Maximize the parallelism between pivot and current utterance

This gives the prediction that where it is possible subject pronouns should have subject antecedents, that optional constituents should be incorporated in ellipsis resolution, that the same quantifier scopes should be preferentially assumed etc. Kehler has however convincingly argued that this is not a general default but one that depends for its operation on the assumption of discourse relations that force parallellism: *List, Formal Contrast* and (cases of) *Concession* and *Narration*. The effects of parallelism can be illustrated by the following examples. In (32) – without special intonation – *she* must be Marian and cannot be Susan.

(With stress on *she*, it is the other way round, due to the distinctness between *she* and *Marian* expressed by the contrastive stress: the most parallel reading that is compatible with contrastive stress on *she*.).

(32) Marian likes Susan. And she likes Tom.

In the second clause of (33), the ellipsed VP is "like Susan at dinner parties" and not "like Susan". In (34), this default is broken by the provision of a different parallel modifier.

(33) Marian likes Susan at dinner parties. And Tom does too.

(34) Marian likes Susan at dinner parties. And Tom does in dancing class.

Kehler's point is that in cases like these, but not with other rhetorical relations the syntax of the connected clauses must be very similar. The effects show up especially in ellipsis. Compare (35) with (36). (36) allows two interpretations: Tom likes himself or Tom likes Marian, interpretations that are both unavailable for (35). ((35) will be repaired to have one of the indicated readings, but *And Tom does too.* is just not the right way to express them.)

(35) Marian likes herself. (?) And Tom does too.

(36) Marian likes herself. Because Tom does too.

Further compare (37) with (38). Here the unexpressed reflexive in the ellipsed clause creates a problem in (37), while this does not seem to matter in (38).

(37) Marian likes Tom. (?) And he does too.

(38) Marian likes Tom. Because he does too.

What seems to be going on is that the *List, Formal Contrast* and (cases of) *Concession* force syntactic parallelism and that the antecedent as a syntactic object must allow the interpretation. This restriction is removed when the relation is not one of *Similarity*.

It is quite tempting to think that this can be analysed with quaestios (von Stutterheim & Klein 1989), discourse topics (Asher 2004) or schemas (Prüst, Scha & van den Berg 1994). *Lists* are then joint answers to a single question (or different elements falling under one discourse topic or sharing a schema). The problem then seems to be that the underlying questions (topic, schemata) in the cases considered are not well-formed. This would block the interpretations that need them. For example, in Prüest, Scha & van den Berg (1994) *And Tom does too*, is expanded to *And Tom likes herself* which cannot be interpreted.

As noted before, the distinctions between *List, Formal Contrast* and *Concession* can be reduced to the kind of question.

(39) List: wh-question
      Contrastive Pair (Parallel): double wh-question
      Formal Contrast: wh-whether question
      Concession: why-whether question

The relations then follow by the assumption that the pivot and the current utterance are in fact distinct for each wh-element.

Explanation, Justification and *Result* and *Narration* cannot be described as connecting two elements that give different answers to the same question and consequently no question needs to be constructed. The parallelism principle should be changed to take Kehler's observations into account.

(40) Parallelism Revised
      If possible assume that the pivot and current answer are (multiply) distinct answers to the same wh-question.

Such an assumption will not be possible with *Restatement, Elaboration, Explanation,* and *Justification*. It is definitional of *List, Formal Contrast, Contrastive Pair* and *Concession*. The question perspective also makes it applicable to *Denial*. Occasionally, it can also be assumed in *Narration*.

5.2 Generation theory

Natural language generation is a branch of computational linguistics which studies the automatic generation of chunks of natural language text for conveying information available to a computational system in an optimal way to a human user. A useful and fairly complete introduction is Reiter & Dale (2000). The aim of the field cannot be given by a correctness notion, e.g. that the available information is in fact coded in the message. That can be met by bizarre and incomprehensible productions. Generation is primarily a matter of quality: the system needs to select the right information and needs to express it in the right way to the user so that the aim of the application is met. Selecting too little or too much information is wrong, it is easy to generate text which will not be understood or is misleading. How to do this is however rather unclear in the abstract – the subject of classical rhetorics is to answer this question in general in the domain of the adversarial legal debate – and it is no wonder that work in this area has largely proceeded empirically, effectively trying to find principles from the study of particular human-generated texts employed in a particular application. In imitating the structure of these texts closely, the system acquires whatever insights the human text writers have into how to present what domain information in a clear and effective way.

This way of proceeding also seems much favoured in the study of rhetorical relations within natural language generation. It is however one of the areas in which principles and structure have been uncovered that are important also outside natural language generation (another area for which useful generalisations have emerged is in NP selection, i.e. pronoun resolution in NL interpretation). Rhetorical relations come in in two different ways. In the first place, as an approach to the problem of presenting more information than will fit in a single sentence. That means that several sentences have to be formed which must be linearised in some way. How to do this? The standard solution is to construct a text plan where messages (corresponding to clauses) and connected blocks of such messages are connected by rhetorical relations. Later processing takes care of how the relations are expressed and of the linear order.

Second, rhetorical relations provide a basis for deciding which messages to put in and the reason for putting them in: context selection and text planning. For example, an inventory of relations can be checked one by one to decide if it is necessary to add further motivation, to provide further elaboration, to generate a concessive clause etc. In practice, this is difficult and often avoided, though it can play a role in local decisions (e.g. whether to insert further detail in a given text plan).

Pioneering work in natural language generation was the background to Rhetorical Structure Theory (RST) (Mann & Thompson 1988; Mann & Matthiessen 1985). These are the first publications about rhetorical relations (if one does not count classical rhetorics, in which rhetorical structure is important but rhetorical relations much less). They are still worth reading. Taboada & Mann (2006) gives an overview and useful discussion of the research in the RST tradition.

In RST rhetorical relations are defined in terms of constraints on the relata and their combination and specify the effect they have, when they are assumed. The constraints can be seen as giving limitations on when the relation can be assumed. The effect is typically the perlocutionary effect: what is the speaker hoping to achieve with the utterance bearing this relation to the pivot. The connection with the perlocutionary effect is important: it makes the connection between rhetorical relations and speech acts. One can say that an utterance in a text, bearing a rhetorical relation to a pivot is just a special kind of speech act: one that tries to achieve something which – in a way specified by the rhetorical relation – depends on the pivot (a point also made in Asher & Lascarides 2003). The perlocutionary effect or rather the speaker's goal of attaining certain perlocutionary effect gives the motive for the speech act and can be identified with the speaker intention of Grice (1957). If it is possible to pursue the programme of identifying particular perlocutionary goals with rhetorical relations, RST becomes a theory of speech acts in which one new parameter is the identity of the pivot and another one the particular relation the pivot bears to it. The perlocutionary effect in principle also provides an interface with text planning. The proper text planner should be able to reason about what perlocutionary effects the generator wants to achieve on the user and to be able to realise these with rhetorically related utterances.

The views on rhetorical structure have not changed much since RST started. So much of the general picture is already there that one starts wondering what the last 30 years have brought. In fact, that is quite a lot. Conspicuously absent in early RST is the RFC and in general the relation between pronominal, temporal and ellipsis resolution and rhetorical relations. Or the relation between information structure and rhetorical structure. The most important shift seems however wanting to deploy rhetorical structure in the study of text interpretation.

5.3 Information structure

There is a seemingly opposite school in the study of rhetorical structure represented by scholars like von Stutterheim & Klein (1989) and van Kuppevelt (1995). In this approach, the starting point is the task of the speaker, conceived as a question. The structure of a text is then a complex answer to this question. This immediately leads to a distinction between partial answers to the question and satellites to such partial answers (which answer questions of their own, raised by their nucleus). The question of a text also leads to the fixation of the topic and foci of the partial answers and the fixation and movement of the referential parameters in these texts. This leads to interesting parallels with treatments of discourse semantics such as Discourse Representation Theory.

One can say from the perspective of this school that RST is just a classification of a set of natural relations that arise in the goal-directed enterprise that is telling a story or producing an overview of some states of affairs or to provide an extended explanation.

A difference with RST is that the question immediately makes a connection with the task of the text as a whole. Moreover, it is possible to develop an account of especially those discourse relations that seem to be governed by information structure rather than by semantic relations almost directly on the basis of the questions structure: especially van Kuppevelt works out this connection and treats both information structure and text structure in terms of questions. This makes it possible to link up with areas such as theories of topic-focus articulation (cf. article 10 [Semantics: Sentence and Information Structure] (Hinterwimmer) *Information structure* or Grosz, Joshi & Weinstein 1995 on centering).

The theory seems to have the potential to serve as a foundation for rhetorical relations and rhetorical structure. Any element of a text needs to be assigned a role with respect to the question of the text or with respect to one of its answers. If this role can be expressed as another question, specific for the particular element, this question will determine both the rhetorical relation and the pivot.

5.4 Text interpretation

While rhetorical relations started in text generation as a theory of how to structure texts, section 5.1. should have made it clear that there is quite a lot of semantic mileage in having a grasp on rhetorical relations in interpretation. The main obstacle for achieving such a grasp is the fact that rhetorical relations quite commonly are not overtly marked at all.

Two remarks are in order. First of all, it is quite normal that there is not a marker in NL for all the conceptual distinctions that are expressed in the sense that speakers are aware of the distinction and hearers are supposed to figure out what it is. The many meanings of common prepositions in English like "with", "of" or "in" are a clear case in point. A natural language understanding system faces the task of filling in the blanks there, if it is aiming for understanding that is comparable with what humans get out of the language input. A lot of ambiguity resolution is necessary.

The second remark is that nonetheless NL is full of markers for rhetorical relations and that texts are full of these markers: various coordinating and subordinating connectors express one or more rhetorical relations, many particles at least rule out some rhetorical relations. (Webber et al. 2003 argues for what seems to be the correct view: the markers are normally just anaphoric elements that express semantic relations: as such they restrict the possibilities of the relations that can be assumed. In this way, particles are not different from other restrictions on rhetorical structure.) The tense and aspect system can play an important role as well and the phenomena discussed in section 5.1. can also be used in reverse: a successful resolution of a VP ellipsis at least identifies a pivot. In fact, low level techniques for parsing rhetorical structure based on cues like particles and other markers have been used successfully in some applications, e.g. in automatic summarizing (Polanyi et al. 2004).

But it cannot be denied that attempts to parse rhetorical structure have been obsessed by this problem to a considerable degree. It has given rise to different approaches. The oldest approach is Jerry Hobbs (Hobbs et al. 1990; Hobbs 1985) which models the hearer trying to explain why a new utterance in the text is coherent with a given one. Rhetorical relations and candidate pivots form different explanation strategies to make the new text coherent. This allows the construction of a set of explanations which can be compared for plausibility. The system recognises the rhetorical relation that belongs to the most plausible explanation. People used to be rather negative about this approach, especially because in toy implementations there is no principled way to assign the weights for the plausibility evaluation, but times seem to have changed dramatically in this respect with the advent of computational systems in natural language processing that assign all kinds of weights to linguistic analyses on an empirical basis. The abduction approach in fact now seems to have a lot of future, not just with respect to rhetorical relations. The work of Kehler in section 5.1., (Kehler 2002) belongs to this tradition.

A more linguistic approach is the Linguistic Discourse Model (Polanyi 1988) and Discourse Grammar (Prüst, Scha & van den Berg 1994; Scha & Polanyi 1988; Polanyi et al. 2004). This approach essentially tries to make the most of information sharing and inheriting as in unification grammar approaches to NL syntax. A full interpretation in this approach resolves the pronouns, the tenses and VP ellipsis and uses all the lexical and syntactic cues that are available. Given that the parameters used in these tasks are controlled by the postulated rhetorical relations, this gives a powerful filter on allowable rhetorical relations and pivots. The quality of the analyis is further improved by having rule priorities, giving priority to certain rhetorical relations over others and a default of the lowest pivot. Similarly oriented work is currently being pursued under the label of DTAG using tree adjoining grammar. This work is currently the most worked out grammatical approach to discourse markers and discourse grammar (Webber & Joshi 1998; Webber, Knott & Joshi 1999; Webber 2004; Webber 2006).

The third approach, Segmented Discourse Representation Theory (SDRT), employs the framework for semantic representation developed by Kamp & Reyle (1993) in combination with a special brand of default logic for inferring rhetorical structure. Using default logic for this task removes the methodological problems noted with respect to abduction, but these seem to come back in the necessity of using a large database of conceptual knowledge which is acquired in ways not less mysterious than the weights in abduction.

All these approaches seem excellent but they should be combined where appropriate and given a proper empirical basis by fully exploiting data-driven computational linguistics. It is necessary on the one hand to have a proper formalisation of all the interactions that obtain in this area as was emphasized in discourse grammar. On the other hand, one needs to be able to compare explanations by a combination of logical and empirical methods to get anywhere at all. It would however not seem that there is anything going on in the area of rhetorical relations that is not just normal computational linguistics. It would therefore seem that further development of empirical computational semantics will bring solutions for asyndetic marking of rhetorical relations.

SDRT has dominated rhetorical structure in recent years. It started as an attempt to get rid of some of the limitations of the treatment of tense and aspect in DRT, a treatment that is largely a refinement of the treatment of tense and aspect in Hinrichs (1986) assuming a very basic narrative structure (Kamp's earlier collaborative work with Christian Rohrer on French tense and aspect (Kamp & Rohrer 1983) – the discovery context for discourse representation theory – was also limited to narration, this time based on Gustave Flaubert's Education Sentimentale). It was however clear to everybody, that the limitation to narration led to generalisations that are not tenable when one considers a wider category of texts. The original work is reported in Lascarides & Asher (1993) and is influenced by attempts at that time to investigate the applicability of default logic to phenomena in natural language semantics and pragmatics. The combination of rhetorical structure and non-monotonic reasoning was not new, since Hobbs had proposed a combination of abduction and his work on text coherence, but SDRT aims for a comprehensive model for the first time. It brought applications to presupposition and the development of a hybrid logical system which separates the logic of rhetorical relations (a propositional non-monotonic logic) from the logic in which the proper natural language semantics is taking place (a variant of standard first order logic). Merging the two logics would lead to an intractable system. While it seems that SDRT can profit as much from empirically acquired statistical data, it requires argument to assume that non-monotonic logic is the most suitable formalism for exploiting it. The aim of SDRT is to develop a implementable logical model of rhetorical structure. And certainly, the work collected in the monograph Asher & Lascarides (2003) comes closer to that goal than any other effort in the area. Moreover, almost all issues in rhetorical structure have come by in this enterprise and no student of rhetorical structure would be wise to ignore SDRT.

6 Outlook

I have tried to show in this overview that rhetorical structure is a necessary ingredient of accounts of text generation and of generalised pronominal resolution, including next to pronouns, tense and aspect, ellipsis and gapping, particles and information structure and therefore an essential part of context-based interpretation of natural language. Here the qualification "context-based" can be safely dropped: there is no natural language interpretation worthy of the name that is not context-based.

With the exception of SDRT, there is no theoretical model of the recognition of rhetorical relations that has been worked out on a larger scale. For SDRT too, the proper recogniser of rhetorical structure has not been achieved yet. With the exception of the rather limited cue-based recognition of rhetorical relations, there is therefore nothing that can be immediately incorporated into natural language understanding systems. In text generation, rhetorical structure is part of most systems. Nonetheless there are many phenomena that need improved understanding. For example, while recent years have seen a substantial improvement in our understanding of the meaning of particles and conjunctions, the question when to deploy these devices in a text generator is still not well understood. It seems that knowing the meaning is not enough, one also needs a proper description of the triggering conditions beyond meaning. For an area that is as central as rhetorical structure, the research investment so far has been very small indeed. As compared e.g. to the investment in the syntax of sentences where hundreds if not thousands of researchers are active there are maybe 75 people altogether who have contributed to the area of rhetorical structure and for a few of them only it has been a substantial part of their career. The intellectual interest of the two problems is hard to compare, but theoretical syntax seems to have only a minor impact on natural language understanding and generation and the potential of rhetorical structure seems to be far greater for both of these areas.

I would gamble on two new impulses into the area in the coming years. One is the advent of corpora that are annotated with rhetorical structure. Such corpora have already been developed and annotation schemes have been provided. For useful references, see http://www.isi.edu/marcu/discourse/. More recent is the Penn Discourse Treebank (http://www.ldc.upenn.edu). They can be combined with the development of more semantic understanding within the stochastic paradigm in NLP in combination with logical techniques. This will lead within the coming years to the possibility of estimating the plausibility of a given interpretation in a context and preferring the most plausible interpretation. This will also allow the recognition of rhetorical relations and thereby liberate research on rhetorical structure from the fixation on the problem of asyndetic expression, a problem outside the reach of current technologies. While these new possibilities will help considerably in other areas of semantics and pragmatics, the improvement of rhetorical understanding will have strong repercussions on the overall quality of semantic and pragmatic understanding.

A second promise is optimality theory. Both generation and interpretation can usefully be seen as a choice between alternatives where the choice is guided by principles, i.e. as optimisation problems. Both generation and interpretation also need blocking and blocking is typical for optimisation problems. Certain interpretations may be obscured by other and better ones, certain possible realisations may be blocked by preferred other realisations. Two interpretational constraints seem directly relevant to rhetorical structure and define defaults there. The first is a principle that maximises the givenness of any element of an interpretation, called *NEW, DOAP, *ACCOMMODATE by different authors. This creates defaults in the interpretation of rhetorical relations as indicated in the following diagram, taken from Zeevat & Jasinskaja (2007).

```
                              List
              Explanation              Contrast
Reformulation > Elaboration >          > Narration >
              Justification            Concession
                              Result
```

The principle also underpins the default in pivot identification: the lowest element on the right frontier that fits.

A good thing about the area of rhetorical relations is that, while schools have been formed, they have not led to divisions other than in general ideology. The Right Frontier Constraint, the general picture of rhetorical structure and most of the analysis of empirical data is shared by all. Where divisions occur, they seem to be about issues that transcend rhetorical structure: How much structure can be captured with unification or tree adjoining grammar? What is the correct way to deal with non-monotonic reasoning? Should the inference of rhetorical structure be entirely situated in semantic representation?

The exciting questions in the field seem concerned with extending the empirical coverage of rhetorical structure, the application of rhetorical structure to linguistic and cognitive problems and the foundational questions about rhetorical structure: where does it come from and why is it the way it is? And the issues connected with the enterprise of further developing the technological potential of rhetorical structure.

7 References

Asher, Nicholas 2004. Discourse topic. *Theoretical Linguistics* 30, 163–201.
Asher, Nicholas & Alex Lascarides 2003. *Logics of Conversation*. Cambridge: Cambridge University Press.

Austin, John L. 1962. *How to do Things with Words: The William James Lectures delivered at Harvard University in 1955*. Oxford: Clarendon Press.
Caesar, Gaius Julius 1869. *Commentaries on the Gallic War*. New York: Harper & Brothers.
Carlson, Lynn & Daniel Marcu 2001. *Discourse Tagging Reference Manual*. ISI Technical Report ISI-TR-545. Marina del Rey, CA, University of Southern California.
Comrie, Bernhard 1999. Tense. In: K. Brown & J. Miller (eds.). *Concise Encyclopedia of Grammatical Categories*. Amsterdam: Elsevier, 363–368.
Danlos, Laurence & Bertrand Gaiffe 2004. Event coreference and discourse relations. In: K. Korta & J. M. Larrazabal (eds.). *Truth, Rationality, Cognition, and Music: Proceedings of the Seventh International Colloquium on Cognitive Science*. Dordrecht: Kluwer, 105–130.
Dowty, David 1989. On the semantic content of the notion of thematic role. In: G. Chierchia, B. Partee & R. Turner (eds.). *Properties, Types, and Meanings, vol. II*. Dordrecht: Kluwer, 69–130.
Ducrot, Oswald 1973. *La preuve et le dire*. Paris: Mame.
Grice, Paul 1957. Meaning. *Philosophical Review* 67, 377–388.
Grosz, Barbara, Aravind Joshi & Scott Weinstein 1995. Centering: A framework for modeling the local coherence of discourse. *Computational Linguistics* 21, 203–225.
Hinrichs, Erhard 1986. Temporal anaphora in discourses of English. *Linguistics & Philosophy* 9, 63–82.
Hobbs, Jerry R. 1985. *On the Coherence and Structure of Discourse*. Technical Report CSLI-85-37. Stanford, CA, Center for the Study of Language and Information, Stanford University.
Hobbs, Jerry, Mark Stickel, Douglas Appelt & Paul Martin 1990. *Interpretation as Abduction*. Technical Report 499. Menlo Park, CA, SRI International.
Jasinskaja, Katja & Henk Zeevat 2008. Explaining additive, adversative and contrast marking in Russian and English. *Revue de Sémantique et Pragmatique* 24, 65–91.
Kamp, Hans & Uwe Reyle 1993. *From Discourse to Logic*. Dordrecht: Kluwer.
Kamp, Hans & C. Rohrer 1983. Tense in texts. In: R. Bäuerle, Ch. Schwarze & A. von Stechow (eds.). *Meaning, Use and Interpretation of Language*. Berlin: de Gruyter, 250–269.
Kehler, Andrew 2002. *Coherence, Reference, and the Theory of Grammar*. Stanford, CA: CSLI Publications.
Knott, Alistair & Chris Mellish 1996. A feature-based account of the relations signalled by sentence and clause connectives. *Language and Speech* 39, 141–177.
Knott, Alistair & Ted Sanders 1998. The classification of coherence relations and their linguistic markers: An exploration of two languages. *Journal of Pragmatics* 30, 135–175.
König, Ekkehard 1991. Concessive relations as the dual of causal relations. In: D. Zaefferer (ed.). *Semantic Universals and Universal Semantics*. Dordrecht: Foris, 435–456.
van Kuppevelt, Jan 1995. Discourse structure, topicality and questioning. *Journal of Linguistics* 31, 109–147.
Lascarides, Alex & Nicholas Asher 1993. Temporal interpretation, discourse relations and commonsense entailment. *Linguistics & Philosophy* 16, 437–493.
Malchukov, Andrej L. 2004. Towards a semantic typology of adversative and contrast marking. *Journal of Semantics* 21, 177–198.
Mann, William C. & Christian M.I.M. Matthiessen 1985. Demonstration of the Nigel text generation computer program. In: J.D. Benson & W.S. Greaves (eds.). *Systemic Perspectives on Discourse*. Norwood, NJ: Ablex, 50–83.

Mann, William C. & Sandra Thompson 1988. Rhetorical Structure Theory: Toward a functional theory of text organization. *Text* 8, 243–281.
Polanyi, Livia 1988. A formal model of the structure of discourse. *Journal of Pragmatics* 12, 601–638.
Polanyi, Livia, Chris Culy, Martin van den Berg, Gian Lorenzo Thione & David Ahn 2004. A rule based approach to discourse parsing. In: M. Strube & C. Sinder (eds.). *Proceedings of the 5th SIGdial Workshop on Discourse and Dialogue*. Stroudsburg, PA: ACL, 108–117.
Prüst, Hub, Remko Scha & Martin van den Berg 1994. Discourse grammar and verb phrase anaphora. *Linguistics & Philosophy* 17, 261–327.
Reichenbach, Hans 1947. *Elements of Symbolic Logic*. New York: Macmillan.
Reiter, Ehud & Robert Dale 2000. *Building Natural Language Generation Systems*. Cambridge: Cambridge University Press.
Scha, Remko & Livia Polanyi 1988. An augmented context free grammar for discourse. In: D. Vargha (ed.). *Proceedings of the 12th International Conference on Computational Linguistics*. Budapest: John von Neumann Society for Computing Scienes, 573–577.
Singh, Dharamjit 1970. *Indian Cooking: A practical guide*. Penguin Books.
Stirling, Lesley 1993. *Switch-Reference and Discourse Representation*. Cambridge: Cambridge University Press.
von Stutterheim, Christiane & Wolfgang Klein 1989. Referential movement in descriptive and narrative discourse. In: R. Dietrich & C. F. Graumann (eds.). *Language Processing in Social Context*. Amsterdam: North-Holland, 39–76.
Taboada, Maite & William C. Mann 2006. Rhetorical Structure Theory: Looking back and moving ahead. *Discourse Studies* 8, 567–588.
Traum, David 2000. 20 questions on dialogue act taxonomies. *Journal of Semantics* 17, 7–30.
Umbach, Carla 2001. Contrast and contrastive topic. In: I. Kruijff-Korbayová & M. Steedman (eds.). *Proceedings of the ESSLLI 2001 Workshop on Information Structure, Discourse Structure and Discourse Semantics*, Helsinki: University of Helsinki, 171–184.
Webber, Bonnie 1988. *Discourse Deixis and Discourse Processing*. Technical report. Philadelphia, PA, CIS, University of Pennsylvania.
Webber, Bonnie 2004. DLTAG: Extending Lexicalized TAG to discourse. *Cognitive Science* 28, 751–779.
Webber, Bonnie 2006. Accounting for discourse relations: Constituency and dependency. In: M. Dalrymple, M. Butt & T. King (eds.). *Intelligent Linguistic Architectures*. Stanford, CA: CSLI Publications, 339–360.
Webber, Bonnie & Aravind Joshi 1998. Anchoring a lexicalised tree-adjoining grammar for discourse. In: M. Stede, L. Wanner & E. Hovy (eds.). *Proceedings of the Coling-ACL'98 Workshop on Discourse Relations and Discourse Markers*. Montreal: Coling/ACL, 86–92.
Webber, Bonnie, Alistair Knott & Aravind Joshi 1999. Multiple discourse connectives in a lexicalized grammar for discourse. In: H. Bunt & E. Thijsse (eds.). *Proceedings of the 3rd International Workshop on Computational Semantics (IWCS-3)*. Tilburg: Tilburg University, 309–325.
Webber, Bonnie, Matthew Stone, Aravind Joshi & Alistair Knott 2003. Anaphora and discourse structure. *Computational Linguistics* 29, 545–587.
Zeevat, Henk & Katja Jasinskaja 2007. *And* as an additive particle. In: M. Aurnague, K. Korta & J. M. Larrazabal (eds.). *Language, Representation and Reasoning. Memorial volume to Isabel Gómez Txurruka*. Bilbao: University of the Basque Country Press, 315–340.

Index

adverbial modification 134, 233–236, 245, 249, 278
anaphora 96, 107, 271–275, 282–289, 303, 322, 333, 340–345, 362–364, 390, 391, 396, 402, 408, 414–419, 427–429
Austinian proposition 274–277, 282, 286, 290, 301, 306, 313

basic level 35–38, 41, 48, 49, 127, 158
Basic Principle of Truth-Conditional Semantics 182–187, 206

categorization 30–32, 35–44, 51, 60, 70, 79, 90, 91, 101, 118, 123, 177
Causal Relations 38, 176, 415, 418–421
cause 25, 58–61, 80, 147, 164–170, 176, 244, 257, 334, 417–421, 425, 427
change of state 154, 156, 159, 163, 164, 167, 169, 173, 258
coercion 22, 86, 105, 106, 114, 131, 132, 138–140, 177, 178, 255–260
– event 255–260
cognition 4, 7, 18, 26, 34, 35, 46–48, 90–94, 98, 102, 140, 141, 146, 174, 271, 299, 313, 437
cognitive
– linguistics 1–4, 7, 18, 21, 24, 26, 158
– recruitment 21
– semantics 1, 4, 26, 92, 115, 155, 159, 160, 166
combinatory meaning variation 132–137
compositionality 90, 91, 105, 108–110, 115, 123, 125, 131–134, 140, 185, 196, 201, 206, 407, 408
conceptual imposition 18, 19, 23
conceptual organization 2, 13–17
Conceptual Semantics 4, 86–105, 110, 115, 116, 123, 155
Conceptual Structure 1–7, 17, 21, 26, 29, 57, 60, 86, 92–96, 100, 101, 110, 114–117, 120, 127, 131, 138, 154, 157, 159, 167, 176, 178
Conceptual System 16, 115, 117, 127, 149
contextuality 407, 409

contextualization 123, 125, 131
context 38, 45, 81, 91, 103, 131, 132, 141–149, 163, 187, 195, 205, 206, 252, 271, 281, 288, 296–308, 311–316, 335–349, 357–363, 367, 386, 388–394, 398–409, 427–437
– dependence 101, 122, 163, 301, 314, 386, 388, 403
– independence 131, 132
Contiguity Relations 419
core abstract theories 160
cultural context of categories 38–40

decomposition 63, 91, 99–101, 115, 123, 131, 157–161, 178, 179, 232–234, 239, 243–245, 255–258
dialogue 283, 287, 288, 295, 296, 303, 304, 307–312, 400, 404, 416, 419
dimensional adjectives 140
direct reference and anchors 374–376
discourse
– context 131, 332, 337, 338, 340, 347, 362, 363
– relations 334, 376, 387, 408, 414–418, 426, 428–430, 433
– structure 376, 409
– tree 416, 428, 437
– understanding 59, 81, 82
Discourse Representation Theory 96, 245, 282, 307, 308, 311, 321–379, 386–391, 396–400, 404, 408, 409, 413, 433–436
distinguishing lexical and world knowledge 173–179
distribution of attention 11–13
donkey sentences 335–340, 388, 395, 401, 402
dot-objects 103–105
dynamic
– binding 394–399, 407
– interpretation 391–394, 398–401, 405, 408, 409
– semantics 282, 302, 307, 314, 323, 377, 378, 385–410
Dynamic Predicate Logic 321, 391–400, 404, 408

ellipsis 86, 108, 303, 308, 323, 376, 419, 427–430, 433–436
embodiment 4, 19–21, 68
events 7–16, 25, 44, 58, 65–68, 73–82, 96–98, 126, 133–136, 156, 159, 163–167, 232–261, 268–270, 286, 299–310, 315, 327–334, 343–354, 368, 387, 400–405, 418–429
– and thematic roles 232–234, 239, 243
eventuality 75, 133–135, 165, 233, 241, 327, 351

factive/fictive organization 13–15
feature analysis in word meanings 99, 100
figure/ground organization 13, 14
File Change Semantics 323, 390
Fillmorean frames 59–73
force dynamics 4, 13, 16, 17, 100
frame semantics 24, 57–82, 154
frames 24, 57–74, 77–82, 141, 154, 169
– vs. lexical fields 70, 71
– vs. relations 68–70

grounding 12, 13, 24, 62, 66, 77, 82, 301, 307–315, 406

inferences 21, 58, 81, 88–95, 105, 123–131, 146–149, 157–165, 172–178, 224, 269, 296, 347–356, 360–363, 377, 413, 438
information structure 86, 95, 96, 108, 278, 376, 396, 402, 413, 414, 419, 422, 425, 433, 434, 437
institution nouns 125–127
intensionality 205–208, 224, 366–370

lexical
– decomposition 99, 123, 131, 161, 178, 179, 243
– fields 57, 68, 70, 71, 140–142
– knowledge 146, 147, 154, 173, 177, 178
– semantics 30, 41, 49, 59, 61, 67, 68, 126, 131, 154, 155, 160, 172–179, 353, 360, 362
lexicography 59, 80, 81
lexicon 59, 122, 147, 352–361
– and inference 147, 352–361
linguistic vs. non-linguistic knowledge 116, 117
locative prepositions 127–130, 132

logical space 181, 189, 193, 194, 197–208, 211–228

material models 183, 195, 198–216, 220
Mathematical Model Theory 203, 228, 229
meaning postulates 115, 147, 215–218, 223–227, 296, 354, 355, 358–361
Meaning Reification 298, 300, 307, 311
mentalism 87–91
metacommunicative interaction 277, 283, 286, 287, 291, 295–317
micro-conversational events 308–310
Minskian frames 71–73
model-theoretic semantics 181–229
model theory 87, 181–229, 268, 275, 327, 348, 373
Montague Grammar 105, 321, 323, 371, 378, 391
Most Certain Principle 182–186

Neo-Davidsonian Paradigm 232–234, 240, 252
non-compositional meaning adjustments 138–140
nucleus and satellite 417, 418, 428, 433

Object Schemata 142, 144
ontological categories and aspectual features 97–99
ontology of natural language 232, 233, 267–291

perspectivalization 69–73, 76–79
perspective point 9–11, 18
plurals 98, 362, 366, 399, 400
polysemy 29, 49, 50, 63, 67, 114, 115, 122, 125, 127, 130, 131
possible worlds 87–91, 181, 189, 193–196, 200–208, 211–213, 221–224, 227, 290, 367–369, 378, 403
– semantics 87, 181, 189–208
presupposition 130, 274, 281, 304–310, 312–315, 323, 338–352, 358–361, 375, 376, 387, 399, 403–408, 413–424, 436
– and binding 341–349, 406
Principle of Compositionality 105, 108, 131, 185
priority of information 268, 297

processing of underlying event structures 176, 257–259
profiling 12, 64–73, 77–81
pronoun 127, 177, 186, 236, 283–289, 322–333, 336–340, 345, 346, 362–365, 378, 387–396, 400–402, 413, 419, 428, 432–436
propositional attitudes 273, 277, 323, 361, 367, 371–376
prototype effects 29, 30, 32–35, 39, 44–47
prototypes 30, 32, 35–49, 52, 158
– and categories 29, 40–44
– and polysemy 29, 49–52
– and the basic level 35–38, 48, 49

Relational Theory of Meaning 295–303, 306, 317
representationalism 268, 407–409
– and dynamism 407–409
Resemblance relations 419
rhetorical relations 334, 413–421, 424–438

saliency 11, 12, 36, 68, 144
schematic structure 2, 7–13
semantic conflict resolution 22–24
Semantic Form 114, 116, 131, 137
semantics of grammar 4–7
semantics/pragmatics interface 138–140
semantic underspecification and coercion 131–140
situations 13, 60, 61, 64, 95, 98, 100, 163, 174, 193, 267–290, 295–301, 336, 388, 400
Situation Semantics 97, 267–274, 282–290, 295–303, 306, 311, 313, 317
situation types 241, 269–285, 290
Spatial Structure 4, 86, 92–101, 110

spatiotemporal entity 238, 239, 280
stage-level/individual-level distinction 232–234, 245–252
state 7–10, 59, 63, 71, 159, 163–173, 232–234, 241–244, 252–258, 270, 277, 282–287, 311, 326, 331, 342, 344, 354–360, 372–373, 378, 386, 403–405, 418–422, 427
Substitution Principle 184–187, 205
syntax 26, 49, 59–68, 78–82, 87–95, 105–110, 133–141, 173–176, 214, 234, 249, 300, 308, 327, 338, 350, 373, 409, 430–437

tense 6, 7, 11, 130, 140, 144, 145, 233, 241, 322–325, 329, 333, 356, 368, 376, 402, 427, 429, 434–436
– in texts 324–335
text interpretation 57, 60, 78, 433, 434
text structure 417, 434
thematic roles 65, 66, 166, 167, 232–234, 239, 243, 245
topological principle for grammar 5, 6
truth-conditional semantics 182–189, 193
type theoretic ontology for interaction 282–290
Type Theory with Records (TTR) 282–291, 297, 301, 311

underspecification 114, 115, 118, 122, 131, 135, 139, 259, 260, 377
updates in discourse 309, 403, 404

word senses 29, 49–51, 60, 167–173
words and the world 47–49
world knowledge 15, 87, 92, 100, 109, 115, 127, 131, 136, 139, 154, 155, 159, 167, 173–178

www.ingramcontent.com/pod-product-compliance
Lightning Source LLC
Chambersburg PA
CBHW031541300426
44111CB00006BA/127